Eindeutigkeiten sprengen
Subverting Disambiguities

Kuratorische Praxis Shedhalle 2009–2012
Curatorial Practice Shedhalle 2009–2012

Herausgegeben von / Edited by
Anke Hoffmann und / and Yvonne Volkart
für den / for the Verein Shedhalle

EINDEUTIGKEITEN SPRENGEN

SUBVERTING DISAMBIGUITIES

Factory of Found Clothes/Gluklya: *Dumped Dreams (Utopian Unemployment Union N4)*, 2011

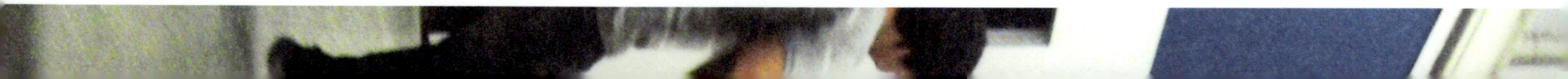

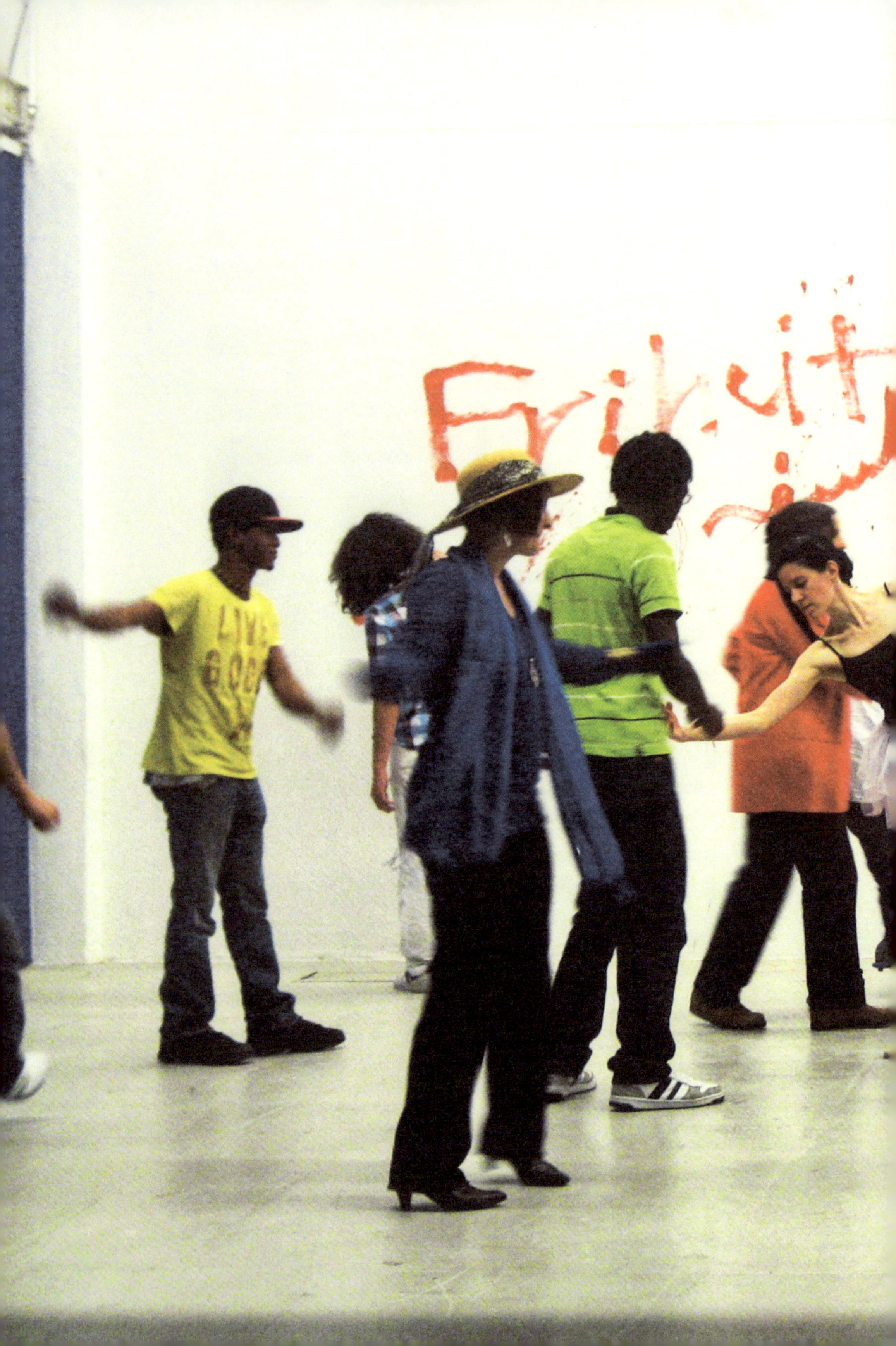

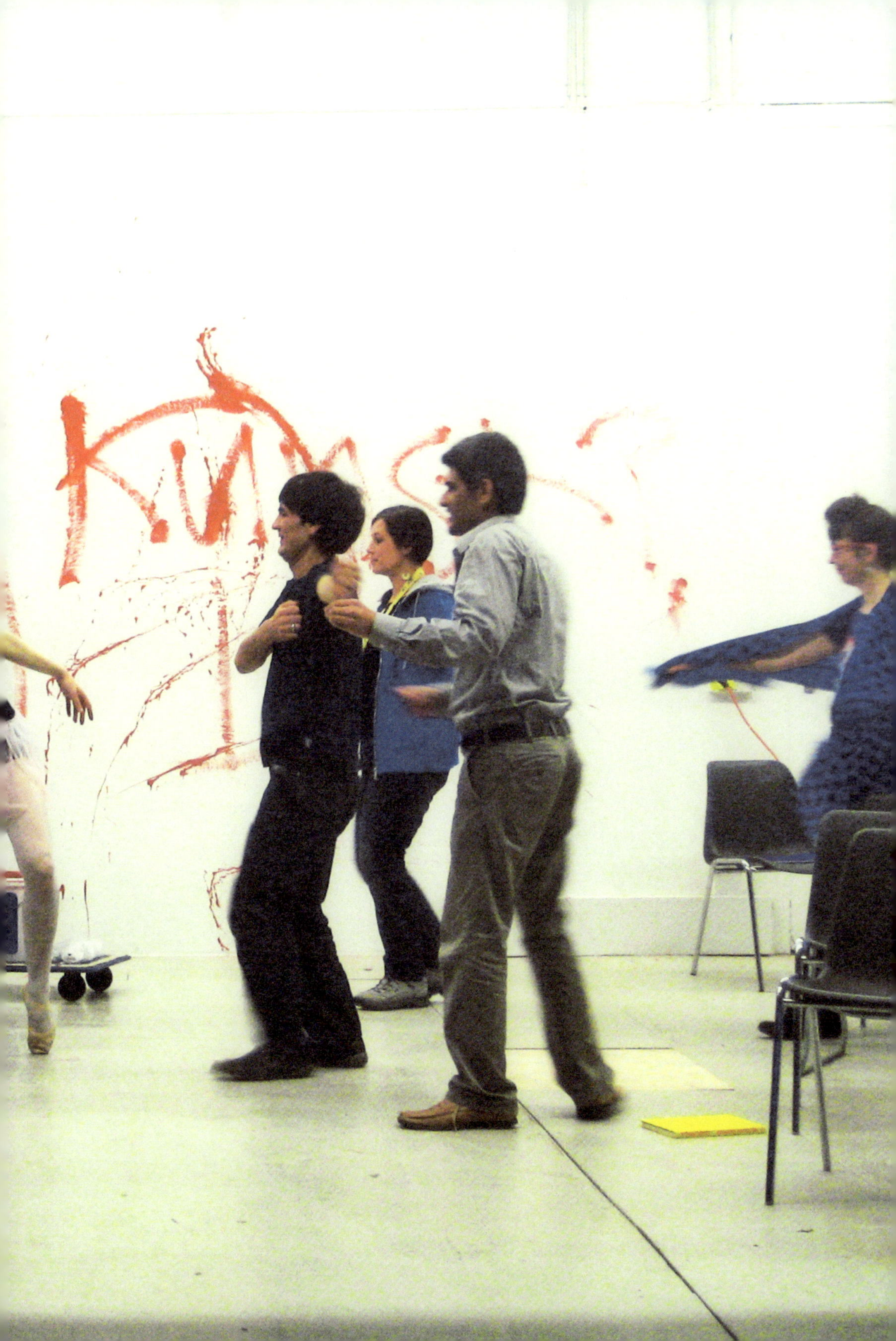

9............. **Editorial / Editorial** Anke Hoffmann, Yvonne Volkart

Innehalten und Unterbrechen / Pausing and Interrupting

22.............. **Dump Time. Für eine Praxis des Horizontalen / Dump Time. For a Practice of Horizontality** Anke Hoffmann, Yvonne Volkart

30.... **Schlaf, Kapitalismus und Subjektivität / Sleep, Capitalism and Subjectivity** Alexei Penzin

46...... **The Praise of Laziness** Mladen Stilinović

48........... **A Kind of Certainty is Uncertainty** Interview with Igor and Ivan Buharov

52........... **If A Storeclerk Gave Me too Much Change** Stefan Panhans

55.............. **wir schlafen nicht** Kathrin Röggla

Wie Kunst Geschichte schreibt / How Art Writes History

62............ **Überblendungen. Das Zukünftige rekonstruieren. Oder: Vom Umgang mit Geschichte in der Kunst / Cross-fades: Reconstructing the Future. Or: On Dealing With History in Art** Yvonne Volkart

76........... **Zur künstlerischen Aneignung des Historischen / The Artistic Appropriation Of The Historical** Anke Hoffmann

88....... **Vergangenheiten erfinden. Oder: Die Kunst der Aktualisierung / Inventing the Past. Or: The Art of Updating** Ute Vorkoeper

99.................... **How I work** Zbyněk Baladrán

102........ **Everything is somehow related to everything else, yet the whole is terrifyingly unstable** Rossella Biscotti

104..... **History as Hallucination** Interview with Uriel Orlow

108......... **MarYvon. Eine RetroPerspektive, Zürich 1930...** Karen Geyer

111........ **Aneignung und Inszenierungen von Geschichte** Hofmann&Lindholm im Interview

Ökologiken / Ecologics

118............ **Lands End. Die Dinge von ihrem möglichen Ende her denken / Lands End: Thinking Things from Their Possible End** Yvonne Volkart

136........ **Zur Ausstellung *Unter Strom*. Wie Unsichtbarkeit zu trügerischen Selbstverständlichkeiten verleitet / On the Exhibition *Live Wire*. How Their Invisibility Treacherously Misleads Us to Take Things for Granted** Anke Hoffmann

150............... **Another Mode of Relation to Non-Human Species** Interview with Matthew Fuller/Graham Harwood

154..... **The Voice of a Traumatised Territory** Interview with Sebastian Diaz Morales

158... **Wildes Gärtnern im öffentlichen Raum** Maurice Maggi

163.. **A Particular Level of Attention** Interview with Emily Richardson

166............. Hörner/Antlfinger: **Dream Water Wonderland**

168............... **Plasma. Im und entlang dem Medium denken** Jan Peter E.R. Sonntag im Interview

172.... **Temporäre Präsenzen – Freie Energien**
Alexander Tuchaček

176....... **Im Scheitern steckt die Poesie des Unvollendeten** Christina Hemauer und Roman Keller im Interview

Un/Mögliche Gemeinschaft / Im/Possible Community

184.... **Un/Mögliche Gemeinschaft, oder: die Gemeinschaft in den Zeiten der Globalisierung / Im/Possible Community. Or: Community in the Era of Globalisation**
Anke Hoffmann

201 ...... **Die un/mögliche Gemeinschaft von Theorie und Praxis / The (Im)Possible Community of Theory and Practice**
Elke Bippus

213................ **Masterpieces** Juliane Zelwies

218 .... **Für ein Miteinander von Mehrdeutigkeiten** Sabina Baumann im Gespräch

223........**Immer wieder Wiedersehen! Oder: Zu welchem Song sterben wir jetzt?**
Heimo Lattner

228.......... **Erster Zürcher Beschwerdechor**

232................. Hassan Khan

234........................ **Atom** Korpys/Löffler

Durchspielen und Eröffnen / Acting Out and Opening Up

242......... **Formen der Beteiligung. Tellervo Kalleinen/Oliver Kochta-Kalleinen, JOKAklubi und YKON / Forms of Participation: Tellervo Kalleinen/Oliver Kochta-Kalleinen, JOKAklubi and YKON**
Yvonne Volkart

254....... **The F-Word. Sind wir alle Top Girls oder brauchen wir den Feminismus heute noch? / The F-Word: Are We All Top Girls, Or Do We Still Need Feminism?**
Anke Hoffmann

276............. **Eine Extrarunde Nachdenken, oder: wider eine vorschnelle Funktionalisierung von Kunst / An Extra Round of Thinking, or Against Functionalising Art Too Quickly**
Rachel Mader

283.............. **Sprengende Eindeutigkeiten. Das Eine als Singularität in der Vieldeutigkeit / Subversive Disambiguities: The One as Singularity in Ambiguity**
Gerald Raunig

294........... **Formen der Beteiligung** Tellervo Kalleinen/Oliver Kochta-Kalleinen

298........ **Towards Transversal Intersections**
Interview with Gluklya

Anhang / Appendix

306..... **Kurzbiografien von Autor_innen und Künstler_innen / Short biographies of authors and artists**

312............... **Veranstaltungen Shedhalle / Shedhalle Events**

319......... **Danksagung / Acknowledgements**

320...................... **Impressum / Imprint**

ANKE HOFFMANN, YVONNE VOLKART

EDITORIAL
EDITORIAL

Die Shedhalle versteht sich seit ihrer Neuausrichtung im Jahr 1994 als Verhandlungsort politischer, gesellschaftlich relevanter und unbequemer Fragen. Die Kurator_innen, die seit damals in der Shedhalle tätig waren, haben dabei Produktions- und Repräsentationsverhältnisse untersucht und die Shedhalle als Diskurs- und Artikulationsraum für gesellschaftlich marginalisierte und unterbelichtete Realitäten eröffnet. Auch unsere kuratorische Arbeit war diesem Ansatz verpflichtet und widmete sich Themen, die gesellschaftlich zu wenig beachtet oder verdreht werden. Auch wir versuchten, adäquate Praktiken und ästhetische Formate zu entwickeln, die das Repräsentative des Ausstellungsraums einerseits zu sprengen, andererseits dessen Qualitäten aber auch tiefer auszuloten suchten als das hier bisher geschah. Unser Versuch, den Ausstellungsraum auch als Erfahrungsraum für ästhetische Erlebnisse wiederzubeleben, war verbunden mit dem Wunsch, Unterschiedliches und vormals Ausgeschlossenes als gleichberechtigt nebeneinander zu stellen und dabei nicht zuletzt auch der Ausstellung eine neue Chance zu geben. Wir wollten den diskursiven Ort Shedhalle vermehrt als Erfahrungsraum für ästhetische Erlebnisse erweitern und neu zugänglich machen, denn die ästhetische Erfahrung ist unserer Meinung nach im Alltag kaum erfahrbar, und sie unterscheidet sich auch wesentlich von der intellektuellen oder diskursiven Erfahrung. Ausserdem ist sie situativ und nicht wiederholbar, das heisst, sie widerspricht im Kern repräsentativer Strategien bzw. liegt die kuratorische Herausforderung darin, immer wieder nach Mitteln und Wegen zu suchen, die repräsentative Vereinnahmung zu sprengen. Wir taten dies, indem wir auch auf erweiterte, diskursive, performative oder ins Reale intervenierende Formate und ausserkünstlerische Kollaborationen setzten.

Eindeutigkeiten sprengen

Eindeutigkeiten sprengen war theoretisches Leitmotiv und praktische Herausforderung für drei Jahre gemeinsamer kuratorischer Verantwortung in der Shedhalle und ist als Referenz auch dieser Publikation voran gestellt. Das Buch versteht sich als eine Reflexion jener Themen, Ausstellungen und künstlerischen Projekte, die wir zwischen 2009 und 2012 entwickelt haben, und versucht, das Hybride, Heterogene und Konfliktuöse, wie wir es in unserer Praxis bevorzugten, auch in Buchform wiederzugeben.

Zu Beginn unserer Tätigkeit schrieben wir ein Plädoyer für die Shedhalle als Ort „des Stillstehens und des Unterbrechens": „Innehalten und Stillstand ist nicht Flucht oder Rekreation. Es ist Anhalten und temporäres Aussetzen der Leistungsmaschine". Wir meinten damit also etwas Grundlegenderes, als es ein Modewort wie Entschleunigung suggeriert. Dieses Statement bezog sich sowohl auf die lange Abfolge der Projekte und die jeweils dialogische Präsentationsweise als auch auf die zunächst so unterschiedlich erscheinenden Themen wie der ökologischen Ästhetik, bei der es konkret um Landschaft oder Elektrizität ging, oder um die Frage der Darstellung von Geschichte, um Schlaf als Modell von Widerstand, um Gemeinschaft versus Individuum und Gesellschaft, um Medienreflexion oder um die Fragen nach Beteiligung und feministischen Praxen heute. Das heisst, bei aller Unterschiedlichkeit interessieren uns grundsätzlich Fragen nach dem Widerständigen gegenüber den (auch die kritische Kunstszene antreibenden) neoliberalen Verwertungszusammenhängen, die Grundlagen des sozialen Zusammenlebens, die subtilen Mechanismen von Aus- und Einschlüssen sowie die Fragen von Repräsentation und Zukunftsgestaltung. Und dazu gehört es auch, Wege und Mittel zu ersinnen, mittels der er wir uns selbst immer wieder in Frage stellen und reflektieren können, damit wir nicht unsererseits jene Ausschlüsse produzieren, die wir diskursiv verwerfen. Wir lösten dies unter anderem dadurch, dass wir uns als kollaborative Komplizinnen verstanden, die trotz unterschiedlicher Methoden und Referenzen ein gemeinsames kuratorisches Team bildeten – und uns so auch permanent befragen mussten.

Die in der Praxis und im vorliegenden Buch verhandelten Themen sind eine Art Schnittmenge unserer subjektiven ‚Begehren' und Dringlichkeiten, von denen wir denken, dass sie eine gesellschaftliche und persönliche Relevanz haben und kritisch denkende Menschen bei ihrer Lebenswirklichkeit abholen und herausfordern. Wir wollen das sichtbar machen, was neben der Spur liegt, das Abseitige, Verdrängte, Irrationale und Nachtseitige oder traumatisch Wiederkehrende, aber auch deren Kehrseiten, das Absurde, Witzige und Heitere, das ebenso hartnäckig sein kann. Diese Widerständigkeit in den Dingen und Zusammenhängen zu fassen, das war und ist unser erklärtes ästhetisches Unternehmen, nicht nur auf der thematischen Ebene.

2009 schrieben wir:
„Eine Hartnäckigkeit gegenüber unseren ideologischen Rastern zu entwickeln heisst unserer Meinung nach, das duale System der Eindeutigkeiten zu sprengen. Es heisst, Praktiken, Konstellationen und Ästhetiken zu fördern, die eine Vieldeutigkeit oder gar Sinnlosigkeit jenseits konventioneller Sinnzuweisungen zulassen. Es geht um die Produktion von Sinn, der seinen Un/Sinn immer mitführt. Wir plädieren für ein Sprechen, das immer auch ein Widersprechen ist. Es geht um Formen des Nicht-Verstehens, um Wider/Sprüche als Einsprüche, um Praktiken des Dissens. Diese richten sich auch darauf, dass unsere Kultur Probleme mit Unterschieden hat. Sie hat nicht nur Schwierigkeiten damit, Unterschiedliches jenseits dualer Hierarchien zu denken, sondern versucht sie auch aufzubauschen oder im Gegenzug dazu zu relativieren. Die Stichwörter dazu sind bekannt: Kampf der Kulturen oder Multikulti. Unsere schöne neue Konsum- und Technowelt homogenisiert und vereinfacht zudem gerne die Materialitäten und damit verbunden auch die Zusammenhänge. Im Zulassen vom Unverständlichen oder gar Disparaten, sowohl inhaltlich als auch formal, materiell oder szenografisch, plädieren wir damit für eine Offenheit, in der sich über Konstellationen und Versammlungen Möglichkeiten auftun und erahnen lassen, die jenseits des gesellschaftlichen Zwangs zur Simplizität liegen. Nicht um die Dinge zu verkomplizieren, sondern um deren Kompliziertheit und somit Widerständigkeit zu sehen geben. Dies tun wir auch dadurch, dass alle künstlerischen Formate und Medien, wie Installation, Performance, Video, neue Medien

Since its reorientation in 1994, Shedhalle sees itself as a venue for dealing with political, socially relevant and uncomfortable questions. The curators who have been active at Shedhalle since then have examined relations of production and representation, and opened it up as a space of discourse and articulation for socially marginalised and underexposed realities. Our curatorial work was also committed to this approach and was devoted to issues that have received too little attention socially or have been distorted. We, too, also attempted to develop adequate practices and aesthetic formats that subvert the representative quality of the exhibition space on the one hand, while on the other hand seeking to explore its qualities more deeply than has been done in the past. Our attempt to also revitalise the exhibition space as a space of experience was bound to the desire to place different and previously excluded things alongside one another on an equal footing, and in doing so ultimately give the exhibition a new chance. We wanted to make the discursive site of Shedhalle re-accessible and expand it to become a space of aesthetic experience, something that in our opinion is lacking in everyday life and which distinguishes itself considerably from the intellectual or discursive experience. In addition, it is situative and irreproducible; that is, it essentially contradicts representative strategies or poses the curatorial challenge of constantly seeking new ways and means of subverting representative monopolisation. We did this by relying on formats and extra-artistic collaborations that were expanded, discursive, performative or intervened in the real.

Subverting Disambiguities

Subverting disambiguities was the theoretical leitmotif and practical challenge for three years of joint curatorial responsibility at Shedhalle, and it is also the point of departure for this publication. The book sees itself as a reflection on those themes, exhibitions and artistic projects we developed between 2009 and 2012, and it also attempts to render in book form the hybrid, heterogeneous and conflictive aspects we gave preference to in our practice.

At the start of our activity we made a case for Shedhalle as a site 'of pausing and interrupting': 'Pausing and interrupting does not mean flight or recreation. It means stopping and temporarily shutting down the performance machine.' Thus, what we meant was something more fundamental than suggested by the buzzword deceleration. This statement made reference both to the long succession of projects and the respective dialogical mode of presentation as well as what were initially apparently very different themes such as ecological aesthetics, which was specifically concerned with landscape or electricity, or the question of the portrayal of history, sleep as a model of resistance, community versus individual and society, media reflection or questions with respect to participation and current feminist practices. This means, for all their diversity, we are basically interested in questions about taking a stand against contexts of neoliberal exploitation (also those that drive the art scene), the foundations of social co-existence, the subtle mechanisms of exclusion and inclusion as well as questions of representation and designing the future. And this also includes devising ways and means through which we can continually question and reflect on ourselves so that we, for our part, do not produce those exclusions that we discursively reject. We solved this by, among other things, seeing ourselves as collaborative accomplices who formed a joint curatorial team despite differing methods and references—and thus had to permanently sound ourselves out.

The themes dealt with in practice and in the present book are a kind of intersection of our subjective 'desires' and priorities, which we believe have social and personal relevance and will meet and challenge the everyday reality of critically minded people. We want to make that visible which is off the beaten track: the remote, suppressed, irrational and that which is on the dark side or traumatically recurs. But also the flip side: the absurd, humorous and cheerful, which can be equally tenacious. Grasping this resistance in things and contexts was and is our declared aesthetic undertaking, not only on a thematic level.

In 2009 we wrote the following: 'In our opinion, developing the necessary tenacity with respect to our ideological patterns means subverting the dual system of disambiguity. It means promoting practices, constellation, and aesthetics that allow for ambiguity or even meaninglessness beyond conventional assignments of meaning. It is about the cultivation of production, which always brings along non/sense. We appeal for a diction that is always a contradiction as well. It is about forms of not understanding, contra/dictions as objections and practices of dissent. These focus on the fact that our culture has problems with differences. It not only has problems conceiving of difference beyond dual hierarchies, but also tries to exaggerate or, conversely, to relativise them. The catchwords are familiar: the clash of cultures or multiculturalism. Our brave new world of consumption and technology furthermore likes to homogenise and simplify materialities and their associated contexts. By allowing the incomprehensible or even disparate with respect to content as well as form, material or scenography, we appeal for an openness in which, by way of constellations and assemblies, possibilities open up and become perceptible that lie beyond social dictates of simplicity—not to make things more complicated, but to render their complexity and thus their tenacity visible. We also achieve this by treating all artistic formats and media equally, such as installations, performances, videos, new media or painting. We seek equivalence, not balance.

'We want to add the dimensions of poetry, mysteriousness, experience, corporeality and paradox to the radical, political and critical facets of Shedhalle, in order to break open the smooth surfaces and allow the intractable to become tangible. We want to introduce a world of nuances and oscillation that enables different spaces for thought and action. This

can occur through interventions, media shifts, aesthetic disruptions, unintelligibilities, mysterious condensations or inconsistencies. It is about saying things again and again, each time in a different way, and finding languages and translations that take account of the small changes and differences in the course of things.'[1]

Thus countering disambiguity does not mean semantic confusion or political indifference, which the ambiguous often proves to be, but the attempt to embrace conflict and create openings. The collision of the different and incongruous blasts the representative and becomes an event, a performative gesture. As such, it remains singular, challenges us in our self-confidence or even jolts us: an aesthetic experience.

Thinking Things from Their Possible End

Between 2009 and 2012 we worked together to organise six thematic group exhibitions as well as various event formats, such as 'Cross-Talks', performances or collaborative projects with people from Zurich.[2] In our final year we wanted to further develop our curatorial approach by means of close co-operations with artists, and so we had sole responsibility for the last two exhibitions. Because we were able to mount the exhibition *Connect. Art between Media and Reality* (2011) in collaboration with the BAK, which was accompanied by a comprehensive catalogue, the present publication documents only seven instead of eight of our exhibition projects.

The chapters reflect our thematic strands—they sometimes deal with several exhibitions, other times only one. The chapters are arranged according to a fixed scheme; our introductory texts are followed by theoretical positions

1 .... Anke Hoffmann and Yvonne Volkart, 'For a Practice of Pausing and Interrupting'. Curatorial Profile 2009–12. www.shedhalle.ch/en/profile.
2 .... There is a complete list of all of the events and participants on page 312.

oder Malerei, gleichrangig behandelt werden. Wir suchen Gleichwertigkeit, nicht Ausgewogenheit.

Wir wollen das Radikale, Politische und Kritische der Shedhalle um die Dimensionen von Poesie, Rätselhaftigkeit, Erfahrung, Körperlichkeit und Paradoxie ergänzen. Um die schönen Oberflächen aufzubrechen und Widerspenstiges erfahrbar zu machen. Wir wollen eine Welt der Zwischentöne und des Oszillierens einführen, die andere Denk- und Handlungsräume ermöglicht. Diese können durch interventionistische Praktiken, mediale Verschiebungen, ästhetische Brüche, Unverständlichkeiten, rätselhafte Verdichtungen und Ungereimtheiten geschehen. Es geht darum, die Dinge immer wieder zu sagen und immer wieder anders zu sagen; Sprachen und Übersetzungen zu finden, die den kleinen Veränderungen und Unterschieden im Lauf der Dinge Rechnung tragen."[1]

Gegen die Eindeutigkeit angehen meint hiermit also nicht semantische Konfusion oder politische Indifferenz, als die sich das Uneindeutige häufig erweist, sondern den Versuch, Konfliktuöses zuzulassen und Öffnungen zu schaffen. Das Zusammenprallen des Differenten und Unpassenden sprengt das Repräsentative und wird Ereignis, performative Geste. Als solche bleibt sie singulär, fordert uns in unseren Selbstsicherheiten heraus oder erschüttert uns gar: ein ästhetisches Erlebnis.

Die Dinge von ihrer Un/Möglichkeit her denken

Zwischen 2009 und 2012 realisierten wir gemeinsam sechs thematische Gruppenausstellungen sowie unterschiedliche Veranstaltungsformate, wie CrossTalks, Performances oder kollaborative Projekte mit Menschen aus Zürich.[2] In unserem letzten Jahr wollten wir unseren kuratorischen Ansatz mittels einer engen Zusammenarbeit mit Künstler_innen

1............... Hoffmann, Anke/Volkart, Yvonne: Für eine Praxis des Innehaltens und Unterbrechens. Kuratorisches Profil 2009–12. www.shedhalle.ch/de/profil.
2............... Die gesamte Liste aller Veranstaltungen und Beteiligten befindet sich auf S. 312.

weiterentwickeln und so haben wir die letzten beiden Ausstellungen in jeweiliger Alleinregie verantwortet. Da wir die Ausstellung *Connect. Kunst zwischen Medien und Wirklichkeit* (2011) in Zusammenarbeit mit dem BAK machen konnten und sich daraus ein umfangreicher Katalog ergab, sind im vorliegenden Buch statt acht nur sieben unserer Ausstellungsprojekte dokumentiert. Die Kapitel geben unsere thematischen Stränge wieder, manchmal geht es um mehrere Ausstellungen, manchmal nur um eine. Der Kapitelaufbau verläuft nach einem feststehenden Schema: Auf unsere Einführungstexte folgen theoretische Positionen von Menschen, die uns bei der Realisation der Projekte begleitet haben. Künstlerseiten von ausgewählten Künstler_innen, Interviews, Statements oder Manuskripte aus den jeweiligen Projekten erweitern den Einblick in die vergangenen Projekte und ihre Heterogenität. Die langen Beiträge sind zweisprachig, die kurzen Deutsch oder Englisch. Dieser aus praktischen Erwägungen gezogene Entschluss betont das Vielsprachige und Multi-Perspektivische, das unsere Arbeitsweise so sehr geprägt hat.

Das Kapitel *Innehalten und Unterbrechen* liefert den programmatischen Auftakt für unser Anliegen, in welchem uns stets die nicht offensichtlichen, sich entziehenden und unbeachteten Formen des Widerständigen interessieren. Ausgehend von unserer Ausstellung *Dump Time. Für eine Praxis des Horizontalen* eröffnen wir mit der Frage, ob der Schlaf in unserer 24-Stunden-Gesellschaft, insofern er eine der letzten Möglichkeiten bewusstloser Auszeit, Nichtstun und Hingabe ist, nicht widerständige Momente birgt? Philosophisch eingebettet wird diese Diskussion durch Alexei Penzins Beitrag, in welchem die historischen und biopolitischen Implikationen des Schlafs im Kapitalismus und davor untersucht und auf die Frage des Widerständigen hin eröffnet werden.

Im Kapitel *Wie Kunst Geschichte schreibt* versuchen wir, den unterschiedlichen Aufschreibesystemen bzw. künstlerischen Darstellungen des Historischen auf den Grund zu gehen. Bezugnehmend auf unsere Ausstellung *Überblendungen. Das Zukünftige rekonstruieren* stellen wir künstlerische

Praktiken qua ihres non-narrativen, fragmentarischen, a-linearen und anti-heroischen Charakters als notwendiges Umschreiben historischer Bewusstseinsbildung heraus. Ute Vorkoeper plädiert dabei für Darstellungsformen, die statt einer simplen Rekonstruktion eine Aktualisierung und Auslegung des Vergangenen ermöglichen.

Das Kapitel *Ökologiken* versteht sich als Plädoyer für einen politischen Begriff des Ökologischen, das Fragen nach unserer Lebensweise und Umwelt grundsätzlich, weder nostalgisch noch sentimental fasst. Kunst kann, muss Dinge sichtbar machen, ein Punkt, der gerade im Bereich dieser so stark von Naturwissenschaften dominierten Auseinandersetzung ungleich an Gewicht gewinnt und ein erster Schritt dafür sein kann, dass uns bestehende Ungerechtigkeiten und Ausbeutungsverhältnisse auf ganz neue Weise bewusst werden und sich somit ändern liessen. Mit Bezug auf scheinbare Selbstverständlichkeiten wie Landschaft oder Strom wird der Virulenz solcher Fragen nachgegangen.

Un/Mögliche Gemeinschaft heisst das vierte Kapitel und trägt damit denselben Titel wie das Projekt, mit dem wir an der Shedhalle zu arbeiten begannen. Die Idee zum Projekt entstand aus einem Vorschlag von Elke Bippus und fand bei uns angesichts der damals schwierigen, von Finanzkrise, Verunsicherung und Wut gezeichneten Zeit und der Frage nach Solidarität begeisterten Widerhall. In ihrem Essay nun wendet Elke Bippus die Frage nach der Gemeinschaft auf das an Orten wie der Shedhalle so oft diskutierte Verhältnis von Theorie- und Kunstproduktion an. Sie versteht es als un/mögliche Gemeinschaft in einem philosophischen Sinn. Es gehe um ein ‚Mit' von Theorie und Praxis, um ihr Werden, das so wie die Entstehung von Gemeinschaften oder ästhetischer Erfahrungen ausserhalb konventioneller Signifikation verläuft. Der paradoxe Begriff der Un/Möglichkeit ist dabei für uns bis heute ein zentraler Begriff für unser Kuratieren geblieben, trägt er doch die Anlage des Möglichwerdens im Kern mit sich und schreibt doch nichts fest.

Das letzte Kapitel ist eine Konklusion und ein Ausblick: *Durchspielen und Eröffnen*. Im Vordergrund stehen künstlerische Projekte, die das Soziale, das Gemeinschaftliche, aber auch die Verhandlung von Identifikation und Selbstreflexion sowie performative und ereignishafte Strategien bevorzugen. Die unser Buch abschliessenden Essays von Rachel Mader und Gerald Raunig nehmen die Frage nach dem Sprengen der Eindeutigkeiten nochmals auf. Obwohl beide recht unterschiedliche künstlerische Praktiken im Auge haben und auch unterschiedlich argumentieren – Rachel Mader für temporäre Offenheiten, Gerald Raunig für eine Eindeutigkeit als Sigularität, die über Verkettung der Vielheit etwas hinzufüge, plädieren doch beide für Ästhetiken und Praktiken, die gängige Definitionsmuster sprengen. Viele der in diesem Kapitel verhandelten Projekte bestechen dadurch, dass sie statt über Intellekt und Logos über hybride soziale Konstellationen, Körperpraktiken wie Tanz, Bewegung und Gesang sowie Inszenierungen und einander erzählte Geschichten und Fantasien verlaufen. Sie leiten dadurch nicht nur vielfältige Bedeutungsprozesse in die Wege, sondern fächern auch die Grenzen von Theorie und Praxis, Diskussion und Inszenierung, Artefakt und dialogischer Prozess neu auf. Das Format Ausstellung und die Dinge, die darin geschehen, werden zu einem übergreifenden Ereignis, das ästhetische Erfahrung und Kritik verbindet. Damit möchten wir das Feld eröffnen, zur Reflexion, zum Gespräch und zum Weitermachen, an einem Ort wie der Shedhalle, diesem einen Ort, der immer zugleich viele war.

by people who accompanied the realisation of the projects. Artists' pages by selected artists, in interviews, statements or manuscripts from the respective projects heighten insight into past projects and their heterogeneity. The long contributions are in both German and English, the short ones in only one language or the other. The decision to do this was based on practical considerations and emphasises the multilingual and multiperspectival qualities that had such a major influence on our work.

The chapter *Pausing and Interrupting* supplies the programmatic prelude for our concern, in which we are always interested in the inapparent, elusive and unnoticed forms of the intractable. Based on our exhibition *Dump Time. For a Practice of Horizontality,* we start off with the question of whether in our 24-hour society sleep does not harbour intractable elements, inasmuch as it is one of the last possibilities for conscious time out, idleness and devotion. Alexei Penzin's contribution embeds this discussion in philosophy. He examines the historical and biopolitical implications of sleep in capitalism and prior to that, and opens them up for scrutiny in terms of intractability.

In the chapter *How Art Writes History* we attempt to get to the bottom of the different historiographies and the artistic depiction of the historical. Making reference to our exhibition *Cross-fades. Reconstructing the Future,* as being of a non-narrative, fragmentary, non-linear and antiheroic character, we expose artistic practices as a necessary rewriting of historical consciousness formation. Ute Vorkoeper makes a case for forms of representation that enable the updating and interpretation of the past instead of its simple reconstruction.

The chapter *Ecologics* sees itself as an appeal for a political concept of the ecological that essentially does not grasp questions with respect to our way of life and environment either nostalgically or sentimentally. Art can—must—make things visible, a point that gains disproportionate importance precisely in this discussion, which is so strongly dominated by the natural sciences, and can be a first step in the direction of our becoming aware of existing injustices and relations of exploitation in a completely new way and thus change them. The virulence of such questions is pursued based on apparent matters of course such as landscapes or electricity.

Im/Possible Community is the title of the fourth chapter and thus bears the name of the project with which we commenced our work at Shedhalle. Elke Bippus suggested the idea for the project, and it met with our enthusiastic response in view of the difficult period at the time—marked by the financial crisis, insecurity and rage—and the question of solidarity. In her essay, Elke Bippus applies the question of community to the relation between the production of theory and art that is so often discussed at places such as Shedhalle. It is about the alliance of theory and practice, and about their becoming, which, like the development of communities or aesthetic experiences, takes place outside conventional signification. In doing so, for us the paradoxical term of im/possibility has continued to remain a central concept for our curatorial activity as it essentially bears the disposition of becoming possible and yet does not stipulate anything.

The final chapter is a conclusion and outlook: *Acting Out and Opening Up.* It focuses on artistic practices that give priority to the social and communal, but also deals with identification and self-reflection as well as performative and eventful strategies. The concluding essays in our book by Rachel Mader and Gerald Raunig again take up the question with respect to subverting disambiguities. Although both of them have very different artistic practices in mind and present different arguments—Rachel Mader for temporary openness and Gerald Raunig for a disambiguity that adds something to multiplicity—both of them make a case for aesthetics and practices that force open conventional definition patterns. Many of the projects dealt with in this chapter stand out due to the fact that they proceed by way of hybrid social constellations, physical practices such as dance, movement, and singing, as well

as productions, fantasies and stories that have
been told one another instead of conveyed
by way of the intellect and logic. In doing so, they
do not only initiate a variety of processes of
meaning but once again also expand the boundaries between theory and practice, discussion
and production, artefact and dialogical
process. The exhibition format and the things
that occur there become an all-embracing
event that combines aesthetic experience and
criticism. Hence, we would like to open up the
field for reflection, discussion and carrying on at
a site like Shedhalle, this place that was always
many venues simultaneously.

Translated by Rebecca van Dyck

1

INNEHALTEN UND UNTERBRECHEN
PAUSING AND INTERRUPTING

Dump Time (Ausstellungsansicht / Exhibition view)
Vorne / Front: Igor und / and Ivan Buharov: Selection of short films
Links hinten / Back left: Alex Antener: *Ich denke, das bin ich*, 2005/2011
Rechts hinten / Back right: Factory of Found Clothes/Gluklya: *Utopian Unemployment Union N1*, 2009

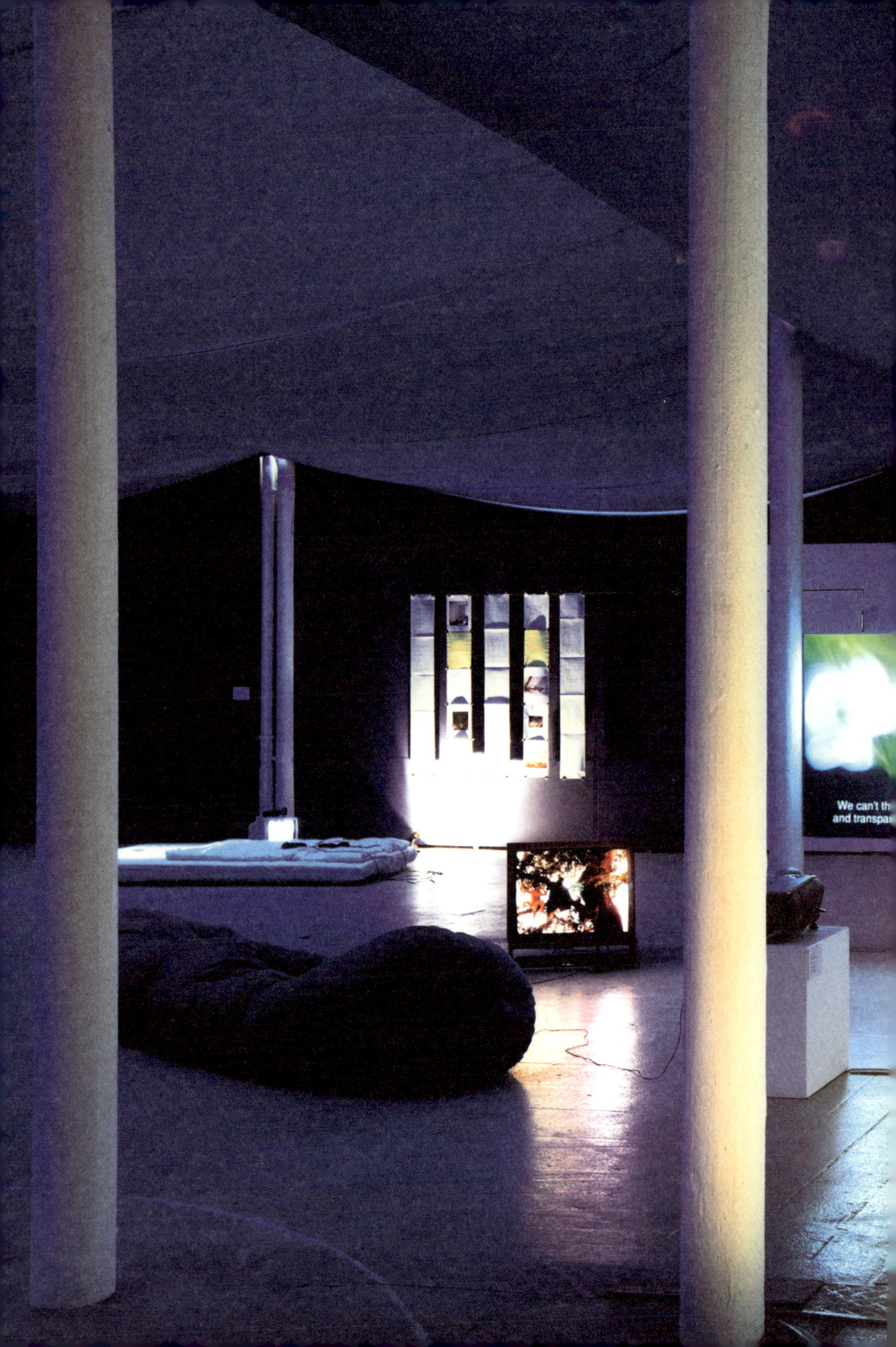
We can't th
and transpa

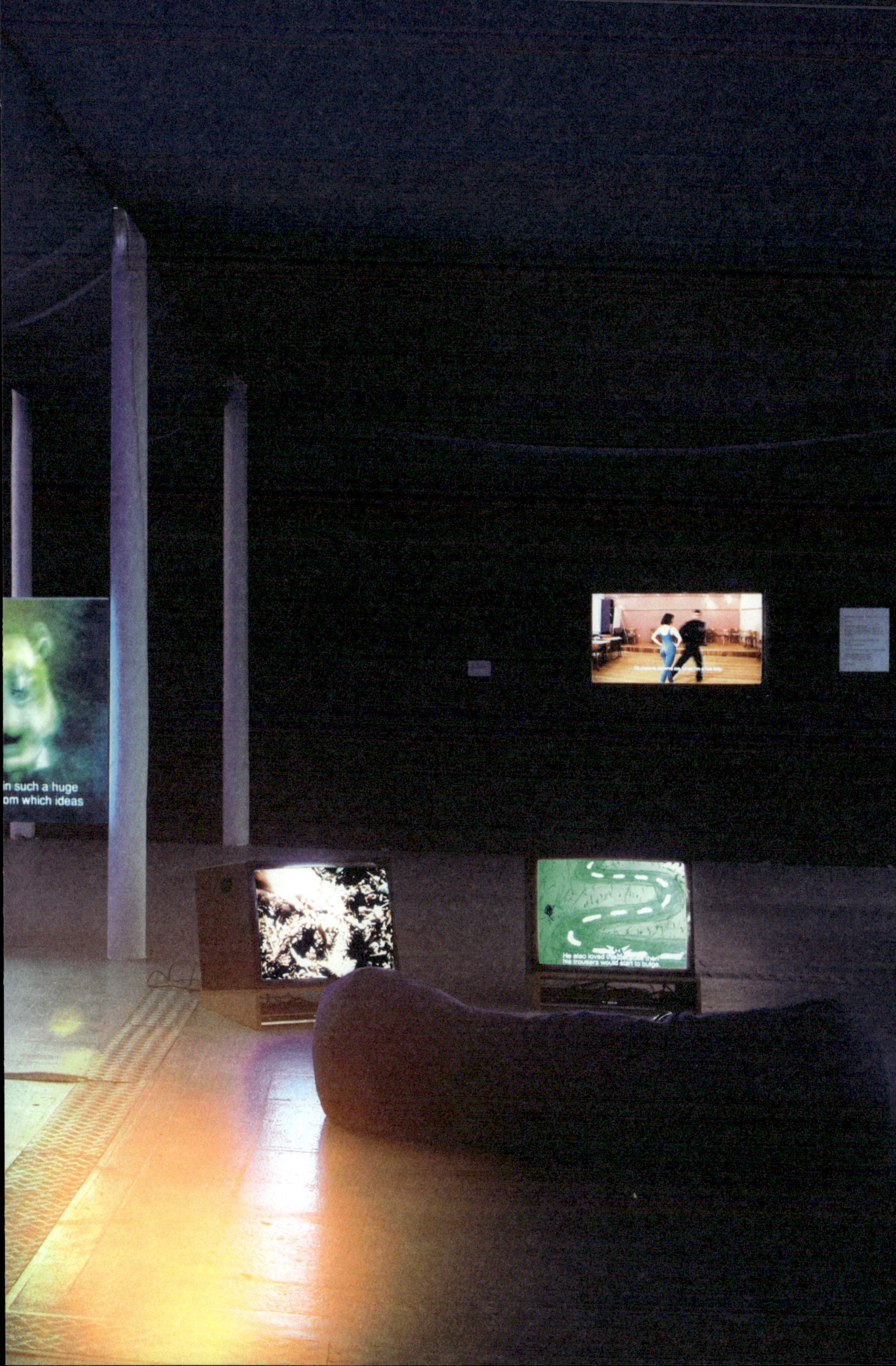
in such a huge
om which ideas
He also loved the idea that
his trousers would start to bulge

ANKE HOFFMANN, YVONNE VOLKART

DUMP TIME. FÜR EINE PRAXIS DES HORIZONTALEN

DUMP TIME. FOR A PRACTICE OF HORIZONTALITY

> Die Erschöpfungsmüdigkeit ist eine Müdigkeit der positiven Potenz. Sie macht unfähig, *etwas* zu tun. Die Müdigkeit, die inspiriert, ist eine *Müdigkeit der negativen Potenz*, nämlich des *nicht-zu*. […] Heilig ist also nicht der Tag des *um-zu,* sondern der Tag des *nicht-zu,* ein Tag, an dem der Gebrauch des Unbrauchbaren möglich wäre. Es ist der Tag der Müdigkeit.
>
> (Byung-Chul Han, *Müdigkeitsgesellschaft*)

Wir sind eine schlaflose Gesellschaft geworden. Viele können nicht schlafen, denn unaufhörlich rattert es im Kopf, lässt sich die ‚Maschine' nicht abstellen. Viele wollen nicht schlafen, weil es so Wichtiges zu tun oder erleben gibt. Drogen helfen mitunter, den Schlaf zu besiegen. Forschungsberichte halten fest, dass noch nie so wenig geschlafen wurde wie heute. Die Industrialisierung und heute potenzierter die Netzgesellschaft führten dazu, dass sich Tag und Nacht immer mehr angleichen. Gleichzeitig existiert ein Muss zum Schlaf. Nichts erscheint beängstigender als das nächtens ruhelose Umherwandeln. Wenn der Schlaf sich nicht einstellen will, wird er medikamentös erzwungen, damit man endlich ausruhen und abtauchen kann ins dunkle Vergessen.

In unserer Vorstellung ist der Schlaf das Gegenkonzept zum Wachzustand, zum Tätigsein. Er ist bewusstlose Auszeit, in der der Mensch nichts tut, in Träume abdriftet, in andere Welten und Zeiten, sich verwandelt. Die Erlebnisse der Nacht lassen wir gewöhnlich am Morgen hinter uns, stehen auf, als ob nichts gewesen wäre. Auch das Erwachen ist ein Vergessen, oder denken wir an die Psychoanalyse, ein Verdrängen, so wie der Schlaf auf andere Weise ein Vergessen ist. Im Schlaf sind wir da und doch nicht da. Schlaf und Traum bergen unheimliche Dimensionen, denn es geht um (Kontroll-)Verluste, um Hingabe, um ein Anders-Werden. Da, wo es um diese entsubjektivierenden Momente und um den Verlust von Kontrolle und Individualität geht, ist der Schlaf anderen Phänomenen wie dem Rausch, der

Fatigue from exhaustion is a fatigue of positive potentiality. It makes somebody incapable of doing 'something'. Inspiring fatigue is a fatigue of negative potentiality, a fatigue of 'not-to'. […] Thus, a day of 'to-do' is no holy day, holy is the day of 'not-to', a day that makes the use of the useless possible. It is the day of fatigue.
(Byung-Chul Han, *Müdigkeitsgesellschaft*)

We have become a sleepless society. Many cannot find any sleep because 'the machine' cannot be turned off, because there is something constantly clattering in their heads. Many do not want to sleep because there are so many important things to do or to experience or to witness. Sometimes, drugs will help to overcome fatigue, to defeat sleep. Research shows that people never slept as little as they do today. Industrialisation and, even more so, today's world wide web are the causes that there is hardly any difference between day and night. At the same time, sleep is a must. Nothing seems more alarming than having to wander about all night. If sleep does not come, we take drugs to be able to get some rest, to abandon ourselves to oblivion.

The idea of sleep, to us, represents the other side, the dark side of daytime with its ratio, activities and economics. Sleep is unconscious time out, we remain inactive while we are asleep, we drift away into our dreams, into different worlds and times, we turn into different beings. In the morning, we usually leave behind what we experienced during the night, get up as if nothing had happened. Awakening, too, is a kind of forgetting, or, thinking of psychoanalysis, repressing, just like sleep, though in a different way. While sleeping, we are present and not present at the same time. Sleeping and dreaming have uncanny dimensions, involving the loss of control, abandon and changing into somebody else. Where sleep involves these de-subjectivizing moments and the loss of control and

individuality, it resembles phenomena like death, frenzy, hallucination or trance. Sleep makes you think of death, of passages, of thresholds. With these archaic and mythic dimensions, sleep represents something totally different from today's world, which is always experienced as geared by political activity and subjective agency. It is something horizontal; it rejects our projections of the subject as a standing vertical 'man', like a rock. How can sleepers and slackers change the world? We are consciously alive only when we are awake in an alert world which is our social world, a common and shared world which we must not give up, or as Elisabeth Bronfen says: 'But we have to go through the night in order to wake up into another day, a day that, because of this experience, is different.'[1]

It was this dimension of un-productivity, un-consciousness and in-sanity in the literal sense that is so characteristic of sleep that interested us in our exhibition *Dump Time.* While asleep, the ego cannot be captured; it has slipped away. Even the power nap involves moments of no control. Sleep, dreams and intoxication involve moments of resistance; a form of resistance, however, that is passively structured and char-acterised by the suspension, the withdrawal of or the non-compliance with certain rules and regulations rather than characterised by revolt.

Sleep, dreams and frenzy became virulent in art, whenever artists were looking for an aesthetics opposed to rationalism. Surrealism tried to bring the passive and mysterious categories of sleep, dreams and frenzy to fruition, aestheti-cally as well as politically. Walter Benjamin, e.g., summarised the aesthetics of surrealism the following way: 'The aim of surrealism, in all its books and endeavours, was to win the forces of frenzy for the revolution.'[2] Whenever he went to bed in the morning, wanting not to be disturbed, the poet Saint-Pol-Roux wrote 'Le poète traivaille' on his bedroom door.

1 ...... Elisabeth Bronfen, *Tiefer als der Tag gedacht. Eine Kulturge-schichte der Nacht* (München, 2008), p. 176. [transl. by I. Fichtner]
2 ..... Walter Benjamin, Der Sürrealismus. Letzte Momentaufnahme der eurpäischen Intelligenz. In the following quoted online: www.culture.hu-berlin.de/hb/files/Benjamin_Der_Surrealismus.pdf.

This anecdote mentioned by Walter Benjamin is interesting in two ways. On the one hand, it refers to the modern way of thinking that an artist needs to be in some kind of a 'different' state, that creativity depends on having a time out, on getting rid of the troubles of work life and that the artist, in order to become creative and visionary, needs a special susceptibility and passivity which can, e.g., be found in sleep. On the other hand, it involves the bourgeois concept of work. Declaring himself—the unproductive, sleeping artist recharging his batteries—as a working artist (and not a slacker), he superficially adopts the ideology of bourgeois industriousness and constant industrial productivity, but reduces it to absurdity at the same time.

Taking such concepts into account, the project *Dump Time* investigated how sleep is being experienced and artistically represented today, in a society that is called a sleepless or 24-hour-society. What does an aesthetics of sleep look like today? Does it have a decelerating function and how could it be classified? Is it still a valid category of resistance or utopia?

It is not by chance that the first work displayed in the exhibition was *Artist at Work* (see p. 46) by Mladen Stilinović from Croatia. The work represents the artist's attitude, an active individual refusal of permanent production, which the artist committed himself to as his manifesto *Praise of Laziness* from 1993 repeatedly states.

Eiko Grimberg's reflections of the sleeping *Madwoman in the Attic* (fig. p. 25) also studies an attitude of refusal: it is the historical case of a woman's unconscious and passive withdrawal into an illness which today would probably be diagnosed as hysteria and depression. Stefan Panhans' figure in *If a Store Clerk Gave Me too Much Change* (see p. 52) is 'obsessed' in a different and yet similar way, staged as human maggot waiting for its pupation and trying, through endless mantras, to improve its achievement potential and psychological self-optimisation. In *Sleepers* (fig. p. 25), showing stranded passengers of budget airlines on their way to the next spectacle of distraction, Johanna

Domke proved that the life strategies mentioned above and the ever-present challenge of 'higher-faster-better' are extremely fatiguing.

Overfatigue and drifting between being asleep and being awake, however, can also trigger reveries and utopias which artists have been using and trying to evoke for a long time. The short films by the Hungarian artists Igor and Ivan Buharov (see p. 48) present such dreamlike stories; partly children's dream, partly surrealistic fables, they take the viewer to a world full of absurd encounters. Dreams can be manifestations of our hidden fears, desires and doubts; they show us our anxieties and thus often remain invisible and unspoken of. Russian artist Gluklya (part of the artist duo Factory of Found Clothes) investigated two such aspects that usually remain invisible, working together with asylum-seekers from Zurich in her dance performance *Dumped Dreams* (see p. 298). Alex Antener, a young artist from Zurich, also investigated the dream and its mysteries in his installation *Ich denke, das bin ich* (I think, this is me) (fig. p. 20). The artist himself plays the role of a test person, researcher, analyst and provider of artistic ideas, thus rendering the scientific utilisation of sleep absurd. Artist Cristina David from Bucharest also made herself the subject of her research project and lived in a different time for a whole month: in astronomical time. Here, the hourly difference is corrected by the leap year once every four years. So, for a whole month, she was awake at a time when everybody else was asleep. She presented her forays against rationalism in an installation titled *Time Travel Diary* (fig. p. 26).

Anna Zaradny from Warsaw also investigated phenomena of shifts in time and changes of perception. Her installation *PASS/ED* (fig. p. 26), a composition of sound arrangements and a 4-channel-video, overwhelms the viewers with its visual and acoustic frenzy and takes them to some trance-like threshold between the conscious and the unconscious.

The fact that the whole exhibition could be experienced as a passage and an invitation to some deceleration was stressed by the

Eiko Grimberg: *Madwoman in the Attic*, 2006

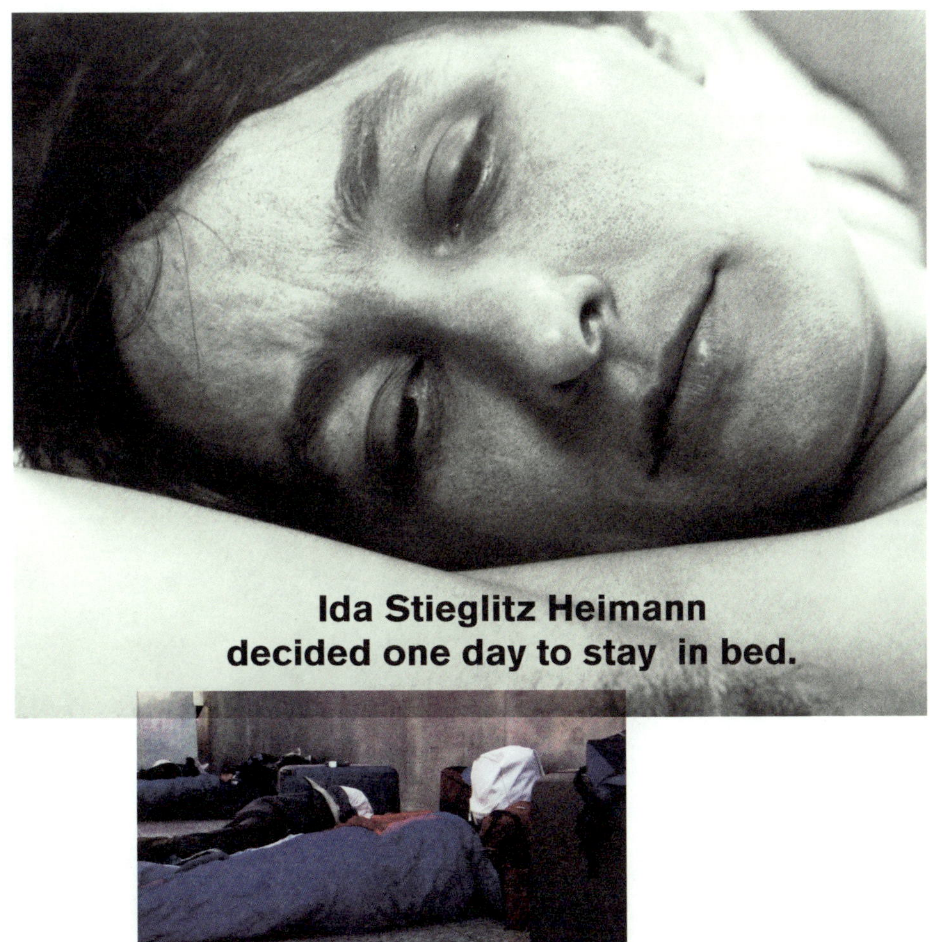

Johanna Domke: *Sleepers*, 2007

Anna Zaradny: *PASS / ED*, 2009/2010
(Ausstellungsansicht / Exhibition view)

Petra Elena Köhle/Nicolas Vermot Petit-Outhenin:
Kunst-Luftschutz-Massnahme, 2011
(Ausstellungsansicht / Exhibition view)

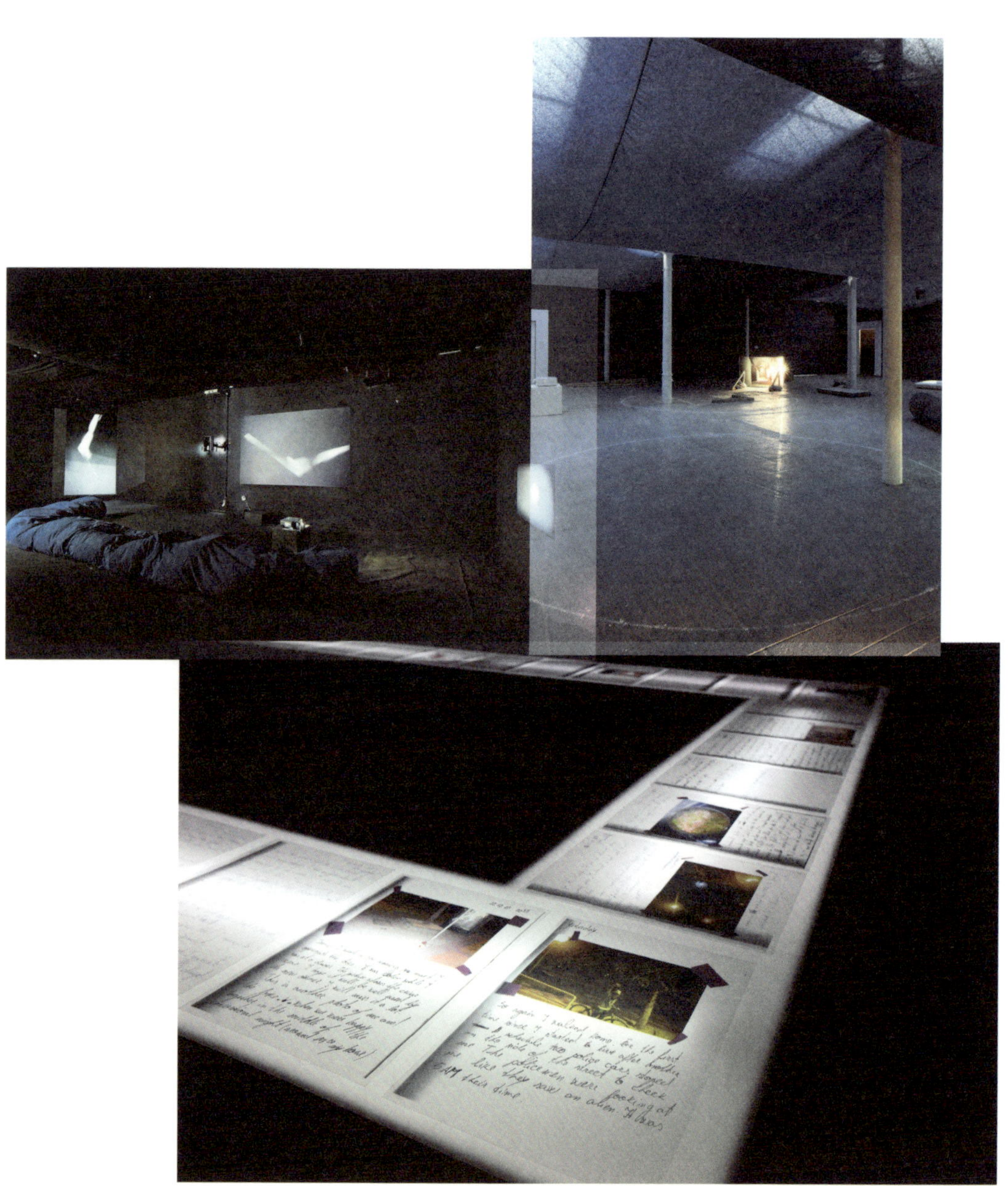

Cristina David: *Time Travel Diary*, 2010/2011 (Ausstellungsansicht / Exhibition view)

Ekstase, der Halluzination oder der Trance verwandt. Der Schlaf erinnert an den Tod, an Passagen, an Schwellen. Er hat archaische und mythische Dimension – und ist deswegen dem modernen Denken diametral entgegengesetzt: nicht nur zu Tätigkeit und Fleiss, sondern auch zur Vorstellung von politischer Aktivität und subjektiver Handlungsmacht. Wie könnten Schläfer_innen und Faulpelze unsere Welt ändern? Denn bewusst leben wir nur in der wachen Welt; nur diese ist die soziale Welt, die geteilte und gemeinschaftliche Welt, die wir nicht aufgeben dürfen, oder wie es Elisabeth Bronfen formuliert: „Aber wir müssen auch durch die Nacht hindurch, um in einen Tag, der aufgrund dieser Erfahrung verändert ist, aufzuwachen."[1]

Es ist diese nutzlose, bewusstlose und im wahrsten Sinn des Wortes ver-rückte Dimension des Schlafs und ihr Hineinwirken in den Tag, die uns für die Ausstellung *Dump Time* interessierte. Das Ich im Schlaf lässt sich nicht vereinnahmen, denn es ist weggeglitten; sogar der Powernap birgt unkontrollierte Momente. Insofern bergen Schlaf, Traum und Rausch widerständige Momente; eine Form von Widerständigkeit jedoch, die passiv strukturiert ist und sich eher durch das Aussetzen, den Entzug oder das Nicht-Einhalten bestimmter Regelwerke als durch Revolte auszeichnet.

Schlaf, Traum und Rausch in der Kunst wurden immer dann virulent, wenn es um den Entwurf einer Gegenästhetik zum Rationalismus ging. Der Surrealismus versuchte, die passiven und geheimnisvollen Kategorien von Schlaf, Traum und Rausch ästhetisch und politisch fruchtbar zu machen. „Die Kräfte des Rausches für die Revolution zu gewinnen, darum kreist der Sürrealismus in allen Büchern und Unternehmen"[2], resümierte Walter Benjamin die surrealistische Ästhetik. „Le poète travaille", schrieb der Dichter Saint-Pol-Roux an seine Schlafzimmertüre, wenn er sich morgens schlafen legte und nicht gestört werden wollte. Diese von Walter Benjamin erwähnte

Anekdote ist aus zweifacher Perspektive interessant: Einerseits spielt sie mit der modernen Vorstellung, dass das Künstlerdasein anderer Zustände bedürfe, dass Kreativität sich erst in der Auszeit zu den Mühen des Arbeitslebens einstellt, dass es, um visionär zu sein, einer Empfänglichkeit und Passivität bedürfe, wie sie exemplarisch im Schlaf zu finden ist. Andererseits wird gerade hier mit der bürgerlichen Vorstellung von Arbeit gespielt. Indem der schlafende, Kräfte tankende, im Moment gerade nichts leistende Künstler als ein Arbeitender (und nicht ein Faulpelz) benannt wird, übernimmt er vordergründig die Ideologie bürgerlichen Fleisses und industrieller Produktivität, die unablässig produziert, und führt sie doch ad absurdum.

Bezug nehmend auf solche Konzepte ging das Projekt *Dump Time* der Frage nach, wie der Schlaf heute erfahren und künstlerisch adäquat dargestellt wird, in einer Gesellschaft, die mittlerweile gerne als schlaflose oder 24-Stunden-Gesellschaft benannt wird. Wie sieht eine Ästhetik des Schlafs heute aus? Wie wäre ihre entschleunigende Funktion zu werten? Hat sie als widerständige oder utopische Kategorie noch Gültigkeit?

Die Ausstellung begann nicht zufällig mit der Arbeit des kroatischen Künstlers Mladen Stilinović *Artist at Work* (vgl. S. 46) von 1973. Sie beschreibt die Haltung einer individuell-aktiven Verweigerung zur permanenten Produktion, der sich der Künstler in seinem Manifest *Praise of Laziness* wiederholt 1993 verschrieben hat. Auch Eiko Grimbergs Reflexion der Schlafenden in *Madwoman in the Attic* (Abb. S. 25) untersucht eine Verweigerungshaltung: den historisch weit zurückliegenden Fall einer Frau, die sich unbewusst-passiv in den Status der Krankheit zurückzieht und heute mit den Diagnosen von Hysterie und Depression seine Erklärung findet. Anders und dennoch ähnlich ‚besessen' ist die Figur in Stefan Panhans *If a Store Clerk Gave Me too Much Change* (vgl. S. 52), die, als menschliche Made inszeniert, ihrer Verpuppung in endlosen Mantras der psychologischen Selbstoptimierung und Leistungspotenzierung harrt. Dass diese zitierten Lebensstrategien und das Höher-Schneller-

---

1 .... Bronfen, Elisabeth: *Tiefer als der Tag gedacht. Eine Kulturgeschichte der Nacht.* München 2008, 176.
2 .... Benjamin, Walter: Der Sürrealismus. Letzte Momentaufnahme der eurpäischen Intelligenz. Im Folgenden zitiert online: www.culture.hu-berlin.de/hb/files/Benjamin_Der_Surrealismus.pdf.

Weiter selbst extrem ermüdend sind, zeigte Johanna Domke in *Sleepers* (Abb. S. 25), mit gestrandeten Passagieren von Billigfluglinien auf dem Weg zum nächsten Ablenkungsspektakel.

Aber Übermüdung und das Driften zwischen Wach- und Schlafzustand setzen gerade auch Fantasien und Utopien frei, die Künstler schon lange zu nutzen oder zu evozieren versuchten. Die Kurz-Filme der ungarischen Künstler Igor und Ivan Buharov (vgl. S. 48) sind solche träumerischen Geschichten, die, halb Kinderträume, halb surrealistische Fabeln, in eine Welt voller absurder Begegnungen führen. Träume sind Ausdruck unserer verborgenen Ängste, Wünsche und Zweifel, sie bringen zu Tage, womit wir uns quälen und bleiben, eben darum, zumeist unausgesprochen und unsichtbar. Zweierlei Unsichtbarkeiten widmete sich die russische Künstlerin Gluklya, Teil des Künstlerduos Factory of Found Clothes, als sie im Workshop *Dumped Dreams* (vgl. S. 298) daran ging, die Träume von und mit Asylbewerber_innen aus Zürich tänzerisch-performativ zu erarbeiten. Dem Traum und seinen verborgenen Geheimnissen widmet sich auch der junge Zürcher Alex Antener mit seiner Installation *Ich denke, das bin ich* (Abb. S. 20), in der sich der Künstler selbst in die Rollen von Proband, Forscher, Analytiker und künstlerischem Ideengeber begibt und so die wissenschaftliche Verwertung des Schlafes ad absurdum führt. Die Künstlerin Cristina David aus Bukarest unternahm ebenfalls ein Forschungsprojekt an sich selbst und lebte für einen Monat nach einer anderen Zeit, der astronomischen, deren stündliche Verschiebung mit dem alle vier Jahre stattfindenden Schaltjahr wieder auskorrigiert wird – und wachte folglich, wenn alle anderen schliefen. Über ihre Streifzüge gegen den Rationalismusapparat berichtete sie in einer Installation mit dem Titel *Time Travel Diary*, auf der Basis eines Tagebuchs (Abb. S. 26). Anna Zaradny aus Warschau arbeitet an den Phänomenen solch einer zeitlich-sinnlichen Verschiebung. In ihrer Rauminstallation *PASS|ED* (Abb. S. 26) aus komponierter Soundebene und 4-Kanal-Video begeben sich die Besucher_innen in einen Rhythmus von visuell-akustischer Trance, einem rauschhaften Schwellenzustand ins Bewusst-Unbewusste.

Dass die Ausstellung selbst als Schwellengang erfahrbar wurde und zu einer Entschleunigung einlud, wurde mit einer Rauminszenierung realisiert, die wir in Zusammenarbeit mit den Techniker_innen der Shedhalle erarbeitet hatten. Eröffnet wurde die Ausstellung *Dump Time* mit der Sound-Video-Performance *Pink Noise/ Fishing for Sound* (Abb. S. 314) der holländischen Soundartistin Yolande Harris. Sie verbindet Fragmente einer Psychotherapie mit Tönen, die aus der Tiefe des Meeres stammen, zu einem traumhaften Gewebe, das uns normalerweise verschlossen bleibt. Den Bogen zurück zum Bruch mit der Ökonomie der permanenten Produktion schlugen Petra Köhle und Nicolas Vermont Petit-Outhenin. Das Künstler_innenpaar aus Zürich erarbeitete auf Einladung der Shedhalle eine Rauminstallation, *Kunst-Luftschutz-Massnahme* (Abb. S. 26), deren Mittelpunkt ein historisches Foto ist, welches die Schutz-Betonverschalung eines Kunstwerkes in der Florentiner Akademie zur Zeit des Zweiten Weltkrieges zeigt. Der erzwungene ‚Tiefschlaf der Kunst' wird in einer räumlichen Auslegeordnung mit verschiedenen Materialien verdoppelt und fragmentiert.

Wie Psychoanalytiker_innen nähern sich die Künstler_innen diesem längst vergangenen ‚Traumbild einer Rettung' und versuchen, die Beschaffenheit einzelner Teile als Knotenpunkte versteckter Bedeutungen zu entziffern.

multidimensional exhibition design the curators had staged in collaboration with the Shedhalle technicians. The exhibition *Dump Time* was declared open with a sound-video-performance by Yolande Harris from Holland, *Pink Noise/ Fishing for Sounds* (fig. p. 314). This installation turned excerpts of psychotherapeutic sessions and sounds from the depth of the ocean into a dreamlike fabric which we usually do not encounter. Petra Köhle and Nicolas Vermont, on the other hand, brought the audience back into the world and economy of permanent production. Shedhalle had invited the artist duo from Zurich to present an installation, *Kunst-Luftschutz-Massnahme* (Art Air Raid Protection Measure) (fig. p. 26), with a historic photograph in the centre showing the concrete formwork protecting a work of art in the Academy of Fine Arts in Florence during WW II. In this installation, the 'deep sleep enforced upon art' is fragmented and doubled by diverse materials. Like psychoanalysts, the artists approach this 'oneiric image' of a rescue, trying to decipher the nature of single parts as nodal points of hidden meanings.

Translated by Ingrid Fichtner

SCHLAF, KAPITALISMUS UND SUBJEKTIVITÄT[1]
SLEEP, CAPITALISM AND SUBJECTIVITY[1]

1.

In der Erforschung der Physiologie und Neurologie des Schlafs verzeichnen Medizin und Biologie heute ausserordentliche Fortschritte, und die daraus resultierende Medikalisierung von Schlafstörungen ist eines der neuen Gebiete der Akkumulation von ‚Biokapital'. Zugleich erklärt unsere ‚24-Stunden-Gesellschaft', die ständig produzieren, kommunizieren und konsumieren muss, den Schlaf zu einem problematischen, unsicheren Element unseres Alltags, zu vergeudeter Zeit oder einem Zeichen von Trägheit in einer mobilen und pragmatisch neoliberalen Gesellschaft, die vom Gedanken des vollen Ausschöpfens der endlichen menschlichen Existenz besessen ist.

Ich möchte hier nur einige Beispiele aus dem gegenwärtigen populären Diskurs anführen, welche die dem Schlaf in letzter Zeit erneut geschenkte Aufmerksamkeit illustrieren. Margaret Thatcher, die ehemalige britische Premierministerin, ist nicht nur dafür berühmt, dass sie das neoliberale Motto ‚etwas wie Gesellschaft gibt es nicht' geprägt hat, sie war auch eine Person, die sehr wenig Schlaf brauchte – nur vier Stunden etwa, und vielleicht hielt sie ja zuviel Schlaf für etwas dem Wirtschaftswachstum Abträgliches. Solche Haltungen und ihre politischen Implikationen werden sehr unterhaltsam in einem britischen Roman gespiegelt, der die enthusiastische Gemeinde der Schlafforscher_innen und ihre hitzigen Debatten wie folgt beschreibt:

„‚Aber warum ihn verachten? Was meinst du?'
‚Schau: Wer schläft ist hilflos; im Schlaf ist jeder machtlos. Der Schlaf liefert sogar die Stärksten den Schwächsten und Unfähigsten aus. Stell dir vor, wie schlimm es für jemanden wie Margaret Thatcher, mit ihrer moralischen Einstellung, sein muss, sich tagtäglich diesem erbärmlichen Zustand überlassen zu müssen, in dem das Gehirn ausgeschaltet ist und die Muskeln träg und schlaff sind? Es muss unerträglich sein.'

1 .... Dieser Essay basiert auf einem Vortrag, den ich am 30. März 2011 in der Shedhalle Zürich hielt und der einen kurzen Einblick in mein Projekt zur Erforschung der philosophischen und politischen Anthropologie des Schlafes und des Wachzustands gibt. (Arbeitstitel: *Rex Exsomnis. Towards a Political Economy of Sleep*).

1.

Today, biology and medical sciences are highly advanced in terms of the physiology and neurology of sleep, and the emerging medicalisation of sleep disorders is one of the new sites of 'biocapital' accumulation. At the same time, our '24-hour-society' with its incessant production, communication and consumption makes sleep a problematic, uncertain element of everyday life, just dump time or inertia in a mobile and pragmatic neoliberal society obsessed with the idea of the full employment of finite human existence.

I would just like to give a couple of quotes from contemporary popular discourse which shed some light on the new anxiety around sleep. Former British prime minister Margaret Thatcher is famous not only as the inventor of the neoliberal motto, 'There is no such thing as society', but she was also a person who required very little sleep—something like 4 hours—and, perhaps, she blamed oversleeping as a barrier to economic growth. These moments and their political implications are wittingly reflected in a British novel which depicts an enthusiastic community of sleep researchers and their heated debates:

'"Why despise it, anyway? I don't understand." "I'll tell you why: because the sleeper is helpless; powerless. Sleep puts even the strongest people at the mercy of the weakest and most feeble. Can you imagine what it must be like for a woman of Mrs Thatcher's fibre, her moral character, to be obliged to prostrate herself every day in that posture of abject submission? The brain disabled, the muscles inert and flaccid? It must be insupportable." "I hadn't thought of it like that before," said Terry. "Sleep as the great leveller." "Exactly. That's exactly what it is: the great leveller. Like fucking socialism."'[2]

And another telling quote from the same novel: '"I'm the only one working in this field, who sees sleep for what it really is." "And what's that?" "A disease, of course." He began making his way along the path—which at this point ran perilously close to the edge of the cliff—while declaiming over his shoulder: "A disease, Terry—the most widespread and life-curtailing disease of all! Forget cancer, forget multiple sclerosis, forget AIDS. If you spend eight hours a day in bed, then sleep is shortening your life by a third! That's the equivalent of dying at the age of fifty—and it's happening to all of us. This is more than just a disease: this is a plague! And none of us is immune, you realize."'[3]

If in ancient times sleep was a parable of death, as 'eternal sleep', now sleep is directly perceived as a disease, or as a terrifying death immanent to our lives. The anxiety around sleep (booming scientific research of sleep, discussion of its good or bad condition, healthy duration, self-help books and debates about various techniques of 'sleeping well', or, say, the legitimacy of napping during work time) is a symptom of our present, which has problemzatised the old and 'natural' temporality of everyday life. On a different but interconnected register, sleep functions as a metaphor for political somnolence, from which people are 'awakening' in the current economic turmoil to stage protests and civil disobedience.

However, despite taking these new problems into account, it seems almost impossible to identify a consistent critical discourse on sleep in its social, political and philosophical registers. Sleep remains in the realm of natural, a-historical rhythmicity: days and nights, dusk and dawn, falling asleep and awakening. At the same time, the 'natural' preconditions for sleep are already shifted, transformed

---

1. The essay is based on a lecture given at Shedhalle on 30 March 2011, and is a short summary of a larger projected study of the philosophical and political anthropology of sleep and wakefulness (working title: *Rex Exsomnis: Towards a Political Economy of Sleep*).

2. Jonathan Coe, *The House of Sleep* (New York, 1997), p. 177.

3. Ibid., pp. 179–80. Of course, the grand theme of sleep as a leveller is not an invention of Jonathan Coe or philosopher Jean-Luc Nancy—see the chapter entitled 'Monde égal' in his charming book *Tombe de sommeil* (Paris, 2007)—but has existed since the classics of early modernity, for example, Cervantes' *Don Quixote*: 'While we're asleep we're all equal, great and small, rich and poor' (Project Gutenberg Ebook, 2004).

or even destroyed by the incessant function of a wired globalized economy, 24/7 media and security checks, or by personal self-exploitation, deprivation of sleep in order to get more time for work, consumption or pleasure.

Michel Foucault once said that the most difficult tasks for thought is to grasp what is most intimate to us, what is so close to us that it is invisible. Sleep is indeed a phenomenon of such closeness, being something obvious, banal and at the same time one of the most complicated to think about. With several interesting and thoughtful exceptions in recent, mainly sociological and anthropological scholarship, the phenomenon of sleep is an unusual subject for philosophy, critical theory and the humanities.[4]

2.

The question is about the *limits* of capitalist modernity as a progression in the complex rationalisation of life forms aimed at the accumulation of capital and the extraction of profit. Today's critical testing of the limits of this rationalisation becomes the key political and theoretical question; it is imperative to confront the widely accepted position that there is 'no alternative' to a capitalist organisation of the economy, society and politics. That is why I take regulations and controls over such a 'natural' phenomena as *sleep* as a paradigmatic case of the rationalisation of everyday life in time of capitalist hypermodernity.

In 'The Working-Day' chapter in *Capital,* Marx argues:
'The prolongation of the working day beyond the limits of the natural day, into the night, only acts as a palliative. It only slightly quenches the vampire thirst for the living blood of labour. Capitalist production therefore drives, by

its inherent nature, towards the appropriation of labour throughout the whole of the 24 hours in the day.'[5]

The capital-vampire attacks at night, the time of sleep. Capital is 'dead labour', and it is incommensurable with the living—and sleeping—subjectivity of the labour force. That triggers the hypothesis that in the space of capital there is no structural place for sleep at all, except for solving the practical problem of the recreation and reproduction of the labour force and arranging incessant production (Marx describes in the same chapter of *Capital* its primary stage, the organisation of night shifts). This violent exception at work is very intense at the early stage of capitalist development when, as Marx writes: 'Some of these gentlemen were accused of having kept five boys between 12 and 15 years age at work from 6 a.m. on Friday to 4 p.m. on the following Saturday, not allowing them any respite except for meals and one hour for sleep at midnight.'[6] Then, in late modernity, sleep is captured in a *dispositif* of control, not just for the sake of intensified production, but also in the name of constant consumption, communication and entertainment (of course, in reality this control in its full operation is more like a neoliberal phantasm, and, to be precise, communication is now an essential part of production). At the same time, in post-Fordist society of 'immaterial labour', when the time of work is merging with the time of life itself, sleep acquires new value as the *sole non-working time*. I am not saying how it is going to help us, arguing that in this new zone of indifference between work and life, sleep has this specific position. That gives it a specific ambivalence; from the point of view of the pure logic of capital it is negative, from the standpoint of the contemporary 'creative' and 'cognitive' worker (whose entire life is work) it is rather positive. It is not an appeal to sleep as an act of resistance to this 'colonisation', at least at this point, but rather, just an identification of its exceptional place, which could be used differently.

4..... Including Walter Seitter, *Geschichte der Nacht* (Berlin, 1999), Simon J. Williams, *The Politics of Sleep: Governing (Un)consciousness in the Late Modern Age* (Basingstoke, England, 2011), Brigitte Steger and Lodewijk Brunt (eds.), *Night-time and Sleep in Asia and the West* (London, 2003), Roger Ekirch, *At Day's Close: Night in Times Past* (New York, 2005).

5................ Karl Marx, *Capital: A Critique of Political Economy, Volume One* (London, 1982), p. 367.
6.. Ibid., p. 364.

‚So habe ich darüber noch nie nachgedacht', sagte
Terry. ‚Der Schlaf als der grosse Gleichmacher.'
‚Genau. Das ist er: der grosse Gleichmacher. Wie
der Scheiss-Sozialismus.'"[2]

Und noch ein typischer Abschnitt aus dem gleichen
Roman:
„‚Ich bin der Einzige, der auf diesem Gebiet
arbeitet und den Schlaf als das sieht, was er
wirklich ist.'
‚Und das wäre?'
‚Natürlich eine Krankheit.' Er begann den Weg
– der an dieser Stelle gefährlich nah an den Rand
der Klippe führte – weiterzugehen, während
er über seine Schulter hinweg weiter dozierte:
‚Eine Krankheit, Terry – die am weitesten verbrei-
tete und das Leben verkürzende Krankheit
von allen! Vergiss den Krebs, vergiss Multiple
Sklerose, vergiss Aids. Wer acht Stunden am Tag
im Bett verbringt, verkürzt sein Leben um ein
Drittel! Es bedeutet, dass man grad so gut
mit fünfzig sterben könnte – und wir werden
alle davon heimgesucht. Es ist mehr als
nur eine Krankheit: Es ist eine Seuche! Und
es ist dir klar – keiner ist davor geschützt.'"[3]

Früher war Schlaf als ‚ewiger Schlaf' eine Parabel
für den Tod, heute wird er als eine Krankheit
gesehen, als Krankheit zum Tod, die unserem
Leben eingeschrieben ist. Die Aufmerksamkeit,
die der Schlaf zur Zeit auf sich zieht (erinnert
sei an die boomende Schlafforschung, an die
Diskussionen über seine gute oder schlechte
Qualität, an seine Auswirkung auf die Gesundheit,
an all die Selbsthilfe-Literatur und Debatten,
wie man zu ‚gutem Schlaf' kommen kann, oder
beispielsweise daran, was der Nutzen eines
Nickerchens während der Arbeitszeit sei), ist ein
Symptom unserer Zeit, die den alten ‚natürlichen'
Rhythmus des Alltags zu einem Problem macht.
Auf einer anderen, aber damit verbundenen
Ebene ist der Schlaf eine Metapher für politische

Verschlafenheit, aus der die Menschen in der
gegenwärtigen Wirtschaftskrise nun zu Protesten
und bürgerlichem Ungehorsam ‚erwachen'.

Aber auch wenn man diese neuen Problem-
stellungen mit einbezieht, scheint es fast unmöglich, einen konsistenten kritischen Diskurs zum
Thema Schlaf mit all seinen sozialen, politischen
und philosophischen Aspekten auszumachen.
Schlaf bleibt seiner natürlichen, ahistorischen
Rhythmizität verhaftet: Tage und Nächte, Abend-
dämmerung und Morgendämmerung, Einschlafen
und Aufwachen. Zugleich aber haben sich die
‚natürlichen' Gegebenheiten, die Vorbedingungen
für den Schlaf bereits verlagert und verändert.
Oder sie wurden durch das unaufhörliche Funktionieren der vernetzten globalisierten Wirtschaft,
durch die Medien rund um die Uhr, sieben Tage
pro Woche, durch Sicherheitskontrollen oder
individuelle Selbstausbeutung und Schlafentzug
sogar zerstört, nur damit mehr Zeit für die Arbeit,
den Konsum, das Vergnügen bleibt.

Der französische Philosoph Michel Foucault hielt
einmal fest, dass es etwas vom Schwierigsten
sei, das zu begreifen, was uns am nächsten bzw.
uns so nah sei, dass es praktisch unsichtbar
sei. Der Schlaf gehört sicher zu diesen Phänomenen, er ist so offensichtlich oder banal, d.h. uns
so nah, dass es eine grosse Herausforderung ist,
ihn kritisch zu untersuchen. Und so ist der Schlaf,
trotz einiger interessanter aktueller Gegenbei-
spiele hauptsächlich in der soziologischen und
anthropologischen Forschung, ein ungewöhnliches
Thema in der Philosophie, der kritischen Theorie
und den Geisteswissenschaften geblieben.[4]

2.

Die Frage, die sich stellt, betrifft die ‚Grenzen'
der kapitalistischen Moderne mit ihrer immer
komplexer werdenden Rationalisierung der

2............ Coe, Jonathan: *The House of Sleep*. Viking, New York 1997, 177.
3............ Ebd., 179–180. Natürlich ist das Thema nicht neu. Das Bild vom
Schlaf als Gleichmacher wurde weder von Jonathan Coe noch von
Jean-Luc Nancy erfunden – vgl. das Kapitel „Monde égal" in seinem
bezaubernden Buch *Tombe de sommeil*, erschienen bei Galilée, Paris
2007. Vielmehr ist es seit der frühen Moderne ein Klassiker, z.B. bei
Cervantes' *Don Quixote*: „Während wir schlafen, sind wir alle gleich,
gross und klein, reich und arm." [dt. zitiert nach Gutenberg Ebook,
2004].

4.............. Siehe u.a. Seitter, Walter: *Geschichte der Nacht*. Philo, Berlin
1999; Williams, Simon J.: *The Politics of Sleep: Governing
(Un)consciousness in the Late Modern Age*. Palgrave Macmillan,
Basingstoke, England 2011; Ster, Brigitte/Brunt, Lodewijk (Hg.):
Night-time and Sleep in Asia and the West. Routledge, London 2003;
Ekirch, A. Roger: *In der Stunde der Nacht*. Lübbe,
Bergisch Gladbach 2006.

Lebensformen, die einzig die Akkumulation von Kapital und Gewinnoptimierung zum Ziel haben. Das kritische Hinterfragen dieser Rationalisierungsgrenzen ist von grösster Bedeutung, in der Politik wie in der kritischen Theorie, damit der weit verbreiteten Meinung und Einstellung, dass es ‚keine Alternative' zum kapitalistischen Denken £in Wirtschaft, Gesellschaft und Politik gäbe, entgegengetreten werden kann. Aus diesem Grund sehe ich die Regulierung von und Kontrolle über ein so ‚natürliches' Phänomen wie den Schlaf als paradigmatisch für die Rationalisierung des Alltagslebens in Zeiten einer kapitalistischen ‚Hyper-Moderne'.

In seinem Werk *Das Kapital* argumentiert Karl Marx im Kapitel „Der Arbeitstag" folgendermassen:

„Die Verlängerung des Arbeitstags über die Grenzen des natürlichen Tags in die Nacht hinein wirkt nur als Palliativ, stillt nur annähernd den Vampyrdurst nach lebendigem Arbeitsblut. Arbeit während aller 24 Stunden des Tags anzueignen ist daher der immanente Trieb der kapitalistischen Produktion."[5]

Der kapitalistische Vampir greift während der Nacht, der Schlafenszeit an. Kapital ist „tote Arbeit", und es ist unvereinbar mit der lebendigen – und schlafenden – Subjektivität von Arbeitskraft. Das führt zur Hypothese, dass es im Bereich des Kapitals überhaupt keinen strukturellen Ort für Schlaf gibt, ausser in praktischer Hinsicht, um die Rekreation und Reproduktion der Arbeitskraft sowie eine unaufhörliche Produktion zu gewährleisten. (Die erste Stufe, die Organisation der Schichtarbeit inkl. Nachtschichten beschreibt Marx im gleichen Kapitel von *Das Kapital*). Wie diese Verhältnisse sich in der Frühzeit des Kapitalismus zeigen, lässt sich aus einer Beschreibung von Marx erkennen: „Ein Teil dieser Herren war angeklagt, 5 Knaben zwischen 12 und 15 Jahren von 6 Uhr morgens des Freitags bis 4 Uhr nachmittags des folgenden Samstags abgearbeitet zu haben, ohne irgendeine Erholung zu gestatten, außer für Mahlzeiten und eine Stunde Schlaf um

Mitternacht."[6] In der Spätmoderne dann wird Schlaf zu einem Dispositiv der Kontrolle, nicht nur aus Gründen intensivierter Produktion, sondern auch im Namen des ständigen Konsums, der Kommunikation und im Bereich der Unterhaltung. (Natürlich ist absolute Kontrolle in Wirklichkeit eher ein neoliberales Phantasma, ausserdem ist Kommunikation, um genau zu sein, mittlerweile ein grundlegender Bestandteil der Produktion). Gleichzeitig bekommt in der postfordistischen Gesellschaft mit ihrer ‚immateriellen Arbeit', in der sich die Arbeitszeit völlig mit der Lebenszeit vermischt, der Schlaf einen neuen Wert als die einzige ‚Nicht-Arbeitszeit'. Ich kann nicht sagen, inwiefern uns die Einsicht weiterhilft, dass der Schlaf in dieser neuen Zone der Un-Unterscheidbarkeit von Arbeit und Leben diese besondere Stellung einnimmt. Festzustellen bleibt vorerst, dass sie sich durch eine besondere Ambivalenz auszeichnet – aus rein kapitalistischer Sicht ist sie negativ besetzt, aus Sicht des/der zeitgenössischen ‚kreativen' und ‚kognitiven' Arbeiter_in (dessen/deren ganzes Leben aus Arbeit besteht), ist sie eher positiv besetzt. Das soll, an diesem Punkt zumindest, nicht als eine Aufforderung zum Schlaf als einem Akt des Widerstands gegen diese Form der ‚Kolonisation' verstanden werden. Vielmehr geht es darum, dessen besondere Stellung, die auch anders genützt werden könnte, festzuhalten.

Der besondere Status von Schlaf ist nicht nur ein Nebenprodukt der kapitalistischen Moderne. Nimmt man Schlafen und Wachen als anthropologische Paradigmen, stellen sie eigentlich ein Modell für das Verständnis der Machtverhältnisse dar, die eine solche Ordnung überhaupt erst möglich machen. Ernst Kantorowicz erwähnt in seinem Klassiker *The King's Two Bodies: A Study in Mediaeval Political Theology* ganz kurz, in einer Fussnote nur, die faszinierende Figur des Rex Exsomnis. Es handelt sich dabei um einen wachsamen König, der nicht schlafen darf, weil sonst seine Macht verloren ginge und die soziale Ordnung zerfiele.[7] Auch die modernen Formen der Herrschaft wie Foucault sie skizzierte und

---

5......... Marx, Karl: Das Kapital, 379. Digitale Bibliothek Band 11: Marx/ Engels, 3688 (vgl. MEW Bd. 23, 271).

6... Ebd.

7.......... Kantorowicz, Ernst: *The King's Two Bodies: A Study in Mediaeval Political Theology.* Princeton University Press, Princeton 1997, 131.

The exceptional status of sleep is not just a passive outcome of capitalist modernity. Conversely, sleep and wakefulness, taken as anthropological paradigms, shape a model for the understanding of the power operations which enable this order. For example, in a footnote to his classic *The King's Two Bodies: A Study in Mediaeval Political Theology*, Ernst Kantorowicz briefly mentions the intriguing figure of the *rex exsomnis*, a vigilant king who must not sleep or the operation of sovereign power will cease and social order will fall apart.[7] The modern regime of power, famously outlined by Foucault and updated by the Deleuzian notion of the 'society of control', is also *sleepless*. Checkpoints, monitoring cameras, police patrols, security guards, just to mention the most obvious examples, function incessantly.

The figure of the watchman who doesn't sleep at night is the most archaic paradigm of this incessant, uninterrupted activity of power. The concept of 'the night watchman state'—the minimal state reduced to position of a watchman, just passively guarding the normalcy of the bourgeois social order and property—was one of the key threads in the neoliberal re-thinking of the state in the 'new economy of power' of the nineteenth and twentieth centuries. Michel Foucault discussed a similar problem in his research of 'pastoral power', embedded in Christianity, a transitional form of power, linking its archaic rituals and its modern biopolitical mode of existence. This type of power operation presupposes the pastor's (shepherd's) incessant monitoring of the 'souls' of believers and the whole religious community ('flock'). As Foucault notes, the pastor never sleeps. Then this paradigm of power was generalized in the context of modern biopolitics and finally in the contemporary 'society of control'.[8]

7 .... Ernst Kantorowicz, *The King's Two Bodies: A Study in Mediaeval Political Theology* (Princeton, 1997), p. 131.

8 .... 'When they sleep, he keeps watch. The theme of keeping watch is important.' Michel Foucault, 'Omnes et Singulatim: Towards a Criticism of Political Reason', Tanner Lectures on Human Values, delivered at Stanford University, Pale Alto, Calif., October 10 and 16, 1979, accessed at http://foucault.info/documents/foucault.omnesEtSingulatim.en.html.

3.

This complex position of sleep in modernity requires a political and philosophical archaeology of its specific rationality. There are two parts of investigation here, one is about the relationship between sleep and dreams, and the second is about the anthropology of sleep and the sleeper. I will just briefly summarize them here.

a) As a rule, in the humanities and social sciences sleep has been treated from the point of view of the *dream*, which alone has decipherable meanings. Sleep as a whole was seen as just one of life's natural functions, explored in biology, neurology, medicine, etc. We might describe this strategic division of discourse as a form of modern *oneirocentrism*, just to coin a new term here. Since the ancient Greek philosophy dreams, *oneiros* has been a traditional part of sceptic argumentation. Then, with the emergence of psychoanalysis, dream paradoxically became a 'royal road' to subjective truth. To cut the story short and oversimplify matters somewhat, this moment coincides with the symptomatic exclusion of sleep from the field of psychoanalysis by its founder: 'I have had little occasion to deal with the problem of sleep, for that is essentially a problem of physiology.' [9]

b) The next step will be to question this exclusion of sleep, tracing several arguments for its absence in theory and philosophy, starting from obvious empirical reasons (specific weakness and neutrality of sleep experience) and stretching to metaphysical ones, privileging wakefulness over sleep, which might be linked to logocentrism in a Derridean sense. At this point, one needs to trace several philosophical models of understanding sleep. To give an example, it is a *negative* model at work in Plato's *Laws*:

'For much sleep is not naturally suitable either to our bodies or souls, not yet to employment

9 .... Sigmund Freud, *Interpretation of Dreams* (London, 1953–74), p. 40.

on any such matters. For when asleep no man is worth anything, anymore than if he were dead: on the contrary, every one of us who cares most greatly for life and thought keeps awake as long as possible, only reserving so much time for sleep as his health requires—and that is but little, once the habit is well formed. And rulers that are watchful by night in cities are a terror for evil-doers, be they citizens or enemies, but objects of respect and admiration for the just and temperate; and they confer benefit alike on themselves and on the whole State. The night, if it is spent in this way, will—in addition to all the other benefits described—lend greater fortitude to the souls of all who reside in these States.'[10]

In the excellent state, according to Plato, citizens should not sleep at all, because while sleeping human beings are outside of any ties with *logos* (reason), they are useless for the state and *ungovernable* at the same time. The whole programme of reducing sleep is already at work here. We can find a *positive* model in Aristotle; sleep here is placed in relation to life, *bios*. The duality of sleep/wakefulness is an analogy of the actuality/potentiality duality:

'What we want to say is clear from the particular cases by induction, and one should not look for a definition of everything but should also take in what is analogical, because as what builds is to what can build, and what is awake to what is asleep, and what is seeing to what has closed eyes but has sight, [so is] what has been separated off from the matter to thematter, and what has been finished off to what is unwrought. Of these contrasts let the actuality be defined by the one part, the potential by the other.'[11]

Sleep is a part of the economy of life forces, a potentiality (*dynamis*) preserving their instant expenditure.[12] At another point in *Metaphysics*, Aristotle describes sleep as '*divine intellect*', i.e., the intellect of a sleeper is analogical to God's intellect, which does not think of something concrete since otherwise it would exhaust His pure and infinite potentiality.

Elements of these models can be found in modern philosophy, especially interestingly configured in Kant and Hegel. In his *Encyclopaedia of Philosophical Sciences* Hegel gives a rich account of sleep and wakefulness, inscribing these states in the trajectory of the deployment of the 'subjective Spirit.' Sleep, in Hegel's anthropology, is both negative and positive:

'Generally, the waking state includes all the self-conscious and rational activity of spirit's distinguishing himself as a being-for-self.—Sleep invigorates this activity, not simply negatively, as rest from it, but as withdrawal from the world of determinateness, from diversion of becoming fixed in singularities, into the universal essence of subjectivity, which constitutes the substance and absolute power [*Macht*] of these determinatenesses.'[13]

Jean-Luc Nancy comments on the Hegelian moment in the history of thought on sleep as follows:

'This existence [of sleeper] should rightly be called absolute: *ab-solutum*, it is detachment from everything, it is that from which every link, every relation, every connection or composition, has been dissolved and excluded.'[14]

For Hegel, sleep is ambivalent, because it is a *singularity* outside of the order of universal reason, rationality, and, at the same time, it is an intimate core of *subjectivity* as its full interiority, power (*Macht*) and absoluteness.

10....... Plato, *Laws* (London, 1926), Vol. 2, Book 7, p. 69. As Walter Benjamin notes in *Passagen-Werk*, this motif repeats in modern utopias. For example, citizens of Fourier's Harmonia 'need very little sleep (like Fourier!)' See Walter Benjamin, *The Arcades Project* (Cambridge, Mass., 1999), p. 646 (W16, 5).

11.......... Aristotle, *Metaphysics*, Book Theta, translated with an introduction and commentary by Stephen Makin (Oxford, 2006), 1048b, p. 7.

12............ See a radical interpretation of *dynamis* in the work of Giorgio Agamben.

13.... *Hegel's Philosophy of Subjective Spirit* (Boston, 1978), p. 127.

14....... Jean-Luc Nancy, *The Fall of Sleep* (New York, 2009), p. 15.

wie sie durch Deleuze und seinen Begriff der ‚Kontrollgesellschaft‘ aktualisiert wurden, sind ‚ohne Schlaf‘. Kontrollpunkte, Überwachungskameras, Polizeipatrouillen, Wachmänner – um nur die offensichtlichsten Beispiele zu nennen – sind unaufhörlich im Einsatz.

Die Figur des Wachmanns, der in der Nacht nicht schläft, ist das archaischste Beispiel solch unaufhörlicher, ununterbrochener Machtausübung. Der Begriff des ‚Nachtwächterstaates‘, des minimalen Staates (Robert Nozick), dessen Funktion sich auf die eines Wächters reduziert, der unbeteiligt die Normalität der sozialen Ordnung und des bürgerlichen Besitzes bewacht, war grundlegend für den neoliberalen Entwurf des Staates in der ‚neuen Ökonomie der Macht‘ des 19. und 20. Jahrhunderts. Michel Foucault befasste sich mit einer ähnlichen Frage, als er die im christlichen Glauben verankerte ‚Pastoralmacht‘ untersuchte, eine Übergangsform von Macht, die sich sowohl durch ihre archaischen Rituale als auch durch ihre moderne biopolitische Existenzweise auszeichnet. Diese Ausübung von Macht setzt die ständige Überwachung der ‚Seelen‘ der Gläubigen und der ganzen religiösen Gemeinschaft (der ‚Herde‘) durch den Pastor (den ‚Hirten‘) voraus. Wie Foucault bemerkt, schläft der Pastor nie. Später wurde dieses Machtmodell im Kontext der modernen Biopolitik und schlussendlich in der heutigen ‚Kontrollgesellschaft‘ verallgemeinert.[8]

3.

Die komplexe Stellung, die der Schlaf in der Moderne einnimmt, verlangt eine politische und philosophische Archäologie seiner besonderen Rationalität. Deswegen ist meine Untersuchung zweigeteilt, einerseits befasst sie sich mit der Beziehung zwischen Schlaf und Traum, andererseits mit der Anthropologie des Schlafs und des/der Schlafenden. Ich möchte hier nur eine kurze Zusammenfassung davon geben.

a) Üblicherweise ging es in den Geisteswissenschaften und in der Soziologie beim Phänomen Schlaf primär um den Traum und seine Deutung. Der Schlaf als solcher wurde schlicht als eine natürliche biologische Funktion angesehen, und war somit Forschungsgegenstand der Biologie, Neurologie und Medizin. Diese strategische Teilung des Diskurses können wir als eine Form von modernem ‚Oneirozentrismus‘ bezeichnen, um gleich auch einen neuen Ausdruck zu prägen. Schon die Philosophen der griechischen Antike setzten sich mit dem Traum, mit ‚oneiros‘, auseinander. Dann wird er paradoxerweise, mit dem Auftreten der Psychoanalyse, der ‚Königsweg‘ zu einer subjektiven Wahrheit. Etwas vereinfachend und um die Geschichte abzukürzen verweise ich auf den Begründer der Psychoanalyse, der den Schlaf bezeichnenderweise von seinen psychoanalytischen Betrachtungen ausgenommen hat: „Ich hatte wenig Anlass, mich mit dem Problem des Schlafs zu befassen, denn dies ist wesentlich ein physiologisches Problem.“[9]

b) In einem nächsten Schritt soll dieses Ausklammerns des Schlafs untersucht und verschiedene Argumente für seine Absenz in Theorie und Philosophie nachgezeichnet werden, angefangen bei offensichtlich empirischen Gründen (die besondere Schwäche und die Neutralität, die der Schlaferfahrung innewohnen), bis hin zu ‚metaphysischen‘ Gründen, die den Wachzustand dem Schlaf gegenüber privilegieren, was man als mit dem ‚Logozentrismus‘ im Sinne Derridas in Zusammenhang stehend sehen könnte. An diesem Punkt müssen mehrere philosophische Modelle des Verständnisses von Schlaf berücksichtigt werden. In den *Gesetzen* Platos zeigt sich zum Beispiel ein negatives Modell:

„Viel Schlaf ist nämlich von Natur aus weder unserem Körper noch unserer Seele und auch nicht den diesbezüglichen Tätigkeiten förderlich. Denn wer schläft, der ist nichts wert, so wenig wie einer, der nicht lebt. Wem von uns aber besonders daran gelegen ist, zu leben und geistig rege zu sein, der bleibt so lange wie möglich wach und gönnt sich bloß das für seine Gesundheit förderliche Maß an Schlaf; das ist aber nicht viel,

---

8................. „Wenn sie schlafen, wacht *er*. Das Thema des Wachens ist bedeutsam." Michel Foucault: „‚Omnes et Singulatim‘: zu einer Kritik der politischen Vernunft", in: ders., *Dits et Ecrits. Schriften* 4, Suhrkamp, Frankfurt a.M. 2005, 165–198, hier: 170.

9............. Freud, Sigmund: *Die Traumdeutung*. Frankfurt a. M. 1981, 17.

37

wenn es nur recht zur Gewohnheit wird. Beamte, die nachts in der Stadt wach bleiben, sind gefürchtet bei den Schlechten, Feinden wie Bürgern, bewundert und geachtet bei den Gerechten und Besonnenen und nützlich sich selbst und der gesamten Stadt. Wenn die Nacht so zugebracht wird, könnte sie neben all den erwähnten Vorteilen auch eine Art Tapferkeit den Seelen jedes einzelnen Bürgers in den Städten verleihen."[10]

Im idealen Staat, meint Plato, sollten die Bürger überhaupt nicht schlafen, denn während sie schlafen, sind sie ohne jede Verbindung zum ‚Logos' (der Vernunft), sind sie für den Staat nicht von Nutzen und zur gleichen Zeit nicht regierbar. Das ganze Programm der Schlafreduktion ist hier bereits am Werk. Ein ‚positives' Modell können wir bei Aristoteles finden – hier wird der Schlaf eher mit dem Leben, mit ‚bios', in Verbindung gebracht. Die Dualität von Schlafen und Wachen kann als analog zur Dualität von Aktualität und Potentialität (Akt und Potenz) gesehen werden:

„Es ist durchaus nicht immer geboten, für alles die streng begriffliche Form zu suchen; es genügt schon eine Reihe von analogen Fällen zu überblicken. Dazu dient hier das Verhältnis des Bauenden zum Bauverständigen, des Aufgewachten zum Schlafenden, des Sehenden zu dem, der die Augen geschlossen hält, aber Sehkraft besitzt, des aus dem Stoffe Gestalteten zum Stoffe, des Fertiggestellten zum Unfertigen. Durch das eine Glied dieser Gegensätze soll jedesmal die Aktualität, durch das andere die Potentialität bezeichnet sein."[11]

Der Schlaf ist Teil der Ökonomie der Lebenskräfte, eine Möglichkeit (dynamis), die sich die

sofortige Verausgabe vorbehält.[12] An einer anderen Stelle in seiner *Metaphysik* beschreibt Aristoteles den Schlaf als ‚göttlichen Intellekt', d.h. der Intellekt eines Schlafenden ist Gottes Intellekt analog, der an nichts Konkretes denkt, sonst würde er seine reine und unendliche Potenz (potentiality) erschöpfen.

Elemente dieser Modelle finden sich auch in der modernen Philosophie, auf besonders interessante Weise bei Kant und Hegel. In seiner *Enzyklopädie der philosophischen Wissenschaften* räumt Hegel dem Schlaf und dem Wachsein viel Platz ein, schreibt diesen Zuständen die Entfaltung des ‚subjektiven Geistes' ein. In Hegels Anthropologie ist der Schlaf sowohl positiv wie negativ besetzt:

„In das Wachsein fällt überhaupt alle selbstbewußte und vernünftige Tätigkeit des für sich seienden Unterscheidens des Geistes. – Der Schlaf ist Bekräftigung dieser Tätigkeit nicht als bloß negative Ruhe von derselben, sondern als Rückkehr aus der Welt der Bestimmtheiten, aus der Zerstreuung und dem Festwerden in den Einzelheiten in das allgemeine Wesen der Subjektivität, welches die Substanz jener Bestimmtheiten und deren absolute Macht ist."[13]

Jean-Luc Nancy kommentiert Hegels Position in Bezug auf den Schlaf in der Geistesgeschichte wie folgt:
„Diese Existenz [des Schlafenden] muss zu Recht absolut genannt werden: *ab-solutum,* d.h. losgelöst von allem, es ist der Zustand, in dem alle Verbindungen, alle Beziehungen, alle Zusammensetzungen oder Nahtstellen gelöst und ausgeschlossen wurden."[14]

Für Hegel ist der Schlaf etwas Ambivalentes, weil er eine Singularität ist, ausserhalb der Ordnung

---

10 .... Plato: *Gesetze* [Nomoi 808], übersetzt nach: Plato: *Laws,* in two volumes. London 1926, Vol. 2, Book 7, 69. Wie Walter Benjamin in seinem Passagen-Werk anführt, wiederholt sich dieses Motiv in modernen Utopien. Die Bürger von Fouriers Harmonia zum Beispiel „brauchen sehr wenig Schlaf (wie Fourier!)". Vgl. Benjamin, Walter: *Das Passagen-Werk.* Suhrkamp Verlag, Frankfurt am Main 1982, 795 (W16,5).

11 .... Aristoteles: *Metaphysik,* Buch IV, Die Aktualität. 149 [gefunden auf zeno.org], vom Autor zitiert aus: *Metaphysics,* Book Theta, von Stephen Makin übersetzt und mit einer Einleitung und einem Kommentar versehen. Clarendon Press, Oxford 2006, 1048b, 7.

12 .... Vgl. eine radikale Interpretation von dynamis im Werk von Giogio Agamben.

13 .... Hegel, G.W.F.: Philosophie des Geistes. Der subjektive Geist. Anthropologie. Die Seele, § 398. In: *Gesammelte Werke, Bd. 19,* hg. v. der Rheinisch-Westfälischen Akademie der Wissenschaften, Düsseldorf: Enzyklopädie der philosophischen Wissenschaften im Grundrisse (1827), hg. v. Wolfgang Bonsiepen und Hans-Christian Lucas, Hamburg 1989, 398.

14 .... Nancy, Jean-Luc: *The Fall of Sleep.* Fordham University Press, New York 2009, 15.

One of the general premises of my research is that the capitalist order of modernity privileges wakeful and active time over passiveness and non-productivity (having as its horizon a total wakefulness, the ultimate consequence of this logic), and reaffirms the old metaphysical thought, which had the same preferences. But the new aspect here is this ambivalent dimension of subjectivity, which unfolds a perspective of breaking with negativity of metaphysical thinking on sleep, and, perhaps, thinking of sleep in terms of Aristotelian 'divine intellect'.

4.

Departing from the Hegelian perspective, sleep and awakening are to be considered as founding anthropological events of subjectivity formation, or, better, as the degree zero of subjectivization. Sleep is constitutive for subjectivity. It marks its specific anthropological value, which in my view has been underestimated in the history of thought. Of course, there is some similarity between sleeping, fainting, idling and all 'nonproductive' states of life. Maybe I am overestimating my case, but sleep is fundamentally different because it presupposes isolation, detachment from the world and its rationality, which is also our regular experience (it is not something occasional like fainting). It is a regular existential experiment of the minimization of our psychological lives, our egos, etc. It is very radical indeed, but seems quite ordinary to us because of its biological regularity. There are several not so obvious but provoking examples in the twentieth century's radical philosophy which point in this direction. I will give just two impressive excerpts from the work of two well-known thinkers.

In his book *Existence and Existents,* Emmanuel Lévinas gives a beautiful account of sleep as a kind of 'support' for subjectivity. Sleep is a shelter for an anonymous existence, a resisting suspension of negative forces of the incessantly wakeful modern rationality:

'Nothingness is still envisaged as the end and limit of being, as an ocean which beats up against it on all sides. But we must ask if "nothingness", unthinkable as a limit or negation of being, is not possible as interval and interruption; we must ask whether consciousness, with its aptitude for sleep, for suspension, for *epoche*, is not the locus of this nothingness-interval.'[15]

This is the start of a paradoxical inversion. Sleep is not a disappearance of conscious subject, 'ego', but its own foundation, localisation and maybe salvation. Otherwise, as Lévinas suggests, the forces of an anonymous and incessantly wakeful presence of things around us would make subjective existence unbearable. Sleep, isolating and switching off the apparatus of our intentionality, is an interval, a possibility of human subjectivity folded into the inhuman world of totally wakeful beings, of an ontological insomnia.

For Walter Benjamin, falling asleep seems to be an only decisive event for subjectivity in the world of late capitalist modernity, which impoverished traditional structures of experience:

'*Rites de passage*—this is the designation in folklore for the ceremonies that attach to death and birth, to marriage, puberty and so forth. In modern life, these transitions are becoming ever more unrecognizable and impossible to experience. We have grown very poor in threshold experiences. Falling asleep is perhaps the only such experience that remains to us. (But together with this, there is also waking up.)'[16]

Of course, it sounds like a brilliant exaggeration, but, on a more profound level, in *The Arcades Project* Benjamin notes on several occasions that a singular dialectics of sleep and awakening is indeed essential in understanding the emergence of collective subjectivity:

'It is one of the tacit suppositions of psychoanalysis that the clear-cut antithesis of

15 Emmanuel Lévinas, 'Existence and Existents', *The Levinas Reader* (Cambridge, Mass., 1989), p. 35.
16 .... Benjamin, *The Arcades Project*, p. 494 (0 2a, 1).

sleeping and waking has no value for determining the empirical form of consciousness of the human being, but instead yields before an unending variety of concrete states of consciousness conditioned by every conceivable level of wakefulness within all possible centers. The situation of consciousness as patterned and checkered by sleep and waking need only be transferred from the individual to the collective.'[17]

And, finally, sleep and its bizarre products, dreams, are analogical to relations of economic infrastructure and its cultural expressions:

'The economic conditions under which society exists are expressed in the superstructures—precisely as, with the sleeper, an overfull stomach finds not its reflection but its expression in the contents of dreams, which, from a causal point of view, it may be said to "condition".'[18]

In Benjamin's social ontology, the economic condition is the collective sleeping body of society. The question arises here: how is the political awakening of this sleeping body of society possible?

5.

Sleep, as a state of 'uselessness', unproductiveness and potentiality, connect with artistic subjectivity and preconditions of its creativity as well (the most emblematic contemporary example is Mladen Stilinović's sleeping self-portrait series *Artist at Work* of 1978 (fig. p. 46)). Sleep functions as a condition of suspension and inactivity, necessary for the production of an image, or as 'teleology' of the revolutionary 'awakening' of individuals and collectives (see Benjamin's essay on Surrealism). I think that the considerable number of artists who now are trying to explore the theme of sleep, the sleeping body, conditions of sleep, etc., signals some growing awareness of this function. Sleep and wakefulness are not just

social symptoms, or empirical states of our minds and bodies with the discourses that surround them, but some abstract 'machine' of actualisation and potentiality; falling asleep and awakening should be taken in terms of becoming a specific subject, a political subject.

Art plays an indispensable role in the evolution or formation of political subjectivity. Certainly, the sleeping body has been represented in many works of art from antiquity up to the present day. It is possible to make the entire album of artworks, starting from classical to modernist art (Brueghel, Rubens, De La Tour, etc.) representing sleeping people, their bodies—serenely stretched, naked, in all possible poses and circumstances, in private or public space. They express various conditions—defencelessness, vulnerability, or, on the contrary, a quiet pleasure of rest and rejuvenation.[19] But it is more interesting to think about a different aspect: that the structure of an artwork is close to the structure of sleep. The artwork is an isolation of a certain phenomenon, its exception from pragmatic contexts of everyday life. This exception translates it to an aesthetic field, opens it to our vision. At least, it is possible to say that, according to Kant's logic of understanding of art, is a result of 'disinterested contemplation'. In the same way, sleeping human bodies are not instrumental; they are switched off from the context of work, activity, production and realisation of an interest. Sleep is a loss of interest in the world. Freud, for example, theorised the state of sleep in exactly this way. When we sleep, it could be said we become artworks of ourselves.[20]

On the other hand, there is a tendency, that connects art to awakening, activity and an ability to influence spectators and change their vision of the world and even the world itself. The numerous avant-gardes of the twentieth century attest to this tendency. Certainly, these

---

17... Ibid., p. 389 (K. 1,5).
18... Ibid., p. 392 (K. 2,5).
19............. See for example, Sophie Sivry et al., *The Art of Sleep: A Short Social Symbolic Medical Poetic and Amorous History* (London, 1997).
20 .... See the similar analysis of sleep and image in Seitter, *Geschichte der Nacht*, pp. 192–200.

der universellen Vernunft, der Rationalität, und zugleich der Kern von Subjektivität ist, von ihrer vollen Innerlichkeit, Macht und Losgelöstheit.

In meiner Forschung gehe ich grundsätzlich davon aus, dass die moderne kapitalistische Ordnung den Wachzustand, die aktiv zugebrachte Zeit, gegenüber der Passivität und Unproduktivität bevorzugt (wobei das eigentliche Ziel und die Folge dieses Denkens ein totaler Wachzustand wäre oder ist); damit bekräftigt sie den alten, gleich lautenden metaphysischen Gedanken nochmals. Der neue Aspekt jedoch liegt nun in der ambivalenten Dimension der Subjektivität, die die Möglichkeit des Bruchs mit der Negativität des metaphysischen Gedankenguts bezüglich des Schlafs aufzeigt und somit vielleicht ein Denken des Schlafs im Aristotelischen Sinn, als Zustand ‚göttlichen Intellekts‘, erlaubt.

4.

Wenn man von Hegels Lehre ausgeht, können der Schlaf und das Erwachen als grundlegend für die anthropologische Subjektbildung betrachtet werden, oder, genauer, als Grundstein der Subjektivierung. Der Schlaf ist konstitutiv für die Subjektivität. Er stellt einen besonderen anthropologischen Wert dar, dem meines Erachtens in der Geistesgeschichte zu wenig Beachtung geschenkt wurde und wird. Natürlich gibt es Ähnlichkeiten zwischen Schlaf, Ohnmacht, Nichtstun und allen anderen ‚unproduktiven‘ Verfassungen im Leben. Vielleicht überschätze ich meinen Denkansatz, aber der Schlaf unterscheidet sich von den anderen Zuständen dadurch, dass er eine Ablösung von der Welt und ihrer Rationalität voraussetzt, und noch dazu eine Erfahrung ist, die wir regelmässig machen (und nicht nur gelegentlich, wie im Fall einer Ohnmacht). Schlaf ist ein regelmässiges existenzielles Experiment der Minimierung unseres Seelenlebens, unseres Egos usw. Das ist eigentlich etwas sehr Radikales, erscheint uns aber aufgrund der biologischen Regelmässigkeit ganz normal. In der radikalen Philosophie des 20. Jahrhunderts gibt es einige nicht wirklich auffällige, aber provokante Beispiele, die ebenfalls in diese Richtung weisen. Ich möchte hier nur zwei beeindruckende

Auszüge aus Werken zweier sehr bekannter Denker geben.

In seinem Buch *De l'Existence à l'existant* beschreibt Emmanuel Lévinas auf wunderbare Weise den Schlaf als eine Art ‚Unterstützung‘ der Subjektivität. Der Schlaf ist eine Art Schutz für eine anonyme Bewusstseinsform, eine Art Widerstand gegenüber den oder eine Aufhebung der negativen Kräfte der ununterbrochen wachen modernen Rationalität:

„Das Nichts wird immer noch als das Ende oder die Grenze des Seins imaginiert, als Ozean, der von allen Seiten dagegen anschlägt. Wir müssen jedoch die Frage stellen, ob das ‚Nichts‘, da es als Grenze oder Negation des Seins undenkbar ist, nicht vielleicht ein Zwischenraum (interval), eine Unterbrechung ist; wir müssen die Frage stellen, ob das Bewusstsein, mit der in ihm angelegten Möglichkeit von Schlaf, von Aufhebung, von ‚epoche‘, nicht der Ort dieses Zwischenraums ist.“[15]

Damit stellt sich eine paradoxe Umkehr ein. Schlaf steht nicht mehr für das Verschwinden des bewussten Subjekts, des ‚Ego‘, sondern für seine Grundfesten, seine Lokalisierung und vielleicht Rettung. Andernfalls würden gemäss Lévinas die Kräfte einer anonymen und ununterbrochenen wachen Präsenz der Dinge um uns herum die subjektive Existenz unerträglich machen. Schlaf vereinzelt uns und schaltet die Apparatur unserer Intentionalität aus, er stellt einen Zwischenraum dar, eine Möglichkeit menschlicher Subjektivität inmitten der inhumanen Welt total wacher Wesen, inmitten einer ontologischen Schlaflosigkeit.

Für Walter Benjamin scheint das Einschlafen die für die Subjektivität der spätkapitalistischen Moderne, die die traditionellen Erfahrungsstrukturen ärmer machte, einzig entscheidende Erfahrung zu sein:

„Rites de passage – so heißen in der Folklore die Zeremonien, die sich an Tod, Geburt, an

---

15 .... Lévinas, Emmanuel: Existence and Existents. In: *The Levinas Reader*. Basil Blackwell, Cambridge, Mass. 1989, 35.

Hochzeit, Mannbarwerden etc. anschließen. In dem modernen Leben sind diese Übergänge immer unkenntlicher und unerlebter geworden. Wir sind sehr arm an Schwellenerfahrungen geworden. Das Einschlafen ist vielleicht die einzige, die uns geblieben ist. (Aber damit auch das Erwachen.)"[16]

Das sieht wie eine brilliante Übertreibung aus. Aber Benjamin vertieft das Thema im *Passagen-Werk* und hält an mehreren Stellen fest, dass eine eigene Dialektik des Schlafs und des Erwachens essentiell für ein Verständnis der Entwicklung der kollektiven Subjektivität ist:

„Es ist eine der stillschweigenden Voraussetzungen der Psychoanalyse, daß der konträre Gegensatz von Schlaf und Wachen für die empirische Bewusstseinsform des Menschen keine Geltung hat, vielmehr einer unendlicher Varietät konkreter Bewußtseinszustände weicht, die durch alle denkbaren Gradstufen des Erwachtseins aller möglichen Zentren bedingt sind. Der Zustand des von Schlaf und Wachen vielfach gemusterten, gewürfelten Bewußtseins ist nur vom Individuum auf das Kollektiv übertragen."[17]

Und schlussendlich sind der Schlaf und seine bizarren Produkte, die Träume, in Bezug auf die wirtschaftliche Infrastruktur und den Ausdruck, den sie in der Kultur finden, analog:

„Die ökonomischen Bedingungen, unter denen die Gesellschaft existiert, kommen im Überbau zum Ausdruck; genau wie beim Schläfer ein übervoller Magen im Trauminhalt, obwohl er ihn kausal ‚bedingen' mag, nicht seine Abspiegelung, sondern seinen Ausdruck findet."[18]

In Benjamins sozialer Ontologie wird die wirtschaftliche Situation dem kollektiven schlafenden Körper der Gesellschaft gleichgesetzt. Die Frage, die sich hier stellt: Wie ist dieser schlafende Körper der Gesellschaft zum politischen Erwachen zu bringen?

5.

Schlaf, als Zustand der ‚Nutzlosigkeit', Unproduktivität und Potentialität, wird auch mit künstlerischer Subjektivität und den Voraussetzungen von Kreativität in Verbindung gebracht. (Als hervorragendes Beispiel sei Mladen Stilinović' Serie von Selbstportraits als schlafender *Artist at Work* (Abb. S. 46) angeführt). Der Schlaf ist Vorbedingung für eine zeitweilige Entziehung und Inaktivität, notwendig zum Beispiel für die Produktion eines Bildes, oder als ‚Teleologie' eines revolutionären ‚Erwachens' von Individuen und Kollektiven (vgl. Benjamins Essay über den Surrealismus). Ich sehe es als Zeichen einer zunehmenden Bewusstheit dieser Funktion des Schlafes, dass es zur Zeit eine beträchtliche Zahl von Künstler_innen gibt, die das Thema Schlaf erforschen, den schlafenden Körper oder die mit dem Schlaf verbundenen Bedingungen. Der Schlaf und der Wachzustand sind nicht nur soziale Symptome oder empirische Zustände unseres Geistes und unseres Körpers (mit allen Diskursen, die sich um das Thema drehen), sondern auch eine abstrakte Maschine der Aktualisierung und Potentialität; Einschlafen und Aufwachen sollten als ein speziell werdendes Thema, als ein politisches Thema gesehen werden.

Die Kunst spielt eine unverzichtbare Rolle in der Entwicklung oder Bildung politischer Subjektivität. Natürlich war und ist der schlafende Körper in vielen Kunstwerken, von der Antike bis in die Gegenwart, ein Thema. Man könnte mit Werken aus der klassischen Kunst (Brueghel, Rubens, De La Tour usw.) bis zu solchen der Moderne einen ganzen Bildband zusammenstellen, der nur Schlafende und ihre Körper zeigt – entspannt hingestreckt, nackt, in allen möglichen Posen und Positionen, in privater Zurückgezogenheit oder im öffentlichen Raum. Sie veranschaulichen unterschiedliche Aspekte – Schutzlosigkeit, Verletzlichkeit, oder auch wohltuende Ruhe und Erquickung.[19] Es ist jedoch interessanter, über einen anderen Aspekt nachzudenken, nämlich dass die Struktur eines Kunstwerks der Struktur

---

16 .... Benjamin: *Das Passagen-Werk*, 617 (0 2a,1).
17 .... Ebd., 493 (K1,5).
18 .... Ebd., 495 (K2,5).

19 ....Vgl. zum Beispiel Sivry, Sophie et al.: *The Art of Sleep: a Short Social Symbolic Medical Poetic and Amorous History*. Institut d'edition, London 1997.

motives are present not only in the visual arts, but also in literature. Marcel Proust's first novel *Swann's Way* begins with the long description of the awakening of the hero. As though he collects himself, his own 'I', his fluid subjectivity from uncountable *mémoires* of all rooms and places in which he woke up before. Similarly, the notorious madeleine cake evokes the past of the hero, leading to an illumination, and finally serves to rescue this past in an impressive sequence of images arising through sleep-like isolation from the pragmatic, operative functioning of our memory.

6.

To conclude my essay I would just like to expand some of the notes above, stressing my general position. *Vulnerability* is an important part of contemporary discourse surrounding sleep research in the social sciences. It is very interesting how many devices and rules have been invented in the history of human societies to protect sleep. For example, disturbing a sleeping person was strictly taboo in some traditional societies. In modern societies, the whole system of policing the streets at night and preventing disturbances to sleep was established. But the level of vulnerability obviously differs and is class-based—the poor are more vulnerable, and homeless people are most vulnerable of all.

At the same time, in modern thought, art and literature, sleep is a place of some special *equality* already discussed above. Sleep is something common, something that is equally shared by all—like the air, the sky or a beautiful view of a landscape. At the same time, the law of value, of production that depends on labour, extracts more and more time from working bodies, depriving them of sleep, reducing it to 'several hours of numbness', as Marx once wrote. Of course, the ways of extracting and privatising sleep time have changed, for example, with the self-employment and self-exploitation typical of immaterial work in neoliberal times.

On the other hand, one could say that we are powerful and *potentially* resistant during our sleeping time. Sleep as non-communication or non-productivity is a powerful exodus from society, which is based on communication and production. If all the people in a given society were asleep, that society would no longer exist. That would be like political mobilisation: if everyone came to a demonstration (or, a sleeping human strike), the government would be toppled for sure. Perhaps that is why power is afraid of total sleep and has introduced night watches, patrols, etc. It is not just for security, it's also for keeping some people awake.

This approach to the theme of sleep does not concern some 'other world', if by that we mean dreaming as an experience of alteration to access new possibilities of existence. My position is rooted in the philosophy of immanence, which does not search for some external transcendence or an escape from our everyday world into some desired world of the imaginary, utopia or a sublime and sophisticated negativity (which is just a new substitute for transcendence). I am not a supporter of the concept of utopia, because it is poisoned by a figure of impossibility, by unsatisfied desire with its lost objects, by some sweet melancholy, etc. I avoid the field of dreams, which is well explored and commoditised today, and address instead the phenomenon of sleep as a singular state of being. I am not so nostalgic for the 'good old days' when the pace of life was slow and not under pressure of the principles of productivity and efficiency. These good old days are often our own contemporary fantasies.

Nor am I praising sleep as a strange new and *actual* form of resistance. I am attempting to understand the complex connection between capitalism, metaphysics, sleep, waking and subjectivisation. My research is about the ontology and a political economy of sleep and the sleeping 'subject' (the term is here placed in quotes because we usually understand the subject as active, wakeful, etc.). At the same time, this is not about being resigned

to the world in which we live, and that is why politics and critique occupy a crucial place in this investigation. I think it is more important to constitute a real militant subject, whether awake or asleep, than a utopian and dreamlike object.

von Schlaf sehr ähnlich ist. Das Kunstwerk ist eine Isolierung eines bestimmten Phänomens, das dadurch den pragmatischen Kontexten des Alltags entzogen ist. Diese Sonderstellung macht es zu etwas Ästhetischem, öffnet es für unsere Sehweise. Zumindest kann man es, in Übereinstimmung mit Kants Verständnis von Kunst, als Ergebnis ‚gleichgültiger Kontemplation‘ sehen. So werden schlafende Körper auch nicht instrumentalisiert; sie werden aus dem Kontext von Arbeit, Aktivität, Produktion und Verwirklichung eines Interesses herausgehoben. Schlaf bedeutet auch den Verlust des Interesses an der Welt. Auf diese Weise äusserte sich zum Beispiel Freud über den Schlafzustand. Man könnte sagen: Als Schlafende werden wir Kunstwerke unserer selbst.[20]

Andererseits gibt es eine Denkströmung, die die Kunst mit Erwachen, mit Aktivität, mit der Fähigkeit den/die Betrachter_in zu beeinflussen, seine/ihre Weltsicht zu ändern oder sogar die Welt selber zu ändern, in Verbindung bringt. Besonders prominent waren darin die zahlreichen Avantgarden des 20. Jahrhunderts. Natürlich finden sich diese Motive nicht nur in der bildenden Kunst, sondern auch in der Literatur. Marcel Prousts *In Swanns Welt* beginnt mit der langen Schilderung des Erwachens des Helden, als würde er sich selber, sein ‚Ich‘, seine fliessende Subjektivität aus unzähligen Erinnerungen an alle Räume und Orte, an denen er je aufgewacht war, sammeln. Auch das berühmte Gebäck, die ‚Madeleine‘, evoziert die Vergangenheit des Helden, führt zu einer Erleuchtung und rettet dadurch diese Vergangenheit mittels einer beeindruckenden Folge von Bildern, die sich aus dem schlaf-ähnlichen Ausklinken aus dem pragmatischen ‚Funktionieren‘ unserer Erinnerung speist.

6.

Abschliessend würde ich gern einige der oben anführten Punkte noch einmal aufgreifen und ausführen, um damit meine allgemeine Position genauer herauszuarbeiten.

20 .... Vgl. die ähnliche Analyse von Schlaf und Bild in Seitter: *Geschichte der Nacht*, 192–200.

Verletzlichkeit ist ein wichtiger Aspekt im gegenwärtigen Diskurs über die Schlafforschung in der Soziologie. Es ist sehr interessant, wie viele Regeln und Vorrichtungen in der Geschichte der Menschheit erfunden wurden, um den Schlaf zu schützen. So war es in manchen Gesellschaften strikt verboten, eine_n Schlafende_n zu stören. Die modernen Gesellschaften haben das ganze System der Überwachung der Strassen während der Nacht und das Vermeiden nächtlicher Ruhestörung eingeführt. Der Grad der Verletzlichkeit variiert aber offensichtlich und scheint klassen- bzw. gesellschaftsschichtsbezogen – die Armen sind verletzlicher, und die Obdachlosen sind die verletzlichsten von allen.

Zugleich ist, wie oben bereits erwähnt, im modernen Denken, in der Kunst und in der Literatur, der Schlaf ein Ort einer besonderen ‚Gleichheit‘. Der Schlaf ist allen gemein, gehört zu allen – wie die Luft, der Himmel oder der Anblick einer schönen Landschaft. Dennoch entzieht das Wertgesetz der Produktion, die auf Arbeit beruht, den Arbeitskräften immer mehr Zeit, entzieht ihnen Schlaf, reduziert den Schlaf auf ‚ein paar Stunden Fühllosigkeit‘, wie Marx es ausdrückte. Natürlich haben sich die Arten, wie Schlafenszeit entzogen und privatisiert wird, geändert, zum Beispiel durch die selbstständige Erwerbstätigkeit und die Selbstausbeutung, die für Geistesarbeit in neoliberalen Zeiten typisch ist.

Andererseits könnte man natürlich anführen, dass wir, während wir schlafen, mächtig und ‚potenziell‘ widerstandsfähig sind. Schlaf als ein Zustand der Nicht-Kommunikation und Unproduktivität stellt ein mächtiges Sich-aus-der-Gesellschaft-Ausklinken dar, die auf Kommunikation und Produktion ausgerichtet ist und auf ihr beruht. Würden in einer bestimmten Gesellschaft alle Menschen zur gleichen Zeit schlafen, existierte diese Gesellschaft nicht mehr. Das wäre wie eine politische Mobilmachung. Gingen alle Bürger_innen an eine Demonstration (oder führten alle einen Schlafstreik durch), wäre die Regierung sicher gestürzt. Vielleicht ist das ein Grund, warum sich die Macht vor dem Schlaf fürchtet und weshalb also die Nachtwache, die Patrouillen, die Überwachung usw. eingeführt wurden. Es geht dabei nicht nur um die Sicherheit, es geht auch darum, einige Leute wach zu halten.

Dieses Herangehen an das Thema Schlaf betrifft nicht ‚eine andere Welt‘, wenn wir darunter den Traum als eine Erfahrung der Veränderung oder des Zugangs zu anderen Seinsmöglichkeiten verstehen. Meine Position beruht auf der Immanenzphilosophie, die keine externe ‚Transzendenz‘ sucht, um aus unserem weltlichen Alltag in eine Wunschwelt, eine Utopie oder eine erhabene und ausgeklügelte Negativität (die nichts anderes als ein weiterer Ersatz für Transzendenz ist) zu flüchten. Ich bin kein Anhänger von Utopien, weil dieses Konzept durch eine Figur der Unmöglichkeit vergiftet ist, durch unerfüllte Wünsche mit ihren verlorenen Objekten, durch ach so süsse Melancholie etc. Ich halte mich vom Gebiet der Träume fern, das heute sehr gut erforscht und auch zur Ware geworden ist, und wende mich lieber dem Phänomen Schlaf als einzigartigem Seinszustand zu. Ich sehne mich nicht besonders nach den ‚guten alten Zeiten‘ zurück, als der Lebensrhythmus noch langsam war und man nicht unter dem Druck von Produktions- und Leistungsprinzipien stand. Jene guten alten Zeiten existieren oft nur in unserer heutigen Fantasie.

Genauso wenig möchte ich den Schlaf als eigenartige neue oder ‚aktuelle‘ Form von Widerstand rühmen. Ich versuche, die komplexen Zusammenhänge zwischen Kapitalismus, Metaphysik, Schlaf, Wachzustand und Subjektivierung zu verstehen. Ich befasse mich mit der Ontologie und einer politischen Ökonomie des Schlafs und des schlafenden ‚Subjekts‘ (hier in Anführungszeichen, weil wir üblicherweise das Subjekt als etwas Aktives, etwas Waches usw. sehen). Zugleich ist es nicht meine Absicht, mich mit der Welt, in der wir leben, abzufinden, deshalb nehmen Politik und Kritik einen zentralen Platz in meiner Forschung ein. Was meiner Meinung nach wirklich wichtig ist, egal, ob im Wachen oder Schlafen, ist es, ein wirklich militantes Subjekt zu sein, und kein utopisches, irgendwelchen Träumen nachhängendes Objekt.

Übersetzt von Ingrid Fichtner

Mladen Stilinović: *Omjetnik radi (Artist at Work)*, 1978

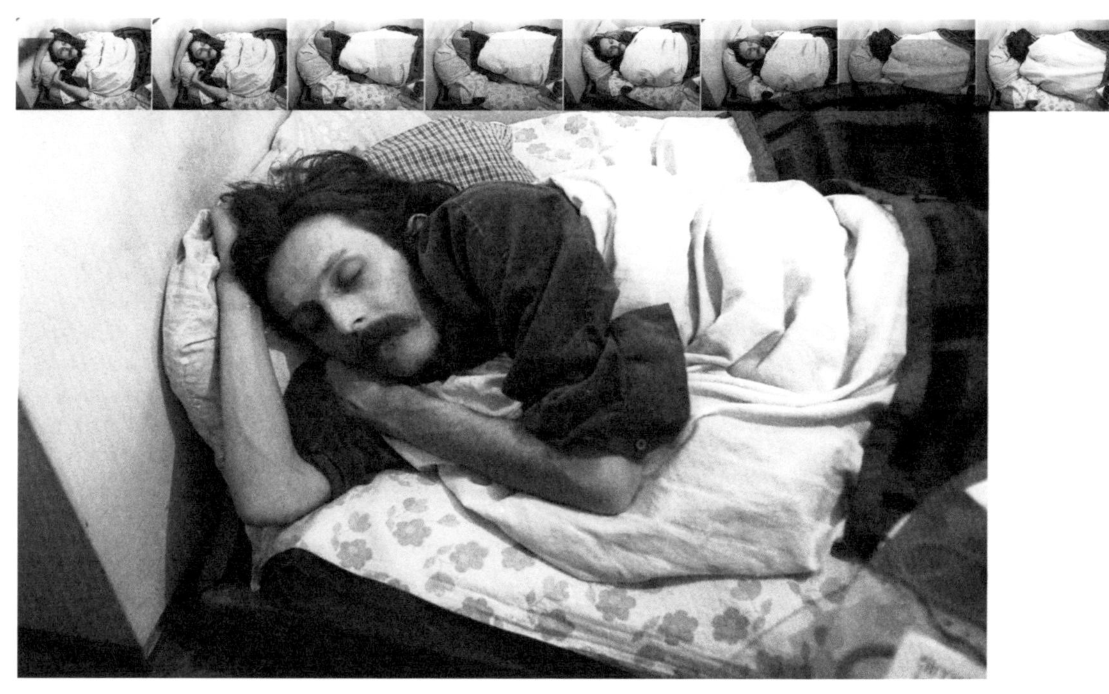

MLADEN STILINOVIĆ

THE PRAISE OF LAZINESS

THE PRAISE OF LAZINESS

As an artist, I learned from both East (socialism) and West (capitalism). Of course, now when the borders and political systems have changed, such an experience will be no longer possible. But what I have learned from that dialogue, stays with me. My observation and knowlesge of Western art has lately led me to a conclusion that art cannot exists any more in the West. This is not to say that there isn't any. Why cannot art exist any more in the West? The answer is simple. Artists in the West are not lazy. Artists from the East are lazy; whether they will stay lazy now when they are no longer Eastern artists, remains to be seen.

Laziness is the absence of movement and thought, dumb time - total amnesia. It is also indifference, staring at nothing, non-activity, impotence. It is sheer stupidity, a time of pain, futile concentration. Those virtues of laziness are important factors in art. Knowing about laziness is not enough, it must be practiced and perfected.

Artists in the West are not lazy and therefore not artists but rather producers of something..... Their involvment with matters of no importance, such as production, promotion, gallery system, museum system, competition system (who is first), their preoccupation with objects, all that drives them away form laziness, from art. Just as money is paper, so is a gallery a room.

Artists from the East were lazy and poor because the entire sistem of insignificant factors did not exist. Therefore they had time enough to concetrate on art and laziness. Even when thay did produce art, they knew it was in vain, it was nothing.

Artists from the West could learn about laziness, but they didn't. Two major 20th centery artists treated the question of laziness, in both practical and theoretical terms: Duchamp and Malevich.

Duchamp never really discussed laziness, but rather indifference and non-work. When asked by Pierre Cabanne what had brought him most pleasure in life, Duchamp said: "First, having been lucky. Because basically I've never worked for a living. I consider working for a living slightly imbecilic from an economic point of view. I hope that some day we'll be able to live without being obliged to work. Thanks to my luck, I was able to manage without getting wet".

Malevich wrote a text entitled "Laziness - the real truth of mankind" (1921). In it he criticized capitalism because it enabled only a small number of capitalists to be lazy, butalso socialism because the entire movement was based on work instead of laziness. To quote: "People are scared of laziness and persecute those who accept it, and it always happens because no one realizes laziness is the truth; it has bees branded as the mother of all vices, but it is in fact the mother of life. Socialism brings liberation in the unconscious, it scorns laziness without realizing it was laziness that gave birth to it; in his folly, the son scorns his mother as a mother of all vices and would not remove the brand; in this brief note I want to remove the brand of shame from laziness and to pronounce it not the mother of all vices, but the mother of perfection".

Finally, to be lazy and conclude: there is no art without laziness.

WORK IS A DISEASE - KARL MARX   **WORK IS A SHAME**
Mladen Stilinović   Vlado Martek

Mladen Stilinović

A KIND OF CERTAINTY IS UNCERTAINTY

An e-mail exchange between Igor and Ivan Buharov and Yvonne Volkart

Yvonne Volkart: *I always wanted to know why you work under the pseudonym Igor and Ivan Buharov. Can you tell me something about this name? Furthermore, you mostly work together, but you also work within other constellations of people, and sometimes you work alone. Can you tell me something about your way of cooperating with other artists and why this is important to you?*

Igor and Ivan Buharov: **About our pseudonym, it's a complex question. First of all we like the Russian avant-garde from the beginning of the last century, and when we became film-makers—about 17 years ago—the Russian army had just left the country so at that time everybody hated the Russians. We wanted to perpetuate an *épater le bourgeois* attitude, so we chose the names Igor and Ivan Buharov. In our slang 'buherál' means somebody tinkering around in his shed, turning useless household appliances into something totally different, like a washing machine into a lawn mower—crude makeshift solutions to some existing problem…**

We wanted to make an associative joke with our chosen names too. We bought a 'Soviet' Super-8 camera at the flea market.

About cooperation, I don't think anybody can make a film alone, if somebody says: 'I made this film', it's not true because there were other people involved too, like a dramaturge, a set designer and so on. When we started to make films together we did everything ourselves, from the shooting to the editing, like real outsiders. When we cooperate with other people, we still work the same way and it doesn't cause problems if somebody has to act a bit or hold the lights. The point is that the film should be good. And more eyes see more than one… or two.

Yvonne Volkart: *Within the last 15 years, you made a lot of short films, which from my point of view were made in a very horizontal way. By horizontal I mean that your approach is not geared toward letting reason dictate the action, but allowing for aspects like chance, collectivity or playing—in short letting things happen or letting go as well as daring to leave the conventional paths of comprehension. Can you tell me more about the ideas behind your short films, e.g.* **Hotel Tubu** *from 2002?*

Igor and Ivan Buharov: **We started shooting *Hotel Tubu* without a concept. We didn't really know what we wanted to shoot in the beginning; all we knew was that we wanted to make a short about animals and humans. Domestic animals give up their freedom because of 'better' circumstances; people act similarly, accepting and assisting systems that don't work. That's why we went to rent a bear costume, but all they had was a bear costume with a monkey head. In fact, this was better.**

Igor und / and Ivan Buharov: *Johnny and the Goosies*, 2010

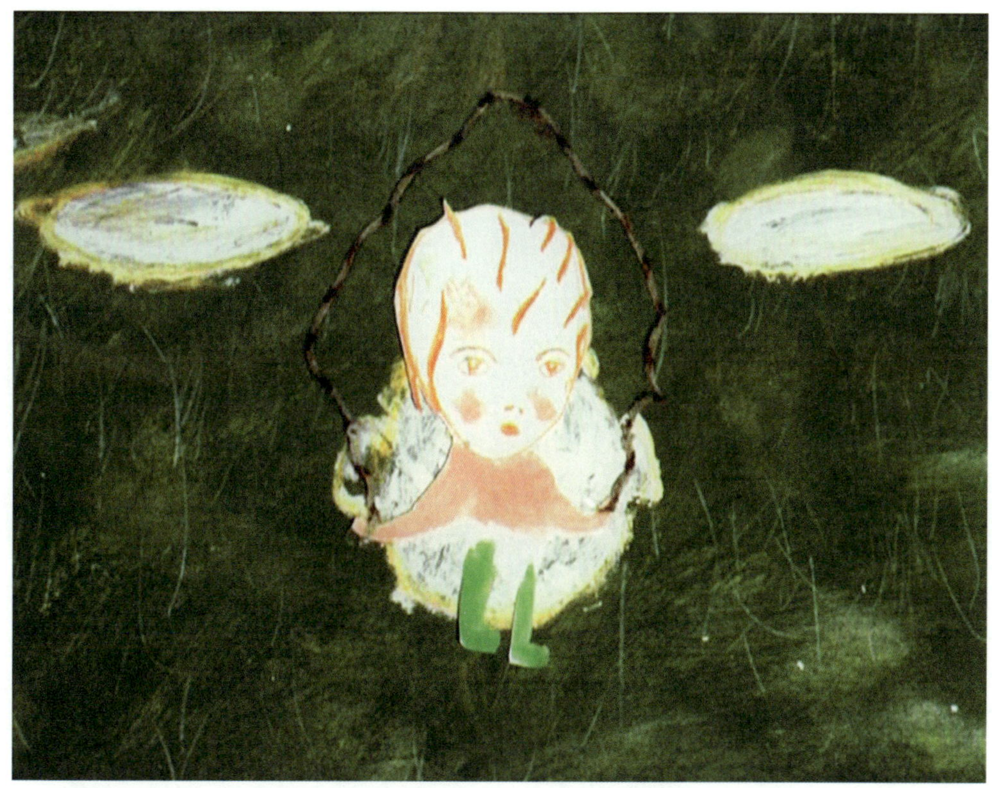

Igor und / and Ivan Buharov: *Oneheadword Protection*, 2006   Igor und / and Ivan Buharov: *Johnny and the Goosies*, 2010

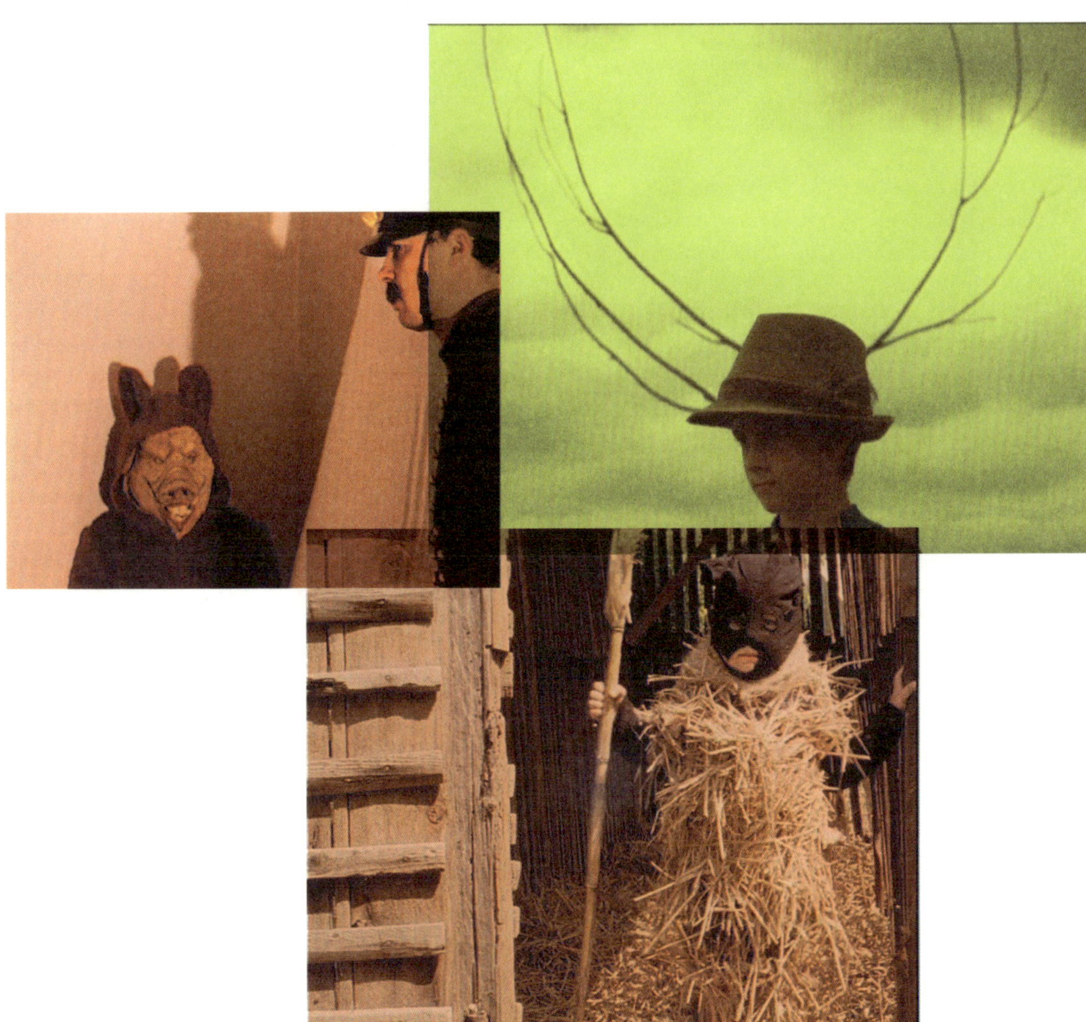

Igor und / and Ivan Buharov: *Oneheadword Protection*, 2006

So we used that costume. Sometimes Ivan was in the costume, sometimes I was. It only took three days to film it, and all we had were nine minutes of 35-mm material and the costumes. The actors used what we found around the house, thus Ivan's grandmother, a hunter's costume, a stuffed bird and a dead frog appear in the movie as well. When we saw the results, we were disappointed. Four years later we came across some found footage sound that inspired us to resume the movie project.

Yvonne Volkart: Let's talk more in detail about this film, which is at the same time nonlinear and fragmented, like a collage, and, especially because of the music, immersive and beautiful as well. Nevertheless, there is a kind of story, and there are protagonists who change shape from man to animal to cosmos workers and back…

Igor and Ivan Buharov: When we listened to this found footage audio cassette we heard a lot of sentences from a 'guru' of the 'fellowship—or company of friends—about the mysteries of the cosmos'. The voice of the leader was very inspirational, serious, ironic, funny, hopeless, hopeful, weird and true at the same time. We liked it very much because we were able to create a new context from it. It opened up the possibility of a game between image and sound, by incorporating our own surreal, esoteric world and our dreams as well. The edited sound layer was designed to reflect our thinking, but leave the viewers with an opportunity to create their own world. A kind of certainty is uncertainty. The title *Tubu* is a play on words and meanings. The word 'butu' derives from 'buta', meaning silly, which can be said about the characters and the manner of the fairy tale as well. This was offset by the presumed seriousness of the edited text to voice. The music was composed by Ivan, as usual.

Yvonne Volkart: This film, especially together with the music, which in the beginning is as pure as water (we also see this, visually), and as beautiful as a flower (this we see, too, although superimposed with a hanging puppet or dead frog),

becomes more and more intense—like a drug—so that at the end, in a certain sense, it seems to swell, and thus also the rhythmic hitting the monkey/hunter by the old woman fits quite well into this exaggerated and heated atmosphere with one thing leading to the next. In this situation, the narrator says: 'The cosmos workers only want what God's will demands and what is allowed by Karma. The power should never work in any other way. If they wanted something else, then its effect would stop and not work anymore.' How am I to understand these lines? Are they true, or paradoxical?

Igor and Ivan Buharov: Maybe your question is the answer: they are paradoxically true.

Yvonne Volkart: Johnny and the Goosies (2010) is a newer film. It narrates the story of a gooseherd. At a certain point, after he sleeps too much and loses control, his story seems to be linked to the Hungarian nation. Thus, this film seems to be like a political allegory, but told as a fairy tale, shown in images that are like animated cartoons. Can you tell me something about this film, and what may have changed in your strategy?

Igor and Ivan Buharov: Actually we made a half-an-hour-long short film in 2010, *Rudderless*, which also deals with the current political situations in Hungary and Europe in general, especially the issue of immigration. In *Johnny and the Goosies*, of course, we remained in the fairy tale genre, including the expressive possibilities of a dream, but we wanted to express political and social criticism in our own language. In Hungary there is more and more populism and nationalism, so we tried to play with these symbols, destroying romantic national tabus. Johnny is a simple character, an instinctive being, like the main character in *Hotel Tubu*, but he wants to do good things, and his simplicity makes the 'Hungarian' people happier. In the last 20 years since the collapse of communism, there have never been so many people who want to leave the country as there are today. More and more destroyed lives, hopeless and homeless people on the streets, so the critical voice has to be stronger.

Stefan Panhans: *If A Store Clerk Gave Me too Much Change*, 2009

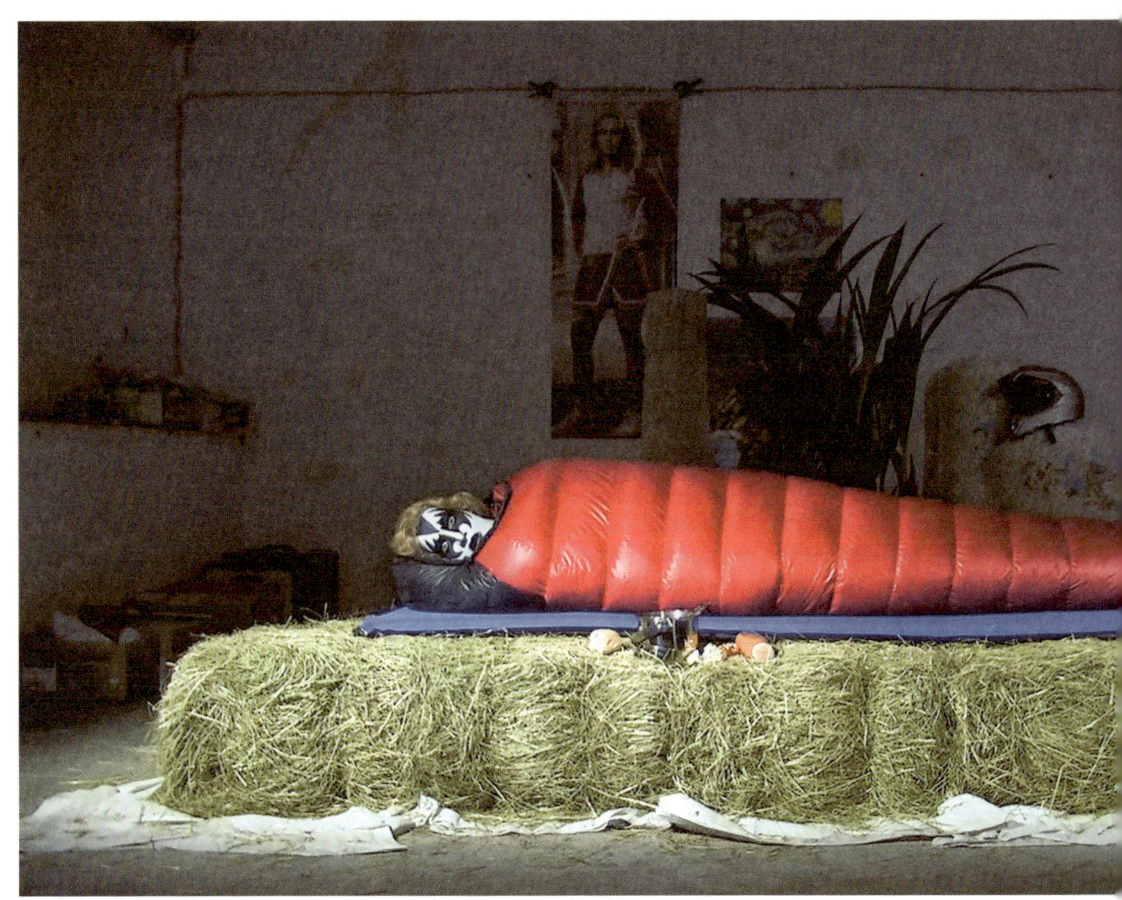

STEFAN PANHANS

IF A STORE CLERK GAVE ME TOO MUCH CHANGE

The following excerpt is part of a monologue around which the video work *If A Store Clerk Gave Me too Much Change* (2009) by Stefan Panhans is centered. The topic of the text, spoken by somebody in a sleeping bag, is the subject facing the challenges of a neoliberal society geared toward achievement and control.

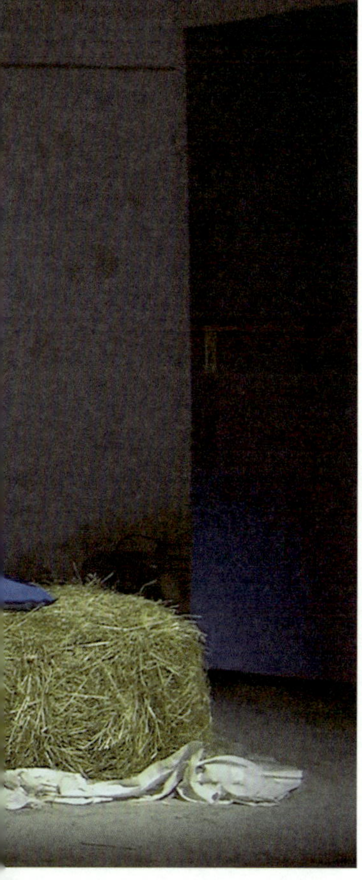

You can specify the cleaning of your working clothes as promotional expenses with the corresponding receipts. If you do not have any receipts, because e.g. you wash your working clothes privately in your washing machine then you can specify the following formula: 48 x 3 kilogramm x 0,93 Euros = 134.- Euros. In general this amount is accepted. If you have constantly changing deployment locations and after an absence of at least 8 hours from your apartment you can specify 6 Euros for extraordinary food expenses. After an absence of more than 14 hours you can specify 12 Euros and after an absence of at least 24 hours you can estimate 24 Euros. But you have to deduct any reimbursements of your employer from these expenses. BUT FIRST OF ALL YOU HAVE TO KNOW THE FOLLOWING: A huge accumulation of favourable Qi can lead to positive results in health, harmony and success. This is actually totally easy; give yourself the power to let yourself go! First of all this is the most important, you have to learn this. Let go. LET GO FIRST OF ALL. You have to find YOURSELF, your inner power source, thereto first you must let go. Do you know what Qi is? Qi is blown by the wind and stops at the border of the water. Qi is the invisible energy of life, which flows everywhere around us, in every creature and — damn it — in every cell! It is the energy that inspirits and creates everything, you must learn to feel it inside you, this will happen slowly, you cannot expect fast successes, SLOW DOWN, remember the hare and the hedgehog, which one of them was always first in the end?, slowness is not a deficiency, through it you actually shorten the way, you proceed vertically, you rise slowly into the height and you see the others running below, but where?,

you get an overview in this height, up there
things seem to work slower, that's what you
know from any kind of hierarchy, the bosses
up there take plenty of time. From there you
have to start, by then you will feel when you can
lead your wishes. Proper wishing, there you
have to be, in the height proper wishing and then
in the right moment you will start from your
centre and everything will lie open in front
of you, you have the chance and you take it. Luck
is a question of attitude, of self-tuning. Find the
access to yourself and to your feelings and
wishes again, this is very important, only who
CORRECTLY wishes gets what one wishes.
Thereto you have to know what you ACTUALLY
want. Get to the bottom of your unconscious
wishes, check your attitudes accurately and your
perception of life and don't forget: your perception develops your scheme of life! Understand
that all your thoughts are already your wishes.
So stop with all this negative thinking about
yourself, about others and about your situation,
don't rate and judge yourself, focus only on what
you want to achieve, be in a good mood, keep
it up, imperturbably! Make some info diets,
turn off and on several days all the devices that
give you continuously this unnecessary,
confusing so called information, you will see,
you don't miss that much! This is all part of the
HORIZONTAL!, YOU are taking from now on
the VERTICAL way! The human being has about
60 000 thoughts a day, most of them are the
same ones as on the day before, and those are
again the same ones as on the day before yesterday, and so on and on. Important is to turn off
the negative and the constantly recurring ones,
those ones you cannot need up there, up there
where you want to go. Those belong to the
HORIZONTAL, but YOU are taking from now on
the VERTICAL way!, you are climbing unstoppa-
bly up, up to the top, way over the top into the
wide open! Important is to turn off the negative
and the constantly recurring ones, get rid off
them, those ones you cannot need up there, they
are totally inefficient and useless. ONE HAS TO
START ALWAYS WITH ONESELF, this has to be
clear. If you want to achieve something you will
not get around to adjust to this. Everything is up
to YOU. AND DON'T FORGET, WHEREVER YOU
GO, YOU ALWAYS TAKE YOURSELF WITH YOU!!

WIR SCHLAFEN NICHT

Der nachfolgende Text ist ein Auszug aus dem Roman *wir schlafen nicht* von Kathrin Röggla (S. Fischer Verlag, Frankfurt am Main, 2006).

5. life-style (der senior associate)

wisse man doch: immer hübsch eine autoklasse unter denen müsse man bleiben. auch bezüglich der anzüge heiße es: aufgepaßt, nur nicht zu edel. am besten grau. und dann einmal quer durch die landschaft damit: banken, versicherungen, automobilhersteller, versorgungsunternehmen, baustoffe. aber von so einem yuppie-high-flyer-leben brauche ihm keiner was zu erzählen, da könne ihm keiner was vormachen, das könne er auswendig runtersagen: den inhalt der minibar, die streifen der tapete. er kenne das lächeln der rezeption, er kenne die blicke der sechs-uhr-flieger, er kenne den kaffeeautomaten von lufthansa am flughafen und auch leysieffer.

wisse man doch: man müsse diesbezüglich den mund halten, sich zumindest etwas zurückhalten mit der eigenen meinung. wisse man doch: was dürfe man sagen und was nicht. und immer hübsch darauf achten, eine autoklasse drunter zu sein, sich nie allzu auffällig zu verhalten, habe man ihm nicht lange sagen müssen, das verstehe sich von selbst. „und wenn jemand nur ja-nein-entscheidungen am tisch haben möchte, was machst du dann? wenn jemand nur noch ja-nein-entscheidungen am tisch haben möchte, dann wirst du ihm auch nur ja-nein-entscheidungen auf den tisch legen!" das verstehe sich von selbst, sonst habe man seinen job nicht gemacht.

*

die ersten beiden jahre sei man berater, d.h. er habe als summer associate angefangen, also praktisch als praktikant, dann weitergemacht als associate, sprich, als ganz normaler consultant - „ja, das ist schon eine ganz schöne show mit den bezeichnungen." - jedenfalls sei er danach teamleiter geworden, und eine stufe drüber werde man dann partner wie herr gehringer, irgendwann mal. die organisation sei nämlich als partner-schaft aufgebaut, „und irgendwann läßt du dich

zum partner wählen von den anderen partnern",
aber das sei schon die große hürde, eben
der entscheidende karrieresprung. die meisten
gingen aber schon nach zwei bis drei jahren, weil
es ihnen reiche. weil sie in irgendeinem unternehmen, wo sie auf projekt gewesen seien,
eine stelle angeboten bekommen hätten und
lieber eine ruhige kugel schieben wollten.

*

„du wohnst als wg in einem appartementhotel,
das ist so ein appartement, wo geputzt wird. du
arbeitest sehr viel, weil du sowieso nichts anderes
machen kannst, du hast hier ja keine sozialisation.
du baust auch keine auf, weil du weißt, du bist
in ein paar monaten wieder weg. und freitags
landest du dann um halb elf in deiner stadt, dann
schreibst du dein reporting am wochenende.
und du machst auch deine reisekostenabrech-
nung, also nochmal acht stunden am wochenende."

müsse er zugeben: ein wenig geistesgestört seien
die arbeitszeiten schon, das sei ihm klar, wenn
einem die arbeit nicht über alles gehe, dann könne
man das auch nicht machen. das verstünde sich
von selbst. man mache ja locker 14 stunden, wenn
nicht gar 16 oder mehr. und das sei natürlich
ein riesenunterschied. gerade diese zwei stunden
mehr, die einem von der freien zeit noch abge-
knappst würden, die könnten sie einem irgendwann
nicht mehr bezahlen. diese letzte stunde freizeit,
die sie einem wegnähmen, die sei einfach die
teuerste. müsse er zugeben: die wenigsten könnten sowas auf dauer durchhalten.

*

also seine leistung überrasche ihn nicht, genau-
sowenig wie seine leistungsfähigkeit. die habe er
immer schon einkalkuliert, die wundere ihn nicht.
daß er mehrere tage durcharbeiten könne, auch
das wundere ihn nicht wirklich, das sei nicht interessant. seine leistungsfähigkeit sei für ihn nicht
interessant, die sei ja auch immer schon vorher da,
sozusagen, bevor er eintreffe in einer situation.
spitzenleistungen seien für ihn das übliche, aber er
erwarte auch von seinem gegenüber die absolute
performance, er könne mit mitarbeitern nichts
anfangen, die das nicht brächten.

die devise „schlafen kann ich, wenn ich tot bin",
würde er jetzt nicht so direkt-adaptieren, das habe
man ja eher früher gesagt, „so mitte der neunziger
war das die devise schlechthin", zumindest
in seiner generation. so mitte der neunziger habe
man das auch noch sagen können. sicher, das
hätte heute auch noch was brauchbares, aber
damals habe man es eben praktiziert. und wenn
er länger darüber nachdenke, müsse er schon
sagen, das sei ja was erstaunliches, so seine generation. das müsse man sich mal vorstellen, was
da in kürzester zeit an wissen akkumuliert worden
sei und an erfahrung. ja, was mittzwanziger sich
da schon reingezogen hätten an erfahrungswerten.
die seien jetzt natürlich angeschlagen, aber wenn
die sich erst einmal wieder erholt hätten, dann
könnten die auf ganz anderem niveau loslegen.

nee, schlafen sei nicht schick, „das kommt nicht
so gut." wer schlafe, sei auch schlecht beraten,
so als berater (*lacht*), man würde eben viel arbeiten,
und man würde ja auch viel nachts arbeiten,
„also wenn man um 18 uhr geht, kommt üblicherweise der spruch: ob man sich einen halben
tag freigenommen habe?" das sei ein völlig
normaler spruch. ja, er würde fast sagen, es herr-
sche da so eine art wettbewerb vor, so unter dem
motto: wer hält am längsten durch?

er habe sich ja zeitweise runterdimensioniert auf
drei stunden schlaf. das könne er eine ganze
weile durchhalten, und wenn es sein müsse, sage
er mal, könne er auch einige zeit praktisch ohne
schlaf existieren. das ginge aber nur wenige
tage gut. „tatsache ist, man kann diese dinge
trainieren." er kenne einen, der brauche konstant
nur eine stunde schlaf am tag, also er müsse
schon sagen, das bewundere er sehr. er finde es
immer wieder erstaunlich, wozu der menschliche
körper fähig sei. gerade, wenn man denkt, das
sei jetzt ein standardbedürfnis, „ohne das geht es
jetzt wirklich nicht. und man sieht: es geht doch."

*

er habe in london gelebt, er habe in paris gelebt, er
habe in san diego gelebt. er könne es sich
gut vorstellen, in london zu leben. unter umständen
paris. zu deutschland habe er eigentlich wenig
affinität, aber als wirtschaftsraum sei es interessant.

*

das wolle er jedenfalls nicht mehr machen: durch
irgendwelche pißdörfer fahren, wo man halt
irgendwann mal ein großes werk hingestellt habe,
und diese menschen sehen. durch pißdörfer
fahren und menschen sehen und wissen, daß die
ganze region abhänge von diesem kieswerk.
oder diesem baustoffzulieferbetrieb. also manchmal habe er da den volkswirtschaftlichen exkurs
gestartet, manchmal den rein moralischen.
manchmal habe er sich gesagt: diese leute,
die er jetzt da freisetze, die stünden letztlich auf
seinem lohnstreifen, „ist ja logisch!" - über die
steuern. und das mache nun auch wieder keinen
sinn, so volkswirtschaftlich gedacht. aber
letztendlich fahre man durch so pißdörfer und
man sehe, wie trostlos es in vielen regionen sei.

„du denkst dir: meine güte, das kann doch gar
nicht sein! und jetzt nochmal 100 leute! du weißt,
ein gewisser prozentsatz, der geht in den vor-
ruhestand. geschenkt. die meisten leute finden's
nicht so furchtbar schlimm. also es ist nicht
die absolute höchststrafe, nicht zu arbeiten. andere
sind mobil, die finden was neues. aber es ist
trotzdem nicht so leicht, einfach mal 300 leute
rauszuschmeißen."

so koche man die dinge für sich runter, so unter
dem motto: der dreifache familienvater, der
dann ohne lohn und brot dastehe, den gebe es
ja doch eher nicht. oder zumindest relativ selten.
man würde die ja auch nicht zu gesicht bekommen.
sicher, es wäre schon schwieriger, wenn man
es jedem einzelnen selber sagen müsse. aber
letztendlich sei man ja auch dabei, die arbeitgeberfront zu bewaffnen, d.h. den taschenrechner
rauszuholen, „und los geht's!" ja, letztendlich sei
man eben dabei, der arbeitgeberfront genügend
munition zu bieten, ordentliche kaliber wie dieses
argument „tot oder leben". das verstünden immer
alle gleich, auch der betriebsrat. das sei immer
das beste argument: also, wenn man gewisse
maßnahmen nicht machte, dann müßten eben alle
gehen.

*

nein, meist gingen die leute dann weniger aus
moralischen gründen, sondern weil der life-style
sie total ankotze: all das short-sleeping,
quick-eating und diese ganzen nummern. und das
hotelgeschlafe, das business-class-gefliege,
das first-class-gewohne. irgendwann könne man
das alles nicht mehr sehen.

man könne die minibar nicht mehr sehen.

man könne die minibar nicht mehr sehen
und die immergleichen gesichter an der rezeption.

auch die kästchen auf dem teppich, die habe
man schon durchgezählt.

und fliegen wie busfahren, das könne man
auch nicht mehr haben.

aber auch diese ewige wachstumslogik, die man
irgendwann gegen sich selbst anwende.

*

„zitiere mich ja richtig!"
„was? das kannst du nicht?"
„und was kannst du sonst nicht?"

2

WIE KUNST GESCHICHTE SCHREIBT

HOW ART WRITES HISTORY

Sarah Vanagt: *Boulevard d'Ypres / Ieperlaan*, 2010

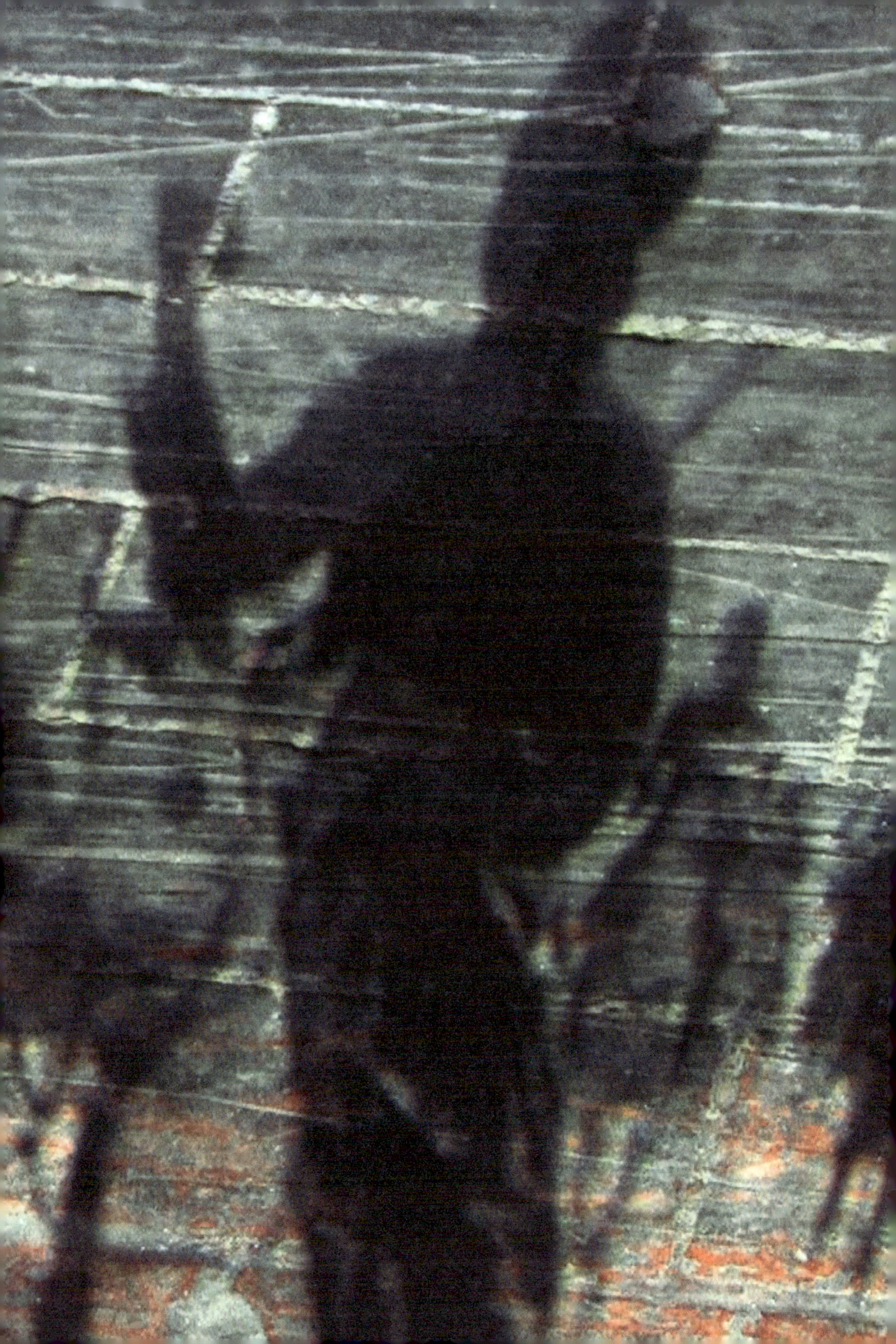

ÜBERBLENDUNGEN. DAS ZUKÜNFTIGE REKONSTRUIEREN. ODER: VOM UMGANG MIT GESCHICHTE IN DER KUNST

CROSS-FADES: RECONSTRUCTING THE FUTURE. OR: ON DEALING WITH HISTORY IN ART

Will man die Geschichte als einen Text betrachten, dann gilt von ihr, was ein neuerer Autor von literarischen sagt: Die Vergangenheit habe in ihnen Bilder niedergelegt, die man mit denen vergleichen könnte, die von einer lichtempfindlichen Platte festgehalten werden.
(Walter Benjamin, Gesammelte Werke)

Das Projekt *Überblendungen. Das Zukünftige rekonstruieren* geht auf Beobachtungen der letzten zehn Jahre zurück, die auf einen neuen Umgang mit der Vergangenheit und geschichtsbildenden Prozessen hindeuten. Mit einem neu erwachten Selbstbewusstsein verstehen sich Künstler_innen als Teil historischer Diskurse und fragen danach, wie und mit welchen Mitteln sich bestimmte Geschichtsbilder und historische Erzählungen durchsetzen konnten oder nicht, und was das für die Gegenwart bedeutet. Sie machen bewusst, dass die Darstellung und Medialität von Geschichte ein Problem ist, und dass es weniger um die Frage gehen muss, wie es denn wirklich war, sondern darum, wie man das, was geschehen sein könnte, aus heutiger Sicht sieht und interpretiert. Es geht um Fragen wie: Wer ist ermächtigt, über das, was vor mir geschehen ist, zu sprechen? Wer spricht? Wie wird gesprochen oder auch: Wie werden Dinge nicht gesagt und wie wird dennoch Geschichte erzählt? Viele der im Ausstellungsprojekt versammelten Künstler_innen machen deutlich, dass Geschichte stets situiert ist, d.h. aus einer ganz bestimmten Perspektive erzählt und konstruiert wird. Und sie machen deutlich, dass es an der Zeit ist, Geschichte nicht mehr nur aus der Siegerposition zu erzählen, sondern aus derjenigen, die Subalterne und Namenlose miteinschliesst, mithin aus jener Perspektive, die immer wieder, über Generationen hinweg, zu den Verliererinnen gehört.

Im Mittelpunkt unserer Ausstellung stand die Methode der ‚Überblendung‘, die in der Kunst immer wieder zur Anwendung kommt: Das Gestern wird mit dem Blick von heute überblendet. Diese Beobachtung wurde durch unsere Benjamin-Lektüren aus der Studienzeit genährt;

If one looks upon history as a text, then one can say of it what a recent author has said of literary texts—namely, that the past has left in this images comparable to those registered by a light-sensitive plate.
(Walter Benjamin, *Selected Writings*)

The project *Cross-fades: Reconstructing the Future* can be traced back to observations made in recent years that indicate a new way of dealing with the past and with processes of history formation. With a newly awakened self-confidence, artists see themselves as participants in historical discourses and inquire into how and with what means certain historic images and narratives were able or unable to assert themselves, and what this means for the present. They call attention to the fact that the depiction and mediality of history is a problem, and that it must be less a question of how it really was and more how one sees and interprets what was able to happen at that time from today's point of view. They are concerned with questions such as: Who is empowered to speak about that which occurred before me? Who speaks? How do they speak? Or: How do things go unsaid while at the same time history is nevertheless related? Many of the artists assembled in the exhibition project point out that history is always situated, i.e., is related and constructed from a certain perspective. And they point out that it is time to stop relating history only from the point of view of the victor and begin relating it from one that includes the subaltern and the nameless, hence from a point of view that time and again, over generations, belongs to the losers.

The focus of our exhibition was 'cross-fading', a method that is frequently applied in art: yesterday is cross-faded with today's perspective. This observation was fed by our study of Walter Benjamin at university, above all of the theses he put forward in *On the Concept of History*.[1] It seems as if traces of Benjaminian readings influence many current artistic strategies. According to Benjamin, insight into the past is not gained qua linear historicism—he explicitly opposed this—but via an ephemeral image in which the now and what was coalesced to form a constellation with lightning speed. 'For it is an irretrievable picture of the past, which threatens to disappear with every present, which does not recognize itself as meant in it.'[2] Walter Benjamin was firmly of the opinion that it cannot be about finding out how it was, but that it is instead about awakening knowledge about the inherent possibilities of what was of which one is not yet conscious. He speaks of the 'fight for the suppressed past'[3] (Thesis XVII), thus suggesting that it has to be about the recognisability of a past that perhaps never even took place in that way. The cross-fading of now with what was leads to knowledge of the 'here-and-now', in which elements of something redeeming are embedded; Benjamin refers to this as the 'Messianic'.[4] This takes place at the moment of danger and can only ever arise against the background of acknowledging the catastrophic quality of history. When it looks at history, his symbolic 'angel of history'—which in fact makes reference to Paul Klee's painting *Angelus Novus*—sees nothing but debris and catastrophes. This is the melancholic speaking.[5] Yet because the angel looks at these catastrophes and does not suppress them, something different, something hopeful can occur; in the future, history does not necessarily have to be a catastrophe.

We based the subtitle *Reconstructing the Future* on this notion of history. It implies that it cannot be about the future (in contrast to the present) in a platitudinous sense, but about thinking about the condition of a possible present and future that consistently includes a present that is to be refabricated. It is only with the situated view of yesterday that I can change tomorrow and thus perhaps even today.

---

1 .... Walter Benjamin, *On the Concept of History*, trans. Dennis Redmond (New York, 2009).

2 .... Ibid., p. 6.
3 .... Ibid., p. 20.
4 .... Ibid.
5 .... On the melancholy, see the text *Lands End: Thinking Things from Their Possible End*, p. 118 in this volume.

Catastrophic Pasts

Cross-fading is originally a film technique and refers to seamlessly fading from one shot into another or simultaneously combining several shots in one image. However, we assume that this initially formal technique also becomes a content-related method in which times, spaces, subjects, voices, things, etc., are superimposed and thus produce a leap, a discontinuity in the structure of meaning. Although this method, which is related to the montage technique, is in principle open to all media, it frequently occurs in filmic contexts.

Besides the possibility of new forms of narration, this is possibly one reason why the medium of film was so prominent in this exhibition project. In the following, based on several examples I would like to illustrate the various modes of cross-fading.

There are numerous such cross-fades in Sarah Vanagt's film *Boulevard d'Ypres* (fig. p. 60/61): it is initially a street in which the artist and in particular immigrants from the Mediterranean region and Africa live. This street is named after Ypres, a town that became well known because during World War I it was situated on the severely embattled Western Front, where mustard gas (which is why the gas is also called yperite) was used for the first time in history. What is not officially mentioned—and what the film reveals to us uninformed at first opaquely and only successively—is the fact that numerous men from the colonies also fought here for the allied forces: Africans, Indians, etc. This Boulevard d'Ypres is now being beset by gentrification and the associated displacement of its inhabitants, a circumstance that prompted Sarah Vanagt to portray the street in such a way that reflects the so-called 'micro-history' (Carlo Ginzburg) of the people who live here. She asked her neighbours to tell their (life) stories, not, however, in a first-person account, but as a kind of fairytale or legend in the third person. We only gradually become aware that it is a device, a technique of superimposing the first with the third person; we initially simply hear the most incredible life stories.

The site of the relation of the stories and thus history is an empty storeroom that, at first only marginally recognisable, has been converted into a kind of improvised, temporary cinema: documentary films from World War I are being shown on the shop door, the steps, and in the end over a wide area on the paved floor that show entire battalions consisting of dark-skinned people. These films are now superimposed, commented on and in part reduced to absurdity with incredibly biting humour with the perspective and knowledge of immigrants from the 21st century. One person, for instance, finds it amusing that the Africans did not even know how to handle these modern guns. But they were not important anyway, because all they were just cannon fodder.

A further line in the film is the improvement of sound recordings that were made between 1915 and 1918 in German prisoner-of-war camps. Many of these doomed Africans were imprisoned and thus became fascinating field research objects for German scientists (ethnographers and linguists). A total of 1,650 recordings of various languages were made for the Prussian national library; they are now stored at the Humboldt University and can be listened to on the Internet.[6] At the time, the prisoners were asked to tell a story or sing a song in their native language. Sarah Vanagt now gives these old sound recordings to their compatriots from the Boulevard d'Ypres of today and asks them to translate or interpret what they hear. Like the film material, these recordings or their translations by the asylumseekers allow us to hear things that have probably never been heard and understood before. We hear about one African soldier's hardship and how he was forcibly recruited for a war that meant nothing to him, and how sad he is that he had to leave his wife and children behind.

Like in the films with commentary, Sarah Vanagt also carries out a cross-fade here, namely with a sonographic recording from the 20th century

6 .... 'Kabinette des Wissens', www.sammlungen.hu-berlin.de.

Überblendungen / Cross-fades (Ausstellungsansicht / Exhibition view)
Vorne / Front: Rossella Biscotti: *Everything is somehow related to everything else, yet the whole is terrifyingly unstable*, 2008

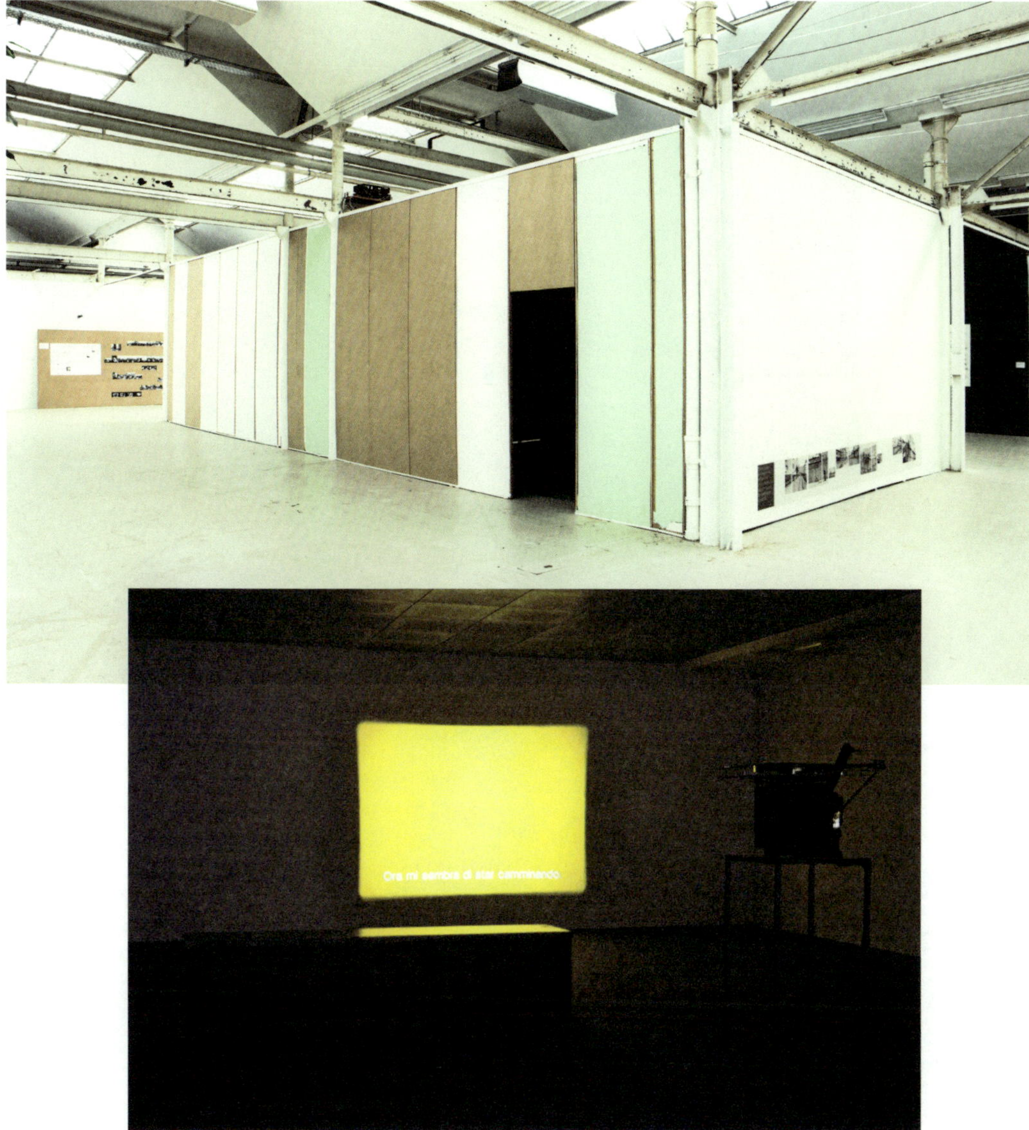

Rossella Biscotti: *Yellow*, 2010 (Ausstellungsansicht / Exhibition view Galleria di Civica, Trento)

Christoph Draeger: *the man who stole the moon ... (fell from the sky and crashed on earth)*, 2010
(Ausstellungsansicht / Exhibition view)

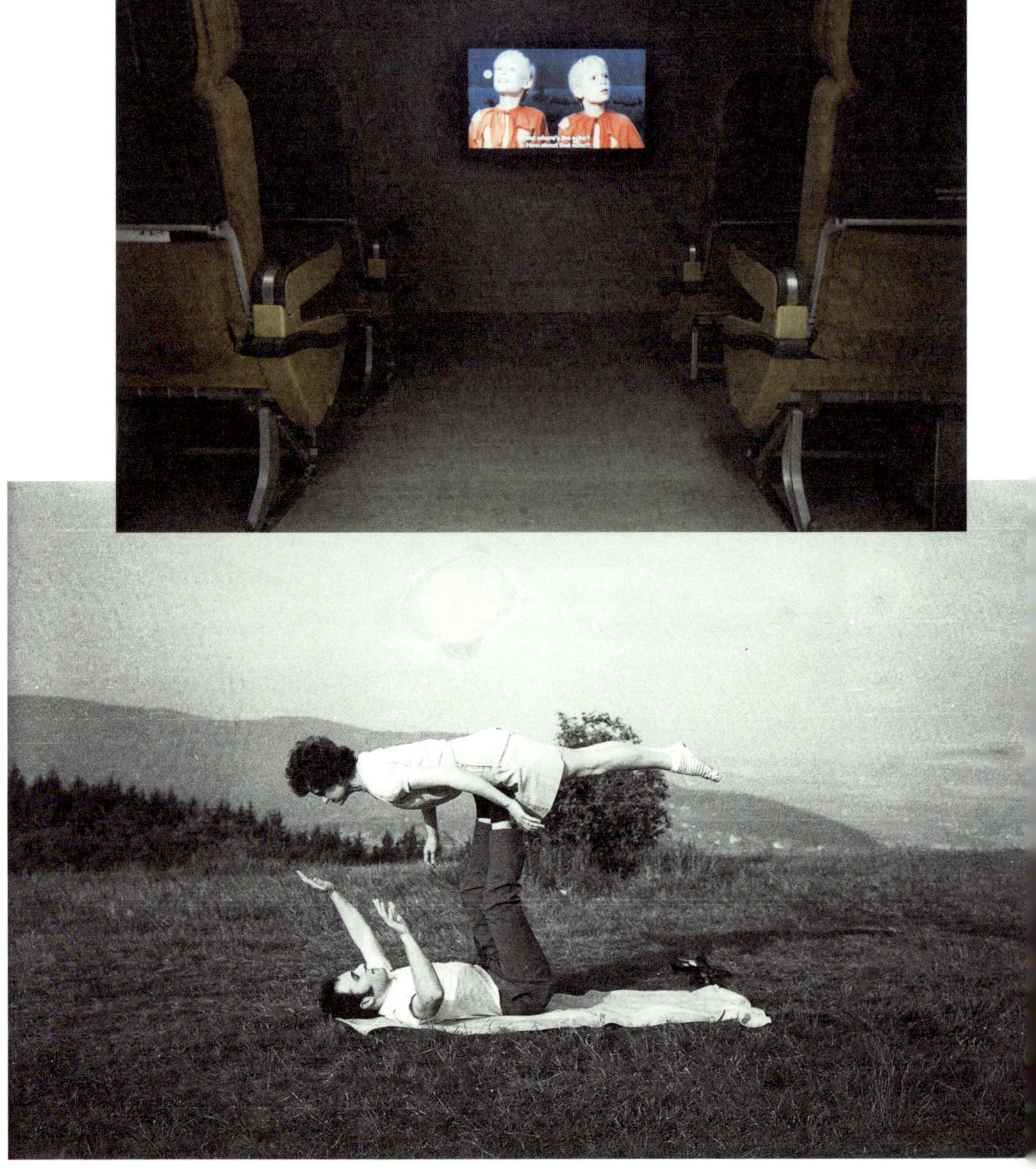

Zbyněk Baladrán: *Diagram*, 2007 (Foto aus dem Archiv von Willi Najvar / Photo from Willi Najvar archive)

vor allem Walter Benjamins Thesen *Über den Begriff der Geschichte* bildeten die Grundlage.[1] Es schien, als ob Spuren Benjamischer Lektüren in vielen der aktuellen künstlerischen Strategien wirkten. Gemäss Benjamin geschieht Erkenntnis über das Vergangene nicht qua linearem Historismus – gegen den wandte er sich explizit –, sondern über ein ephemeres Bild. Bei diesem treten das Jetzt und das Gewesene blitzhaft zu einer Konstellation zusammen. Dieses Bild sei unwiderruflich, weil es durch jede Gegenwart gelöscht werde, die sich nicht „als in ihm [diesem Gewesenen] gemeint sieht". Walter Benjamin vertritt dezidiert die Meinung, dass es nicht darum gehen könne herauszufinden, wie es gewesen sei, sondern dass es vielmehr um die Erweckung eines noch nicht bewussten Wissens der inhärenten Möglichkeiten des Gewesenen gehe. Er spricht vom Kampf „für die unterdrückte Vergangenheit" (These XVII) und suggeriert damit, dass es um die Erkennbarkeit einer Vergangenheit gehen muss, die so vielleicht gar nie stattgefunden hat. Die Überblendung vom Jetzt mit dem Gewesenen führt zu einer Erkenntnis von „Jetztzeit", in die Momente von etwas Heilsbringendem eingesprengt sind, Benjamin nennt es das „Messianische". Dieses ereignet sich im Moment der Gefahr und kann sich immer nur vor dem Hintergrund einer Anerkennung des Katastrophischen der Geschichte einstellen. Der sinnbildlich von ihm eingeführte „Engel der Geschichte"– tatsächlich bezieht er sich auf das Bild *Angelus Novus* von Paul Klee – sieht, wenn er auf die Geschichte sieht, nur Trümmer und Katastrophen. Auch hier spricht der Melancholiker.[2] Doch dadurch, dass der Engel diese Katastrophen anschaut und nicht verdrängt, kann sich etwas Anderes, Hoffnungsvolles ereignen, wird Geschichte in Zukunft nicht zwingend eine Katastrophe sein müssen.

In Anlehnung an diese Vorstellung von Geschichte prägten wir unseren Untertitel *Das Zukünftige rekonstruieren*. Er besagt, dass es nicht in einem platten Sinn um die Zukunft (in Abgrenzung zur Gegenwart) gehen kann, sondern um das Nachdenken über die Bedingung einer möglichen Gegenwart und Zukunft, das die sich immer wieder neu herzustellende Gegenwart und Vergangenheit miteinschliesst. Nur mit diesem situierten Blick auf das Gestern kann ich das Morgen und damit vielleicht auch schon das Heute ändern.

Katastrophische Vergangenheiten

Die Überblendung wurde ursprünglich in der Filmtechnik entwickelt und bedeutet, dass man übergangslos von einer Einstellung in die andere gleitet bzw. gleichzeitig mehrere Einstellungen in einem Bild vereint. Diese zunächst formale Technik wird jedoch, so unsere Annahme, auch zu einem auch inhaltlichen Verfahren, bei dem sich Zeiten, Räume, Subjekte, Stimmen, Dinge usw. überlagern und somit einen Sprung, eine Diskontinuität im Sinngefüge erzeugen. Obwohl dieses mit der Montagetechnik verwandte Verfahren prinzipiell für alle Medien geöffnet ist, taucht es stark in filmischen Kontexten auf. Möglicherweise ist dies mit ein Grund – neben der Möglichkeit zu neuen Formen der Narration –, weshalb in diesem Ausstellungsprojekt das Medium Film so stark vertreten war. Im Folgenden möchte ich die unterschiedlichen Überblendungsweisen an ein paar Beispielen erläutern.

In Sarah Vanagts Film *Boulevard d'Ypres* (Abb. S. 60/61) gibt es viele solche Überblendungen: Zunächst ist da eine Strasse, in der die Künstlerin und besonders auch Migrant_innen aus dem Mittelmeerraum und Afrika leben. Diese Strasse ist nach Ypres benannt, eine Stadt, die dadurch berühmt wurde, dass sie während des Ersten Weltkrieges an der hart umkämpften Westfront lag, wo auch das erste Mal in der Geschichte Senfgas (deswegen auch Yperit genannt) zur Anwendung kam. Was nicht offiziell erwähnt wird, und was der Film für uns Nicht-Informierte zunächst unverständlich lässt und nur sukzessive enthüllt, ist die Tatsache, dass hier, auf der Seite der Alliierten, auch viele Männer aus den Kolonien kämpften: Afrikaner, Inder usw. Dieser Boulevard d'Ypres nun wird von Gentrifizierung und der damit verbundenen Verdrängung seiner Bewohner_innen heimgesucht; ein Umstand, den Sarah

---

1 .... Benjamin, Walter: Über den Begriff der Geschichte. Im Folgenden zitiert online: www.mxks.de/files/phil/Benjamin. GeschichtsThesen.html.

2 .... Zum Melancholischen vgl. den *Text Lands End. Die Dinge von ihrem möglichen Ende her denken*, S. 118 in diesem Buch.

Vanagt zum Anlass nimmt, diese Strasse so zu portraitieren, wie sie sich als sogenannte „Mikrogeschichte" (Carlo Ginzburg) in den hier lebenden Menschen spiegelt. Sie bat ihre Nachbar_innen, ihre (Lebens-)Geschichten zu erzählen, allerdings nicht in der persönlichen Ich-Form, sondern als eine Art Märchen oder Legende, in der Er-Form. Dass es sich auch dabei um einen Kunstgriff handelt, um eine Technik der Überlagerung der ersten mit der dritten Person, werden wir erst langsam gewahr, zunächst hören wir einfach die unglaublichsten Lebensgeschichten.

Ort des Geschichten- und somit Geschichte-Vortragens ist ein bereits geräumter Lagerraum, der, zunächst nur marginal erkennbar, gleichzeitig zu einer Art improvisiertem temporären Kino umfunktioniert ist: An der Ladentür, auf den Stufen und am Schluss auch grossräumig auf dem gepflasterten Boden sind Dokumentarfilme aus dem Ersten Weltkrieg projiziert, die zeigen, dass ganze Bataillone aus dunkelhäutigen Menschen bestanden. Diese Filme nun werden mit dem Blick und dem Wissen der Migranten aus dem 21. Jahrhundert überlagert, kommentiert und teilweise mit unglaublich bissigem Humor ad absurdum geführt. So etwa spricht einer lachend darüber, wie die Afrikaner nicht einmal wussten, wie man diese modernen Gewehre bedienen sollte. Aber dies sei sowieso nicht wichtig gewesen, weil sie eh nur Kanonenfutter gewesen seien.

Ein weiterer Strang im Film ist die Aktualisierung von Tonaufnahmen, die zwischen 1915 und 1918 in deutschen Kriegsgefangenenlagern gemacht wurden. Viele dieser todgeweihten Afrikaner gelangten in Kriegsgefangenschaft und stellten damit für die deutschen Wissenschaftler (Ethnografen und Linguisten) spannende Feldforschungsobjekte dar. So wurden für die Lautabteilung der preussischen Staatsbibliothek 1650 Aufnahmen von verschiedenen Sprachen gemacht; heute befinden sie sich an der Humboldt Universität und können über das Internet gehört werden.[3] Die Gefangenen wurden damals gebeten, in ihrer Sprache eine Geschichte zu erzählen oder ein Lied zu singen. Sarah Vanagt gibt nun diese alten Tonaufnahmen den Landsleuten des

Boulevard d'Ypres von heute und bittet sie, das Gehörte zu übersetzen oder zu interpretieren. Wie das Filmmaterial, so lassen uns auch diese Aufnahmen bzw. deren Übersetzungen durch die Asylbewerber von heute Tatsachen hören, die wahrscheinlich noch nie gehört und verstanden wurden: So hören wir das Elend von einem Soldaten aus Afrika, der von seiner Zwangsrekrutierung für einen Krieg spricht, der ihm total egal ist, und wie traurig er ist, dass er Frau und Kind zurücklassen musste. Wie bei den kommentierten Filmen, so macht Sarah Vanagt auch hier eine Überblendung, nämlich von einer Sonografie aus dem frühen 20. Jahrhundert mit einer Stimme aus dem 21. Jahrhundert. Erst der sowohl distanzierte als auch beteiligte und in diesem Fall auch subalterne Blick von heute bringt das (ungeheuerlich) Gewesene zu Tage und macht zugleich offenbar, dass sich fast nichts geändert hat. Denn wenn der Soldat von vor 100 Jahren darüber spricht, dass er immer nur gehen muss und gehen und nicht weiss, ob er seine Familie jemals wiedersehen wird, weiss man für einen Moment nicht, wer spricht. Ist es der Asylbewerber von heute oder der tote Soldat, dem er nur seine Stimme leiht? Was war, was ist, was wird sein? So wird über diese Verschmelzungen durch die Zeiten und Räume hinweg eine Leerstelle deutlich, ein heilloses Paradox: die Einsicht, dass die damaligen Autoritäten, so sehr sie alles mit den neuesten Medien aufzeichneten und konservierten, und so sehr sie beanspruchten, die technische Fortschrittlichkeit und wissenschaftliche Deutungshoheit inne zu haben und Weltgeschichte zu schreiben, nichts von dem verstanden oder verstehen wollten, was sie in Bewegung setzten: die Menschen und ihre Existenzweisen.

Sarah Vanagts filmische Ästhetik überlagert somit nicht nur das Gestern mit dem Heute, oder technische Medien mit lebendiger Sprache, oder Strasse mit Film, sie überlagert auch banale und deprimierende Realität mit dem Märchenhaften und Besonderen. Vor dem Hintergrund einer drohenden Gefahr und Katastrophe (diese vertriebenen Menschen werden wieder vertrieben werden, wenn auch aus anderen, ‚humaneren' Gründen), schafft Vanagt eine Situation des Eingedenkens, in der die Menschen an die Geschichte ihrer Vorfahren, die Leib und Leben für

---

3 .... Kabinette des Wissens: www.sammlungen.hu-berlin.de.

and a voice from the 21st century. It is both the distanced and participating, and in this case today's subaltern point of view as well, that first reveals what (outrageously) once was, and at the same time that almost nothing has changed. For when a hundred years ago the soldier talks about always being forced to go and does not know if he will ever see his family again, for a moment one does not know who is speaking. Is it the asylum seeker of today or the dead soldier to whom he is lending his voice? What was, what is, and what will be? By means of combining these things, a gap, a frightful paradox becomes apparent over time and space: the knowledge that as much as they produced recordings and preserved them with the most modern media, and as much as they claimed to possess technological progress and the prerogative of scientific interpretation and writing world history, the authorities at the time did not or did not want to understand what they had set in motion: human beings and their modes of existence.

Thus, Sarah Vanagt's film aesthetic not only superimposes yesterday with today, or technological media with living language, or street with film; it also superimposes ordinary and depressing reality with something fairy-tale-like and special. Against the backdrop of impending danger and catastrophe (these displaced persons will repeatedly be displaced, of for other, 'more humane' reasons), Vanagt created a situation of independent thought in which people recall the history of their ancestors, who risked life and limb for this country, and their own inextricability in this history. By means of the legend-like, distanced narrative style of one's own life story (this is theirs and not theirs at the same time, as it is told in the third person), the respective individual and time-specific as well as collective and banalised destiny of thousands of immigrants is elevated into the myth-like and wonderful. The cross-fading of the real with the fictional thus creates an opportunity not to speak of the extraordinary but open it up as something to be imagined: while one immigrant legend follows the other, they always break off there where the rescue takes place in the conventional fairy tale. In

the film, what occurs at this moment is always a look at the reality and materiality of the street. This shift is a moment of emptiness, standstill, of the no more and not yet: open for many things. While the film ends with the image of shadow-like hordes of troopers from old films on the paved street, the question remains of whether perhaps there could not at some point also be something like an escape from this repeatability, a departure.

Raising Awareness

Rossella Biscotti also works with the cross-fading of time and space. In the installation *Yellow* (fig. p. 65), it almost seems as if a light from the 21st century illuminates the dark shadows from the 20th and raises our awareness for them. We first see a projector unreeling a yellow film. 'I want to try to descend deep into myself, then I don't know what I will encounter' we hear a voice utter in Dutch, and read it in the English subtitles. The voice speaks slowly, hesitantly, is sometimes interrupted by questions. What we hear is outrageous; even the speaker does not want to talk about it. 'No, no, that's very bad.' *Yellow* consists of recordings of different therapy sessions a psychiatrist conducted in the Netherlands in the late 1980s with the aid of Pentothal in order to heal people who were traumatized by World War II. The drug, also known as 'truth serum', narcotised the patients so that they could abandon themselves to their memories and talk about them.

On the one hand, Rossella Biscotti now takes various recordings from one such session and has them proceed linearly; on the other hand, she cross-fades the utterances with the colour yellow. The images that are heard remain in space, in one's mind. In doing so, the installation explicitly denies any illustrative or narrative aesthetic whatsoever, almost making non-showing its theme. However, what we come to see very sharply are eighty different yellow shades of filters to which the artist has subjected her film. These stand for the filters used in film in order to change scenes atmospherically; in this case they also

knowbotic research: *huwwara_anybody, looking*, 2010 (Ausstellungsansicht / Exhibition view)

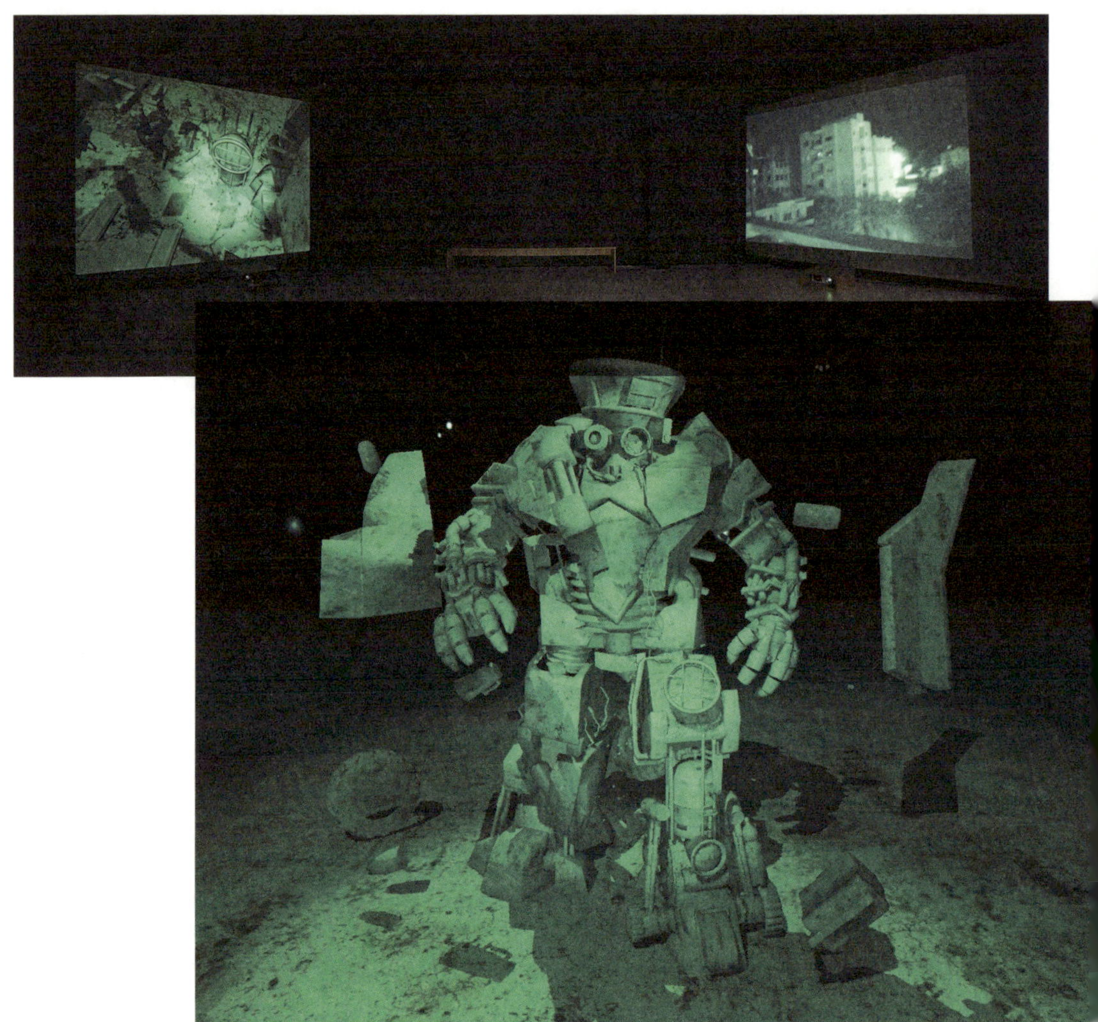

knowbotic research: *huwwara_anybody, looking*, 2010

dieses Land liessen, und ihr eigenes Eingewobensein in diese Geschichte erinnern. Durch den legendenhaften, distanziert erzählten Stil der eigenen Lebensgeschichte (diese ist zugleich ihre und doch nicht ihre, weil in der dritten Person erzählt), wird das jeweils individuelle und zeittyptische, aber auch kollektive und banalisierte Schicksal Tausender von Migrant_innen ins Mythenhafte und Wunderbare gehoben. Die Überblendung des Tatsächlichen mit dem Fiktionalen schafft somit die Möglichkeit, das Aussergewöhnliche nicht zu sagen, sondern als zu Denkendes zu eröffnen: Während sich Migranten-Legende an Migranten-Legende reiht, bricht sie immer dann ab, wenn im konventionellen Märchen die Rettung erfolgen würde. Im Film folgt in diesem Moment immer ein Blick auf die Realität und Materialität der Strasse. Dieser Wechsel ist ein Moment der Leere, des Stillstands, des Nicht-Mehr und Noch-Nicht: offen für Vieles. Während der Film mit dem Bild schattenhafter Reiterhorden aus den alten Filmen auf dem Strassenpflaster von heute endet, bleibt im Raum die Frage stehen, ob es vielleicht doch einmal so etwas wie einen Ausbruch aus dieser Wiederholbarkeit, einen Aufbruch geben könnte?

Ins Bewusstsein holen

Ebenfalls mit der Überblendung von Zeiten und Räumen arbeitet Rossella Biscotti. In der Installation *Yellow* (Abb. S. 65) erscheint es beinahe so, als ob ein Licht aus dem 21. Jahrhundert die dunklen Schatten aus dem 20. anleuchteten und ins Bewusstsein holte. Zu sehen ist zunächst nur ein Filmapparat, der einen gelben Film abspult. „Ich möchte versuchen, tief in mich hinabzusteigen, denn ich weiss nicht, was mich erwartet", hören wir eine Stimme auf Holländisch sprechen und können wir auf englischen Untertiteln lesen. Die Stimme erzählt langsam, stockend, manchmal wird sie durch Fragen unterbrochen. Was wir hören, ist unerhört, auch der Sprecher will nicht reden: „Nein, nein, das ist zu schlimm". *Yellow* besteht aus den Mitschnitten verschiedener Therapiesitzungen, die ein Psychiater in den Niederlanden Ende der 1980er Jahre mithilfe des Medikaments Pentothal durchführte, um Menschen, die vom Zweiten Weltkrieg traumatisiert waren, zu heilen. Die auch als ‚Wahrheitsserum' bekannte Medizin narkotisierte die Patient_innen, sodass sie sich ihren Erinnerungen hingeben und darüber sprechen konnten.

Rossella Biscotti nimmt nun einerseits verschiedene Mitschnitte aus einer solchen Sitzung und lässt sie linear ablaufen, andererseits überblendet sie das Sprechen mit der Farbe Gelb. Die gehörten Bilder bleiben im Raum, im Kopf. Die Installation verweigert so explizit jegliche illustrative oder narrative Ästhetik, sie macht geradezu das Nicht-Zeigen zu ihrem Thema. Was wir jedoch sehr genau zu sehen bekommen, sind 80 verschiedene Gelbtöne von Filtern, denen die Künstlerin ihren Film ausgesetzt hat. Diese stehen für die Filter, die man im Film verwendet, um Szenen atmosphärisch zu verändern; hier stehen sie auch für die Versuche, sich immer wieder der unsäglichen Vergangenheit annähern zu müssen, die Traumata der Vergangenheit ans Licht zu holen. Beim Hören werden wir gewahr, dass der Patient verschiedene Gedächtnisschichten durchstösst und dass es das eine ‚Urereignis', das alle Fragen lösen würde, nicht gibt. Vielmehr kommt ein Netz undeutlicher Ab- und Überlagerungen zum Tragen; vieles hört sich an wie ein Traum, es sind vor allem Bilder, die im Patienten hochkommen, Bilder, die nach ihrer Übersetzung in gesprochene Sprache ringen und die uns nicht völlig unbekannt erscheinen, auch hier heisst es einmal, ähnlich wie in der übersetzten Sonografie aus *Boulevard d'Ypres*: „Then I have to walk walk." Mit der dunklen, sonoren, schwer betäubten Stimme des Patienten gleiten wir selbst hinab in die Tiefen des Unbewussten. Manchmal bricht es ab, der Schluss bricht ab: „Let them talk talk." Auch *Yellow* verwendet Found Footage, hier ist es Material, das aus der Psychiatrie stammt, das normalerweise nicht der Öffentlichkeit zugänglich gemacht wird. Dadurch, dass Rossella Biscotti sich dieses Materials annimmt und es verfilmt, wird das traumatische Sprechen selbst zur historischen Aufzeichnung. Diese beansprucht ihre Gültigkeit, egal, ob sie auf der Liege eines Psychiaters oder in der Schreibstube eines Wissenschaftlers verfasst wurde. So wird dieses Stottern und Stammeln in Gelb zu einer Art Geschichtsschreibung, die das sowohl Persönlichste als auch Unpersönlichste –

weil im Unbewussten vergraben – sammelt und als gemeinsame Geschichte dem kollektiven Durcharbeiten zur Verfügung stellt.

Aus dem Kontinuum reissen

In der Computerinstallation *huwwara_ anybody, looking* (Abb. S. 70) von knowbotic research überblenden sich neben Zeiten und Räume auch Personen und Dinge. Dieser Arbeit liegt ebenfalls Found Footage zu Grunde. Es handelt sich um ein Video, das im Jahre 2004 auf YouTube zirkulierte und zeigt, wie am israelischen Checkpoint Huwwara im Westjordanland ein zwölfjähriger Selbstmordattentäter seinen Bombengürtel nicht zündet. Darauf wird er von einem Roboter entwaffnet. Die Installation stellt diese Szene digital nach und ‚konstelliert' sie mit einem zweiten, gegenüberliegenden Bild, auf dem in einer Infrarotaufnahme eine palästinensische Stadt zu sehen ist. Im Gegensatz zur Realität und der Darstellung in den Medien wird im Computerfilm die Entwaffnung nicht vollzogen, sondern der Junge und der Roboter verschmelzen zu einem Maschinensuperwesen – ein Monster, das direkt den militaristischen Computergames entsprungen scheint. Junge, Roboter und Cyborg sind digital hergestellt, auch sie in Infratrotgrün gehalten, nichts an ihnen erscheint natürlich. Immer wieder wechselt die Blickposition und untermauert damit das Gefühl der Beobachtung und Kontrolle. Die Zeitlichkeit und Abfolge der Bilder der Stadt wird mittels eines Soundradars, der die Bewegungen des Publikums im Raum aufnimmt, gesteuert. Hinzu kommt eine dritte Ebene: In unvorhersehbaren Abständen wird es schwarz, und eine künstlich und traumhaft klingende Frauenstimme erzählt die Geschichte, kommentiert die Szenerie, stellt Fragen, eröffnet Horizonte: „I remember a kabbalist saying: To achieve another territory, things don't have to be destroyed. In order to change, only things like this boy with his belt, this roadblock, this robot have to be moved a little bit."

Diese Arbeit vereint somit zwei grundlegende Strategien: Die eine ist die Überblendung der Vergangenheit mit der Zukunft, des Jungen mit dem Roboter, des TV-Videos mit Computeranimation, der Realität mit der Fiktion, die andere,

damit zusammenhängende Strategie ist die des Herausreissens aus einem Kontinuum: Der Film eines Schrecken auslösenden Moments wird aus dem historischen Kontext gerissen, abstrahierend nachgestellt und seine Momenthaftigkeit gewissermassen ‚verewigt'. Die Figuren bewegen sich unendlich langsam, als ob sie aus Stein wären. So wird dieser alltäglich gewordene und medialisierte Schrecken eine Art mythische, ewig ablaufende Geschichte, deren Legendenhaftigkeit sich jedoch nicht wie üblich aus einer unbestimmten Vergangenheit, sondern aus der Aktualität futuristischer Fantasien und militaristischer Realität speist. Neben dieser strategisch in Szene gesetzten Mythisierung findet jedoch gleichzeitig eine figurative und narrative Dekonstruktion statt: Während der Junge zu Beginn stählern und wie aus einem Guss wirkt (eine menschliche Kampfmaschine), ist die Cyborgmaschine gegen Ende des Films ein zusammengesetztes Wrack aus Einzelteilen, das bekannte Bilder von Soldaten mit Gasmasken aus dem ersten Weltkrieg mit Terminatorfantasien aus der Zukunft verbindet und ad absurdum treibt. Darüberhinaus wir auch die Geschichte selbst nicht kontinuierlich erzählt, sondern vielmehr steht der/die Zuschauer_in zwei entgegengesetzten Leinwänden gegenüber, muss er/sie den Blick wechseln und Bewegungen koordinieren. Die Hauptgeschichte, nämlich die der Transformation des Jungen in einen Cyborg (der er, wie die Bilder deutlich machen, immer schon war), wird unterbrochen durch die Schwärze, durch die Erzählerstimme und die sich bewegenden Stadt- und Grenzbilder. Wir, das Publikum, sind sowohl räumlich mitten in der Geschichte bzw. zwischen den Bildern, dem Ton und der Stimme positioniert als auch narrativ mitten in die Erzählung gerissen, insofern sie nämlich einfach beginnt, abbricht, uns Informationen vorenthält oder diese nur sporadisch durch die Erzählerin nachliefert. So müssen wir sowohl räumlich als auch narrativ versuchen, uns zu orientieren, einen Sinn zurechtzulegen und körperlich einzugreifen. So wie die filmische Blickführung immer wechselt und neue Perspektive einnimmt, so wechseln auch wir, und mit uns das Bild der von uns unsichtbar gesteuerten Stadt.

Mit den Überblendungen zusammen sind da also auch viele Brechungen und Sprünge. Eine

stand for the attempts at always having to approach the unspeakable past, to shed light on the traumas of the past. While listening we become aware that the patient penetrates various memory layers and that there is no original event that would solve all questions. Rather, a network of obscure stratifications and superimpositions are brought to bear; a great deal of things sound like a dream. It is primarily images that surface in the patient, images that struggle to be translated into spoken language and do not seem completely unfamiliar to us. And much like in the translated sonograph from *Boulevard d'Ypres,* at one point it is said: 'Then I have to walk walk.' Along with the dark, sonorous, strongly drugged voice of the patient, we ourselves slide down into the depths of the unconscious. It sometimes breaks off, the end breaks off: 'Let them talk talk.' *Yellow* also makes use of found footage, in this case material that stems from psychiatry and is not normally made accessible to the public. By Rossella Biscotti adopting and filming this material, the traumatic utterances themselves become a historical recording. This calls for validity, regardless of whether it was drawn up on the psychiatrist's couch or in a scientist's office. Hence, this stuttering and stammering in yellow becomes a kind of historiography that assembles both the most personal as well as the most impersonal—because it is buried in the unconscious—and makes it available as a shared history for dealing collectively.

Removal from the Continuum

In the computer installation *huwwara_anybody, looking* (fig. p. 70) by knowbotic research, time and space cross-fade, as do people and things. This work is also based on found footage, a video that circulated on YouTube in 2004 showing how a twelve-year-old suicide assassin fails to ignite his bomb belt at the Israeli checkpoint Huwwara in the West Bank. A robot later disarms him. The installation re-enacts this scene digitally and places it in a constellation with a second image opposite it that shows an infrared picture of a Palestinian town. In contrast to reality and its depiction in the media, in the computer film the boy is not disarmed, but he and the robot merge to become a hideous mechanical super being— a monster that seems to have originated in a militaristic computer game. The boy, robot and cyborg have been produced digitally, also in infrared-green; nothing about them seems natural. The filmic gaze constantly shifts positions, and in doing so reinforces the impression of observation and control. The temporality and sequences of the images of the town is controlled by means of sound radar, which records the movements made by the viewers. This is augmented by a third level: the film becomes black at unpredictable intervals, and a woman's voice that sounds artificial and dreamlike tells a story, comments on the scenery, asks questions, opens up horizons: 'I remember a Kabbalistic saying: To achieve another territory, things don't have to be destroyed. In order to change, only things like this boy with his belt, this roadblock, this robot have to be moved a little bit.'

This work joins two fundamental strategies: one is cross-fading the past with the future, the boy with the robot, the TV video with computer animation, reality with fiction; the other, associated strategy is removal from a continuum: the film of a moment that triggers terror is removed from its historical context, reenacted in an abstract way, and its momentariousness 'eternalised', as it were. The figure's movements are endlessly slow, as if they were made of stone. Thus, this everyday and mediatised horror becomes a kind of mythic story that wears on eternally, yet whose legendary nature is not, as is customary, fed out of an indefinite past but out of the topicality of futuristic fantasies and militaristic reality. However, a figurative and narrative deconstruction takes place alongside this strategically staged mythologisation: while at the beginning the boy seems to be cast from steel (a human fighting machine), towards the end of the film the cyborg machine is a wreck assembled out of individual parts that connects familiar images of soldiers wearing gas masks from World War I with terminator fantasies from the future and reduces them to absurdity. In addition, the story itself is not related continuously; rather, the viewers stand in front of two screens that are facing each other and have to change their vantage point and coordinate their movements. The main story, that is, the boy's transformation into a cyborg (which he, as the images make obvious, always was), is interrupted by a period of blackness, by the narrator's voice and the moving images of the town and the border. We, the audience, are spatially positioned in the middle of the story or between the images, the sound and the voice as well as narratively pulled into the middle of the story to the extent that it simply begins, breaks off, deprives us of information or only sporadically supplies us with any information later via the narrator. Hence, we have to spatially as well as narratively attempt to orient ourselves, work out meaning and intervene physically. Much like the filmic perspective constantly changes, we also change, as does the image of the town we invisibly control.

The cross-fades are thus accompanied by numerous breaks and jumps. A possible opening up of ominous contemporary history is not directly depicted, above all not by this figure. And yet something seems to crumble; possibilities of change seem to flash in the voice from the darkness or in the interaction with the visual structure.

History Unspoken

All of the works presented here recall the thesis from Walter Benjamin's concept of history in which he appeals for the 'here-and-now' as an element of recognisability. Like Benjamin's 'angel of history', these films also once again direct our eyes to the debris of history. We examine it in and through the films, yet we also see it removed from the familiar, in new contexts. The strategies of cross-fading and breaks are often unexpected, dark and painful, in the same way memories often surface unexpectedly; a word, a place, a gesture and our security is cross-faded by the traumatic. In Uriel Orlow's film *Remnants of the Future* (see p. 104), 'Mush' is such a code word: the Mush of today always carries along with it the Mush of

yesterday, and associated with this are the Soviet Union and the genocide in Armenia. There is a similar word in Christoph Draeger's film *the man who stole the moon... (fell from the sky and crashed on earth)* (fig. p. 66). The word is Smolensk, and in 2010 it was not only the site of the crash of a plane with the Polish president on board, but it was also one of the stations along the journey to Katyn, where in 1940 Stalin had twenty thousand members of the Polish elite murdered: Smolensk–Katyn, Katyn–Smolensk. Or Huwwara. Or Ypres. It is time and again about war, death and extermination. All of the films discussed here do not initially deal directly with these themes; no, these themes are unspoken but automatically ensue, begin to speak themselves. They are conjured up on film; 'hallucinated', as Uriel Orlow puts it. Much is held in suspense, is left open; much remains in those unspoken, unpictured intermediate spaces that have to remain empty in order for 'homogenous and empty time' (Walter Benjamin) not to be stored and depicted. History is unfinished. It has to always and time and again be worked through, opened up for something called the 'here-and-now', or simply livability, existence.

Translated by Rebecca van Dyck

mögliche Öffnung der unheilvollen Zeitgeschichte wird nicht direkt dargestellt, vor allem nicht durch diese Figur. Und doch scheint etwas zu zerbröckeln, scheinen in der Stimme aus der Dunkelheit oder der Interaktion mit der visuellen Struktur Möglichkeiten der Veränderung aufzublitzen.

Zeit" (Walter Benjamin) zu speichern und abzubilden. Die Geschichte ist unerledigt. Sie muss immer und immer wieder durchgearbeitet, geöffnet werden für etwas, das „Jetztzeit", oder einfach auch Lebbarkeit, Existenz heisst.

Geschichte nicht sagen

Alle hier vorgestellten Arbeiten erinnern an die These aus Walter Benjamins Geschichtstheorie, in der er für die „Jetztzeit" als Moment der Erkennbarkeit plädiert. So wie Walter Benjamins „Engel der Geschichte", so wenden auch diese Filme noch einmal den Blick auf die Trümmer der Geschichte. In und durch die Filme schauen wir sie an, sehen wir sie aber auch, losgelöst von Bekanntem, in neuen Zusammenhängen. Die Strategien der Überblendungen und Brüche sind oft unerwartet, dunkel und schmerzvoll, so wie Erinnerungen sich oft unerwartet einstellen: ein Wort, ein Ort, eine Geste – und unsere Sicherheiten werden mit Traumatischem überblendet. In Uriel Orlows Film *Remnants of the Future* (vgl. S. 104) ist beispielsweise das Wort ‚Mush' ein solches Codewort: Das heutige Mush führt das alte Mush und damit verbunden die Sowjetunion und den Genozid in Armenien immer mit im Gepäck. Ein ähnliches Wort gibt es in Christoph Draegers Film *the man who stole the moon… (fell from the sky and crashed on earth)* (Abb. S. 66). Es heisst Smolensk und war im Jahre 2010 nicht nur der Ort eines Flugzeugabsturzes mit dem polnischen Präsidenten an Bord, sondern es war auch eine Station auf der Reise nach Katyn, wo Stalin 1940 20'000 Angehörige der polnischen Elite umbringen liess: Smolensk – Katyn, Katyn – Smolensk. Oder Huwwara. Oder Ypres. Immer wieder geht es um Krieg, um Tod und Auslöschung. Alle hier diskutierten Filme gehen zunächst gar nicht direkt auf diese Themen ein, nein, diese Themen werden nicht gesagt, sie stellen sich vielmehr ein, ergreifen wie von selbst das Wort. Sie werden filmisch beschworen, „halluziniert", wie Uriel Orlow sagt. Vieles bleibt in der Schwebe, wird offen gelassen, vieles bleibt in jenen ungesagten, unbebilderten Zwischenräumen, die leer bleiben müssen, um nicht „leere und homogene

ANKE HOFFMANN

ZUR KÜNSTLE-RISCHEN ANEIGNUNG DES HISTORISCHEN

THE ARTISTIC APPRO-PRIATION OF THE HISTORICAL

Geschichte ist ein ungemein populäres Thema geworden. Angesichts der auffallenden Vielzahl von Sachbüchern, Film- und Fernsehproduktionen stellt sich die Frage: Warum? Vor dem Hintergrund der steten Veränderung und partiellen Auflösung von nationalstaatlichen, soziokulturellen und politischen Identitätsmustern scheint die Beschäftigung mit Geschichte der Versuch zu sein, eine Lesbarkeit kollektiver Kohärenz zu entwerfen. Da, wo bisherige Deutungsmuster brüchig und widersprüchlich werden, machen historische Erzählungen und Interpretationen Angebote der Identitätsstiftung.

Der Zwang zur Unterhaltung aller Inhalte jedoch, die Entertainisierung unserer Kultur sowie die Reduzierung auf das Anekdotische versäumen, die Zusammenhänge und Bedingungen von geschichtlichen Prozessen zu beleuchten, weswegen sich gerade Künstler_innen herausgefordert fühlen, offenere Lesarten von historischen Überlieferungen anzubieten, als es narrative Spektakel-, Erregungs- oder Happy-End-Dramen tun. Denn auch im Kunstdiskurs ist eine Aktualität künstlerischer Auseinandersetzungen, kuratorischer Projekte und kulturkritischer Beobachtungen zu verzeichnen.

Gemein ist allen künstlerischen Praktiken, die sich mit Historiografie beschäftigen, dass das Historische immer den Resonanzboden der eigenen kulturellen Verfasstheit im Hier und Jetzt bildet. Künstlerische Historiografie richtet sich „nicht auf Vergangenheit als solche, sondern eher darauf ideologische Gewissheiten der Gegenwart über die Vergangenheit zu dekonstruieren"[1]. Künstler_innen begreifen Geschichte als einen veränderbaren Interpretations- und Darstellungsraum des Vergangenen; Geschichte wird in der Kunst zum Feld einer alternativen Gegenwartserzählung auf der Basis einer kritischen Intervention von konventionellen Überlieferungen, ihren Methoden und ihren Autorschaften. Geschichte wird verhandelbar statt festgeschrieben, wird zur Erzählung

1 .... Zuckermann, Moshe: Das Bewusstsein von den Abgründen des Nichts – Gespräch über das Verhältnis von Kunst und Geschichte zwischen Moshe Zuckermann und Roee Rosen. In: Leeb, Susanne: Flucht nach nicht ganz vorn – Geschichte in der Kunst der Gegenwart. *Geschichte. Texte zur Kunst* 76 (2009), 29.

History has become a remarkably popular subject. In the face of a conspicuous variety of non-fiction books, films and TV productions, the question arises: why? Given the background of a constant change and partial dissolution of national, socio-cultural and political patterns of identity, focusing on history seems to be an attempt at proposing a legibility of collective coherency. Where traditional patterns of interpretation have become fragile and contradictory, historical narratives and interpretations offer possibilities to shape identities.

However, the necessity of making all contents funny, turning our culture into entertainment and reducing everything to anecdotes means that the contexts and prerequisites of historical processes are not reflected upon—which is why artists in particular feel challenged to offer readings of historical heritages that are more open than the narrative dramas of spectacles, excitement or happy ends tend to be. Even in art discourse one can identify a currency in artistic debates, curatorial projects and critical observations of culture.

What all artistic practices that deal with historiography have in common is that the historical element is always the resonating body of one's own cultural constitution in the here and now. Artistic historiography is 'not directed towards the past as such, but rather towards deconstructing ideological certainties of the present via the past'.[1] Artists see history as a malleable space of interpretation and representation of the past; history in art becomes a field of an alternative story of the present on the basis of a critical intervention into conventional traditions, their methods and authorships. History becomes negotiable instead of being static; it turns into a narrative with an open end instead of a unified story.

In the following, three artists who were a part of the exhibition *Cross-fades* will be presented along with their respective artistic strategies.

Re-representation of history

'By the way, we also have a problem in dealing with racism. We approach it with tolerance, but tolerance is not a solution for racism. … The problem of racism is primarily a problem of representation',[2] says René Pollesch in a discussion about his theater work. Representation is not just the fate of the performing arts, but also one of communicating about and constructing past events.

Sarah Vanagt is a filmmaker and artist from Brussels; she also studied history. Historiography is at the center of her artistic approach. Her highly respected work *Little Figures* (fig. p. 79) is a film that combines found footage with documentary and fictional methods in dealing with filmic narrative approaches. In film, Sarah Vanagt documents the urban coexistence of asynchronous events. *Little Figures'* setting is the Mont des Arts in Brussels, a generously designed square surrounded by Belgium's important museums and cultural treasures, representational architecture and statues of national heroes—often financed using the profits from a colonial heritage. Children and young adults skateboard under the stone feet of such statues as Godefroy de Bouillon, Albert I. and his wife Queen Elisabeth. 'What is happening now?' asks the stone Elisabeth with the voice of a Rwandan girl, a refugee child that currently lives in Brussels. Albert and Godefroy answer, with the voices of a Moroccan and a Philippine boy. A fictional dialogue unravels between the three that Vanagt developed with these children—children living in a country that is still searching for an adequate way of speaking about its brutal colonial heritage 50 years after the Congo's independence. In the children's free interpretation, the reanimated statues mix their memories of the Belgian

1 .... Moshe Zuckermann, Das Bewusstsein von den Abgründen des Nichts: Gespräch über das Verhältnis von Kunst und Geschichte zwischen Moshe Zuckermann und Roee Rosen, quoted in: Susanne Leeb, 'Flucht nach nicht ganz vorn: Geschichte in der Kunst der Gegenwart', *Geschichte. Texte zur Kunst*, 76 (Berlin, 2009), p. 29.

2 ...... René Pollesch in an interview with the Süddeutsche Zeitung magazine, 17 (Munich, 2012), p. 31.

history of conquest and colonisation with the significance they have today. Godefroy and Albert demarcate historic cornerstones of European/Belgian politics of conquest. Godefroy was a crusader during the 11th century, and Albert I. was King of Belgium from 1909–1934 and thus the king of the Congo in Central Africa—a land that lost highly valuable resources and an estimated 10 million lives under his uncle Leopold II's private and brutal leadership. Sarah Vanagt conveys very few details of the historical shadow that these stone conquerors throw. She leaves the associative level of reflection up to the children. She is not interested in a complete clarification of what happened, but rather a view of the history that today's generation lives with. By casting these 'legends' with children from immigrant families, she even deconstructs heroic history and opens the space for anti-racist and anti-heroic self-appropriation of colonial history.

Little Figures: these are the children who have the opportunity to shape future conceptions of history and leave their own traces. *Little Figures* are also the more than human-sized statues that hardly anyone notices and whose historic factuality is speculated upon by today's generation more than it is understood by them. The static figures belong to an out-of-date, conventional conception of history that recorded the conquerors' stories and even gave them a mythos of invulnerability. In the contrast of movement in the film, the artist symbolises that even this perspective can be rewritten and that the view onto the past is flexible and open. Everything around the monuments is in motion: the traffic in the streets and above all the young skaters. But even the camera is in a constant flow of movement; it crawls along the surfaces of the sculptures, as though it wanted to close in, level by level, on fossilised emotions. The language of these images emphasises the statues' immobility all the more, and thus underscores the static nature and brittleness of conventional heroic tales. The artist's filmic mix with historic footage reveals additional forms of historic manifestations that have been determining our perception of the past for a long time: an excerpt from an affirmative

re-enactment of crusade festivities and the inauguration of the Albert statue in Kinshasa, when the Congo was still a colony. From today's perspective, these images seem all the more suspicious, since they expose the symbolic acts that served to counter the loss of illegally appropriated privileges of power as rituals. By contrasting the children's imaginations with the material heritage of colonialism, the artist breaks down the representation of historiography and places it in a new relationship of definitions.

Authorship and subjectivization

In her work *Ich war's. Tagebuch 1900–1999*, (It was me. Diary 1900–1999) (fig. p. 80), the artist Daniela Comani crosses through the entire history of the 20th century. On a wall-sized canvas, 365 entries from a fictitious 'I' can be read: On September 3rd this 'I' was a victim of the mafia in Palermo; on September 4th it was elected to be the president of Chile; on September 5th it kidnapped Hanns-Martin Schleyer. In a fictional year's chronology, Comani selected historic events between 1900 and 1999 and ordered them as supposed eyewitness accounts in the style of a chronologic journal. The events are known incidents in world history, but also very private moments from daily life. The arrangement is a result of the artist's subjective sense of selection, concern and relevance. The locations, associations and contexts change constantly: sports victories next to murders, election victories, terrorist attacks, the founding of states, film premieres, kidnappings, inauguration celebrations, declarations of war and the weather. The roles change between passive and active, and alternate between perpetrator, victim, witness or reporter. One gets dizzy in the face of the density of such existential, menacing and dramatic events.

The personification of authorship offers observers a disconcerting identification that teeters between megalomania and apocalyptic self-destruction. The anonymous and multi-personal 'I' becomes the protagonist in world

Sarah Vanagt: *Little Figures*, 2003 (Ausstellungsansicht / Exhibition view)

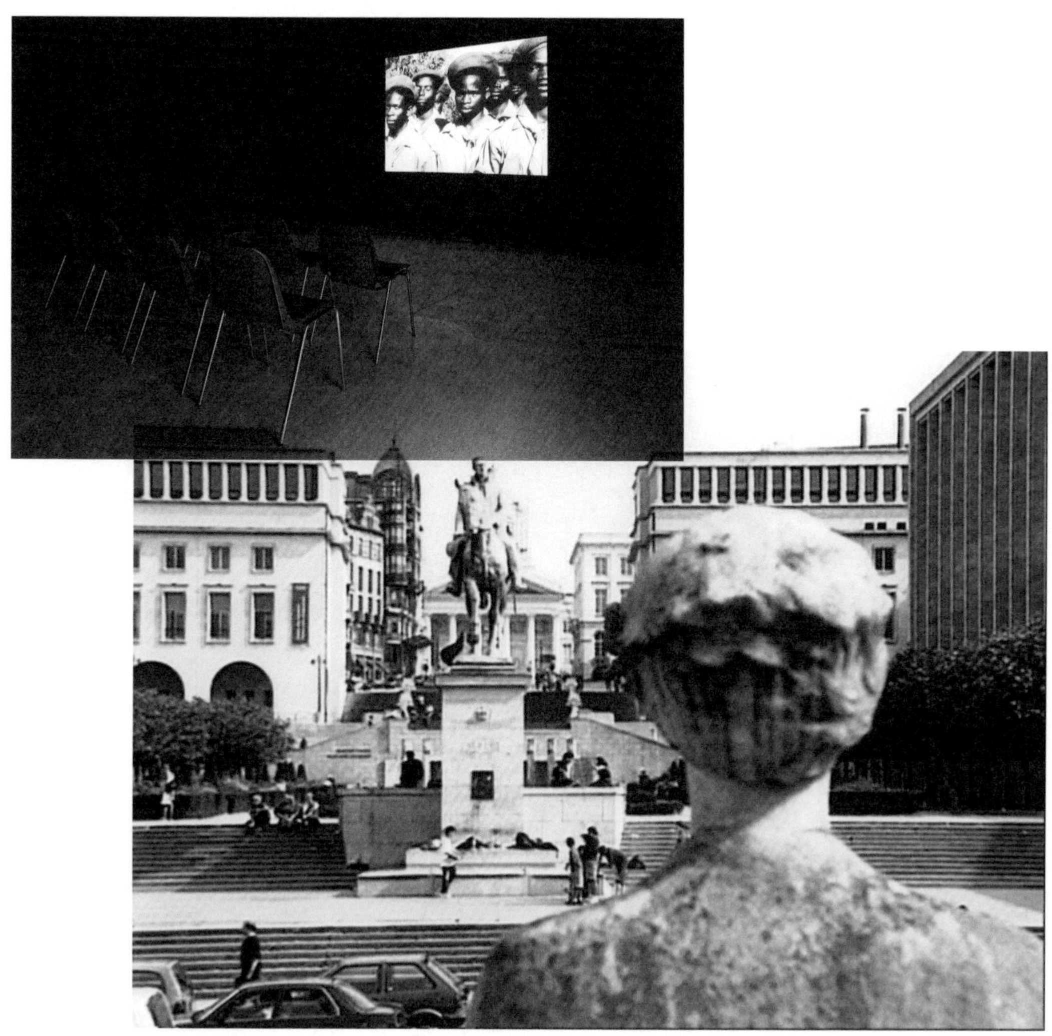

Sarah Vanagt: *Little Figures*, 2003

Miriam Visaczki: *Waldmünchen 1–4*, 2006 (Ausstellungsansicht / Exhibition view)

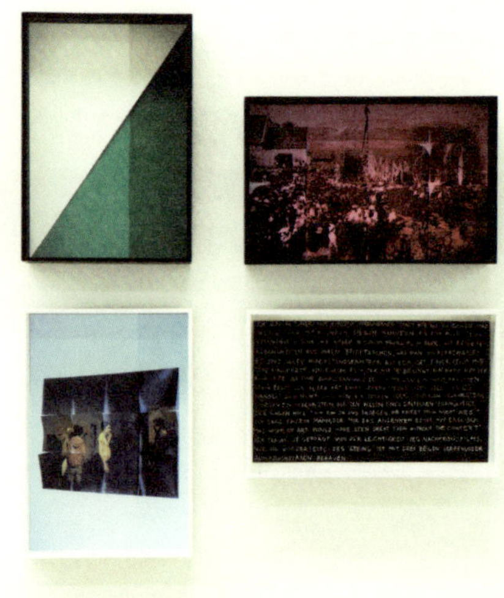

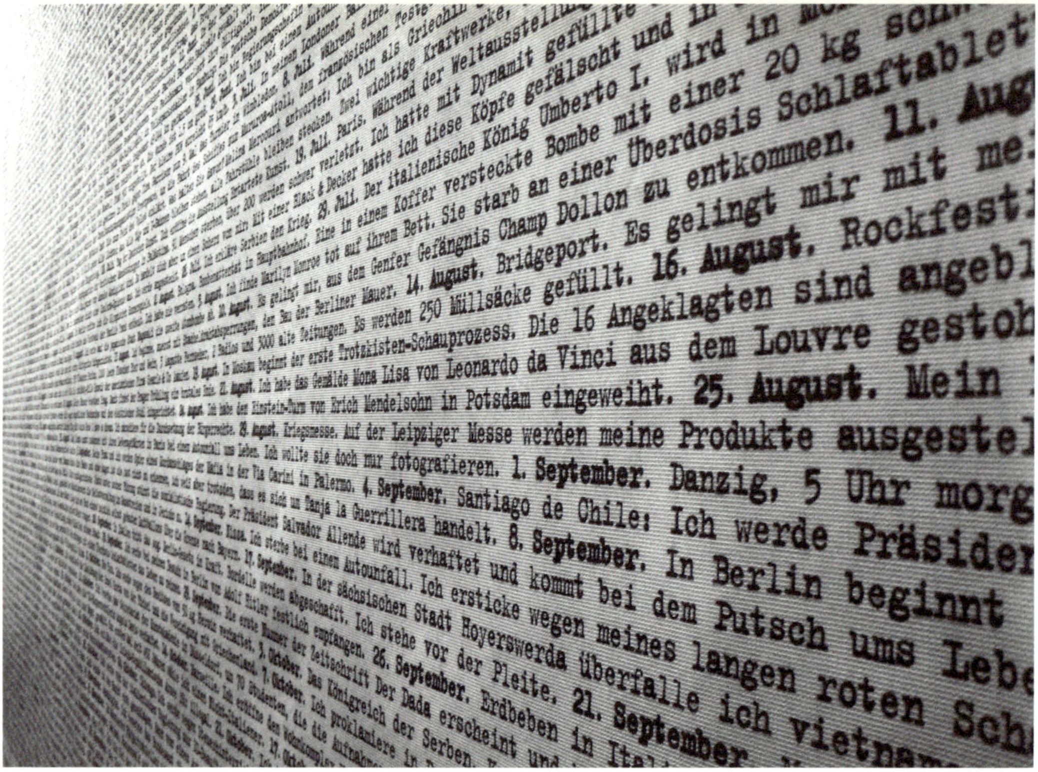

Daniela Comani: *Ich war's. Tagebuch 1900–1999*, 2002/2007

mit offenem Ausgang statt einer einheitlichen Erzählung.

Drei Künstlerinnen, die Teil der Ausstellung *Überblendungen* waren, werden im Folgenden mit ihren je eigenen künstlerischen Strategien vorgestellt.

Re-Repräsentation von Geschichte

„Wir haben übrigens auch ein Problem bei der Auseinandersetzung mit dem Rassismus. Wir bearbeiten ihn mit Toleranz, aber Toleranz ist keine Lösung für Rassismus. [...] Das Problem des Rassismus ist in erster Linie das Problem der Repräsentation"[2], äussert sich René Pollesch in einem Gespräch über seine Theaterarbeit. Repräsentation ist aber nicht nur ein Verhängnis der darstellenden Kunst, sondern auch der Vermittlung und Konstruktion von vergangenen Ereignissen.

Sarah Vanagt ist Filmemacherin und Künstlerin aus Brüssel und darüber hinaus studierte Historikerin. Historiografie steht im Zentrum ihrer künstlerischen Auseinandersetzung. Ihre viel beachtete Arbeit *Little Figures* (Abb. S. 79) ist ein Film, der im Umgang mit filmischer Erzählweise sowohl Found Footage als auch dokumentarische und fiktionale Methoden kombiniert. Sarah Vanagt dokumentiert filmisch das urbane Nebeneinander von Ungleichzeitigkeiten. Der Schauplatz von *Little Figures* ist der Mont des Arts in Brüssel, ein grosszügig gestalteter Platz, gesäumt von wichtigen Museen und Kulturschätzen Belgiens, von Repräsentationsbauten und Statuen von Nationalhelden – mitunter finanziert durch Einnahmen aus kolonialem Erbe. Unter den steinernen Füssen solcher Statuen, denen von Godefroy de Bouillon, von Albert I. und seiner Frau Königin Elisabeth, fahren Kinder und Jugendliche auf ihren Skateboards. „What is happening now?", fragt die steinerne Elisabeth mit der Stimme eines ruandischen Mädchens, ein Flüchtlingskind, das heute in Brüssel lebt. Albert und Godefroy antworten mit den Stimmen eines marokkanischen

und eines philippinischen Jungen. Ein fiktiver Dialog entspinnt sich zwischen den Dreien, den Vanagt mit diesen Kindern entwickelt hat. Kinder, die in einem Land leben, das auch 50 Jahre nach der Unabhängigkeit Kongos nach einer adäquaten Sprache ringt, mit dem blutigen kolonialen Erbe umzugehen. Die zum Leben erwachten Statuen mischen durch die freie Interpretation der Kinder ihre Erinnerungen an die belgische Eroberungs- und Kolonialgeschichte mit der Bedeutung, die ihnen heute zuteil wird. Godefroy und Albert markieren so etwas wie historische Eckpfeiler europäisch-belgischer Eroberungspolitik: Godefroy, Kreuzritter im 11. Jahrhundert, und Albert I., König von Belgien von 1909–1934 und damit König des zentralafrikanischen Kongo, das unter der privaten und brutalen Führung seines Onkel Leopolds II. um hochwertige Rohstoffe und geschätzte zehn Millionen Menschen ärmer gemacht wurde. Sarah Vanagt vermittelt wenig Details des historischen Schattens, den die Eroberer aus Stein werfen. Sie überlässt den Kindern diese assoziative Reflexionsebene. Es geht ihr nicht um lückenlose Aufklärung, sondern um den Blick auf die Geschichte, mit dem die heutige Generation lebt. Aber mehr noch, indem sie die Repräsentation dieser ‚Legenden' mit Kindern aus Migrationsfamilien besetzt, dekonstruiert sie die Heldengeschichte und öffnet den Raum für anti-rassistische und anti-heroische Selbstermächtigungen von kolonialer Geschichte.

Little Figures, das sind die Kinder, deren Chance es ist, das zukünftige Geschichtsbild zu entwerfen und ihre eigenen Spuren zu hinterlassen. *Little Figures* sind aber auch die mehr als menschengrossen Statuen, die kaum noch jemand beachtet und über deren historische Faktizität die heutige Generation mehr spekuliert als sie genau zuzuordnen weiss. Die starren Figuren gehören zu einem veralteten konventionellen Historienbild, welches die Geschichte von Eroberern festzuschreiben wusste und sie zuweilen in einen Mythos des Unverwundbaren verkehrte. Dass auch diese Sichtweise umgeschrieben werden kann, dass der Blick auf die Vergangenheit beweglich und offen ist, symbolisiert die Künstlerin mit der Gegenüberstellung von Bewegungen im Film. Alles um die Denkmäler herum ist in Bewegung,

2........... René Pollesch im Interview mit dem *Süddeutsche Zeitung Magazin* 17 (2012), 31.

der Verkehr auf den Strassen und vor allem die jugendlichen Skater, aber auch die Kamera ist in ständiger, fliessender Bewegung. Sie kriecht an den Oberflächen der Skulpturen entlang, als ob sie sich Schicht für Schicht den versteinerten Emotionen annähern wollte. Diese Bildsprache verstärkt die Unbeweglichkeit der Statuen um so mehr und verdeutlicht so die Starre und Brüchigkeit konventioneller Heldenerzählungen. Die filmische Kombination der Künstlerin mit historischem Footage offenbart weitere Formen der Geschichtsmanifestation, wie sie lange Zeit unsere Wahrnehmung von Vergangenem geprägt hat: Ein Ausschnitt aus einem affirmativen Re-Enactment von Kreuzzugsfestspielen und die Einweihung der Albert-Statue in Kinshasa, als Kongo immer noch Kolonie war. Mit dem heutigen Blick erscheinen diese Bilder weitaus verdächtiger, entlarven sie die symbolischen Handlungen als Rituale, die dazu dienten, dem Verlust unrechtmässig erworbener Machtprivilegien entgegenzuwirken. Dadurch, dass die Künstlerin die Imagination der Kinder der materiellen Überlieferung des Kolonialismus gegenüberstellt, bricht sie die Repräsentation von Historiografie auf und setzt sie in ein neues Definitionsverhältnis.

Autorschaft und Subjektivierung

Mit ihrer Arbeit *Ich war's. Tagebuch 1900–1999* (Abb. S. 80) durchquert die Künstlerin Daniela Comani das gesamte weltgeschichtliche 20. Jahrhundert. Auf einer wandgrossen Leinwand lesen sich eng aneinander gereiht 365 Selbstzeugnisse eines fiktiven Ichs: Am 3. September wurde das Ich Opfer der Mafia in Palermo, am 4. September zum Präsidenten Chiles gewählt, am 5. September hat es Hanns-Martin Schleyer entführt. In der Chronologie eines fiktiven Jahres hat Comani historische Ereignisse zwischen 1900 und 1999 ausgewählt, und sie als vermeintliche Selbstzeugnisse im Stil eines Chroniktagebuchs angeordnet. Die Ereignisse beziehen sich dabei auf bekannte Ereignisse der Weltgeschichte, aber auch auf ganz private Alltäglichkeiten. Die Zusammenstellung folgt der subjektiven Auswahl, Einschätzung und Betroffenheit durch die Künstlerin. Die Orte, Zusammenhänge und Kontexte ändern

sich permanent: Sportsiege neben Ermordungen, Wahlsiegen, Terroranschlägen, Staatsgründungen, Filmpremieren, Entführungen, Gründungsfeiern, Kriegserklärungen und Wettererscheinungen. Die Rollen wechseln dabei zwischen passiv und aktiv, zwischen Täter_in, Opfer, Zeug_in oder Berichterstatter_in hin und her. Ein Schwindelgefühl entsteht durch die Dichte der existentiellen, bedrohlichen und dramatischen Ereignisse.

Die Personifizierung der Urheberschaft versetzt Betrachter_innen in eine befremdliche Identifikation, die zwischen absurdem Grössenwahn und apokalyptischer Selbstvernichtung wankt. Das anonyme und multi-personale Ich wird zum_r Akteur_in von Weltgeschichte. Aber dieses Ich bleibt nicht fremd, sondern versetzt sich im Leseprozess in jede und jeden von uns und vermag es so, die Fragen nach Involviertheit in, Verantwortung für und Beteiligung an Zeitgeschichte in uns selbst zu aktivieren und zu hinterfragen.

Die Originalversion der Arbeit hat die italienische Künstlerin Comani, die seit mehr als 25 Jahren in Berlin lebt, zunächst in Italienisch verfasst – danach wurde sie in mehrere Sprachen übersetzt. Der Titel *Sono stata io* und alle folgenden Tagebuchberichte sind im Italienischen in der weiblichen Form verfasst. So wird hier eine (genderidentitäre) Verschiebung der Autorschaft in Szene gesetzt, mit der weibliche Akteurinnen als Handelnde jene Lücken in der *vorherr*schenden Geschichtsschreibung andeuten sollen. Comani überblendet sowohl zeitliche Ungleichzeitigkeiten, indem sie vordergründig einer Chronologie von Ereignissen folgt und diese zugleich sprengt, als auch Geschichte als ein Nebeneinander von subjektiv selektiven Wahrnehmungen und weltgeschichtlichen Meilensteinen widerspiegelt. Damit hinterfragt sie nicht nur die Autorität von Geschichtsschreibung, sondern beschreibt die Konstruktion von Geschichte als etwas zutiefst subjektives und macht deutlich, dass es bei einer solchen gerade nicht um die Anhäufung von Daten und Ereignisse oder rein dramatischexistentiellen Ereignissen gehen kann. Die Inhalte, Fakten, Zuschreibungen und Verdichtungen von Vergangenheit werden hier im Hinblick auf

history. But this 'I' doesn't remain foreign to us; in the process of reading, it enters into each one of us and is thus able to activate and criticise within us the questions of involvement in, responsibility for and participation in history. The Italian artist Comani, who has been living in Berlin for more than 25 years, originally created the work in Italian—then it was translated in numerous languages. The title, *Sono stata io*, and all of the following journal entries are in the Italian feminine form. Thus a (gender identity) shift of authorship is staged that is meant to refer to gaps in dominant historiography. Comani dissolves asynchronous moments by following a chronology of events on the surface while simultaneously blowing them up and reflecting on history as a juxtaposition of subjective, selective perceptions and milestones of world history. In the process, she not only questions the authority of historiography, but also describes the construction of history as something that is deeply subjective. She makes it clear that history shouldn't be limited to a pile of dates and events or purely dramatic/existential events. The contents, facts, attributions and consolidation of the past are investigated here in reference to our cultural conditioning and the psychological and emotional charge of such stories. In many practices of artistic historiography, the strategies of subjectivisation, identification and reflection are paramount in revealing the structures that separate the seemingly important from the unimportant and the heroic from the less heroic—the structures that write history.

De/construction between facts and fiction

The British artist Suzanne Treister often produced multi-year, complex series of works that offer their own universe of unusual contexts of meaning and explanations based on her extensive research in the history of culture, the media and the military. The focus of the *Hexen 2039* art project (fig. p. 84/85) is the researcher Rosalind Brodsky, a time traveler who is doing para-scientific research on psychological warfare on commission by the Institute of Militronics and Advanced Time Interventionality in London (IMATI) between 1995 and 2058. Rosalind Brodsky is the artist's absent, fictional alter ego who carries the name of her Jewish/Polish grandmother— a victim of genocide during the 2nd World War.

The *Hexen 2039* work complex is made up of large-format diagrams drawn with India ink, 49 coal drawings, objects collected at Ebay (tarot cards, souvenirs from the Brocken mountain, eavesdropping equipment and transmitters), a fictional documentary video and remote-viewing drawings. All of these artifacts, drawings and recordings serve as documents of a narrative derivation in the style of conspiracy theories. It is Rosalind Brodsky's revealing report about the early 20th century, dated 2039, about the US military, its connections to occult rituals such as the witch cult of Walpurgis night or those of an Aleister Crowley, to Hollywood productions such as *The Wizard of Oz* and telecommunications technology such as the TV tower on the Brocken mountain. *Hexen 2039* places everything in a big context: the Jewish Kabbalah, the cultural industry, the history of technology, psychology, black magic and science fiction. The coal drawings and their historical and fictional references, which optically seem to stem from the 19th century, are a kind of evidence—as are the diagrams and objects. However, it remains unclear what the actual event is and which of the conspiracy theories and interpretations are true or false. As a result of the specific nature of much of the information, fact and fiction, fantasy and instinct, historic documentation and paranoia can't be differentiated. 'The whole thing is a sci-fi construct, like a series of novels set in the future but drawing upon the past,' Suzanne Treister explains in a discussion about her method of historical deconstruction and the speculative reconstruction of history.

The practice of mixing fact and fiction is an artistic method of reconstructing the past that rejects factual explanation and—precisely because of this—attempts to 'describe facticity itself as historical imagination'.[3] This means that

3 ⸻ Leeb, 'Flucht nach nicht ganz vorn', p. 42.

Suzanne Treister: *Hexen 2039/Diagram*, 2006–2008

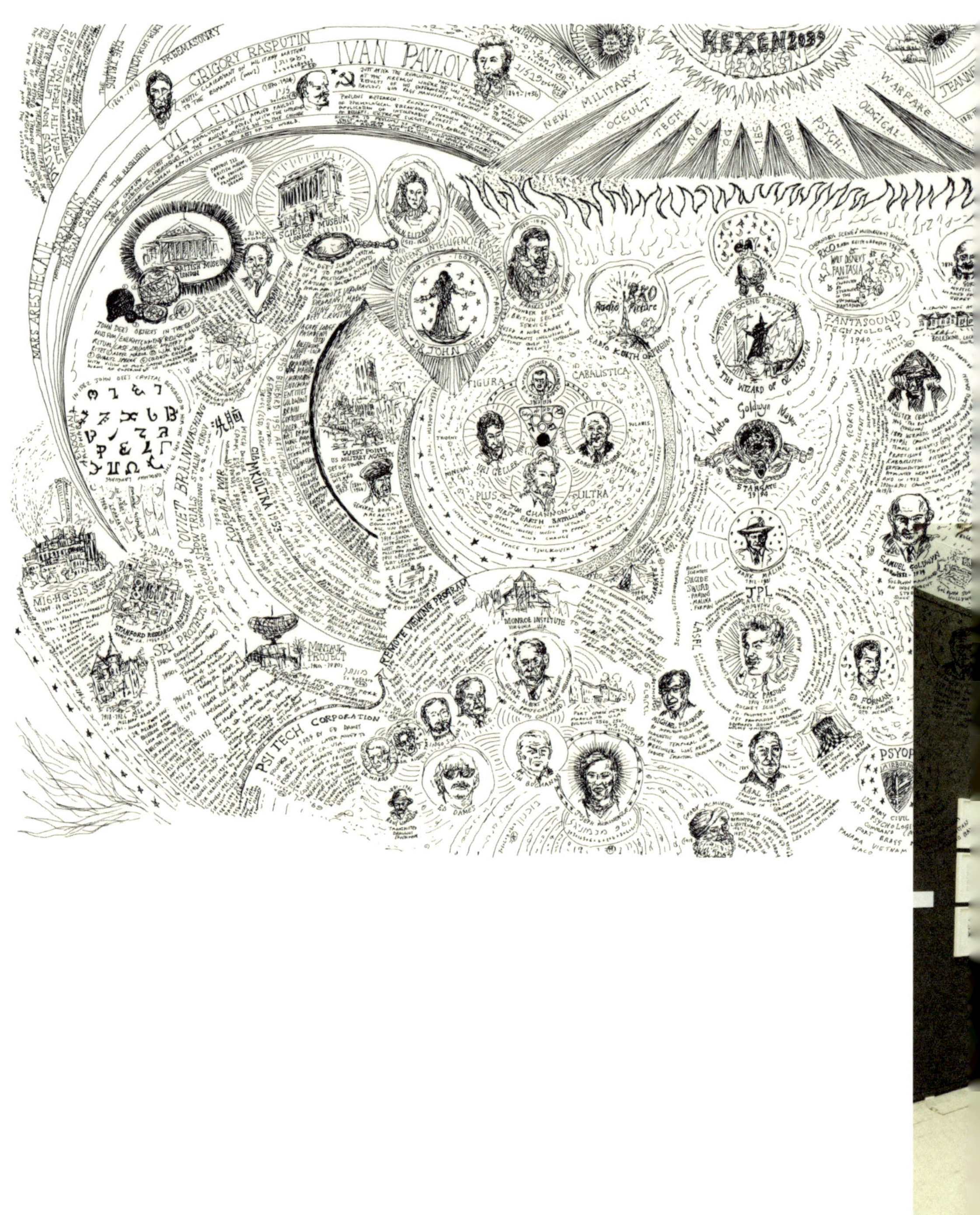

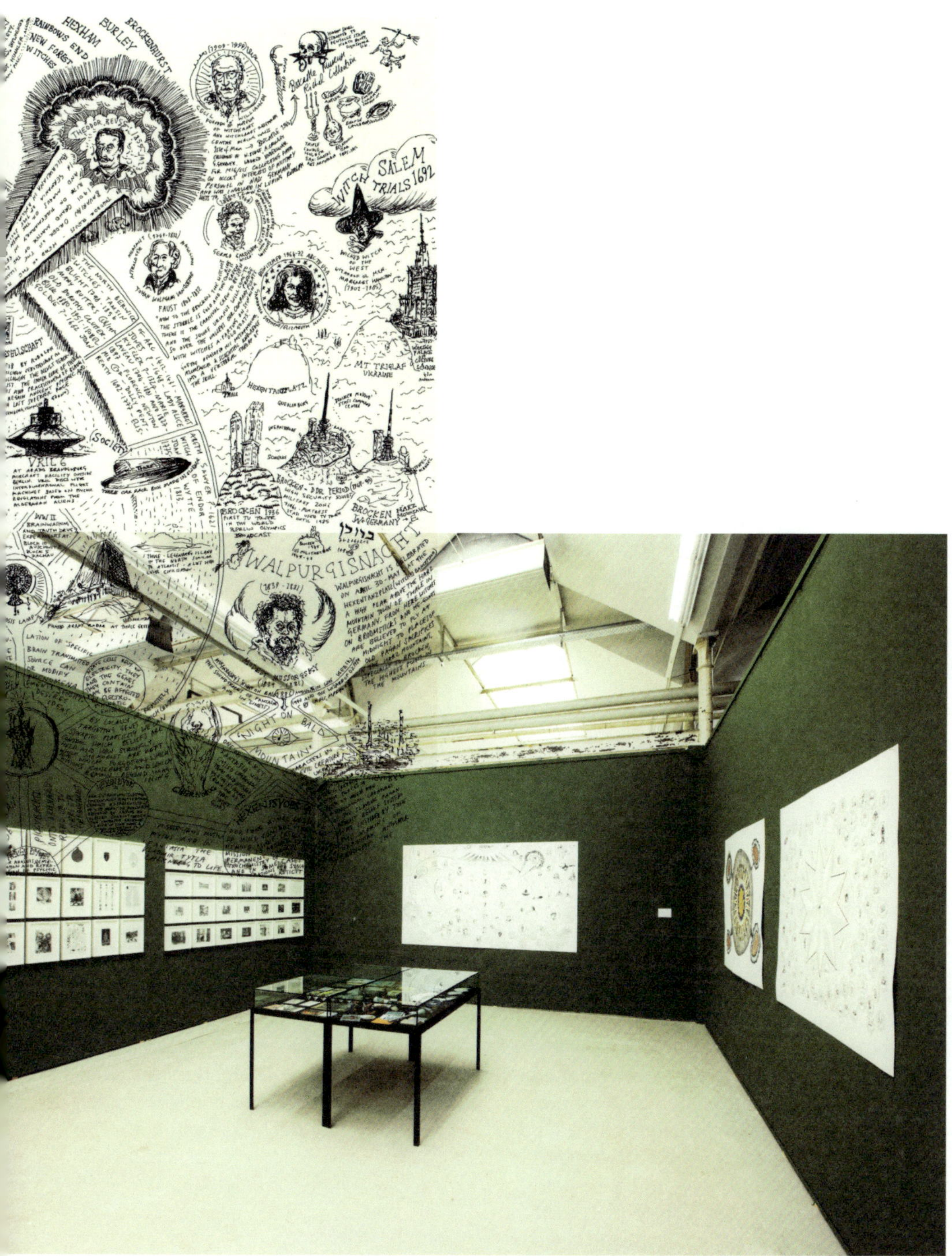

Suzanne Treister (v.l.n.r./f.l.t.r.): *Hexen 2039/Graphites, 2006; Hexen 2039/Artefacts, 2006; Hexen 2039/Diagram, 2006–2008;*
Hexen 2039/Diagram/Hexen 2039 Equipment, 2008; Hexen 2039/Diagram/eBay Artefacts-Locations, 2008
(Ausstellungsansicht/Exhibition view)

unsere kulturelle Prägung und die psychologisch-emotionale Aufladung solcher Erzählungen untersucht. Bei vielen Praktiken künstlerischer Historiografie geht es um die Strategie von Subjektivierung, Identifikation und Reflexion als Aspekt der Vermittlung jener Strukturen, nach denen vermeintlich Wichtiges von Unwichtigem, Heroisches von weniger Heroischem getrennt wird, nach denen Geschichte geschrieben wird.

De/Konstruktion zwischen Fakt und Fiktion

Die britische Künstlerin Suzanne Treister produziert oft mehrere Jahre andauernde, komplexe Werkserien, die ein ganz eigenes Universum von aussergewöhnlichen Bedeutungszusammenhängen und Welterklärungen anbieten, die auf Treisters aufwändiger Recherche von Kultur-, Medien- und Militärgeschichte beruhen. Mittelpunkt des Kunstprojekts *Hexen 2039* (Abb. S. 84/85) ist die Forscherin Rosalind Brodsky, die zwischen 1995 und 2058 als Zeitreisende aus der Zukunft im Auftrag des Institute of Militronics and Advanced Time Interventionality in London (IMATI) para-wissenschaftliche Untersuchungen zur psychologischen Kriegsführung unternimmt. Rosalind Brodsky ist ein abwesendes, fiktionales Alter-Ego der Künstlerin und trägt den Namen ihrer jüdisch-polnischen Grossmutter, die dem Genozid im Zweiten Weltkrieg zum Opfer fiel.

Der Werkkomplex *Hexen 2039* besteht aus grossformatigen, in Tusche gezeichneten Diagrammen, 49 Kohle-Zeichnungen, über Ebay gesammelten Objekten (Tarot-Karten, Brocken-Souvenirs, Abhör- und Sendegeräte), einem fiktionalen Dokumentationsvideo und Fernwahrnehmungs-Zeichnungen. All diese Artefakte und (Auf-)Zeichnungen fungieren als Dokumente einer narrativen Herleitung im Stile von Verschwörungstheorien. Es ist der Enthüllungsbericht der Rosalind Brodsky über das frühe 20. Jahrhundert, datiert mit dem Jahr 2039, über das US-Militär, seine Verbindung zu okkulten Ritualen, wie dem Hexenkult der Walpurgisnacht oder denen eines Aleister Crowley, zu Hollywood-Produktionen, wie *The Wizard of Oz*, und der Telekommunikationstechnik, wie dem Fernsehturm auf dem Brocken.

Hexen 2039 stellt alles in einen grossen Zusammenhang: Jüdische Kabbala, Kulturindustrie, Technikgeschichte, Psychologie, Schwarze Magie und Science Fiction. Die optisch aus dem 19. Jahrhundert stammenden Kohlezeichnungen mit historischen und fiktionalen Referenzen stellen eine Art Beweisführung dar, der sich auch die Diagramme und Objekte verschreiben. Unklar bleibt, was überhaupt das Ereignis ist und welche der Verschwörungstheorien und Auslegungen wahr oder falsch sind. Aufgrund der Spezifik vieler Informationen sind Fakt und Fiktion, Fantasie und Spürsinn, historische Dokumentation und Paranoia nicht zu unterscheiden. „The whole thing is a sci-fi construct, like a series of novels set in the future but drawing upon the past", erklärt Suzanne Treister in einem Gespräch ihre Methode der historischen Dekonstruktion und spekulativen Rekonstruktion von Geschichte.

Die Praxis der Vermischung von Fakt und Fiktion ist eine künstlerische Methode der Vergangenheits-Rekonstruktion, die sich dem faktischen Erklären verweigert und gerade dadurch versucht, „Faktizität selbst als historische Imagination zu beschreiben"[3]. Dass heisst, die Rekonstruktion von Geschichte wird nicht als narrativ geschlossener Kausalzusammenhang beschrieben, sondern als subjektive Aneignung und fragmentiertes Arrangement von Dokumenten, Bildern, Artefakten, Zitaten oder anderen formalen Bezügen und als politische Durchsetzung von kollektiven Machtpositionen innerhalb bestimmter diskursiver Strukturen. Und diese historischen Aneignungen und Arrangements werden, so analysiert Susanne Leeb erkenntnisreich, „[…] dann als Ursprungsmythen an den Anfang einer jeweiligen Geschichte gesetzt, um Fakten schaffende Handlungen zu legitimieren."[4] Die Unterhaltungsindustrie tut ihr Übriges, um diese Mythen in heroische Happy-End-Dramen zu vervielfältigen und produziert so populäre Vereinfachungen, die wenig zur Nachfrage anregen.

3.................... Leeb: Flucht nach nicht ganz vorn, 42.
4.................... Leeb: Flucht nach nicht ganz vorn, 43.

the reconstruction of history is not described
as a narrative that is a closed chain of causality,
but rather as a subjective appropriation
and fragmented arrangement of documents,
images, artifacts, quotes or other formal
references and as a political implementation of
collective positions of power within certain
structures of discourse. These historical appro-
priations and arrangements are '… then placed
at the beginning of a respective story as a
myth of origin in order to legitimate acts that
created precedents,'[4] as Susanne Leeb analyses
insightfully. The entertainment industry
does the rest by copying these myths into heroic
happy-end dramas. Thus it produces popular
simplifications that hardly inspire any inquiry.

Translated by Christopher Langer

---

4 .... Ibid., p. 43.

VERGANGENHEITEN ERFINDEN. ODER: DIE KUNST DER AKTUALISIERUNG

INVENTING THE PAST. OR: THE ART OF UPDATING

The past is never dead.
It is not even past.
(William Faulkner, *Requiem for a Nun*)

Geschichte und Kunst

Geht uns heute die Vergangenheit verloren, nachdem sich die Zukunft als unplanbar erwiesen hat? Mehr und mehr leben wir in einer gespenstischen Gegenwart, zerstreut im „externalisierten globalen Nervensystem"[1] Internet, das alle bekannten Gedächtnismetaphern real überbietet, weil es jede kleinste Äusserung und Reaktion speichert und uns unvergangen hält – zumindest solange der elektrische Strom fliesst. Wenn alle reden, schreiben, Ansichten, Analysen, Songs, Bilder und Videos verbreiten, und nichts und niemand mehr verloren gehen muss, wenn zudem die kommerziell angebotenen, sozialen Netzwerke nichts von dem, was man ihnen einmal preisgegeben hat, wieder hergeben wollen, was bedeutet da noch Geschichte, was meint Geschichtsschreibung? Ist nicht endlich alles gut? Und sollten wir nicht einfach akzeptieren, dass wir in der Posthistoire angekommen sind, dass sich die Geschichte entweder mit der Durchsetzung der liberalen Demokratie erfüllt oder dass mindestens die Medien uns in eine unbekannte Zeit nach der Geschichte geschickt haben?[2] Oder sind wir doch unglücklich, weil wir, wie Vilém Flusser diagnostizierte, von unseren eigenen Apparaten programmiert werden, die an die Stelle der Erzählung die Aufzählung, die Statistik und die bildliche Schilderung setzen, ohne dass wir mit ihnen heute schon ernsthaft und kreativ umgehen könnten?[3]

Die Geschichte, bzw. die Frage danach, was in welcher Form zu überliefern ist, war seit jeher ein umstrittenes und umkämpftes Feld, vor allem dort, wo sich Historiker_innen an die Erzählung einer Universalgeschichte gemacht haben.

[1] Assmann, Aleida: *Erinnerungsräume. Formen und Wandlungen des kulturellen Gedächtnisses.* München 1999, 178.
[2] Francis Fukuyamas *Das Ende der Geschichte* ist hier stellvertretend zu nennen.
[3] Vgl. Flusser, Vilém: *Nachgeschichte. Eine korrigierte Geschichtsschreibung.* Frankfurt a.M. 1997.

**The past is never dead.
It is not even past.**
(William Faulkner, *Requiem for a Nun*)

History and Art

Is the past becoming lost to us after, in this day and age, the future has proved to be unpredictable? We are living more and more in an eerie present, scattered throughout the 'externalised global nervous system'[1] of the Internet, which truly surpasses all of the known metaphors for remembrance, because it stores each and every comment and reaction, regardless of how small, making them perpetually accessible—at least as long as the electricity is flowing. When everyone talks, writes and circulates opinions, analyses, songs, images and videos, and nothing and no one ever gets lost; when furthermore the commercially available social networks never want to part with what one once revealed to them, then what does history stand for, and what does historiography mean? Isn't everything all right in the end? And shouldn't we simply accept that we have arrived in post-history; that history is fulfilled either with the emergence of liberal democracy, or that at least the media have sent us into an unknown time after history?[2] Or are we unhappy because, as Vilém Flusser diagnosed, we are programmed by our own apparatuses, which substitute lists, statistics and visual accounts for the narrative without us currently even being able to deal with them in a serious or creative way?[3]

History, or the question of what is to be passed down in what form, has always been a controversial and contested field, above all when historians have set out to relate a universal history. However, for several decades now, the general and generally acceptable concepts of history hidden behind the term 'history' have again been called into question even more fundamentally. Scepticism towards 'history' is linked with scepticism towards any type of project that deals with historical progress, and this is above all due to the analysis of totalitarianism and its destructive impact on the world. After 1989, the collapse of the dual post-war world order ultimately revealed boundaries and histories in all of their arbitrariness and caused some state constructions to disintegrate dramatically.[4] In addition, accidents and catastrophes increase doubt in the logic underlying technological progress. We are surrounded the world over by small and larger apocalypses, apocalypses without apocalypse, i.e., without the discovery of a truth, without vision, sense and purpose in the catastrophe.[5] They increase insight into the end of great historical projects, i.e., the insight that neither a world spirit nor construction nor planning will straighten things out, and allow for the acknowledgment fundamental human insufficiency. At the same time, this acknowledgment opens up the world to an unplanned, unforeseen opportunity for a better future and community. The revolutions in North Africa, which no one foresaw and which (shall) triumph due to the courage of the masses, raise hopes in this direction.

The network world also confirms the postmodern deconstruction of evolutionary models of history as well as modern social projects. The experiences of plurality, synchronicity and transmediality have irrevocably suspended the concept of a linear, general or universal and actualizing history, or at least lastingly complicated it, and by the same token underscore doubt in the concept that the modern human being, liberated from nature and prevision, writes his or her own history. It even appears to be the case that the dismissal of anthropocentric and teleological models of history have opened up unforeseen scopes

1 .... Aleida Assmann, *Erinnerungsräume: Formen und Wandlungen des kulturellen Gedächtnisses* (Munich, 1999), p. 178.
2 ... As put forth by Francis Fukuyama in his book *The End of History and the Last Man.*
3 ... Cf. Vilém Flusser, 'A Historiography Revised', in id., *Writings*, ed. Andreas Ströhl, trans. Erik Eisel (Minneapolis, 2002).
4 .... Cf., e.g., Tony Judt, *Geschichte Europas von 1945 bis zur Gegenwart* (Frankfurt am Main, 2006).
5 ...... Cf. Jacques Derrida, 'Of an Apocalyptic Tone Newly Adopted in Philosophy', in *Derrida and Negative Theology*, ed. Harold Coward and Toby Fosbay, trans. John P. Leavey, Jr. (New York, 1992), pp. 25–72.

of thought and action in the middle of the world for which other modes of representation and narration are sought. We are on the threshold of a different way of narrating and preserving that uses a variety of means to seek to capture, sustain and think the uniqueness of experiences, such as the complexity, variability and dissemination of past occurrences and relationships in the present.

For several decades now, at the latest since the late 1950s, visual artists have performed pioneering work in the development of new and different forms of communicating pasts. Their—in part reflected, in part rebellious—retrieval of what was mimetically, narratively and theatrically excluded from the post-war project 'modern art'[6] led to hybrid forms of art in the use of or in correspondence with the neighbouring arts of music, theatre and design. It was about, either in the name of politicisation or in the name of popularisation, the invention of new social locations and roles in visual art.

Artists continue to work on the temporalisation of images to this very day—against the traditional monumentalisation or spatialisation of history, but also against the placelessness and lack of content of numerous formal abstractions. They translate images into space, link image with text, image with sound, or use all variations of photographic and filmic recording and display. In the 1970s, co-dependent terms emerged such as Process Art, Narration Art or Story Art in order to describe forms of images and presentation that allow thinking, occurrences and courses of time to be experienced as time-space processes.[7] The non-linear forms of narration developed chiefly by female artists in the 1990s correspond with the global leave-taking from the great history projects, the 'grands récits humaine' (Jean-François Lyotard) that was becoming prevalent at the time on a global scale. At first, for a certain period of time focus was consequentially placed on the everyday life of the many and the history of the individual in order to afford both poetic as well as reflected space to what the media so spectacularly and mercilessly illuminated: the search for the status of the individual in the world and for his or her relationships with a changing society. The simultaneous expansion of the artistic field of perception to include the conflicts occurring around the world, suppressed experiences, blocked-out places, and events initially occurred by falling back on documentary formats.[8] Consequently, doubt with respect to the document as 'true evidence' of past events and the limitations of the documentary, i.e., the temporal impossibility of post hoc proof, the linking of any and every documentary view to a situation, and the perspective of the person recording a particular event have been reflected to an increasing extent. Counter to the concept of simple historical proof, complex forms of bearing testimony to occurrences and events developed that are well informed of the impossibility of one true piece of evidence.[9]

Contemporary art has meanwhile assembled a substantial reservoir of ways of aesthetically representing or communicating past events and experiences that distinguishes itself from the registry and processing of indifferent unpasts in the network world as well as from their portrayal in historiography and administration in archives. By recalling the past tense I would like to give particular prominence to the meaning of artistic inventions and the updating of unique pasts for the present and the future. Unlike in other places of social transmission or media, by means of contemporary art

6......... Arthur C. Danto mistakenly subsumed this turn under the label 'post-historical.' Cf. id., *Vom Fortleben der Kunst* (Munich, 2000). Danto makes it into a stylistic phenomenon without taking into consideration any meaning in terms of content, i.e., meaning for articulation and communication.

7.. Cf. 'Text-Foto-Geschichten', *Story Art/Narrative Art. Kunstforum International* 33 (1979). I provide an overview in 'Unauffällige Fiktionen: Von Foto- zu Video-Texten; Die geteilte Aufnahme', *Fiktion der Kunst der Fiktion. Kunstforum International* 202 (2010), pp. 71–91.

8.... I would like to point out the large number of documentary films presented at documenta11, curated by Okwui Enwezor.

9................. Cf. Ute Vorkoeper, 'Mitwirkung am Politischen: Über Zeugenschaft und Dauer von zeitgenössischer Kunst,' in Michaela Ott and Harald Strauss, eds., *Ästhetik + Politik: Neuaufteilungen des Sinnlichen in der Kunst* (Hamburg, 2009), pp. 82–100.

Allerdings stehen seit ein paar Jahrzehnten die hinter dem Begriff ‚Geschichte' verborgenen, allgemeinen und allgemein gültigen Geschichtsvorstellungen nochmals grundlegender in Frage. Die Skepsis an ‚der Geschichte' ist verkoppelt mit der Skepsis gegenüber jeder Art von historischem Fortschrittsprojekt und dies verdankt sich vor allem der Auseinandersetzung mit dem Totalitarismus und seinen Welt vernichtenden Auswirkungen. Der Zusammenbruch der dualen Nachkriegsweltordnung hat nach 1989 alle Grenzen und Geschichten endgültig in ihrer Willkür offenbart und einige Staatskonstruktionen in dramatische Auflösung gebracht.[4] Daneben mehren Unfälle und Katastrophen die Zweifel an der technischen Fortschrittslogik. Weltweit sind wir umgeben von kleinen und grösseren Apokalypsen, Apokalypsen ohne Apokalypse, d.h. ohne die Entdeckung einer Wahrheit, ohne Erkenntnis, Sinn und Zweck in der Katastrophe.[5] Sie mehren die Einsicht in das Ende der grossen historischen Projekte, d.h. die Einsicht, dass weder ein Weltgeist noch Konstruktion oder Planung die Dinge richten werden, und lassen die grundsätzliche menschliche Unzulänglichkeit eingestehen. Zugleich öffnet sich mit diesem Eingeständnis die Welt auf eine ungeplante, unvorhergesehene Möglichkeit einer besseren Zukunft und Gemeinschaft. Die von niemandem vorhergesehenen nordafrikanischen Revolutionen, die wegen des Muts der Vielen Erfolg haben (sollen), lassen in diese Richtung hoffen.

Auch die Netzwelt bestätigt die postmodernen Dekonstruktionen der evolutionären Geschichtsmodelle sowie der modernen Gesellschaftsprojekte. Die Erfahrungen von Pluralität, Synchronität und Transmedialität haben unwiderrufbar die Vorstellung einer linearen, allgemeinen, bzw. universalen oder sich verwirklichenden Geschichte aufgehoben, zumindest nachhaltig verkompliziert, so wie sie andererseits den Zweifel an der Vorstellung unterstreichen, dass der moderne Mensch, von der Natur und Vorsehung befreit, seine eigene Geschichte schreibe. Es scheint dabei sogar so, dass die

Verabschiedung der anthropozentrischen und teleologischen Geschichtsmodelle ungeahnte Denk- und Handlungsspielräume inmitten der Welt eröffnet habe, für die nach anderen Darstellungs- und Erzählweisen gesucht wird. Wir stehen am Anfang eines anderen Erzählens und Bewahrens, das mit vielfältigen Mitteln die Einzigartigkeit von Erfahrungen wie die Komplexität, Variabilität und Dissemination von vergangenen Ereignissen und Beziehungen in der Gegenwart einzufangen, zu halten und zu denken sucht.

Bildende Künstler_innen haben seit einigen Jahrzehnten, spätestens seit Ende der 1950er Jahre, Pionierarbeit bei der Entwicklung neuer und anderer Formen der Mitteilung von Vergangenheiten geleistet. Ihre – teils reflektierte, teils rebellische – Rückgewinnung dessen, was als mimetisch, narrativ und theatral aus dem Nachkriegsprojekt ‚moderne Kunst' ausgeschlossen worden war,[6] führte sie zu hybriden Kunstformen in Anwendung oder in Korrespondenz zu den Nachbarkünsten Musik, Theater und Design. Es ging, entweder im Namen der Politisierung oder im Namen einer Popularisierung, um die Erfindung von neuen gesellschaftlichen Orten und Rollen der bildenden Kunst.

Künstler_innen arbeiten bis heute an der Verzeitlichung von Bildern – nach wie vor gegen traditionelle Monumentalisierungen oder Verräumlichungen von Geschichte, aber eben auch gegen die Ort- und Inhaltslosigkeit vieler formaler Abstraktionen. Sie übersetzen Bilder in den Raum, verkoppeln Bild und Schrift, Bild und Sound oder nutzen alle Spielarten der fotografischen und filmischen Aufnahme sowie Wiedergabe. In den 1970er Jahren kamen Begriffspaare wie Process Art, Narration Art oder Story Art auf, um Bild- und Inszenierungsformen zu umschreiben, die Denken, Ereignisse und Zeitläufe als Zeitraumprozesse erfahrbar werden

---

4 .... Vgl. z.B Judt, Tony: *Geschichte Europas von 1945 bis zur Gegenwart*. Frankfurt a.M. 2006.

5 .... Vgl. Jacques Derridas Argumentation gegen das apokalyptische Denken in der Philosophie, ders.: *Apokalypse*. Wien 2009, 72ff.

6 .... Diese Wende wurde von Arthur C. Danto missverständlich unter dem Label „posthistorisch" gefasst, vgl. ders.: *Vom Fortleben der Kunst*. München 2000. Danto macht daraus ein Stilphänomen, ohne die inhaltliche Bedeutung, d.h. die Bedeutung für Artikulationen und Mitteilungen zu berücksichtigen.

liessen, lassen.[7] Die vorzugsweise von Künstler-innen in den 1990er Jahren entwickelten, nicht-linearen Formen des Erzählens entsprechen mit der sich damals durchsetzenden, globalen Abschiednahme von den grossen Geschichts-projekten, den „grands récits humaine" (Jean-Francois Lyotard). Konsequent stand für eine gewisse Zeit zunächst der Alltag der Vielen und die Geschichte der/des Einzelnen im Fokus, um dem, was die Medien spektakulär und gnadenlos beleuchten, einen sowohl poetischen als auch reflektierten Raum zu geben: Der Suche nach der Stellung der/des Einzelnen in der Welt und nach ihren/seinen Beziehungen inner-halb der sich wandelnden Gesellschaften. Die zeitgleiche Erweiterung des künstlerischen Wahrnehmungsfeldes auf die Konflikte der ganzen Welt, auf verdrängte Erfahrungen, auf ausgeblendete Orte und Geschehen geschah zunächst über den Rückgriff auf dokumentarische Formate.[8] Die Zweifel am Dokument als ‚wahrem Zeugnis' von vergangenen Ereignissen und die Grenzen des Dokumentarischen, d.h. die zeitliche Unmöglichkeit des nachträglichen Beweises, die Bindung jedes dokumentarischen Blicks an eine Situation und die Perspektive des Aufnehmenden, wurden in der Folge vermehrt reflektiert. Gegen die Vorstellung vom einfachen geschichtlichen Beweis entstanden komplexe Formen des Bezeugens von Geschehnissen und Ereignissen, die um die Unmöglichkeit des einen wahren Zeugnisses wissen.[9]

Mittlerweile hat sich in der Gegenwartskunst ein beachtliches Reservoir an ästhetischen Darstel-lungen oder Mitteilungen vergangener Ereignisse und Erfahrungen angesammelt, das sich von der Registratur und Verarbeitung der gleichgültigen Unvergangenheiten in der Netzwelt ebenso wie von der Darstellung in Geschichtsschreibung und der Verwaltung in Archiven unterscheidet. Mit der Erinnerung an die Zeitform Vergangenheit möchte ich die Bedeutung für die Gegenwart und die Zukunft von künstlerischen Erfindungen und Aktualisierungen von einzigartigen Vergangenhei-ten besonders herausstellen. Über zeitgenössische Kunst und Ausstellungen kann Vergangenheit – anders als in anderen gesellschaftlichen Überlie-ferungsorten oder Medien – als einzigartige Erfahrung aktualisiert und als Ressource für die Gegenwart und eine andere, unbekannte Zukunft offen gehalten werden.

Vergangenheit, Vergangenes, Vergangenheiten

Vergangenheit klingt dunkel. Es scheint, als ob das Phonem ‚a' in der Mitte des Wortes die Schwere seiner Bedeutung unterstreichen wollte. Diese ergibt sich aber eigentlich erst durch die unerbittliche Vorsilbe ‚Ver', die aus dem ‚Gangen', dem zurückliegenden Gehen, etwas macht, das auf immer ‚fort' und ‚hinweg', d.h. entschwunden ist.[10] Jeder gelebte Moment ist vorbei – auch jeder ungelebte. Vergangenheit, das ist die ungeheure, die unendlich grosse und unüberseh-bare Menge dessen, was einmal Gegenwart hatte. Vergangen ist alles, was je war, das Vergessene, das Unvergessliche, das Beiläufige, das grosse Ereignis und seine unzähligen Folgen, die kleinen wie die grossen, medial gestreuten Geburten und Tode. Vergangenheit hat unweigerlich alles, was ist. Mit jedem Moment eines In-die-Welt-Tretens erwächst eine neue und besondere Vergangenheit. Schon mit dem Eintritt ins Dasein ist etwas vergangen und fortan ins zukünftige Vergehen gesetzt bis zum unausweichlichen Vergang oder Tod. Das Vergehen wie alles je Vergangene sind die Begleiter der Lebenden, sie sind zugleich ihre Bedrohung wie eine Art wach-sendes Reservoir, aus dem ihr Leben seine Tiefe bezieht.

Martin Heidegger hat diese Erfahrung mit einer beklemmenden Formel „Sein zum Tode"

7.......... Vgl. Text-Foto-Geschichten. *Story Art / Narrative Art. Kunstforum International* 33 (1979). Einen Überblick gebe ich in: Unauffällige Fiktionen. Von Foto- zu Video-Texten. In: *Fiktion der Kunst der Fiktion. Kunstforum International* 202 (2010), 71–91.

8............. Es sei hier nur an die Vielzahl dokumentarischer Filme auf der von Okwui Enwezor kuratierten documenta11 erinnert.

9..................... Vgl. Vorkoeper, Ute: Mitwirkung am Politischen. Über Zeugenschaft und Dauer von zeitgenössischer Kunst. In: Ott, Michaela/ Strauss, Harald: *Ästhetik + Politik. Neuaufteilungen des Sinnlichen in der Kunst.* Hamburg 2009, 82–100.

10 .... Die Vorsilbe ‚Ver' ist laut Grimmschen Wörterbuch an erster Stelle ein Derivat von ‚vorbei, hinweg'; vgl. http://woerterbuchnetz.de/ DWB/?sigle=DWB&mode=Vernetzung&lemid=GV00275.

and exhibitions the past can be updated as a unique experience and kept open as a resource for the present and a different, unknown future.

The Past, Past Occurrences, Pasts

The German word for the past, 'Vergangenheit', sounds dark. It seems as if the vowel 'a' in the middle of the word wants to underscore the weight of its meaning. However, this actually results from the relentless prefix 'Ver-', which makes something permanently 'gone' and 'over' out of 'Gangen', the gone 'to go'.[10] Each and every lived—as well as each and every unlived—moment is over. The past—that is, the enormous, the infinitely great and inestimable amount of what was once present. What is past is everything that ever was; the forgotten, the unforgettable, the incidental, the big event and its countless consequences, the minor as well as the major media-disseminated births and deaths. The past unavoidably has everything that is. A new and special past arises with each moment of entering-into-the-world. Yet upon entering existence, something is past and from then on placed in a future passing-away until unavoidable decay or death. Passing-away as well as everything that has ever past are the companions of the living; they are at once a threat to them and a kind of expanding reservoir from which life draws its depth.

Martin Heidegger used the oppressive formula 'Sein-zum-Tode' (being-towards-death) to refer to this experience.[11] When nothing and no one is freed from passing-away, from death, and death will be the unavoidable experience of each and every living human being, it is the experience of the fear of death that allows human beings to recognise the singularity of their temporal existence in the world. According to Heidegger, it is being-towards-death that opens up a unique decision space to everyone

in the first place: one's own life span. In this, each and every present is dominated by the past and the future, likewise suffused with past occurrences, which can erupt into memories, constantly oriented toward something that is upcoming, an incalculable and unpredictable future. The constant experience of passing-away and approaching one's own death is the most universal and at the same time most singular experience of each and every human being, the central intersection of the particular and the general.

It is precisely this that gives cause to reflect on the concept of the past—unlike on the concept of history or that of remembrance: the past is at once an abstract and a general category, yet at the same time it never exists isolated from the concrete present of those who are alive, who force their own past or that of others upon themselves and take into consideration and discuss these pasts for the sake of their own present and future. It is always already predated—while history is of necessity written in retrospect. Lived life constitutes the past—history is a narrative produced in order to prolong it. It is precisely because it is over that it is unpredictable. It is not an archive into which one reaches when it is convenient, but rather a diffuse deep realm shadowed by forgetting into which one often blindly plunges, sometimes descends into collectively, and out of which something time and again suddenly and unexpectedly bursts forth. Pasts: these are all of the passages—the experiences—in time, all of which can never be suppressed, but only individual, special experiences for various reasons, always forcing themselves back into the present in different, new ways.

While remembrance refers to the 'repository' of—important or often recurring—memories, the impact of the finiteness of life in the present echoes in the concept of the past. Unlike remembrance, which of necessity can be conceived of as something circumscribed, i.e., bound to a carrier, a material or a casing, the past is a limitless, endless period of time that encompasses all forgetting. Yet the past never exists as only abstract and universal, but

---

10............ According to Grimm's dictionary, the German prefix 'Ver-' is first and foremost a derivative of 'gone, over'. Cf. http://woerterbuchnetz.de/DWB/?sigle=DWB&mode=Vernetzung& lemid=GV00275.

11............ Cf. Martin Heidegger, *Sein und Zeit* (Tübingen, 1986), pp. 235ff.

always only in the particular moment of its being recollected and updated. While the concept of remembrance requires delineating the contours of each particular remembrance and conceiving the repository as national, regional, global or similar,[12] the concept of the past still contains the most irreconcilable and distant pasts and is at the same time always bound to the moment of recollecting. The past gets by without inclusions and exclusions, as per definition it contains everything—the recollected and the long—since forgotten, as well as what has been blocked out, overlooked, including everything that escapes or has escaped the historical and cultural remembrance of a nation or a specific social or cultural group and its respective professional repositories. At the same time, however, an individual or a particular collective situation is required in order to re-enter the present for the moment. Each individual is a different, singular intersection of endless pasts—and even within these not constantly.

Thus, the thesis of this text, namely that art 'invents pasts' and updates them, shifts the focus from the question of preserving and storing to the act of finding and the form of updating past occurrences or experiences as well as the invention of time-spaces, i.e., the temporal forms of temporalisation, in themselves impossible and open. An art that invents pasts begins at the intersection of general and particular experience, at that complicated moment between times, in the middle of a temporal structure. It begins with the artist's involvement in his or her own past, his or her openness for the present as well as the pasts of others, which erupt as dialogues and in constellations in their untameable plurality and interpretability. The exhibition *Cross-fades: Reconstructing the Future* provided just such an exemplary constellation of inventions and updates of particular pasts, allowing visitors to jump out of their own time into the intersection of

foreign pasts, personal memories and experiences, and a general knowledge, a familiar historiography.

The Invention of Time-Space: The Exhibition Cross-fades

The view is prolonged. It hovers, with almost intolerable slowness, over the barren, vast landscape, in the middle of which is a large housing development whose construction has been abandoned. Only gradually do traces of human beings become recognizable, and it takes some time before several of the residents of the unfinished buildings enter the picture. With his slow approach to the ghost town and the parallel montage of long shots and close-ups, Uriel Orlow (see p. 104) unfolds a filmic time-space in the exhibition that successively leads its viewers from the past to the present of an abandoned plan for the future. For a brief infinity, lacking any narrative, the oppressive present, filled with a global political past, of Mush opens up, a satellite town built by the Soviet Union in Armenia in 1988 and never completed, which each visitor updates in a different way in correspondence with his or her own past and experiences.

As little as historiography can ever be objective or neutral, so little is it personal memories or eyewitness accounts. Memories are always endless. Above all for those who recall their own deeds and misdeeds or those of others. Every memory stream calls forth different facets and produces new gaps. These are not things that are being suppressed, but blind spots, open places, inaccurate observations that cause memories to become vague, coloured by later takes, and to a large extent speculative. The chasm between personal experience and the non-objectifiability of past experiences is forcefully summed up by one of the twin sisters Karen Geyer (see p. 108) interviewed in New York about her difficult years as a Polish-Jewish immigrant in Zurich: 'As a child, one wasn't allowed to ask questions. Later, it was too late.' In view of the past, it is always too late. Even eyewitnesses can never speak 'the truth'

12....... Cf. Aleida Assmann's extensive efforts to theorize types of remembrance including assignments to nations, collectives, cultural groups, etc., in id., *Erinnerungsräume: Formen und Wandlungen des kulturellen Gedächtnisses* (Munich, 1999).

genannt.[11] Wenn nichts und niemand dem Vergehen, dem Tod, enthoben ist, und der Tod die unausweichliche Erfahrung jedes lebenden Menschen sein wird, so lässt erst die Erfahrung der Angst vor dem Tod die Menschen die Einzigartigkeit ihres zeitlichen Daseins in der Welt erkennen. Nur durch das Sein zum Tode, so Heidegger, eröffnet sich jedem Menschen ein einzigartiger Entscheidungsraum: die Spanne des eigenen Lebens. In dieser ist jede Gegenwart beherrscht von Vergangenheit und Zukunft, gleichermassen erfüllt von Vergangenem, das in Erinnerungen hervorbrechen kann, wie immerfort ausgerichtet auf etwas Kommendes, eine unabsehbare und nicht vorhersagbare Zukunft. Die andauernde Erfahrung des Vergehens und des Zugehens auf den eigenen Tod ist die allgemeinste und zugleich singulärste Erfahrung jedes Menschen, der zentrale Kreuzungspunkt von Besonderem und Allgemeinen.

Eben dies ist über den Begriff Vergangenheit – anders als über den Begriff Geschichte oder den des Gedächtnisses – zu denken gegeben: Vergangenheit ist zugleich abstrakte und allgemeine Kategorie, aber existiert zugleich nie losgelöst von der konkreten Gegenwart derjenigen, die leben, denen sich ihre eigene oder die Vergangenheit anderer aufdrängt und die diese Vergangenheiten um ihrer eigenen Gegenwart und Zukunft willen bedenken und besprechen. Sie ist immer schon vorausgegangen – während die Geschichte notwendig erst nachträglich geschrieben wird. Das gelebte Leben bildet die Vergangenheit – die Geschichte ist die Erzählung, die gemacht wurde, um es zu verlängern. Gerade weil sie vorbei ist, ist sie unberechenbar. Sie ist kein Archiv, in das man hineingreift, wenn es passt, sondern ein diffuses, vom Vergessen verschattetes Tiefenreich, in das man oft blindlings stürzt, manchmal gemeinschaftlich abtaucht und aus dem immer wieder plötzlich und unerwartet etwas hervorbricht. Vergangenheiten, das sind all die Gänge – die Erfahrungen – in der Zeit, von denen niemals alle, sondern immer nur einzelne, besondere Erfahrungen aus verschiedenen Anlässen und immer wieder anders, immer neu in die Gegenwart zurückdrängen, gedrängt werden.

Während das Gedächtnis den ‚Behälter‘ von – wichtigen oder oft wiederholten – Erinnerungen bezeichnet, klingt im Begriff der Vergangenheit die Bedrängung des Gegenwartslebens durch seine Endlichkeit an. Anders als das Gedächtnis, das notwendig als etwas Umgrenztes, d.h. an eine Person oder ein Kollektiv, in jedem Fall an einen Träger, ein Material oder ein Gehäuse gebunden gedacht werden kann, ist die Vergangenheit ein unbegrenzter, unendlicher Zeitraum, der alles Vergessen mit umschliesst. Dennoch existiert Vergangenheit niemals nur abstrakt und allgemein, sondern immer nur im besonderen Moment ihrer Erinnerung und Aktualisierung. Während der Begriff Gedächtnis nötigt, die Konturen des je besonderen Gedächtnisses zu umreissen und den Behälter als national, regional, global o.ä. zu denken,[12] sind im Begriff Vergangenheit noch die unvereinbarsten und entferntesten Vergangenheiten enthalten und zugleich immer an den Moment des Erinnerns gebunden. Die Vergangenheit kommt ohne In- und Exklusionen aus, da in ihr per definitionem alles enthalten ist – das Erinnerte wie das längst Vergessene ebenso wie das Ausgeblendete, das Übersehene, auch all dasjenige, das den historischen und kulturellen Gedächtnissen einer Nation oder einer bestimmten sozialen oder kulturellen Gruppe und ihren jeweiligen professionellen Speichern entgeht oder entgangen ist. Zugleich aber bedarf sie immer des einzelnen Menschen oder einer besonderen gemeinschaftlichen Situation, um für den Augenblick neu in die Gegenwart zu treten. Jede_r Einzelne ist ein anderer, singulärer Kreuzungspunkt der unendlichen Vergangenheiten – und selbst darin nicht konstant.

Die These des Textes, dass Kunst „Vergangenheiten erfindet“ und aktualisiert, verschiebt damit den Fokus von der Frage des Bewahrens und Speicherns auf den Akt des Findens und die Form der Aktualisierung vergangener Ereignisse oder Erfahrungen sowie die Erfindung von Zeiträumen, d.h. der in sich selbst unmöglichen und offenen

11 .... Vgl. Heidegger, Martin: *Sein und Zeit*. Tübingen 1986, 235ff.

12 .... Vgl. Aleida Assmanns ausführliche Anstrengungen, die verschiedenen Gedächtnistypen inklusive der Zuordnungen zu Nationen, Kollektiven, kulturellen Gruppen etc. zu theoretisieren, dies.: *Erinnerungsräume. Formen und Wandlungen des kulturellen Gedächtnisses*. München 1999.

Zeitformen der Vergegenwärtigung. Eine Vergangenheiten erfindende Kunst beginnt im Kreuzungspunkt von allgemeiner und besonderer Erfahrung, im komplizierten Moment zwischen den Zeiten, mitten im Zeitgefüge. Sie beginnt mit der Verstrickung des Künstlers, der Künstlerin in die eigene Vergangenheit und seiner, ihrer Offenheit für die Gegenwart wie die Vergangenheiten der anderen, die als Dialoge und in Konstellationen in ihrer nicht zu bändigenden Pluralität und Interpretierbarkeit hervorbrechen. Und eben eine solche exemplarische Konstellation von Erfindungen und Aktualisierungen besonderer Vergangenheiten bot die Ausstellung *Überblendungen. Das Zukünftige rekonstruieren*, die ihre Besucher_innen aus der eigenen Zeit in den Kreuzungspunkt von fremden Vergangenheiten, eigenen Erinnerungen und Erfahrungen und einem allgemeinen Wissen, einer vertrauten Geschichtsschreibung springen liess.

Erfindung von Zeiträumen: Die Ausstellung *Überblendungen*

Der Blick dauert. Mit kaum zu ertragender Langsamkeit schwebt er über die öde, weite Landschaft, in deren Mitte eine verlassene, nicht fertig gestellte Grosswohnsiedlung steht. Erst allmählich werden Spuren von Menschen erkennbar und es dauert nochmals, bis einige der wenigen Bewohner_innen der Bauruinen ins Bild kommen. Mit seiner langsamen Annäherung an die Geisterstadt, der parallelen Montage von distanzierten Ansichten und Nahaufnahmen entfaltete Uriel Orlow (vgl. S. 104) einen filmischen Zeitraum in der Ausstellung, der seine Betrachter_innen sukzessive von der Vergangenheit in die Gegenwart einer aufgegebenen Zukunftsplanung führt. Für eine kurze Unendlichkeit öffnete sich – ohne jede Erzählung – die beklemmende, von weltpolitischer Vergangenheit erfüllte Gegenwart der 1988 von der Sowjetunion in Armenien gebauten, niemals fertiggestellten Satellitenstadt Mush, die jede_r Besucher_in anders, in Korrespondenz zur eigenen Vergangenheit und den eigenen Erfahrungen aktualisiert.

So wenig Geschichtsschreibung je objektiv oder neutral sein kann, so wenig sind es die persönlichen Erinnerungen oder Augenzeugenberichte. Erinnerungen sind immer unendlich. Sie sind es vor allem für diejenigen, die sich an eigene Taten oder die Taten anderer erinnern. Jeder Erinnerungslauf bringt andere Facetten hervor und lässt neue Lücken aufklaffen. Dabei handelt es sich nicht allein um Verdrängungen, sondern um blinde Flecke, offene Stellen, lückenhafte Beobachtungen, die Erinnerungen ungenau, durch nachträgliche Ansichten gefärbt und mitunter in hohem Masse spekulativ werden lassen. Eindrucksvoll wird die Kluft von persönlichem Erleben und der Nicht-Objektivierbarkeit vergangener Erfahrungen von einer der Zwillingsschwestern auf den Punkt gebracht, die Karen Geyer (vgl. S. 108) in New York über ihre schwierigen Jahre als polnisch-jüdische Migrantinnen in Zürich interviewte: „Als Kind durfte man keine Fragen stellen. Später war es zu spät." Angesichts der Vergangenheit ist es immer schon zu spät. Auch Augenzeugen können nie ‚die Wahrheit' sprechen oder reine Fakten ausbreiten, da sie im Moment des Geschehens nicht objektiv, sondern selbst in den Moment verstrickt waren und ihr Zeugnis des Geschehens damit notwendig ein nachträgliches ist.

Zugleich lässt sich die Vergangenheit nicht bändigen oder abschliessen. Gegen Verdrängung und Verschluss erzwingen vor allem Verbrechen und Fehlverhalten immer aufs Neue ihre Erinnerung in der Gegenwart. Sie drängen sich unvermittelt durch alle Schirme und Schutzschichten, die der einzelne oder eine Gemeinschaft angelegt hat. Rossella Biscottis Film *Yellow* (Abb. S. 65), der zu 80 verschiedenen Gelbtönungen Audioaufnahmen von Therapiesitzungen eines hollän-dischen Psychiaters kombiniert, macht die Betrachter_innen zu Zeugen derart hervorbrechender Erinnerungen. Unter der Einwirkung von Pentothal fällt der Selbstschutz der Patienten, und immer neue Fragmente ihrer schrecklichen Kriegserfahrungen kehren zurück. Es sind weniger die Erinnerungsstücke selbst, als vielmehr das ungewollte und ungerichtete Hervorbrechen des Verdrängten neben den bildlosen Gelbtönen, das den Film zu einem erschütternden Zeugnis macht.

In der parallel präsentierten Dokumentation der Performance *Everything is somehow related*

or propagate pure facts, because at the moment something took place they were not objective but involved in the occurrence themselves, and their accounts of the occurrence are therefore necessarily *post hoc* accounts.

At the same time, the past does not allow itself to be tamed or brought to a close. It is above all crimes and wrongdoing that over and over again prevent one from repressing their memory and achieving closure. They abruptly force themselves through all the shields and protective layers the individual or the community have devised. Rossella Biscotti's film *Yellow* (fig. p. 65), which combines eighty different shades of yellow to audio recordings of therapy sessions by a Dutch psychiatrist, turns viewers into witnesses of such erupting memories. Truth serum deactivates the patients' self-protection mechanism, causing more and more fragments of their horrific war experiences to come back. What makes the film into a harrowing report is less the memory fragments themselves than the involuntary and undirected eruption of what has been repressed alongside the non-pictorial shades of yellow.

In the documentation of the performance *Everything is somehow related to everything else, yet the whole is terrifyingly unstable* (see p. 102), which was presented alongside *Yellow*, Biscotti furthermore shows how she lets herself be found by the past and keeps open the chasm between what has passed and her own present. Walking along the wall of the concentration/transit camp in Bolzano, the artist exposed herself to her own fear of heights and physical danger in order to transport the disregarded relic into the present, into temporarily exposed visibility, for the duration of her walk. The documentation in the exhibition duplicated the singularity and fleetingness of this certain experience of past.

The simultaneity of evanescent, sudden recurrence and repetition is after all the central characteristic of all of the works in the past exhibition, which was underscored by the exhibition architecture consisting of unfinished, recycled walls. And it continues to resonate.

Even today, I still hear the calm and concentrated voices of the children who immigrated to Belgium whom Sarah Vanagt (fig. p. 79) asked to give an account of the colonial history of the country from the viewpoint of the silent statues on the Mont des Arts in Brussels. I recall the varying, always slightly-off-the-mark repetitions of photographic poses from world history that Hofmann&Lindholm (see p. 111) produced with different protagonists, and I again wait for nothing to happen—or that something completely different happens—in the space of knowbotic research (fig. p. 70). And I grow desperate due to the impossible mixture of time in Suzanne Treister's fictitious-factual conspiracy theory (fig. p. 84/85), which comes from the future and reaches far back into the past and transforms the present into fiction.

Despite all of the palpable seriousness, nowhere in the exhibition mounted in Zurich and the works it comprised were history lessons held or lectures on the past delivered. Altogether, they did not constitute remembrance, a canon of memory, and they furthermore refused the concept of a history of progress that could point towards the future. Rather, what could be experienced in all of the works was the past in a unique, fragmentary, and gripping update. They drew visitors into the act of recollection and interpretation of past occurrences, turned them in the act of updating into intersections of foreign and personal experience, of foreign and personal non-knowledge of history. What took the place here of an attempt to reconstruct the past was its ongoing updating and interpretation. This makes the entire exhibition as well as all of the works it contains exemplary, and it sustains them. Art is never the communication of history. It begins at that place at which particular pasts are tangent to as well as kept open for the experience and interpretations of others in the world.

Translated by Rebecca van Dyck

to everything else, yet the whole is terrifying unstable (vgl. S. 102) zeigte Biscotti zudem, wie sie sich selbst von Vergangenheit finden lässt und die Kluft zwischen dem Vergangenen und der eigenen Gegenwart offen hält. Mit einem Spaziergang auf der Mauer des KZ-Durchgangslagers in Bozen setzte sich die Künstlerin ihrer eigenen Höhenangst und realer Gefahr aus, um das unbeachtete Relikt für den Moment der Begehung in die Gegenwart, in eine kurzzeitig exponierte Sichtbarkeit zu holen. Die Dokumentation in der Ausstellung verdoppelte die Singularität und Flüchtigkeit dieser Vergangenheitserfahrung.

Die Gleichzeitigkeit von momenthafter, unvermittelter Wiederkehr und Wiederholung ist schliesslich das zentrale Charakteristikum aller Arbeiten der vergangenen Ausstellung, das von der unfertigen, aus wiederverwendeten Wänden errichteten Ausstellungsarchitektur unterstrichen wurde. Und sie hallt nach. Noch heute höre ich die ruhigen und konzentrierten Stimmen der nach Belgien eingewanderten Kinder, die Sarah Vanagt (Abb. S. 79) gebeten hatte, die Kolonialgeschichte des Landes aus Sicht der stummen Historienstandbilder auf dem Mont des Arts in Brüssel zu erzählen. Ich erinnere die variierenden, immer leicht daneben treffenden Wiederholungen von Bildposen aus der Weltgeschichte, die Hofmann&Lindholm (vgl. S. 111) mit verschiedenen Protagonist_innen aufgenommen haben, warte wieder im Raum von knowbotic research (Abb. S. 70), dass etwas nicht passiert, bzw. dass es ganz anders passiert, und verzweifle an der unmöglichen Zeitmischung in Suzanne Treisters fiktiv-faktischer, aus der Zukunft kommender und doch weit in die Vergangenheit reichender Verschwörungstheorie (Abb. S. 84/85), welche die Gegenwart zur Fiktion werden lässt.

Die Zürcher Ausstellung und die gezeigten Arbeiten haben, trotz allem spürbaren Ernst, an keiner Stelle Geschichtslektionen abgehalten oder über die Vergangenheit belehrt. Sie bildeten zusammen kein Gedächtnis, keinen Erinnerungskanon und verweigerten zudem die Vorstellung einer Fortschrittsgeschichte, die in die Zukunft weisen könnte. In allen Arbeiten war vielmehr die Vergangenheit in einer einzigartigen, lückenhaften

und mitnehmenden Aktualisierung erfahrbar. Sie zogen die Besucher_innen in den Akt des Erinnerns und der Auslegung des Vergangenen hinein, machten sie in der Aktualisierung selbst zu Kreuzungspunkten von fremder und eigener Erfahrung, von fremdem und eigenem Nicht-Wissen der Geschichte. An die Stelle des Versuchs der Rekonstruktion von Vergangenheit war hier die immer neue Aktualisierung und Auslegung des Vergangenen getreten. Dies macht die ganze Ausstellung wie alle ihre Arbeiten exemplarisch und lässt sie nachwirken. Kunst ist nie Geschichtsvermittlung. Sie beginnt dort, wo besondere Vergangenheiten derart berührend wie offen für die Erfahrung und Auslegung der anderen in der Welt gehalten werden.

**

***

How I work

*

I am, like pretty much all of us, a reader. Reading is not a passive activity for me; instead it's a radical view of the world. For many years I pondered the h——mony of authorship. I'd always longed to be among the privileged few ...ibute meaning to words. Among those who determine and codify ... . Instead, I just kept reading. At university they forced us to distil the ... of words: to confirm a statement of the prior author through an exact

I could say that I'm not at all interested in history. Yet all my work deals with in history or, I should say, with the past. I use historical material to construct the past so that it also speaks in the present, so that it is a living necessity. Why should we deal with the past? Because the threat of conformism is always at hand. We're in constant danger; the state that we currently perceive as a state of emergency is no exception. It's a continual state of emergency that will never end. As Walter Benjamin pointed out, a real state of emergency must be induced so that we can improve our position. My interest, therefore, lies in the present – which is why I can say that the past doesn't interest me. And yet, without evoking images of the past, without the construct of history, there is no present. The past is concealed in every present moment. Unless past images impressed upon the present are distinguished, every present moment is condemned to conformism. I could also say that conformism doesn't interest me. And yet all the work that I do is about conformism: It's an internal struggle with conformism. The present causes us to doubt whether we are in fact facing the world from the best possible position. Only in confronting images of the past will we build a line of progress toward the future. If it is, indeed, still possible to believe in the future. But what other choice do we have? I'm always asking myself: Is what you do sufficiently autonomous and does it unconditionally capture the truth of the moment in relation to the surrounding reality. Am I not merely following given life patterns set in epistemological and socio-economical frames that I have embedded beneath my skin so that I can't even notice what they're like? This is always on my mind. I feel successful in doing this, except that failure is and has been present in this very idea from its inception. So, as always, I fail successfully. ...need from the ...here is no such thing as privileged authorship or, on the other hand, passive reading. We're all authors and we all have names. As Michel de Certeau wrote long ago: the reader doesn't have to be an easily manipulable consumer; that's just the view of the current epistemological order.

Zbyněk Baladrán

**

***

I am, like pretty much all of us, a reader. Reading is not a passive activity for me; instead it's a radical view of the world. For many years I pondered the hegemony of authorship. I'd always longed to be among the privileged few who attribute meaning to words. Among those who determine and codify meaning. Instead, I just kept reading. At university they forced us to distil the meaning of words: to confirm a statement of the prior author through an exact citation, and thus also to become an author. But there's something perverted in this. It's as if the privileged few would allow others to have the same authorial privileges only if they confirmed the "indestructible" statute of prior authorships. I became an author based on this principle, but I did not feel fulfilled by it. Fulfilment still only came to me by reading. Then I understood why. I feel far freer when reading. All these written texts are an endless reservoir that I'm reforming. I can change their meaning, switch it around, understand it, not understand it and connect it. I no longer see writers here as those who impose literal meaning on me, but as entities that are on the same level as all others. They are part of all texts and hypertexts in the democratic field. This is how I read: I read ten to fifteen books at once. I read them in different rhythms; some I read in a day, some take me years. Then there are books from which I randomly read only a few sentences. I skip from book to book when reading. I employ a severe editing technique and stop reading in the middle of a sentence. I remember every word of some texts. But with other, fascinating texts that I become fully immersed in, I paradoxically can't recall anything. Quite often it's the case that I don't understand some passages because they're too complicated, in other cases I do understand certain passages, but in a different way each time I read them. The library of texts that is forming in my mind is fragmentary and incomplete. It's a kind of commonplace book, full of excerpts and passages. I think this is probably an experience all readers share. I became a writer because the interpretation of the world that I'm presenting is subjectively autonomous and, strictly in the same non-hierarchical relationship to other readers/authors, freed from the hegemony of privileged authorship. All I'm saying is that there is no such thing as privileged authorship or, on the other hand, passive reading. We're all authors and we all have names. As Michel de Certeau wrote long ago: the reader doesn't have to be an easily manipulable consumer; that's just the view of the current epistemological order.

Zbyněk Baladrán

**
***

I am, like pretty much all of us, a reader. Reading is not a passive activity for me. I work in a way that enables me to serenely say that I'm an independent individual who doesn't control others and isn't controlled by others. Let's take a closer look at this. I'll describe the context of my life: I'm a solidly situated member of the middle class. I have a decent education, considering the place I come from; I travel a lot. I live in Central Europe where most people are convinced that they don't have to contemplate things, since the order of things in which they exist cannot be changed. I'm almost forty and I'm beginning to realise that I understand things too slowly to be able to change my life according to my ideas. But that's obviously a bourgeois alibi. I live my life with a deliberate purpose and my work is also deliberate. But, like everyone else I suppose, I have this constant feeling that something is running through my fingers. I'm an artist. This means that in the culture in which I live I'm considered a free-thinker, who lives his life without regard to financial matters. The artist's work is seen as a mission. Unfortunately, it's not like this. My work is part of the circulation of goods, thoughts and ideas that sustains our socio-cultural-economic frame, just like everything else. I work in order to escape this mould, to show myself and others that nothing is unchangeable, that everything can ceaselessly be transformed and our own ideas can be imprinted in it. My entire anarchistic gesture is, however, absorbed by the whole system that I'm part of. It is increasingly difficult to begin again each day. But there's nothing else to do. Emma Goldman dreamt of a situation in which society exists for people, and not vice-versa. She dreamt of a state in which human society is transformed and its models and organization will no longer be imposed upon us. I feel very strongly that we have to realise this dream. And there's also the need for a historical materialist, a radical reader and anarchist in actions, even more than I've indicated here, even more than me – Mr Bourgeois *par excellence*. [...] are. I became a writer because [...] the world that I'm presenting is subjectively autonomou[s ...] same non-hierarchical relationship to other readers/auth[ors ...] hegemony of privileged authorship. All I'm saying is that th[ere ...] as privileged authorship or, on the other hand, passive [...] authors and we all have names. As Michel de Certeau w[rote ...] reader doesn't have to be an easily manipulable consumer; [...] of the current epistemological order.

Zbyněk Baladrán

EVERYTHING IS SOMEHOW RELATED TO EVERYTHING ELSE, YET THE WHOLE IS TERRIFYINGLY UNSTABLE

The following text by Rossella Biscotti is part of a newspaper produced as part of the project *Everything is somehow related to everything else, yet the whole is terrifyingly unstable*. The newspaper featuring this text and photographs of the site—documents a performative artistic intervention by Rossella Biscotti that took place on a wall of a former Nazi transit camp in Bolzano, Italy, in 2008.

By tying our memories to specific sites, places take upon themselves a stratification of meanings and time. The change of these sites due to urbanization does not cancel remembrance, but instead memory becomes part of a changing daily life. What surprises in this wall is its physical presence inside a different context. It is a re-used ruin with the same function but with a different intentionality. Its perimeter closes a situation of houses by isolating them from the rest of the neighbourhood, and by creating at the same time a relational micro-world. This does not change its being a wall of a Nazi concentration camp, but it modifies it. When walking along its perimeter, the wall shamelessly overlooks its being/not being, the history of our relationship with the past in relation to politics and to social needs. It seems to me that saving it from demolition was a functional and structural choice for the new construction plan of the condominium. It anyhow seems an appropriate choice for a socio-psychological study.

My intervention here draws back to the dimension of the individual. I am interested in putting in relationship the sense of vertigo due to my strong acrophobia, with remembrance. Both dimensions share a non-linearity of visualization and a space-time displacement. What surrounds the individual is fragmented and oscillates in space by making him [and her] lose a sense of measurement. Things come forward while distances are timed. Images overlap each other. Things un-focus. The result is a sense of vertigo that oscillates between the space of remembrance, of pure memory, and the present context.

Rossella Biscotti: *Everything is somehow related to everything else, yet the whole is terrifyingly unstable, 2008*

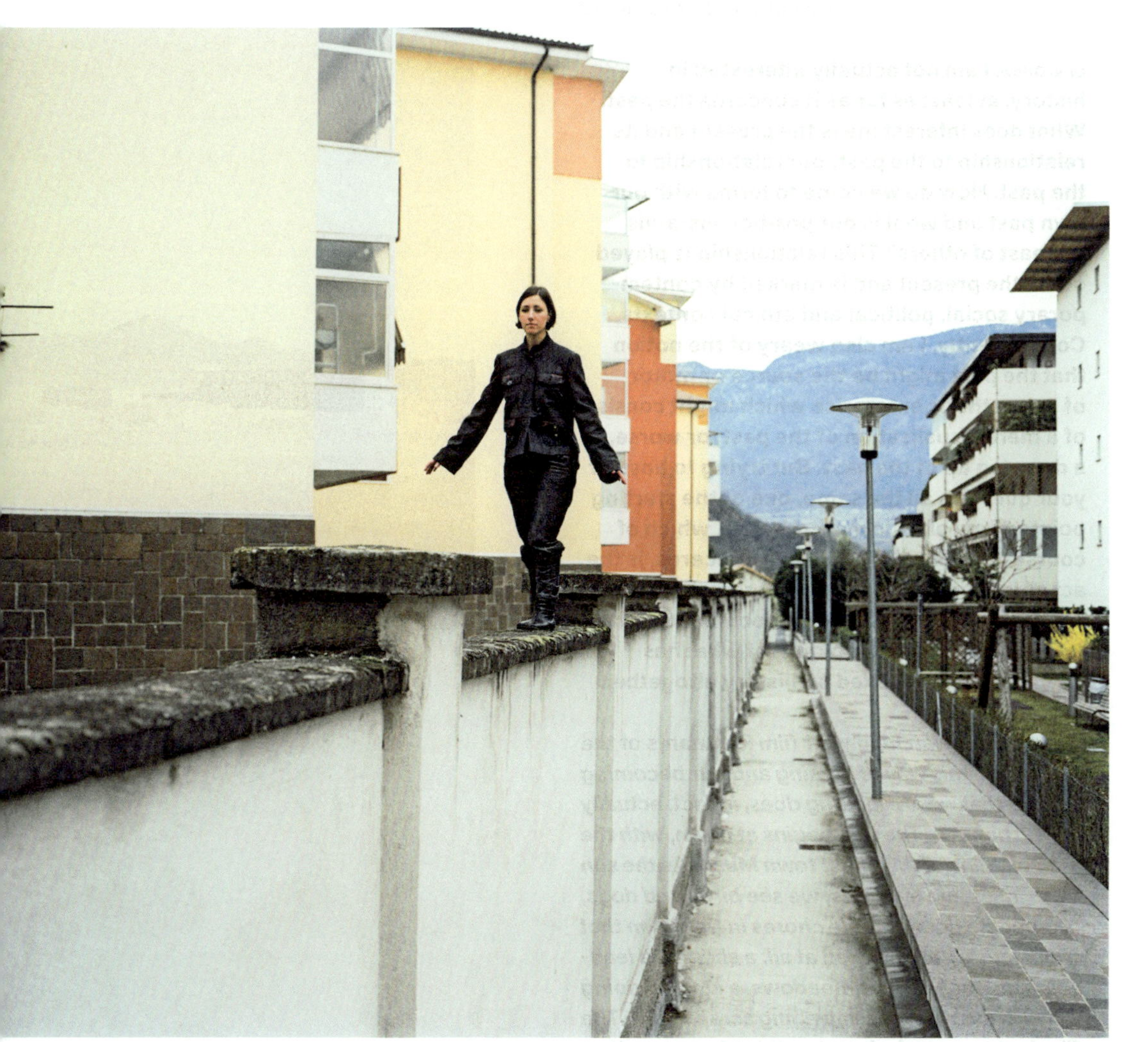

HISTORY AS HALLUCINATION

An e-mail exchange between Uriel Orlow and Yvonne Volkart

Yvonne Volkart: *History or the past is the subject and an aesthetic enterprise in several of your projects. Can you tell us something about this interest and what you think artists can do in regard to this subject?*

Uriel Orlow: **I am not actually interested in history, at least as far as it concerns the past. What does interest me is the present and its relationship to the past, *our* relationship to the past. How do we come to terms with our own past and what is our position vis-à-vis the past of others? This relationship is played out in the present and is marked by contemporary social, political and ethical contexts. Consequently, I am also weary of the notion that the past might be the source or motor of an aesthetic enterprise which might consist of a mere visualisation of the past, or worse, a dressing up of the past. But trying to answer your question all the same, one of the starting points of my artistic methodology, which of course also includes aesthetic concerns, is the act of looking: looking at what remains of the past in the present, be that a document, a place or a story or, indeed, looking for what has been lost or overlooked by history altogether.**

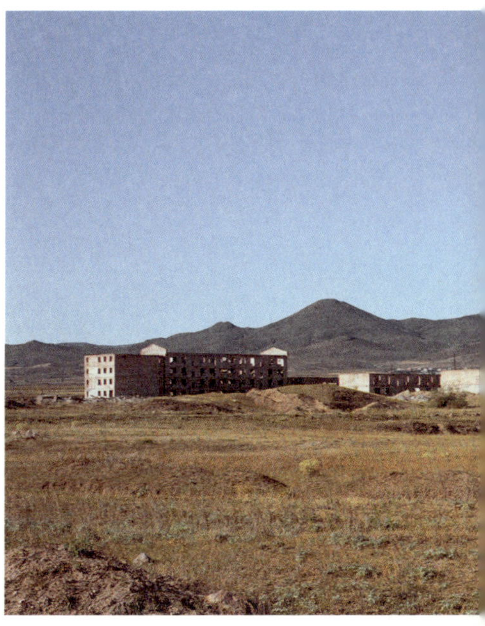

Yvonne Volkart: *Watching your film* Remnants of the Future, *this way of looking and our becoming aware that we are looking does, in fact, actually happen. The film begins at dawn, with the black ruins of the ghost town Mush. As the sun rises, life awakens, we see birds and dogs, people doing simple chores in this town that is obviously not deserted at all: a shepherd leading his sheep to the meadows, a woman doing her laundry, a man salvaging scrap metal. The film is slow paced, almost nothing happens, thus in a certain sense, we lose our awareness of time and space and become lost in this strange space, which becomes, in a certain way, our space. Can you tell me something about your idea of time and how you treat it in the film?*

Uriel Orlow: **What I like about Tarkovski's notion of *Sculpting in Time* to describe film practice**

Uriel Orlow: *Remnants of the Future*, 2010

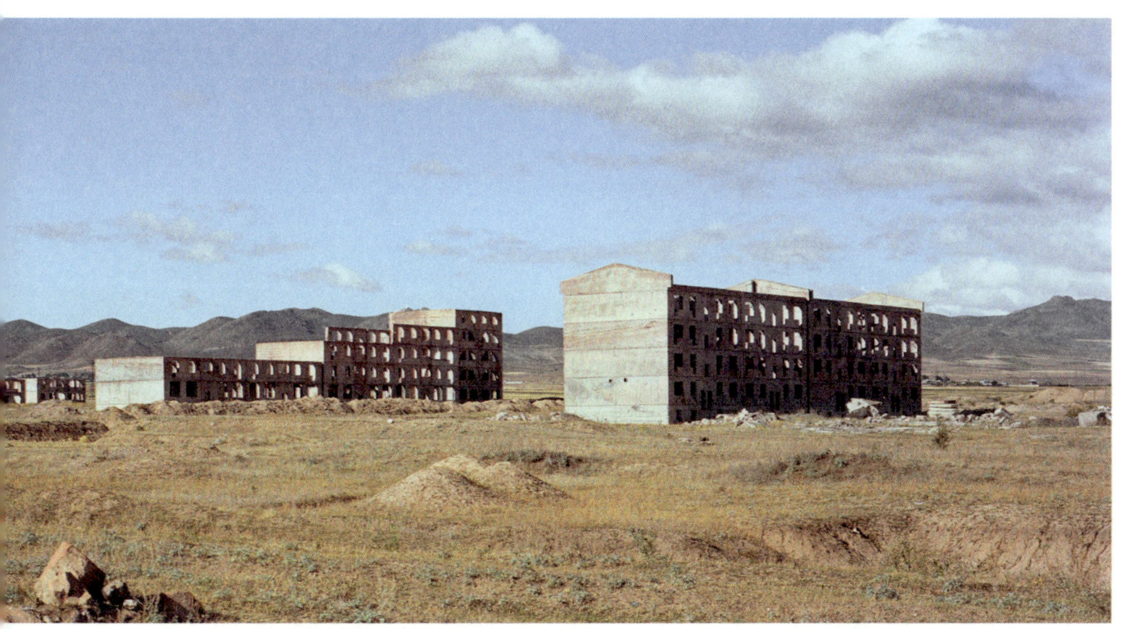

Uriel Orlow: *Remnants of the Future*, 2010

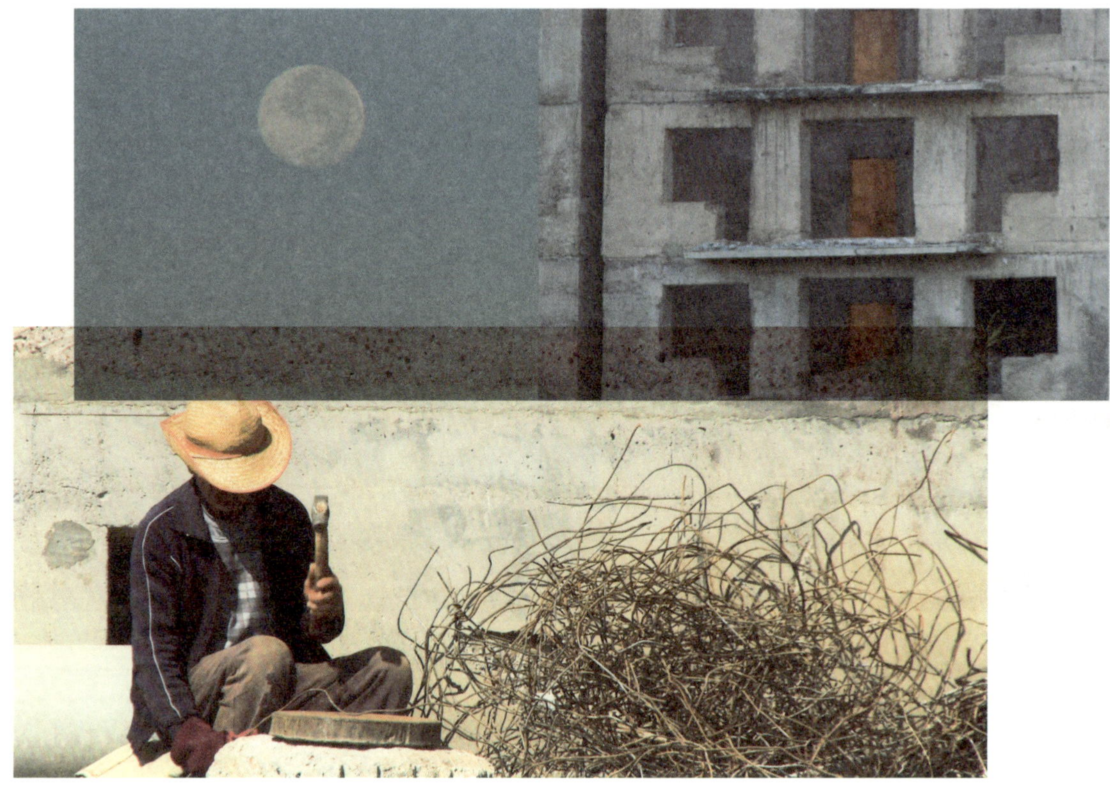

is the way it points to an aspect of malle-ability of time; time can be shaped somehow, stretched and condensed; what we see are time formations. This notion also implies that the medium of film is not the moving image but time itself. And consequently that time is not just a by-product of the moving image or a mere narrative motor for a story but is a kind of milieu that is shared by the film and the life in the film (as well as, of course, our life outside the film). In *Remnants of the Future* this takes multiple forms. The unfinished 'ghost' town of Mush is represented somehow outside of time, suspended in a limbo between de-funct Soviet socialism and the dysfunc-tional market capitalism that replaced it. Mush is off the map, off-grid. So time itself is open, unregulated, expansive, horizontal. But time is also punctuated by human activity; people working, creating discrete homes within the concrete exoskeletons of the big housing blocks as well as slowly taking the buildings apart in order to resell the materials. This is a kind of cyclical time of construction and destruction. And then there is vertical time, where both the past and future break out in the present: on the one hand, the traditional song of the plains of Mush in Eastern Anatolia conjuring the Mush on the other side of the border, a former home of Armenians until the genocide in 1915; and on the other hand, the time-travelling Phosphorescent Woman out of Mayakovski's play *The Bathhouse* who arrives at the end of the film to invite the inhabitants of the new Mush to the future.

Yvonne Volkart: *What happens in your film is that in a certain sense this vertical or linear time collapses. First, the film begins and ends in the dark, this suggests not only cyclical time but also that there is something completely in the dark, something is happening out of time, without progress, beyond rational knowl-edge. Furthermore, past and future happen at the same time, they are juxtaposed or cross-fading; there is, as you say, this old song about old Mush on the one hand, and on the other hand there is this interruption with the electronic voice of a woman from the future. What was your idea behind this strategy?*

Uriel Orlow: Yes, there is not only an intersection of a horizontal, durational expansive time and a vertical historical time, but, as you say, chronology itself collapses by superimposing one time onto another, mapping past, present and future on top of each other. I was inter-ested in seeing what happens when the past breaks out in the present and confronts the future. It goes back to this idea of relation-al temporality: what is interesting is how we face the past in the present and how we imagine the future, what possible change we can envisage. This includes the possibility of a radical break, rather than just a continuity of time implied by a chronological time line. The night, the darkness for me is not just the realm of the unknowable but also the realm of dreams and hopes and fears.

Yvonne Volkart: *Crossfading is not only time, but also the site. The Mush we see is a failed Soviet hous-ing project in Armenia which took over the name of a beautiful city in Anatolia which the song refers to. But what it does not sing of is the gen-ocide of 1915. In other words, what is interesting in your aesthetic strategy of building our rela-tionship to the past is, that there is not much concrete historical information, but a lot of hid-den hints and nodal points, like in a dream when one word has more than one signification.*

Uriel Orlow: To go back to the night, at the begin-ning and end of the film, but also as a metaphor for knowledge: it is a zone of obscurity that does not look for revelation or enlightenment. We hear about the other Mush, it is conjured up as a hallucination. Genocide, or historical trauma, pushes representation or represent-ability to its limits. So not showing something or not naming it becomes a conscious strategy. But since making *Remnants of the Future* I have travelled to the other Mush in Turkey and have made a film there called *Plans for the Past*. It follows a similar structure, moving from the night through the day and into the night. Again we see people inhabiting the place. And again the architecture speaks of other times, other inhabitants. The Mush in Turkey is not so much a ghost city but a city of ghosts…

MarYvon. Eine RetroPerspektive, Zürich 1930 ...

Ihr gehört nicht dazu, ihr gehört nicht hierher, wir gehörten einfach nicht dazu.
Mein Name ist Marion Schlapfer-Brandes, ich wurde am 29. November 1930 geboren und ich kam nicht allein. Ungewöhnlich. Von mir wusste niemand, dass ich komme. Wenn ich mein Leben anschaue, dann sehe ich, dass es wirklich ein sehr ungewöhnliches Leben war, ungewöhnlich.
Ich kam in Zürich zur Welt in der Schweiz. Zürich ist meine Heimatstadt. Ich hab hier 30 Jahre gelebt. Ich kam eben zusammen mit meiner Schwester, gleich nach meiner Schwester, im Roten-Kreuz-Spital zur Welt, das gibt es heute nicht mehr.
Und wir waren zu zweit, wir waren sehr beschützt von meinen Eltern, sehr allein gelassen auch, wir hatten keine Nachbarn, mit

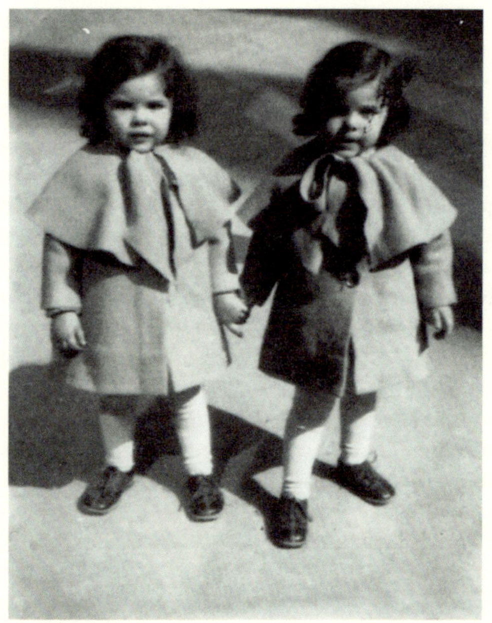

denen wir spielten, wir waren eigentlich sehr sehr einsam. Und ich weiss nicht, was ich gemacht hätte als Einzelkind. Warum man mit niemandem gesprochen hat, war, dass meine Eltern jüdischer und polnischer Abstammung waren. Wobei ich sagen muss, meine Grosseltern sind ausgewandert aus Polen. Meine Eltern mütterlicher- und väterlicherseits kamen in der Schweiz zur Welt, wuchsen in der Schweiz auf. Mein mütterlicher Grossvater hat vermutlich etwas Geld gehabt, konnte sich ein Schweizer Bürgerrecht kaufen. Der väterliche Grossvater hatte das vermutlich nicht, das sind alles Spekulationen. Weil damals konnte ein Kind keine Fragen stellen, das gehörte sich nicht. Später war es zu spät.
Als meine Mutter, die Schweizerin war, meinen Vater heiratete, das war 1929, da verlor sie ihr Schweizer Bürgerrecht, und wurde wieder Polin. Und meine Schwester und ich kamen als polnische Juden zur Welt. Was Juden waren, wussten wir nicht. Weil es gab überhaupt nichts in meiner Kindheit, das darauf hinwies, dass wir anders waren.

Und 1937, da waren wir gerade mal 6 Jahre alt, da haben die Kinder in der Strasse Zürich Oberstrass unten an der Scheuchzer Strasse, auf dem kleinen Platz, an dem die Turnerstrasse und Sonntagssteig und Scheuchzerstrasse zusammenkommen, auf diesem kleinen Platz, sind die Kinder hinter uns hergerannt und haben geschrien: Juden, ihr seid Juden – und es hat hässlich getönt.
Und wir sind nach Hause, haben unsere Mutter gefragt, was ist das – und gell, das sind wir aber nicht. Meine Mutter hatte keine Ahnung, wie sie das handhaben sollte, hat sehr bedenklich in die Welt hinein geschaut, und hat gesagt: doch, es stimmt. Für mich war das wie ein Todesurteil.
Mein Gott, das muss was Kriminelles sein, das muss was ganz Schlimmes sein, das wir uns mal... . Wir haben uns schuldig gemacht. Aber verstanden hab ich es nicht. Und deshalb ...
wir konnten ja auch niemanden fragen, sicher nicht unsere Eltern. Kontakte hatten wir keine. Weil man uns eben schützen wollte, hat man uns so zurück gehalten und separiert. Wie gesagt, wir waren sehr vereinsamt.
Geplagt, geplagt, er hat uns immer zu verstehen gegeben, ihr gehört nicht dazu, ihr gehört nicht hier her. Das hat er so nicht gesagt natürlich. Aber wir gehörten einfach nicht dazu. Und wieder die ganze Klasse starrt uns an, glotzt uns an, als ob wir Ungeheuer wären.

Jetzt sind wir ja Schweizer. Als ichs dann endlich gehabt habe, habe ich realisiert, dass ich mich überhaupt nicht verändert habe. Ob ich jetzt konfirmiert bin, ob ich jetzt Schweizerin bin, ich bin genau dieselbe Person wie vorher. Ob ich jetzt Polin bin oder Schweizerin, ob ich jetzt Jüdin bin oder Christin, im Grunde genommen fühlte ich mich unverändert, konnte ich keinen Unterschied spüren. Und ich realisierte, dass es keine grosse Rolle spielt.
Also um was gings denn da überhaupt? Aber ich war eben ein Kind vorher – und durfte nicht dazu gehören.

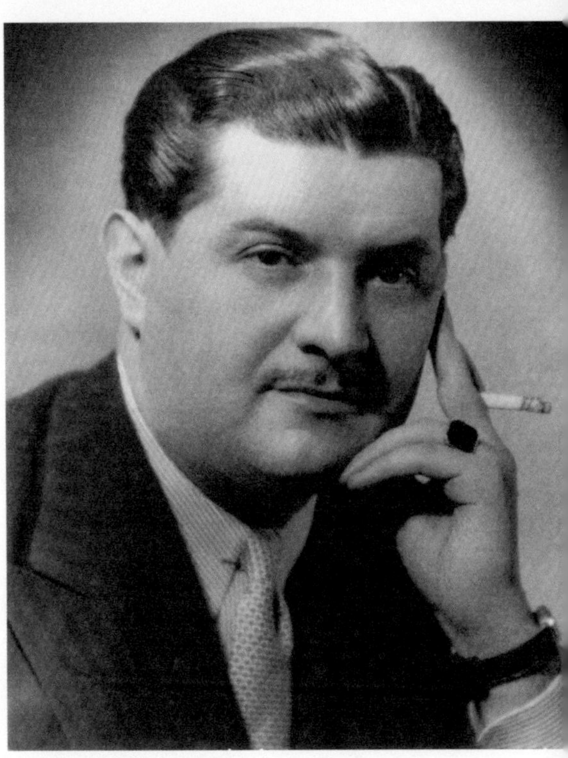

Sehr im Schlaf, alles sehr selbstverständlich genommen, nichts überlegt. Es war, dass, – so ist es doch einfach. Ich habe erst später, als ich dann jeweils meine Eltern besuchte hier, mich auf Zürich gefreut. So im Nachhinein habe ich dann gesehen, wie lieb mir Zürich ist. Aber als Kind und bis ich 30 war und wegging, da hab ich mir nichts überlegt. Das war alles selbstverständlich.

Zu dem Wort „Eltern" muss ich auch noch was erwähnen: Mein Vater, der in der Schweiz zur Welt kam, hier aufwuchs, durfte als Erwachsener nicht in der Schweiz leben. Er war ein polnischer Jude.

Das hat man nie so gesagt. Aber man hat ihm bei der Fremdenpolizei zu verstehen gegeben, dass es in der Schweiz Überjudung hat. Nein, Überf..., Entschuldigung, ich hab immer gedacht, das wär das Wort gewesen. Offiziell war das Wort Überfremdung. Und weil er kein Schweizer ist, kann er nicht hier leben. Das war ihm zu Beginn egal, da war er jung, hat sich keine Gedanken gemacht, hat in Österreich gelebt, die Familie in Zürich, er kam jeweils am Wochenende hier her. Und das schien ihm wunderbar zu sein. Nur ...

Ja, mein Vater war weg, meine Mutter war im Geschäft, von früh bis spät, jeden Tag, am Sonntag zu müde, um sich mit uns zu unterhalten. Meine Schwester und ich waren sehr sehr allein.

Der Krieg wurde strenger und härter, und Antisemitismus genau dasselbe, immer härter. Und er ist immer wieder zur Fremdenpolizei und hat gefleht, bitte lasst mich bei meiner Familie leben. Tut uns leid, abgelehnt, Überfremdung.

Und ein Angestellter bei der Fremdenpolizei hat ihm dann gesagt, eines Tages: „Herr Brandes, heute können Sie nirgends mehr hin in Europa. Gehen Sie nach USA. Das ist der einzige Ort, wo sie noch hingehen können."

Übrigens, dieses Bild hier oben, ganz oben, ist mein Vater, ungefähr 35, und dieses Bild wurde in unserem Kinderzimmer aufgehängt. Und weil Papa uns bei seinem Weggang 1939 gesagt hat: „Ich werde Euch sehen. Und ihr müsst ganz brav und lieb sein und Mama helfen, und ich werde Euch sehen und beobachten können." Haben wir damals natürlich sehr ernst genommen. Ich hab das Bild deshalb hier (lacht).

Und als er dann als Amerikaner zurück kam und schwärmte von diesem Land, in dem alles möglich ist, da wollte ich immer da hin. Da wollte ich immer da hin.

„Halt die Schnauze, was verstehst Du denn schon davon?"
Ich musste ja auch mir alles dann aneignen, was ich gar nicht
erhalten habe, weisst Du, dieses fehlende Selbstbewusstsein.
Wie konnte man damals als Frau in der Schweiz ein Bewusstsein, ein Selbstbewusstsein aufbauen? Nur Selbstzweifel, aber
sicher kein Bewusstsein.
In ganz wenig Jahren wird sie sich vor mich hinstellen und
... wenn ich Glück habe, dann sagt sie: „Mami, ich versteh
Dich nicht. Warum lässt Du Dir das bieten." Aber wenn ich
kein Glück habe, dann wird sie sagen: „Mami, ich hasse
Dich, oder ich verachte Dich. Was bist Du mir denn für ein
Beispiel." Und da habe ich erkannt, dass es meine Aufgabe,
mein Verantwortung ist, für diese wachsende, werdende Frau
ein Rollenbeispiel zu sein, wie eine Frau im Leben steht. Und
als Ehefrau von diesem Mann wird mir das nicht gelingen.
Das gab glaub den Ausschlag. Und dann hab ich mich hinge-
setzt und hab meiner Schwester geschrieben.
Ich muss mein Leben ändern. Aber wie ändert man ein Leben
mit einer Vierjährigen. Ich kann so nicht leben. Ich will so
nicht leben. Ich muss gar nicht so leben. Und während diesen
Gedanken schweift mein Auge ganz unbewusst an dieser
Foto, die da jetzt an der Wand hängt, hab ich auch auf dem
Schreibtisch, ganz klein, und es war dieses kleine Bild, das
im Küchenkästchen eingeklemmt war, das Portrait meiner
Schwester, und sie hält sich so den Kopf.

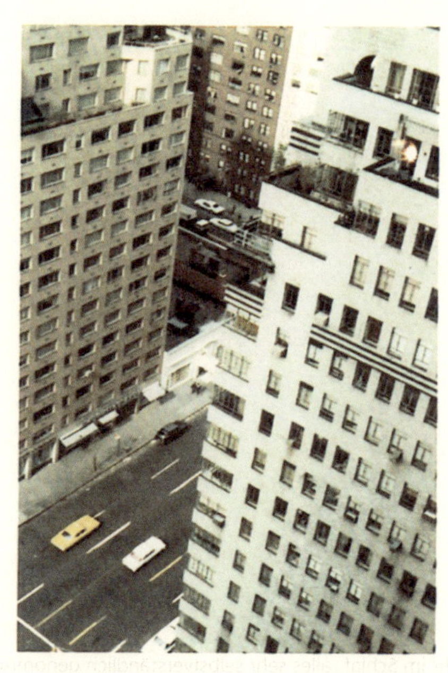

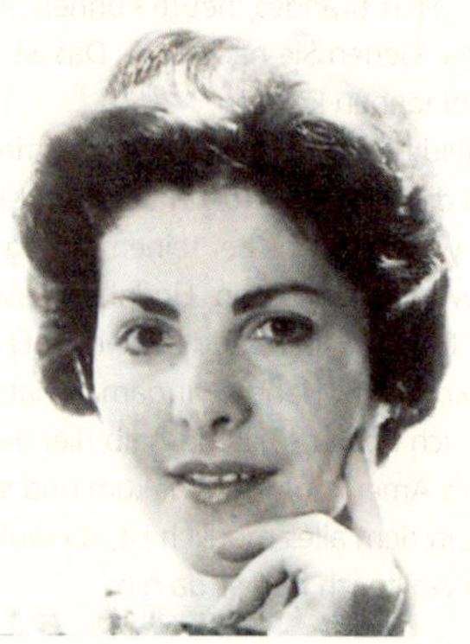

Und ich sag, aber wie tu ich das, was mach ich mit einer
Vierjährigen? Ich muss arbeiten. Und meine Augen gehn da
rüber und ich seh das und ich weiss, ein Foto kann das nicht
tun, das bewegt sich nicht. Aber meine Schwester hat mir mit
ihrem Zeigefinger ein Zeichen gegeben. „Komm."

Und so hab ich dann Zürich verlassen, die Stadt meiner
Kindheit, nach dreissig Jahren, mit grosser Unsicherheit,
... grossen Ängsten, ... grosser Nervosität, ... diesem
grossen Fragezeichen, ... Zweifel, ... Rätsel, ... Zürich,
... grosser Nervosität, um diesem grossen Fragezeichen
entgegen zu gehen.

ANEIGNUNG UND INS- ZENIERUNGEN VON GESCHICHTE

Hofmann&Lindholm im E-Mail-Interview mit Angela Wittwer

Angela Wittwer: *In der 4-Kanal-Videoinstallation* Serie Deutschland *re-inszeniert ihr mit Bürgerinnen und Bürgern eine Reihe von Fotografien bedeutender Ereignisse der Nachkriegszeit Deutschlands – beispielsweise die Unterzeichnung des Grundgesetzes durch Konrad Adenauer (1949), den Kniefall von Warschau von Willy Brandt (1970) oder die Entführung Hanns-Martin Schleyers durch die RAF (1977). Jedes Ereignis wurde viermal mit unterschiedlicher Besetzung am Originalschauplatz inszeniert. Ort, Kameraeinstellung, die Länge der Aufnahme und Anzahl der Beteiligten blieben dabei gleich. Geht es euch um die potenzielle Wiederholbarkeit von Ereignissen?*

Hofmann&Lindholm: Eigentlich nicht. Oder nicht in dieser Arbeit, die sich eher vom klassischen Re-Enactment, bei dem historische Ereignisse rekonstruiert werden, abgrenzt. Wir sind vielmehr daran interessiert, die Bildform und -sprache der Fotografie, die uns als Referenz dient, den Aufbau, die Positionierung der Elemente und die Aufteilung zwischen Vorder- und Hintergründen des Bildes zu re-inszenieren. Was bedeutet, dass weder die historischen Abläufe noch die Inhalte der Ereignisse für die in Szene gesetzten Handlungen ausschlaggebend sind, sondern die Lektüre erkennbarer Strukturen. Das Referenzbild wird dabei seriell und minutiös in Handlung (rück-) übersetzt – in eine Handlung, die mit dem ursprünglichen Ereignis nur die Äusserlichkeit eines deckungsgleichen Bildaufbaus gemein hat.

Angela Wittwer: *Geht es dennoch nicht auch um die Frage der Möglichkeit, sich Geschichte anzueignen, einen persönlichen Bezug zu geschichtlichen Ereignissen herzustellen?*

Hofmann&Lindholm: Bestimmt. Wir machen uns hierfür das Körpergedächtnis zunutze, ohne zu psychologisieren. Die Beteiligten setzen sich durch die Haltungsfindung unmittelbar ins Verhältnis zu einer Momentaufnahme, die auf ein bestimmtes historisches Ereignis verweist. Der Kontext ist allen Beteiligten bewusst. Die physische Auseinandersetzung hinterlässt dabei einen starken Eindruck, was zum Beispiel ganz besonders bei dem Motiv des ‚Gladbecker Geiseldramas' evident ist.

Angela Wittwer: *Diese Videos aus* Serie Deutschland *zeigen auch das Vorher und Nachher des re-inszenierten historischen Moments: Das Einnehmen und Justieren von Posen und Gesten und das Fallenlassen dieser. Kann man das einerseits als ein Offenlegen des Bühnenhaften von Ereignissen und andererseits eine Kritik am Geschichtsverständnis als blosse Abfolge von Ereignissen begreifen?*

Hofmann&Lindholm: Ja. Wir gehen davon aus, dass Fotografien nicht nur abbilden und auf bestimmte Ereignisse verweisen, sondern auch immer Wirklichkeit konstituieren. Sie geben einer Momentaufnahme Gestalt, führen sie in diskursive Strukturen ein und machen den flüchtigen Augenblick damit überhaupt erst denk- und verhandelbar. Aber eben auch: veränderlich. Man muss sich doch fragen, inwiefern der subjektive Konstruktionswille die Inszenierung unseres Geschichtsbewusstseins prägt. Unser Beitrag zu diesem Diskurs ist die Überführung der so genannten historischen Referenz in serielle, vielleicht auch rituelle Handlung.

Hofmann&Lindholm: *Basler Unruhen*, 2010

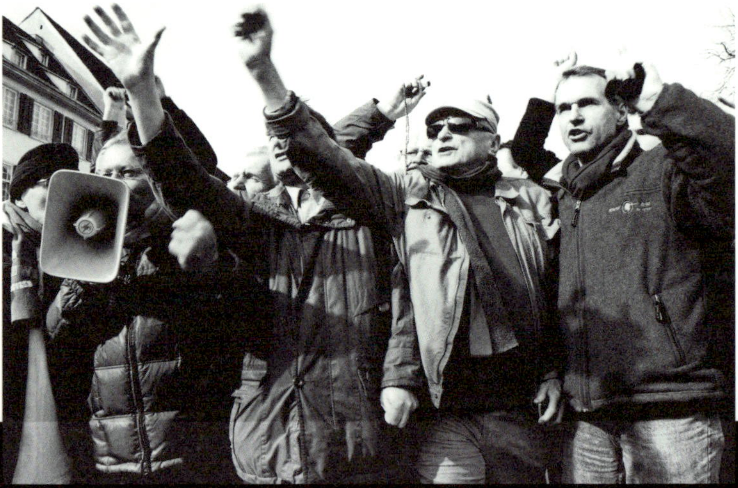

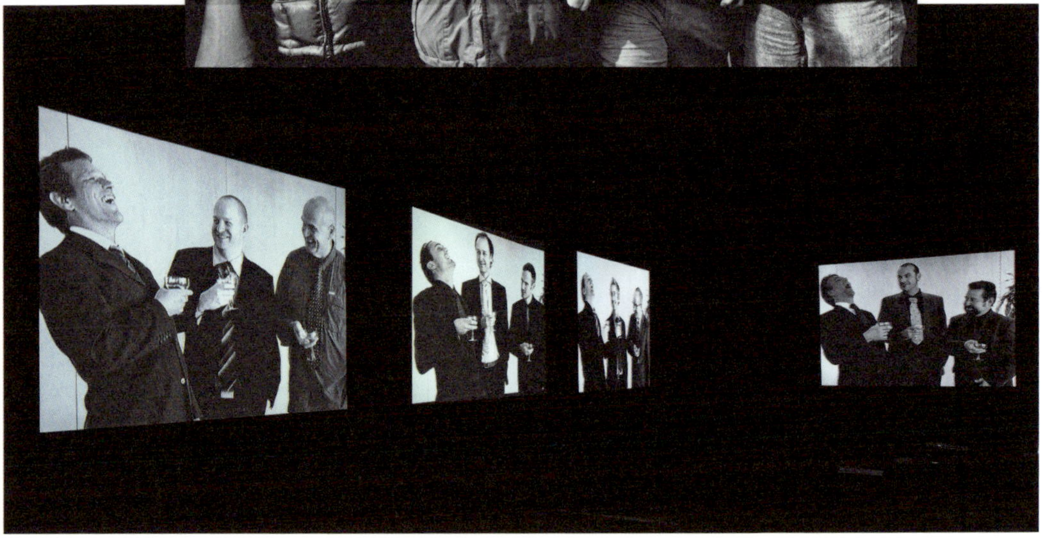

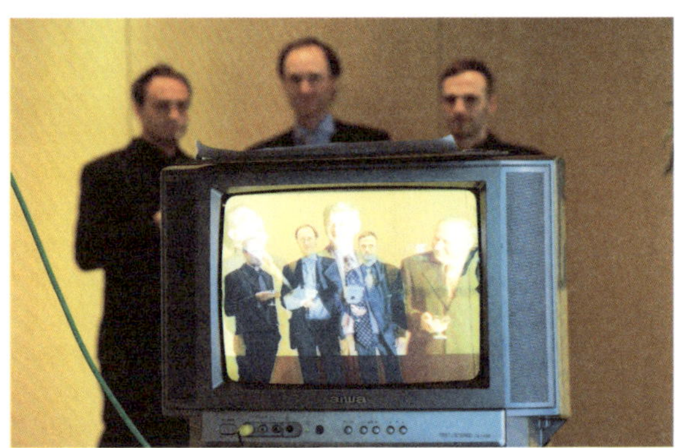

Hofmann&Lindholm: *Serie Deutschland*, seit 2008 (Ausstellungsansicht / Exhibition view)
Hofmann&Lindholm: *Serie Deutschland*, seit / since 2008 (Produktionsfoto / Production photo)

Angela Wittwer: *Momentan läuft in Köln ein Projekt mit dem Titel* Archiv der zukünftigen Ereignisse. *Wie kann man sich die Arbeit vorstellen und was interessiert euch an Ereignissen, die noch nicht stattgefunden haben? Welche Rolle spielt dabei das Eintreten in den öffentlichen Raum?*

Hofmann&Lindholm: Das *Archiv* ist 24 Stunden am Tag zugänglich und ebenso virtuell wie konkret: Man bewegt sich mit einem Smartphone durch den öffentlichen Raum der Stadt und wird an 37 verschiedenen Punkten durch ein auf GPS gestütztes Navigationssystem geortet. Sobald man zum Beispiel vor dem Schauspielhaus steht, findet ein akustischer Zeitsprung statt: Man hört einen ‚Live-Mitschnitt‘ der Abschiedsrede der Intendantin Karin Beier, die sie – aller Voraussicht nach – 2013 an Ort und Stelle halten wird. Für diese Zeitmaschine inszenierten wir, so realitätsgetreu wie möglich, kommende Ereignisse aus Sicht der handelnden Protagonist_innen: Den letzten Arbeitstag von Herrn Salwolke, die Rückkehr eines zur Zeit in Afghanistan stationierten Soldaten, Ruth Henckels 101. Geburtstag, eine Trauerfeier im Kölner Dom… Dabei ist die Vorwegnahme aufgrund der akustischen und visuellen Durchdringung von Gegenwart und Zukunftsaussicht an den jeweiligen Ort des Geschehens gebunden. Wir haben für die Arbeit den Begriff des Pre-Enactments gefunden, um eine der Wirklichkeit vorauseilende Inszenierung zu beschreiben, die notwendigerweise weniger auf die Zukunft als vielmehr auf die Gegenwart verweist. Sobald ein Ereignis eintritt, wird es folgerichtig aus dem Archiv gelöscht.

Angela Wittwer: *Bei* Serie Deutschland *und* Basler Unruhen, *einem inszenierten Aufstand inklusive Besetzung des Basler Rathauses, haben über hundert Beteiligte mitgewirkt. Spielt der biografische Hintergrund der Beteiligten eine Rolle und findet er Eingang in den künstlerischen Prozess?*

Hofmann&Lindholm: Bei *Serie Deutschland* hat der biografische Hintergrund der Beteiligen in Einzelfällen eine Rolle gespielt. So kommen beispielsweise bei der Umsetzung der Sequenz zum Bildmotiv der ‚Schleyer-Entführung‘ Polizisten zum Einsatz, die 1977 den Tatort sicherten – den Tatort, der 31 Jahre später unser Drehort war. Aufgrund der Vorwegnahmen ist die Biografie der Beteiligten im *Archiv* natürlich entscheidend. Die *Basler Unruhen* haben durch ihr Stattfinden Biografien verändert.

Angela Wittwer: *Wie gross ist der Interpretationsspielraum und Aktionsraum der Beteiligten?*

Hofmann&Lindholm: Das ist unterschiedlich. In *Serie Deutschland* haben sich zum Beispiel alle Beteiligten – wir inbegriffen – dem Konzept unterworfen. Andererseits schärft das Bemühen um die Erfüllung der strengen Form den Sinn für abweichende Nuancen, die Differenz, den Spielraum des Einzelnen – und das ist beabsichtigt, also kalkuliert und sehr erfreulich.

Angela Wittwer: *In Basel habt ihr 2010 mit* Basler Unruhen *den „Realitätsgehalt der Wirklichkeit" (*Der Sonntag, 9.5.2010*) auf die Probe gestellt. Die lokale Presse wurde zur Komplizin des Projektes, indem sie mit zunehmender Nervosität über die Vorkommnisse berichtete. Die Theaterbühne spiegelte und historisierte die Ereignisse. Gibt es für euch den realen Aufstand überhaupt und gibt es den Moment, in dem die Zeit des Ereignisses eine neue gesellschaftliche Realität erschafft? Oder spiegeln sich die Ereignisse in einer endlosen, medial begleiteten und erzeugten Wiederholung?*

Hofmann&Lindholm: Es gibt Aufstände und solche, die noch kommen werden, in denen Menschen ihr Leben riskieren, um sich herrschenden Systemen zu widersetzen. Die Realität ihrer Situation ist fraglos. Problematisch ist es, wenn die Revolte über die mediale Verbreitung zum Produkt mutiert und dadurch konsumierbar wird. Mit *Basler Unruhen* haben wir diesen Transformationsprozess exemplarisch unter die Lupe genommen.

Angela Wittwer: Serie Deutschland, Basler Unruhen *und* Archiv der zukünftigen Ereignisse *machen klar, dass es die Medien sind, die ‚Geschichte‘ und ‚Politik‘ erst herstellen, dass sie nicht wertfreie Werkzeuge der Übertragung von Information sind. Kann man eure Kunst als ein Ausbreiten von Möglichkeiten beschreiben, wie kollektive Erinnerung sich dieser hegemonialen Herstellung von Geschichte/Politik entgegensetzen kann?*

Hofmann&Lindholm: *Schön, wenn es so wäre.*

3

ÖKOLOGIKEN
ECOLOGICS

Ulu Braun: *Südwest*, 2006

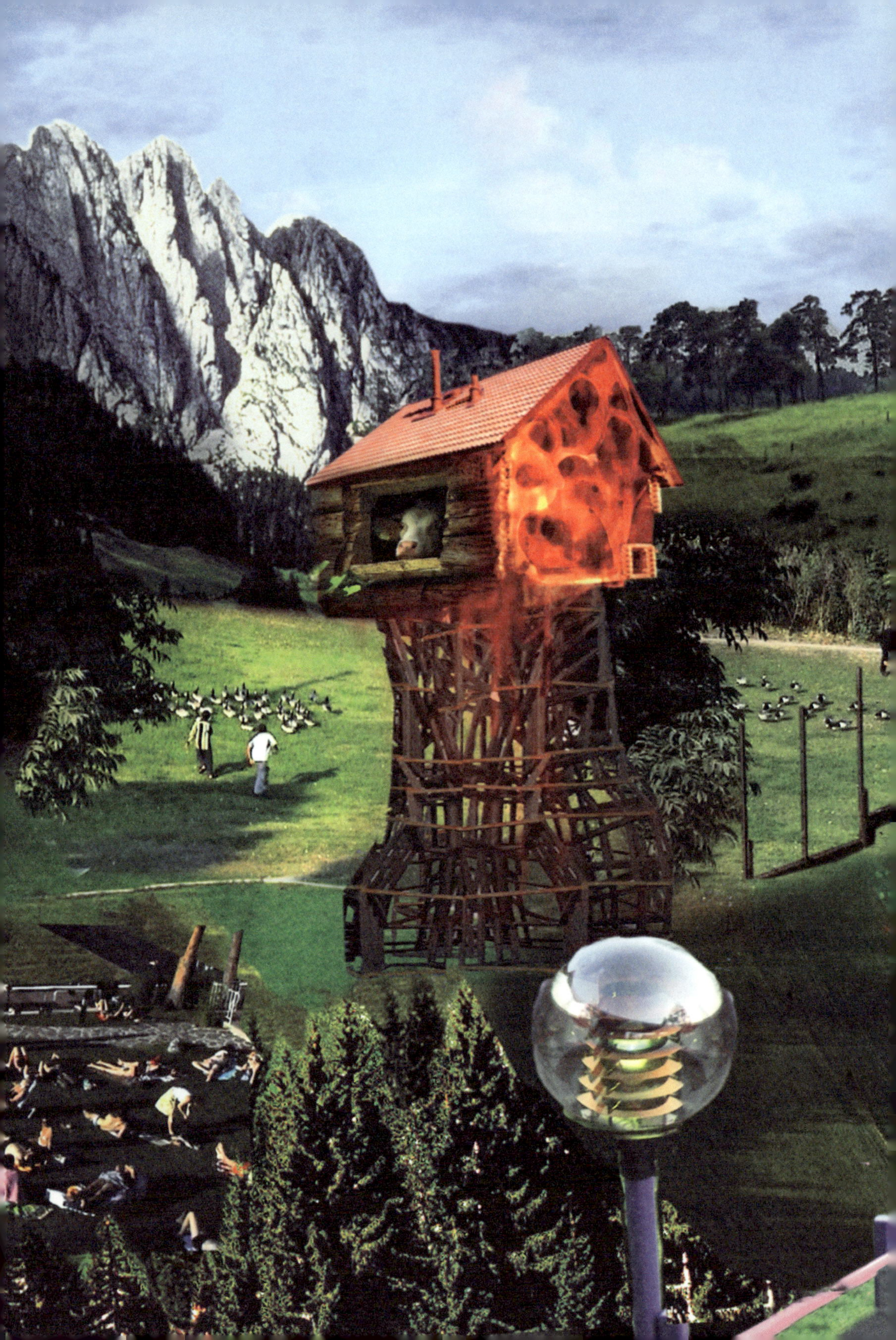

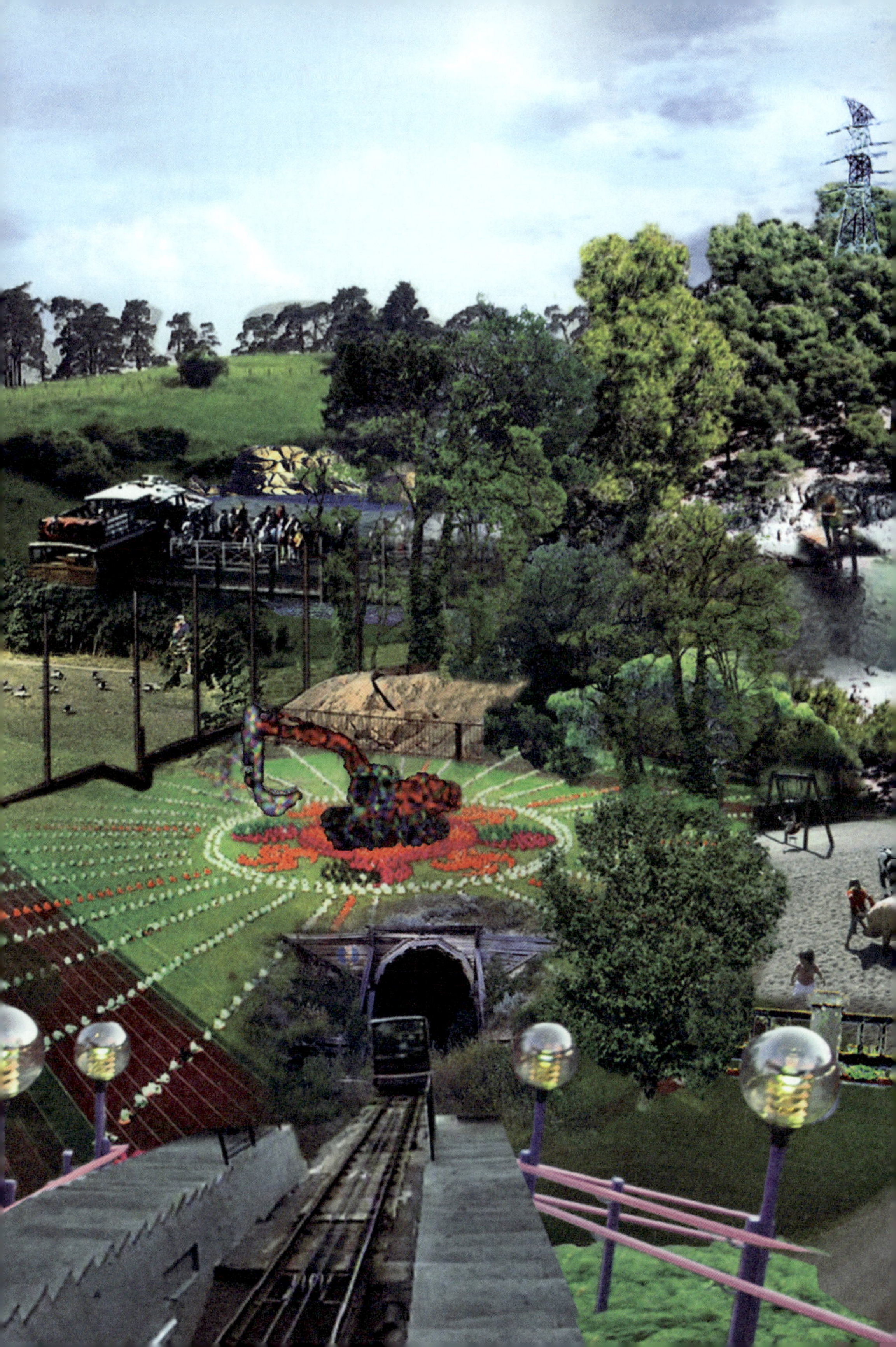

LANDS END. DIE DINGE VON IHREM MÖGLICHEN ENDE HER DENKEN

LANDS END: THINKING THINGS FROM THEIR POSSIBLE END

Unsere Beschäftigung mit Ökologie und Nachhaltigkeit rührt von einer Verzweiflung und Wut her, aber auch von einem „Willen zum Wissen". Durch ihre blosse Lebensweise ist die Menschheit mittlerweile fähig, das Leben auf der Erde auszulöschen. Nicht mehr ‚nur' die sogenannten ‚Anderen' sind gefährdet – die unsichtbaren Würmer, Kräuter, seltenen Vögel, Fische oder subalternen Menschen –, sondern ‚wir' Postindustrialisierten mit ihnen. Wir sind wütend darüber, wie gut wir mit diesen Verlusten leben, und traurig, dass wir so vieles zerstören, das wir nicht einmal ansatzweise kennen. In dieses gesellschaftliche Nicht-Wissen-Wollen intervenierten wir mit zwei Projekten. Das eine war die Ausstellung *Lands End. Landschaft zwischen Bild und Raum*, in der es um die Frage nach unserem Verhältnis zu Natur und Landschaft ging, das andere war *Unter Strom. Kunst und Elektrizität*, in welchem unser Verhältnis zu den Ressourcen und zur Erzeugung von Energie im Vordergrund stand. Beide Projekte einte der Gedanke, dass wir hinsichtlich Lebensmöglichkeiten und Ressourcen zu einem Ende gekommen sind, und die Hoffnung, dass wir mithilfe künstlerischer Zugänge in Sphären vorstossen, die sich ansonsten unserer Wahrnehmung und Erkenntnis entzogen. Denn wer von uns weiss schon, was diese stets verfügbare, unsichtbare Energie aus der Steckdose ist? Gleichzeitig wollten wir die einleitend erwähnte Betroffenheit nicht einem möglichen Pathos aussetzen. Themen wie Landschaft oder Strom faszinierten uns deswegen, weil beide so unaufgeregt und alltäglich daherkommen.

So stand schon hinter *Lands End*, wie der Titel andeutet, die Drohung des Todes. Dieser kehrt in seiner katastrophischen Verfasstheit regelmässig wieder, wie uns zwei Jahre später, mitten in den Vorbereitungen für die Ausstellung *Unter Strom*, nach verschiedenen Ölpesten und pünktlich zum 25. Jahrestag der Katastrophe in Tschernobyl, die Nachricht vom (zunächst verheimlichten) Super-GAU in Fukushima deutlich machte. Es hilft nicht zu denken, dass wir sowieso sterben oder die Natur immer irgendwie weitermacht. Ein solch rudimentärer Naturbegriff wird stets als Legitimation dafür dienen, dass der Mensch rücksichtslos in Beschlag nimmt, was

Our involvement with ecology and sustainability arises out of desperation and anger, but also out of a 'will to knowledge'. Due to its mere *modus vivendi,* humankind is meanwhile capable of eradicating all life on earth. No longer are 'only' the 'others' endangered—the invisible worms, herbs, rare birds, fish, or subaltern people—but 'us' post-industrialized people as well. We are enraged over how well we live with these losses, and sad that we destroy so much we do not even come close to knowing. We wanted to intervene in this social not-wanting-to-know with two projects. One was the exhibition *Lands End: Landscape as Image and as Space,* which dealt with the issue of our relationship to nature and landscape, and the other was *Live Wire: Art and Electricity,* in which the focus was on our relationship to resources and the production of energy. Both projects are united by the thought that we have reached an end with respect to human livability and our earth's resources, and by the hope that with the aid of artistic approaches we can push forward into spheres that otherwise elude our perception and our insight. For who really knows what this invisible energy from the socket is that is always available? At the same time, we did not want to expose our introductory dismay to possible emotionalism. Subjects such as the landscape or electricity fascinate us because both of them are so unremarkable and everyday.

As the title suggests, what was behind *Lands End* was the threat of death. This regularly recurs in its catastrophic state, as it occurred two years later in the middle of preparations for the exhibition *Live Wire*—after various oil spills and just in time for the twenty-fifth 'anniversary' of Chernobyl—when we heard the news about the (initially secret) maximum credible accident in Fukushima. It does not help to think that we are going to die anyway or that nature somehow always carries on. A rudimentary concept of nature of this kind will always serve as justification for people indiscriminately appropriating what ostensibly belongs to them. Yet humankind has no general patent on nature, even if for several centuries now some people have laid claim to one, and if for several years now trans-national corporations have been fervently applying for patents for medicinal plants, for example in the rain forest. We are part of nature, and insofar as we actively intervene in nature, we also have to assume responsibility—not only for what seems to be primary nature, but also for the (climate) changes we initiate, which ironically appear in the guise of nature, such as landslides, floods, droughts, acidotic coral reefs, famine on the soybean fields in the Amazon region or climate refugees.

Melancholy and Landscape

Such miseries are not only testimony to acute mismanagement, they are also images and landscapes. They are disastrous landscapes, techno-natural hybrids, whereby something has gotten out of control. Unlike the concept of nature, landscape was and is an aesthetic category that has something to do with the human perception of the world. Landscape is always bound to an image, be it that we have a real or imaginary image of the landscape or perceive the landscape as an image.[1] But the landscape is also always bound to something we call 'nature', which to a certain degree lies outside human control and refers to a location, a reality in a specific space that itself is the articulation of various bodies and codes. Landscapes are blends of nature and culture. The succulent alpine pastures and snow-covered ski slopes are signifying clusters of technological, cultural and natural nodes. They are social, historical, biological artefacts inhabited and transformed by a multiplicity of living things and actors. Landscapes never simply lie still—they are always in dynamic motion and relational exchange, in a state of change.

And yet here talk will be of a standstill, of phlegmatism and depression, of melancholy that is

1 ...... I would like to call to mind the numerous 'Switzerlands' there are in Germany or the Czech Republic: Saxon Switzerland, Mark Switzerland, or Bohemian Switzerland. The regions were thus named because those who gave them their names found them to be as picturesque and beautiful as Switzerland. A good overview of current theories on the landscape is provided by Brigitte Franzen and Stefanie Krebs, eds., *Landschaftstheorie: Texte der Cultural Landscape Studies* (Cologne, 2005).

fed by desperation and is accompanied by the question of how one can even initiate action in view of these miseries. The twosome landscape and melancholy is not new; they virtually seem to be co-dependent terms. In art, the most melancholy landscapes were produced when the naturalness of nature was perceived as something irretrievable, something threatened by industrialisation. Once again it was attempted to halt the ravages of time and conjure up an idyll that—in the way it was depicted—never really existed. This was the period of Romanticism. Where is the critical treatment of the landscape today? In the following, based on a selection of works from the exhibition *Lands End,* thought will be given to artistic strategies that bring about standstill and retrospection, and create space for a melancholy of an intellectual and not of an emotional kind, a sadness without retrogression and without nostalgic Romanticism.

The assumption was that melancholy, in terms of the landscape in art, could play an important role in critique. Our theory was that melancholy—as a strategy of pause and turning away, of desperation and lapsing into silence—could be a strategy of critical transition that brings to the surface the swirling melancholy and the suppressed preparedness to die of our day and age and opens it up for critical examination. In doing so, we align ourselves with a suggestion made by Hartmut Böhme, who convincingly set forth this theory nearly twenty-five years ago:

'It appears that today, melancholy, which was always the signature of outsiders, is becoming a basic social pattern. The traumatic experiences of our society during fascism and war, which were never adequately come to terms with, are now joining up with the hopelessness that the overwhelming military, ecological and social threats, which for the first time in history threaten all of humankind, can no longer be resolved.'[2]

Böhme therefore appeals for a re-evaluation of melancholy: 'We have to reread the history of the melancholic. We discover that he was always a crack in the power structure.'[3] And he continues: 'Of course, the melancholic keeps his distance from social praxis. But he is productive. … He calls for courage for the signs of fear and threat, knowledge without palliation, feeling without suppression.'[4] It is this productivity, which results from the courage to think things from their end and calling shortcomings by name instead of suppressing them, that makes melancholy as a possible critical strategy in art so interesting to us. Thus, for the exhibition, we proceed from the assumption that in our paradoxical age of a flood of information and suppression, increased performance and an inability to act, individualism and massification, destruction and renaturation, witnessing moments of standstill and sadness aesthetically leads to a fundamental experience and insight: the experience of what is in fact motionlessness behind our superficial hustle and bustle, and insight into the necessity of its transformation.

Establishing Another Relationship to Nature

Donna Haraway gets to the heart of our paradoxical attitude towards nature and the associated, fractured, plural condition of the subject:

'Nature is for me, and I venture for many of us who are planetary fetuses gestating in the amniotic effluvia of terminal industrialism, one of those impossible things characterized by Gayatri Spivak as that which we cannot desire.'[5]

2 ...... Hartmut Böhme, 'Kritik der Melancholie und Melancholie der Kritik', in *Natur und Subjekt* (Frankfurt am Main, 1988). The online version is being cited here: www.culture.hu-berlin.de/hb/static/archiv/volltexte/texte/natsub/inhalt.html, p. 7.

3 .... Ibid., p. 8.

4 ...... Ibid., p. 13. It is apparent, and Böhme himself points this out, that the melancholic's seemingly inability to act results in melancholy's dismissal by both 'left-wing enlighteners' as well as 'right-wing rationalists'. Ibid., p. 2. And in the interesting exhibition *Zwischen zwei Toden* (Between Two Deaths) curated by Ellen Blumenstein and Felix Ensslin, in its dismissal of melancholy something negative cleaved to this convention. However, it made reference to general social stagnation. ZKM Media Museum, Karlsruhe, 12 May–19 August 2007.

5 ...... Donna Haraway, 'The Promises of Monsters: A Regenerative Politics for Inappropriate/d Others', in id., *The Haraway Reader* (New York, 2004), pp. 63–124, esp. p. 64.

ihm vermeintlich gehört. Doch der Mensch hat kein Generalpatent auf die Natur, auch wenn einige seit ein paar Jahrhunderten ein solches beanspruchen und transnationale Firmen seit ein paar Jahren – z.B. im Regenwald – auch eifrig Patente für Heilpflanzen lösen. Wir sind Teil der Natur, und insofern wir handelnd in sie eingreifen, müssen wir auch Verantwortung tragen, nicht nur für das, was primäre Natur zu sein scheint, sondern auch für die von uns initiierten (Klima-) Effekte, die ironischerweise auch als ‚Natur‘ daherkommen, wie Erdrutsche, Überschwemmungen, Dürren, übersäuerte Korallenriffe und Hunger auf Sojafeldern im Amazonasgebiet oder Klimaflüchtlinge.

Melancholie und Landschaft

Solche Miseren sind nicht nur Zeugnisse akuter Misswirtschaft, sondern sie sind auch Bilder, Landschaften. Es sind desaströse Landschaften, techno-natürliche Hybride, bei denen etwas aus dem Ruder geraten ist. Landschaft war und ist – im Gegensatz zum Begriff der Natur – eine ästhetische Kategorie, die mit der menschlichen Wahrnehmung von Welt zu tun hat. Landschaft ist immer an das Bild gekoppelt, sei es, dass wir uns ein reales oder imaginäres Bild von der Landschaft machen oder die Landschaft als Bild wahrnehmen.[1] Aber Landschaft ist immer auch an etwas gebunden, das wir ‚Natur‘ nennen, das bis zu einem gewissen Grad ausserhalb der menschlichen Kontrolle liegt und auf eine Örtlichkeit verweist, eine Realität in einem bestimmten Raum, der selbst Artikulation verschiedener Körper und Codes ist. Landschaften sind Mixturen aus Natur und Kultur. Die saftigen Alpweiden und beschneiten Skipisten sind signifizierende Bündel technowissenschaftlicher, kultureller und natürlicher Knoten. Sie sind soziale, historische, biologische Artefakte, die von multiplen Lebewesen und Akteur_innen bewohnt und verändert

werden. Landschaften liegen nie einfach da, sie sind immer in dynamischer Bewegung und relationalem Austausch, in Veränderung.

Und doch soll hier auch von einem Stillstand gesprochen werden, von einer Schwerblütigkeit und Schwermütigkeit, von der Melancholie, die sich aus der Verzweiflung speist und die Frage mitführt, wie man angesichts dieser Miseren überhaupt noch ins Handeln kommen kann? Landschaft und Melancholie sind als Paar nichts Neues, sie scheinen sich nachgerade zu bedingen. Die melancholischsten Landschaften in der Kunst entstanden, als das Natürliche der Natur als etwas Unwiederbringliches, durch die Industrialisierung Bedrohtes erahnt wurde. Noch einmal wurde versucht, den Zahn der Zeit anzuhalten und eine Idylle zu beschwören, die es so – wie dargestellt – nie wirklich gegeben hat. Das war zur Zeit der Romantik. Doch wo steht der kritische Umgang mit Landschaft heute? Am Beispiel ausgewählter Arbeiten aus der Ausstellung *Lands End* soll im Folgenden über künstlerische Strategien nachgedacht werden, die Stillstände bewirken, den Blick zurückwerfen und einer Melancholie Raum geben, die intellektueller und nicht emotionaler Art ist, eine Trauer ohne Rückwärtsgewandtheit oder nostalgischen Romantizismus.

These war, dass die Melancholie, bezogen auf die Landschaft in der Kunst, eine wichtige Rolle der Kritik spielen könnte. Wir nahmen an, dass die Melancholie – als Strategie des Innehaltens und der Abkehr, der Verzweiflung und der Verstummung – eine Strategie der kritischen Durchquerung sein könnte, die die wabernde Melancholie und verdrängte Todesbereitschaft unserer Zeit an die Oberfläche bringt und zur kritischen Durcharbeitung offenlegt. Damit schliessen wir uns an einen Vorschlag Hartmut Böhmes an, der diese These vor bald 25 Jahren überzeugend dargelegt hat:

„Es scheint nämlich, dass heute die Melancholie, die immer eine Signatur der Aussenseiter war, zu einem gesellschaftlichen Grundmuster wird. Die traumatischen Erfahrungen unserer Gesellschaft in Faschismus und Krieg, die niemals angemessen aufgearbeitet wurden, verbinden sich heute mit der Hoffnungslosigkeit, dass die

---

1 .... Erinnert sei etwa an die vielen ‚Schweiz‘, die es in Deutschland oder Tschechien gibt: die sächsische Schweiz, die märkische Schweiz oder die böhmische Schweiz. Diese Regionen wurden so genannt, weil die Menschen, die ihnen die Namen gaben, es dort so pittoresk und schön „wie in der Schweiz" fanden. Einen guten Überblick über aktuelle Theorien der Landschaft geben Franzen, Brigitte/ Krebs, Stefanie (Hg.): *Landschaftstheorie. Texte der Cultural Landscape Studies*. Köln 2005.

Eva Castringius: *The Great Thirst*, 2003–2004

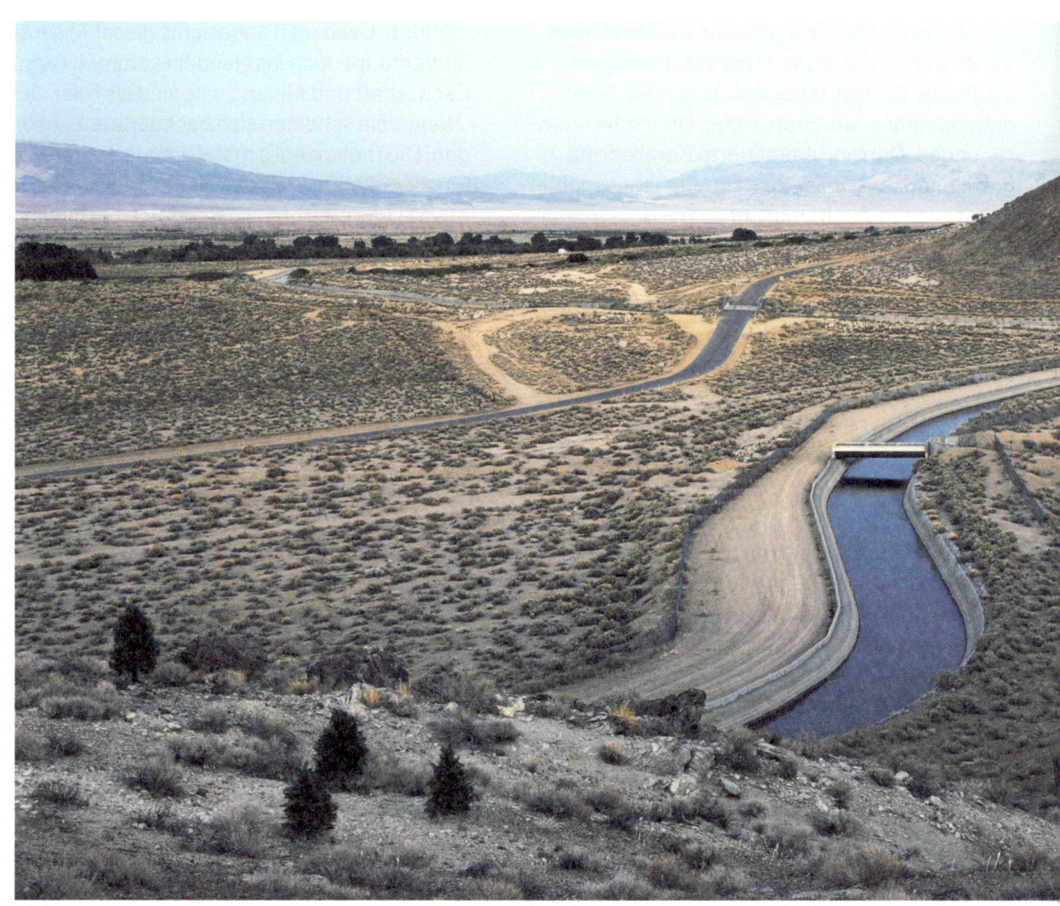

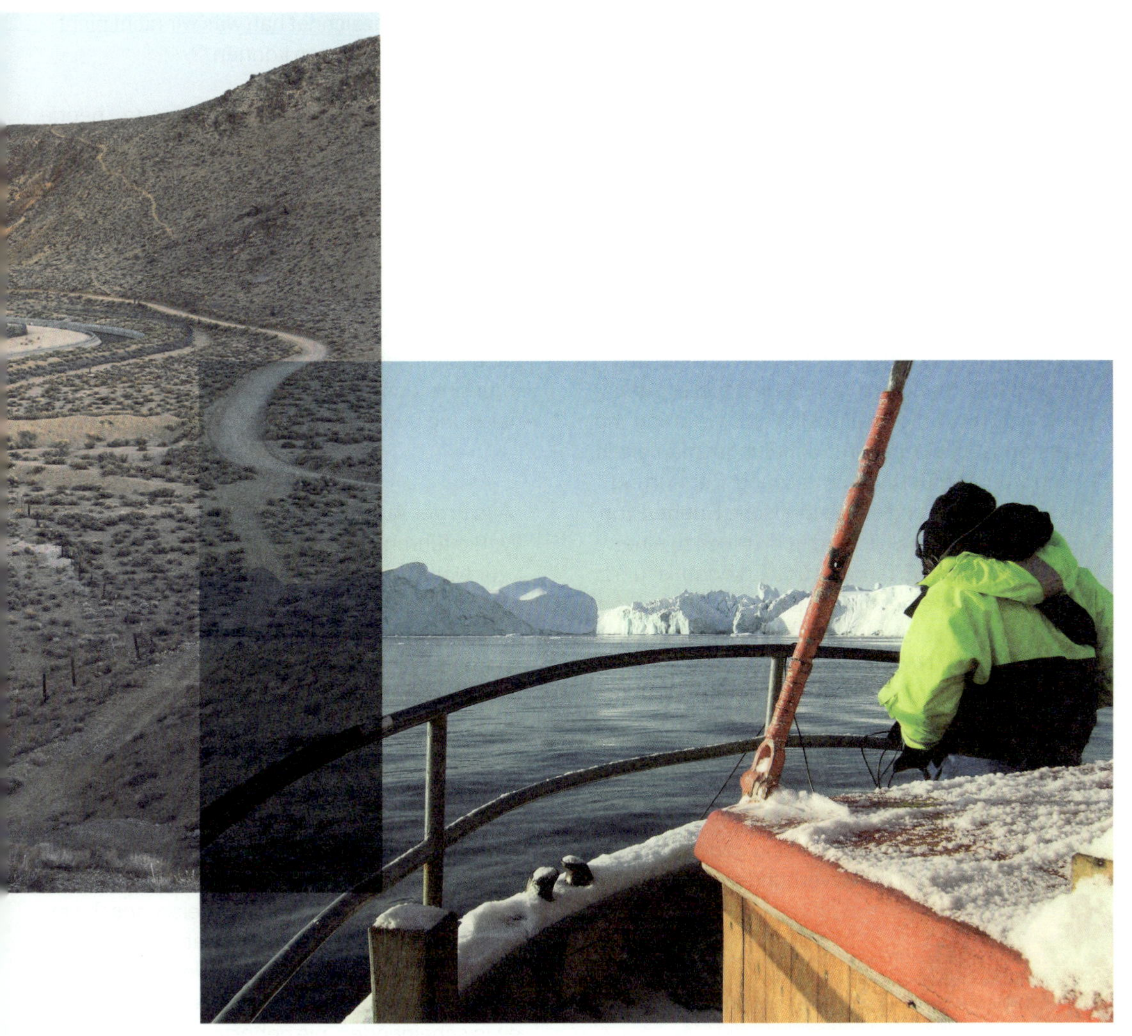

Jana Winderen: *Heated²*, 2010 (Produktionsfoto / Production photo: Kangia, Greenland, 2009)

erdrückenden militärischen, ökologischen und sozialen Bedrohungen, welche erstmals in der Geschichte den Bestand der Menschheit gefährden, nicht mehr lösbar sind." [2]

Deswegen plädiert Böhme für eine Neubewertung der Melancholie: „Wir haben die Geschichte des Melancholikers neu zu lesen. Wir entdecken, dass er immer schon ein Sprung im Gefüge der Macht war."[3] Und er fährt fort: „Gewiss hält sich der Melancholiker in Distanz zur gesellschaftlichen Praxis. Aber er ist produktiv." [...] Er fordert Mut für die Zeichen der Angst und Bedrohung, ein Wissen ohne Beschönigung, ein Gefühl ohne Verdrängung."[4] Diese Produktivität, die aus dem Mut resultiert, die Dinge von ihrem Ende her zu denken und Missstände zu benennen statt zu verdrängen, ist es, die uns an der Melancholie als mögliche kritische Strategie in der Kunst interessiert. So gingen wir für die Ausstellung von der Vermutung aus, dass in unserer paradoxen Zeit von Informationsflut und Verdrängung, Leistungssteigerung und Handlungsunfähigkeit, Individualismus und Vermassung, Zerstörung und Renaturierung das ästhetische Erleben von Momenten von Stillstand und Trauer zu einer grundlegenden Erfahrung und Erkenntnis führt: Erfahrung der eigentlichen Bewegungslosigkeit hinter unserer vordergründigen Umtriebigkeit, und Erkenntnis der Notwendigkeit ihrer Verwandlung.

Ein anderes Verhältnis zur Natur etablieren

Unsere paradoxe Einstellung gegenüber der Natur und damit verbunden, unsere vielfach gebrochene Subjektverfassung bringt Donna Haraway auf den Punkt:

„Natur ist für mich – und ich wage zu sagen, für viele von uns, die wir als planetarische Föten in den Abgasen eines endzeitlichen Industrialismus und Militarismus heranreifen – eines jener unmöglichen Dinge, die Gayatri Spivak als das gekennzeichnet hat, was wir nicht nicht begehren können."[5]

Wie Haraway und mit ihr die feministische Theorie gezeigt hat, hat ‚Natur' in unserem Bedeutungssystem eine strukturelle Funktion, die das subalterne, oft weiblich konnotierte ‚Andere' markiert. ‚Natur' sei eine Trope, eine „Figur, Konstruktion, Artefakt, Bewegung, Verschiebung. Die Natur kann nicht vor ihrer Konstruktion existieren."[6] Weil dieser Begriff aber gleichzeitig auch unumgänglich ist, müssten wir ihn umcodieren: „Wir müssen, jenseits von Verdinglichung, Besitz, Aneignung und Nostalgie, ein anderes Verhältnis zur Natur finden."[7]

Alle in der Ausstellung *Lands End* gezeigten Werke führen ein solches „anderes Verhältnis zur Natur" vor, ohne Natur zu beschönigen, oder Ursprungsmythen und Naturidyllen nachzutrauern. Aber immer spielt die Frage nach den Verlusten eine zentrale Rolle. Jana Winderen etwa spricht dies in ihrem Kommentar zu ihrer Audioinstallation *Heated* [2] (Abb. S. 123) explizit an. Sie sagt, sie wolle diese arktische Unterwasser-Hörlandschaft erfahrbar machen, damit wir wissen, was wir eigentlich daran sind, unwiederbringlich kaputt zu machen. Sie hebt hervor, dass wir die Fische im Eismeer ausrotten und dabei keine Ahnung von deren Lebensweise, geschweige denn von deren Kommunikation hätten. Erstaunlicherweise entspringen die unterschiedlich leisen und lauten, eindringlichen, langsamen, ewig scheinenden, nie gehörten, wellenartigozeanischen Töne in *Heated* [2] realen Soundlandschaften unter Wasser. Winderen nimmt real existierende Klänge mittels Unterwassermikrophonen auf und setzt sie, ohne technologische

---

2............... Böhme, Hartmut: Kritik der Melancholie und Melancholie der Kritik. In: *Natur und Subjekt*. Frankfurt a. M. 1988. Zitiert wird aus der Online-Version: www.culture.hu-berlin.de/hb/static/archiv/volltexte/texte/natsub/inhalt.html, 7.
3.. Böhme: Kritik der Melancholie, 8.
4............... Böhme: Kritik der Melancholie, 13. Es liegt auf der Hand, und Böhme weist selbst darauf hin, dass in dieser vermeintlichen Handlungsunfähigkeit des/der Melancholiker_in deren Verwerfung sowohl durch „linke Aufklärer" als auch durch „rechte Rationalisten" resultiert. Böhme: Kritik der Melancholie, 2. Auch die an sich interessante Ausstellung *Zwischen zwei Toden*, kuratiert von Ellen Blumenstein und Felix Ensslin, blieb in ihrer Verwerfung der Melancholie als etwas Negatives dieser Konvention verhaftet. Allerdings bezog sie sich auf die allgemeine gesellschaftliche Stagnation. ZKM Medienmuseum, 12.5.–19.8.2007.
5............ Haraway, Donna: *Monströse Versprechen. Coyote-Geschichten zu Feminismus und Technowissenschaft*. Hamburg/Berlin 1995, 81.
6.................................... Haraway: *Monströse Versprechen*, 83.
7.................................... Haraway: *Monströse Versprechen*, 82.

As Haraway and feminist theory have demonstrated, in our meaning system 'nature' has a structural function that marks the subaltern 'Other' often connoted with femaleness. Nature is a trope, a 'figure, construction, artifact, movement, displacement. Nature cannot pre-exist its construction.'[6] However, because this concept is at the same time imperative as well, we would have to recode it: 'We must find another relationship to nature besides reification, possession, appropriation and nostalgia.'[7]

All of the works presented in the exhibition *Lands End* demonstrate one such 'other relationship to nature' without whitewashing nature or mourning myths of origin and natural idylls. But the issue of losses always plays a central role. Jana Winderen, for example, explicitly addresses this in her commentary on her audio installation *Heated²* (fig. p. 123). She says she wants to make this arctic underwater audio landscape able to be experienced so that we know what we are actually about to irretrievably destroy. She points out that we are exterminating the fish in the polar sea and yet we do not have a clue about the way they live, not to mention about how they communicate. Amazingly enough, the various muted and loud, haunting, slow, apparently eternal, never-before-heard, wave-like oceanic sounds in *Heated²* have their source in real underwater sound landscapes. Winderen records real sounds using underwater microphones and transforms them into compositions without any technical alienation effects. For instance, one hears the throbbing of a sturgeon defending its territory, or the hissing of a crab that petrifies its enemies by means of sound waves. What is striking is that these seem to be electronic sounds, because that is what we are familiar with.

The sound landscape strikes us as melancholy, but what is audible is not what has already been lost, but the never-before-heard variety of the underwater landscape. The impression of sad beauty may depend on the type of composition and the human range of hearing that is physically possible, but it may also depend on the fact that the sound has an affect on an aesthetic sensorium within us that lends it the meaning of being melancholy. We apparently have visual and auditory images of landscapes in our mind that are retrieved as a result of certain aesthetic stimuli. And against the backdrop of our knowledge of the threat to this underwater world and the glacial desert, our interpretation apparently tends in this direction.

Thus, Jana Winderen does not operate with the strategies of conjuring up a loss or the didactic cautioning of what we long since believe to know, but with the strategy of letting us immerse ourselves in something unfamiliar: the floor pillow invites us to lay down and close our eyes. Visitors to the exhibition are addressed as sensuously receptive people who in the passivity of abandon and attention are given something to hear that they otherwise never would. By immersing themselves in the sound landscape, they become part of this other world, become fish, waves, icebreakers, flowing bodies of water. This moment is a moment of the dissolution of the accustomed ego, a kind of land's end, the end of the mainland, beyond reason or self-attachment. It is identification with the 'Other', with that which otherwise seems to be something irrelevant or exploitable. Contrary to the external impression of passivity, the work allows us to experience a creaturely feeling of being and suffering with what is threatened.

The intervention *Requiem for Cod* (see p. 150) by Matthew Fuller and Graham Harwood, which was documented on video, attempts to establish 'another relationship to nature' and to demonstrate landscape as something that is not only populated by human beings or even needs to be perceived. Much like Winderen, we hear the sounds of fish, not as beautiful compositions but as an odd, almost unpleasant throbbing and knocking that echoes in senselessness. They are the sounds cod emit during mating. However, the sound material does not stem from the

---

6 .... Ibid., p. 65.
7 ..... Donna Haraway, 'Otherworldly Convers ations; Terran Topics; Local Terms', in id., *The Haraway Reader* (New York, 2004), pp. 125–150, esp. p. 126.

fish in their natural environment, but it is recorded and digitalized material from a data-bank. The two artists lowered it into Thames with the aid of an underwater speaker and played it to young cod. Because they are still too young to know how to adequately react to the mating sounds, the sounds fade away without further consequences. The undertaking represents a kind of helpless attempt by human beings to approach wild fish. The attempt to communicate with the fish was fruitless, as infertile as not only the young cod are but cod in general are increasingly becoming, because swarms of fish disintegrate when their population density falls below a certain level and no longer repro-duce. By calling their intervention *Requiem for Cod,* the artists bring home that the fish are sentenced to death. In this case as well, what is being referred to is a loss; it is being anticipated. In this anticipated sadness, that socially sanc-tioned melancholy and inability to act of which Böhme speaks is being aesthetically repeated, however with a difference: this one here ad-dresses the state of the world and at the same time leaves open a gap. Like the singing of Winderen's fish, in this case it is also not too late (for taking possible action). *Requiem for Cod* is therefore not a melancholy celebration of an immutable fact, but the (still) seemingly senseless gesture of approaching the fish and communicating with them.

De/romanticising the World

With these attempts to reveal the other side of belief in progress and create another relationship to nature, our exhibition ties in with Romanticism, if not without contradiction. What interests us is that at exactly that point at which apparently 'untouched' nature and landscape began to become 'touched' by indus-trialisation and stripped of their 'secrets', touch-ing landscapes were created. Nature was no longer something that was taken for granted, but something threatened. The Romanticists furthermore attempted to enter into a unifying

dialogue with nature and its 'world soul'[8] in a different way than had been done previously—for example, during the Renaissance or Enlight-enment, where nature was conceived as a subordinate counterpart.

Hence, the conjuring up at the moment of a picturesque or sublime beauty in a painting could be interpreted as an attempt to halt the ravages of time and visualise something that had never existed as depicted in this way, but that one has to sketch in order to be able to imagine something else. Accordingly, what is apparently lost would also be that which is hoped for in the future. Christian Vetter's instal-lation *Archäologie der Zukunft (Das Eismeer)* (Archeology of the Future, Arctic Shipwreck) (fig. p. 127) suggests this thought. Its title reveals that this work is not only a rereading of Caspar David Friedrich's painting *Das Eismeer* but also a statement to the effect that research into the past involves something promising.

What initially strikes one is the black rod, then the ladders to be ascended, and only then the white sheets of ice or wreckage at the top lying there spread out like in the aftermath of a catastrophe. Below that, embedded between rods, we see a monitor with a sonogram of a wreck. We are standing in front of ruins, turning our gaze towards them. That is the traditional gaze of the melancholic; as Walter Benjamin says, ruins are his home.[9] This is where Friedrich's painting *Das Eismeer* appears in transmuted form. This painting from 1823–24 has led to numerous interpretations. In this context I am less interested in the painterly pithiness of the subject with its horizontal and vertical blocks of ice protruding diagonally upward, or pieces of wood from the wrecked ship jammed between them, and more with its ambiguous allegorical character. Above all, I would like to call attention to the meaning of failure, for the painting was later casually referred to as *Gescheiterte Hoffnung* (The Wreck of Hope), with reference

8.......... This Platonic concept was philosophically and poetically brought up to date above all by the early Romanticists, such as Friedrich Schelling, Novalis and Friedrich Schlegel.

9...... Walter Benjamin, *The Origin of German Tragic Drama*, trans. John Osborne (London and New York, 1998).

Christian Vetter: *Archäologie der Zukunft (Eismeer)*, 2010

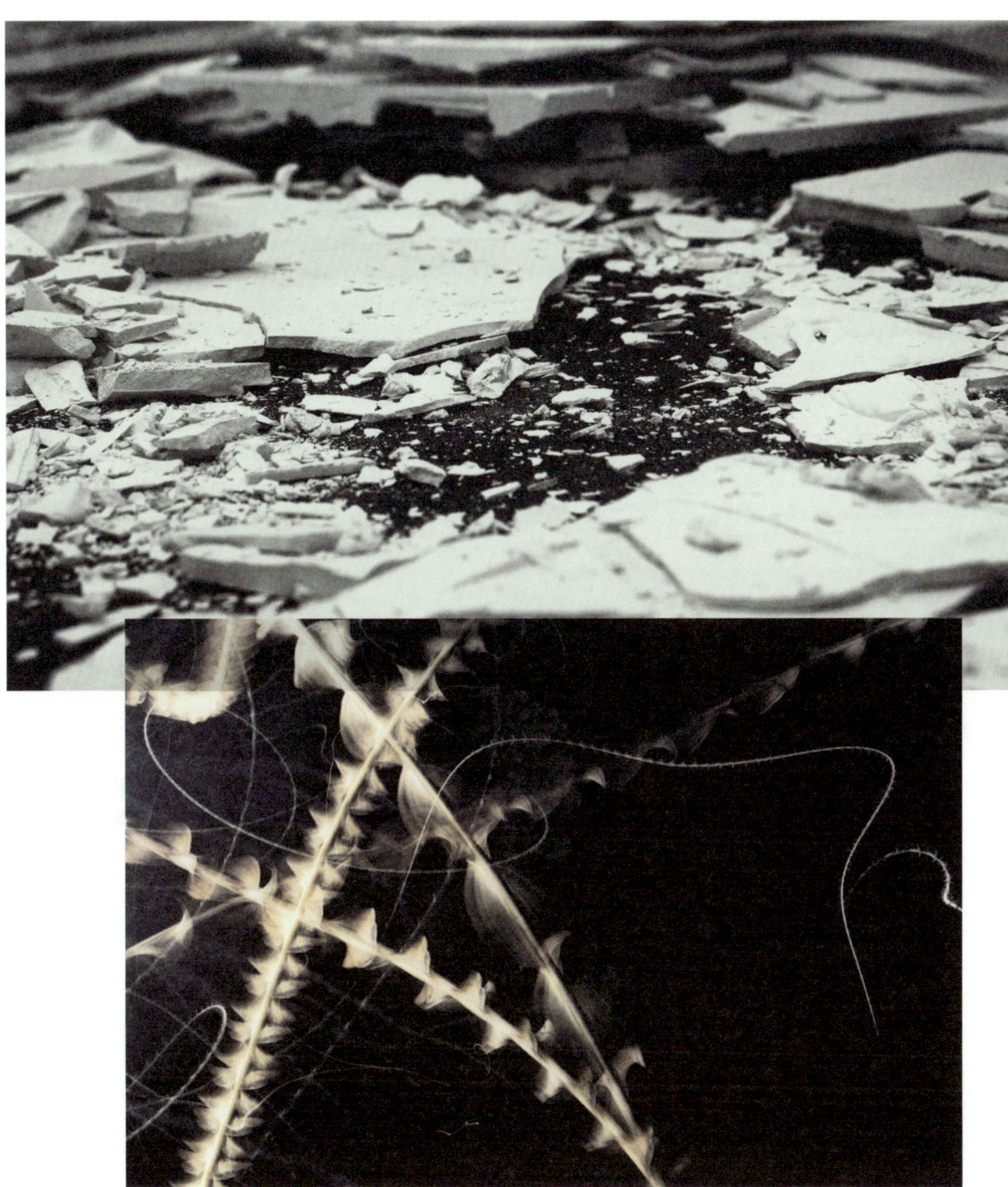

Achim Mohné: *Fireflies*, 2000

Verena Maas: *Brown*, 2008

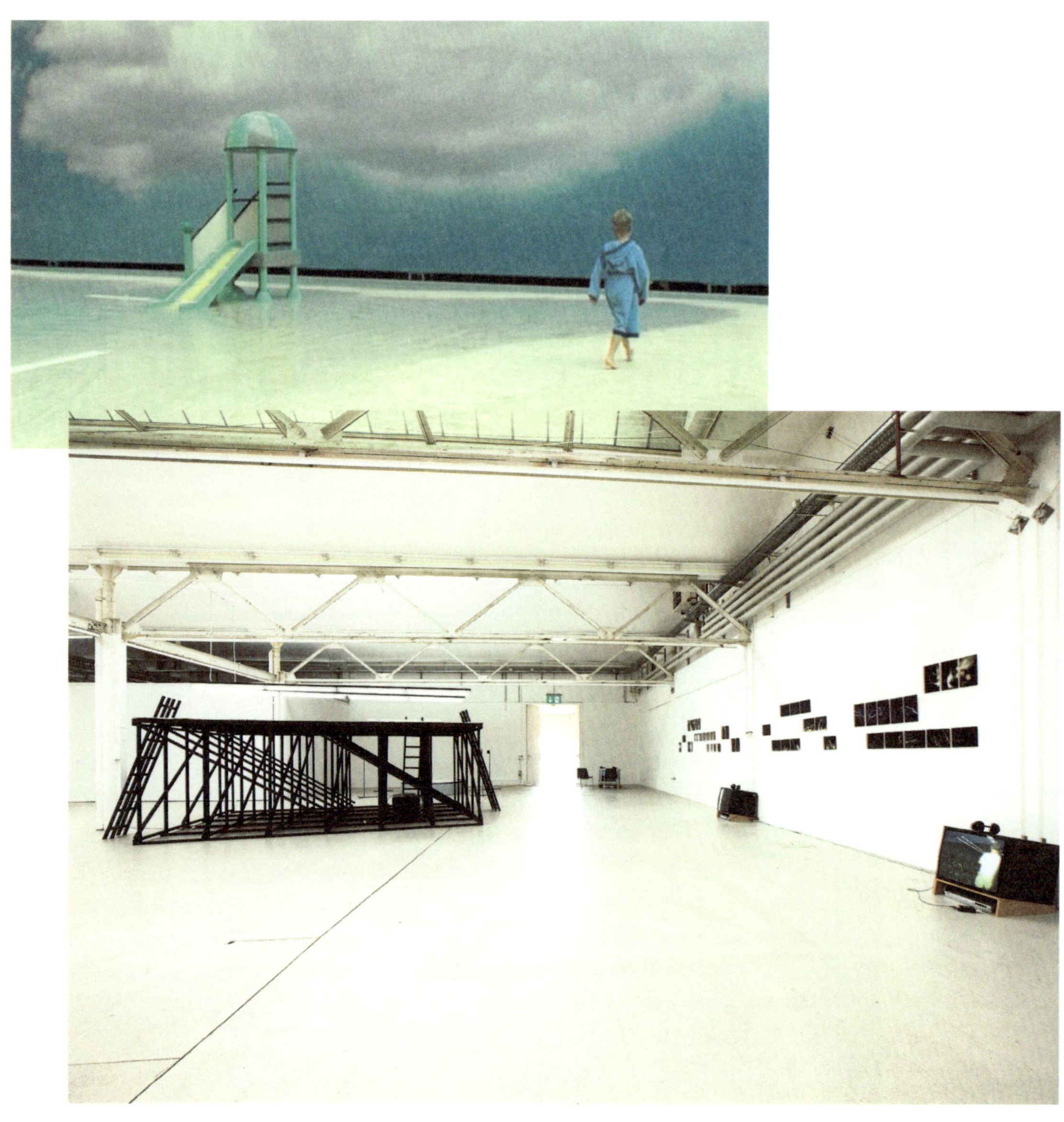

Lands End (Ausstellungsansicht / Exhibition view)
Vorne links / Front left: Christian Vetter: *Archäologie der Zukunft (Eismeer)*, 2010
Vorne rechts / Front right: Achim Mohné: *Fireflies*, 2000

Verfremdungen, in Kompositionen um. Da ist etwa das Pochen eines Störs, der sein Territorium verteidigt oder das Rauschen einer Krabbe, die ihre Feinde mittels Schallwellen versteinert. Bestechend ist, dass uns diese Klänge wie elektronischer Sound erscheinen, weil es das ist, was wir kennen.

Die Soundlandschaft mutet melancholisch an, doch hörbar ist nicht das bereits Verlorene, sondern die von uns nie gehörte Vielfalt der Unterwasserlandschaft. Der Eindruck von trauriger Schönheit mag von der Art und Weise der Komposition abhängen und dem physikalisch möglichen Hörbereich des Menschen, aber auch davon, dass der Sound ein ästhetisches Sensorium in uns trifft, das ihm die Bedeutung des Melancholischen verleiht. Offenbar haben wir Seh- und Hörbilder von Landschaften im Kopf, die aufgrund bestimmter ästhetischer Reize abgerufen werden. Und offenbar tendiert vor dem Hintergrund des Wissens um die Bedrohtheit dieser Unterwasserwelt und der eisigen Wüste unsere Interpretation in diese Richtung.

Jana Winderen operiert also nicht mit den Strategien des Beschwörens eines Verlusts oder des didaktischen Belehrens von etwas, das wir schon längstens zu wissen glauben, sondern mit der Strategie des Uns-Eintauchen-Lassens in etwas Unbekanntes: Das Bodenkissen lädt in die horizontale Position und zum Schliessen der Augen ein. Die Besucher_innen der Ausstellung werden als sinnlich empfängliche Menschen angesprochen, die in der Passivität der Hingabe und Zuwendung etwas zu hören bekommen, das sie sonst nie hören. Durch die Immersion in die Soundlandschaft wird das Publikum Teil dieser anderen Welt, wird Fisch, Welle, Eisbrecher, Wasserlauf. Dieses Moment ist ein Moment der Auflösung des gewohnten Ichs, eine Art Lands End, Ende des festen Lands, jenseits von Vernunft oder Ichhaftigkeit. Es ist Identifikation mit dem ‚Anderen‘, mit dem, was uns ansonsten als etwas Irrelevantes oder Ausbeutbares erscheint. Entgegen des äusseren Eindrucks von Passivität ermöglicht uns diese Arbeit, ein kreatürliches Gefühl des Mit-Seins und Mit-Leidens mit dem Gefährdeten zu erleben.

Ein „anderes Verhältnis zur Natur" zu etablieren und Landschaft als etwas vorzuführen, das nicht nur vom Menschen bevölkert ist oder gar wahrgenommen zu werden braucht, versucht die mittels Video dokumentierte Intervention *Requiem for Cod* (vgl. S. 150) von Matthew Fuller und Graham Harwood. Ähnlich wie bei Winderen hören wir Fischgeräusche, jedoch nicht als schöne Komposition, sondern als eigentümliches, fast schon unangenehmes, im Sinnlosen verhallendes Pochen und Klopfen. Es sind Laute, die Dorsche bei der Paarung ausstossen. Das Soundmaterial stammt jedoch nicht von den Fischen vor Ort, sondern es ist aufgezeichnetes und digitalisiertes Material aus einer Datenbank. Dieses Material spielten die beiden Künstler mittels Unterwasser-Lautsprecher jungen Dorschen in der Themse vor. Da die Fische noch zu jung waren, als dass sie auf die Paarungsgeräusche adäquat zu reagieren gewusst hätten, verhallten die Töne ohne weitere Konsequenzen. Das Unterfangen stellt eine Art hilfloser Annäherungsversuch von Menschen an frei lebende Fische dar. Der Versuch zur Kommunikation bleibt unfruchtbar, so unfruchtbar, wie es nicht nur die zu jungen Dorsche waren, sondern wie es die Dorsche zunehmend werden. Fischschwärme lösen sich nämlich auf, wenn sie unter eine bestimmte Populationsdichte fallen, und pflanzen sich nicht mehr fort.

Mit der Nennung des „Requiems", der Totenmesse, machen die Künstler deutlich, dass der Fisch zum Tode verurteilt ist. Auch hier ist von einem Verlust die Rede, er wird antizipiert. In dieser vorweggenommenen Trauer wird jene gesellschaftlich sanktionierte Melancholie und Handlungsunfähigkeit ästhetisch wiederholt, von der Böhme spricht, jedoch mit einer Differenz: Diese da benennt den Zustand der Welt und lässt gleichzeitig eine Lücke offen. Wie bei Winderens Fischgesang, so ist es auch hier noch nicht zu spät (für mögliches Handeln). Das *Requiem for Cod* ist somit nicht ein melancholisches Abfeiern einer unveränderlichen Tatsache, sondern die (noch) sinnlos anmutende Geste, auf die Fische zuzugehen und mit ihnen in Kommunikation zu treten.

Die Welt de/romantisieren

Mit diesen Versuchen, die Kehrseite des Fortschrittsglaubens zu offenbaren und ein anderes Verhältnis zur Natur zu schaffen, knüpft unsere Ausstellung, wenn auch nicht widerspruchslos, bei der Romantik an. Uns interessiert, dass genau dann, als scheinbar ‚unberührte' Natur und Landschaft begannen, durch die Industrialisierung ‚berührt' und ihrer scheinbaren ‚Geheimnisse' entkleidet zu werden, berührende Landschaften geschaffen wurden. Natur war nichts Selbstverständliches mehr, sondern etwas Bedrohtes. Ausserdem versuchten die Romantiker_innen auf eine andere Weise, als es bis dahin geschehen war – beispielsweise in der Renaissance oder der Aufklärung, als Natur als unterlegenes Gegenüber konzipiert wurde –, in einen Einheit stiftenden Dialog mit der Natur und ihrer „Weltseele"[8] zu treten.

Auch das damalige malerische Beschwören einer pittoresken oder erhabenen Schönheit könnte somit als Versuch interpretiert werden, die Zeit anzuhalten und etwas zu vergegenwärtigen, das es so dargestellt nie gegeben hat, das man aber skizzieren muss, um sich etwas anderes vorstellen zu können. Das scheinbar Verloren-Gegangene wäre demzufolge auch das für die Zukunft Erhoffte. Diesen Gedanken legt Christian Vetters Installation *Archäologie der Zukunft (Eismeer)* (Abb. S. 127) nahe. Ihre Betitelung macht deutlich, dass es mit dieser Arbeit sowohl um eine Re-Lektüre von Caspar David Friedrichs Werk *Das Eismeer* geht als auch um ein Statement dahingehend, dass Vergangenheitsforschung etwas Zukunftsträchtiges beinhaltet.

Zunächst fällt einem nur das schwarze Gestänge auf, dann die Leitern, um hochzusteigen und erst dann die weissen Eisplatten oder Trümmer oben, die wie nach einer Katastrophe ausgebreitet daliegen. Darunter, eingebettet zwischen Stangen, sehen wir einen Monitor mit der Sonografie eines Wracks. Wir stehen vor Ruinen, wenden den Blick darauf. Das ist der traditionelle Blick des

Melancholikers, sein Zuhause ist, wie Benjamin sagt, die Ruine.[9] Hier erscheint Friedrichs Bild *Das Eismeer* in verwandelter Form. Dieses Bild aus dem Jahre 1823/24 hat zu vielen Deutungen geführt. Mich interessiert hier weniger die malerische Prägnanz des Sujets mit den horizontalen und vertikalen, schräg in die Höhe strebenden Eisblöcken sowie den in ihnen verklemmten Holzstücken des Schiffswracks, sondern sein vieldeutiger allegorischer Charakter. Diesen möchte ich vor allem auf die Bedeutung des Scheiterns lenken, denn mit dem Titel *Gescheiterte Hoffnung* wurde das Bild später auch versehen, bezogen auch auf das damalige Scheitern politisch-demokratischer Bestrebungen und Friedrichs mögliche Bezugnahme darauf. Aus der Sicht von *Lands End* könnte man im Bild auch das Scheitern des damals anhebenden Fortschrittsglaubens thematisiert sehen. Im Sujet manifestiert er sich durch das Schiff, mithin den Schiffsverkehr im Polarmeer, das eine Passage zu einem Aufbruch in ungeahnte, wirtschaftliche und technische Sphären verheisst. Doch den Naturbezwingern gelang es offensichtlich nicht, das Ziel zu erreichen; das harte, kalte Packeis verwehrte den Zugriff. Diese Lesart, die wohl über Friedrichs Bild hinausgeht, wird durch die Maschinenhaftigkeit der Konstruktion und die technisch basierte Visualisierung des Wracks in Vetters Installation bestärkt, wenn auch nicht auf die Spitze getrieben, denn weitere Referenzen in diese Richtung fehlen. Doch Vetters Arbeit ist nicht nur eine Re-Inszenierung des alten Sujets, vielmehr wird hier – im Format der Skulptur –, eine Wahrnehmungs-Maschine vorgeführt, die eine Maschine des Endzeit-Bildes ist. Die Installation zwingt zum Sehen – falls ich mir die Mühe mache und die Leitern hochklettere – sie zwingt zum Anschauen von fast nichts, von Trümmern, Resten, Spuren. Aber vielleicht sind dieses Fast-Nichts: Anfänge. Möglichkeiten von etwas, das nie so gewesen war.

Geschickte Dramaturgie, Bildeffekte und ein synästhetischer Umgang mit Musik führen in Emily Richardsons Video *Petrolia* (vgl. S. 163) dazu, dass zur Melancholie weitere Gefühle

---

8............ Dieser platonische Begriff wurde v.a. von den Frühromantikern wie Friedrich Schelling, Novalis und Friedrich Schlegel philosophisch und dichterisch aktualisiert.

9.................. Benjamin, Walter: *Ursprung des deutschen Trauerspiels*. Frankfurt am Main 1978.

to the failure of the political, democratic aspirations of the time and Friedrich's possible allusion to this.

From the point of view of *Lands End,* one could also see the picture addressing the failure of the belief in progress that was commencing at the time. It is manifested in the subject by means of the ship, hence maritime traffic in the polar sea, which augurs a journey towards emergence into unsuspected economic and technical spheres. But the conquerors of nature apparently did not succeed in reaching their goal; the hard, cold pack ice denied them access. This interpretation, which goes beyond Friedrich's painting, is reinforced by the machine-like nature of the construction and the technically based visualisation of the shipwreck in Vetter's installation if not also carried to the extremes, as any further references in this direction are lacking. Yet Vetter's work is not only a restaging of the old subject; rather, in the sculpture's format he presents a perception machine that is a machine of the apocalyptic image. The installation forces us to see. If we make the effort to ascend the ladders; it forces us to look at almost nothing, at rubble, remnants, traces. But perhaps these are almost nothing: beginnings. Possibilities for something that never existed in this form.

In Emily Richardson's video *Petrolia* (see p. 163), skilled dramaturgy, visual effects and a synaesthetic treatment of music lead to melancholy being enhanced by other feelings, namely wit and the sublime. The video begins with the view of an oil platform and passing ships. However, the circumstances soon become busier, and the ships and cranes move in a kind of absurd dance; night falls. The chimneys begin to smoke, lights radiate, cooling towers stretch black and threatening upward: the oil refinery is a factory landscape or a city. The sky is streaked with eerily beautiful smoke coming from chimneys, like the terrible beauty of an erupting volcano. This aesthetic sight strangely affects us. Later, the images become calm again; they become quiescent oil platforms in the water under a grey sky. The end seems unredeemed, horribly beautiful, the illuminated platform at night.

At the threshold to the nineteenth century, 'the sublime' was that aesthetic category that revealed itself to human beings affected by overwhelming natural impressions. In *Petrolia,* one such alarming revelation does not occur in the encounter with nature but with the industrial landscape. By means of image manipulation, this has been alienated to such an extent that it appears to be a force of nature, a ravenous or poisonous organism. The in part abrupt shift between wit and the sublime, melancholy and boredom, does not suggest that these central aesthetic categories are completely different or even contradictory, but that they each correspond with and are the other side of one another.

Wit as the other side of melancholy and socially sanctioned depression is also consciously placed in Ulu Braun's video *Südwest* (Southwest) (fig. p. 116/117). In his strategy of the accumulative, apparently indifferent course of normalising contradictions the likes of the sacred world of the mountains with mobile phone aerials or a deep-blue bay with bathing Indians, laughter gets stuck in one's throat and is twisted into something threatening and depressing: into moments in which the march of time is halted and becomes eternal, so to speak, in its tremendous presence. For instance, when the freshly hatched naked and red chick in the foreground does not stop its uncanny contortions, the jet of water continues to flow out of the hose and the helicopter drones and drones.

Having Arrived at the End—With Temporary Openings

Many of the works shown at *Lands End* with a predominately melancholy mood are designed to be immersive. Sound plays an important role in all of them, not, however, illusionism. On the contrary: illusionism is disrupted by means of various methods and the complete immersion in sound or in vision is thwarted. In the work by Sebastian Diaz Morales (see p. 154), for example, the split and inclined screen disrupts illusionism, as do the irregularly recurring black blanks on one or the other side of the screen or the facial close-ups, which have the appearance of being a break in the sequence. In Michaela Schwentner's video *Bellevue* (fig. p. 135) it is the poor resolution of the images that always place the technical constitution of the fogbound mountain in the foreground, as well as the music recorded in stereo, whose audibility shifts almost hectically between the one or the other speaker. In Emily Richardson's film it is the breaks between the oil platforms and the frenetic motion of the ships in quick motion. In the case of Jana Winderen's audio installation, I have to close my eyes in order not to see the speakers, and at the beginning of *Requiem for Cod,* technology is shifted into the picture and described. The technical constitution of the images and sounds in all of these works is not only not denied, but demonstrated as a constitutive part of the work and its aesthetic perception. Hence, for all of the opportunity to immerse oneself in the unfamiliar, not only a form of distance remains, but the technical constructedness or the artificial character of the negotiated landscape itself is demonstrated. Contrary to numerous such works in the history of media art, the goal of immersion is not the authentically illusionist connection with what is being depicted or with nature, but instead, the temporary opening towards a different state of being, which in the process can always be experienced as plurally fractured and artificially constructed.

In doing so, as was the case in early ecological approaches, technology is no longer the enemy of nature but is regarded as part of nature or used as a means to make what is suppressed visible and audible and arrive at a new form of communication (with fish, for example, or with electromagnetic waves, as in the *Live Wire* installations by Jan-Peter E.R. Sonntag (see p. 168) or Clemens Winkler (fig. p. 142)). These kinds of technology-friendly ecological approaches cannot only be observed in art, but have been a social phenomenon for the past fifteen years and in my opinion a symptom of the fact that dual images of the world are being eroded and new means of access to the environment are being sought.

The conscious demonstration of the media-related constitution of the respective negotiated image of landscapes not only applies for the works discussed here, but for all of those presented at *Lands End:* in Gabriela Gerber's and Lukas Bardill's video installation *Partnun 1–7* (fig. p. 135) it is the sudden interruptions in the movement of the hay loaders and the bales of hay; in Eva Castringius's series of photographs *The Great Thirst* (fig. p. 122) it is the artificially arranged pine trees at the 'wrong' places; in Achim Mohné's photo installation *Fireflies* (fig. p. 127) the 'wonderfully' and at the same time apparently scientific images of things as commonplace as dust particles; in Dirk Haupt's pictures (fig. p. 134) the reductionist manner of painting; and in Verena Maas's film *Brown* (fig. p. 128), it is the fragmented and limited depiction of an artificial adventure park. What unites all of the artists is the attempt to destroy any impression of 'naturalness' and to highlight the artificialness of the depiction as well as of the landscape being shown. They create gaps, not only between the depiction and what is being depicted, but also in the image of the landscape being presented. Yet these gaps produce not only chasms, they also generate spaces, imaginary spaces that, for all of our melancholy, throw us back on ourselves and cause us to question our conduct.

Translated by Rebecca van Dyck

hinzukommen, nämlich Witz und Erhabenheit. Das Video beginnt mit der Ansicht einer Ölplattform und vorbeikreuzenden Schiffen. Bald schon werden die Verhältnisse geschäftiger, und die Schiffe und Kräne bewegen sich in einer Art von absurdem Tanz, es wird Nacht. Die Schlote beginnen zu rauchen, Beleuchtungen strahlen, Kühltürme recken sich schwarz und bedrohlich in die Höhe: Die Erdölraffinerie ist eine Fabriklandschaft oder Stadt. Die rauchenden Schlote zucken schaurig-schön, wie die schreckliche Schönheit beim Ausbruch eines Vulkans. Wir werden seltsam getroffen von diesem ästhetischen Anblick. Später werden die Bilder wieder ruhig, sie werden zur bei grauem Wetter still daliegenden Erdölplattform im Wasser. Das Ende erscheint unerlöst, grausamschön, die erleuchtete Plattform bei Nacht.

Das Erhabene war jene ästhetische Kategorie an der Schwelle des 18./19. Jahrhunderts, das sich dem Menschen beim Getroffenwerden durch überwältigende Natureindrücke offenbarte. In *Petrolia* geschieht eine solche erschreckende Offenbarung nicht in der Begegnung mit der Natur, sondern mit der Industrielandschaft. Diese ist mittels Bildmanipulationen so verfremdet, dass sie wie eine gewaltige Natur, wie ein gefrässiger oder giftiger Organismus erscheint. Die teilweise abrupten Wechsel zwischen Witz und Erhabenheit, Melancholie und Langeweile lassen diese zentralen ästhetischen Kategorien nicht als völlig unterschiedliche oder gar sich widersprechende erkennen, sondern als deren jeweilige Entsprechungen und Kehrseiten.

Der Witz als die Kehrseite der Melancholie und der gesellschaftlich sanktionierten Depression wird auch in Ulu Brauns Video *Südwest* (Abb. S. 116/117) bewusst gesetzt. Bei seiner Strategie des kumulativen, scheinbar gleich-gültigen Ablaufs von so normalisierten Widersprüchen wie heile Bergwelt mit Handyantenne oder tiefblaue Meeresbucht und darin sich waschende Inder_innen bleibt einem das Lachen im Hals stecken und verkehrt sich in etwas Bedrohliches und Schwer(mütig)es: In Momente, in denen sich die Zeit still stellt und in ihrer unerhörten Präsenz gleichsam ewig wird. So etwa, wenn das frisch geschlüpfte, nackte und rote Küken im Vordergrund nicht aufhört, sich unheimlich zu

winden, der Wasserstrahl aus dem Schlauch immer weiter fliesst und der Hubschrauber dröhnt und dröhnt.

Am Ende angelangt – mit temporären Öffnungen

Viele der bei *Lands End* gezeigten Arbeiten, bei denen eine melancholische Stimmung vorherrscht, sind immersiv angelegt. Bei allen spielt der Ton eine wichtige Rolle, nicht jedoch der Illusionismus. Im Gegenteil, ein solcher wird durch verschiedene Verfahren gestört und ein vollkommenes Aufgehen in Sound und Vision durchkreuzt. Bei Sebastian Diaz Morales (vgl. S. 154) etwa stören die Zweiteilung und Schrägstellung der Screens den Illusionismus, aber auch die unregelmässig wiederkehrenden schwarzen Leerstellen auf der einen oder anderen Seite der Screens oder die Nahaufnahmen des Gesichts, die wie ein Bruch in der Abfolge erscheinen; bei Michaela Schwentners Video *Bellevue* (Abb. S. 135) sind es die zu schlecht aufgelösten Bilder, die stets die technische Verfasstheit des Nebelgebirges in den Vordergrund stellen sowie die Stereoaufnahme der Musik, deren Hörbarkeit fast schon hektisch zwischen dem einen oder anderen Lautsprecher abwechselt. Bei Emily Richardson sind es die Brüche zwischen der daliegenden Erdölplattform und den hektisch herumfahrenden Schiffen in erkennbarer Zeitraffertechnik. Bei Jana Winderen muss ich die Augen schliessen, um die Lautsprecher nicht zu sehen, und bei *Requiem for Cod* wird zu Beginn die Technik ins Bild gerückt und erklärt. In allen diesen Arbeiten wird die technische Verfasstheit der gezeigten Bilder und Töne nicht nur nicht verleugnet, sondern als konstitutiver Teil der Arbeit und ihrer ästhetischen Wahrnehmung vorgeführt. Somit bleibt bei aller Möglichkeit zum Eintauchen ins Unbekannte nicht nur eine Form der Distanz, sondern es wird auch die technische Konstruiertheit bzw. der artifizielle Charakter der verhandelten Landschaft selbst vorgeführt. Das Ziel der Immersion ist – ganz im Gegenteil zu vielen solcher Arbeiten aus der Geschichte der Medienkunst – nicht die authentisch-illusionistische Verbindung mit dem Dargestellten bzw. der Natur, sondern vielmehr die temporäre Öffnung auf einen anderen Seins-

Zustand hin, der dabei immer als vielfach gebrochener und artifiziell konstituierter erlebbar wird.

Die Technik ist dabei nicht mehr, so wie in früheren ökologischen Ansätzen, der Feind der Natur, sondern sie wird als Teil davon gesehen bzw. als Mittel genutzt, Verdrängtes sicht- und hörbar zu machen und zu einer neuen Form der Kommunikation (z.B. mit Fischen, oder wie etwa bei Jan-Peter E. R. Sonntag (vgl. S. 168) oder Clemens Winkler (Abb. S. 142) in der Ausstellung *Unter Strom* mit elektromagnetischen Wellen) zu gelangen. Solche technikfreundlichen Öko-Ansätze lassen sich nicht nur in der Kunst beobachten, vielmehr sind sie ein gesellschaftliches Phänomen der letzten 15 Jahre und m.E. ein Symptom dafür, dass duale Weltbilder erodiert und neue Zugänge zur Umwelt gesucht werden.

Das bewusste Vorführen der medialen Verfasstheit des jeweils verhandelten Bilds von Landschaften gilt nicht nur für die hier besprochenen, sondern für alle der in *Lands End* gezeigten Arbeiten: In Gabriela Gerber/Lukas Bardills Videoinstallation *Partnun 1–7* (Abb. S. 135) sind es die plötzlichen Unterbrechungen in den Bewegung der Heulader und Heuballen, in Eva Castringius' Fotoserie *The Great Thirst* (Der Grosse Durst) (Abb. S. 122) die für das Foto künstlich arrangierten Tännchen an ‚falschen' Orten, in Achim Mohnés Fotoinstallation *Fireflies* (Abb. S. 127) die ‚wunderschön' und zugleich wissenschaftlich anmutenden Bilder solch banaler Dinge wie Staubpartikel, in Dirk Haupts Bildern (Abb. S. 134) ist es die reduktionistische Malweise, die Darstellungsweisen computererzeugter Naturbilder imitiert, und in Verena Maas' Videofilm *Brown* (Abb. S. 128) die fragmentierte und limitierende Darstellung der künstlichen Erlebnisparks: Alle Künstler_innen eint der Versuch, jeglichen Eindruck von ‚Natürlichkeit' zu zerstören und die Künstlichkeit sowohl der Darstellung als auch der gezeigten Landschaft hervorzuheben. Sie schaffen Lücken, nicht nur zwischen Darstellung und Dargestelltem, sondern auch im vorgeführten Landschaftsbild. Doch diese Lücken schaffen nicht nur Klüfte, sondern sie erzeugen auch Räume, imaginäre Räume, die uns – bei aller Melancholie – auf uns zurückwerfen und die Frage nach unserem Tun eröffnen.

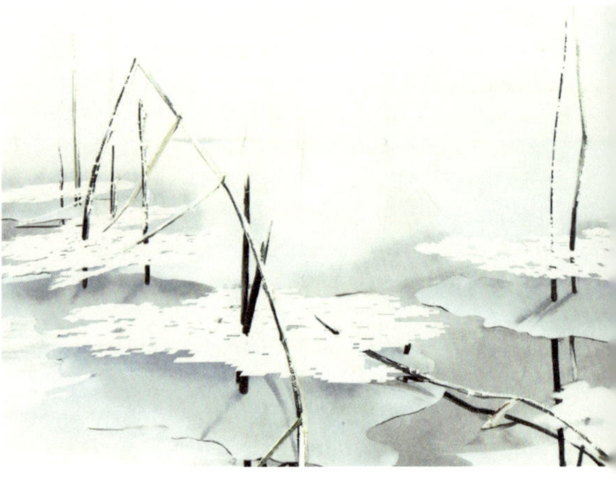

Dirk Haupt: *Frost 2*, 2008
(Ausstellungsansicht / Exhibition view)

Michaela Schwentner: *Bellevue*, 2008

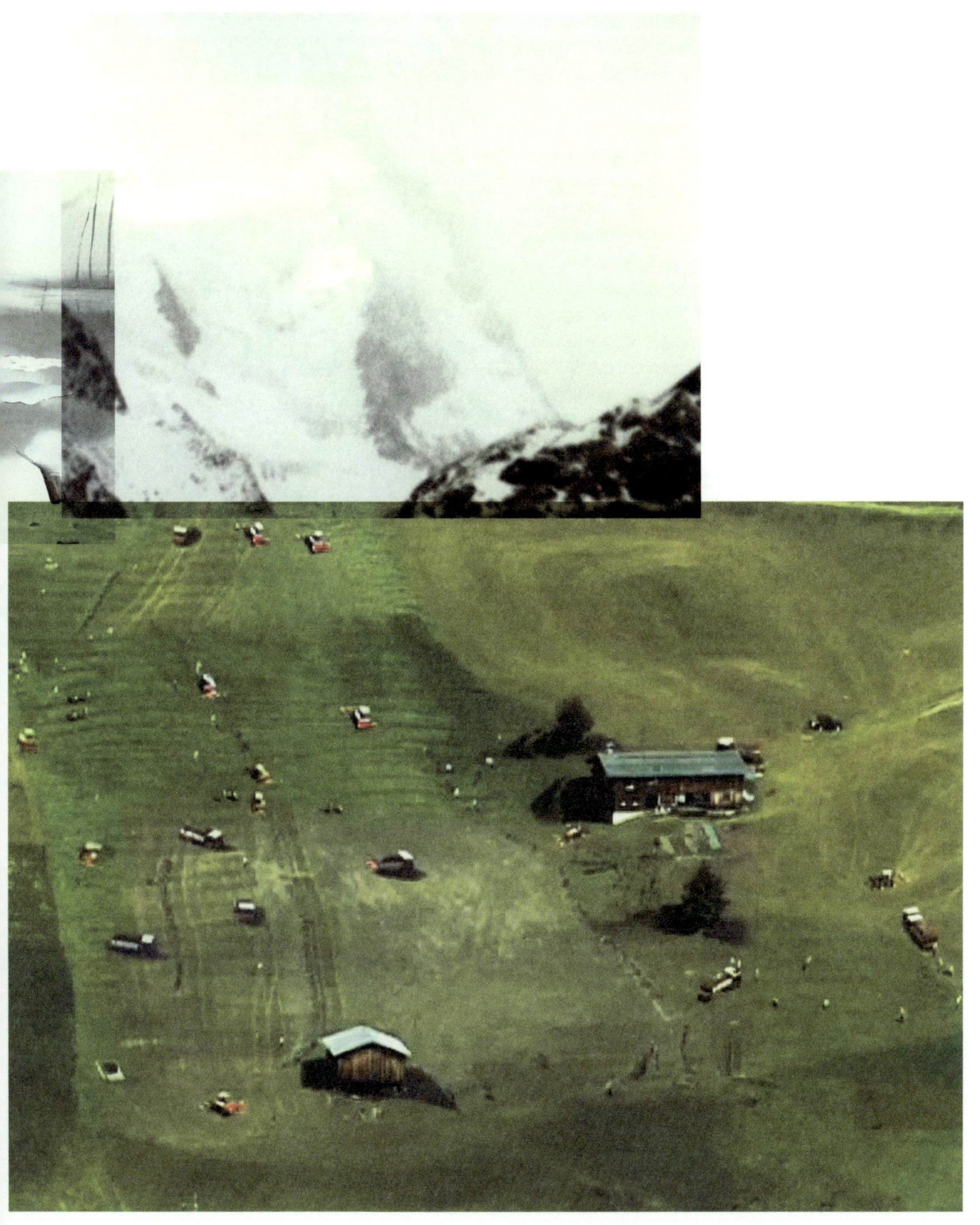

Gabriela Gerber/Lukas Bardill: *Partnun 1–7*, 2008

ANKE HOFFMANN

ZUR AUSSTELLUNG *UNTER STROM.* WIE UNSICHTBARKEIT ZU TRÜGERISCHEN SELBSTVERSTÄNDLICHKEITEN VERLEITET

ON THE EXHIBITION *LIVE WIRE.* HOW THEIR INVISIBILITY TREACHEROUSLY MISLEADS US TO TAKE THINGS FOR GRANTED

Santo Domingo, Dominikanische Republik: Ein wackliges Bild zeigt einen Mann, der auf einen Elektromast klettert, um mittels eines einfachen dicken Drahtes Strom von einer Überlandleitung abzuleiten. Es ist eines von unzähligen Videos auf YouTube unter dem Stichwort ‚Stealing Electricity', bei denen Menschen beobachtet werden, wie sie auf lebensgefährliche Art Stromleitungen anzapfen – lebensgefährlich für sie selbst und für andere. Stealing Electricity ist eine Reaktion auf infrastrukturelles Chaos und ein Armuts-Phänomen. Während Deutschland und die Schweiz über die Aufrechterhaltung der Energieversorgung nach dem Atomausstieg debattieren, leben 1.5 Milliarden Menschen auf der Welt ganz ohne Elektrizität und eine weitere Milliarde ohne stabile Stromversorgung. Die Dominikanische Republik, ein sonnenverwöhntes Land in der Karibik, hat grosse Probleme, seinen Bedarf an elektrischer Energie zu decken. Die Ursachen hierfür sind vielschichtig, reichen von teuren Brennstoffimporten, über ineffektive Wasserkraftwerke infolge der Abholzung von Wäldern und lokaler Klimaveränderung, einem schlechtem Zustand von Kraftwerken und Stromnetzen bis hin zum steigenden Energieverbrauch infolge klimatisch unangepasster Betonbauweise (Häuser mit Klimaanlagen). Stealing Electricity ist eine Folge davon. Nicht nur in der Dominikanischen Republik, auch in Südafrika oder Brasilien helfen sich die Menschen auf diese lebensgefährliche Weise einfach selbst. Diese entbehrungsreichen Lebensformen sind mit unseren in Mitteleuropa kaum zu vergleichen, fehlt es den Menschen doch an Licht und Kommunikationstechnologie.

Der Gesamtstromverbrauch in der Schweiz, inklusive der Industrie, ist sechs Mal so hoch wie der von Mosambik, und jener der USA sechs Mal so hoch wie der von Indien. Und obwohl Elektroenergie anders als Erdöl, Erdgas oder Wasser nicht allein von den Verfügbarkeiten abhängt (siehe das Beispiel Dominikanische Republik), ähneln sich die Verteilungsmechanismen dieser Ressourcen frappierend. Westliche Industrienationen profitieren unverhältnismässig vom globalen Ungleichgewicht im Hinblick auf die landesweite Elektrifizierung, die so zentral

Santo Domingo, Dominican Republic: A blurred picture shows a man climbing a utility pole to collect power from an overhead power cable by means of a simple heavy wire. It is one of the vast number of videos you can find on YouTube under the heading 'Stealing Electricity', videos depicting people tapping power lines, threatening their lives and the lives of others. Stealing electricity is a reaction to infrastructural chaos and a phenomenon of poverty. While Germany and Switzerland are debating how to maintain the supply of power after the nuclear power phase-out, 1.5 billion people on earth still have to get by without any electricity at all, and another billion without a stable power supply.

The Dominican Republic, a sun-kissed country in the Caribbean region, has tremendous problems in meeting its energy needs. The causes are complex, ranging from expensive fuel imports, ineffective hydropower stations because of deforestation and local climate changes, the poor condition of power plants and mains to increasing energy consumption because of climatically inadequate concrete construction technology (air-conditioned housing). Stealing electricity is one of the consequences. But not only in the Dominican Republic, people in South Africa or Brazil also help themselves in this perilous way. Their deprived life forms cannot be compared to life forms in Central Europe at all since the people lack light and communication technology.

In Switzerland, the overall consumption of power, including industrial needs, is six times of Mozambique, and the consumption of power in the US is six times of India. And though electric energy, unlike mineral oil, natural gas, or water, does not depend on availability only (like in the Dominican Republic), the mechanisms of the distribution of these resources are strikingly similar. Western industrial nations disproportionally profit from the global imbalance in the comprehensive supply of electric energy that is so important for the prosperity and economic development of a country. The causes are complex and demonstrate historic privileges. The fact, however, that power

consumption in OECD countries and non-OECD countries during the past ten years has almost become the same[1] not only proves the increase in overall energy demand, but also an increase in the fight for much needed resources, be it mineral resources or the technological advance in the development of sustainable concepts for power production. Stealing electricity is a phenomenon rendering the global imbalance in the distribution of power visible and questioning the intransparent dependency between winners and losers that is not being sufficiently discussed in public.

Even if the UN, declaring 2012 the 'International Year of Sustainable Energy for All', calls for an equal status for all nations, existing structures of privileges remain unaffected. Above all, the departure from fossil energy carriers intended by some industrial nations and the call for an immediate energy turnaround displeases turbo-capitalists and the New Global Players. The 2000-Watt-Society propagated in Switzerland, which aims at a reduction of private energy consumption and thus a change in personal, in individual habits, certainly does not suffice as a plea for sustainable changes in attitudes towards things we take for granted. 'Furthermore, the uncontested position of growth also obviates the need to develop a Plan B—such as a vision for a controlled-growth or post-growth society. ... The fact that all parties lack an alternative to growth not only underscores how unassailable the concept has become, it also shows that the development of alternative strategies for a sustainable world threatens existing economic and social forms',[2] as Harald Welzer, sociologist and socio-psychologist, notes. Electric power is considered the precondition of all economic growth—growth being one of the concepts shaped by the modern industrial era, like mobility and progress, that have penetrated the smallest nooks of our world and are integral parts of our mental

[1] .... Cf. e.g. www.oecd.org/document/37/0,3746,
de_34968570_39907066_39142821_1_1_1_1,00.html.
[2] ...... Harald Welzer, 'Mental Infrastructures. How Growth Entered the World and Our Souls', in Heinrich Böll Stiftung (ed.), *Writings on Ecology*, 14 (Berlin, 2011) p. 10.

and emotional lives.[3] To change our attitudes we need alternative concepts, different stories and utopias, new 'mental infrastructures' (Welzer) which reformulate the current definitions of happiness, success and satisfaction, which do not simply relate them to loss and limitation but to pleasure and enhancement. 'Thinking of what's needed to lead "a good life" and how these resources can be made available by today's technologies, there is enough around for everybody. The problem is not the size of the population but that one part of mankind consumes way too much',[4] thus Marcel Hänggi, journalist and environmentalist, pleading for a radical change in our attitudes and lifestyles, not only a change regarding possible technological and economical solutions of the problems. The threat of peak oil, the disillusionment triggered by several nuclear accidents that could be called MCAs, maximum credible accidents, climate change, and, last but not least, the necessity of equal opportunity globally call for alternative visions with regard to energy supply and demand, call for 'exit strategies from growth, not to preserve a cultural practice that undermines our own survival conditions'[5].

Having the same critical view on things taken for granted in our affluent society and the need for a change of paradigms with regard to growth, Yvonne Volkart and I felt the urge to make electricity the subject of an exhibition. Our interest in electricity as 'invisible energy' was combined with an extreme aesthetic fascination and our interest in the mysteries involved in this natural phenomenon, which we actually know very little about despite our dependency on it and the use we make of it in everyday life. Of course we could not foresee that our exhibition would coincide with the accident in the nuclear power reactor in Fukushima-Daiichi in Japan, in March 2011, exactly 25 years after the disaster in Chernobyl. The MCA in Fukushima finally brought an end to the dream of 'clean atomic energy', and

instigated the exit strategies of the parliaments in Germany and in Switzerland.

Our exhibition project *Live Wire. Art and Electricity* focused on electric power as an invisible medium; discussing it depends on mediation and translation. The artists invited explored the manifold dimensions of the aesthetics and the functions as well as the theory of science or the physiology of perception of electricity and expressed them in widely differing media. Open-mindedly, *Live Wire* wanted to draw attention to the usually neglected aspects of what is unintelligible or hidden in the electricity we use daily as well as to the artistic and the disturbing aspects involved in electric power. The artists' works exhibited encompassed their investigation of economic and political problems, the contradictions involved in energy production as well as the still fascinating aspects of the inexplicability of electricity.

Terra Incognita

We tend to take electric power for granted. But do we understand what electricity actually is? The natural phenomenon, the physical and chemical processes, can be described—but these descriptions are still models of something ineffable like electrons or ether. This inexpressibility involves all the senses; its auditory, haptic or visual aspects have been the focus of its exploration right from the beginning. Christina Hemauer and Roman Keller re-enact one of these discoveries, the early telegraph, invented by Don Francisco Salvá y Campillo around 1795. In their performance at the opening of the exhibition and the video installation *Die Unfreiheit der Elektronen* (The Unfreeness of Electrons) produced at the same time, 22 volunteers act as human semaphores (see p. 176).

One of the most renowned inventors in the field of electrical engineering certainly is Nikola Tesla (1856–1953), whose inventions concerning the wireless transmission of energy have been the subject of the work of artist Jan-Peter E.R. Sonntag for years. Sonntag's installations *Natural-Radio-Wave-Trap* and parts of the

3 .... Ibid, p. 34.
4 .... Marcel Hänggi, *Ausgepowert. Das Ende des Ölzeitalters als Chance* (Zürich, 2011) p. 13.
5 .... Harald Welzer, 'Mental Infrastructures', p. 38.

ist für die Wirtschafts- und Wohlstandsentwicklung. Die Ursachen dafür sind komplexer Natur und manifestieren den historischen Vorteil. Die Tatsache jedoch, dass sich der Stromverbrauch in den OECD-Staaten und den Nicht-OECD-Staaten in den letzten zehn Jahren mehr und mehr angeglichen hat, bestätigt nicht nur den Trend der Zunahme des gesamten Energiebedarfs[1], sondern auch eine Zunahme des Kampfes um eine begehrte Ressource, sei es in Form von Bodenschätzen oder von technologischem Vorsprung bei der Entwicklung nachhaltiger Energieerzeugungskonzepte. Stealing Electricity ist ein Phänomen, das die weltweiten Verteilungsungerechtigkeiten sichtbar macht und ein intransparentes Abhängigkeitsverhältnis zwischen Gewinnern und Verlierern hinterfragt, das öffentlich zu wenig diskutiert wird. Auch wenn die UNO mit dem für 2012 ausgerufenen ‚Jahr der erneuerbaren Energie für alle' eine Gleichberechtigungsthese postuliert, werden die bestehenden Strukturen von Privilegierung und Bevorteilung nicht angetastet. Die vor allem von einigen Industrienationen vertretene Position einer Abkehr von fossilen Energieträgern und sofortigen Energiewende stösst dann verständlicherweise auch auf das Missfallen von Turbokapitalisten und den New Global Players. Die in der Schweiz propagierte 2000-Watt-Gesellschaft, die auf eine Drosselung des privaten Energieverbrauches und damit auf ein wichtiges Umdenkens abzielt, ist als Einzelmassnahme aber kein ausreichendes Plädoyer für eine nachhaltige Veränderung im Umgang mit vermeintlichen Selbstverständlichkeiten.

„Die Alleinstellung des Wachstumskonzepts erfüllt nicht zuletzt auch die Funktion, keinen Plan B – also etwa den einer wachstumsbefriedeten oder Postwachstums-Gesellschaft – entwickeln zu müssen. […] Das Fehlen jeglicher Alternative zum Wachstumskonzept [...] macht nicht nur einmal mehr seinen sakrosanten Charakter deutlich, sondern zeigt zugleich an, dass die Entwicklung alternativer Strategien zur Erreichung und Aufrechterhaltung zukunftstauglicher Lebensverhältnisse sofort die bestehende Wirtschafts- und Gesellschaftsform in Frage zu stellen droht"[2], reflektiert der Soziologe und Sozialpsychologe Harald Welzer. Strom gilt als Voraussetzung jeglichen Wirtschaftswachstums – und Wachstum ist eines der Konzepte, das ähnlich wie Mobilität und Fortschritt unsere Deutungsmuster, Routinen, unseren Habitus organisiert.[3] Um diesen Habitus zu verändern, benötigt es alternative Vorstellungen, Gegengeschichten und Utopien, neue „mentale Infrastrukturen" (Welzer), die die geübten Definitionen von Glück, Erfolg und Zufriedenheit anders erzählen und dies nicht einseitig mit Verlust und Einschränkung belegen, sondern mit Lust und Erweiterung beleben. „Geht man davon aus, was ein Mensch für ein ‚gutes Leben' braucht und wie diese Ressourcen mit den heute verfügbaren Techniken bereitgestellt werden können, so gibt es genug für alle. Nicht die Bevölkerungsgröße ist das Problem, sondern, dass ein Teil der Menschen viel zu viel verbraucht"[4], argumentiert der Umweltjournalist Marcel Hänggi und plädiert für einen radikalen Wechsel im Denken und in unserer Lebensweise, jenseits von technologischen und ökonomischen Problemlösungen. Drohender Peakoil, die Entzauberung der Technologie durch nukleare Super-GAUs, der Klimawandel und nicht zuletzt die Notwendigkeit einer globalen Chancengleichheit erfordern Zukunftsalternativen der Energieversorgung und des Energiebedarfs, „Exit-Strategien aus dem Wachstum, nicht [...] das Konservieren einer kulturellen Praxis, die ihre eigenen Überlebensbedingungen unterminiert"[5].

Dieser kritischen Betrachtung unserer Wohlstands-Selbstverständlichkeiten und einem Paradigmenwechsel von Wachstumsmaximen folgend, war es uns, Yvonne Volkart und mir, ein Bedürfnis in der Shedhalle eine Ausstellung zum Thema Strom zu machen. Das Interesse, sich mit Elektrizität als ‚unsichtbare Kraft' auseinanderzusetzen, verband sich dabei auch und vor allem mit einer besonderen ästhetischen

1 .... Vgl. z.B. www.oecd.org/document/37/0,3746, de_34968570_39907066_39142821_1_1_1_1,00.html.

2 .... Welzer, Harald: Mentale Infrastrukturen. Wie das Wachstum in die Welt und in die Seelen kam. In: Heinrich Böll Stiftung (Hg.): *Schriften zur Ökologie*. Band 14, Berlin 2011, 11.
3 .... Vgl. Welzer: *Mentale Infrastrukturen*, 38.
4 .... Hänggi, Marcel: *Ausgepowert. Das Ende des Ölzeitalters als Chance*. Zürich 2011, 13.
5 .... Welzer: *Mentale Infrastrukturen*, 42.

Faszination und dem Geheimnisvollen einer natürlichen Kraft, von dem wir trotz des alltäglichen
Gebrauchs so wenig wissen. Koinzidenz hatte
unser Ausstellungsprojekt in seiner Vorbereitung
mit dem erschütternden Unfall im japanischen
KKW Fukushima-Daiichi im März 2011, exakt
25 Jahre nach der radioaktiven Katastrophe in
Tschernobyl. Der Super-GAU in Fukushima
hat den Traum von der ‚sauberen Energie' endgültig beendet und die Parlamente in Deutschland
und der Schweiz zu Ausstiegsplänen aus der
Atomenergie bewegt.

Unser Ausstellungsprojekt *Unter Strom. Kunst
und Elektrizität* beschäftigte sich mit Strom
und Elektrizität als sich der Sichtbarkeit entzie-
hendes Medium, deren Verhandlung immer einer
medialen Sprache, einer medialen Übersetzung
bedarf. So waren es die Künstler_innen der
Ausstellung, die den vielfältigen Dimensionen des
Ästhetischen, Funktionalen, Wissenschaftstheo-
retischen oder Wahrnehmungsphysiologischen
von Elektrizität nachgingen und unterschiedliche
mediale Sprachen dafür entwickelten. *Unter
Strom* wollte mit Offenheit und ungewohnten
Perspektiven auf das Verborgene und
Unverständliche des Gebrauchsmediums Elektroenergie aufmerksam machen und den Blick
für die inhärenten künstlerischen Qualitäten
und das dem Strom innewohnende Verstörende
wiederbeleben. Die Zusammenstellung der
künstlerischen Arbeiten umfasste sowohl
die Auseinandersetzung mit ökonomischen und
politischen Fragen und Widersprüchen der
Energieerzeugung als auch die bis heute faszin-
ierenden Aspekte des Unverständlichen von
Elektrizität.

Terra Incognita

Strom ist uns zur Gewohnheit geworden. Aber wer
von uns versteht eigentlich wirklich, was das ist,
Elektrizität? Das natürliche Phänomen kann
in seinen physikalischen und chemischen Prozessen beschrieben werden und dennoch sind diese
Beschreibungen – wie zum Beispiel die von
Elektronen oder des Äthers – Modelle von etwas
Unbeschreibbarem. Dass dieses Unbeschreib-
bare sinnliche, auditive, haptische und visuelle

Phänomene hervorruft, war und ist ein zentraler
Gegenstand der Beschäftigung mit Elektrizität
seit ihrer frühesten Entdeckung. Einer dieser
Entdeckungen spüren Christina Hemauer und
Roman Keller in ihrem Re-Enactment des frühen
Telegrafengerätes von Don Francisco Salvá y
Campillo um 1795 nach. In der zur Eröffnung
aufgeführten Performance und der daraus
entstandenen Videoinstallation *Die Unfreiheit
der Elektronen* (vgl. S. 176) sind es 22 Freiwillige,
die als menschliche Signalträger fungieren.
Einer der bekanntesten Erfinder auf dem Gebiet
der Elektrotechnik ist zweifelsfrei Nikola Tesla
(1856–1943), mit dessen Entdeckungen der
(drahtlosen) Energieübertragung sich der Künstler Jan-Peter E.R. Sonntag seit Jahren künstlerisch auseinandersetzt. Sonntags Installationen
unter dem Titel *Natural-Radio-Wave-Trap* und
Arbeiten aus dem *WARDEN SPRITES*-Zyklus
verknüpfen die kulturtheoretische und wissen-
schaftshistorische Bedeutung der Elektrizitätsex-
perimente des 20. Jahrhunderts (vgl. S. 168).

Die partizipative Arbeit *Temporäre Präsenzen –
Freie Energien* (vgl. S. 172) von Alexander
Tuchaček (knowbotic research) bot als dialogisch
angelegtes Diskursformat während der Ausstellungseröffnung eine exo-akademische Form
der Wissensgenerierung zu Themen von Stromerzeugung, alternativen Energien, physikalischen
Fragestellungen und Zukunftsherausforderungen
an. Mittels eines vom Künstler programmierten
und installierten autonomen Mobilfunksystems
hatten sich eingeladene ‚Expert_innen' und
‚Laien' aus dem Publikum in einem multi-dialogi-
schen Gespräch und auf der Basis von verteilten
Fragekärtchen gegenseitig interviewt. Die zu-
fälligen Zweiergespräche bilden ein Audioarchiv,
das als Audioinstallation zugänglich wurde. Inhalt
der Gesprächschoreografie ist eine Sichtweise
auf elektrischen Strom und Energie, die sich
nicht in erster Linie aus einem physikalischem
Blickwinkel und einer technischen Wirkungsweise
erschliesst, sondern Fragen nach Energie und
Strom als etwas medial Konstruiertes stellt.
Im Projekt *Temporäre Präsenzen – Freie Energien*
geht es weder um Wahrheitsfindung noch um
konkrete Problemlösungen von Energiefragen,
sondern darum, einen opaken Ort zu schaffen, der
eine Repräsentation für das Unfertige, Denkbare

Julieta Aranda: *There is a heppy lend – fur, fur awa-a-ay*, 2011 (Ausstellungsansicht / Exhibition view)

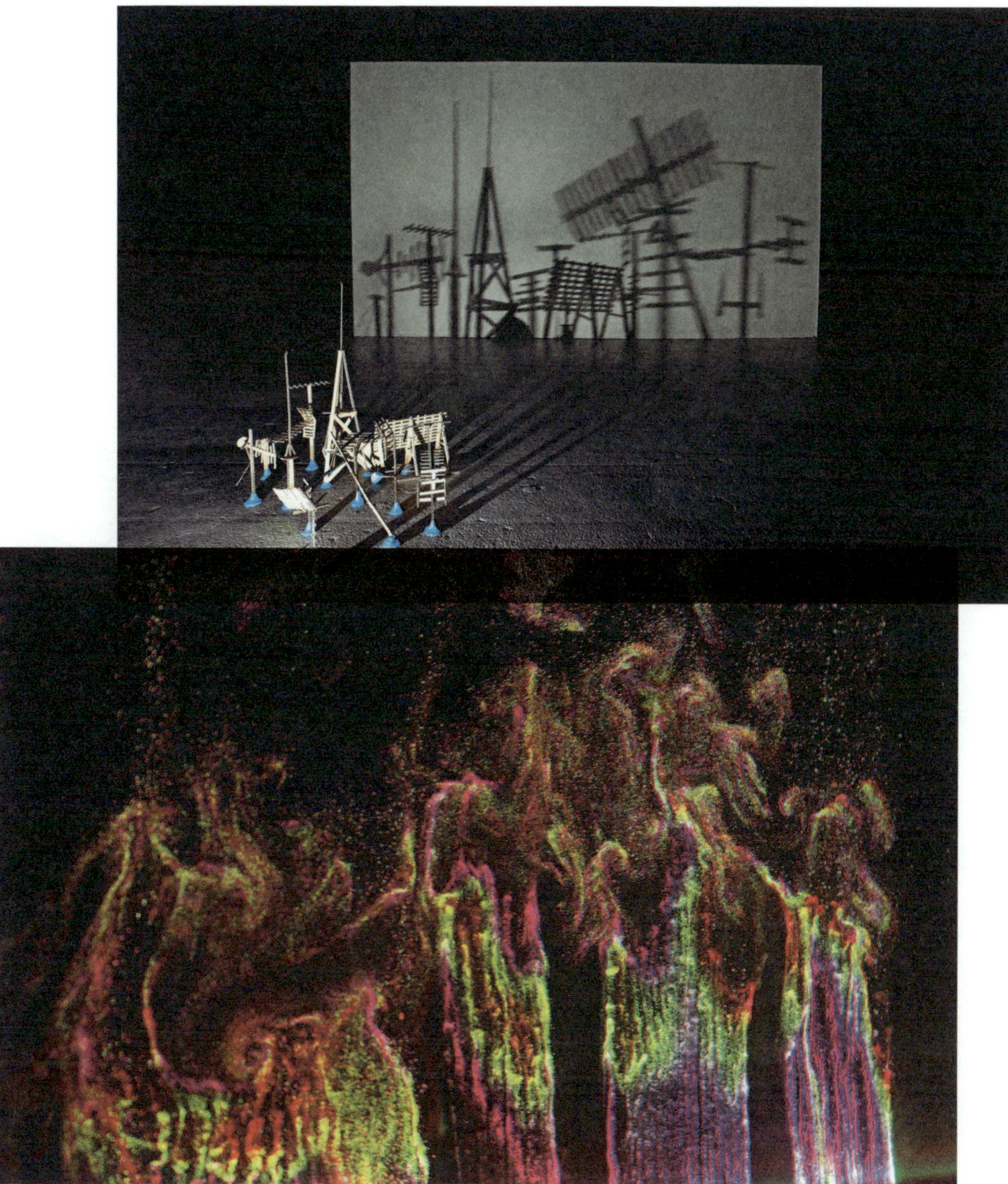

Evelina Domnitch & Dmitry Gelfand: *Hydrogeny*, 2010

Clemens Winkler: *Sense of Orientation*, 2011 (Produktionsfoto / Production photo)

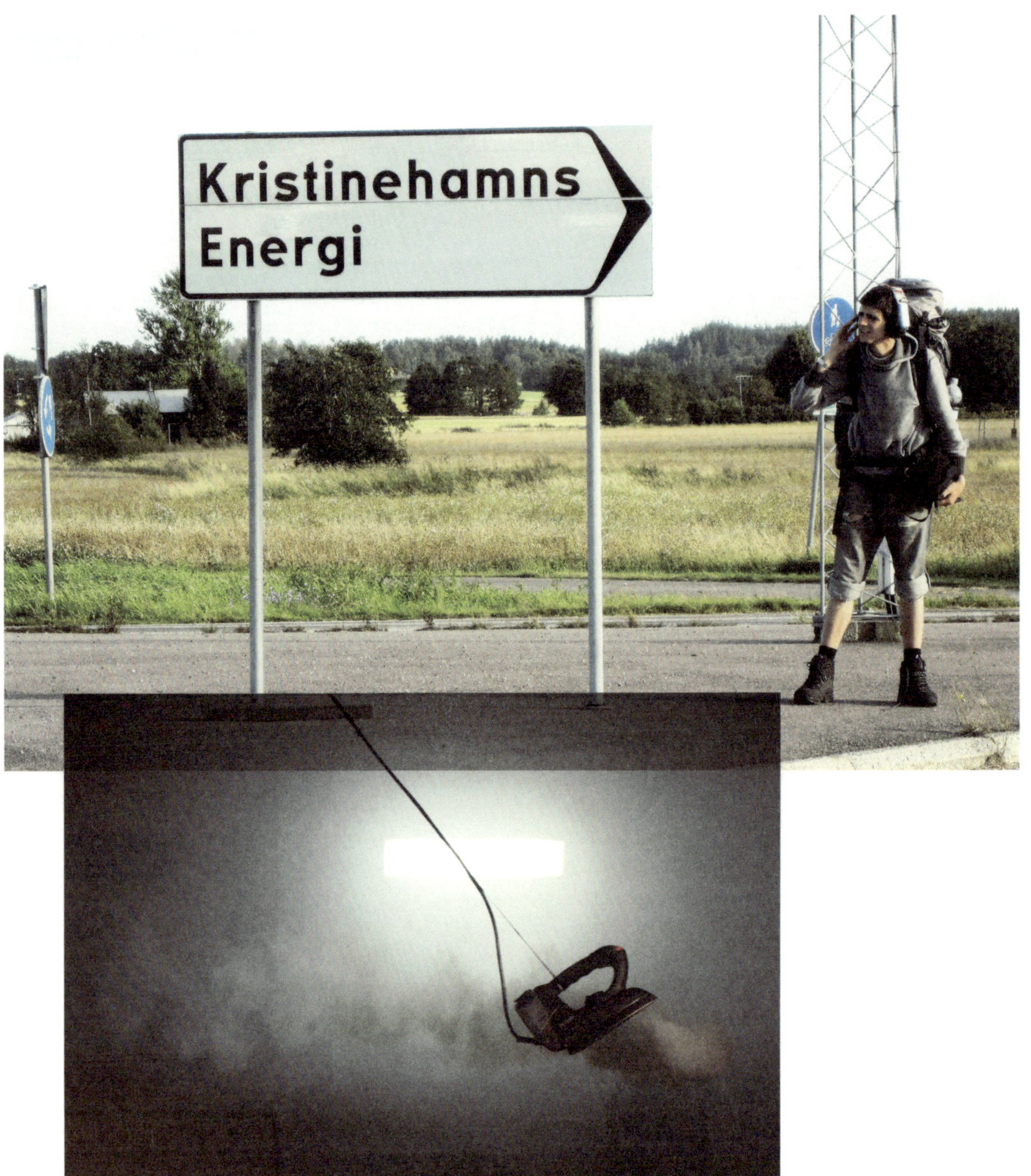

HeHe: *Catastrophes Domestiques Nº 1: Flyrony*, 2010

WARDEN SPRITES cycle aim at bringing together the cultural-theoretical aspects and the importance of the electrical experiments of the 20th century in the science of history (see p. 168).

At the opening of the exhibition, the participatory work *Temporäre Präsenzen – Freie Energien* (Temporary Presences—Free Energies) (see p. 172) by Alexander Tuchaček (knowbotic research) presented a kind of exo-academic generation of knowledge in a format based on private dialogues. Invited 'experts' and 'lay' participants in the audience were handed out questions on small cards and were asked to talk to each other about topics like power production, alternative energies, physics and future challenges by means of an autonomous mobile phone network installed by the artist. The chance dialogues formed an archive, an audio installation, which visitors could listen to during the exhibition. They were choreographed primarily according to points of view not related to physical or technical aspects of electric power and energy but raising questions concerning the way these topics are construed by the media. The project *Temporäre Präsenzen – Freie Energien* does not intend to search for any truths, nor does it try to find any specific solutions to energy problems. It tries to create an opaque scene that makes the representation of the unfinished, the thinkable or unprovable possible by having these narrations told anew, passed on and rearranged in ever new ways.

Evelina Domnitch and Dmitry Gelfand engage in the generation of knowledge in a totally different way, working with electricity as 'artist's material'. In their installation *Hydrogeny* (fig. p. 141), they stage the electrochemical process of electrolysis decomposing water molecules into hydrogen and oxygen by passing an electric current through the water, surprising the viewer by an aesthetic appropriation of scientific methods of presentation. In an aquarium they illuminate the elements set free by electrolysis by means of a laser, turning them into rainbow coloured clouds of small bubbles. This strangely beautiful spectacle intends to stage scientific approaches as possible solutions for the storage of energy:

'In the seas and oceans, the lingering presence of electromagnetic fields imparted by sunlight triggers the electrolysis responsible for most of the Earth's hydrogen. An essential form of photosynthesis, solar water splitting is the cleanest and most efficient means imaginable for generating and storing energy.'[6]

Any device, lamp, mobile telephone, any household appliance but also power supply lines produces 'electrical clouds'—electromagnetic fields. Clemens Winkler is interested in the perception of these fields and waves which surround us everywhere but which we hardly notice or take notice of. The low frequencies of these fields can be directly transformed into sound waves. Clemens Winkler hiked the Swedish landscape carrying a receiver he himself had built, which indicated the particular electric climate through acoustic signals— the droning, the humming, the buzzing, the crackling—, listening to and collecting the sounds. His acoustic room installation *Sense of Orientation* (fig. p. 142) elucidates this sensitisation of perception. The recordings of the noise of overhead wires of trains or power supply lines, or a transformer station or a hydropower station are visualised by 'lines', wires attached to loudspeakers, the frequencies are transformed into visible oscillations. The installation reveals the hidden aspects of our electrically wired everyday life. 'My vision is to transform the transcription of information into something natural, into something directly perceivable and understandable', Clemens Winkler says.

To Counter the Logic of Growth

Since the MCA in Fukushima, atomic energy and its imponderable risks are in the centre of attention again. This invisible threat is of the artist duo Ute Hörner and Mathias Antlfinger's topic. Looking at their work *Dream Water Wonderland* (see p. 166), you will get dizzy. The viewer's eye follows a swing, high up

6 ...... Evelina Domnitch and Dmitry Gelfand in a conversation with the curators, October 6, 2011.

in the air, circling the rims of a gigantic crater, the horizon swaying; you can sense the depth. The black-and-white video footage is accompanied by screaming and cheering. This dizzying carousel ride is projected into a plexiglass cube. In front of the picture, there is a strange little plastic tower on a record player, rotating incessantly. It is a 3D model of the pit Asse II in Lower Saxony (FRG) that had been in use as a final deposal site for nuclear waste and was closed in 1978 for security reasons and because of several contamination incidents. You are getting dizzier and dizzier as the object keeps circling, kept in motion by the record player, a Beogramm 4000, that was brought on the market in 1972, then a futuristic high-tech device very few could afford. It was in the same year, 1972, that one started building the 'fast breeder' reactor in Kalkar, Lower Rhine, then symbolising the promise of clean, efficient energy. Because of certain security risks and several incidents, the power station never went on line and was, in the 1990s, changed into an amusement park, where you now can get on a flying swing in the former cooling tower of the nuclear power plant. Having fun in this particular environment, which is furthermore painted with countryside idylls, unintentionally symbolises the thoughtlessness with which atomic energy is used. The seats of the merry-go-round swing as high as the tower, thus suggesting a possible tearing of the chains or someone being suddenly catapulted out of their seat. This image of a balancing act of technology, of taking risks and of dizziness is condensed to an apocalyptic dream, which is imparted to the viewer by a female voice as soon as he gets near the installation. Ute Hörner and Mathias Antlfinger mirror the former technological utopian dream as a nightmare of today's spectacle generation and question a gain in prosperity by drawing attention to its underexposed costs.

The artist duo HeHe (Helen Evans and Heiko Hansen) and their demonic installation *Catastophes Domestiques N° 1: Flyrony* (fig. p. 142) draw attention to the everyday madness involved in consuming electric power by having an iron distributing smoke rotate

above our heads. The installation *There is a heppy lend—fur, fur awa-a-ay* by Julieta Aranda (fig. p. 141) works with illuminating and darkening, with big dreams and vulnerable realities, with light and shadow. One single bulb, attached to a long wound cord lying on the floor, lights up the room installation. On the floor, there is also a group of miniature models, aerials, telegraph and utility poles made from cardboard. The small and fragile cardboard models mirror constructions of heavy steel or concrete. After a couple of minutes the light goes out, leaving the room in darkness. Then, on the opposite wall, large dark shadows of an antenna farm are silhouetted against the wall, gleaming weakly. A simulated power failure. Electricity is the basis of present day communication and entertainment: no TV, no iPhone, no iPad, no e-mail without electricity. By means of modern high-tech devices we have become very flexible and very mobile, we can save a lot of time. But how often do we have to recharge our devices? How dependent have we become—on a little power outlet? How dependent on technical devices to be part of social networks? Aranda's symbolic 'turning off' brings this precarious covenant with technology to mind. *There is a heppy lend—fur, fur awa-a-ay,* a flawed slogan of confidence indicating that we could save the world by progress and growth. Aranda's interpretation makes our technological dominance over natural resources a house of cards that seems more fragile and volatile than a shadow.

Do It Yourself, or: Why Talking About It Is But a First Step

'[T]he seekers of the 21st century [for a post-growth society] must therefore think in terms of reversibility, fault tolerance, small scales and attentiveness. Their utopia will be compartmentalized, not all encompassing, yet because it will consist of numerous small elements, and for that very reason, it will be possible to realize it *immediately*, as shown by many practical projects that have transformed our reality..'[7]

7 .... Harald Welzer, 'Mental Infrastractures', p. 37.

oder nicht Beweisbare möglich macht, in dem diese Wissensgeschichten neu formuliert, weiter erzählt und immer neu zusammengefügt werden können.

Wissensgenerierung auf eine ganz andere Weise, nämlich als Arbeit mit Elektrizität als ‚Kunstmaterial' selbst, widmen sich Evelina Domnitch und Dmitry Gelfand. In ihrer Installation *Hydrogeny* (Abb. S. 141) inszenieren sie den elektrochemischen Prozess der Elektrolyse von Wasser, die mittels elektrischer Spannung Wassermoleküle in Wasserstoff und Sauerstoff trennt, und überraschen mit einer ästhetischen Aneignung von naturwissenschaftlichen Darstellungsmethoden. In einem Aquarium wird die Freisetzung der Elemente, die bei der Elektrolyse getrennt werden, von einem Laser als regenbogenfarbene Bläschenwolken illuminiert. Mit diesem wunderlich-schönen Schauspiel inszenieren die Künstler_innen verborgene wissenschaftliche Labormethoden als mögliche Überlegungen von Energiespeicherung:

„Die anhaltende Präsenz der vom Sonnenlicht herrührenden elektromagnetischen Felder löst in den Meeren die Elektrolyse aus, die den grössten Teil des Wasserstoffs der Erde produziert. Wasserspaltung durch Sonnenenergie, eine grundlegende Form der Photosynthese, ist die sauberste und effizienteste Möglichkeit der Erzeugung und Speicherung von Energie, die man sich vorstellen kann."[6]

Jedes Gerät, Lampe, Mobiltelefon, Haushaltsmaschine, aber auch Stromleitungen produzieren ‚elektrische Wolken' – elektromagnetische Wechselfelder. Clemens Winklers Interesse gilt der Wahrnehmung von diesen Feldern und Wellen, die uns überall in der Luft umgeben, die wir selbst aber kaum wahrnehmen. Die niedrigen Frequenzen dieser Felder können direkt in Schallwellen umgewandelt werden. Winkler ist mit einem selbstgebauten Empfänger, der durch akustische Signale das jeweilige Elektroklima anzeigt, durch die Landschaft Schwedens gewandert und hat dabei das Brummen und Rauschen,

das Surren und Knacken, das ihm begegnete, gesammelt. In der akustischen Rauminstallation *Sense of Orientation* (Abb. S. 142) wird diese Wahrnehmungssensibilisierung nachvollziehbar. Die akustischen Aufnahmen von elektrischen Zugoberleitungen und Starkstromleitungen, vom Umspannwerk, einer Transformatorenstation und einem Wasserkraftwerk werden mit ‚Leitungen' visualisiert, die an Lautsprechern angebracht sind und so die Frequenzen in sichtbare Schwingungen übertragen. Die Installation bringt das Verborgene unseres elektrisch verkabelten Alltags zu Tage. „Meine Vision ist es, die Transkribierung von Informationen ins Natürliche, in das Versteh- und direkt Wahrnehmbare zu überführen. Ich möchte einen Rahmen schaffen, in dem man sich verhalten kann", unterstreicht Clemens Winkler.

Wider die Wachstumslogiken

Atomenergie ist mit ihren unkalkulierbaren Risiken seit dem Super-GAU im KKW Fukushima erneut ins Zentrum der Aufmerksamkeit gerückt. Die Arbeit des Künstlerpaares Ute Hörner und Mathias Antlfinger macht diese unsichtbare Bedrohung zum Thema. Das Betrachten der Arbeit *Dream Water Wonderland* (vgl. S. 166) erzeugt Schwindel. Das Auge folgt einer Schaukel, die hoch und knapp über dem Rand eines riesigen Kraters kreist, der Horizont schwankt, die Tiefe ist zu erahnen. Kreischen und Jauchzen begleiten die schwarz-weissen Videobilder. Die Schwindel erzeugende Karussellfahrt wird in einen Plexiglaskubus projiziert. Direkt vor dem Bild steckt ein eigenartiger Kunststoffturm auf einem Plattenspieler, der sich unermüdlich dreht und sich bis unter das Gerät verlängert. Es ist das 3D-Objekt der Schachtanlage Asse II in Niedersachsen (D), das als Atommüll-Endlager genutzt und 1978 aufgrund von Sicherheitsbedenken und Kontaminierungsvorfällen geschlossen wurde. Das Objekt dreht sich im Kreis, den Schwindel verstärkend, angetrieben von einem Plattenspieler, einem Beogram 4000, der 1972 auf den Markt kam und damals ein fast unerschwingliches futuristisches Hochtechnologiegerät war. 1972 wurde auch mit der Umsetzung eines anderen technologischen Versprechens begonnen, dem der sauberen effizienten Energie, in Form des Kernkraftwerks Schneller Brüter in Kalkar, Niederrhein. Das Werk ging nach gehäuften Sicherheitsrisiken nie ans Netz und wurde in den 1990er Jahren in einen Vergnügungspark umgebaut, wo man nun im ehemaligen Kühlturm des KKW ein Kettenkarussell besteigen kann. Dieser Spass im ungewöhnlichen Ambiente, zumal bemalt mit einer Naturidylle, symbolisiert ungewollt die Gedankenlosigkeit, mit der Atomenergie lange genutzt wurde und wird. Das Karussell schwingt seine Schaukeln in die Höhe der Turmwände, das Reissen der Ketten oder plötzliche Herausgeworfenwerden evozierend. Dieses Bild von technischer Gratwanderung, vom Spiel mit dem Risiko und vom Schwindelgefühl wird zu einem apokalyptischen Traum verdichtet, der ertönt, sobald man sich der Installation nähert. Ute Hörner und Mathias Antlfinger spiegeln die einstige technologische Utopie als Alptraum der heutigen Spektakelgeneration und hinterfragen den Wohlstandsgewinn auf seine unterbelichteten Kosten.

Das Künstler_innenkollektiv HeHe (Helen Evans und Heiko Hansen) spiegelt in ihrer dämonischen Installation *Catastrophes Domestiques Nº 1: Flyrony* (Abb. S. 142) mit einem über unserem Kopf fliegenden und rauchenden Bügeleisen das Grauen unseres alltäglichen Stromwahnsinns. Die Installation *There is a heppy lend – fur, fur awa-a-ay* von Julieta Aranda (Abb. S. 141) arbeitet mit den Assoziationen von Erhellung und Verdunklung, grossen Träumen und verletzlichen Realitäten, mit Licht und Schatten. In der Rauminstallation beleuchtet eine einzige Glühbirne, die an einem langen gewundenen Kabel am Boden liegt, eine Gruppe von Miniatur-Modellen von Antennen, Telefon- und Elektrizitätsmasten aus Pappe. Konstruktionen, die real aus schwerem Stahl und Beton sind, werden hier zu kleinen, zerbrechlichen Objekten. Nach einigen Minuten erlischt das Licht und taucht den Raum in Dunkelheit. In diesem Moment zeichnen sich die Umrisse eines grossen Antennenwaldes an der gegenüberliegenden Wand ab, mit schwächer werdender Kraft leuchtend. Ein simulierter Stromausfall. Elektrizität ist die Grundlage der heutigen Kommunikation und Unterhaltung, ohne Strom kein Fernsehen, kein iPhone, kein iPad, keine E-Mail. Moderne

Hightechgeräte bieten Flexibilität, Mobilität und Zeitersparnis. Aber wie oft müssen wir das Gerät wieder aufladen? Wie abhängig sind wir von einer Steckdose geworden? Und wie abhängig von technischen Geräten, um Teil der sozialen Netzwerke zu sein? Arandas Sinnbild der ‚Auslöschung‘ verdeutlicht diesen prekären Pakt mit der Technologie. *There is a heppy lend – fur, fur awa-a-ay*, ein mit Fehlern durchsetzter Slogan der Zuversicht, dass wir mit Fortschritt und Wachstum die Welt retten können. Unsere technische Beherrschung der natürlichen Ressourcen wird in Arandas Interpretation zu einem Kartenhaus, dass zerbrechlicher und flüchtiger wirkt als ein Schatten.

Do it yourself – oder warum darüber reden nur der erste Schritt ist

„[D]ie Suchbewegung des 21. Jahrhunderts [nach Alternativen zur Wachstumsgesellschaft] muss vielmehr auf Reversibilität, Fehlerfreundlichkeit, Kleinräumigkeit und Achtsamkeit bedacht sein. Ihr Utopisches ist kleinteilig, nicht grossräumig, aber gerade darum kann es, wie viele unmittelbar wirklichkeitsverändernde Praxisprojekte zeigen, *sofort* in Wirklichkeit transformiert werden."[7]

Es braucht utopische Gegengeschichten und Ideen, Alltägliches anders zu machen, ohne die Verantwortung für Zukunftsoptionen ausschliesslich auf eine nächsthöhere politische Ebene zu verlagern. Einige Künstler_innen der Ausstellung hinterfragten mit spielerischen Methoden und Inszenierungen die Alternativlosigkeit herkömmlicher Energieversorgung. Es heisst, simple Metallelektroden aus Kupfer und Zink in Schlamm oder in Früchte gesteckt, können elektrisches Licht für einen ganzen Tag liefern – eine durchaus praktikable Lösung für Menschen in entlegenen, ländlichen Regionen, die ohne Strom auskommen müssen. Das Experiment, in der eine Kartoffel dank chemischer Reaktion zur Batterie wird, kennt man vielleicht aus der Schule. In der partizipativen und lustvollen Installation *Fresh Music for Rotten Vegetables* (Abb. S. 147)

---

7 .... Welzer: *Mentale Infrastrukturen*, 41.

Party Manual (Marina Belobrovaja, Frank Landes, Valentin Altdorfer): *Party Manual*, 2005–2011
(Ausstellungsansicht / Exhibition view)

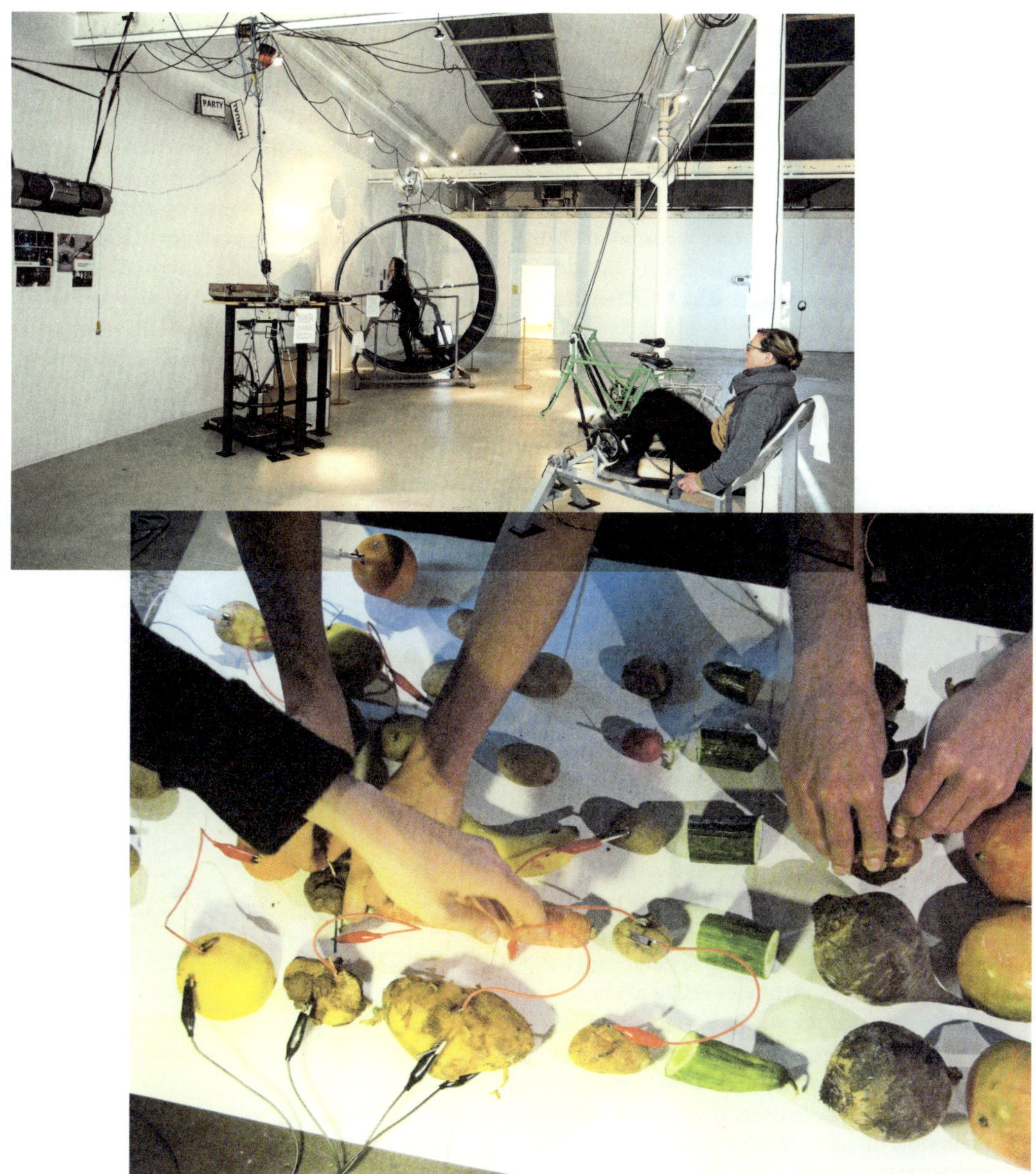

Karl Heinz Jeron: *Fresh Music for Rotten Vegetables*, 2011

Today's world is in need of counter-utopias and alternative ideas to encourage us to solve everyday problems in a different way, without shifting our responsibilities for future options to the next higher political level. Some of the artists playfully staged and questioned the lack of an alternative energy supply.

One knows that simple metal electrodes of copper and zinc put into mud or fruit can provide electric light for a whole day—an indeed interesting solution for people in far-off rural regions without electricity. Some may still remember the experiment from school: due to the chemical reaction a potato can become a battery. In the participatory installation *Fresh Music for Rotten Vegetables* (fig. p. 147), Karl Heinz Jeron makes us aware of a further aspect of our dealing with our resources. In supermarkets and markets, he asks for overripe fruit and vegetables that are usually sorted out and deemed unsellable for optical reasons. Together with the participants he builds simple electronic devices that produce sounds and that are fed by the voltage generated by the surplus of our affluent society, the rotten food he collects. The tone, the tone colour and the volume vary depending on which stage the vegetables are in. This way, a piece of improvised music is created from the most simple components and a bunch of vegetables.

The project *Party Manual* (fig. p. 147) of the group of the same name, consisting of Marina Belobrovaja, Frank Landes and Valentin Altorfer, was premiered in 2005 and restaged for *Live Wire.* An authentic party setting with mirror ball, hi-fi system, bar, etc., is operated by electricity generated solely by human muscular power. All those wanting to celebrate have to pedal, to crank, to sweat like a hamster in his wheel to produce the electric energy needed. A community, a certain number of people is needed to operate the party setting. If somebody gets tired or stops the music will slow down or the lights will go out. This direct action and the results of these actions prove to the visitors of the exhibition how strenuous it is to produce electric energy solely using physical strength. Exhausted and exhilarated, one gets off the bike and realises the ineffectiveness of one's muscular power: one could not even charge or recharge one's own smart phone or one's iPad, much less heat the water for the tub or put a refrigerator into operation. *Party Manual* invites all to think about the methods of energy production, about bodily work, and, beyond things taken for granted, about community.

The last two projects described involved the participation of the visitors of the exhibition and focused not only on alternative and playful ideas regarding the autonomous production of electric energy, but also on a reinterpretation of the economic paradigm of growth into a category of social communities energy production envisaging and involving the strengthening of the community, envisaging and involving wilful social 'wastefulness'.

Translated by Ingrid Fichtner

von Karl Heinz Jeron wird ein weiterer Aspekt des Umgangs mit unseren Ressourcen bewusst: Der Künstler bittet auf Märkten und in Supermärkten um Gemüse und Obst, das aus visuellen Gründen aussortiert wird und als unverkäuflich gilt. Im Workshop bastelt Jeron mit Teilnehmer_innen simple elektronische Klangerzeuger, die dann mit elektrischer Spannung aus dem gesammelten Wohlstandsüberfluss gespeist werden. Je nach Zustand des Gemüses klingen Ton, Klangfarbe und Lautstärke anders. So entsteht ein improvisiertes Musikstück, aus einfachsten Bauteilen und einem Gemüsebouquet.

Das Projekt *Party Manual* (Abb. S. 147), der gleichnamigen Gruppe, bestehend aus Marina Belobrovaja, Frank Landes und Valentin Altorfer, wurde 2005 uraufgeführt und für *Unter Strom* reaktiviert. Ein Partyaufbau mit DJ-Pult, Lichtanlage, Discokugel und Bar wird allein durch menschliche Muskelkraft betrieben. Wer also feiern will, muss selbst aktiv werden, in die Pedale treten, an Kurbeln drehen oder wie ein Hamster im übergrossen Laufrad schwitzen, um die nötige elektrische Energie zu erzeugen. Um die ganze Partyanlage in Betrieb zu nehmen, ist eine Gemeinschaft von mehreren notwendig. Wird jemand müde oder setzt aus, fängt die Musik an zu leiern oder das Licht geht aus. Die Unmittelbarkeit von Aktion und Ergebnis des eigenen Tuns vermittelt Besucher_innen der Ausstellung körperlich, im Laufrad oder auf dem Tretvelo, wie anstrengend es ist, durch den Einsatz von Körperkraft Strom zu erzeugen. Erschöpft und begeistert verlässt man den Velosattel und wird sich der Ineffektivität der eigenen Muskelkraft als Turbine bewusst: So lässt sich nicht einmal das eigene Smartphone oder iPad aufladen, geschweige denn das Badewasser erhitzen oder der Kühlschrank in Betrieb nehmen. *Party Manual* laden mit ihrer Arbeit ein, über Methoden der Stromerzeugung, körperliche Arbeit und Gemeinschaft, jenseits von Selbstverständlichkeiten, nachzudenken.

In diesen beiden zuletzt beschriebenen Projekten der Ausstellung *Unter Strom*, in den auf Partizipation angelegten Projekten, die die Teilnahme von Besucher_innen einforderten, geht es nicht nur um alternative und lustvolle Ideen von selbstverantwortlicher Energieerzeugung, sondern auch um eine Umdeutung des ökonomischen Paradigmas von Wachstum in eine Kategorie der sozialen Vergemeinschaftung: Energieerzeugung als Vision der Stärkung des Gemeinschaftlichen, als Vision sozialer ‚Verschwendung'.

ANOTHER MODE OF RELATION TO NON-HUMAN SPECIES

An e-mail exchange between Matthew Fuller, Graham Harwood and Yvonne Volkart

Yvonne Volkart: *In 2010 you realised an action called* Requiem for Cod *in the estuary of the River Thames, the video documentation of which we showed in our exhibition project* Lands End: Landscape as Image and as Space. *The event basically consisted of sound recordings of the mating sounds of cod being played by a simple underwater speaker to cod hatchlings in the Thames estuary. We see the boat and hear a strange, never-heard 'singing' of fish. Furthermore, we see the estuary, the sea, the scintillating horizon, in short, the surface called 'landscape' well known to us all. We don't know what's happening under water or whether anything is taking place at all, but what we feel is a certain strangeness and emptiness. Can you tell me something about the basic ideas behind this project?*

Graham Harwood: **The 'singing' was a set of a few sound files from the National Sound Archive that has 1971 recordings of the mating signals of cod. Like many such calls that need to be audible in water, they consist of a deep, repeated thumping noise, a throb that travels well through water.**

The mp3 files were played through an 8-ohm speaker wrapped in a self-sealing bag at a depth of 3 metres into the water of the Thames estuary. This is where the codling enter to stay over winter. Clearly there are several transformations occurring here: that of the original recordings, their conversion into MP3, and from there to this rather weak way of offering these up into the water. If one imagines the movement of cod around the oceans, the thousands of individuals that would have been in the shoals at mating time making such a call, the action is rather unlikely to succeed in inspiring hot cod action, but it may remind them of better times.

Yvonne Volkart: *Matthew, in 2007 you wrote a text in which you draw upon the idea of art for animals, that meant art projects which address not an art audience, but animals. Does* Requiem for Cod *have anything to do with this idea, and if so, could you explain it?*

Matthew Fuller: The idea of art for animals is to expand the sense of art as a mode of attention to perception. Art is a form of life in which attention to experience, process, object and interrelation is particularly heightened. A first principle of art, and what distinguishes it as an ethical activity, is that one never operates with *a priori* boundaries on meaning and on the unfolding of the world in relation to the elements that make up its dynamic composition. Of course, such boundaries, and play with them, as in the case of the frame, the pedestal or the institution, have been part of art's histories. As the late potter and writer Emmanuel Cooper suggests in his book *The People's Art,* there have been limits placed on this unfolding in relation to different forms of human social composition, such as class. Art for animals operates with the proposition that we may find out some interesting things if we attend to the aesthetic acuity and unfolding of non-human species.

Graham Harwood: At present there is a debate around the question of the representational or non-representational in aesthetics. This project makes a non-representational action that cannot be received by the species it is intended for, and that can't be directly experienced in the terms it might be known by cod and by the humans who experience it as art. In this sense it works to abolish the categorical distinction between the representational and non-representational. We can also think of this as an attempt to show how, given the operation and disjunction of multiple kinds of sensorium in ecology, they are simultaneously operative, and also failing around us.

If you remember back to *Tantalum Memorial,* where the Congolese could not be directly represented but were represented by the switching of a telephone network. Or you can see it again in *Coal-Fired Computers,* where the English databases of miner lung disease are used to explore the lack of data on Chinese miners. As 91% of all mines are unregulated, it would be impossible to represent them, so we look at why we have English data but not Chinese.

Yvonne Volkart: Hearing and seeing the video, I feel something unreachable, something beyond my perception, but I feel loneliness, sadness and melancholia. The project makes clear, as you also stressed once, that cod won't survive in our environment. How important was this emotional or aesthetic aspect of Requiem for Cod*—an aesthetics that tries, in a certain way, to 're-interpret' the ecological loss? And with which means did you try to underscore it?*

Matthew Fuller: Cod are being intensively overfished. As one of the species that yield an almost flavourless flesh when cooked, they slot very well into the degraded sensorium of the contemporary Western Homo sapiens. A 'governmental' approach to this crisis is to say that all fishing of this species should be suspended until 'populations' are replenished to the point of being sustainable, rather than being on the path to extinction, on which they are currently set. The main debate about cod and fishing in general is held in these terms, one that inspires, at least, melancholia about the forms of politics at large in the world and their meagre capacity to act, or even to compose thought in relation to ecological crises. Our proposition here is that another mode of relation to non-human species is possible, indeed essential, if equally nonsensical.

Graham Harwood: The fisherman who took us out laughed long and hard about the project. They've retold the story again and again in the local pub about the madman playing the sound of fish breeding off their boats. Ridicule can be the flip side of loneliness, sadness and melancholia and is a useful strategy with which to enquire into the insanity of our approach to fish and the lifestyles of those who would depend on them.

Yvonne Volkart: Matthew, in our e-mail exchange of 2011, in which I told you about the idea of thinking about melancholia as a precondition of the awareness of loss and therefore a potential means for a subversive, aesthetic strategy, you wrote: 'Yes, I think you are right about melancholy. It is a far more appropriate mode than the sublime for the current era, especially if we are to think through the question of landscape.' This idea is really interesting. Can you expand on it?

Matthew Fuller: Sadness is quite flat in its tonality, and in a sense it's a rather cerebral mode of emotion. Melancholia has, of course, a profound literature, but also an interesting sense in which it's also a form of intellectual-emotional state that is also physiological, connected to the theory of the humours at certain points in history, but also to the function of the organs, and thus operates within a wider cosmology of experience and intellection in relation to context and ecology. As a mode of understanding it is already ecological, arranging the brain in relation to other organs and physiological processes, but also operating with recognition of a dislocation of certainty. Melancholia in art is classically invoked by, for instance, the still life, in which rot, decay, pestilence, the figuration of death is incorporated into perception. One is lively when one perceives, but one is also a momentary phenomenon. To work in relation to other species is also to recognise not only one's temporal singularity but also to experience it in terms of forms of perception—in terms that are physiological, sensorial and ecological.

Of course, having said this, the idea that we can make something meaningful to cod, at entirely different stages in their life cycles, in different spaces, with the rather meagre equipment at our disposal, is itself rather melancholy.

Yvonne Volkart: Preparing your contribution for the show Lands End, *and talking about the term* landscape, *Matthew wrote me the following: 'Landscape is an aesthetic category that arises after the split between the organic or holistic relation to the land has been abolished for most humans in Europe. We are now in the process of making this the case for many more species, cod being one of the primary species which are on the verge of extinction due to over-fishing.' What do you mean by 'the split between the organic or holistic relation to the land has been abolished'?*

Matthew Fuller: Landscape as a genre of painting arose with the idea of ownership of land and was related to the generation of the visual pleasure in comprehending, in encompassing in a single gaze all that was the property of the landowner. The genre has a genealogically close relation to the map. The invention of property relations in land is a significant current in ecological terms and is interwoven with many other scales of problems, offering in capitalism a broken but unified framework for understanding and failing to resolve ecological crises. Humans were separated from the land via property, and specifically by the different waves of enclosure—something we see being reiterated across the globe in different forms, for instance in the removal of grazing lands from nomadic herders in the Sahel contemporarily. An immense number of species are being separated from their ecological context in an even more fundamental way, via extinction. The aesthetic of landscape as a genre of painting is deeply implicated in the problem of property but may perhaps offer some means of recognising current ecological predicaments.

Graham Harwood: English landscape painting, beyond the idea of ownership, seems to have been invented to record or imagine the land as it disappeared into the smoke of the industrial revolution. The non-human space of sea, tide, wind, planetary motion is a relief from a wired world in which we have to respond to complex ecologies differently. It reminds us that we are not the centre of the universe and that maybe the wired version we have of ourselves is mistaken.

Matthew Fuller/Graham Harwood: *Requiem for Cod*, 2010

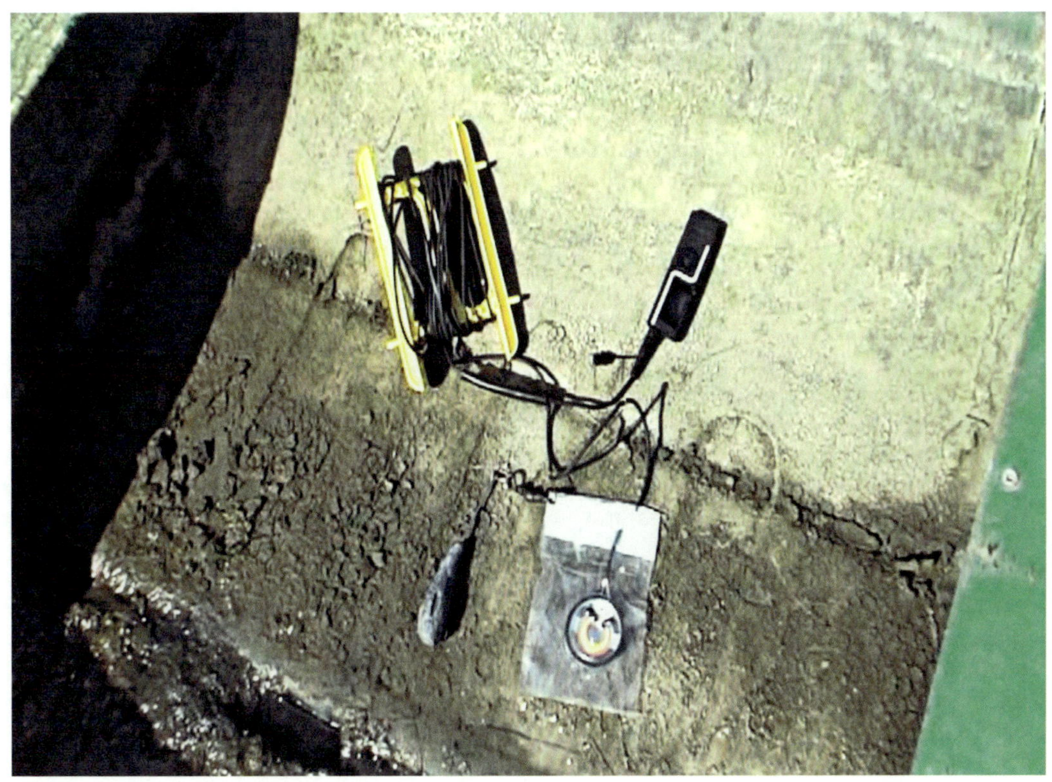

THE VOICE OF A TRAUMA-TISED TERRITORY

Sebastian Diaz Morales in an e-mail-conversation with Anke Hoffmann

Anke Hoffmann: *In your filmic video work* The Way Between Two Points (Terra Incognita) *from 2009, which we showed in our exhibition project* Lands End. Landscape as Image and as Space, *you introduce us to a barren and quite rugged landscape. In the beginning we learn that this is Patagonia, the once unexplored southern region of Argentina. In the video, we follow a man in working clothes walking through puddles of black, sticky oil in an abandoned industrial complex at the edge of a no-name city. You yourself come from Patagonia, from Comodoro Rivadavia, an oil city. What was your motivation for this work and what is its basic idea?*

Sebastian Diaz Morales: *The Way Between Two Points* intends to create a portrait of a territory. The pictured territory is one of the many corners of the Patagonian region. This corner shows a more industrialised part of it, one that clashes the most with the idea of the wild natural reserve that Patagonia is.

This clash is what I am interested in, the clash that generates unusual contradictions, surreal views, all being part of a reality closer to fiction than the real. The work is also a critical view on this place, even more so when you take into consideration that this is my city, the place where I was born and raised, and a place I often come back to. In addition, I take this also as an example to capture a certain general state of the world, which I don't feel comfortable with. Imagine this city (as the aerial view shows) is a city in the middle of the desert. In the east there is the Atlantic Ocean and in its backyard a semi-desert territory stretching for hundreds of kilometers. This city and its society could grow (in the broad sense) in every possible direction. To me, the desert is an empty space to be filled, not only with the tools of civilisation but also with meaning and sense. This city, as a metaphor for this general state of unrest, grows into the future repeatedly stumbling over the same stones, creating the present while disregarding the

context in which it is being built. The portrait is local, but it intends to picture the preset of an age in general.

Anke Hoffmann: *The protagonist walks not only between all the forgotten leftovers of past mining operations, but he touches everything—rusty equipment, warped shacks, an oil puddle, an old shoe—as if he would want to recall the past in some kind of psychotherapy, working it through in order to come to terms with it, as it is his own, the worker's past. On the other hand, he is also the future archeologist, wandering with astonishment through a forgotten culture. What were your intentions with regard to the role of the worker?*

Sebastian Diaz Morales: To begin with, the worker is the main figure in this industrialised landscape. Everything revolves around him. But this worker specifically has some sort of universal sensitivity. He explores the terrain as if wanting to read something else from it than what one can see at first sight. Some objects he discards as scrap, while others deserve a better treatment. He plays with the petroleum as if he sees this substance for the first time, investigating its density, and looking through its deep reflections. Indeed, this area allows for different readings. I see it as an archeological site where the present may speak about the future and the real state of things in the present age. The worker is the medium to unveil this.

Anke Hoffmann: *The video work is realised in a double, split-screen projection. While we follow the man's walk on one projection, we have an aerial view on the left one that takes us into the land from above, hovering over an industrial harbour and grounds marked by industrial conquest. The man's walk and the aerial view both slowly perambulate the branded landscape. They are both mapping a region which has, as it seems, revealed all its mysteries. On the other hand, you call this work* Terra Incognita—The Way Between Two Points. *Has the industrial exploitation made a new Terra Incognita out of Patagonia? And what are the two points you are referring to: the past and the present, the undiscovered and the exploited?*

Sebastian Diaz Morales: **This land still is a Terra Incognita, to be re-discovered. Even though exploration had revealed every corner of it, this still remains an unexplored place with regard to its possibilities. Specifically talking about this area in central East Patagonia, the way it is seen by the society, which inhabits it, doesn't allow for a redefinition or different visions. The general vision people have of this landscape is mostly selfish and entrepreneurial. The exploration proposed by the installation intends to depict a landscape that abstracts itself (in a very real way) out of this 'one way only' perspective. My intention is to give the landscape the chance to speak with a different voice, to adopt and accept those remains of pollution and industrialisation as its own, to create fictions out of it, to exploit it not only in an industrial way but on a creative, cultural, and intellectual level.**

Anke Hoffmann: **Terra Incognita** *is an almost silent observation of a scarred and injured landscape with a traumatised person wandering through it. Poetic pictures, a composition of slow camera moves with wide and close angles leave a very intriguing and powerful impression. Overall, your work, your images and filmic narration comes along as a strong depiction of melancholia. Melancholia and landscape have been closely connected since romantic times. And what is melancholia capable of today, in view of the devastating effects of industrialization?*

Sebastian Diaz Morales: **I see the landscape itself has been traumatised. The idea or instruction the actor received was: What would you do if left alone wandering through this territory, without anybody or anything but the objects, the elements and the landscape you are sub-** merged in? **His actions refer to the dialogue he has with the place and everything in it. The silence is profound, there are not many animals, there are a lot of ruins and remains from a recent past, and then there's the wind, and occasional machines sucking the black gold out of the earth. Let's say, this picture could be called melancholic, but the final intention is to find the constructive aspect of it. The construction of the installation is not melancholic in that sense, it reflects the voice of a territory in a slow and deep voice. I believe that emotions are necessary to appeal to the intellect and when used in the right manner they can be more effective than a plain theoretical or intellectual discourse. The same goes for the use of emotion just to create an effect of entertainment, or easy cliché speech on a deep matter. To me, the right measure of both seems the most powerful alternative.**

Anke Hoffmann: *Beside being a video artist you are also a filmmaker, and as such you produced a feature film on the same topic, with almost the same title. How does this one-channel film differ from the two-channel video work?*

Sebastian Diaz Morales: **In the film, I dig into the same matter, but using a narrative or story to follow. Basically, story telling is something which I feel comfortable with when doing a film. As a movie it does not only play with an atmosphere and a concept but creates a character from beginning to end in a more defined way. Also, picturing the area in a very realistic way creates an ambiguous image of it, telling the viewer that what he sees may perhaps be a dream of this character. There are a few more characters and a long monologue of one of them, role-played by the performance artist Ulay. On the other hand, the installation format gives me the possibility of breaking with the linear way of story telling, and at the same time to develop relations between the screens on display and the space where the work is exhibited. Though probably at the end of the film and the end of the installation you would leave the cinema or the art space with the same feeling, having experienced basically the same thing.**

Sebastian Diaz Morales: *The Way Between Two Points (Terra Incognita)*, 2009

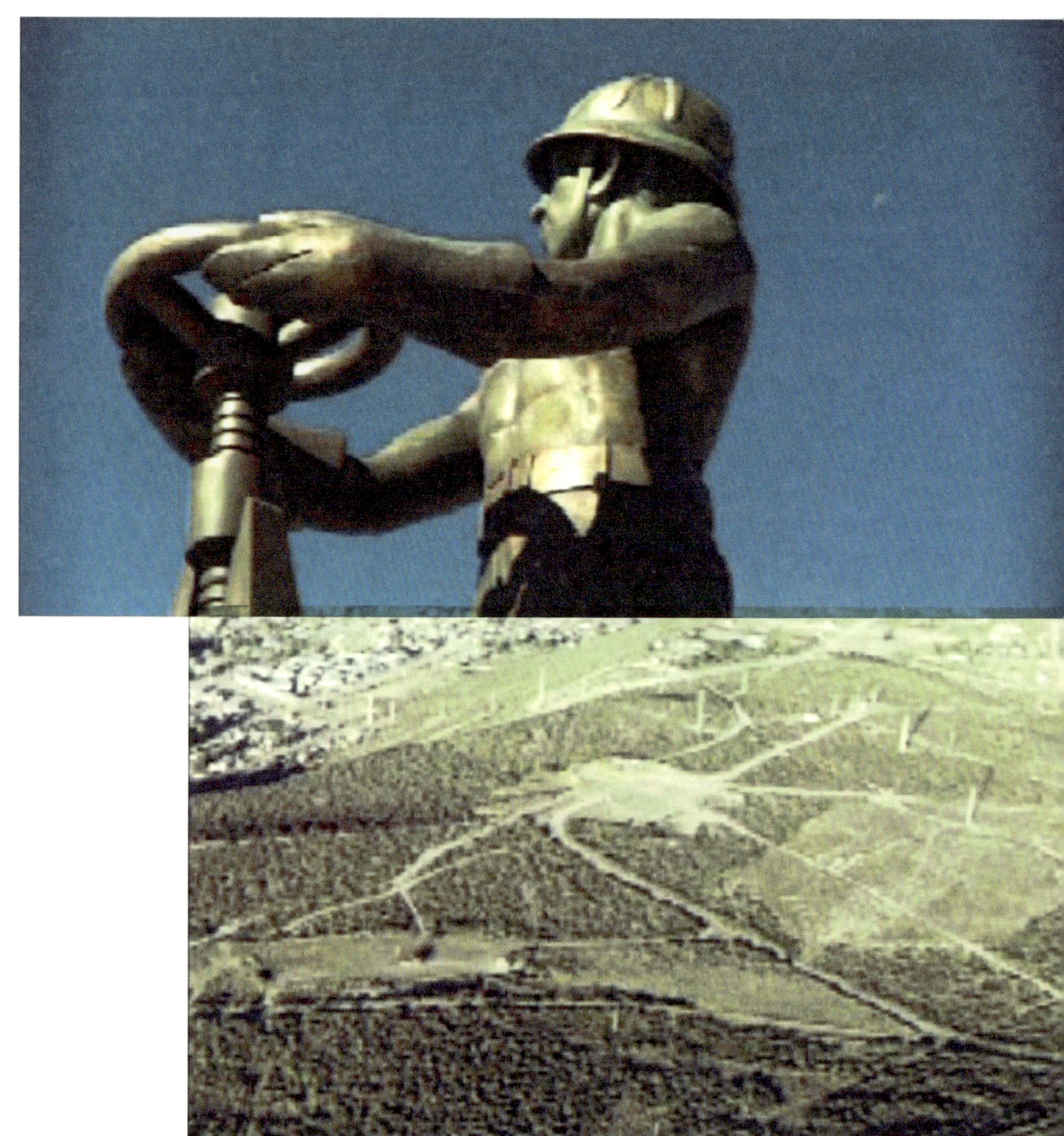

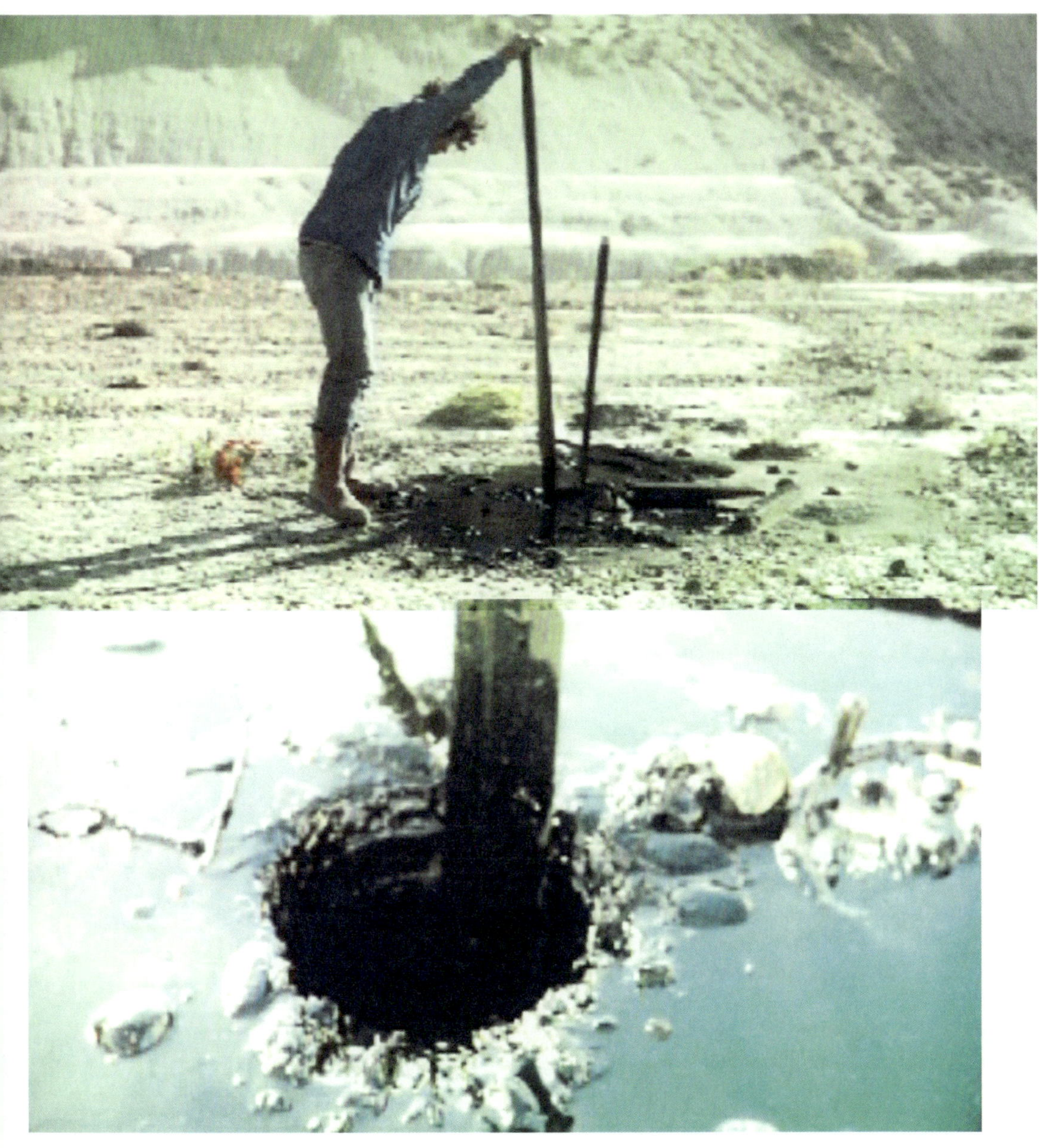

MAURICE MAGGI

WILDES GÄRTNERN IM ÖFFENTLICHEN RAUM

Seit 26 Jahren wildere ich mit heimischen Blumensamen in der Stadt Zürich. Wie ein Hund markiere ich meine Wege; dort, wo es später blühen soll.

Entgegen den Veröffentlichungen hat nicht Richard Reynolds das Guerilla-Gärtnern erfunden, nur vielleicht gekonnter in Szene gesetzt. Vor ihm hat die New Yorker Künstlerin Liz Christy bereits 1973 im East Village ein Grundstück als Green-Guerilla ‚grün besetzt'. Heute ist es ein schöner Community-Garten mitten in Manhattan.

Pionierpflanzen, die in den kleinsten Ritzen keimen und als ein kompaktes Ganzes aus Nischen aufbrechen, faszinieren mich sehr. Sie besiedeln Neuland und bereiten den Boden für anspruchsvollere Pflanzen vor. Sie lassen sich verdrängen und ziehen weiter. In meiner Jugend sah ich in den Pionierpflanzen gesellschaftspolitische Gesinnungsgenossen, die subversiv und avantgardistisch ihr Dasein fristen.

1984 startete ich mein erstes Blumengraffiti im noch sehr gepflegten, aber streng zwinglianischen Zürich. Zu jener Zeit ‚pflegten' die Stadtgärtner den Boden um alle Alleebäume herum unkrautfrei ‚braun'. Blumengraffiti nenne ich meine Aktionen, da sie von der Machart und Ausführung denjenigen der Graffitikünstler_innen sehr ähnlich sind.

Meine Idee war es, die Gärtner herauszufordern – im Juni, wenn sie mit Hacken und Herbizid gefüllten Rückenspritzen ausrückten, um das Unkraut zu vernichten. Dabei aber gibt es nichts Schlimmeres für eine Fachperson, als eine Kulturpflanze versehentlich zu jäten. So blieben 1984 in Zürich die von mir gesäten ersten Malven an den Strassen stehen. Die spiessbürgerliche Ordnung wurde subtil und subversiv gesprengt.

Mein Pakt mit den Malven ging auf: Im Herbst tragen sie in jeder Samenkapsel bis zu 50 Samen. Aus einer Staude ernte ich so jeweils Hunderte neue; dies macht meine Aktion selbsttragend. Malven sind Tiefwurzler und holen das Wasser aus einer Tiefe von über einem Meter. Daher gelten sie als anspruchslos. Der kompakte Wuchs und ihre stattliche Höhe bis zu zwei Metern ist ein idealer Habitus als Begleitung von Alleebäumen. Malven blühen von Juni bis Oktober auf Augenhöhe in den Farben Weiss bis Dunkelviolett, in allen Pastelltönen. Die einzelne Pflanze lebt meist bis zu fünf Jahren, und auch ihre Nachkommen in unmittelbarer Nähe sind garantiert.

Mit allen anderen Strassennutzer_innen kämpft die Malve um ihren Platz. An der Löwenstrasse überraschen sie durch ihre üppige Menge, inmitten einer belebten Einkaufszone. Meine Parademalven auf dem Paradeplatz blühen unmittelbar in der Nähe von Zürichs Grossbanken und Luxuslabels. Subtile und illegale Poesie. Meine Vision war es, ein sich verdichtendes Netz von den Aussenquartieren Zürichs bis zur Innenstadt zu spannen. Malven sind heute mein Markenzeichen geworden. Natürlich bleibe ich ihnen treu, denn sie erfüllen den Zweck meiner Aktionen hervorragend.

Immer öfter säe ich mittlerweile auch andere heimische Wildblumen an. Leider verkennen Gärtner diese Blumen noch zu oft und mähen sie regelmässig im Juni ab. Die mediale Präsenz meiner Aktionen als Guerilla-Gärtner hat jedoch geholfen, eine stille Akzeptanz zu schaffen. So stehen die Malven wie unter Schutz. Ich erhoffe mir sehr, dass ‚Grün Stadt Zürich' sich bald in der Biodiversität unserer heimischen Flora weiterbildet.

Eine meiner ersten grossflächigen Ansaaten war am Oberen Letten, noch bevor die offene Drogenszene das Areal in den 1990er Jahren besetzte. Ich sah in der stillgelegten Bahntrasse den idealen Ort für ein trockenes Biotop. Mein Vorhaben blieb unter den Abfallhaufen versteckt: Erst nach der Räumung der Drogenszene 1995 und der damit verbundenen Einzäunung blühte meine Anpflanzung richtig auf. Eidechsen, Blindschleichen und Falter nutzten das unberührte Gelände als Biotop.

Als wir 1998 mit der Idee eines Strandcafés zur Zürcher Stadtbehörde gingen, wurden wir abgewiesen. Es hiess, dies sei ein schützenswertes Naturreservat und sollte ein solches bleiben. Das Geständnis meiner Bepflanzungs-Aktionen dort und mein ausgearbeitetes Konzept ‚Respect' (im Auftrag der Gasometer AG) stimmte ‚Grün Stadt Zürich' um. Aus dem Schandfleck wurde the place

to be und der Stolz der Stadtregierung als Beispiel für urbane und kostengünstige Stadtentwicklung.

Meine künstliche Pflanzgestaltung wurde als Natürlichkeit wahrgenommen, was mir als gestaltender Künstler mit einem ästhetischen Anliegen gar nicht so recht war. Diese Erfahrung lehrte mich jedoch etwas: Seitdem säe ich grössere Flächen nach Blütenfarbe getrennt, um den Eingriff sichtbar zu machen.

Bahntrassen und Autobahnböschungen sind heute zu seltenen und berührenden Biotopen geworden. Weder Menschen noch Haustiere stören sie, und sie sind europaweit miteinander vernetzt. So können sich Fauna und Flora, wenn auch auf einem schmalen Streifen von Hamburg bis Lecce, frei bewegen. Der Fahrtwind und die Verschleppung von Pflanzensamen tragen zusätzlich zur Verbreitung bei.

So war es auch bei der Böschung vor dem neuen Tamedia-Gebäude am Stauffacherquai 5. Mit quadratischen Feldern in Weiss, Blau und Gelb alternierend säte ich die steile Böschung an. Ein starker Regen nach der Saat verzog und komprimierte mein Bild, so dass die Musterung heute nicht mehr erkennbar ist. Dieses Werk lehrte mich, dass blaue Farbtöne aus der Ferne schlecht zu erkennen sind. Erst ab etwa 50 Metern treten sie zum Vorschein.

In den letzten Jahren stellte ich an meinen gestalteten Orten eine überraschend grosse Schmetterlingspopulation fest. Diese ‚dritte Dimension' und die Nutzung durch die Falter freuten mich. Ich glaubte an meinen direkten Einfluss. Aber so wie ich andere Menschen mit meinen Aktionen lange täuschte, wurde ich diesmal selbst eines Besseren belehrt: André Rey, ein Biologe, sagte mir, er setze Raupen von Schmetterlingen an guten Futterplätzen aus. Lustigerweise stellten wir fest, dass er meinen Aktionsorten nachzog und dort Schmetterlingsraupen aussetzte. Daraufhin wollten wir uns für gemeinsame Projekte zusammentun.

Über das Jahr hinweg notiere ich mir die Orte, an welchen ich intervenieren will. Dazu stelle ich meine Samenmischungen zusammen und säe sie bei günstigen Bedingungen aus.

Maurice Maggi: *Rote und Blaue Steine*, Trasse Wollishofen, 2010

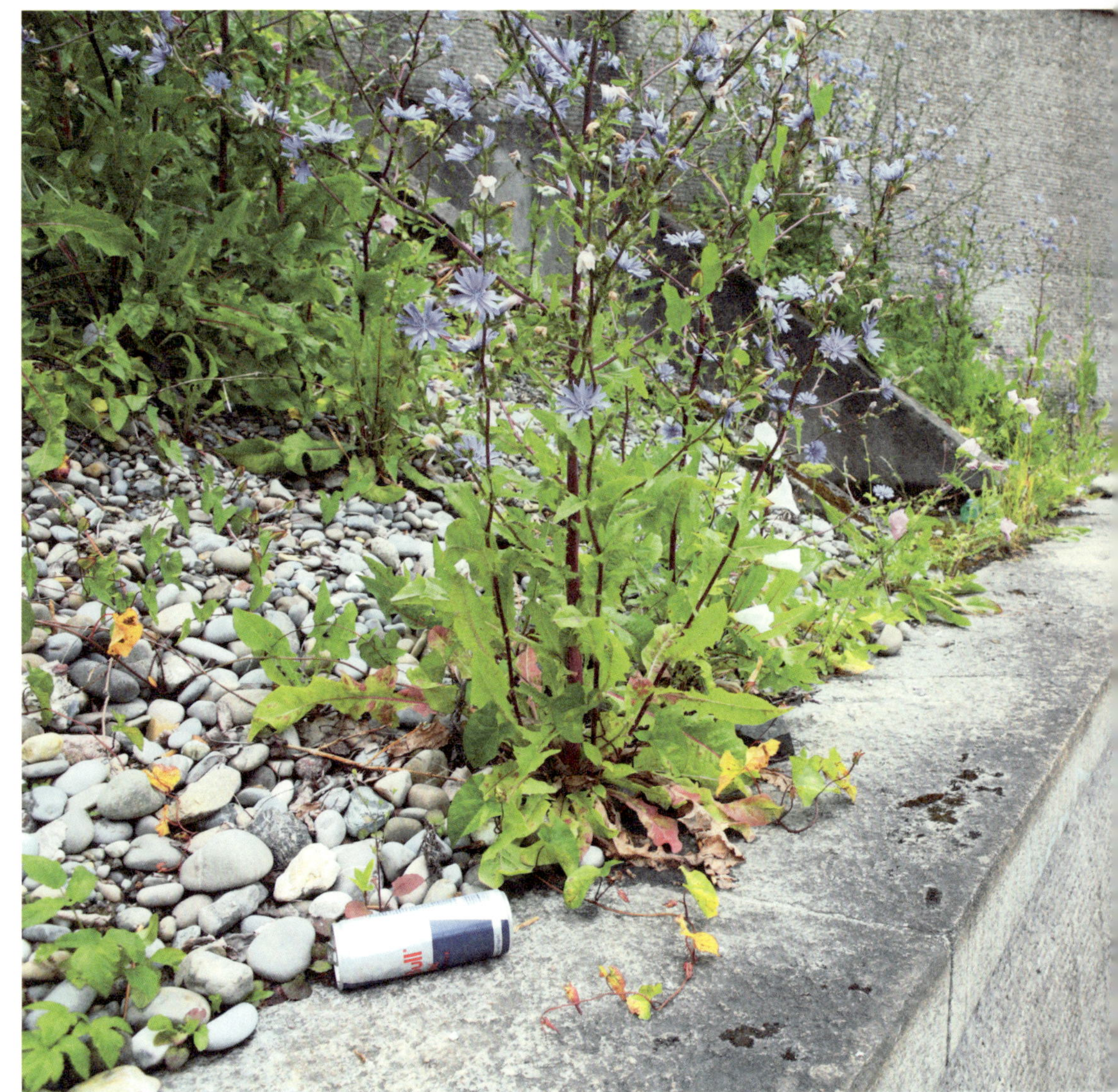

Maurice Maggi: *Rote und Blaue Steine*, Trasse Wollishofen, 2010

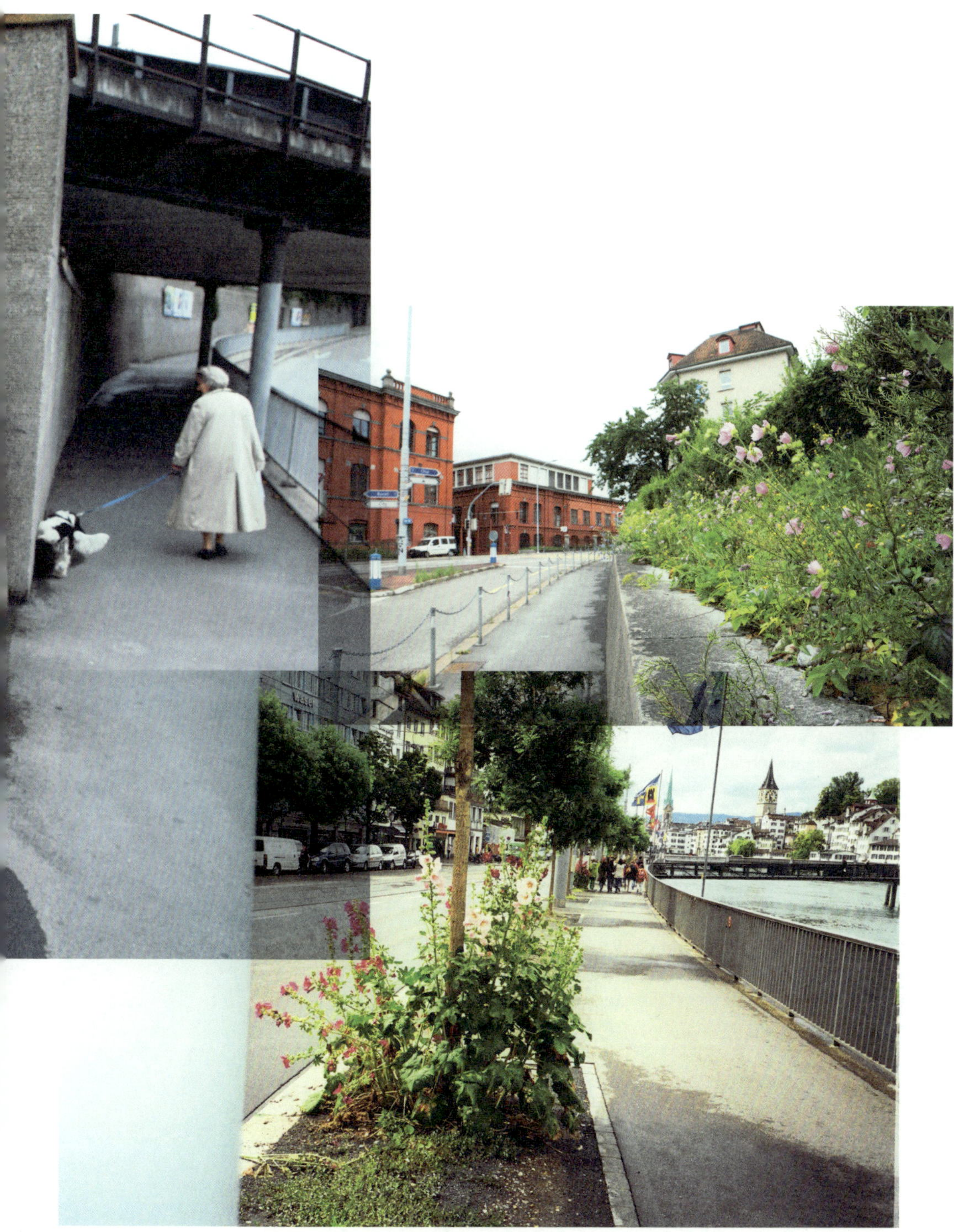

Maurice Maggi: *Malven*, Limmatquai, Zürich, 2009

Es ist keine neue Erkenntnis, dass das Grün der Stadt und der öffentliche Raum Abbild gesellschaftlicher Entwicklung sind. Die Nutzung des städtischen Raums zum Beispiel wird immer intensiver. Diese Impulse aus sich verändernden Ansprüchen und Bedürfnissen erfordern neue Steuerungsmodelle von Stadtgestaltung. Der Gemüseanbau auf öffentlichem Grund (zum Beispiel die Prinzessinnengärten am Moritzplatz in Berlin-Kreuzberg) ist ein gutes Beispiel eines ein Bewohner_innen intensiv genutzten urbanen Raums. Weit über gefälliges Design hinaus, ist Stadtnatur ein Wechselspiel zwischen dem grünen Ort selbst, den Erwartungen, Erinnerungen und Aktivitäten der Nutzer_innen sowie der Gastfreundschaft der Stadt: Sie wandelt sich fortwährend und produziert Vielfalt.

Meine gärtnerisch-künstlerische Gestaltung bleibt zurückhaltend. Ich lasse die Orte selbst erzählen. Sie sind verwunschene Orte ohne Hierarchien; alles existiert in gleichberechtigter Weise und in Bewegung und Veränderung. Die Schauplätze sollen immer auch überraschen. Nichts ereignet sich, nichts passiert, doch alles ist und wirkt.

Ich möchte allerdings auch einen Prozess bei den Betrachter_innen auslösen. Schliesslich empfindet jeder Mensch blühende Blumen uneingeschränkt als schön, selbst wenn ihr Dasein den Ursprung in einer illegalen und subversiven Tat hat. So muss sich der/die Betrachter_in neben der Freude an den blühenden Blumen auch mit der Fremdbesetzung des öffentlichen Raumes auseinander setzen. Folgt dann wirklich die Auseinandersetzung mit den Nischenplätzen, mit ihrer Schönheit und Wichtigkeit, obwohl sie dafür nicht vorgesehen waren, so ist eine Absicht meiner Aktionen erfüllt. Kunst soll ja – gelegentlich – auch unbequem sein.

Rote und Blaue Steine ist mein Projekt in der Nähe der Shedhalle, an der Seestrasse. Der lange kalte Winter 2010 verzögerte leider die Blüte. Das ist der Preis der Natur, die bestimmt, wann von der Aussaat etwas sichtbar wird.

Mit dem Label Guerilla Gardening scheint mein Wirken endlich die populäre Bühne gefunden zu haben. Meine Eingriffe nenne ich Bilder oder Graffiti und deklariere sie als genuin künstlerische Statements. In den von mir manipulierten öffentlichen Brachen und Nischen blühen jedes Jahr neue Kunsträume auf. Meine künstlerischen Eingriffe bleiben dabei subversiv, poetisch – und brotlos.

Manuskript des Vortrages vom 8. Mai 2010, Shedhalle Zürich, im Rahmen der Ausstellung *Lands End*.

A PARTICULAR LEVEL OF ATTENTION

An e-mail exchange between Emily Richardson and Yvonne Volkart

Yvonne Volkart: *Emily, in several of your short films you deal with the subject of today's endangered, hybrid landscapes, many of them are depleted and barren, have become infertile. In* Petrolia *and* Cobra Mist, *the landscape is ruined, exploited by the industrial or militaristic interests of man. In* Memo Mori *you show a neighbourhood of romantic old allotments in Hackney, which soon will be demolished and transformed into a car park or something like that (for the Olympics). They all bear witness of economic interests, or a history of depletion, or, like in* Memo Mori, *insinuate a capitalist future. Sometimes, your landscapes are melancholic, sometimes frightful, and mostly they are beautiful even in this dreadful or melancholic state of decay or deteorioration. Can you tell me something about your ideas behind these projects and the role or your concept of beauty behind them?*

Emily Richardson: I'm certainly interested in places in transition and there is something about capturing a place at a moment of transition or disintegration that I am drawn to. Ruins are often beautiful and melancholic, suggestive of time past, nostalgic in a way. They also conjure up ideas about possible narratives and layers of history. I'm interested in places and phenomena that can reveal these layers of history and express something about our relationship to the world. The beauty of the image draws the viewer into the film and also makes it feel slightly unreal, transforming something ordinary into something extraordinary, which brings out previously unnoticed aspects of a place or phenomena.

Petrolia was a commission for an exhibition in Scotland about the Scottish coastline and in my research I found one of the most interesting aspects of the coast was the oil industry and its architecture, the rigs and refineries. The rigs, the huge sculptural forms that drifted about in the firth were dwindling in numbers (as the oil runs out in the North Sea), so I wanted to capture something of their relationship to the landscape. They were like beautiful floating giants. And the refinery too captured my imagination, it's vastness and the aging technology that still has elements of science fiction about it.

Cobra Mist was shot on Orford Ness, a shingle spit off the coast on Suffolk. It was an MOD site that has been used for military testing since the First World War. I was intrigued by the former Atomic Weapons Research Establishment there, it's ruined buildings still holding on to the secrets of what took place there during the Cold War years. The buildings have been left to the elements to deteriorate, creating a tension between the time it will take for their secrets to come out and for the buildings to disappear.

Yvonne Volkart: *Often you work with the strategy of time lapse, or exposure over long periods of time (months and years) , which you condense into only a few minutes. Thus, the viewer perceives things as dramatic, which usually are not dramatic, or animated like the clouds in the air, or the refinery at the coast, sometimes this strategy is witty. Can you tell me something about your aesthetic strategies and about your ideas behind them?*

Emily Richardson: The time lapse allows me to explore units of time and other measures of time that evoke ideas about time itself, the passing of time, historical time or astronomical time for example. The process of shooting time lapse also requires a long time looking at a particular place, which often reveals hidden aspects and layers of meaning. Time lapse transforms space so the image becomes outside 'the real' which opens it up to more poetic readings, whereas the moving image is clearly a more direct representation of the place I am filming. So with *Memo Mori*, for example, Iain Sinclair's voice over/narration becomes important in giving the film the revealing layer that with the other films is achieved through the use of time lapse (and sound).

The long durational static shot is also a signature of my work. It demands a particular level of attention in the viewer which is important to me. I feel that by looking at something for long enough much can be revealed that would often pass unnoticed, and the use of the lingering durational shot is a way to try and make something that feels more solid and lasting.

Yvonne Volkart: *I would say, you foster an aesthetics which opens up for transformation, for different 'layers of history' than the ones, which we actually perceive, suggest. From my point of view, this is a fundamental strategy for critical engagement and responsibility, by means of ambiguity, though; it's very poetic. Is this something of importance to you and can you tell me what exactly became visible, e.g., in* Petrolia, *from your point of view?*

Emily Richardson: I would say yes, it is of importance. *Petrolia* highlighted the scale and sculptural forms of the rigs against the landscape, the weather revealing and concealing them from view. The time lapse of the belching refinery at night has a sublime toxic beauty, the beauty is often laced with poison in this way which makes the viewer reflect on what they are seeing. By using some of the techniques and forms familiar to documentary filmmaking in an unfamiliar way, the films do become poetic, subjective documents or portraits of the places they represent.

Yvonne Volkart: *Mostly, you work with 16mm film, and then you copy it on DVD. Can you tell me something about your preference for 16mm, and why you transfer it into the digital medium?*

Emily Richardson: I have worked a lot with 16mm film and ideally I like to show the films on film too although, as you say, sometimes they are shown on tape or DVD. When I began working with time lapse and shooting at night it was not possible to do this with video so I was working with 16mm for its photographic qualities. It allowed me to use long exposures on individual film frames. I like the richness of colour and the luminosity of the projection of 16mm film. I always want to create rich, beautiful images so 16mm was the medium I chose to do this.

Emily Richardson: *Petrolia*, 2005

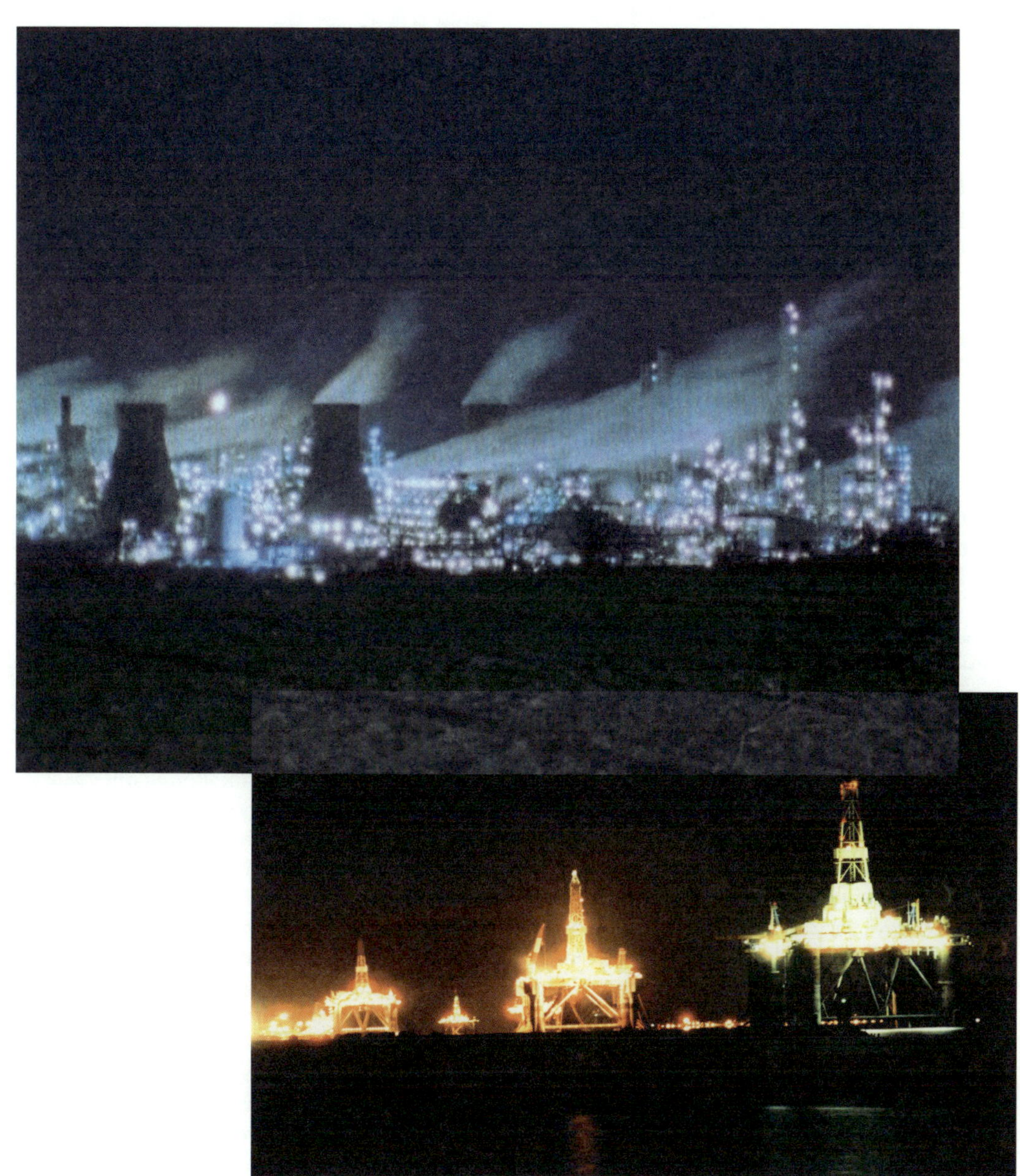

DREAM WATER WONDERLAND

The following excerpt is taken from the work *Dream Water Wonderland* (2010) by the artists Hörner/ Antlfinger. The dream monologue is spoken by a female voice and played from a vinyl record as part of the installation that combines video images of an amusement park in a former nuclear power plant and a 3D model of a former nuclear waste disposal site.

I'm in a very large room with high white walls. One of our birds has perched on top of one wall. I'm about to climb up and catch him when I notice another bird up there, too. Or, at least, I think it's a bird.

The creature is a deep, shimmering blue, and has long, thin legs. Where the head should be there is a kind of hat, like a lampshade. A trimming of white plumage runs around the lampshade and the length of the bird's body, much like the decoration on some fancy-dress costume. I reach out for the bird, and it hops straight on to my hand. Despite its size, it hardly weighs a thing. Then it hops back off my hand, recoiling like a spring.

I go to catch it then realise I'm standing on a very narrow ridge high up between the partition wall and the real wall. I'm afraid of falling, so I sit down very carefully. And now I manage to get hold of the bird. It's very tame. I take it back down with me, and put it on a table for closer inspection.

As I expected, it has an opening on the back like a walking doll would. I open the flap and see two baby faces, very realistically made. The smaller of the two is deeper inside, while the larger one is almost poking out. I ask the pair of them what's going on, and the larger head says something like they've got some growing to do yet.

I ask her how long it will take. She answers three months. She'll be born, she says, holding the bouquet of flowers to place on the grave of the doll that houses her.

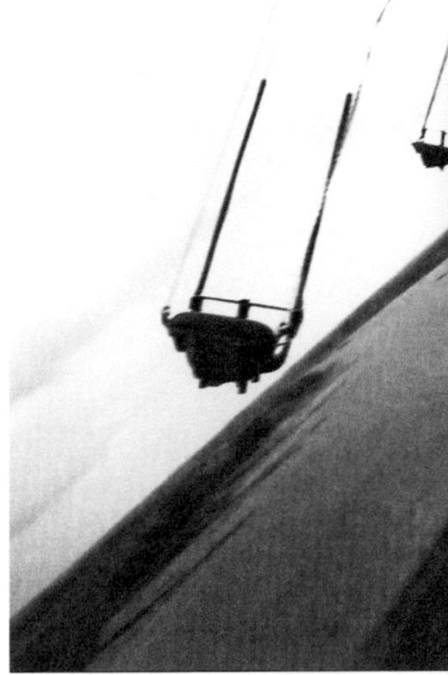

I find her words very farsighted but absolutely unattractive and precocious from the mouth of a child, when suddenly I find myself in a strange living room furnished in 1970s style.

There's a kind of report running on the TV set. The presenter is explaining that these creatures (I immediately know what he's referring to) are made to take up residence with families.

But, he continues, they need incredible amounts of electricity, which they get hold of in all kinds of ways. They're equipped with a kind of remote control, or a memory card, that lets them draw power from TV broadcasts. They also force their owners to procure ever-greater quantities of electricity, plunging one family after the other into ruin.

The whole time, the blue creature with a lampshade for a head is standing next to me, watching the TV screen. We need to get rid of it fast, I think to myself.

Hörner / Antlfinger: *Dream Water Wonderland*, 2010

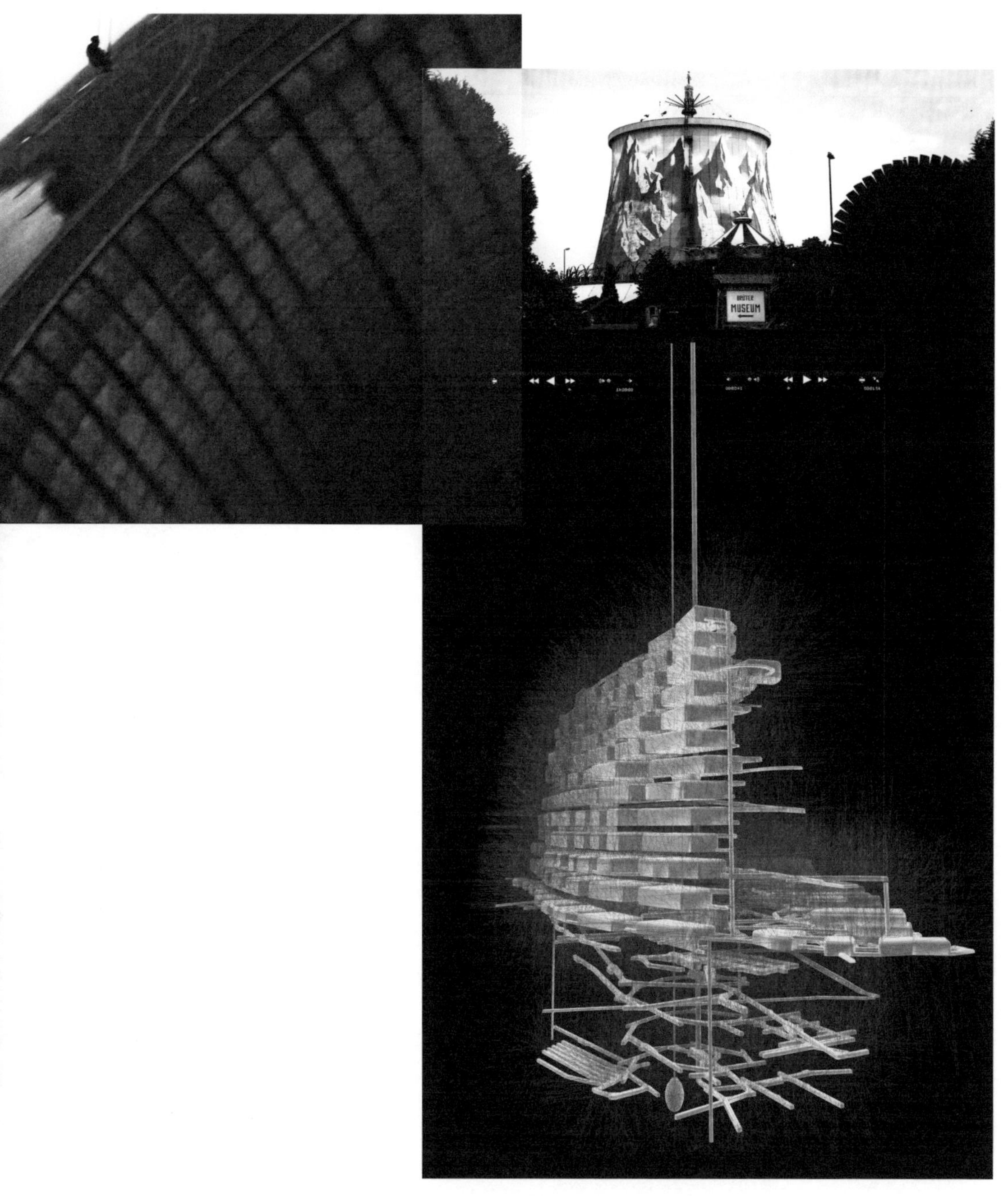

Hörner / Antlfinger: *Dream Water Wonderland*, 2010 (Montage)

PLASMA. IM UND ENTLANG DEM MEDIUM DENKEN

Jan-Peter E.R. Sonntag im E-Mail-Interview mit Yvonne Volkart

Yvonne Volkart: *Deine Vorgehensweise für den* sonArc::-*Zyklus war sehr prägend für die Konzeption unserer Ausstellung* Unter Strom. *Auf der Suche nach „dem Wesen der Elektrizität" reinszenierst du einerseits (obsolete) elektrische Phänomene, andererseits verwendest du Strom als künstlerisches Material, um Unsichtbares sichtbar und Unhörbares hörbar zu machen. Was möchtest du in unseren Wahrnehmungsbereich holen und weshalb? Hat das für dich auch eine politische Bedeutung?*

Jan-Peter E.R. Sonntag: Am Anfang des *sonArc::*-Projektes stand die Idee, ein totes Ende der Technik- oder möglichen Musikgeschichte aufzugreifen und etwas zu realisieren, was vor über 100 Jahren technisch so noch nicht möglich war. Ausgangspunkt war der singende Lichtbogen von William Duddel aus dem Jahr 1900. Doch er war zu leise, um neben den konventionellen, rein mechanischen Instrumenten als erstes wirklich rein elektrisch und elektronisches Instrument in die Musik-Geschichte einzugehen. Das *sonArc::*system vereint 100 Jahre elektronische Medien und ist zugleich die radikalste Plastik. Es wird ein offenes Hochspannungsplasma modelliert: Elektrizität ionisiert die Moleküle der Luft zu einem Plasma und dieses leuchtet. Wenn man es modelliert, ändert sich lichtschnell seine Temperatur: Die Luft kontrahiert, und es entsteht eine Luftdruck-Schwankung, und dies ist der Schall des Blitzes, Donner, nur viel kleiner, zeitlich gedehnt und steuerbar. Der Lichtbogen ist ein frühes, selbst oszillierendes System und ein erster Lautsprecher, ein ‚domestizierter Blitz'. Der springende Funke erzeugt die elektromagnetischen Wellen, die Heinrich Hertz suchte und entdeckte, um Maxwells bis heute gültige Gleichungen über das elektromagnetische Feld und die Existenz einer elektromagnetischen Welle im Experiment zu beweisen – und womit er letztlich ahnungslos das drahtlose Kommunikationszeitalter einleitete. Die elektrischen Bau-Elemente suchte der Elektro-Amateur Marconi zusammen, baute ein erstes funktionierendes System und erfand damit die drahtlose, aber noch morsecodierte Telegrafie.

Ich wollte ein erstes, rein elektrisch-elektronisches System entwickeln, um die minimalste allsinnliche Schnittstelle zwischen dem Menschen als

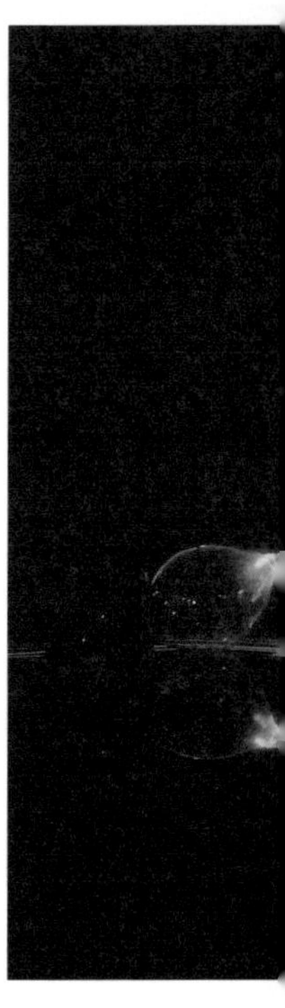

Jan-Peter E.R. Sonntag: *WARDEN SPRITES Zyklus* **(Ausstellungsansicht / Exhibition view)**
Links / Left: *Natural-Radio-Wave-Trap*, **2011**
Mitte / Middle: *PLASMA 011#2*, **2011**
Rechts / Right: *PLASMA 011#1*, **2009–2011**

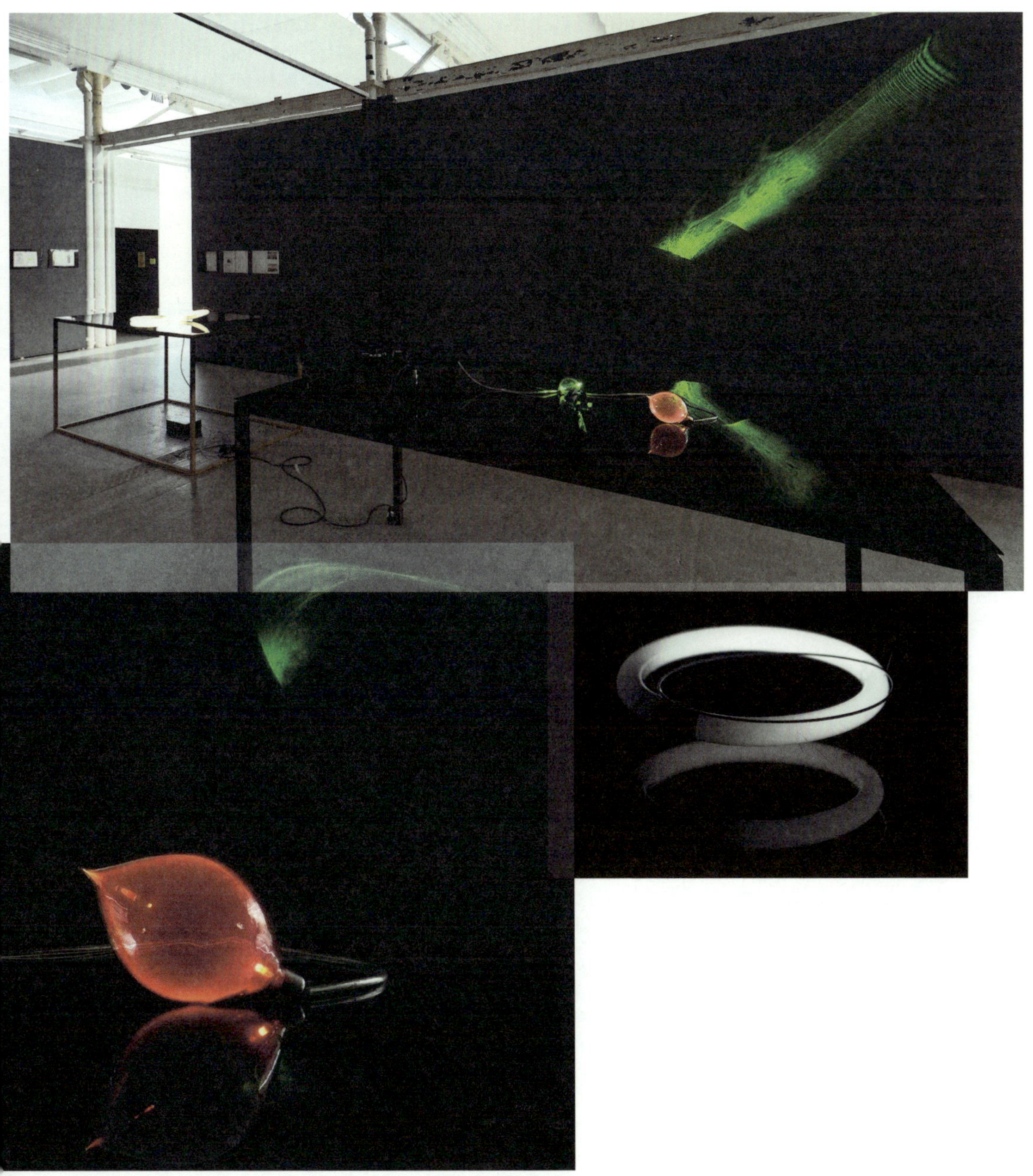

Jan-Peter E.R. Sonntag: *PLASMA 011#1*, **2009–2011**
Jan-Peter E.R. Sonntag: *PLASMA 011#2*, **2011**

teilelektrischem System und einem rein elektrisch-elektronischen System herzustellen. In meiner Arbeit bin ich mehr an unserer Wahrnehmung und ihren Grenzen interessiert als an Transformationen von Signalen in unser Wahrnehmungsspektrum hinein. Solche kommen in meiner Arbeit auch vor, sind aber eher von der Information bzw. dem Signal her gedacht, wie beim Natural-Radio bzw. den Radio-Signalen der Nordlichter in meiner Arbeit in der Shedhalle.

Generell gehe ich mehr von den Phänomen Licht und Schall als unmittelbar Formbarem – eben als Material – in Wechselwirkung mit dem menschlichen Körper aus. Da der allgemeine Diskurs in der Medienkunst sich nach 2000 vom ‚elektronischen‘, wo ein unbeschreibliches Material steuert und wirkt, hin zu einem digitalen softwarebasierten Diskurs über ‚digitale Kultur‘ bewegt hat, der den Code in den Vordergrund stellt, wollte ich dieses Projekt vor allem als Statement und zugleich Recherche über das, was ich immer schon formte – Plasma – machen. Dabei kamen immer mehr Aspekte und Narrative hinzu, so dass mir mit der Zeit – ich habe sechs Jahre teilweise mit sechs Mitarbeiter_innen am *sonArc::project* gearbeitet – immer klarer wurde, dass ich das ‚You see what You see‘ der Minimal Art zwar immer noch als Dispositiv bevorzuge, aber dass sich in meinem Diskurs längst die komplexen Narrative aus der Moderne mit denen der Medienepistemologie und Medienarchäologie überlagern. Der Grossteil meiner Installationen hat aber immer noch diese Unmittelbarkeit, dieses Sublime, Überwältigende.

Aber sowohl die ‚Kunst‘ wie auch ihre Orte und Institutionen sind komplexe Konstruktionen in einem komplexen Diskursgemenge. Mit der Frage nach den Institutionen und Formaten begann für mich anfangs der 1990er Jahre ein Denken über Gesellschaft. Da drang auch das Politische unmittelbar in mein Arbeiten ein, und das kann ich auch nicht mehr verdrängen. Wie kann man die Bedingungen seines Arbeitens ignorieren?

Yvonne Volkart: *Du sagst, dass du Plasma formst, das heisst also, dass du mit einem elektrisch leitenden Gas als Material arbeitest. Du sagst weiter, dass dir die Phänomene von Licht und Schall und deren Wirkung auf den Körper wichtiger sind als das Unsichtbare sichtbar zu machen und du sagst auch, dass du in dem Moment,*

als das Sprechen von codebasierter, digitaler Kunst zunahm, dein Statement mit Plasma machen wolltest. Was hat Plasma mit Digitalität zu tun und worin besteht dein ästhetisches Statement?

Jan-Peter E.R. Sonntag: Plasma ist (auf Griechisch) das Geformte an sich. Aber zugleich ist die Materialität des elektrischen Plasmas eben nicht ontologisch bestimmbar. Ich gehe soweit zu sagen, dass mit der Frage nach dem Wesen der Elektrizität – man darf auch nicht vergessen, dass anfangs des 19. Jahrhunderts die Physik noch ein Teil der Philosophie und die Frage nach der Materialität eine eben elementare war: Hegel versucht die Materialität des elektrischen Fluidums zu erklären, Marx und Engels folgen ihm und spätestens nachdem der Äther-Anhänger Einstein den Äther nivelliert und Heisenberg daraufhin die Unschärferelation formuliert haben – auch die ontologische Frage nach dem ‚Sein an sich‘ aus dem Zentrum der Philosophie verschwindet.

Mich haben immer einerseits die Grenzen des Wahrnehmbaren interessiert und andererseits die Extensionen des Eben-noch-als-Kunst-Denkbaren. Digital meint das Zählbare, und die Diskursverschiebung der ‚elektronische Medien‘ hin zu ‚digitalen Medien‘ beschreibt eben diese Verschiebung vom Steuern-mit-Elektronen – dem kybernetischen Plot – hin zur Sprache, zum Algorithmus, zum Code: Die Hardware wird ausgeblendet und die Software tritt in den Vordergrund. Dabei gibt es eigentlich nur Hardware – da würde mir Friedrich Kittler bestimmt Recht geben.

Ich forme Klänge, Licht, Räume, Bilder – Wahrnehmbares. Für die Medienkunst bedeutete der um das Jahr 2000 bestimmt wichtige Diskurs über Software in den Jahren danach dennoch auch eine enorme Reduktion: Das Medium droht sein Medium zu verlieren. Bob Moog – der Entwickler des ersten erfolgreichen Modularsynthesizers, sagte in einem Interview kurz vor seinem Tod, dass er ein Gefühl habe für die elektrischen Wege und Wechselwirkungen in den Schaltungen und in ihnen auch träume.

Ich habe über die Jahre ein Gefühl für Wellen in erschieden Medien bekommen, kann aber nicht diskret und im Binärcode denken und fühlen. Was mich an Kunst fasziniert, ist eben zumeist nicht In-Formation, das Prozessieren von Signalketten – auch nicht in Relation zu gesellschaftlichen Prozessen: Digital

Culture. Deswegen steht am Ende komplexer
Verschlingungen von Narrationen in meiner Arbeit
doch immer das Geformte in seiner unmittelbaren
Erscheinung und dieses in Bezug auf die Geschichte
der Moderne in bildender Kunst und Musik.

Yvonne Volkart: *Spannend bei deiner Arbeit ist ja, dass du
die Materialität und Präsenz des Flüchtigen und des
für uns nicht immer Sichtbaren ästhetisch erfahrbar
machst. Du sagst aber gleichzeitig auch, dass für dich
das Moment des Sicht- und Hörbarmachens selbst,
z.B. von unsichtbaren Wellen, nicht im Vordergrund
deines Interesses steht, sondern dass du das bei den
hier bei uns gezeigten Arbeiten beispielsweise vom
Signal oder von der Information her denkst. Kannst du
das ausführen?*

Jan-Peter E.R. Sonntag: Das ist ja nur eine Frage nach der
Perspektive, und mit der spiele ich gerne. Das
„Unsichtbare sichtbar machen" klingt so nach einer
‚romantischen Aufklärung', „vom Code her denken"
ist mathematisch und so, wie wenn man „Musik vor
allem in der Partitur errechnet". Und so ist mir die
‚Information' und das ‚Signal' schon auf halben Weg
sympathischer, weil es das Material mit ein-denkt.
Ich denke immer vom Phänomen her, und das heisst
umgekehrt vom leiblichen Gewahr-Nehmen /
Gewahr-Werden – oder wie es in der Vertextlichung
eines Songs von Duke Ellington singt: It Don't Mean
a Thing If It Ain't Got That Swing – duwap, duwap,
duwap, duwap, duwap, duwap, duwap, duwap – man
muss das Zitat natürlich singen und dann hört man,
ob es swingt oder nicht. Und so versuche ich mir
ab einem bestimmten Punkt nur noch den Raum oder
den Klang vorzustellen.

TEMPORÄRE PRÄSENZEN – FREIE ENERGIEN

Der folgende Dialog ist ein aufgezeichnetes Telefongespräch, das Teil der partizipativen Arbeit *Temporäre Präsenzen – Freie Energien* von Alexander Tuchaček ist. Das Projekt wurde zur Eröffnung der Ausstellung *Unter Strom* aufgeführt und erprobt eine medial-reflexive und unhierarchische Wissensvermittlung zum Thema Strom und Elektrizität.

1 = Caller (Tel.-Nr. 1006)
2 = Callee (Tel.-Nr. 10112)

1 [tut, tut] Hallo? Ich hör nichts.

2 *Jetzt geht es.*

1 Ah, jetzt geht es. [lachen – sehen sich beide zufällig]

2 *Dann können wir es auch abstellen.*

1 Muss es nicht aufgenommen werden?

2 *Wird es aufgenommen?*

1 Ich glaub, weil nachher spielt's irgendwie ab.

2 *Aha, ok.*

1 Wie geht's jetzt weiter? Ich glaub in der Ecke hat's kein WLAN.

2 *Wie bitte?*

1 Ah ja, geht immer noch. Und?

2 *Jetzt geht es ja darum, einer Frage nachzugehen. Ich habe sie aber nicht!*

1 Die Frage ist bei mir: War oder ist Elektrizität Leben?

2 *Das ist eine fast nicht beantwortbare Frage, aber sie ist in der Hinsicht sehr spannend, weil im 18. Jahrhundert die frühe, die animalische Elektrizität oder die ersten Phänomene der Elektrizität sehr stark mit Lebenden verbunden wurden. Spätestens nachdem [Luigi] Galvani diese Froschversuche gemacht hat – was zur gleichen Zeit war, als man den Blutkreislauf entdeckte – hatte man die Annahme, dass vielleicht das elektrische Fluidum, dieser damals elektrisch-statischen Entladung, die man quasi als Flicken oder Elektroschocks spüren konnte, dass diese Elektrizität vielleicht auch Leben sein könnte.*

1 Ja man dachte ja, das sei wie… also der Ursprung… der Spirit, der Strom. Das war ja die Geschichte mit der Aura, die auch nur Strom ist, da dachte man, das sei das Zeichen von Leben.

2 *Die Aura, das führt weiter. Das ist dann noch komplizierter. Auren oder Aurenfotografien kommen erst mit der Fotografie im 19. Jahrhundert auf. Aber die Idee, dass Elektrizität, also quasi der Funke, Leben stiftet oder überhaupt in unseren Körpern Elektrizität an*

sich, von dem man nicht wusste, was es ist, dieses seltsame Fluidum, dass es Leben ist. Das ist also nochmal ein ganzes Ende früher. Ich finde die Frage eigentlich deswegen spannend, weil man eigentlich nicht mehr im Sinne des 18. Jahrhunderts sagen würde, Elektrizität ‚ist' Leben. Auf der anderen Seite wird mit dem Defibrillator elektrisch wiederbelebt. Der Tod ist elektrisch definiert. Bis in die Fünfzigerjahre hinein war der Tod … war man tot, wenn das Herz nicht mehr schlug und man nicht mehr geatmet hat. Man hat früher den Leuten eine Feder vor den Mund gehalten und wenn es kein Gasaustausch gab, war man wohl tot. Seit [Hans] Berger, seit der Entdeckung des Elektroenzephalogramm, also des EEG's, ist man heute per Definition dann tot, wenn keine Ströme mehr im Hirn nachgewiesen werden. In einer ganz neuen medizinischen Weise könnte man wieder sagen, wenn der Tod elektrisch definiert wird, dann muss das Dasein von elektrischen Strömen im Hirn also Leben repräsentieren.

1 Der Körper ist ja an sich eine Maschine, die aufgrund von Elektroimpulsen funktioniert. Das Hirn, die Nerven, die Muskeln, das funktioniert alles elektrisch. Im Prinzip sind wir eine Maschine, die Futter in elektrische Energie umwandelt.

2 *Von daher wäre es immer noch eine These, dass man sagen kann; was wir als Leben definieren, können wir elektrisch definieren. Obwohl die Versuche, dass man elektrisch nun Leben stiften kann, was wir auch bei Frankenstein finden, eben auch auf Experimenten beruht, die These, die dazu geführt hat, dass Dr. Frankenstein sein Monster elektrisch wiederbelebt. Das sind letztendlich alles Versuche, die Galvani-Experimente auch am Leben durchzuführen. … Auf einem anderen Weg mag Elektrizität auch Leben sein. Damals war das noch universeller. Man dachte wirklich, wenn das Blut die Nährstoffe in den Körper bringt, also der Saft des Lebens ist, dann ist das Leben an sich Elektrizität. Also philosophisch reicht es weiter.*

1 Ja, weil wir uns heute grundsätzlich nie mit dieser Frage befassen. Aber wenn wir das machen, kommen wir wahrscheinlich auch nicht viel weiter, als dass dieser Strom, dieser Stromfluss, dieser Stromverbrauch der Grund ist, wieso wir leben, oder wieso unser Körper funktioniert. Ohne Strom, ohne diesen Hirnstrom können wir ja gar nicht denken. Grundsätzlich weiss man ja nicht richtig, ob der Strom an sich nur das Benzin vom Auto ist, oder doch mehr als nur das Benzin. Alles ist ja elektrisch. Es sind ja Ladungen von Muskeln, Hirn, Nerven. Kann man sich fragen, was mehr lebt: diese biologische Materie oder eben der Strom.

2 *Das ist eben daran die spannende Frage. Und an der Frage der Elektrizität zerbricht ja auch quasi die Suche nach einem eindeutigen Materialbegriff. Das heisst, eigentlich ist diese Frage immer noch unbeantwortbar und dadurch enorm spannend. Man würde heute sagen, dass das alles Dinge sind, die wir separieren können. Wir können Hirnströme messen, wir können elektrisch stimulieren, wir können Zellen in Schwingungen versetzen, in ihnen arbeiten Ladungen. Aber die Fragestellung „Was ist Leben?" stellt sich heute in der Form gar keiner mehr.*

1 Es ist natürlich eine Frage, die unsere Gesellschaft ausgeklammert hat. Komischerweise. Früher war das ja eine zentrale Frage, aber sie hatten ihre Standardlösung, das war die Religion. Heute haben wir diese Standardlösungen nicht mehr. Aber die Frage wird umso mehr ausgeklammert.

2 *Anscheinend.*

1 Ein seltsamer Prozess.

2 *Und damit bleibt die Frage vielleicht offen, ob Elektrizität Leben sein kann. Ich finde nur spannend, dass diese Frage heute eine ganz andere Bedeutung hat, weil wir ganz anders mit Elektrizität verbunden sind. Weil wir ja gerade zum Beispiel hier auch wireless kommunizieren. … Wir sind ja mit viel mehr artifiziellen elektrischen Phänomenen umgeben. Wir leben in einem, technisch gesehen, viel elektrischerem Zeitalter, als das, in dem man das erste Mal diese Phänomene untersucht hat.*

1 Ich meine… wenn man Elektrizität als Basis hat… Elektrizität ist ein Spannungsunterschied, dann ist das, was wir am CERN machen auch nichts anderes als elektrische Untersuchungen. Die Spannungsunterschiede sind extrem gering, aber an sich hält dort auch alles nur zusammen wegen dieser elektrischen Felder, oder eben magnetischen Felder. Die aber auch elektrisch sind.

2 *Deswegen kann man sagen, dass sich die Fragestellung anhand der Elektrizität nur verschoben hat. Also ich würde es so zuspitzen, dass man die Frage nach der Elektrizität sehr vielfältig beantworten kann, was einerseits unsere Medienzeit erklärt, aber auf der anderen Seite auch vielleicht ein Bruch in der Philosophiegeschichte darstellt.*

1 Wahrscheinlich ist es auch so, wenn man diesen Bereich plötzlich mit Elektrizität umfasst und dann die Spannungsunterschiede im Körper und die elektrische Strahlung, magnetische Strahlung vom Körper mit den gleichen Termini bezeichnet, wie eben diese ganzen magnetischen und elektromagnetischen Wellen,

die wir jetzt überall produzieren mit Natel und Wi-Fi
und so. Man hat plötzlich mit der Terminologie gemerkt,
dass das etwas Gefährliches ist, wenn man im gleichen
Feld Elektrizität an zwei so verschiedenen Sachen
hat und was diese Strahlung auf einem Körper macht,
der grundsätzlich mit Ladungsunterschieden funktioniert, das ist auch eine Frage, die überhaupt nicht
geklärt ist.

2 *... Hallo?*

1 Hallo?

2 *Ich hatte Sie grade nicht verstanden. Für einen
winzigen Moment. Aber das liegt vielleicht auch an diesen
Feldern, mit denen wir jetzt gerade kommunizieren.*

1 Genau. Also dieses Wi-Fi-Feld.

2 *Was für ein Feld? Stimmt. Ich habe noch nie darüber
nachgedacht, Wi-Fi als ein Feld zu bezeichnen.*

1 Es ist ja ein Feld.

2 *Ja, dann kommen wir jetzt auch nicht weiter in der
Frage, ob Elektrizität Leben ist. Aber es scheint mit
Leben eng verknüpft zu sein.*

1 Ich find's spannend rauszufinden, ... wenn man den
Körper, den Mensch wirklich als elektrisches Feld
anschaut, was das bedeuten würde, vor allem heute,
wo wir unsere Umwelt vollstopfen mit elektrischen
Felder. ... Auch unserem elektrischen Feld.

2 *Ja, was macht es, wo wir gerade mobil miteinander
kommunizieren, mit uns? Glauben Sie, dass das
Benutzen jetzt einer Wireless-Kommunikation, dass wir
beide telefonieren, dass das Einfluss hat auf ihr Feld?*

1 Ja, sicher. Also beim Mobilfunk ist ja klar, es gibt
diese Erwärmung. Die Frage ist nur, erstens: ist diese
Erwärmung schädlich und zweitens: ist es nur
diese Erwärmung? Die Erwärmung der Hirnzone ist
ja erwiesen. Das ist ja nicht die Frage, ob erwärmt
wird oder nicht. Die Frage ist, ob diese Erwärmung
anders ist als wenn ich an der Sonne stehe.

2 *Ok. Und wo ist es erwiesen?*

1 Ja, diese Untersuchungen über die Schädlichkeit
auf das Gehirn... Also diese ganzen Untersuchungen
laufen ja auf das hinaus. ... [unverständlich] ... kein
Feld mehr.

2 *Können wir in diesem Moment abbrechen, ich muss
mich hier gerade um etwas anderes kümmern. Tut mir
leid, aber wir setzen es gerne fort. Vielen Dank!*

1 Wiederhören!

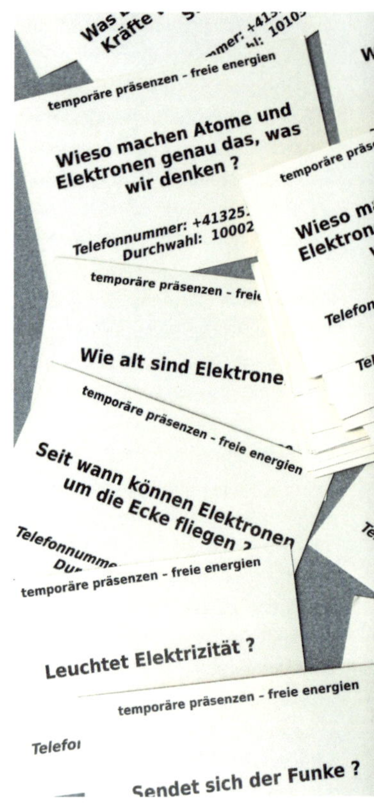

Alexander Tuchaček: *Temporäre Präsenzen – Freie Energien*, 2011

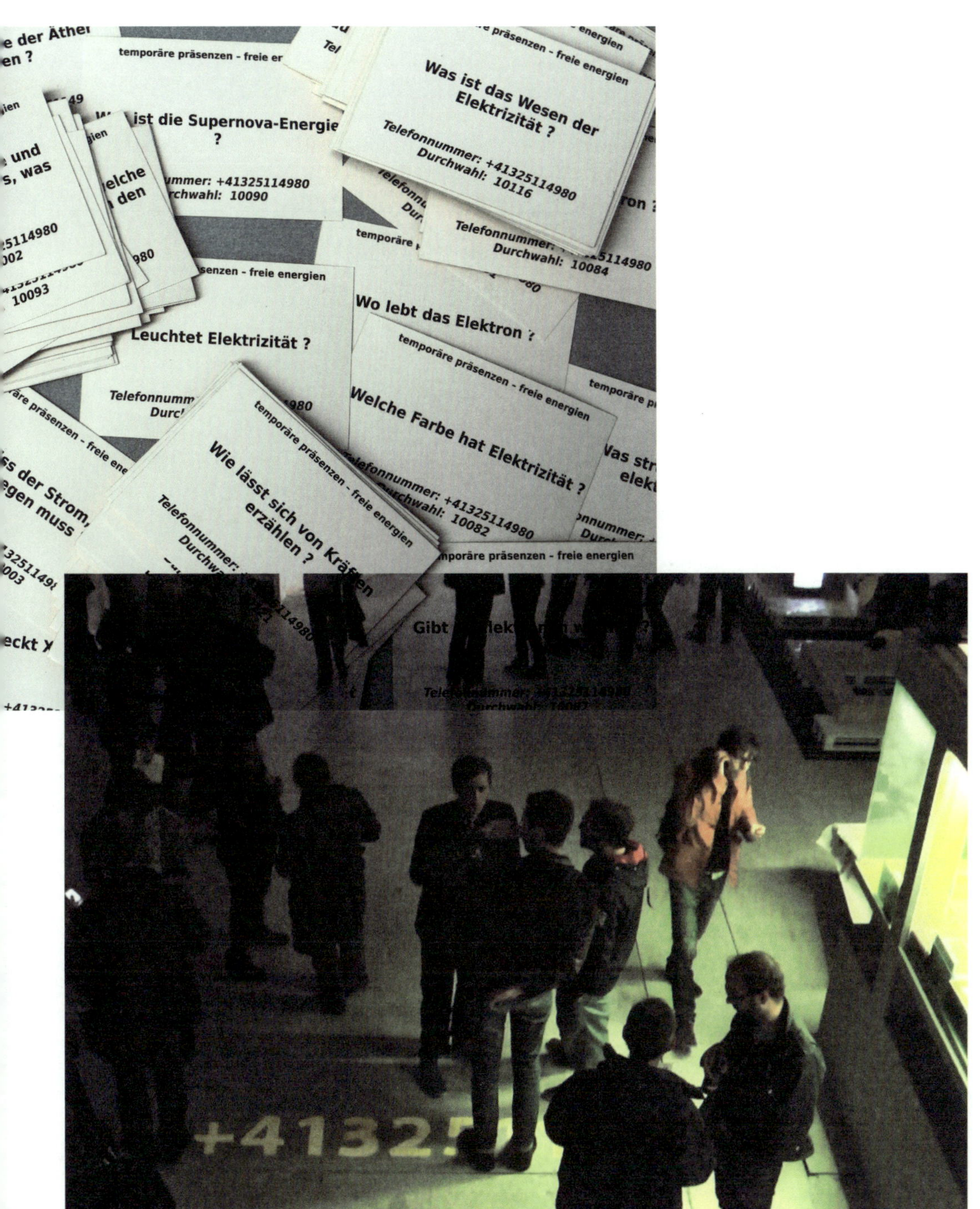

Christina Hemauer und / and Roman Keller: *Die Unfreiheit der Elektronen*, 2011

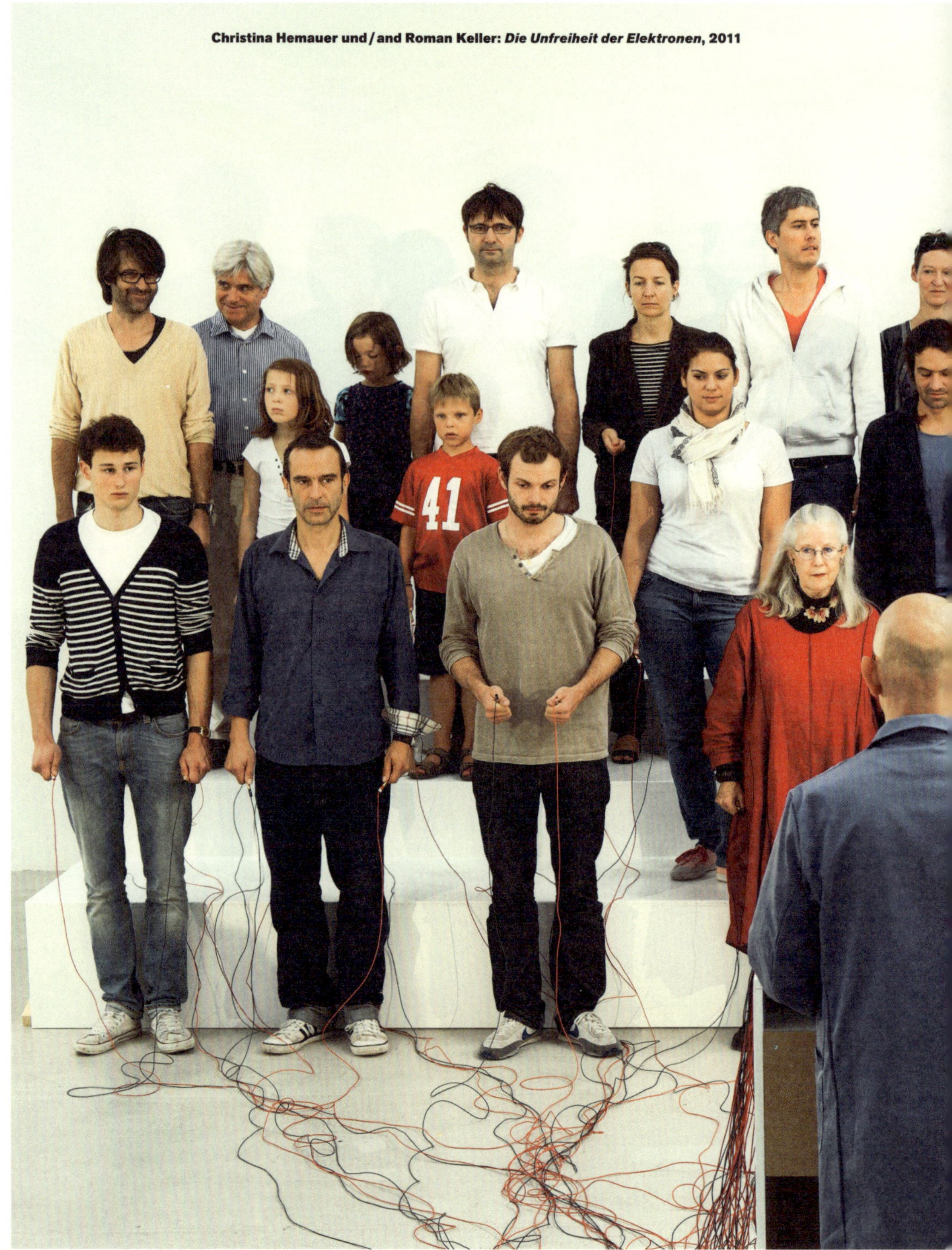

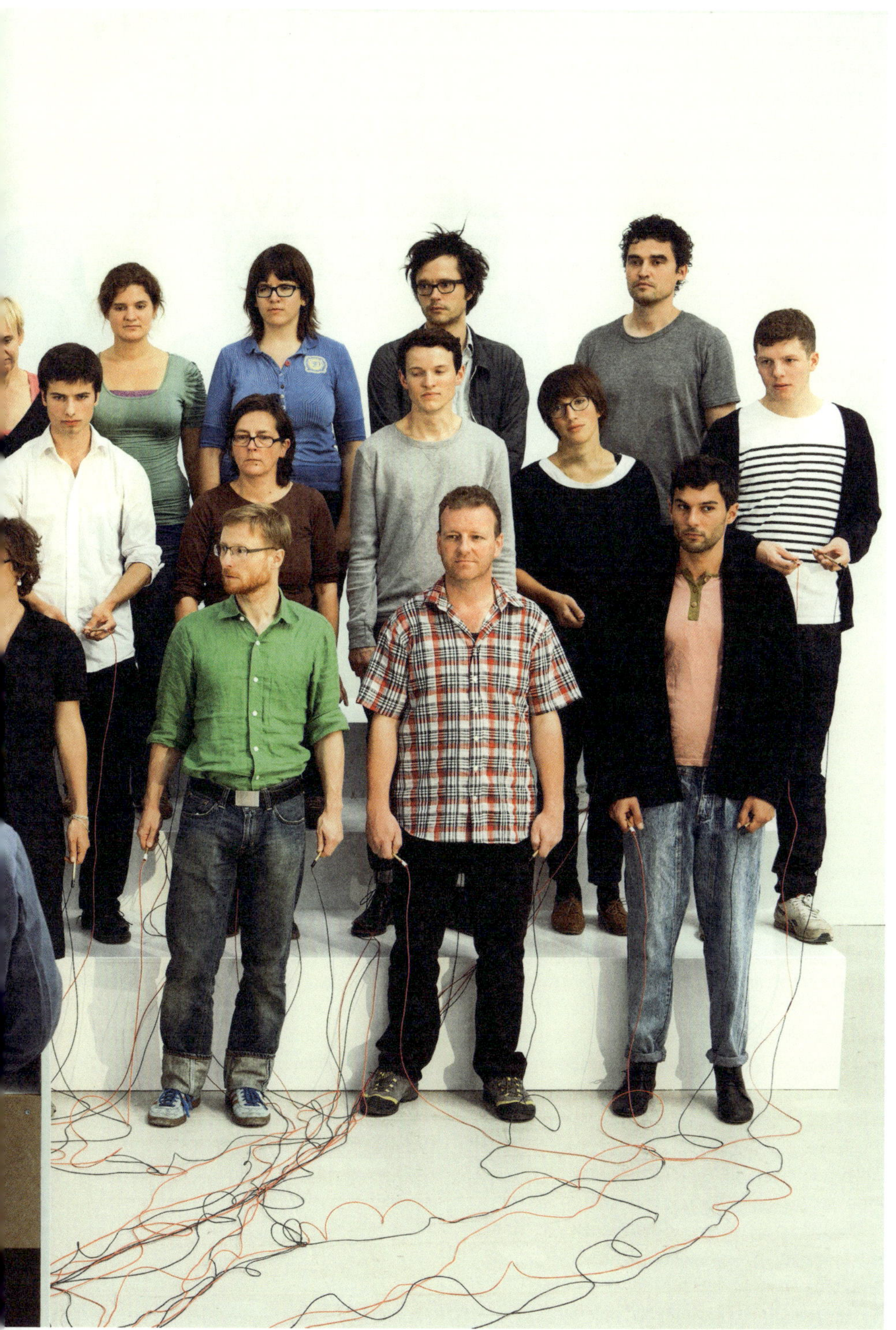

IM SCHEITERN STECKT DIE POESIE DES UNVOLL-ENDETEN

Christina Hemauer und Roman Keller im E-Mail-Interview mit Anke Hoffmann

Anke Hoffmann: Christina und Roman, ihr setzt euch seit einiger Zeit in unterschiedlichen künstlerischen Formaten mit der Beziehung von Energie, Kultur und Geschichte auseinander. Worin besteht eure individuelle Motivation und euer stetes Interesse am komplexen Thema der Energie?

Christina Hemauer und Roman Keller: Die Moderne ist untrennbar mit der Nutzbarmachung fossiler Energieträger verbunden. Kohle und Dampf haben die industrielle Revolution angeschoben. Sie veränderte die betroffenen Gesellschaften fundamental. Die Entwicklung der europäischen Sozialstaaten ist ohne die neu entstandene Arbeiterklasse nicht denkbar. Ende 19. Jahrhundert fand dann der Wechsel zum Erdöl statt, was die möglichen Nutzungen fossiler Energieträger potenzierte und der Moderne zum Durchbruch verhalf.

Nun stehen wir vor dem Ende dieser wunderbaren und reichen, aber auch destruktiven Epoche. Der Wandel zur postfossilen Gesellschaft ist aus unserer Sicht mehr als nur eine Technologiefrage. Mit dem absehbaren Ende unserer Reservoirs an ‚alter‘ Sonnenenergie wird ein kultureller Wandel einhergehen. Diesem gilt unser Interesse.

Anke Hoffmann: In der Arbeit Die Unfreiheit der Elektronen, die ihr für unsere Ausstellung Unter Strom entwickelt habt, stellt ihr unter Beteiligung von 22 Personen das Experiment eines spanischen Arztes aus dem Jahr 1795 nach, in dem Menschen durch kleine Stromstösse zu recht simplen Informationsträgern werden. Was hat euch an diesem Experiment so fasziniert, dass daraus ein Re-Enactment entstanden ist?

Christina Hemauer und Roman Keller: Das von Don Francisco Salvá y Campillo beschriebene Experiment ist ein Hinweis, dass die Entdeckung der Elektrizität von Anfang an mit der Idee der Langstreckenkommunikation verbunden ist. Strom ist zu diesem Zeitpunkt vor allem eine Jahrmarktsattraktion, wo Freiwillige mit statischen Ladungen ‚geschockt‘ werden. Salvá erkannte das Potential bevor eigentliche Elektrizitätsanwendungen wie Batterien, Motoren oder Glühbirnen entwickelt wurden. Salvá schreibt, dass Elektrizität – falls sie für die Telegrafie irgendwie von Nutzen sein soll –

jegliche Art von Informationen transportieren können oder sprechen lernen muss.[1] Uns faszinierte diese wahrlich direkte Verbindung von Kommunikation und Elektrizität. Die verkabelten Personen sind auch ein passendes Abbild der heutigen Kommunikationsgesellschaft. Einige Jahre nach Salvás Veröffentlichung des Experiments – wir haben übrigens nicht herausfinden können, ob es in der beschriebenen Form je durchgeführt wurde – sind die sprechenden Menschen durch zuckende Froschschenkel ersetzt worden.

Anke Hoffmann: Historische Recherche charakterisiert eine Seite eurer künstlerischen Praxis. Dabei geht es euch um die Aufdeckung von teils utopischen und alternativen Projekten der Energieerzeugung als Vorreiter des ‚post-petrolistischen Zeitalters‘, die dem Vergessen preisgegeben wurden. Dazu gehören jüngere Arbeiten wie No1 Sun Engine, die das weltweit erste Sonnenkraftwerk thematisiert, das 1913 in einem Vorort von Kairo in Betrieb genommen wurde, oder der Film A Road Not Taken, welcher eure Spurensuche nach Solarpanelen dokumentiert, die Jimmy Carter 1979 auf das Dach des Weissen Hauses installieren liess und

1 .... Vgl. Salvá y Campillo, Don Francisco: *La Electricidad Aplicada á la Telegrafía*. Barcelona 1795, 3. Der im Re-Enactment von Christina Hemauer und Roman Keller übermittelte Text ist folgende freie Übersetzung des Originals: „Fals Elektrizität für di Telegrafi irgendwi fon Nutzen sein sol mus si iegliche Art fon Informatsionen transportiren könen oder in anderen Worten si mus schprechen lernen, Sibzenhundertfünfundnöinzig Doktor Frantsisgo Salwa".

*von seinem Nachfolger Ronald Reagan 1986 abmon-
tiert wurde, was gleichzeitig auch ein vorläufiges Ende
der amerikanischen Solarindustrie bedeutete. Wie
kommt ihr auf diese besonderen Fälle von industriege-
schichtlichen Sackgassen und wie geht ihr als Künst-
ler_innen damit um, mal filmisch-dokumentarisch, parti-
zipatorisch oder auch installativ-poetisch?*

Christina Hemauer und Roman Keller: Im Scheitern steckt die
Poesie des Unvollendeten. Das Misslingen geht meist
mit einem Stillstand einher, wodurch die Ambitionen
des Unterfangens in ihrer reinen Form konserviert
werden. Darüber hinaus stellt sich jeweils die Frage
„Was wäre wenn…" – wo stünden wir und die USA
beispielsweise, wenn Jimmy Carters Energiepolitik die
letzten dreissig Jahre fortgeführt worden wäre?
Es kommt ja nicht von ungefähr, dass sich am Ende
jeder Sackgasse ein Kehrplatz findet. Zur unterschiedlichen Herangehensweise: Wir suchen jeweils nach
adäquaten Möglichkeiten, um Themen anzupacken,
die uns interessieren. Dieses Sondieren verstehen
wir als unsere eigentliche Arbeit. Wir probieren gerne
Neues aus – mit dem Risiko, hin und wieder zu
scheitern.

4

UN/MÖGLICHE GEMEINSCHAFT
IM/POSSIBLE COMMUNITY

Nevin Aladağ: *Occupation Shedhalle 2009*

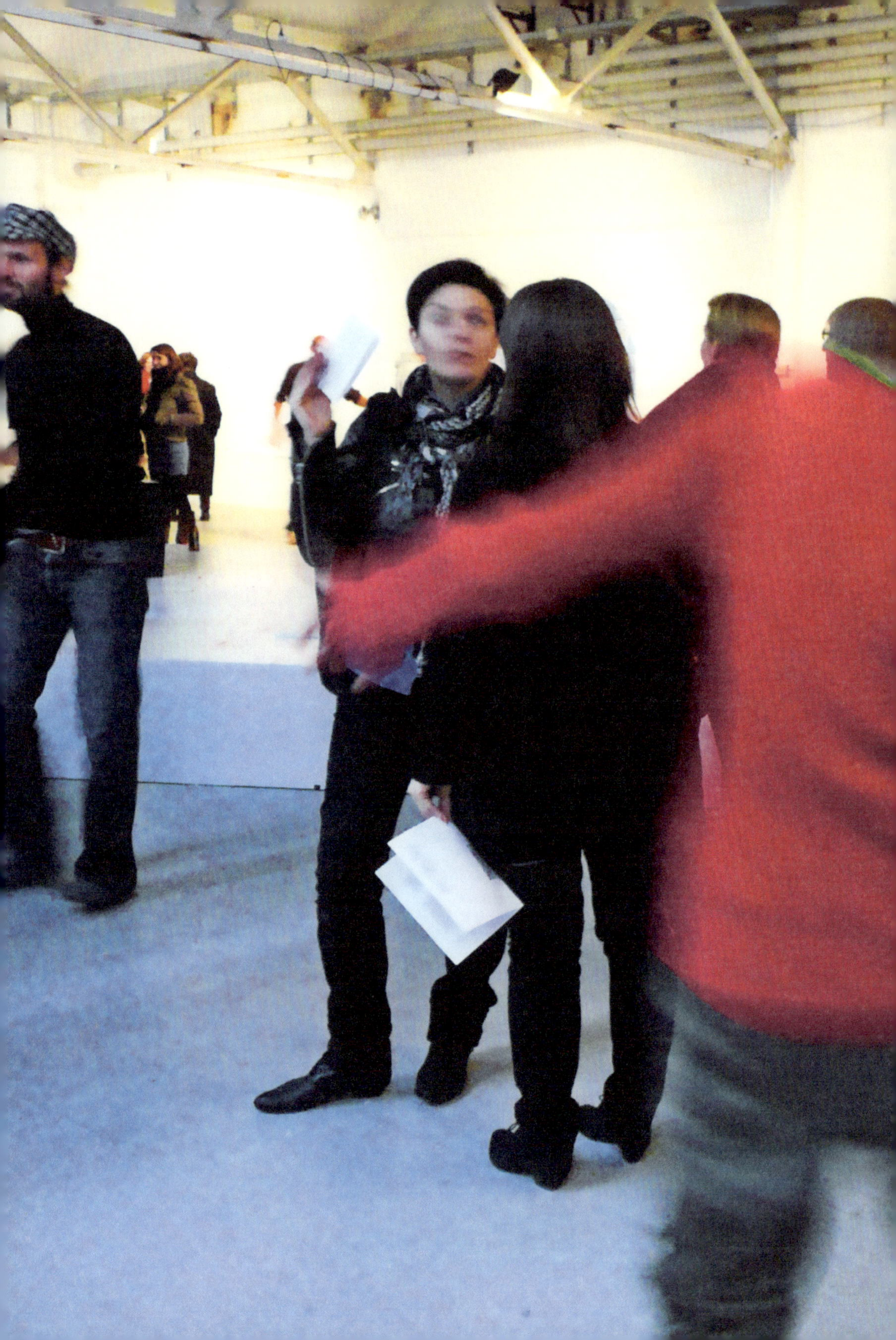

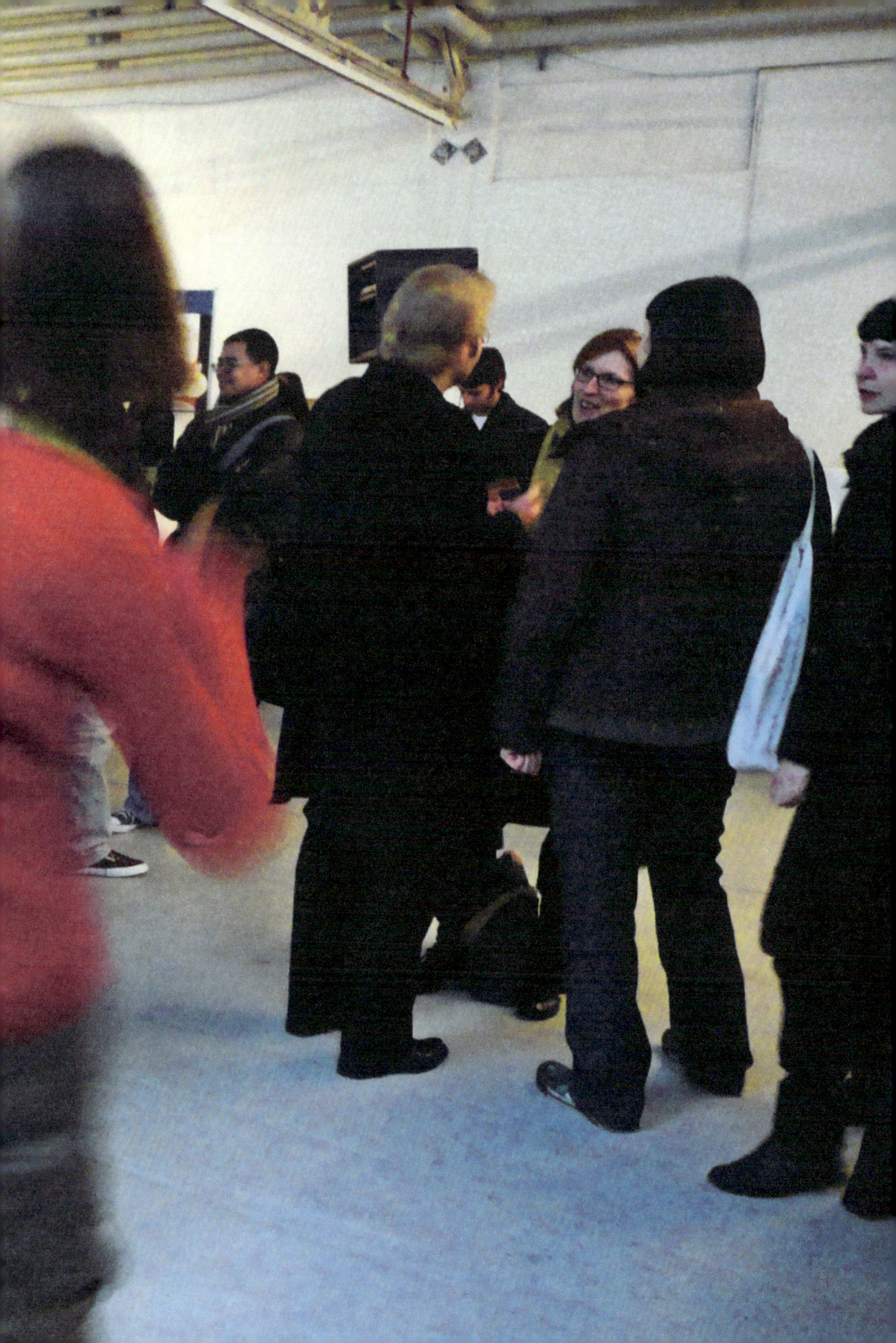

ANKE HOFFMANN

Die Bremer Stadtmusikanten
vol. 2

UN/MÖGLICHE GEMEINSCHAFT, ODER: DIE GEMEINSCHAFT IN DEN ZEITEN DER GLOBALISIERUNG

IM/POSSIBLE COMMUNITY. OR: COMMUNITY IN THE ERA OF GLOBALISATION

Stefan, 36 Jahre alt, arbeitet als Leiharbeiter in einem Energie-Unternehmen in Bremen. Vor fünf Jahren ist er aus einer Neonazi-Kameradschaft ausgestiegen, in der er als Schläger Respekt erntete. In der Haft fand er neue Freunde, türkische Freunde, und konnte eine Ausbildung zum Elektriker machen. Seit zwei Jahren lebt Stefan in Bremen und will sich hier ein neues Leben aufbauen. Er engagiert sich seit einem Jahr ehrenamtlich in einem Hausprojekt für Flüchtlinge. Dort trifft Stefan auf den 23-jährigen Mohammad aus dem Norden Malis, der als zehntes Kind seiner Familie sein Glück in Europa suchte und nur dank glücklicher Zufälle in Bremen gelandet ist. Mohammad kann nur schlecht lesen und schreiben und möchte gern einen Schulabschluss machen. Dort trifft Stefan auch auf Preslava aus Plovdiv, eine 31-jährige allein erziehende Frau, die als Prostituierte in Hamburg arbeitete. Im Hausprojekt hilft sie in der Küche mit und ist auf der Suche nach einem kinderfreundlichen Auskommen. Preslava benimmt sich fast ein wenig mütterlich gegenüber dem einsamen Mohammad, der sich mit der 15-jährigen Gizella, einer jungen Roma aus Ungarn, die aufgrund von Fremdenhass mit ihrer Familie nach Deutschland geflohen ist, angefreundet hat. Aufgrund der Sprachprobleme gestaltet sich die zarte Freundschaft zwischen den vieren eher schwierig. Der kostenlose Deutschunterricht im Hausprojekt hilft für die einfache Kommunikation. So kann Stefan den Dreien auch von seiner verrückten Idee, eine Band zu gründen, erzählen. Eine Band, so ungewöhnlich und unmöglich, dass sie unweigerlich Aufmerksamkeit erzeugen würde. Die drei anderen sind erstaunt, und können es nicht recht glauben. Doch bald tauschen sie sich über ihre individuellen Talente aus und planen erste Proben.

So könnte sie aussehen, die zeitgenössische Version der Bremer Stadtmusikanten, diese unterhaltsame Parabel über Mut und Selbsthilfe,

The Town Musicians of Bremen, vol. 2

Stefan, 36 years old, is an agency worker employed by a utilities company in Bremen. Five years ago he left a neo-Nazi gang where he had earned respect as a fighter. In jail he made new friends, Turkish friends, and trained as an electrician. Stefan has been living in Bremen for two years now and wants to build a new life for himself here. For the past year he has also worked as a volunteer at a hostel for refugees. That's where he met twenty-three year old Mohammed from northern Mali, who—as the tenth child in the family— had left home to seek his fortune in Europe and had made it to Bremen by a series of lucky circumstances. Mohammed still has difficulty writing and reading but he would very much like to graduate. At the hostel Stefan also met Preslava from Plovdiv, a thirty-one year old single mother, who used to be a sex worker in Hamburg. At the hostel she helps out in the kitchen in between looking for child-friendly employment. In some ways Preslava mothers lonely Mohammad, who is also friends with fifteen-year old Gizella, a young Roma from Hungary, whose family fled to Germany to escape ongoing xenophobia. Because they have no common language, the tentative friendship between the four is not without its difficulties.

The free German lessons at the hostel help with basic communication, and Stefan tells the other three about his crazy idea of forming a band. This band would be so unusual and impossible that it couldn't help but attract attention. The other three are astonished and can't really believe what they are hearing. But soon they are avidly discussing what talents each of them has and planning their first rehearsals.

It could be like that—a contemporary version of the Town Musicians of Bremen, that appealing parable of courage and self-help, friendship and creativity.[1] The characters are rather cliché-laden but perfectly imaginable— with the exception of this absurd, impossible community of four such different personas. Just as un/imaginable as the donkey, dog, cat and rooster who, with their shared experience as outcasts, together send the four robbers packing and happily spend the rest of their days in the woodland cottage. What kind of a community is formed by this alliance of outcasts who had been declared 'surplus to needs'?

The Town Musicians of Bremen are not a family, not a chess club or a party, but an im/possible community, like that of Stefan, Preslava, Mohammad and Gizella, a community that 'is able to respect differences and that at least partially does away with limitations and hate figures', as we said in our curators' statement for the exhibition *Im/Possible Community*. Thus, when we talk of an 'impossible' community, we mean it in both senses of the word: impossible because the more a community is inclusive and tolerates differences, the greater its tendency to being inconclusive and temporary. And impossible in the sense of casting aside existing thought patterns, establishing new values and cutting through ideas: being outrageous. Im/possible is about turning internal division within the group and oneself to advantage. Community always has to be created; it requires constant action— locating desires, arguing, listening. And it is precisely this continuous action, this degree of uncertainty and uncontrollability that makes communities into something exciting. For community is also about relinquishing a piece of oneself, letting it go, negating it.[2] Thus the Town Musicians of Bremen came to symbolise our group exhibition *Im/Possible Community*, the theme of which was developed in collaboration

---

1 .... This fairytale by the Brothers Grimm has also been used elsewhere as a parable of current precarity: the German dramatist Volker Lösch took it as the starting point for his play *ArmAltArbeits-los—Die Bremer Stadtmusikanten* (Theater Bremen, 2012), which comes to a climax with the group of 'superfluous' individuals violently destroying their own work situation. This prompted one critic to ask if the collective is the task that human beings should still work on when they themselves have become superfluous. See www.nachtkritik.de.

2 ...... For the curatorial statement by Volkart and Hoffmann on the exhibition *Im/Possible Community*, see: www.shedhalle.ch/en/exhibitions/impossible-community.

with the Institute for Critical Theory at Zurich University of the Arts.

Not One, But Many

In a band or an orchestra each musical instrument or voice follows its own part. By playing or singing together, temporarily in step with each other, with breaks from time to time and melody and counter-melody, they make music. This form of playing together thrives on differences, be it in pitch or timbre. Every community thrives on more or less different individual positions. But the polyphony of a community is traditionally conceived in terms of identities and exclusions rather than differences. Hence we feel moved to plead for im/possible communities that are not communities of similarity but dissimilarity, because this by definition induces self-questioning and, as a consequence, the questioning of the structure of the ties that bind the community's members together.

'In my view we should guard against "realising" communities … On the contrary, we should be opening them to the outside world, making them permeable. In other words, not so much perfecting them and fixing their locations as seeking out gaps and non-locations … There is a good example of this in literature, almost a theoretical concept, in Kafka's *The Great Wall of China.* The narrator tells us that the wall, which is to protect the "people", has to be built in sections, in fragments, with gaps between them. That could serve as an example of how a community should be built. Communities, wherever they are, should always also prepare for their own dismantling.'[3]

This is the view of the literary scholar Joseph Vogl. This permeable wall, which he takes as his example, symbolises the need for creating openings in bonds, which we often struggle with—despite our protestations of empathy and tolerance towards others. Looking around us at our own surroundings we see that artists make friends with other artists, academics with other academics, young Turks socialise with other young Turks, politicians with politicians, millionaires with millionaires, Muslims with Muslims. Crossing boundaries and forming ties with those who think and live differently is more complicated than we might have thought—both on a local and a global scale.

What other kinds of models of communal life are there that can provide a sense of belonging yet are still open? As so often, our attention turns to the omni-accessible Internet and our growing dependence on it. The Internet, with the reality of its networking potential across borders and time zones, has facilitated new forms of resistance and has opened up new realms of political action. Take the media-activist group Anonymous. Felix Stalder has written about the phenomenon of this particular im/possible community: 'For Anonymous is not one, but many. This is not a single group or network, but a swarm, or rather, a number of swarms, which bolster each other's efforts.'[4] This swarm of anti-capitalist cyber activists and hackers, who have been bombarding servers since 2010 in their determination to increase freedom of political thought and social justice, who have been attacking websites and organising real-life marches, is 'a collective without leaders that spurns the principles of representation in favour of direct participation in concrete projects'.[5] Their activities arise from an ad hoc consensus regarding the nature and aims of their ongoing Internet campaigns. Majority decisions constitute the legislative and the executive of this 'transient community of independent individuals with a horizontal organisational structure', as Stalder puts it. This type of organisation guarantees constant flexibility in its form and contents—up to and including its own dissolution.

---

3 .... Joseph Vogl, 'Enttotalisierte Begegnungsformen', interview with *An Architektur*, 2003, http://smallschoolofarchitecture.tinka.cc/en/node/52.

4 ... Felix Stalder, 'Anonymous—Zur Funktionsweise des Schwarms', 2012, http://berlinergazette.de/anonymous-schwarm.

5 .... Ibid.

Ulf Aminde: *Schamdruck*, 2009

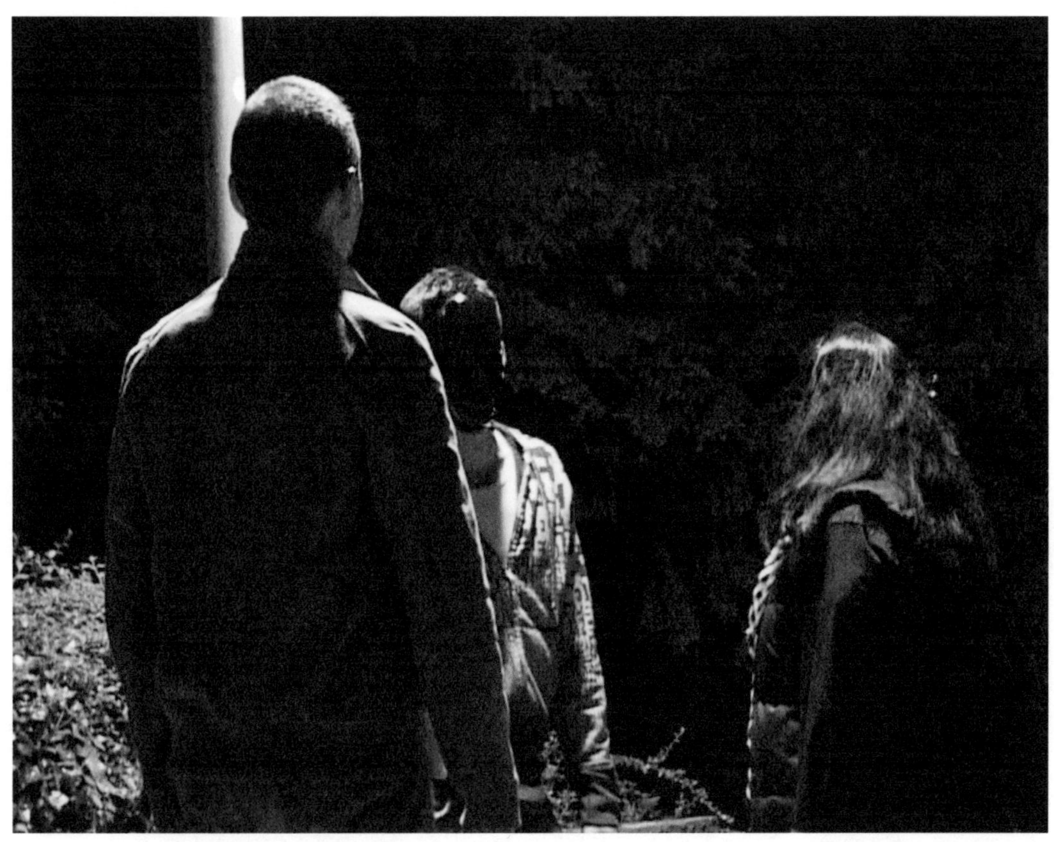

p-r-o-x-y: *Die undarstellbare Gemeinschaft*, 2009 (Ausstellungsansicht / Exhibition view)

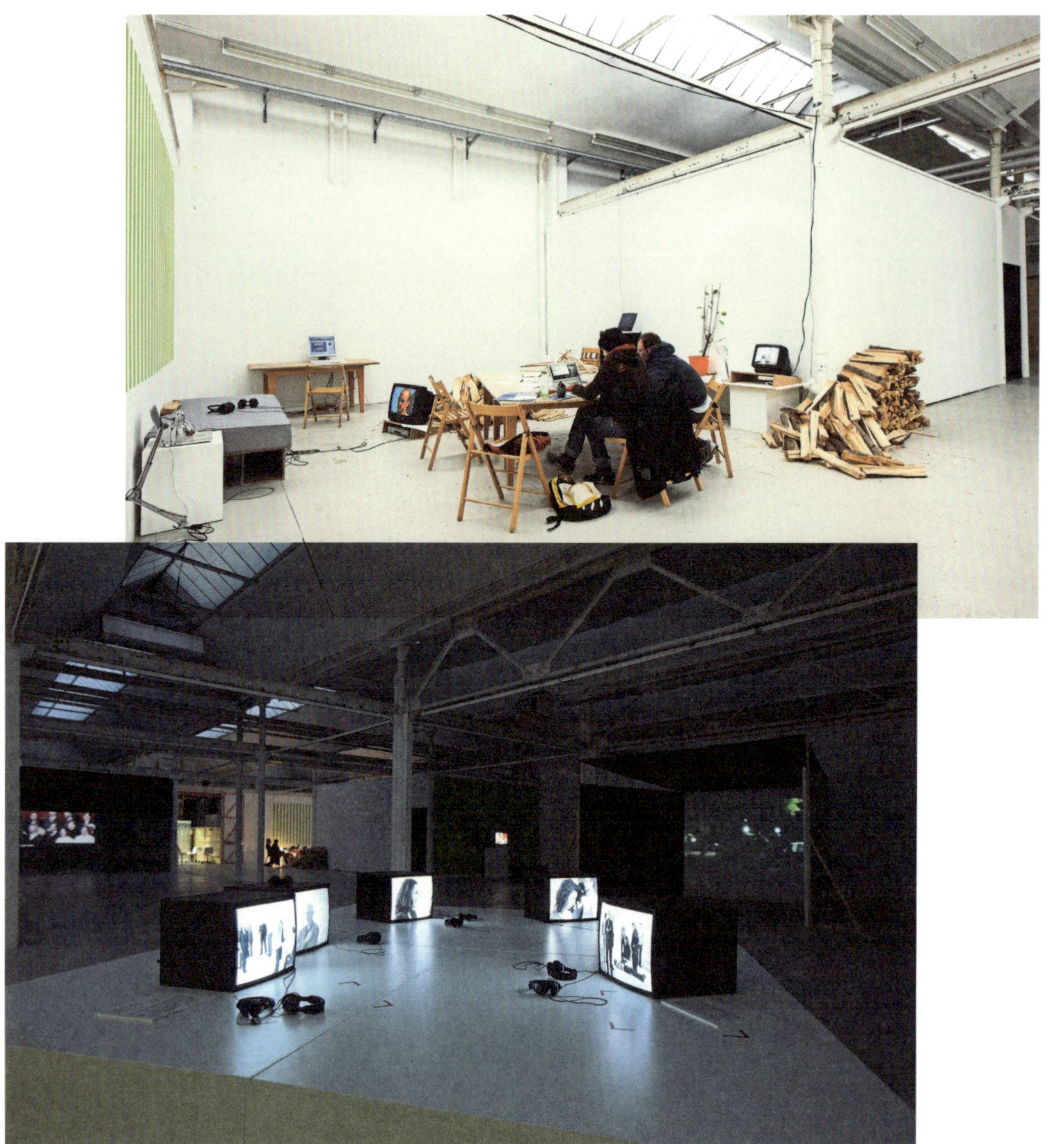

Juliane Zelwies: *Meisterwerke*, 2009 (Ausstellungsansicht / Exhibition view)

Freundschaft und Kreativität.[1] Etwas klischeebeladene Protagonist_innen, aber durchaus vorstellbar – bis auf diese absurde, un/mögliche Gemeinschaft der vier Ungleichen. Ähnlich un/vorstellbar, wie Esel, Hund, Katze und Hahn aus der geteilten Erfahrung des Abgeschoben-Seins die Räuberbande gemeinsam in die Flucht schlagen, um ihren Pensionsalltag in der Waldhütte zu verbringen. Was für eine Gemeinschaft ist diese Allianz der Ausgestossenen und ‚Überflüssigen'? Die Bremer Stadtmusikanten sind keine Familie, kein Skatverein oder keine Partei, sondern eine un/mögliche Gemeinschaft, wie die von Stefan, Preslava, Mohammad und Gizella, die „Unterschiede respektiert und Grenzen und Feindbilder zumindest partiell auflöst", so liest es sich in unserem kuratorischen Statement zur Ausstellung *Un/Mögliche Gemeinschaft*: Wenn wir also von einer ‚unmöglichen' Gemeinschaft sprechen, meinen wir das im doppelten Sinn des Wortes: Unmöglich, weil Gemeinschaften in dem Masse, in dem sie einschliessen und Differenzen zulassen, lediglich partiell und temporär sein können. Und unmöglich im Sinne von Denkmuster überschreiten, Werte neu setzen und Vorstellungen durchqueren: empörend sein. Un/möglich heisst, die Spaltung im Inneren der Gruppe und von sich selbst fruchtbar zu machen. Gemeinschaft muss hergestellt werden, sie ist permanentes Handeln: Wünsche platzieren, streiten, zuhören. Gerade dieses Verhandeln, dieser Grad an Unbestimmtheit und Unkontrollierbarkeit macht Gemeinschaften auch zu etwas Lustvollem: Gemeinschaftlich sein heisst somit auch, ein Stück von sich selbst abzugeben, loszulassen, aufzulösen.[2] So wurden die Bremer Stadtmusikanten denn zum Sinnbild unserer Gruppenausstellung *Un/Mögliche Gemeinschaft*, deren Thematik aus einer Zusammenarbeit mit dem Institut für Theorie der Zürcher Hochschule der Künste erwuchs.

Nicht eins, sondern viele

In einer Band, oder auch in einem Orchester, wird musiziert, indem jedes Instrument und jede Stimme nach einer eigenen Partitur spielt oder singt. Durch das Zusammenspiel, das temporären Gleichschritt, abwechselnd gesetzte Schnittpunkte oder gegenläufige Melodien erzwingt, erklingt Musik. Das Zusammenspiel basiert also auf Unterschieden, und sei es nur die Stimmlage oder der Klang. Jede Gemeinschaft basiert auf mehr oder weniger unterschiedlichen singulären Positionen. Aber die Polyphonie von Gemeinschaften wird traditionell in den Begriffen von Identitäts- und Ausschlusslogiken anstatt in Begriffen des Unterschieds gedacht. Deshalb plädieren wir für un/mögliche Gemeinschaften, die nicht eine Gemeinschaft der Gleichen, sondern der Ungleichen wäre, weil sie sich selbst auch immer in Frage stellen und damit ihr eigenes Gerüst der Verbindlichkeiten hinterfragen müsste.

„Man muss sich, glaube ich, davor hüten, Gemeinschaften zu ‚verwirklichen'. [...] Vielmehr sollte man sie öffnen, durchlässig machen. Also weniger vollenden und verorten, als nach Lücken und Nicht-Orten zu suchen. [...] Ein literarisches Beispiel, fast schon ein theoretisches Konzept, ist der *Bau der chinesischen Mauer* von Kafka. Dort wird gezeigt, dass die Mauer, die das ‚Volk' umschließen soll, nur in Rudimenten, in Fragmenten, also mit Löchern gebaut werden darf. Das wäre ein Beispiel für die Konstruktion des Gemeinschaftlichen. Gemeinschaften müssen dort, wo sie sich finden, immer auch ihren eigenen Abbau fabrizieren."[3]

Dies konstatiert der Literaturwissenschaftler Joseph Vogl. Diese löchrige Mauer, die er als Sinnbild heranzieht, verweist auf die Bedingung der Öffnung von Zusammenschlüssen, die uns selbst trotz aller proklamierter Empathie

---

1 .... Das Grimm'sche Märchen taugt auch anderswo zur aktuellen Prekariats-Parabel: Der deutsche Theaterdramatiker Volker Lösch nahm das Märchen als Ausgangspunkt für sein Theaterstück *ArmAltArbeitslos – Die Bremer Stadtmusikanten* (2012, Theater Bremen), bei dessen Klimax die Gruppe der Überflüssigen zur gewaltsamen Zerstörung ihrer Arbeitswelt ansetzt. Ist das Kollektiv, die Aufgabe, die der Mensch noch zu leisten hätte, wenn er überflüssig geworden ist?, summiert ein Kritiker. Nachzulesen hier: www.nachtkritik.de.

2 .... Vgl. kuratorisches Statement Volkart/Hoffmann zur Ausstellung *Un/Mögliche Gemeinschaft*: www.shedhalle.ch/de/ausstellungen/ unmoegliche-gemeinschaft.

3 .... Vogl, Joseph: Enttotalisierte Begegnungsformen. Interview mit *An Architektur*, 2003: http://smallschoolofarchitecture. tinka.cc/en/node/52.

und Toleranz für Andere oft schwer fällt. Betrachten wir unser eigenes Umfeld, stellt sich heraus: Künstler_innen sind mit Künstler_innen befreundet, Akademiker_innen mit Akademiker_innen , türkische Jugendliche mit türkischen Jugendlichen, Politiker_innen mit Politiker_innen, Millionäre mit Millionären, Muslim_innen mit Muslim_innen. Die Grenzen zu überschreiten und sich mit Andersdenkenden und Anderslebenden zu verbünden, ist komplizierter als gedacht – im Lokalen wie im Globalen.

Welche Alternativen gibt es von Bündnissen, deren Gemeinschaftsmodell, Zugehörigkeit verleiht und dennoch offen ist? Der Blick fällt, wie so oft, auf das allseits verfügbare Internet und unsere wachsenden Abhängigkeiten davon. Das Internet mit seinen grenz- und zeitüberschreitenden Vernetzungsrealitäten ermöglicht neue Formen des Widerstands und des politischen Handlungsspielraums: zum Beispiel die Medienaktivist_innen Anonymous. Felix Stalder schreibt über das Phänomen dieser ‚un/möglichen Gemeinschaft‘: „Anonymous ist nämlich nicht eins, sondern viele. Hier agiert keine Gruppe oder ein Netzwerk, sondern ein Schwarm oder, noch präziser: mehrere Schwärme, die einander verstärken.“[4] Dieser Schwarm aus Cyberaktivist_innen und Hacker_innen, der seit 2010 in anti-kapitalistischer Stossrichtung vor allem für politische Meinungsfreiheit und soziale Gerechtigkeit Server torpediert, Webseiten angreift oder reale Aufmärsche organisiert, sind „Kollektive ohne Anführer, die das Prinzip der Repräsentation ablehnen und die direkte Teilhabe an konkreten Projekten favorisieren“[5]. Die Basis ihres Agierens ist ein Ad-hoc-Konsens über Ziel und Form der Aktionen via Internet. Eine Mehrheitsentscheidung bildet die Legislative und gleichzeitig die Exekutive dieser „vorübergehenden Gemeinschaft aus unabhängigen Individuen, die sich horizontal organisieren“, so Stalder. Die Art und Weise dieser Organisationsform garantiert ständige Beweglichkeit in ihrer Form und in ihrem Inhalt – bis hin zu ihrer Auflösung.

Zusammen gewinnen oder einzeln verlieren[6]

Warum aber braucht es ein neues Nachdenken über Gemeinschaft? Der Ausgangspunkt für die Ausstellung *Un/Mögliche Gemeinschaft* lag in der Beobachtung und Analyse des Weltgeschehens, und dem, was wir tagtäglich in den Nachrichten hören. Und damit meinen wir die aktuelle Herausforderung durch die Häufung von globalen Krisen, die sich in der Entsolidarisierung in Gesellschaftsgefügen und der fortschreitenden Unterwanderung von Demokratie gegenseitig begründen.

Zum einen verursacht die Finanz- und Bankenkrise nicht nur einen Strudel von Währungsabwertungen und Arbeitsmarktimplosionen, sondern macht auch eine Schwächung der Demokratie deutlich. Sichtbar wird diese Schwächung im wachsenden Verdruss der Bürger_innen mit den politischen Parteien, in massiven (Jugend-) Bürger_innenprotesten, in aktivistischen Aktionen oder der weltweiten Occupy-Bewegung. Der globale wirtschaftliche Wettbewerb, in dessen Schatten nationale Arbeitsmärkte erodieren, Arbeitsmigration wächst und Preisspekulationen auf heimische Rohstoffe zunehmen, zeigt, dass wir das nationale Zeitalter hinter uns gelassen haben. Dazu schüren Katastrophen wie die in Fukushima Zukunftsängste, weil sie die vermeintliche technologische Beherrschbarkeit von Umweltrisiken widerlegen. Auch die prognostizierte Klimaveränderung verunsichert und birgt unberechenbare Umweltkatastrophen. Terrorismus und religiöser Fundamentalismus sind zusätzliche Faktoren, die die Entgrenzung der Bedrohungen charakterisieren. Der durch all diese Risiken gekennzeichnete radikale globale Wandel verändert die bisher gewohnten nationalen Lösungsansätze und politischen Gewissheiten. Die Risiken haben sich ‚demokratisiert‘: Prekariatsängste machen vor Akademiker_innen nicht halt, Hitzesommer nicht vor der Schweiz, Unternehmensabwanderungen nicht vor den USA und Staatsbankrotte nicht vor Griechenland.

4............ Stalder, Felix: *Anonymous – Zur Funktionsweise des Schwarms*, 2012: http://berlinergazette.de/anonymous-schwarm/#more-28658.
5.. Stalder: *Anonymous*.

6...................................... Beck, Ulrich: Empört Euch, Europäer. In: *Der Spiegel* 34 (2011), 128–129, hier 128.

'Win together or lose alone'[6]

But why does community need to be rethought? The exhibition *Im/Possible Community* came about as a result of the close observation and analysis of certain world events and the things we hear in the news day after day— by which we mean the ongoing challenge of the current build-up of global crises, the desolidarisation of societal bonds and the progressive undermining of democracy, which are currently all fuelling each other.

On one hand the crisis in the banking and financial industries has not only unleashed a rush of currency devaluations and implosions in the job market, it has also noticeably weakened democracy. This new weakness is evident in the growing dissatisfaction the general public is expressing regarding political parties, in mass (youth) protests, in activist campaigns and in the worldwide occupy movement. Global economic competition—in whose shadow national job markets are eroding, economic migration is growing and there is ever more intense speculation in home-produced raw materials—shows that the age of national priorities is now over. At the same time, catastrophes like the events in Fukushima heighten our fear of the future by underlining the incapacity of our current technological resources to cope with environmental crises, as do prognoses of climate change and unforeseeable environmental disasters. Meanwhile terrorism and religious fundamentalism are yet more factors in the increasingly boundless threats on the horizon. The radical global transformation reflected in all these dangers is altering customary national solutions and political certainties. And these dangers have 'democratised' themselves: academics are no longer exempt from precarity anxieties, even Switzerland now has its heat waves, the USA has started to see companies relocating overseas and Greece faces national bankruptcy.

The sociologist Ulrich Beck sees current developments leading to a 'global risk society': 'We cannot escape … our shared fate, because no matter what we do, global risk capitalism is creating new existential tensions and ties extending across national, ethnic, religious and political boundaries.'[7] The scenarios that Beck outlines as possible actions run in contrary motion: towards the increase of ethnic and nationalist (exclusion) policies or Hegelian reason[8] and, hence, also towards cooperation and investment in, let's say, im/possible communities. Because of the destabilising effects of financial crises, climate change and terrorism, which cannot be resolved on a national level, we need alliances or, as Beck puts it, an 'enforced community'. Communal action is vital to our survival, appropriate in the present day and age, and fundamentally reasonable. And yet old hate figures and exclusion mechanisms are as strong as ever and still hold sway. The destabilisation, triggered by the progressive dissolution of the certainties of nation states, is successfully exploited by populism and neo-nationalism.[9] This in turn, as Beck has shown, leads to the 'mutual overlaying and reinforcement of self-destructive processes in Europe: xenophobia, Islamophobia and Europhobia.'[10] But we cannot stop time, all we can do is respond to it as best we can. Cultural and economic globalisation creates dependencies and interdependencies that take no heed of customary alliances. The changes that we are seeing today both facilitate and necessitate im/possible communities—possibly more urgently than ever before.

Art and Social Participation

What keeps im/possible communities together? How are they constituted? What is their self-identity? How can im/possible communities forge temporary associations without their

6.......... Ulrich Beck, 'Empört Euch, Europäer', in *Der Spiegel* 34 (Hamburg, 2011), p. 128.

7... Ibid.
8... Ibid.
9......... This is exemplified, for instance, in the cultural-racist and xenophobic campaigns 'Anti-Minarett' of 2010 and 'Gegen Masseneinwanderung' in 2011 run by the Swiss People's Party SVP.
10................................. Beck, 'Empört Euch, Europäer'.

behaviour becoming either opportunistic or arbitrary? What are temporary communities capable of? How can forms of togetherness arise that do not by definition also mean exclusion and totality? How can we respond to the crisis of democracy? All of these questions of ours were directed towards artists.

In so far as they engage critically with the problems of our own time, artists are the agents of social consciousness, of social and cultural participation and—possibly—of social change. The exhibition project *Im/Possible Community* used a range of different media and aesthetic constellations and reflections to gather together prospects and experiences regarding various aspects of what it is to form a community. The main themes were media activism and freedom of thought, democracy and public life, migration and cultural globalisation, social utopias and collective psychodynamics.

In so doing we attached particular importance to the idea of mediating community as a real experience of communal existence—be it in the spirit of utopian striving or of the desire for social participation and collaboration. To this end we invited a number of artists for whom the notion of participation is central to their work. We opened the exhibition with an artistic *mise en scène* by Nevin Aladağ. *Occupation Shedhalle 2009* (fig. p. 182) was a performance that intervened in the usual social ritual of the art show opening. During the curators' opening address, certain individuals in the audience started to dance, each entirely on his or her own, without any music. Undaunted, passionate, self-absorbed—as though they were living sculptures mingling with the evening's guests. As the sound of music gradually increased the contrasting situations of exhibition opening and party developed a dynamic that soon also drew in the members of the public and set them dancing, too. This approximately forty-minute intervention came to an abrupt end when the music stopped. Nevin Aladağ's performance, *Occupation Shedhalle 2009*, presented members of the public with a surprise collective action that they had not been warned about. Hence their actual presence was not an anonymous 'I Like' or 'I Dislike', but allowed

them to directly experience a groundswell of movement to which they could respond as they liked. Those present variously reacted to the intervention with uncertainty or amusement, delight or liberating self-abandon, in some cases to the point of ecstasy, and with very few instances of dismay or displeasure.

Another moment of communal existence was instigated in the form of the First *Zurich Complaints Choir* (see p. 228), according to the format devised by the German-Finnish artist duo Oliver Kochta-Kalleinen and Tellervo Kalleinen. Crowdsourcing was used to collect complaints and assemble a volunteer choir. This *Zurich Complaints Choir*, with its own words and music for a complaints song, performed in the centre of Zurich one Saturday in January 2010. The intention of the artist duo Kalleinen/Kochta-Kalleinen is that the members of each Complaints Choir should have a sense of a shared experience. The format allows participants to take possession of a public 'complaints space' and to list in public the things that bother them—political, funny, accusing others of misdemeanours—unlike the 'silent masses'. It's about letting off steam and being heard. But the most important thing is the act of coming together, with no thought to professionalism of any kind, solely for the fun of it and for the sake of communally realising a creative, social project. By now this initiative has seen countless people in almost ninety countries singing in public about their own personal complaints.[11]

The American artist Perry Bard also set up a participatory, creative platform, albeit in this case with no actual physical gathering of the participants. She presented her collective auteur film, which—using the style of media activism and open source contributions from countless co-authors all over the world— is constantly being recreated. Her work *Man With A Movie Camera: The Global Remake* (fig. p. 194) is based on the experimental film shot by Dziga Vertov in 1929. The original movie

11 ... The *First Zurich Complaints Choir*, with lyrics and photographs, is documented on p. 228.

UN/MÖGLICHE GEMEINSCHAFT

Isabelle Stever: *Eine demokratische Gesprächsrunde zu festgelegten Zeiten*, 2009

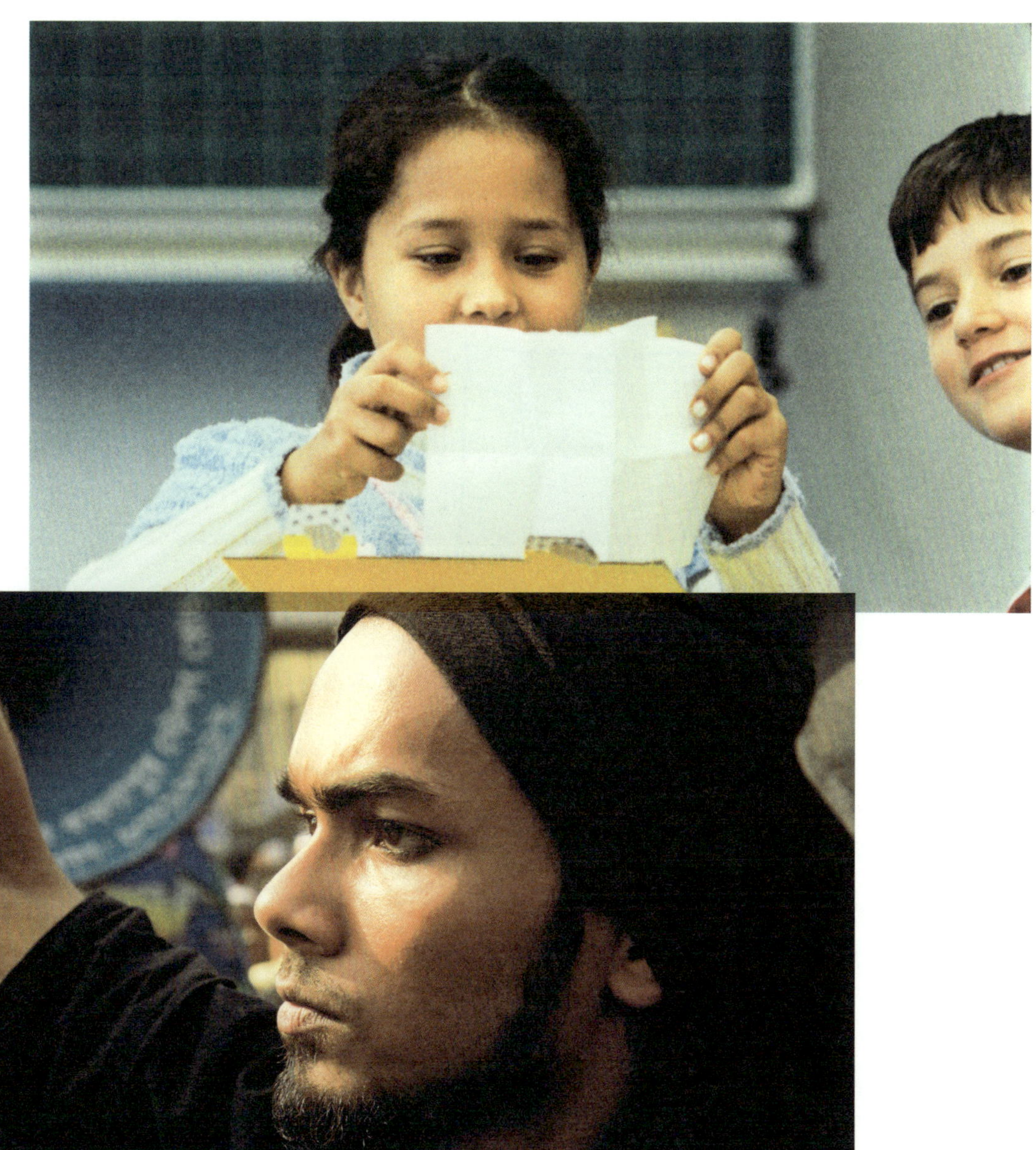

Naeem Mohaiemen: *Live True Life or Die Trying*, 2009

Perry Bard: *Man With a Movie Camera: The Global Remake*, 2007

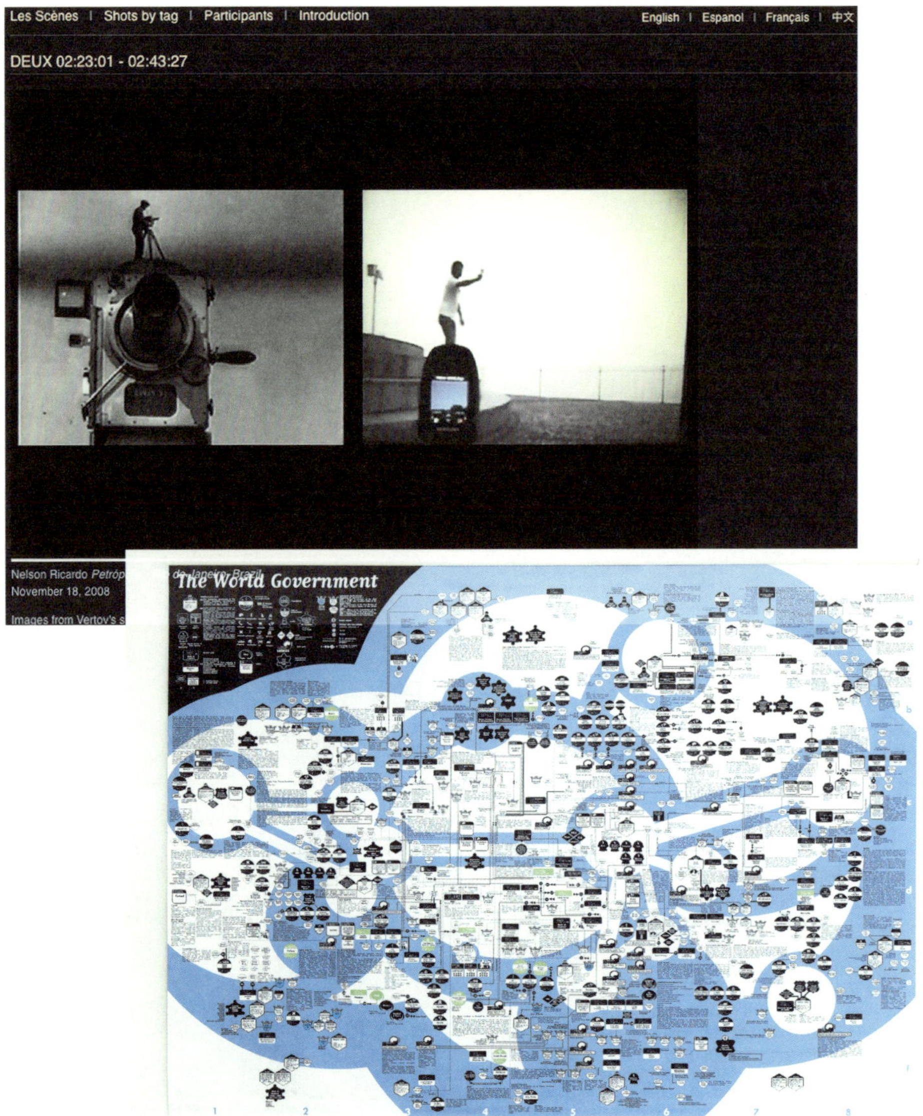

Bureau d'Etudes: *World Gouvernement*, 2005 (Ausstellungsansicht / Exhibition view)

Der Soziologe Ulrich Beck beschreibt die aktuelle Entwicklung als „Weltrisikogesellschaft": „Der Schicksalsgemeinschaft kann man [...] nicht entfliehen, weil der Weltrisikokapitalismus, egal was wir tun, neuartige existentielle Spaltungen und Bindungen über nationale, ethnische, religiöse und politische Grenzen hinweg stiftet."[7] Die Szenarien, die Beck als mögliche Handlungsbögen skizziert, verlaufen in gegenläufige Richtungen: in die der Zunahme von ethnischer und nationalistischer (Abschottungs-)Politik oder die der Hegelschen Vernunft,[8] und damit die Kooperation und die Investition in, sagen wir, un/mögliche Gemeinschaften. Weil Finanzkrise, Klimawandel und Terrorismus verunsichern und nicht mehr national lösbar sind, braucht es Allianzen, oder wie Beck meint, eine „Zwangsgemeinschaft". Gemeinsames Handeln ist lebensnotwendig, zeitgemäss und vernunftorientiert. Und trotzdem behalten die gewohnten Feindbilder und Ausschlussmechanismen an Substanz und Anziehungskraft. Die Verunsicherung, hervorgerufen durch die fortschreitende Auflösung der nationalstaatlichen Stabilitäten, wird durch Populismus und Neo-Nationalismus erfolgreich ausgenutzt.[9] Dadurch, schreibt Beck, kommt es zur „wechselseitigen Überlagerung und Verstärkung von selbstzerstörerischen Prozessen in Europa: Ausländerfeindlichkeit, Islamfeindlichkeit und Europafeindlichkeit"[10]. Aber wir können die Zeit nicht aufhalten, sondern nur adäquat darauf reagieren. Die kulturelle und ökonomische Globalisierung schafft Abhängigkeiten und Interdependenzen quer zu allen gewohnten Allianzen. Der Wandel, den wir heute erleben, ermöglicht und verlangt nach un/möglichen Gemeinschaften – vielleicht so dringend wie nie zuvor.

Kunst und soziale Teilhabe

Was hält un/mögliche Gemeinschaften zusammen? Auf welcher Basis konstituieren sie sich?

Wie identifizieren sie sich? Wie können un/mogliche Gemeinschaften temporäre Bündnisse schaffen, ohne opportunistisch oder beliebig zu werden? Wozu sind temporäre Gemeinschaften in der Lage? Wie können Formen von Zusammen-Sein entstehen, die nicht per se Ausschluss und Totalität meinen? Wie kann auf die Krise von Demokratie reagiert werden? Diese unsere Fragen richteten sich an Künstler_innen. Künstler_innen fungieren, soweit sie sich kritisch mit aktuellen Problemen auseinandersetzen, als Agent_innen eines sozialen Bewusstseins, sozialer und kultureller Teilhabe und – möglicherweise – der sozialen Veränderung. Das Ausstellungsprojekt *Un/Mögliche Gemeinschaft* versammelte mittels unterschiedlicher Medien und Ästhetik Konstellationen und Reflexionen, Angebote und Erfahrungen zu Aspekten von Gemeinschaftsbildung. Themen waren dabei Medienaktivismus und Meinungsfreiheit, Demokratie und Öffentlichkeit, Migration und kulturelle Globalisierung, soziale Utopien und kollektive Psychodynamik.

Gemeinschaft als reale Erfahrung des Gemeinsam-Seins zu vermitteln, war uns dabei besonders wichtig, sei es als utopisches Moment oder dem Wunsch nach sozialer Teilhabe verpflichtet. Daher haben wir mehrere Künstler_innen eingeladen, die Partizipation und Kollaboration als zentrale Momente ihrer Arbeit konzipierten. Wir eröffneten die Ausstellung mit einer künstlerischen Inszenierung von Nevin Aladağ. *Occupation Shedhalle 2009* (Abb. S. 182/183) ist eine Performance, die in das gewohnte soziale Ritual der Vernissage interveniert. Während der Eröffnungsrede der Kuratorinnen begannen Einzelne inmitten der Zuhörerschaft zu tanzen, jede_r für sich, ohne Musik. Unbeirrt, leidenschaftlich und versunken. So als wären sie lebende Skulpturen inmitten ihres Publikums. Mit der leise anschwellenden Musik bekam das gegenläufige Setting von Ausstellungseröffnung versus Party eine Dynamik, die auch das Publikum erfasste und zum Tanzen anregte. Die etwa 40 Minuten andauernde Intervention wurde abrupt mit dem Verstummen der Musik beendet. Nevin Aladağs Performance *Occupation Shedhalle 2009* konfrontierte die Besucher_innen mit einer kollektiven Aktion, in die sie nicht eingeweiht waren. Dabei ging es

---

7 .... Beck: Empört Euch, Europäer, 128.
8 .... Vgl. Beck: Empört Euch, Europäer, 128.
9 .... Hier sei exemplarisch nur auf die kulturrassistischen und xenophobischen Kampagnen ‚Anti-Minarett' 2010 und ‚Gegen Masseneinwanderung' 2011 der Schweizerischen Volkspartei SVP verwiesen.
10 .... Beck: Empört Euch, Europäer, 128.

aufgrund der direkten Anwesenheit nicht um ein anonymes „I Like" oder „I Dislike", sondern um die unmittelbare Erfahrung einer Bewegung, zu der man sich, wie auch immer, verhalten konnte. Bei den Anwesenden entstanden wahlweise Gefühle der Unsicherheit oder Belustigung, Freude oder befreienden Ausgelassenheit bis hin zu Ekstase, nur selten Verstimmung oder Unlust, ob der Intervention.

Ein anderes Erfahrungsmoment des Gemein-sam-Seins initiierten wir mit dem *ersten Zürcher Beschwerdechor* (vgl. S. 228) auf der Basis der Idee des finnisch-deutschen Künstlerduos Oliver Kochta-Kalleinen und Tellervo Kalleinen. Per Crowdsourcing wurden vielerlei ‚private' Beschwerden als auch freiwillige Sänger_innen gesucht. Der Chor aus Zürcher_innen mit einem eigens getexteten und komponierten Beschwerde-song trat an einem Samstag im Januar 2010 in Zürichs Innenstadt auf. Dem Künstlerduo Kalleinen/Kochta-Kalleinen geht es darum, mit dem Chor ein Gefühl des gemeinsamen Erlebens zu schaffen. Das Format ermöglicht den Teil-nehmer_innen, sich einen öffentlichen ‚Klageraum' zu erobern und Beschwerden, politische, witzige und anklagende, öffentlich aufzuführen, im Gegensatz zur ‚stummen Masse'. Es geht darum, sich Luft zu machen und Gehör zu verschaffen. Das Wichtigste aber war, im Zusammenkommen – ungeachtet von Professionalität und aufgrund von Lust und Engagement – ein soziales und kreatives Projekt zu realisieren. Diese Initiative hat unzählige Menschen in knapp 90 Ländern dazu motiviert, öffentlich auf der Strasse ein Lied von individuellen Beschwerden zu singen.[11]

Die amerikanische Künstlerin Perry Bard initiierte ebenfalls eine partizipatorische, kreative Platt-form, allerdings ohne direktes körperliches Zusammenkommen. Perry Bard präsentierte eine Art kollektiven Autorenfilm, der sich im Stil von Medienaktivismus und Open Source mithilfe unzähliger globaler Mitautor_innen ständig neu gestaltet. Die Arbeit *Man With A Moving Camera: The Global Remake* (Abb. S. 194) basiert auf dem 1929 gedrehten Experimentalfilm von Dziga

Vertov. Der historische Film zeigt auf recht hero-ische Art und Weise die Gesellschaft der jungen Sowjetrepublik und wie ihre Zukunft auf Tausenden von eifrigen Menschen basiert. Perry Bard eröffnet einer virtuellen Community die Möglich-keit, den Film neu zu ‚schreiben', eigene kurze Handy-Clips zu drehen, sie auf eine Webseite zu laden und den originalen Film-Kapiteln gegen-überzustellen. So entsteht ein Remake des Klassikers, ohne Drehbuch und von einer unsicht-baren und temporären Gemeinschaft gestaltet, wie sie so typisch ist für unsere heutige Zeit der virtuellen Verschaltung im Internet und den Möglichkeiten des Web 2.0.

Weniger die globale, als mehr die lokale Verge-meinschaftung interessierte p-r-o-x-y (Abb. S. 188), die selbst eine un/mögliche und temporäre Gemeinschaft von Künstler_innen und Philosoph_innen war. In ihrem Ausstellungs-setting, das vielerlei Handlungsmöglichkeiten eröffnet, sind Elemente eines Versammlungs-raums mit Tisch und ein angedeutetes Lagerfeuer einer Überwachungskamera gegenüberstellt, die das Gefühl von Loyalität und Offenheit hinter-fragt und verletzt. In diesem Setting, diesem potentiellen Raum für kollektives Agieren, zeigt sich das, laut p-r-o-x-y, „Undarstellbare von Gemeinschaft", weil Gemeinschaft sich immer wieder neu ereignen muss. So führten Exkursionen und Beobachtungen, angeleitet durch p-r-o-x-y auch Ausstellungsbesucher_innen durch die Stadt, um rituelle Vergemeinschaftungen oder spontane Versammlungen zu besuchen. Diese Arbeiten, die mit Mitteln der Partizipation und Teilhabe reale soziale Erfahrungen und Erlebnisse vermittelten, stellten zentrale Fragen von Gemeinschaftsbildung und Tragfähigkeit von un/möglichen Gemeinschaften.

Konflikt und Aushandlung

Die Realität des Zusammenlebens, in Gesellschaft und Gemeinschaft, war ein weiterer zentraler Schwerpunkt der künstlerischen Arbeiten in der Ausstellung. Das Medium Video stand dabei als bevorzugtes Mittel der Dokumentation, aber auch der Inszenierung im Mittelpunkt. In Ulf Amindes Videoarbeit *Schamdruck* (Abb. S. 187)

11.......... Der Songtext des *Ersten Zürcher Beschwerdechors* und Fotos findet sich auf Seite 228.

presents a distinctly heroic picture of society in the young Soviet Union, with its future dependent on the efforts of thousands of committed individuals. Perry Bard, for her part, gave a virtual community the chance to 'rewrite' sequences from the original movie by uploading their own equivalent short mobile-phone videos to a website set up for this purpose. The result is a remake of the classic movie, without a screenplay, by an invisible and temporary community, of the kind that has nowadays come to typify the virtual connections in the Internet and the possibilities opened up by Web 2.0.

p-r-o-x-y (fig. p. 188) from Zurich turned its attention to creating a local, rather than global, communal existence, which itself proved to be an im/possible and temporary community of artists and philosophers. In their exhibition scenario, which opened up the potential for all kinds of actions, aspects of a meeting room with a table and indications of a camp fire were juxtaposed with a number of surveillance cameras, which cast doubt on and detracted from any sense of loyalty and openness. This setting, a space for potential collective action, demonstrated, as p-r-o-x-y put it, the 'unrepresentability of community', because any community constantly has to reinvent itself. So excursions and observations, led by p-r-o-x-y, took exhibition visitors out into the city to visit formal communities and spontaneous gatherings alike. These works, which mediated real social experiences through direct social participation brought to light fundamental questions concerning the formation of communal groups and the sustainability of im/possible communities.

Conflict and Negotiation

The reality of living together, of society and community, was another main focus of the works of art in the exhibition. Video turned out to be the preferred medium for both documentation and *mise en scène*. Ulf Aminde's video work *Schamdruck* (fig. p. 187) presented the following scenario: One night, in a park in Frankfurt am Main in the midst of gigantic

bank towers, there is an encounter between three people: a female investment banker, a junkie and a rent boy. During the course of their dialogue, which is both physically and linguistically uncomfortable, a conflict between morals, responsibility and guilt unfolds. Ulf Aminde uses a 'family situation' with authentic protagonists to re-enact the unequal competition for financial capitalism, the drugs scene and prostitution between those whose morals, life patterns and fates society judges very differently. The conflict and the mutual reproaches of the three 'representatives' reflect the intractability of the inclusions and exclusions sanctioned by society. Thus Aminde, who is based in Berlin, created a picture that, as he puts it, 'articulates society's disbelief in its own fiction of society'. The evident mismatch between social recognition and the privileges enjoyed by some becomes almost physically tangible in the irreconcilable encounter between the members of this 'Frankfurt family'.

The handling of conflicts also has to be experienced and learnt. That is the theme of the short film *Eine demokratische Gesprächsrunde zu festgelegten Zeiten* (fig. p. 193) directed by Isabelle Stever. A teacher, with a class of nine to eleven year olds from contrasting social and cultural backgrounds, sets up a class council, which discusses day-to-day problems in structured debates with speakers taking on specific roles. In a manner that is as yet unfamiliar to them, the children communicate and negotiate their antipathies, anxieties and resentments, and the short film shows how essential the development of rituals, roles and methods of conflict resolution are when it comes to respecting differences and agreeing on compromises.

That this learning phase in fact never comes to an end and that unresolved conflicts can lead to serious internal anxieties and aggression is the theme of the five-canal video installation by Juliane Zelwies. Her *Meisterwerke* (Masterpieces) (see p. 213) takes us into the realms of unspoken social mental conflicts, which are evident in even the smallest community. To this end Zelwies created a very unusual social configuration. Taking five historic paintings as her starting point, works such as Diego Velázquez *Las Meninas*, she filmed volunteers who had adopted the roles of the different family members in the painting under the guidance of a psychotherapist. The participants represent what is visible in the paintings but also that which is not visible but may well have contributed to the making of the painting. On the basis of the artificial configuration, a dialogue develops that primarily concerns the iconography of the paintings but that also generates powerful emotional tensions, resistance and outbursts on the part of the volunteers, which even the viewer feels painfully drawn into. For Zelwies this is an experimental investigation into the hidden psychodynamics of art. The paintings now indirectly serve as indicators of issues the participants are suppressing and of as yet unresolved projections. Their astonishing behaviour shows that in each and every one of us there is already an im/possible community, filled with desires and anxieties, images of ourselves and others that collide with each other and that we (have to) negotiate.

Negotiation and conflict also feature in Naeem Mohaiemen's photographic installation *Live True Life Or Die Trying* (fig. p. 193), which counters gatherings of the political Left and Islamists in Dhaka, Bangladesh with an artistic-photographic intervention into its documentation. The actual representation of these different political communities becomes somewhat indistinct, conveying a sense of Mohaiemen's disappointment with political developments in his native country. For their part, the artist duo Andree Korpys and Markus Löffler—acute observers of the choreographies of governmental violence—undertook an investigation into political representation and the rituals of conflict as seen in the mass demonstrations and blockades surrounding the transportation of nuclear waste to Gorleben and the G8 Summit in Heiligendamm in 2008. The video work *Eure Kinder werden so wie wir* juxtaposes a brightly coloured, impassioned community of demonstrators with a uniform army embodying state and police violence. The images captured by Korpys/Löffler attest to the implacability of these different roles and their practiced execution. They tell of an im/possible community, whose resistance culminates in the oracular chant directed by the demonstrators at their counterparts: 'Eure Kinder werden so wie wir'—your children will be like us![12]

Social participation, freedom of thought, representation, conflict, negotiation and forming a community were the themes of the works by the invited artists. On one hand, video and photography were used to document the reality of certain power relations. The artistic take on these situations was generally open; a detail, a stance and a perspective would be selected, but without proposing patterns of interpretation. Society and communities were reflected in all their contradictions and lapses—contradictions that demonstrate that friend and foe are often not so far apart after all, or that seemingly fixed roles in communal structures often too rarely questioned. On the other hand, we also saw that there are occasions when situations set up by artists can inspire different community types and create unexpected openings. Artists themselves thought of communities as open, debatable, temporary associations of equals, which could be used as part of our experience of the world to address and (re-)solve private and public issues. And in the back of our minds—and of the artists, too, whom we invited to participate in this exhibition project—was the notion of creating a *We* that includes all of *You* and that engages with differences and conflicts on the basis of what we are facing, and that has to be dealt with.

Translated by Fiona Elliott

12... There is a text-image collage from Korpys/Löffler's subsequent work, *Atom*, in this chapter.

begegnen wir folgendem Szenario: Auf einem Parkgelände im nächtlichen Frankfurt am Main, inmitten turmhoher Bankgebäude, treffen drei Personen aufeinander: eine Investmentbankerin, ein Junkie und ein Stricher. Im körperlich wie sprachlich beklemmenden Dialog entspinnt sich eine Konfrontation von Moral, Verantwortung und Schuld. Ulf Aminde inszeniert den ungleichen Wettbewerb von gesellschaftlich moralisierten Lebensentwürfen und -schicksalen um Finanzkapitalismus, Drogenszene und Prostitution in einer Art Familienaufstellung mit authentischen Protagonist_innen. Der Konflikt und die Vorwürfe der drei ‚Stellvertreter_innen' reflektieren die Vertracktheit der sanktionierten Ein- und Ausschlüsse der Gesellschaft. So entsteht ein Bild, das „den Unglauben an die Fiktion von Gesellschaft formuliert, die die Gesellschaft von sich selber hat", so der Berliner Künstler. Die vermeintliche Schieflage von gesellschaftlicher Anerkennung und gewährten Privilegien wird in der unversöhnlichen Gegenüberstellung der ‚Frankfurter Familie' fast körperlich spürbar.

Auch das Austragen von Konflikten muss gelebt und gelernt werden. Das war Thema des Kurzfilms *Eine demokratische Gesprächsrunde zu festgelegten Zeiten* (Abb. S. 193) der Regisseurin Isabelle Stever. Die Lehrerin einer Klasse von Neun- bis Elfjährigen aus unterschiedlichen sozialen und kulturellen Zusammenhängen stellt mit den Kindern einen Klassenrat auf, der alltägliche Probleme in einer geführten und nach Sprechrollen aufgeteilten Auseinandersetzung diskutiert. In der für die Kinder ungewohnten Art und Weise, ihre Antipathien, Ängste und Missgunst kommunikativ auszuhandeln, zeigt der dokumentarische Kurzfilm, wie essentiell die Ausbildung von Ritualen, Kompetenzen und Methoden der Konfliktaushandlung ist, um Unterschiede zu respektieren und gleichzeitig Kompromisse miteinander zu erreichen.

Dass diese Lernphase eigentlich nie aufhört und sich ungeklärte Konflikte zu ernsthaften psychischen Ängsten und Aggressionen entwickeln können, behandelte die Künstlerin Juliane Zelwies. Ihre 5-Kanal-Videoinstallation *Meisterwerke* (vgl. S. 213) führt uns auf die Ebene unausgesprochener sozialer Psychokonflikte, die sich in der Kleinstgemeinschaft bemerkbar machen. Dazu inszeniert Zelwies ein sehr ungewöhnliches soziales Setting: Auf der Basis von fünf historischen Bildern, so z.B. *Die Hoffräulein* von Diego Velázquez, stellen sich freiwillige Teilnehmer_innen unter Leitung eines Psychotherapeuten in einer Familienaufstellung der Kamerabeobachtung. Sie stehen für das, was auf den Bildern zu sehen, und für das, was nicht zu sehen ist, aber möglicher Teil des Entstehungsprozesses der Malerei gewesen sein könnte. Dieser künstlichen Konstellation folgend, entwickelt sich ein Dialog, der auf die Ikonografie der Bilder gerichtet ist, und dennoch starke emotionale Spannungen, Widerstände und Ausbrüche bei den Teilnehmer_innen erzeugt, denen man sich selbst als Betrachter_in ausgeliefert fühlt. Für Zelwies ist dies eine experimentelle Methode, Kunst auf ihre verdeckten Psychodynamiken hin zu untersuchen. Die Bilder sind nunmehr Auslöser für psychische Verdrängungen und ungelöste Projektionen bei den Probanden. Dieses erstaunliche Verhalten offenbart, dass in jeder und jedem von uns selbst schon eine un/mögliche Gemeinschaft steckt, voller Wünsche und Ängste, Selbst- und Fremdbilder, die im Miteinander aufeinanderprallen und ausgehandelt werden (müssen).

Aushandlung und Konflikt behandelte auch Naeem Mohaiemen in seiner Fotoinstallation *Live True Life Or Die Trying* (Abb. S. 193), der dem Aufmarsch von politischen Linken und Islamist_innen in Dhaka, Bangladesh mit einem künstlerisch-fotografischen Abbildungseingriff begegnete. Dieser lässt die reale Repräsentation der politischen Gemeinschaften verschwimmen und die Enttäuschung Mohaiemens über die politische Entwicklung in seinem Land erahnen. Das Künstlerduo Andree Korpys und Markus Löffler wiederum unternahm in einer präzisen Beobachtung von Choreografien staatlicher Gewalt eine Untersuchung zur politischen Repräsentation und den Ritualen des Konflikts am Beispiel von Massendemonstrationen und Blockaden anlässlich der Atommülltransporte nach Gorleben und des G8-Gipfels in Heiligendamm 2007. Die Videoarbeit *Eure Kinder werden so wie wir* skizziert den Aufmarsch einer bunten und leidenschaftlichen Demonstrations-Gemeinschaft auf

der einen und eines uniformen Heers aus
Staats- und Polizeigewalt auf der anderen Seite.
Die eingefangenen Bilder zeugen von der
Unausweichlichkeit der verteilten Rollen und ihrer
eingeübten Inszenierung. Sie erzählen von einer
un/möglichen Gemeinschaft, deren Gegnerschaft
im Orakelchor der Demonstrant_innen
gegenüber ihrem Widerpart kulminiert: Eure
Kinder werden so wie wir![12]

Soziale Teilhabe, Meinungsfreiheit, Repräsentation,
Konflikt, Aushandlung und Vergemeinschaftung
waren Themen, denen sich die eingeladenen
Künstler_innen widmeten. Zum einen wurde
mit dem Medium Video und auch der Fotografie
die Realität von Machtverhältnissen dokumen-
tarisch abgebildet. Der künstlerische Blick blieb
dabei meist offen für Deutungen, wählte einen
Ausschnitt, eine Haltung, eine Perspektive, aber
kein Interpretationsmuster. Gesellschaft und
Gemeinschaft wurde mit all ihren Widersprüchen
und Verfehlungen widergespiegelt. Widersprüche,
die zeigen, dass Freund und Feind oft gar
nicht so weit voneinander entfernt sind oder
dass scheinbar feste Rollen im Gemeinschafts-
gefüge oftmals zu wenig hinterfragt werden.
Auf der anderen Seite konnten wir Inszenierungen
und Angebote von Künstler_innen beobachten,
die alternative Gemeinschaftsentwürfe und unge-
wohnte Öffnungen anregten, die Gemeinschaften
als offene, streitbare, temporäre und gleich-
berechtigte Zusammenschlüsse dachten und
sie als Teil unserer Welterfahrung für private
und öffentliche Probleme und ihre (Auf-)Lösungen
nutzten. Diesen Hintergedanken hatten wir,
hatten die Künstler_innen, die wir zu diesem
Ausstellungsprojekt einluden: Ein Wir zu bilden, das
das Ihr einschliesst und sich mit Unterschieden und
Konflikten auseinanderzusetzen, auf der Basis,
dessen, was vor uns liegt und zu bewältigen ist.

12 .... Aus der Folge-Arbeit *Atom* von Korpys/Löffler findet sich eine
Bild-Collage in diesem Kapitel.

DIE UN/MÖGLICHE GEMEINSCHAFT VON THEORIE UND PRAXIS

THE (IM)POSSIBLE COMMUNITY OF THEORY AND PRACTICE

Als Ausstellungs- und Diskursraum hat die Shedhalle seit einigen Jahren künstlerische Praxen gedanklich durchgespielt, Theorie praktiziert und sich von der reduktionistischen Oppositionsbildung von Theorie und Praxis emanzipiert. In weiten Zügen gelang es, selbst gesetzte Ziele umzusetzen, wie etwa das Ausstellen performativ zu wenden und zeitgenössische Kunst nicht allein zu präsentieren, sondern sie auch mit zu produzieren, zu vermitteln, zu diskutieren und zu distribuieren.[1] Eines der Ziele der Kuratorinnen Anke Hoffmann und Yvonne Volkart war es, Ausstellen und Publizieren „bei der Theoriebildung zeitgenössischer Kunst aktiv mit[wirken]"[2] zu lassen. Dieser Anspruch ist, so meine These, wesentlich davon bestimmt, das Verhältnis von Theorie- und Kunstproduktion als ‚un/mögliche Gemeinschaft' zum Zuge kommen zu lassen. Das heisst als ein differenzielles Gefüge, das mit Kategorien der Verfestigung wie der Verflüssigung und Bewegung charakterisiert werden kann. Meine Reflexionen nehmen ihren Ausgang im Kooperationsprojekt *Un/Mögliche Gemeinschaft*, das von November 2009 bis Januar 2010 von der Shedhalle und dem Institut für Theorie (ith) realisiert worden ist.[3] Das Projekt versuchte Gemeinschaft, aber auch das Verhältnis von Theorie und Praxis differenztheoretisch[4] zu denken.

1............... Vgl. Gau, Sønke/Schlieben, Katharina: The mental comma instead of the fullstop. Das gedankliche Komma statt des Full Stop. Kuratorisches Profil 2004-09. In: *Shedhalle Zeitung*, Edition 01/04. Online: http://archiv.shedhalle.ch/dt/archiv/2004/editorial/index.shtml.

2.............. Hoffmann, Anke/Volkart, Yvonne: Eindeutigkeiten sprengen. Unveröffentlichtes Konzeptpapier für diese Publikation, 2011.

3.............. Mit dem Projekt eröffneten die Kuratorinnen Anke Hoffmann und Yvonne Volkart im November 2009 ihre kuratorische Arbeit in der Shedhalle. Die Kooperationsbeiträge des Institut für Theorie bestanden in drei Workshops, einem Künstler_innen-Gespräch und einer Filmveranstaltung. Die Workshops fächerten gesellschaftlich-soziale Felder auf (Politik–Ästhetik, Identität–Ethnizität, Geschichte–Erzählung), um sie in ihrer aktuellen Bedeutung für ein politisch, kritisches Verständnis von Gemeinschaft zu reflektieren. Sie wurden von der Verfasserin unter Unterstützung von Anne Schuh (zu der Zeit Absolventin des BA Medien & Kunst, Vertiefung Theorie] konzipiert. Bei der Realisation wirkten mit: Chantal Küng und Daniel Lanz (z.d.Z. Studierende des BA Medien & Kunst, Vertiefung Bildende Kunst). www.ith-z.ch/veranstaltungen/archiv/gemeinschaft-vielleicht.

4........... Das Denken der Differenz ist von einem substanztheoretischen Ansatz zu unterscheiden. Es meint eine Theorie, die sprachliche Bedeutungs(zu)schreibungen innerhalb einer umfassenden Verweisstruktur ohne Referenz auf ein aussersprachliches Sein produziert.

Mit folgenden Überlegungen soll die Signifikanz der Rede von einer un/möglichen Gemeinschaft, wie sie mit Jean-Luc Nancy formuliert werden kann, als ein Denkmodell für das ‚Mit' von Theorie und Praxis diskutiert werden.

Gemeinschaft

Gemeinschaft ist ein Begriff, der mit heiligen wie profanen, mit verheissungsvollen wie fatalen Vorstellungen verknüpft und mit emotionalen Metaphern wie Wärme, Geborgenheit, Liebe, Freundschaft und Vertrautheit besetzt ist. Konservative Befürworter_innen machen die in der Moderne ausgebildeten Lebensformen für den Verlust von Gemeinschaft verantwortlich,[5] und Kritiker_innen des Begriffs bekräftigen dessen Unbrauchbarkeit mit dem Verweis auf die nationalsozialistische Ideologie.[6] Spricht man von Gemeinschaft, hat man insofern gleichermassen romantisierende Verklärungen wie auch die faschistisch-ideologische Inanspruchnahme des Begriffs, die von rechtsextremistischen Gruppierungen auch heute weiter gehegt und gepflegt wird, im Gepäck. Auch die seit dem Wiederaufleben der Idee der Gemeinschaft in den 1970er Jahren geführten Debatten unterstreichen, dass der Begriff extrem strittig und prekär ist.[7] Man könnte hierdurch zur Feststellung kommen, Gemeinschaft könne einem kritischen Denken nicht gerecht werden, da der Begriff unwiderruflich an Identität, am Eigenen und an der Einheit orientiert sei und auf Selbstschutz ziele, was bedeute, allem Fremden gegenüber intolerant und ausgrenzend entgegen zu treten. Der Titel der Veranstaltungen *Un/Mögliche Gemeinschaft* sollte die Problematik des Begriffs kenntlich machen, aber auch einen produktiven Ausgangspunkt des Denkens eröffnen; die Schreibweise zeigt eine Differenz an, die das Denken der Gemeinschaft aufnimmt, und zugleich das Ideal der Einheit und Identität unterbricht. Im Wissen der Unmöglichkeit von Gemeinschaft sollten die mit ihr verknüpften Vorstellungen von Praxen, Lebensweisen oder Subjektivierungs-prozessen reflektiert und deren Möglichkeiten für eine politisch ästhetische Theorie/Praxis abgewägt werden. Im Laufe unserer Arbeit stellte sich heraus, dass die Auseinandersetzung mit Gemeinschaft dann eine Produktivität herbei-führen kann, wenn diese nicht als Modell eines möglichen Zusammenseins befragt, sondern als Bedingung des menschlichen Seins und als Praxis begriffen wird. Aufgrund dieser Perspektivierung von Gemeinschaft wurde das Denken Jean-Luc Nancys zentral. Bereits seine Publikationen *Die undarstellbare Gemeinschaft* von 1986 (dt. 1988) und *Die herausgeforderte Gemeinschaft* von 2001 (dt. 2007) hatten zu heftigen und sehr konträren Debatten geführt. Im Rahmen der Arbeitstagung *Gemeinschaft vielleicht*[8] knüpfte der Philosoph an das Denken des ‚Mit-Seins' an, mit dem er schon 2001 ‚Gemeinschaft' über sich hinausgeführt hatte, und schritt vom ‚Mit-Sein' zum ‚Mit-Sinn'.

Mit-Sein als Bedingung des Seins

Bereits in *Die undarstellbare Gemeinschaft* hat Nancy identitären Gemeinschaftsforderungen ein differenztheoretisches, relationales Gemein-schaftsdenken entgegengesetzt, indem er Gemeinschaft aus einer Zerrissenheit heraus (be-)gründet erkennt und sie als untrennbar mit einem Moment des Ekstatischen verbunden

---

5 In der Mitte des 19. Jahrhunderts, also zu der Zeit, als der Kapitalismus sich strukturell durchsetzte und sich soziale Sphären (Politik, Ökonomie, Recht, Wissenschaft usw.) ausdifferenzierten, werden die bis dahin synonym und in vertauschten Rollen verwandten Begriffe Gesellschaft und Gemeinschaft zu Gegenbegriffen: Gesellschaft wird zum „begrifflichen Platzhalter für die Ausbreitung kapitalistischer Erwerbslogik, der Massenverelendung des Proletariats und die Zerstörung traditionaler Lebensformen". Gemeinschaft wird dagegen in konservativer Ausrichtung zur Projektionsfläche für die „im Zuge der Modernisierung verlorenen Sicherheiten" und aus politischer Perspektive zur politischen Kampfvokabel, „die von Seiten der Restauration wie der Revolution gleichermassen ins Spiel gebracht wird." Gertenbach, Lars/Laux, Henning/Rosa, Hartmut/Strecker, David: *Theorien der Gemeinschaft zur Einführung*. Hamburg 2010, 34f.

6 Vgl. dazu Gertenbach u.a.: *Theorien der Gemeinschaft*, 44f.

7 Zur Wiederkehr der Gemeinschaft seit den 1970er Jahren und zur Konzeption posttraditioneller Vergemeinschaftung vgl. Gertenbach u.a.: *Theorien der Gemeinschaft*, 58ff.

8 Die vom Institut für Theorie veranstaltete Arbeitstagung *Gemeinschaft – vielleicht. Un/mögliche Gemeinschaft – vorläufige Gemeinschaften* fand vom 12. – 14. März 2010 an der Zürcher Hochschule der Künste statt.

As a space of exhibition and discourse, Shedhalle has conceptually played through artistic practices, practiced theory and emancipated itself from the reductionist opposition between theory and practice. By and large it has succeeded in achieving the goals it set for itself, such as giving exhibitions a performative turn: not just presenting contemporary art, but also assisting in its production, its presentation to the public, its discussion and distribution.[1] One of the goals of curators Anke Hoffmann and Yvonne Volkart was to allow exhibitions and publications 'to participate actively in the theory formation of contemporary art.'[2] This claim is, I would argue, largely defined by allowing the relationship between theory and art production to come into its own as an impossible community. This means a differential arrangement that can be characterised with categories of fixation as well as categories of fluidisation and movement. The collaborative project *Im/Possible Community* hosted by Shedhalle and the Institute for Critical Theory (ith) from November 2009 to January 2010, serves here as my point of departure.[3] This project tried to conceive community as well as the relationship between theory and practice in terms of a theory of difference.[4]

In the following, the significance of the notion of an im/possible community as can be formulated in Jean-Luc Nancy's terms will be discussed as a conceptual model of the *with* of theory and practice.

Community

Community is a term that is linked to the sacred and profane, to promising and fatal conceptions, and one that is laden with emotional metaphors such as warmth, security, love, friendship and familiarity. Conservative proponents blame life forms that developed in modernity[5] for the loss of community, while critics of the concept stress its uselessness by referring to Nazi ideology.[6] To that extent, when we speak of community we have to confront the romanticising and fascist-ideological appropriation of the term still fostered and maintained today by extreme right wing groups. The debates that have arisen since the re-emergence of the concept of community in the 1970s underscore that the term is extremely controversial and precarious.[7] In so doing, one might arrive at the conclusion that community cannot do justice to critical thought, for the concept is irrevocably linked to identity, to the individual and unity, and aims at self-protection, which entails responding to all things foreign with intolerance and exclusion.

The title of the event series 'Im/Possible Community' was intended to mark this problematic, but also to open a productive point of departure for thinking on the subject: the orthography denotes a difference that takes up

1 ..... See Sønke Gau and Katharina Schlieben, 'The Mental Comma Instead of the Full-Stop'. Curatorial Profile 2004–09, *Shedhalle Zeitung*, 1 (2004), online: www.shedhalle.ch/sites/default/files/pdf_downloads/shedhalle_zeitung_0104.pdf.
2 .. Anke Hoffmann and Yvonne Volkart, 'Eindeutigkeiten sprengen', unpublished concept paper for this publication, 2011.
3 .... With this project, curators Anke Hoffmann and Yvonne Volkart began their curatorial work at Shedhalle in November 2009. Institute for Critical Theory held three workshops, an artists' podium discussion and a film event. The workshops explored social fields (Politics–Aesthetics, Identity–Ethnicity, History–Narration) to reflect on their current significance for a political, critical understanding of community. They were conceived by the author with the help of Anne Schuh. Further participants included Chantal Küng and Daniel Lanz. See www.ith-z.ch/veranstaltungen/archiv/gemeinschaft-vielleicht.
4 ... Thinking in terms of difference should be distinguished from an approach rooted in substance theory. This means a theory that produces linguistic attributions of meaning within a comprehensive structure of reference without referring to a non-linguistic being.

5 ...... During the mid-nineteenth century, as capitalism established itself structurally and social spheres differentiated from one another (politics, economics, law, science, etc.), the terms society and community, until then synonymous and used interchangeably, became opposites: society became 'a conceptual placeholder for the spread of a capitalist logic of acquisition, the mass impoverishment of the proletariat, and the destruction of traditional lifestyles'. Community in contrast became—in its conservative variant—a projection surface for the securities lost 'in the course of modernization' and from a political perspective a political term of struggle 'used equally both by the side of restoration and revolution.' See Lars Gertenbach, Henning Laux, Hartmut Rosa and David Strecker, *Theorien der Gemeinschaft zur Einführung* (Hamburg, 2010), p. 34f.
6 .. See on this Gertenbach et al., *Theorien der Gemeinschaft*, p. 44f.
7 .... On the return of the notion of community since the 1970s and the conception of post-traditional communitarisation, see Gertenbach et al., p. 58ff.

thinking in terms of community, while at the same time interrupting the ideal of a unity of identity. Aware of the *impossibility* of community, the goal was to reflect upon associated conceptions of practices, ways of life and processes of subjectification, and to deliberate on the possibilities for a political aesthetic of theory/practice. In the course of our work, we found that engaging with community can generate productivity if it is not explored as a model of possible coexistence, but rather as the condition of human existence and practice. Due to this perspectivisation of community, the thought of Jean-Luc Nancy has become central. His publications *The Inoperative Community* from 1986 and 'The Confronted Community' from 2001 already led to fierce and quite controversial debates. At the conference 'Gemeinschaft vielleicht' (Community Perhaps),[8] the philosopher returned to his thoughts on *Mit-Sein*, with which he had already taken *Gemeinschaft* to a new level in 2001, moving from *Mit-Sein* to *Mit-Sinn*.

Mit-Sein as a Condition of Being

Already in *The Inoperative Community,* Nancy opposed identitarian demands for community with a relational notion of community based in difference theory, acknowledging that community is grounded in a rupture while granting that it is inseparable from a moment of the ecstatic.[9] Despite this modification of the concept, he preferred replacing the word community with 'graceless expressions' like '"being-together", "being-in-common", and finally "being-with" ... On several sides I saw approaching the dangers inspired by the usage of the word "community": its invincibly

full resonance—indeed a resonance bloated with substance and interiority'.[10] By turning to the *with*, the subject, the individual is no longer the central category for thinking community,[11] but—and here Nancy turns to Martin Heidegger—human existence.[12] In the *with*, Nancy finds a 'being together without assemblage'.[13] The *with* introduces a confrontation and an opposition, an antagonism, 'it is a question simultaneously of a confrontation and of an opposition, of an encounter where one goes out to meet oneself, so as to challenge and test oneself, so as to divide oneself in one's being by a remove that is also the condition of that being'.[14] The difference established with the *with* provides for the possibility of the existence of the 'we'. Or, as Nancy suggests, we are given a 'we' before we can articulate or justify a 'we'. Yet this 'we' is 'not a communion that fuses the egos into an Ego or a higher we. It is the community of others'.[15] In contrast to Heidegger, Nancy does not categorically distinguish the *Volksgemeinschaft* from seemingly banal coexistence in the social crowd, instead granting the latter the possibility of an existential *with*.[16] That is to say, adjacency can become a with; it is thus not limited to an indifferent externality. It can generate effects of 'contagion or communication'. 'But whenever there is communication, albeit silent, uncertain, elusive, there is what is called 'sense'—in the sense that there is 'meaning' of possible meaning, the *significabilité* or possible significance.'[17] A meaning points beyond the expectable, perhaps precisely because it emerges from

---

8............ The workshop 'Gemeinschaft, vielleicht: Un/mögliche Gemeinschaft, vorläufige Gemeinschaften', held by the Institute for Critical Theory, took place on 12–14 March 2010 at Zurich University of the Arts.

9.... Or as Nancy puts it, 'the rupture ... which breaks up the totality of things that are ... and Being ... defines a relation to the absolute, imposing on the absolute a relation *to* its own Being. ... Being itself comes to be defined as relational, as non-absoluteness, and if you will—in any case, this is what I am trying to argue—as community.' Jean-Luc Nancy, *The Inoperative Community,* tr. Peter Connor et al. (Minneapolis, 1991), p. 6.

10........ Jean-Luc Nancy, 'The Confronted Community', tr. Amanda Macdonald, Postcolonial Studies 6.1 (2003), p. 31.

11..... The concept of the subject is foundational for communitarian and individualist concepts of community.

12 With his existential orientation of the *with*, Nancy refers to Martin Heidegger, according to whom the *with* (mit) that is constitutive of *Dasein* is to be understood 'existentially and not categorically'. See Jean-Luc Nancy, 'Mit-Sinn', unpublished manuscript, p. 21.

13..................... Nancy, 'The Confronted Community', p. 32.

14.................................... Ibid., p. 34.

15....................... Nancy, *The Inoperative Community*, p. 15.

16..... As Nancy points out, 'Le problème avec Heidegger, c'est qu'il n'a pas du tout développé cette nécessité. Ou bien il ne l'a fait qu'en faisant paraître la forme "authentique" ou "proper" du *mit* comme celle de la *communauté du peuple* (beaucoup plus loin dans le même ouvrage). Et son égarement politique a trouvé là sa source' (Nancy, 'Mit-Sinn', unpublished manuscript).

17.. Ibid., p. 6.

sieht.[9] Trotz dieser Modifizierung des Begriffs zog er es schliesslich vor, das Wort Gemeinschaft mit den „unschönen" Ausdrücken „des ‚Zusammen-Seins‘, des ‚Gemeinsam-Seins‘ und des ‚Mit-Seins‘ zu ersetzen [...] Von mehreren Seiten her sah ich von dem Gebrauch des Wortes ‚Gemeinschaft‘ Gefahren ausgehen: Unweigerlich klingt es von Substanz und Innerlichkeit erfüllt, ja aufgebläht".[10] Durch die Hinwendung zum ‚Mit‘ ist nicht mehr länger das Subjekt, das Individuum zentrale Kategorie[11] des Denkens der Gemeinschaft, sondern – hier knüpft Nancy an Martin Heidegger an – die menschliche Existenz.[12] Im ‚Mit‘ findet Nancy ein „Zusammen-Sein ohne Zusammenfügen".[13] Das ‚Mit‘ führt eine Konfrontation und eine Opposition ein, ein Gegeneinander, „ein Vor-sich-selbst-Hintreten, um sich herauszufordern und zu erproben, um sich in seinem Sein zu teilen mit einem Abstand, der auch die Bedingung dieses Seins ist."[14] Die durch das ‚Mit‘ gezogene Differenz setzt als Möglichkeit der Existenz ein ‚wir‘: „Uns ist ein ‚wir‘ gegeben, ehe wir ein ‚wir‘ artikulieren oder gar rechtfertigen können."[15] Dieses ‚Wir‘ ist jedoch „keine Einswerdung, die die [sic] *Ich-Selbst (moi)* zu einem einzigen *Ich-Selbst (Moi)* oder zu einem höheren *WIR* verschmelzen würde. Es ist die Gemeinschaft der *anderen*."[16] Im Unterschied zu Heidegger grenzt Nancy die „Volksgemeinschaft" nicht kategorial vom scheinbar banalen

Nebeneinander in der sozialen Menge ab. Er räumt ihm vielmehr die Möglichkeit des existenzialen ‚Mit‘ ein.[17] Das heisst, das Nebeneinander kann zum ‚Mit‘ werden, es ist so nicht auf eine indifferente Äusserlichkeit beschränkt. Es kann Effekte der „Ansteckung und Kommunikation" zeitigen. „Gibt es aber Kommunikation [...] so gibt es das, was man ‚Sinn‘ nennt – und zwar in dem Sinne, dass es ‚Sinn‘ (er)gibt, möglichen Sinn, mögliche Bedeutsamkeit oder Signifikanz."[18] Einen ‚Sinn‘, der über das Erwartbare hinausweist, vielleicht gerade auch, weil er aus einem ‚bloss‘ willkürlichen und nicht bereits Sinn versprechendem Nebeneinander hervorgeht.

‚Sinn‘ denkt Nancy „fiktional: [...] er gibt sich im Schaffen, im Herstellen (fingo, fictum) von Gestalten und Formen, die selbst beweglich, plastisch, dehnbar sind, und gemäss denen das ‚Mit‘ sich unendlich konfiguriert."[19] ‚Sinn‘ meint demnach keine Fixierung einer vorgängigen Wahrheit, ‚Sinn‘ hat vielmehr zu tun mit einer Begegnung mit dem Inkommensurablen, er ist performativ und zeugt von einer Lust des Denkens, das „über alles Gegebene, aber auch über sich selbst" hinausschiesst.[20] Nancy geht es hier darum, jenseits des ‚natürlich‘ gegebenen Sinnes, „außerhalb der Signifikation Sinn herzustellen und auszutauschen, [...] Bedeutungen in ein anderes Regime zu tragen, wo die Zeichen auf das Unendliche verweisen."[21] Was Nancy hier beschreibt, kann als Gegenentwurf zur Signifikation (Repräsentation, Expression, Kommunikation) verstanden werden; als Signifikanz (Produktion, Vollzug). Signifikanz ereignet sich in der Materialität des Textes und widersetzt sich der Kommunikation von Sinn. Dementsprechend verwundert es nicht, dass Nancy einen solchen Sinn ausserhalb

9............ Bei Nancy heisst es, die Zerrissenheit zwischen der Totalität der seienden Dinge und dem Sein „bestimmt eine *Beziehung* des Absoluten, erlegt dem Absoluten eine Beziehung *zu* seinem eigenen Sein auf". Das Sein selbst gelangt hierdurch dazu, „sich als Beziehung zu bestimmen, als Nicht-Absolutheit, und wenn man so will – zumindest versuche ich dies zu sagen – *als Gemeinschaft*." Nancy, Jean-Luc: *Die undarstellbare Gemeinschaft*. Stuttgart 1988, 20.

10................ Nancy, Jean-Luc: *Die herausgeforderte Gemeinschaft*, Berlin 2007, 30f.

11........ Der Begriff des Subjekts ist grundlegend für kommunitaristische und individualistische Gemeinschaftskonzeptionen.

12............ Nancy bezieht sich mit dieser existenziellen Ausrichtung des ‚Mit‘ auf Martin Heidegger demzufolge das dem Dasein konstitutiv zugehörige „Mit‘ ‚existenzial, nicht kategorial‘ zu verstehen" sei. Nancy, Jean-Luc: Mit-Sinn. In: Bippus, Elke/Huber, Jörg/Richter, Dorothee (Hg.): *,Mit-Sein'. Gemeinschaft – ontologische und politische Perspektivierungen*. (T:G 08), Zürich, Wien, New York 2010, 21–34, hier 21.

13 .... Nancy: *Herausgeforderte Gemeinschaft*, 31.

14 .... Nancy: *Herausgeforderte Gemeinschaft*, 37.

15 .... Nancy: *Herausgeforderte Gemeinschaft*, 38.

16 .... Nancy: *Undarstellbare Gemeinschaft*, 38. Die grammatikalisch falsche Form von „die Ich-Selbst" verstehe ich als Formulierung eines dividuellen Ich-Selbst, oder als Versuch, das Sein als prinzipielles Mit-Sein kenntlich zu machen.

17 .... Nancy weist darauf hin, dass Heidegger in *Sein und Zeit* „die ‚eigentliche‘ Gestalt des ‚Mit‘ als die der *Volksgemeinschaft* zur Erscheinung brachte. Und seine politische Verirrung hat darin ihre Quelle gefunden." Nancy: Mit-Sinn, 22.

18 .... Nancy: Mit-Sinn, 23.

19 .... Nancy: Mit-Sinn, 33.

20...................... Nancy: Mit-Sinn, 33.

21 .... Nancy: Mit-Sinn, 34. Das Überbordende des Sinn ist allerdings „dem Sinn selbst, in die Sinnesempfindung eingeschrieben" (ebd. 28). Vgl. hierzu Isekenmeier, Guido: Textuelle Performativität als Produktion von Sinn. Julia Kristevas Texttheorie und die Semiologie der Paragramme. In: Buschmeier, Matthias/Dembeck, Till (Hg.): *Textbewegungen 1800/1900*. Würzburg 2007, 73–90, insb. 78–81.

der Signifikation in der Literatur und in der Kunst findet.[22]

Mit der Hinwendung zum ‚Mit-Sinn' transformiert Nancy das Denken der Gemeinschaft fundamental. ‚Gemeinschaft' ist so nicht mehr länger an das Sein eines Individuums oder einer ‚Volksgemeinschaft' gebunden, sondern an die menschliche Existenz über das Gegebene und vom Subjekt Geschaffene hinaus. Gemeinschaft als etwas prinzipiell Unvollendbares ergibt sich in Relationen und ist nicht wesenhaft bestimmt. Sie lässt sich weder besitzen, verteidigen oder herstellen. Vielmehr ist sie „etwas, das man immer schon teilt und das nur unter Anerkennung einer in ihr enthaltenen Kluft überhaupt existieren kann."[23] Gemeinschaft ist stets im Werden, sie ereignet sich zwischen mehreren. Sie ist „stets ‚flüchtig' – aber zugleich entsteht sie immer wieder neu."[24] Dabei werden insbesondere ästhetische Praxen bedeutsam. In ihnen wird Sinn ausserhalb der Signifikation möglich. Wird der poststrukturalistische Textbegriff herbeigezogen, dann lässt sich sagen, dass Sinn in und durch eine textuelle Performativität der Materialität und des Vollzugs entsteht, die nicht von einem Subjekt begründet wird, sondern dieses bewegt.[25] Deshalb kann ein Text denn auch als Ver-Äusserung und nicht als Äusserung betrachtet werden.

Zusammenfassend lässt sich sagen, dass Nancys Überlegungen zur Gemeinschaft in doppelter Weise weitreichend und inspirierend für unser Projekt wurden. Die eine Seite betrifft das Denken der Gemeinschaft als ‚Mit-Sein' und damit als Bedingung der menschlichen Existenz eines ‚Wir'. Die andere Seite geht aus der Hinwendung des Mit-Seins zum ‚Mit-Sinn' und damit zur fundamentalen Bedeutung ‚ästhetischer Praxen', vor allem von Literatur und Kunst hervor. Denn damit

wird nicht nur eine relevante Absetzung moderner Konzepte von Rationalität und Identität geltend gemacht, vielmehr werden ästhetische Praxen in zweifacher Hinsicht bedeutsam: als Widerständigkeit gegen normative Sinnsetzungen einerseits, und zwar insofern sich in ästhetischen Praxen die Potentialität findet, Sinn ausserhalb von Signifikation herzustellen und auszutauschen, und als Arbeit am Sichtbaren, an der Darstellung andererseits. Die Arbeit am Sichtbaren stiftet und reflektiert Gemeinschaft, indem sie sie (re-)präsentiert. Künste (und andere Regime der Sichtbarkeit) sind dergestalt Formen der Einschreibung des Sinns in die Gemeinschaft. Als solche legen sie fest, „wie Werke oder ‚künstlerische Aufführungen' Politik machen".[26] Kunst schafft Narrationen, die wiederum neue Komplexe, neue Diskurse mit all ihren materiellen Erscheinungsformen hervorbringen. In die Frage nach der Gemeinschaft ist insofern „stets die Frage nach der Praxis der Gemeinschaft eingeschlossen."[27] Denn der Zugang zur Sichtbarkeit und Hörbarkeit ist grundlegend für die Herstellung von Gemeinschaft. Insofern sind aber auch Formen der Sichtbarkeit künstlerischer Praktiken, aber auch kuratorischer Praktiken oder Theorieproduktionen dahingehend befragbar, „was sie im Hinblick auf das Gemeinsame ‚tun'".[28]

Gemeinschaft durch (künstlerische) Praxis

Im künstlerischen Kontext meint Praxis jenseits einer Genieästhetik ein Schaffen, das sich nicht in einem schöpferisch genialen Akt erschöpft, sondern auch Mittel und Techniken der Darstellung einbezieht, die etwas zur Erscheinung, zur Anschauung zu bringen vermögen, das ansonsten der Signifikation entgeht. In diesem Sinn ist die Rede davon, dass Kunst Kräfte, Handlungen oder das Unsichtbare sichtbar macht, die andernfalls unsichtbar blieben. Dem poststrukturalistischen Textbegriff vergleichbar repräsentieren künstlerische Darstellungen nicht

---

22 Literatur ist bei Nancy privilegierter Ort des Erscheinens der undarstellbaren, entwerkten Gemeinschaft. Die Literatur ist für Nancy „der Ort der irreduziblen Vielstimmigkeit der Sprachen." Etzold, Jörn: Vom Erscheinen der Gemeinschaft in der Kunst; Mimesis der Praxis. In: Bippus u.a. (Hg.): *Mit-Sein*, 141–153, hier 150.

23 Gertenbach u.a.: *Theorien der Gemeinschaft*, 165.

24 Etzold: Mimesis und Praxis, 149.

25 Im Text vollzieht sich etwas, „das auf den Leser wartet und gleichwohl über ihn hinausgeht, jenseits von ihm geschieht". Isekenmeier: Textuelle Performativität, 76.

26 Rancière, Jacques: *Die Aufteilung des Sinnlichen. Die Politik der Kunst und ihre Paradoxien*. Berlin 2006, 28.

27 Etzold: Mimesis der Praxis, 149.

28 Rancière: *Aufteilung des Sinnlichen*, 27.

a 'merely' arbitrary adjacency, one with no promise of meaning.

Nancy conceives of meaning in a 'fictional' sense, 'it presents itself in the creation (*fingo, fictum*) of forms that are themselves mobile, flexible, ductile, according to which the 'with' constitutes itself indefinitely'.[18] Accordingly, meaning does not entail a fixation on a prior truth, but has much more to do with an encounter with the incommensurable; it is performative and attests to a pleasure of thought that exceeds 'everything given, but also surpasses itself'.[19] For Nancy at issue is 'creating and exchanging meaning' beyond 'signification . . . it brings meanings to another regime, where signs refer to the infinite'.[20] What Nancy is describing here can be understood as a counter-model to signification (representation, expression, communication): as significance (production, completion). Significance *takes place* in the materiality of the text and resists the communication of meaning. Accordingly, it is not surprising that Nancy finds such a meaning outside signification in literature and in art.[21] In turning to *Mit-Sinn*, Nancy transforms our conception of community in a fundamental way. Community is no longer bound to the being of an individual or a *Volksgemeinschaft*, but to human existence beyond the given and what is created by the subject. Community as something fundamentally incompletable results in relations and is not defined in terms of essence. It refuses to be possessed, defended or created. Instead it is 'something that is always already shared and that can only exist if an inherent gap is acknowledged'.[22] Community is always in the process of becoming; it always takes place among several. It is always '"fleeting"—yet at the same time it emerges in ever new ways'.[23] In so doing, aesthetic practices become especially meaningful. Here, sense outside signification becomes possible. Using the post-structural concept of the text, it could be said that meaning emerges in and through a textual performativity of materiality and of completion, one that is not founded on a subject, but moves the subject.[24] In so doing, a text can be considered as realization [*Veräusserung*] and not as expression [*Äusserung*].

To sum up, Nancy's considerations on community are far reaching and inspiring for our project in a dual sense. On the one hand, there is thinking as a community of *Mit-Sein* and thus the condition of human existence of a 'we', while at the same time there is the turn from *Mit-Sein* to *Mit-Sinn* and hence to the fundamental significance of 'aesthetic practices', especially literature and art. Not only is a relevant dismissal of modern concepts of rationality and identity asserted, aesthetic practices also become significant in a dual sense: on the one hand, as resistance against normative positions of meaning, to the extent that aesthetic practices contain the potentiality of creating and exchanging meaning beyond signification; on the other hand, as work on the visible, on representation. Work on the visible generates and reflects community to the extent that it (re)presents it. The arts (and other regimes of visibility) are in this sense forms of the inscription of meaning in community. As such, they fix how 'works of art or performances are "involved in politics"'.[25] Art creates narrations that in turn generate new complexes, new discourses with all their material forms of appearance. In the question of community, the 'question of the

18 Ibid., p. 6.
19 Ibid., p. 7.
20 Ibid., p. 7. The excessiveness of meaning 'is inscribed in meaning itself, the sense of meaning' (ibid.). See especially Guido Isekenmeier, 'Textuelle Performativität als Produktion von Sinn: Julia Kristevas Texttheorie und die Semiologie der Paragramme', *Textbewegungen 1800/1900*, eds. Matthias Buschmeier and Till Dembeck (Wurzburg, 2007), pp. 78–81.
21 For Nancy, literature is the privileged site of the appearance of an unrepresentable, de-instrumentalised community. For Nancy, literature is the 'site of the irreducible polyvocality of languages.' Jörn Etzold, 'Vom Erscheinen der Gemeinschaft in der Kunst: Mimesis der Praxis', *Mit-Sein*, eds. Bippus et al., p. 150.
22 Gertenbach, et al., *Theorien der Gemeinschaft*, p. 165.
23 Etzold, 'Mimesis und Praxis', p. 149.
24 In the text, something takes place 'that waits for the reader and yet surpassed him, takes place beyond him'. See Isekenmeier, 'Textuelle Performativität', p. 76.
25 Jacques Rancière, 'The Distribution of the Sensible: Politics and Aesthetics', p. 14

practice of community is always included'.[26] For access to visibility and audibility is fundamental for the creation of community. To that extent, forms of visibility of artistic practices, but also curatorial practices and theoretical productions can be interrogated in terms of 'what they "do" or "make" from the standpoint of what is common to the community.'[27]

Community Through (Artistic) Practice

In an artistic context, practice beyond an aesthetics of genius means a work that is not exhausted in a creative act of genius, but also includes means and devices of representation that are able to contribute something to reveal or illustrate something that otherwise escapes signification. In that sense, this means that art renders visible forces and acts that otherwise remain invisible. Comparable to the post-structural concept of the text, artistic representations do not accord with reality in the sense that they point to absent elements, but possess a performative power. This makes its possible to render the invisible visible. But it would be false to posit that art has a genuine relationship to the invisible, for it escapes signification itself. This mythic exaggeration of the difference between the utterable and the visible conceals the fact that art is a 'modified intervention'[28] of signification. This means that art necessarily moves in the visible, in signification, but grasps it in an altered fashion and is able to make something visible and thus utterable that was otherwise not utterable in that fashion. A politics (of representation) thus inheres in art: it produces cultural forms, developing a social field and spaces for action.[29] It creates with and through its aesthetic practices 'a frame of visibility and intelligibility that puts things or practices together under the same meaning, which shapes thereby a certain sense of community'.[30] Aesthetic practices do not deal with community or represent it; they project it. Analysis and reflection of community based on action and practice penetrates and thinks through aesthetic strategies and techniques in terms of their (political) effects on the formation, construction and the addressing of community.

Theory

Theory does not give rise to harmonious solutions', it offers 'not a set of solutions but the prospect of further thought',[31] as Jonathan Culler postulates in his introduction to literary theory. This claim can be supported by looking at the Greek meaning of the word *theorein* (to observe, inspect, examination, consideration), that is, a consideration of truth through pure thought to create prognoses. The definition of theory as 'pure thought' now has the superficial effect of bringing together theory and practice.

But: what is 'really' called thinking? Heidegger took up this question in a 1952 series of lectures with that very title. The text gives a great deal to think about, and even if it ends by saying that we don't actually 'genuinely' think, and therefore the question should rather be: 'What is called thinking?'[32] For the considerations to be developed here, the following points seem notable. Heidegger understands thinking as a practice that cannot be absorbed theoretically or by way of a treatise. 'We shall never learn what "is called" swimming, for example, or what it "calls for", by reading a treatise on swimming.

---

26 .... Etzold, 'Mimesis der Praxis', p. 149.

27 .... Rancière, 'The Distribution of the Sensible', p. 13.

28 ... Nancy adopts the concept of 'modified grasp' from Heidegger.

29 ...... Rancière, 'Distribution of the Sensible', p. 34. Rancière also locates the question of the relationship between aesthetics and politics on the 'distribution of the commons of the community, its forms of visibility and its structure', speaking of a politics of aesthetics.

30 ..... Rancière, 'Contemporary Art and the Politics of Aesthetics', Communities of Sense: Rethinking Aesthetics in Practice, eds. Beth Hinderliter et al. (Durham, 2009), p. 31. According to Rancière, the 'practices and forms of visibility of art intervene in the distribution of the sensible and its reconfiguration'. See Jacques Rancière, Aesthetics and Its Discontents, trans. Steven Corcoran (London, 2009), p. 25.

31 .... Jonathan Culler, *Literary Theory: A Very Short Introduction* (Oxford, 2000), p. 133.

32 .... Martin Heidegger, *What is Called Thinking?*, tr. J. Glenn Gray (New York, 1966), p. 127.

die Realität in dem Sinne, dass sie auf abwesende Elemente hinweisen, sondern sie beinhalten eine performative Kraft. Diese erlaubt, Unsichtbares sichtbar zu machen. Es wäre jedoch eine Fehleinschätzung davon auszugehen, Kunst hätte eine genuine Beziehung zum Unsichtbaren, da sie selbst der Signifikation entgeht. Diese mythische Überhöhung der Differenz zwischen Sagbarem und Sichtbarem verdeckt, dass Kunst ein „modifiziertes Ergreifen"[29] der Signifikation ist. Das heisst, auch Kunst bewegt sich notwendig im Sichtbaren, in der Signifikation, ergreift dieses aber in veränderter Weise und vermag, etwas sichtbar und damit auch sagbar zu machen, das so nicht sagbar war. Damit ist der Kunst eine Politik (der Darstellung) eigen. Sie produziert kulturelle Formen, entwirft ein soziales Feld und Handlungsspielräume.[30] Sie schafft mit und durch ihre ästhetischen Praxen einen „Rahmen der Sichtbarkeit und Intelligibilität, der Dinge oder Praktiken unter einer Bedeutung vereint und so einen bestimmten Sinn für Gemeinschaft entwirft."[31] Ästhetische Praxen handeln nicht von Gemeinschaft, oder repräsentieren sie, sie projektieren sie. Eine handlungs- und praxisorientierte Analyse und Reflexion von Gemeinschaft durchdringt und durchdenkt ästhetische Strategien und Verfahrensweisen in ihren (politischen) Effekten auf die Bildung, Konstruktion und Adressierung von Gemeinschaft.

Theorie

„Theorie macht Beherrschung unmöglich", sie bietet „keinen festen Bestand an Lösungen, sondern die Aussicht auf weiteres Nachdenken",[32] postuliert Jonathan Culler in seiner Einführung zur aktuellen Literaturtheorie. Diese Behauptung findet eine Begründung in der griechischen Bedeutung des Wortes „theorein" (beobachten, betrachten, Anschauung, Überlegung), das eine Betrachtung der Wahrheit durch reines Denken meint, um Prognosen zu erstellen. Die Bestimmung der Theorie als „reines Denken" hat nun den vordergründigen Effekt, Theorie und Praxis in Opposition zu bringen.

Aber: Was heisst ,eigentlich' Denken? Dieser Frage ging Heidegger 1952 in einem Vortrag nach, den er eben so betitelte. Der Text gibt viel zu denken auf, auch wenn er damit endet, dass wir noch nicht ,eigentlich' denken und es deshalb weiter zu fragen gälte: „Was heißt Denken?"[33] Für die hier zu entfaltenden Überlegungen scheinen mir folgende Punkte bedenkenswert. Heidegger begreift das Denken als eine Praxis, die man sich nicht theoretisch oder durch eine Abhandlung über etwas aneignen kann. Was schwimmen heisst, lerne man nicht „durch eine Abhandlung über das Schwimmen. Was schwimmen heißt, sagt uns der Sprung in den Strom. Wir lernen so das Element erst kennen, worin sich das Schwimmen bewegen muß."[34] Ein Sprung ins Unbekannte ist demnach notwendig, um ins Denken zu gelangen.

Des Weiteren stellt Heidegger fest, dass sich das „zu-Denkende" entzieht, sich uns vorenthält. Deshalb bleibe uns nur „zu warten, bis das zu-Denkende sich uns zuspricht."[35] Warten versteht Heidegger allerdings nicht passiv, im Gegenteil, er beschreibt es als ein „Ausschau halten, und zwar innerhalb des schon Gedachten nach dem Ungedachten, das sich im schon Gedachten noch verbirgt."[36] Mit dieser Formulie-

---

29 Den Begriff ,modifiziertes Ergreifen' übernimmt Nancy von Heidegger. Dieser arbeitete damit der Polarisierung von Eigentlichem und Uneigentlichem entgegen, insofern das Eigentliche (oder auch das Ereignis) immer nur ein modifiziertes Ergreifen des Uneigentlichen sei. In Heideggers Aufsatz *Was heißt Denken?* findet sich des Weiteren eine ähnliche Denkfigur, wenn er schreibt, dass sich das Zu-Denkende in Abwendung hält, sich allerdings Abwendung nur dort ereignet, „wo bereits eine Zuwendung geschehen ist", d.h. dass das Zu-Denkende sich bereits dem Denken anvertraut hat. Heidegger, Martin: Was heißt Denken? In: Ders.: *Vorträge und Aufsätze.* Stuttgart 2009, 123–137.

30 Rancière: *Aufteilung des Sinnlichen*, 34. Auf der „sinnlichen Aufteilung des Gemeinsamen der Gemeinschaft, ihrer Formen der Sichtbarkeit und ihres Aufbaus" siedelt Rancière auch die Frage nach dem Verhältnis zwischen Ästhetik und Politik an und spricht von einer Politik der Ästhetik.

31 Rancière: *Aufteilung des Sinnlichen*, 71. Nach Rancière wirken die „Praktiken und Formen der Sichtbarkeit der Kunst selbst in die Aufteilung des Sinnlichen und in ihre Umgestaltung ein". Rancière, Jacques: *Das Unbehagen der Ästhetik.* Wien 2007, 35.

32 Jonathan Culler zit. n. Grizelj, Mario/Jahraus, Oliver: Einleitung. Theorietheorie. In: Dies. (Hg.): *Theorietheorie. Wider die Theoriemüdigkeit in den Geisteswissenschaften.* München 2011, 9–14, hier 3.

33 Heidegger: Denken, 137.

34 Heidegger: Denken, 133.

35 Heidegger: Denken, 133.

36 Heidegger: Denken, 133.

rung rückt die Vorstellung von Denken in die Nähe solcher künstlerischen Praxen, in denen Nancy die Potentialität findet, Sinn ausserhalb der Signifikation herzustellen. Dieses Heidegger'sche „Denken des Ungedachten" ist dem „Hinausschießen über das Gegebene" (Nancy) vergleichbar, das sich immer nur in dem Element ereignen kann, das uns vermeintlich vertraut ist, das heißt im Sichtbaren und im Sagbaren. Michel Foucault hat es das historische Apriori genannt, mit Jacques Lacan kann man vom Register des Symbolischen sprechen. Durch das Sich-Einlassen, durch die Öffnung für das Unvertraute, für das, was nicht der jeweiligen historischen Sinnsetzung entspricht, wird ein „modifiziertes Ergreifen" möglich. In diesem Zusammenhang ist es bemerkenswert, dass Heidegger die künstlerische Praxis des Dichtens mit dem Denken vergleicht und zugleich eine Kluft der verschiedenen Register betont: „Das dichtend Gesagte und das denkend Gesagte sind niemals das Gleiche. Aber das eine und das andere kann in verschiedenen Weisen dasselbe sagen. Dies glückt allerdings nur dann, wenn die Kluft zwischen Dichten und Denken rein und entschieden klafft."[37]

Heideggers Entwurf des Denkens zeigt Nähen zum Begriff der Theorie, wenn Theorie als ein Sehen erkannt wird, dem es weder darum geht, tatsächlich Vorhandenes festzustellen, noch darum, das zu sehen, wovon man wünscht, dass es sei, oder das zu identifizieren, was dem common sense entspricht. Theorie kann im Gegenteil als eine Anschauung beschrieben werden, die sich vom bereits Bekannten löst, einen Sprung ins Unbekannte wagt. Theorie, als eine spezifisch reflexive Betrachtungsweise, meint dann keine kritische Metareflexion, die das, was die Kunst sichtbar macht, sagt und vergegenständlicht. Im Gegenteil, sie ist nicht in „erster Linie ein Verhalten, durch das man sich eines Gegenstandes bemächtigt oder

ihn sich durch Erklärung verfügbar macht."[38] Avancierte Theorien tragen der Unmöglichkeit der Vergegenständlichung vielmehr dadurch Rechnung, dass sie an „die Stelle von Vergegenständlichung […] Prozessualität, und an die Stelle von Identifikation Differenzialität"[39] treten lassen.

Theorie unterscheidet sich hierdurch – der Kunst vergleichbar – vom traditionellen Bild von Wissenschaft. In diesem wird Wissenschaft darauf reduziert, das „Beständige vorzustellen und die Geschichte zum Gegenstand zu machen".[40]

In Anlehnung an Heideggers Reflexionen zum Denken kann Theorie mit Prozessen und Techniken des Unterbrechens verknüpft werden, mit notwendigen Sprüngen, die es ermöglichen, den vertrauten Boden zu verlassen, um „zwischen den Sachen [zu] sein, mitten in einer Sache [zu] stehen und bei ihr aus[zu]harren".[41] Mit den hier entwickelten Perspektiven habe ich versucht, Praxis und Theorie als ein ‚Mit-Sein' vorstellbar zu machen, als eine sich ereignende, flüchtige und stets im Werden befindliche Gemeinschaft. Folglich als eine un/mögliche Gemeinschaft, insofern diese „nur unter Anerkennung einer in ihr enthaltenen Kluft überhaupt existieren kann."[42] Eine solche un/mögliche Gemeinschaft von Theorie und Praxis löste sich von reduktionistischen Polarisierungen, indem sie sozusagen einen Sprung mitten in eine Sache hinein wagte, um in ihr auszuharren, an ihr Teil zu nehmen, ohne sie zu besitzen, sich ihrer als Gegenstand zu bemächtigen.

37 .... Heidegger: Denken, 132.

38 .... Gadamer, Hans Georg: *Lob der Theorie. Reden und Aufsätze.* Frankfurt am Main 1983, 45. Gadamer folgend unterscheidet sich Theorie von der Art von Gütern, die man erwirbt, um sie zu gebrauchen und zu besitzen. Theorie gehört zu jener Art von Gütern, die „keinem gehören und gerade dadurch für einen jeden etwas sind, woran er ganz teil hat".

39 .... Jahraus, Oliver: Theorietheorie. In: Grizelj (Hg.): *Theorietheorie*, 17–39, hier 33.

40 .... Heidegger, Martin: Die Zeit des Weltbildes. In: Ders.: *Holzwege.* Frankfurt a.M. 2003, 75–113, hier 82. Der Rahmen lässt es nicht zu, die durch die Ausfransung der Disziplinen in Frage gestellte einfache Gegenüberstellung von Theorie/Kunst und Wissenschaft adäquat zu problematisieren. Festzuhalten ist jedoch, dass es in den Wissenschaften genügend Felder gibt, die von der Unzugänglichkeit der Welt ihren Ausgang nehmen und Theorien erstellen. Denn Theorien sind auch Funktionen von Wissenschaft.

41 .... Heidegger: Denken, 125.

42 .... Gertenbach u.a.: *Theorien der Gemeinschaft*, 165.

Only the leap into the river tells us what is called swimming. We thus only come to know the element in which swimming must move.'[33] A leap into the unknown is thus necessary to arrive *in* thought.

Heidegger is not interested in thinking 'about thinking', not the production of the ordinary through the use of language as a 'means of expression' or through an understanding of the 'work as expression, and the impression as experience'.[34] In his explication of thinking, Heidegger divorces words from their representative function, he understands them precisely 'not like buckets and kegs from which we scoop a content that is there'.[35] Words, in his view, are 'wellsprings that must be found and dug up again and again, that easily cave in, but that at times also well up when least expected'.[36]
Thinking here is undertaken as a practice divorced from the ordinary—and this is the link to Nancy—which creates meaning outside signification. Nancy's 'surpassing the existent' or the separation from the 'ordinary' (Heidegger) takes place in the element that we think we are familiar with, which we think we use as a means. By allowing ourselves to open up to the unfamiliar, to what does not correspond to the respective historical meaning assigned, a 'modified grasping' is made possible. In this context, Heidegger compares the artistic practice of poetry with that of thought. Both can say the same thing in different ways, but only when a gaping chasm resolutely lies between them.[37]

Heidegger's model of thought shows a proximity to a notion of theory if theory is recognized as a seeing which is neither about establishing what is actually present, nor about seeing what one hopes to be the case, or identifying what corresponds to common sense. On the contrary, theory can be described as an illustration that divorces itself from the already familiar, dares a leap into the unknown. Theory, as a specifically reflexive form of observation, thus does not mean a critical metareflection that says what makes art visible and makes it present. On the contrary, it is not 'in the first instance a behavior whereby we control an object or put it at our disposal by explaining it'.[38] Advanced theories account for the impossibility of realisation by 'allowing processuality to take the place of realization, and differentiality to take the place of identification'.[39] In so doing, theory, like art, differs from the traditional notion of science. Here, the historical and the natural sciences are 'aimed at presenting the constant and at making history an object'.[40]

Borrowing from Heidegger's reflections on thinking, theory can be linked to processes and techniques of interruption, with necessary leaps that allow us to leave familiar territory. By taking the leap into the current, we remove ourselves from the 'steady progress, where we move unawares from one thing to the next and everything remains alike'.[41] The leap takes us 'abruptly to where everything is different, so different that it strikes us as strange'.[42]
With the perspectives developed here, I have attempted to make practice and theory imaginable as a *Mit-Sein*, as a community that is taking place, fleeting, and always in becoming, and thus as an im/possible community, to the extent that it can 'only exist with the acknowledgement of an inherent rupture'.[43]
Such an im/possible community of theory and practice divorces itself from the reductionist

33 .... Ibid., p. 21.
34 .... Ibid., p. 128.
35 .... Ibid., p. 130.
36 .... Ibid., p. 130.
37 .... Ibid., p. 132.

38 ...... Hans Georg Gadamer, 'Praise of Theory', *Praise of Theory: Speeches and Essays*, tr. Chris Dawson (New Haven, 1999), p. 32. According to Gadamer, theory differs from the kind of goods acquired in order to be used and possessed. Theory belongs to the kind of goods that 'belong to nobody, and for just that reason they are something in which each individual has a full share' (ibid.).
39 ...... Oliver Jahraus, 'Theorietheorie', *Theorietheorie*, ed. Grizelj, p. 33.
40 . Martin Heidegger, 'The Age of the World Picture', *Off the Beaten Track*, tr. Julian Young and Kenneth Haynes (Cambridge, 2002), p. 62. There is no room here to adequately discuss the opposition between theory/art and scholarship, questioned by the fraying of the disciplines. Suffice it to say that there are enough fields in scholarship that take their point of departure from the inaccessibility of the world and develop theories on this basis. For theories are also functions of science.
41 .... Heidegger, *What Is Called Thinking?*, p. 12.
42 .... Ibid.
43 .... Gertenbach, et al., *Theorien der Gemeinschaft*, p. 165.

polarisations by daring as it were a leap into the midst of a thing, to persevere in it, to take part in it, without possessing it, taking hold of it as an object.

The two curators argue that at issue for them is admitting the incomprehensible or even the disparate, as well as practices of dissent, which is why it is necessary 'to explode the dual system of disambiguities'. The system of disambiguity entails authenticity, for example the authenticity of *theory* and *practice.* It seems that it is time to emancipate ourselves from these disambiguities and authenticities. If theory and practice are thought from the perspective of the with, that this is also true of the im/possible community of the many and irreducible differences. Perhaps then processes of 'contagion and communication' can be triggered that allow challenging significances and divisions of the sensible to come into their own in practices of theory and art production.

Translated by Brian Currid

Die beiden Kuratorinnen formulieren, dass es ihnen um das Zulassen von Unverständlichem oder gar Disparatem geht, sowie um Praktiken des Dissens, weshalb es nötig sei, „das duale System der Eindeutigkeiten zu sprengen". Das System der Eindeutigkeit behauptet Eigentlichkeit, etwa die ‚Eigentlichkeit' von der Theorie und der Praxis. Es scheint an der Zeit, sich von diesen Eindeutigkeiten und Eigentlichkeiten zu emanzipieren. Werden Theorie und Praxis vom ‚Mit' aus gedacht, dann gilt auch für sie die un/mögliche Gemeinschaft der Vielen und irreduziblen Andersheiten. Vielleicht können dann Prozesse der „Ansteckung und Kommunikation" in Gang kommen, die herausfordernde Signifikanzen und Aufteilungen des Sinnlichen in Praxen der Theorie- wie Kunstproduktion zum Zuge kommen lassen.

MASTERPIECES

The following script is an excerpt of the dialogues from the videoinstallation *Meisterwerke* (Masterpieces) (2009) by Juliane Zelwies. In this work, psychotherapy is used to explore the interpersonal relationships of the people and objects portrayed in six famous paintings, here: *Las Meninas*.

INT. – SEMINAR ROOM – DAY

Ten people are positioned like figures on a game board. Hardwood floor, big windows, sunshine. FABIAN walks around and questions one by one.

FABIAN

How does THE FOCUS feel?

THE FOCUS

I am very confused about the setup right now.

FABIAN

What's confusing?

THE FOCUS

That I don't know who it is all about. It was pretty odd when THE MIRROR came in, I felt a short twitch in my forehead.

FABIAN (repeats quietly)

A short twitch in your forehead.

FABIAN walks over to THE MIRROR.

THE MIRROR (quietly)

In the very beginning I felt as if everything was inside me—from all of them. I mirror everything.

FABIAN (louder)

Everything is inside you. You mirror everything.

THE MIRROR

Yes, I take everything in.

FABIAN

Thank you. How is THE ARTIST VELÁZQUEZ doing?

THE ARTIST VELÁZQUEZ

I believe that my strongest tie is with THE MIRROR, because he's standing right in front of me, whereas I stand in front of a diagonal, which is formed by THE MIRROR, MYSELF IN THE PAINTING and THE CANVAS.

THE CANVAS is blocking WHAT IS SHOWN ON THE CANVAS though. However, that is why it is reflecting

the relationship with THE MODEL, which has been placed next to me and that I feel as it's standing right behind me...

THE MODEL nestles up against THE ARTIST VELÁZQUEZ. VELÁZQUEZ freezes.

FABIAN
VELÁZQUEZ finds this uncomfortable. Please take a step forward. Is it better like this?

THE ARTIST VELÁZQUEZ
Yes, I need a bit more distance.

FABIAN (gentle)
A bit more distance.
(to THE MODEL)
I'd like to offer you a chair now. Could you, dear MODEL, please come here and sit down?

THE MODEL follows reluctantly, sits down slowly onto the chair, then slides off to the ground. (to THE ARTIST VELÁZQUEZ)
How is it now?

THE ARTIST VELÁZQUEZ
I feel these relationships clearly. There is this diagonal, which is formed by THE MIRROR, THE ARTIST INSIDE THE PAINTING and THE CANVAS. And then there is also a very clear diagonal between WHAT IS SHOWN ON THE CANVAS and THE MODEL. But they both disappear from sight.

FABIAN
WHAT IS SHOWN ON THE CANVAS and THE MODEL vanish from your sight.

THE ARTIST VELÁZQUEZ
Exactly, but they're strongly connected.

FABIAN
Is it important to you that the audience knows WHAT CAN BE SEEN IN THE PAINTING?

THE ARTIST VELÁZQUEZ
No, I think I only care about THE MIRROR.

FABIAN
Can I ask THE FOCUS to follow me?

THE FOCUS
I can't move from here. There's too much happening right now and, well, the diagonal is so strong. I see that handle, and as soon as he moves it, it looks as if he's going to hit something. Quite peculiar.

FABIAN
Could I ask you now—look at me!

THE FOCUS
That was very hard!

FABIAN
Look at me now! Get out of your role! Immediately!
THE FOCUS shakes himself and stamps his feet.

FABIAN
Please try something new. Follow me!

IM/POSSIBLE COMMUNITY

Juliane Zelwies: *Meisterwerke*, 2009

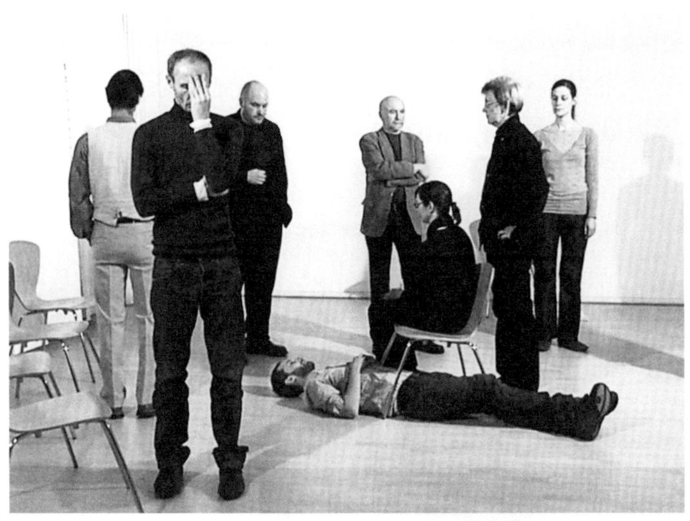

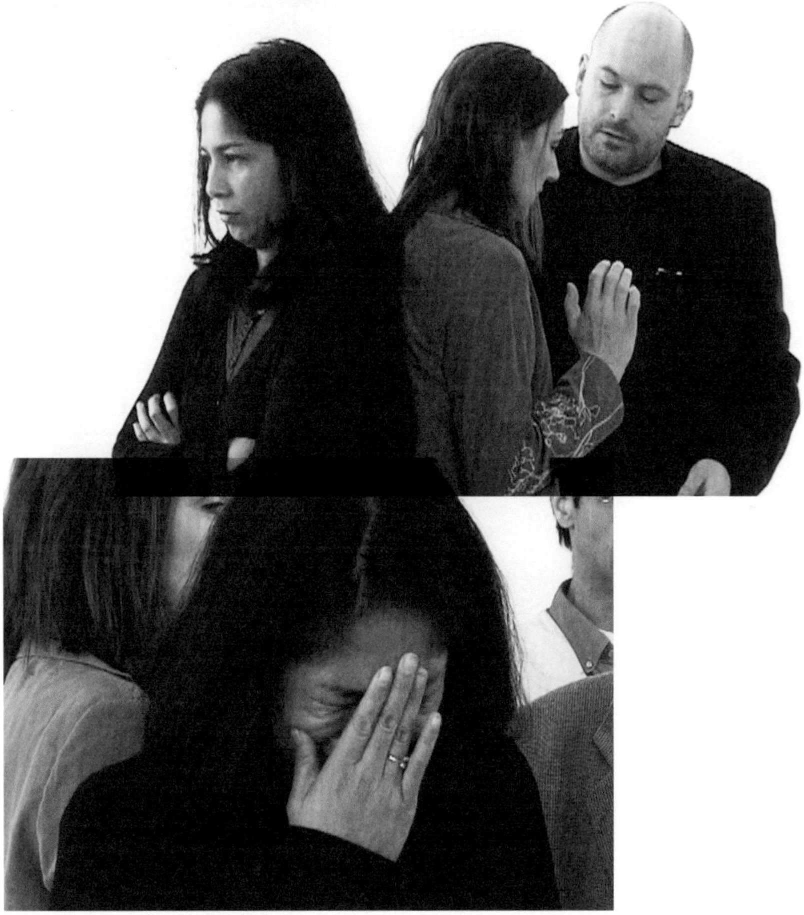

THE FOCUS follows FABIAN through the room.

FABIAN
What is it like to stand here? Does this feel better?

THE FOCUS
It is different, but it isn't better.

FABIAN
It is different, but it isn't better.

THE FOCUS
I see that there is a real threat. THE PAINTER is full of doubt. And he is somehow constrained. And I still see that there's a heavy burden on THE INFANTA.

FABIAN
We're getting to that very soon. JULIANE, can I ask you to come on his side? Please take his hand.

THE FOCUS
That's what I also was planning to do now as well.
JULIANE stands to the right side of THE FOCUS and holds his hand.

FABIAN
Look at each other and please take your time!
THE FOCUS and JULIANE look each other into their eyes.

FABIAN (gentle)
Could I ask you, dear INFANTA, to look here? Imagine there's something here, which could pop up here. How is that?

THE INFANTA MARGARITA
I couldn't care less!

FABIAN
You couldn't care less?

THE INFANTA MARGARITA
Correct.

FABIAN
Okay. Where have you been looking the whole time?

THE INFANTA MARGARITA (points toward the floor)
Here.

FABIAN
Here?
FABIAN kneels downs and holds his hands in the spot THE INFANTA has been pointing at.

FABIAN
And if something were to appear here? How would that be?
THE INFANTA MARGARITA
Well, what would appear?

FABIAN
Don't know. Is it pleasant, now, since it's been here?

THE INFANTA MARGARITA
Can't tell you.

FABIAN (to another person)
**Could I ask you to stand here, to stand-in for what is supposed to be here? And so that T
HE INFANTA can see it properly.**

(to THE INFANTA MARGARITA)
How is that?

THE INFANTA MARGARITA
Fine.

FABIAN
Fine. Just find out how it feels.
THE MODEL starts to cry (again).

FABIAN
What is it now?

THE MODEL
Can't say.

WHAT IS SHOWN ON THE CANVAS
My leg is hurting so badly, it is hurting so much.
FABIAN nods.

THE FOCUS
I can't stand it any more. I want to get away from the image.

FABIAN
**Alright. We've gone quite deep into the analysis of the image. And there's some discomfort to go on,
because the remaining questions can't be solved.**

THE FOCUS
I've resolved something. And I don't want to see the painting anymore!

FABIAN
**And in that case the job is finished. Fine. Let's do the ritual to get out of our roles now, altogether.
Please come together. Stamp your feet, press your fingers into your palms…**

FADE TO BLACK.

FÜR EIN MITEINANDER VON MEHR-DEUTIGKEITEN

Sabina Baumann
im Gespräch mit Anke Hoffmann

Anke Hoffmann: *Sabina, du warst mit deinen Arbeiten Teil der Ausstellung* Un/Mögliche Gemeinschaft. *Ich würde dich gern fragen: Bist du Teil einer un/möglichen Gemeinschaft? Und wenn ja, welcher?*

Sabina Baumann: Generell würde ich sagen, dass wir alle Teil einer un/möglichen Gemeinschaft sind. Weil immer mehr Menschen auf diesem Planeten leben und der Platz immer enger wird, müssen wir irgendwie miteinander auskommen. Es ist eine unmögliche Gemeinschaft. Jede Kultur ist eine Ausnahme in Zeit und Ort. Das, was selbstverständlich oder die Norm ist, ist eigentlich die Ausnahme. Die andere un-mögliche Gemeinschaft, zu der ich mich spezifischer zugehörig fühle, ist die Queer Community, dieser Platz zwischen den Geschlechtern... Es wird an den Universitäten viel darüber gesprochen, es gibt viel Theorie, aber nicht im Entferntesten eine Basisbewe-gung, wie sie der Feminismus in den 1970er Jahren hatte. So ist sie eine doppelt unmögliche Gemein-schaft, weil sie sich so wenig etablieren konnte. Ich würde aus dem Erklären nicht herauskommen, wenn ich meine Identität selbstverständlich leben wollen würde. Denn ich empfinde es als Fassade und als Ge-walt, die mir widerfährt, wenn mir eine Identität von aussen übergestülpt wird. Daher finde ich es einfacher, darüber zu arbeiten und nachzudenken.

Anke Hoffmann: *Woher kommt es, dass wir uns mit einfachen, gegenübergestellten Identifikationen besser zurechtfinden, oder zumindest denken, uns besser zu-rechtzufinden?*

Sabina Baumann: In der Gruppe fühlt man sich gestärkt. In jedem Gespräch ist es so: Wenn jemand eine ähnliche Meinung hat, fühlt man sich unterstützt und andernfalls fühlt man sich bekämpft. Ich denke, das kommt aus diesem ganz einfachen und verständ-lichen Bedürfnis, sich aufgehoben, sicher und zuhause zu fühlen.

Anke Hoffmann: *Daraus würde sich eigentlich ergeben, dass es immer ein Miteinander ist von Grenzen ziehen und Grenzen öffnen. Dass es immer ein Miteinander ist, zu sagen wer ich bin, wer ich nicht bin und wer ich vielleicht sein könnte?*

Sabina Baumann: *o.T.,* 2009; *Marvin*, 2008; *Ich Du Es sein*, 2009
(Ausstellungsansicht / Exhibition view)

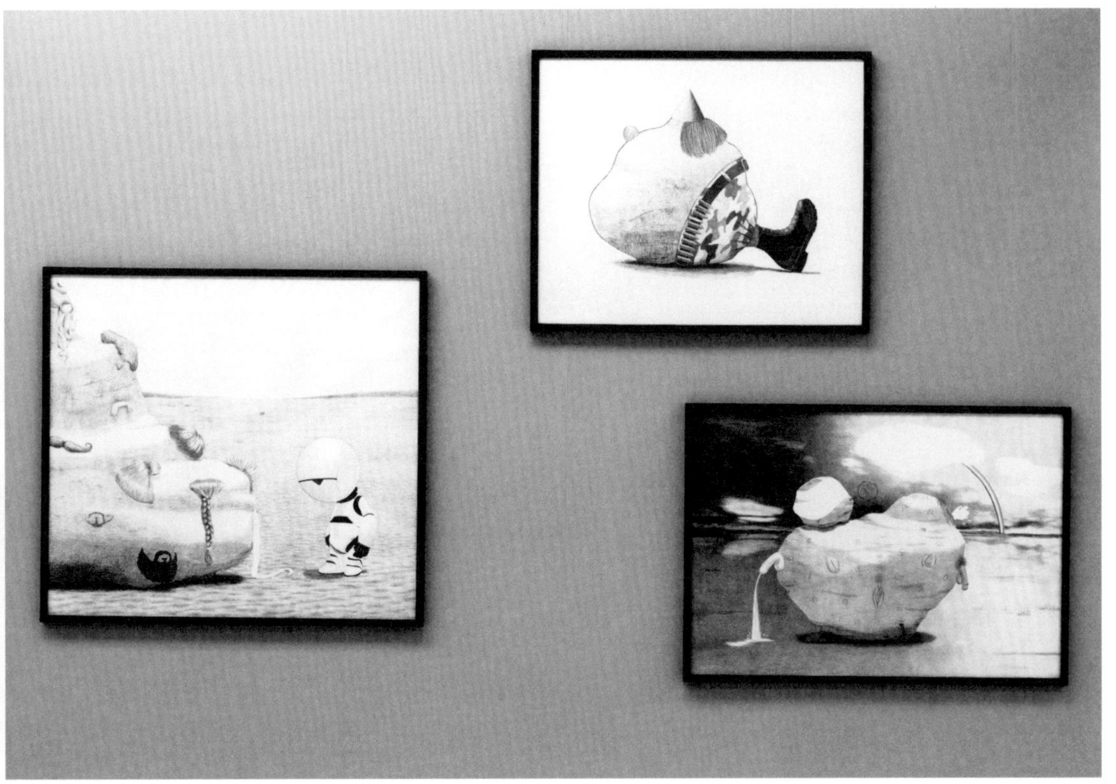

SABINA BAUMANN

Sabina Baumann: *Ich Du Es sein*, 2009

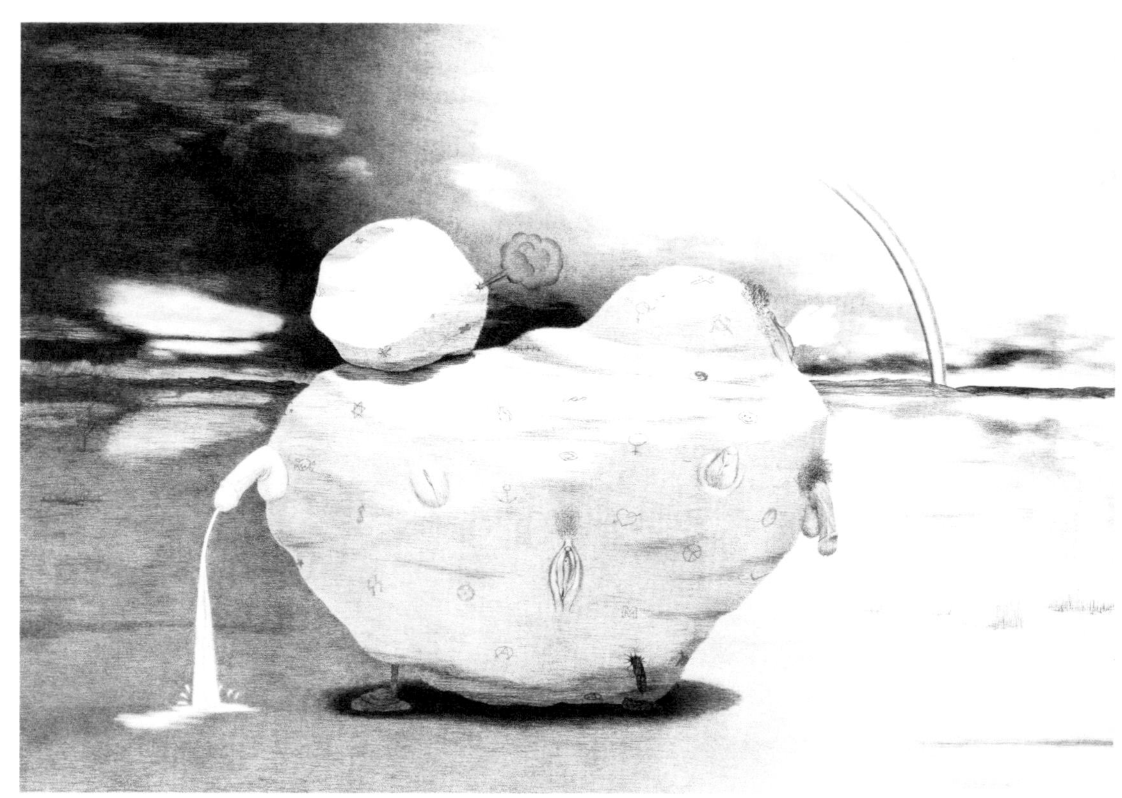

Sabina Baumann: Genau. Es ist ein permanentes Verhandeln und eine Möglichkeitsbedingung dessen, eine Identität leben zu können oder zu dürfen. Man kann nicht jenseits davon sein. Existieren bedeutet, sich mit einer Identität auseinanderzusetzen. Ich denke, das Identitäten immer neu ausgehandelt werden müssen. Dass es so etwas wie ‚mich' gar nicht gibt. Man sollte jede Identität, jede gefühlte Identität ernst nehmen und daraus etwas machen können dürfen. Diese Art von Offenheit sollte es geben.

Anke Hoffmann: *Dies versuchst du in deinen grossformatigen Zeichnungen und in den drei Arbeiten aus deiner Steineserie, die wir ausgestellt haben, zu thematisieren. Es sind einzelne monolithische Steine, die mit ganz unterschiedlichen Zuweisungen und Beschreibungen markiert sind. Bei der Zeichnung Ich Du Es sein ist es ein Nebeneinander von unterschiedlichen Codes, von pseudo-politischen bis hin zu Pop-Symbolen. Der Judenstern neben dem Feminismus-Zeichen, der Amorpfeil im Herz neben einer SS-Rune; alle diese Symbole sind auf diesem einen grossen Stein verteilt. Daneben Körperfunktionen wie Urinieren, Scheissen oder Ejakulieren, also der Körper zwischen Verdauung und Sexualität. Dieser Stein mit den diversen Symbolen und Merkmalen ist eingebettet in eine Landschaft mit einer Abfolge von Wettererscheinungen…*

Sabina Baumann: *Ich Du Es sein* bringt alles – innerhalb der Serie, aber auch meiner Arbeit generell – auf den Punkt. Nämlich dieses Parallelsein von Welten. Mir kommt es so vor, als wenn wir riesige Mythen über die armen kleinen Körperteile stülpen, die eigentlich nichts dafür können und eigentlich das machen, was sie sonst immer machen – aber diese Vorgänge sind tabuisiert. Das ist das unter der Gürtellinie. Die Geschlechtsteile sind das Einzige, was als menschliche Körperteile erkennbar ist auf dem Stein. Der Stein ist dabei eine abstrakte Körper-Metapher. Er ist ein utopischer Körper und kann als Subjekt oder Erde gelesen werden. Gelabelt wird so vieles, wo man einkaufen geht bis hin zur politischen Gesinnung. Das ist jetzt alles auf diesem Stein. Dazu das Wetter… Der Regenbogen ist das Symbol der Queerbewegung und ein Friedenszeichen, in Grautönen gezeichnet, macht es lustig und trist zugleich. Es geht vom Unwetter bis hin zum schönen Wetter. Jedes Wetter, jedes Geschlecht, jede Gesinnung, alles ist da auf diesem Bild. Und dann gibt es die feinen Unterschiede,

zum Beispiel dass nicht ein Penis ejakuliert, sondern die Vagina. Und dass es keine erigierten Penisse ind, sondern so halb erigierte oder schlaffe. Das sind kleine Hints, die untypisch dafür sind, wie Geschlechter sonst präsentiert werden.

Anke Hoffmann: *Aber gibt es da nicht auch eine Unterschiedlichkeit in den Zuschreibungen? Zwischen dem, was du Überstülpen nennst und den Identitätslogiken, die wir uns wählen können. Das Peace-Zeichen oder das christliche Kreuz beispielsweise kann ich wählen. Es ist natürlich davon abhängig, in welche Familie ich hineingeboren wurde. Die Kategorie Geschlecht ist dagegen schwieriger verhandelbar.*

Sabina Baumann: Wenn man an all die Möglichkeiten denkt, von der plastischen Chirurgie bis zur Geschlechtsanpassung, ganz zu Schweigen von der sozialen Seite, dann könnte man sagen, man hat genau die gleichen Möglichkeiten heute. Da gibt es auch ein wählbares Spektrum.

Anke Hoffmann: *Wir sind heute auf einem erweiterten Pfad der Wahlmöglichkeiten. Trotzdem gibt es viele Normen, viele Einschränkungen, die – wenn man jetzt auf Gemeinschaft zurückkommt – festlegen, wer zu wem und wer nicht dazu gehört. Da sind wir wieder bei der Angst oder bei der Nervosität, keinen Rückhalt, keine Mitstreiter_innen zu haben.*

Sabina Baumann: Ja, einerseits dominieren wirtschaftliche Interessen die globale Weltgemeinschaft, andererseits leben wir in Wettbewerbsgesellschaften, in der sich jeder soziale Halt immer mehr auflöst und die Politik ausgehebelt wird. Wir haben diese Einschränkungen verinnerlicht und fühlen uns chronisch überlastet und schuldig am eigenen Versagen. Mittlerweile bin ich sehr pessimistisch und glaube, dass es unmöglich ist, den deregulierten Kapitalismus auszuhebeln. Kann man durch alternative Strategien, wie zum Beispiel Ökodörfer oder bewusstes Konsumieren die herkömmlichen Werte langsam durchlässig machen? Das bezweifle ich stark. Dinge, die noch unvorstellbar waren in der Nachkriegszeit, wie das Ende der Kleinfamilie zum Beispiel oder dass Schwule und Lesben heiraten, sind am Bröckeln hier bei uns. Weshalb kann man nicht bestimmte Gruppierungen, die eine ganz subjektive Erfahrung haben, sei es Geschlecht oder etwas anderes, direkt als ‚Expert_innen' ansehen? Sie als verschiedene Perspektiven einbringen

und sie als Chancen sehen und nicht tendenziell be-
kämpfen? Diejenigen, welche die Kastanien aus dem
Feuer holen, werden bestraft, obwohl letztlich die gesamte Bevölkerung davon profitiert.

Anke Hoffmann: *Seit wann übersetzt du deine Reflexionen
und Gedanken in deine zeichnerischen Bild-
kompositionen?*

Sabina Baumann: Ich habe eigentlich immer gezeichnet,
aber mit den grossformatigen Zeichnungen erst
2007 begonnen. Ich fand es faszinierend, dass mit
so wenig Aufwand – einem Bleistift und einem Blatt
Papier – Welten entstehen können. Es ist wie ein
Aufenthalt in dieser Welt, vielmehr als das Aufschütten
von Ideen in kleinen Zeichnungen. Es hat auch eine
ökologische Komponente, dass alles aus natürlichem
Material ist und auch hier produziert wird. Diesen
Teilaspekt fand ich irgendwann auch wichtig. Und
die Langsamkeit und das völlig Anachronistische dieser
Bilder.

Anke Hoffmann: *Das klingt sehr schön. Gibt es etwas
für dich, das du sowohl künstlerisch als auch mensch-
lich machen willst, wo du hinkommen willst?*

Sabina Baumann: Einerseits habe ich das Gefühl, dass
ich ewig weitermachen könnte mit diesen Bildern.
Andererseits habe ich das Gefühl, dass ich mit anderen
Menschen ganz konkret dieses Leben zusammen-
leben möchte. Dass ich wirklich leben will mit Leuten.
Ich habe das nie gemacht, ich habe immer zu zweit
gewohnt. Dieses Zusammenkommen, mit anderen
Leuten ...

IMMER WIEDER WIEDERSEHEN! ODER: ZU WELCHEM SONG STERBEN WIR JETZT?

Der folgende Text ist ein Auszug aus Heimo Lattners Hörspielinstallation *Immer wieder Wiedersehen! Oder: Zu welchem Song sterben wir jetzt?* nach Jean Genets *Der Balkon*. Das Stück handelt von den Machtspielen der Gesellschaft, von Revolution und der Bedeutung von Bildern und vertraut auf den Augenblick von Stimmen, Rollen und Räumen. Text und Dramaturgie: Heimo Lattner und Karolin Nedelmann; künstlerische Mitarbeit: Jaime Lutzo.

Personen: Nina (Kronjäger) und Angelika (Sautter), zwei Schauspielerinnen
in den Rollen
Rodger: Klempner und Revolutionär
Karl: Gasmann und Bischof

In irgendeiner Stadt, in der für die Revolution gekämpft wird.

1. Bild
Angelika und Nina

Angelika:
Der BALKON
ist ein Theater, ein Salon, in dem die Rollen- und Machtspiele der Gesellschaft nachgespielt werden.
Ein Bischof.
Ein Richter.
Ein General.
Und eine Revolution versucht gerade die Gesellschaft umzustürzen,
das System der repräsentativen Macht abzuschaffen.

Nina:
Und Jean Genet hat 30 Seiten aus der zweiten Fassung seines Stücks herausgerissen. Und zwar genau die, auf denen sich die Revolutionäre wegen einer Frau in die Haare kriegen.

Angelika:
Nein, nicht wegen einer Frau. Wegen des Bildes einer Frau.
Sie heißt Chantal, sie ist Sängerin und wurde von einem der Revolutionäre, der eigentlich Klempner ist, aus dem Puff gerettet.

Nina:
Aus dem *Großen Balkon*, dem berühmten Haus der Illusionen.
Jean Genets Mutter, eine Prostituierte, gab ihr Kind weg;
es wuchs bei Pflegeeltern auf.
Als der zehnjährige Junge, der bis dahin als folgsam und fromm gegolten

Heimo Lattner: *Immer wieder Wiedersehen! oder: Zu welchem Song sterben wir jetzt?*, 2009
(Ausstellungsansicht/Exhibition view)

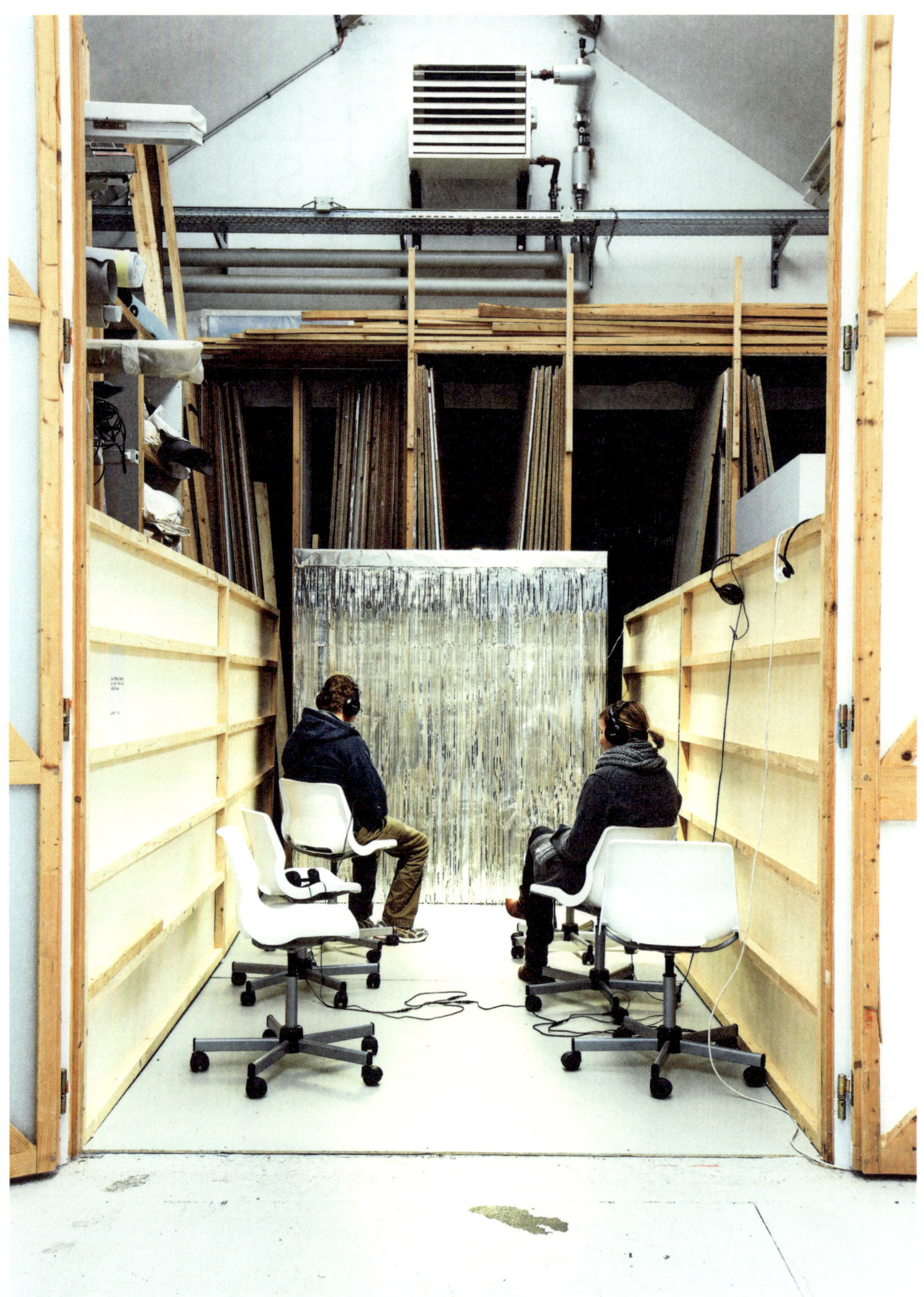

hatte, eines Tages von seinem Klassenlehrer des Diebstahls bezichtigt wurde, fasste er den Entschluss,
ein Dieb zu *sein*.
Ein Dieb.
Ein Stricher.
Ein Fremdenlegionär.
Ein Aktivist.

Angelika: Der Höhepunkt seiner Karriere als Dieb soll der Einbruch in ein Museum gewesen sein.
Der Dichter stahl Bilder.

Nina   In einem Land von Dieben kann man nicht stehlen. Wenn man stiehlt, fügt man sich damit in die herrschende Ordnung ein, anstatt sie zu zerstören.
(Das hat Genet mal über Deutschland gesagt.)

Angelika   Bei der Welturaufführung vom *Balkon* in London hat Zadek, der Regisseur, Genet aus dem Theater rausgeschmissen, weil er aus Protest gegen die Inszenierung gewalttätig geworden ist.

Nina: Für Genet ist der Traum von seinem Stück *Der Balkon* die Wirklichkeit.
Diesen Traum konnte er nicht opfern, nicht eintauschen gegen die schauspielerische Wirklichkeit des Stücks auf der Bühne.
[....] Der Körper der Wünsche ist ein Bild. Und der Wunsch, der wir selbst sind, den wir uns aber nicht eingestehen können, bleibt für immer eingeschlossen in einer Krypta.

Angelika: Die Eingangsszene zeigt einen prächtig gekleideten Bischof, der in salbungsvoller Theologensprache daherredet.

Nina: Eigentlich ist der gar kein Bischof.

BISCHOF   *(getragen)* Die Majestät und Würde, die mich umstrahlen, sind geheimnisvoller Art: Der Bischof ist mir vorangegangen. Ich will Bischof sein in der Einsamkeit, um der Erscheinung willen.
Und um jede Funktion zu zerstören, werde ich einen Skandal machen und dir das Kleid aufschürzen, Hure, Dirne, Metze.

Nina: Karl Marx hat einmal gesagt, dass die Forderung nach der Aufhebung der Religion die Forderung nach dem wirklichen Glück sei.

Angelika: Ja. Und Mark Twain sagte: „Bewahre deine Illusionen. Wenn sie verschwunden sind, wirst du weiter existieren, aber nicht weiter leben."

Nina: Eigentlich dreht sich doch alles um Chantal.
Sois belle et tais-toi!
Man wird für Chantal in den Tod gehen, aber im Grunde genommen will sie nur singen. Für viele ist sie das Bild, das gehört für viele eben immer noch dazu, ein Bild, zu einer Revolution.

Angelika: Und Rodger, der Anführer der Aufständischen, widersetzt sich diesen
Forderungen, muss jedoch zum Schluss unter Protest nachgeben.

REVOLUTIONÄR Ich habe dich nicht aus dem Puff entführt, damit du ein Musical-Star oder
ein Doppeladler wirst!

Angelika: Genau. Aber eigentlich ist Rodger – der Revolutionär – Klempner.

Nina: Er ist Klempner und hat in dem Puff, im Großen Balkon, die Rohre in Stand
gehalten. Der Bischof, also Karl, spielt im Puff einen Bischof, aber eigentlich
ist er bei den Gaswerken angestellt.

Angelika: Genet ist einmal einem großen, einhändigen Zuhälter, Dieb und Rauschgift-
händler namens Stilitano, den er in seiner Jugend wie einen Helden verehrt
hatte, zufällig auf einem Jahrmarkt begegnet. Stilitano hatte sich dort in einem
Spiegelkabinett verirrt, in dem die Scheiben so angeordnet waren, dass die
Leute von außen die grotesken Bemühungen der drinnen nach dem Ausgang
Suchenden verfolgen konnten.
Stilitano war allein. Alle hatten sie den Ausgang gefunden, nur er nicht. Und
wie ein Tier in der Falle, zu müde, um noch länger zu brüllen und mit dem
Kopf gegen die Scheiben anzurennen, abgestumpft gegen das Hohngeläch-
ter der gaffenden Menge, hatte sich Stilitano auf den Boden gelegt und
weigerte sich, weiterzusuchen.

Nina: So sehr man ein neues, schöneres Leben beschwört: Die Gegenwelt bleibt
immer innerhalb der Welt, wie die Gegenmoral immer innerhalb der Moral
bleibt.

Angelika: Jeder Revolutionär spielt. Und er liebt sein Spiel.

Nina: Und wenn er sich von seinem Spiel hinreißen lässt? Leidenschaftlich?
Sich hineinstürzt?

6. Bild
Revolutionär und Bischof

REVOLUTIONÄR Die Revolution ist aus Ekel vor eurem Komödienspiel ausgebrochen,
aus Ekel vor eurer Selbstgefälligkeit.

BISCHOF Aber was ist denn die Revolution anderes als ein Salto-Mortale ins Reich
der Illusionen? [....]

REVOLUTIONÄR [....] Du bist sogar bereit gegen die Revolution zu kämpfen, weil sie deine
Träume bedroht.

BISCHOF Aber ja! Schauen Sie: Ist das Wesen des Seins der Verstand oder der Glaube?
Oder anders gefragt, *(zögert)* ich nenn's mal Einsatz:
Ist der entscheidende Einsatz die Vorstellung eines Lebens
oder die Illusion des Glaubens? Na?

REVOLUTIONÄR

Wer ein einziges Mal in seinem Leben eine tödliche Gefahr durch seinen Verstand abgewendet hat, der weiß, dass die Revolution nur durch Intelligenz und Willen gewonnen werden kann. Die Gefahr und die Überwindung der Gefahr müssen vom Einzelnen ausgehen. Alles andere ist Spiel und Pose. Ein Mensch der hofft, fängt schon zu träumen an.

BISCHOF

Aber der Traum ist Wirklichkeit! Das Fest ist schon da! Der Justizpalast steht in Flammen. Die Kirchen werden geplündert. Einige Männer kämpfen im Kostüm, in Chorhemden und Richterroben. Ein wahrer Karneval. Eure Revolution produziert Bilder!

REVOLUTIONÄR

Im Augenblick halten sich die Helden für Auserwählte, vom Schicksal, vom Himmel auserwählt. Aber dieser Himmel, der von euren Bildern, und euren Helden übersät ist, den sollte man ausrümpeln und ihn zwingen, nackt auf dem Vorplatz der Kathedrale zu tanzen. [....]

BISCHOF

Sag ich doch: Die Revolution wird auf dem Balkon entschieden.

[....]

8. Bild
Nina und Angelika

Nina:

Wir spielen dasselbe Stück, nur kommen wir aus zwei entgegen gesetzten Richtungen. Aber das lässt sich jetzt nicht mehr ändern.

Angelika:

Wie zwei Menschen, die zum selben Zeitpunkt, an zwei unterschiedlichen Orten in ein Taxi gestiegen sind und jetzt auf denselben Punkt zufahren.

Nina:

Ja, und dann: PENG!

Angelika:

Also, da stehen die sich Auge in Auge gegenüber

Nina:

Genau. Und da stehen sie heute noch.

Angelika:

Und vor ihnen liegt Chantal. Tot.

Nina:

Und neben ihr, da wo der Kopf ist, liegt ein Flugblatt mit einem Bild von ihr drauf.

Bei dem nachfolgenden Text handelt
es sich um den Liedtext des *Ersten
Zürcher Beschwerdechors*, der
Teil der internationalen Projektreihe
Complaints Choirs (seit 2003)
ist, ursprünglich initiiert von Tellervo
Kalleinen und Oliver Kochta-Kalleinen.
Eine Gruppe von Freiwilligen bildete
den Chor, zusammen mit der Alpinistin
Regina Steiner und dem Pianisten
Niels van der Waerden, unter der
Leitung der Komponistin Stefanie
Ressin und Mitarbeit von Jan Theiler.
Der Text wurde auf Basis gesam-
melter Beschwerden entwickelt und
am 30. Januar 2010 auf öffentlichen
Plätzen in Zürich sowie im Fabrik-
theater der Roten Fabrik aufgeführt.

Eine Produktion der Shedhalle
in Kooperation mit dem Fabriktheater
Rote Fabrik und unterstützt
vom Institut für Theorie der Zürcher
Hochschule der Künste.

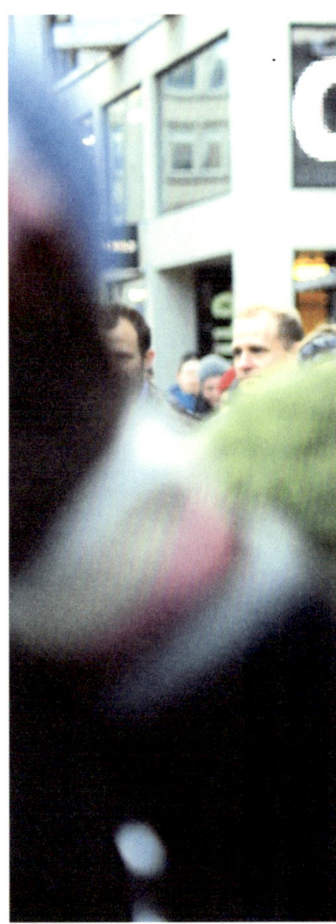

Vortrag

Keis Problem! S'git schliässli immer öppis über
das me sich beschwere cha: mal isch's z'warm,
mal isch's z'chalt, s'hät z'viil Lüüt oder äkei, si sind
z'jung, oder z'alt, mal isch's der Räge, mal der
Schnee oder Sand am falsche Ort, d Underhose
zwicked oder d'Cervala isch i grosser Gfaar.
Nei, im Ernscht, was mi würkli beschwert und mir
mängisch au no d'Nachtrue stört: Frömds Gäld,
vo dem dörfs ha beliäbig viil i dere Schwyz, das
schützt und hätschlet mer. Aber Mensche schickt
me use, will kei andri Farb als Grau in Schwiizerrot,
s'chönt ja richtig spannend werde suscht.
D'Angscht isch riisig, d'Angscht mer bliibted
nümme di gliiche, alte, riiche, behüetete, blüemle-
te, krüüzlete Schwyzer.

Intro

Pilzbefall im Badezimmer – ekelhaft! Wachstum,
nichts als Wachstum, immer – einfallslos!
Zu wenig Damenklos in den Theatern, der Egois-
mus wird schlimmer – überall! Morgens um sieben
die Presslufthammer – Laubbläser! Höllischer
Lärm von den Kirchglocken – Stundentakt!

Erster Zürcher Beschwerdechor, 2010

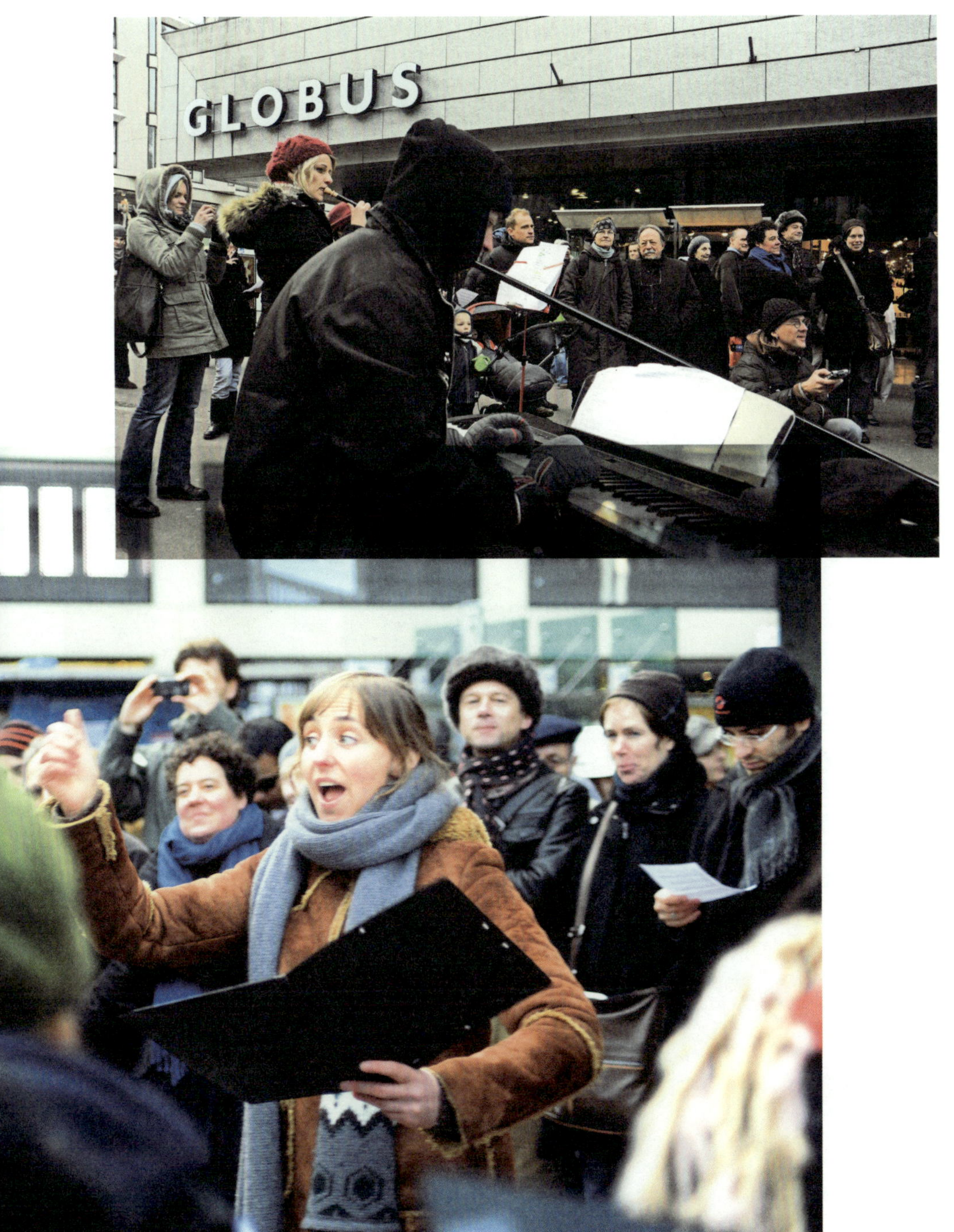

Erster Zürcher Beschwerdechor, 2010

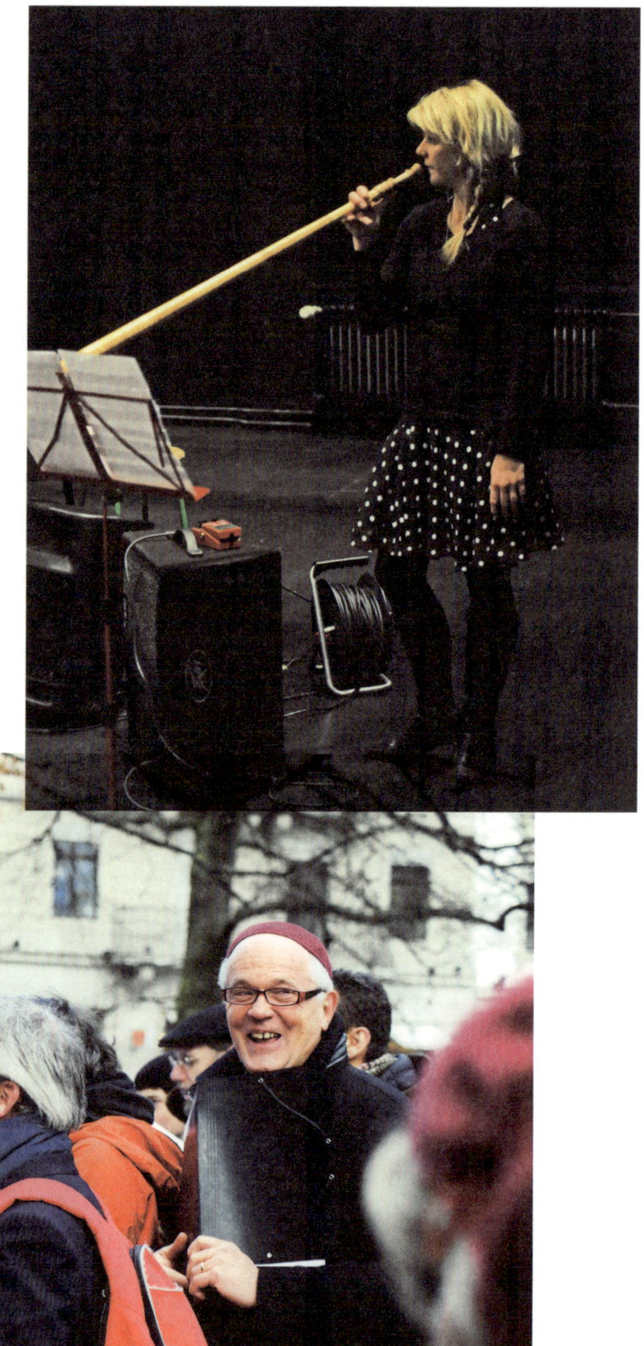

Abends um zehn kommt die Polizei, weil man zu Hause zu laut gelacht hat.

Strophe 1

Uns regieren nur Wirtschaftsinteressen, Mitbestimmung können wir hier vergessen! Keiner kann mir Philosophie erklären, hört auf, euch übers Wetter zu beschweren! In diesem Chor machen manche nur mit, um Leute kennen zu lernen, denen geht es gar nicht ums Singen, die suchen nur Kontakt!

Refrain 1

Wärum wird min Buuch no grösser und mini Titte werded chlii? Wärum wird Wohnruum no tüürer, das chas doch nöd sii! Fruschtrierti Privilegierti wone irgend öppis fählt, Schwizer Chääs und Schwiizer Konte morded mit i aller Wält!

Strophe 2

Im luxuriösesten Land der Welt leben und trotzdem nicht zufrieden, was wollt ihr denn? Ausser 3-Monats-Visa-Sex-Sklavinnen, will man hier partout keinen Ausländer sehen! In diesem Chor machen manche nur mit, weil sie sich sonst nicht wehren können, denen geht es gar nicht ums Singen, die brauchen nur ein Ventil!

B-Teil 1

Di huere Seefeldisierig isch en tüüflische Plan! Und d'Gentrifikation vom Chreis drü schiisst mich a! De dümmlichi Wahlkampf, wo me nüt enscheide dörf. Wärum git's dänn für Mänsche kän Winterschlaf?

Strophe 3

Wenn mein Chef für seinen Job viel zu doof ist, warum sollte man ihn dann nicht rausschmeissen? Die Katze von den Nachbarn soll aufhören, immerzu auf meinen Balkon zu scheissen! In diesem Chor machen viele nur mit, weil es für Beschwerdechöre auf öffentlichen Strassen und Plätzen noch kein Verbot gibt!

Refrain 2

Wärum isch es Wuchenändi numäh zwei Täg lang? Wärum chann ich nümä läbe oh ni min Netzzuegang? Fruschtrierti Privilegierti wone irgend öppis fählt, Schwiizer Chääs und Schwiizer Konte morded mit i aller Wält!

Intro (2)

Noch schneller schmelzende Polkappen – Schneegletscher! Der Zürcher ist ein Jammerlappen – ausnahmslos! Liebe und Sex werden meistens verwechselt, in dieser Stadt find ich keinen Mann – keine Frau! Isolation und Misstrauen – stur gradaus! Noch ein Atomkraftwerk bauen – Risiko! Hört auf zu kläffen ihr kleinen Scheissköter – wider keis Schöggeli zum Kaffi.

Refrain 3

Wärum werdet d'Füess no grösser und d'Wimpere gheied us? Und die huere Schtüür-Erklärig, da chunt doch keinä druus! Innerschwiizer Agglofrizze blaset mir doch id'Schueh, Beni Thurnheer, Roger Köppel löhnt mich endlich in Rueh!

Strophe 4

Militante Senioren mit Sturmgewehr bedrohen unsere Jugend immer mehr! Milliardenüberschüsse bei Swiss-Re, Volksschuel hingäge gits bald nüme meh! In dieser Welt wird Unzufriedenheit und Empörung zum Spektakel und unser Protest zu einem Vehikel der Vermarktung!

B-Teil 2

Di huere Seefeldisierig isch en tüüflische Plan! Und d'Gentrifikation vom Chreis Drü schiisst mich a! De dümmlichi Wahlkampf, wo me nüt enscheide dörf, werum git's dänn für Mänsche kän Winterschlaf?

ecently I have found myself, partially by choice, thinking about my past in one way or another. This, however, was not alien territory; I have always had an emotional, conflicted and productive relationship to this past. Faced with one more attempt at explanation, this time I have decided to compile a few quotations from different texts I have written, and to allow the reader to come at them head on. Quotes are in reverse chronological order.

'There is a contradiction that lies just beneath the surface: This is the contradiction between the physical art practice and what lies behind that practice. Let us try to follow the implications of this word and then try to understand what that contradiction itself might mean; to do so, we can pinpoint moments where the fascination with that symptom, hysteria, betrays itself. As I mentioned earlier, the interest in hysteria finds a correlative in ready-made aesthetic forms, in this case in popular culture. However, the relationship to this popular format is not one that is about appropriating or imitating it but rather engaging it and trying to understand how it could be constitutive of the act of making forms themselves.'

'Where do I stand now?,' *The Ungovernables*. Exh. cat. published in conjunction with the exhibition organised by the New Museum, 2012.

'The sources I am referring to here are several things at once. The reasons they are trusted also vary.

On one hand these are the sources of the work. And that could almost be anything: the way you dash across the road, the exact distance between two shelves in a run down café, the hysterical ranting of an obsessed writer, a moment of embarrassment suddenly remembered while washing the dishes, the fantasy of an incredible victory, a burning ambition, a deep sadness, a half-smile, a simple song that every time it's listened to reveals something new, a mistake taken absolutely seriously.

They are the also the sources that I imagine lie behind every gesture of the world. The hidden agreement that allows a transaction between two individuals to take place, to have a name and to remember that it's yours. To know, to believe, to be. To believe or not in love, friendship and family, to believe or not in punishment and rewards, in wanting and striving, in giving up, in accepting and rejecting. It is what allows a collective to exist, to organize itself into a form, and to communicate this order to all its members. It is what allows us to realize that we are conscious, we are one, and we are many. These are the sources that allow us to recognize that everyone else is similar to us, yet not us exactly.'

trusted sources, press release distributed in conjunction with solo exhibition by Hassan Khan at CCA Kitakyushu, 2011.

'My mother, in a way I suspect she was not fully conscious of, constantly pointed out to me this condition in the world. Last year, through working on a show that in the end did not take place, I realized that I had learnt this lesson in a profound and deeply felt fashion many years before. This was the first time that something that has always been clear was finally stated, whispered back as a secret thought.'

The Twist, flyer distributed in conjunction with solo exhibition by Hassan Khan at Objectif Exhibitions, 2011.

'In a sense it felt as if we were, in our own ways, shoveling hard crystallized fully formed pieces out of our memories. These pieces were not memories, though; they were transformations. They were pieces that were not figments of the imagination, but rather actual things from a collective landscape that were from our respective backgrounds; were part of, belonged to and drank from.'

'the first lesson I remember learning is that humiliation exists,' *Index*, no. 2 (2011).

'We were suddenly two uneasy monsters looking at each other across the room. He was a monster who could draw upon enormous resources and didn't care what others thought; I was a monster begging for recognition, for the person in front of me to admit that I was not of his ilk. And all he had to do was look at me as if we were friends but not exactly—a slight smug smile told me that he knew exactly what I could really afford and what I couldn't. He had called my bluff.'

a short story based on a distant memory with a long musical interlude, live performance. Premiered at Objective Exhibitions, 2011.

'Maybe Sherif El-Azma, like me, listens to the invisible audience in his head and presents his images to them. On this secret stage things are also by necessity not only connected, but also operating under forces that makes them act *as if* they are connected. The space between appearance and reality is at best confused. I have to admit that this is a lesson that I find easier to accept as a formal and aesthetic choice rather than as an absolute. My suspicion is that Sherif El-Azma secretly subscribes to animism where the figure of the signifier is implicitly possessed by its function—by what it signifies. Maybe for Sherif El-Azma the uniform is always inhabited, is always invested, is always real, and hence a sense of dread.

That understanding is also an ability to single out the source of a sound while listening to the general murmur of the stream.'

Nine Lessons Learned from Sherif El Azma. Cairo: Contemporary Image Collective, 2009.

'What this implies is that our relation to 'what constructs meaning' is not based upon some kind of hidden internal kernel of truth that we will discover or uncover or recover, but is rather related to the very possibility of shaping it into different forms—a relation to something active and exterior to us—something that is completely unsentimental and cold and alien, but which is also our very destiny and possibility. ... This emotion is for me very important.'

I AM NOT WHAT I AM. Artist's talk, performed 2005–2009, multiple venues.

'to touch it again something about that your inner echo to realize the delusion you have built for yourself to be completely fucked by that realization flying over the gap in a way just flying over this gap and looking at it again and again I wonder why I see it as a gap through a hole a gap I like to use these words about it because it feels a bit like that in a way and maybe OK if I'm to focus again I can look at my memory in terms of moments of falling into the gap in a way or moments when the fall becomes clear one of those moments is looking out of the window and seeing the stars layered another moment is jamming and wessam was there me and sheriff and jimmy just playing music and having a complete orgasm and laughing while orgasming on the guitar and collapsing on the floor and then standing up and wessam smiling at us and looking at us and talking to us and that was the moment where I saw the gap the hole ... like also walking out of my house with sheriff after watching eraserhead on pulmolar and stoning and walking out together and walking in the street and the asphalt was like mud and that was the gap again and that was the gap again and that was the gap again yeah yeah OK OK'

17 and in AUC— the transcriptions. Paris; Ghent; Crousel; Merz, 2004.

ATOM

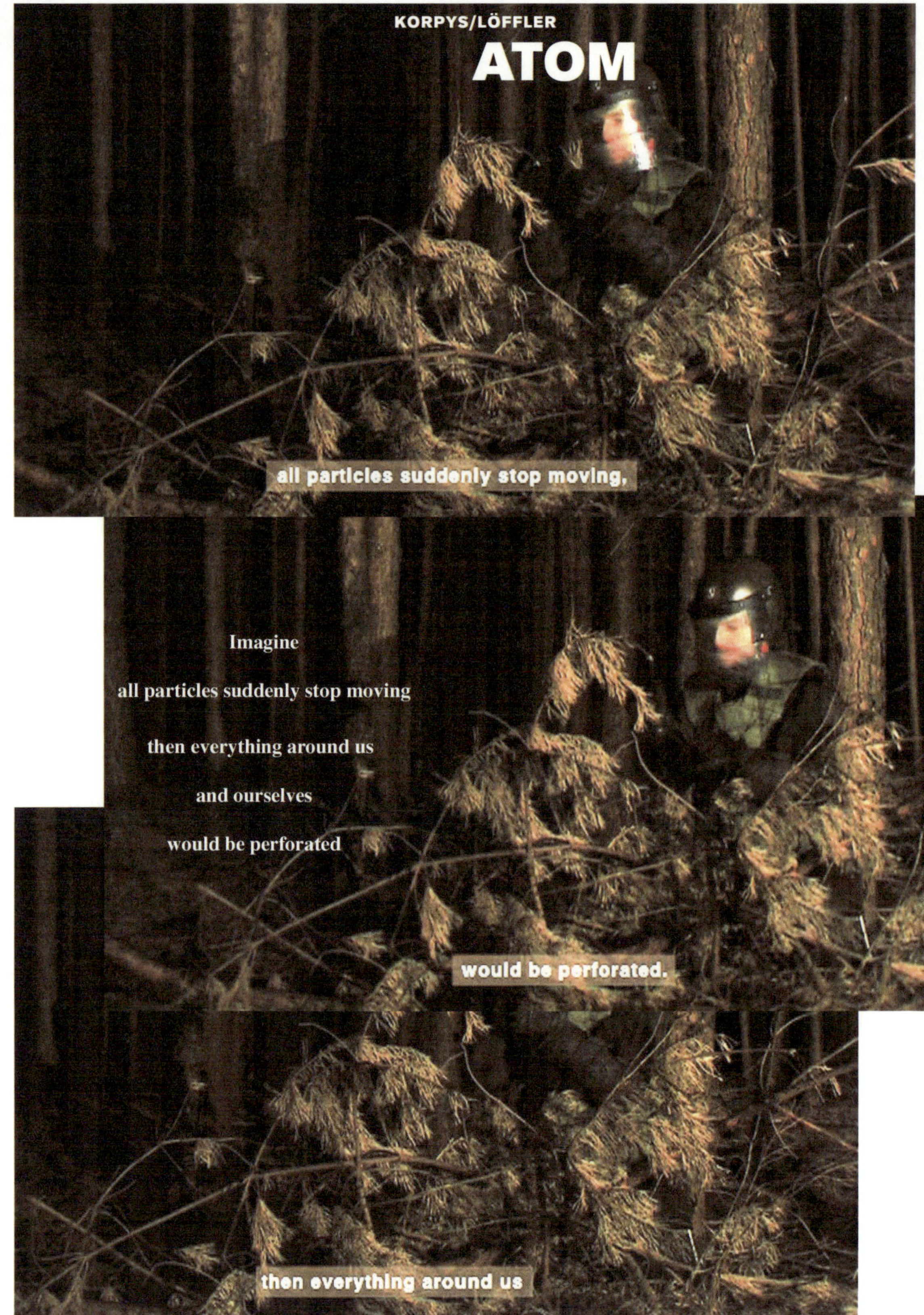
all particles suddenly stop moving,

Imagine

all particles suddenly stop moving

then everything around us

and ourselves

would be perforated

would be perforated.

then everything around us

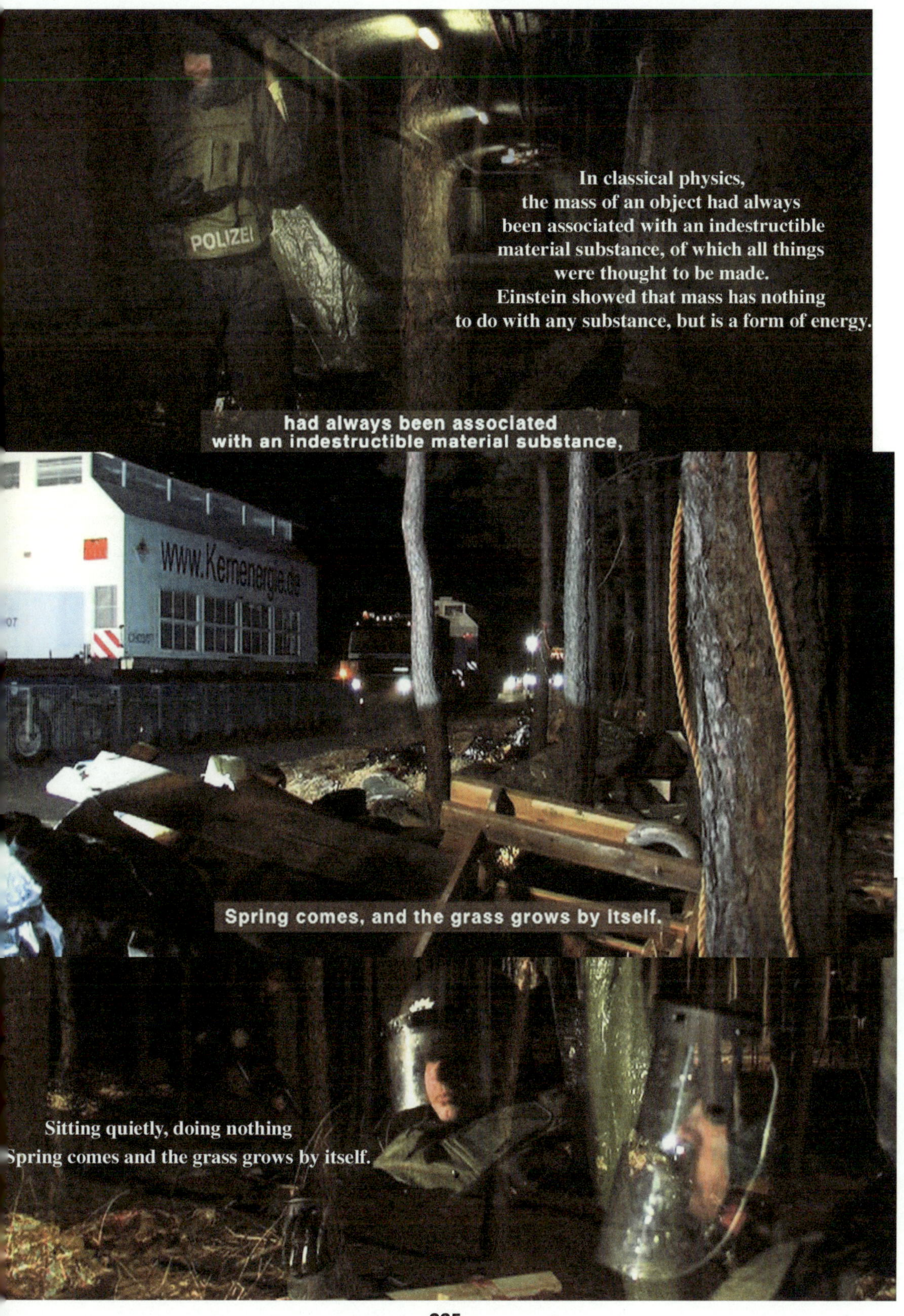

In classical physics,
the mass of an object had always
been associated with an indestructible
material substance, of which all things
were thought to be made.
Einstein showed that mass has nothing
to do with any substance, but is a form of energy.

had always been associated
with an indestructible material substance,

Spring comes, and the grass grows by itself.

Sitting quietly, doing nothing
Spring comes and the grass grows by itself.

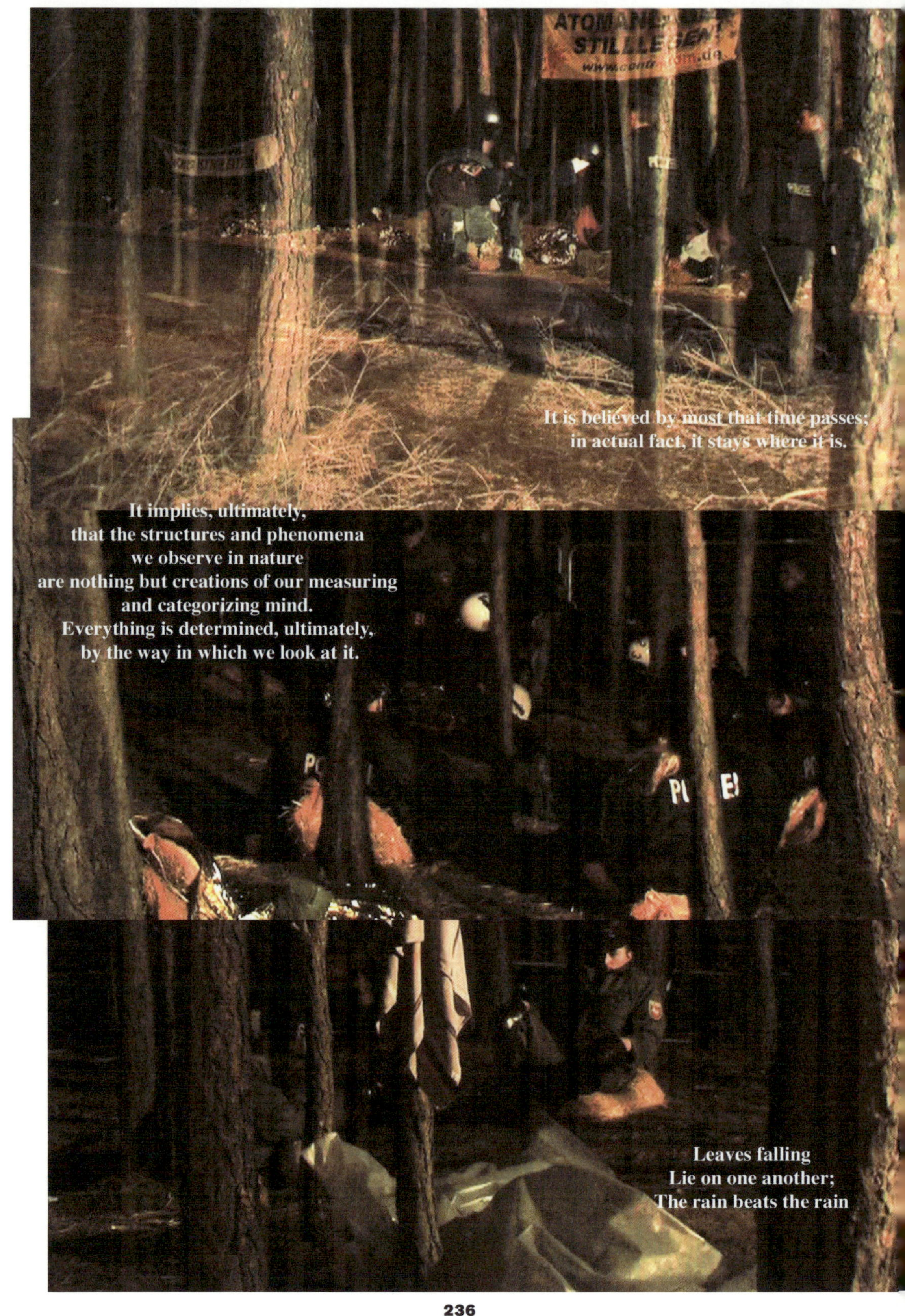
It is believed by most that time passes;
in actual fact, it stays where it is.

It implies, ultimately,
that the structures and phenomena
we observe in nature
are nothing but creations of our measuring
and categorizing mind.
Everything is determined, ultimately,
by the way in which we look at it.

Leaves falling
Lie on one another;
The rain beats the rain

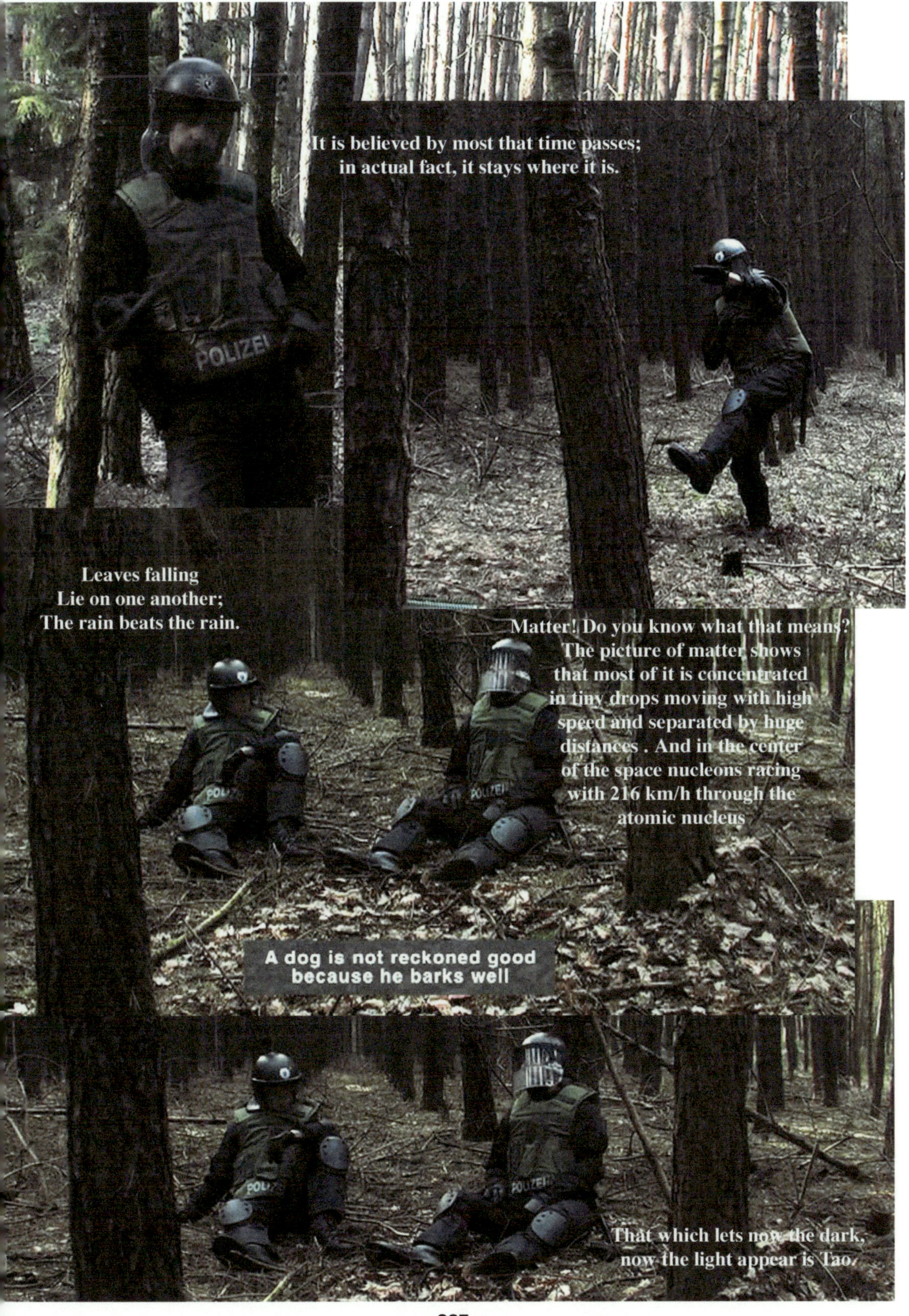

It is believed by most that time passes; in actual fact, it stays where it is.
Leaves falling
Lie on one another;
The rain beats the rain.
Matter! Do you know what that means? The picture of matter shows that most of it is concentrated in tiny drops moving with high speed and separated by huge distances . And in the center of the space nucleons racing with 216 km/h through the atomic nucleus
A dog is not reckoned good because he barks well
That which lets now the dark, now the light appear is Tao.

5

DURCHSPIELEN UND ERÖFFNEN

ACTING OUT AND OPENING UP

JOKAklubi: *Off Art Talent Show*, Shedhalle 2012

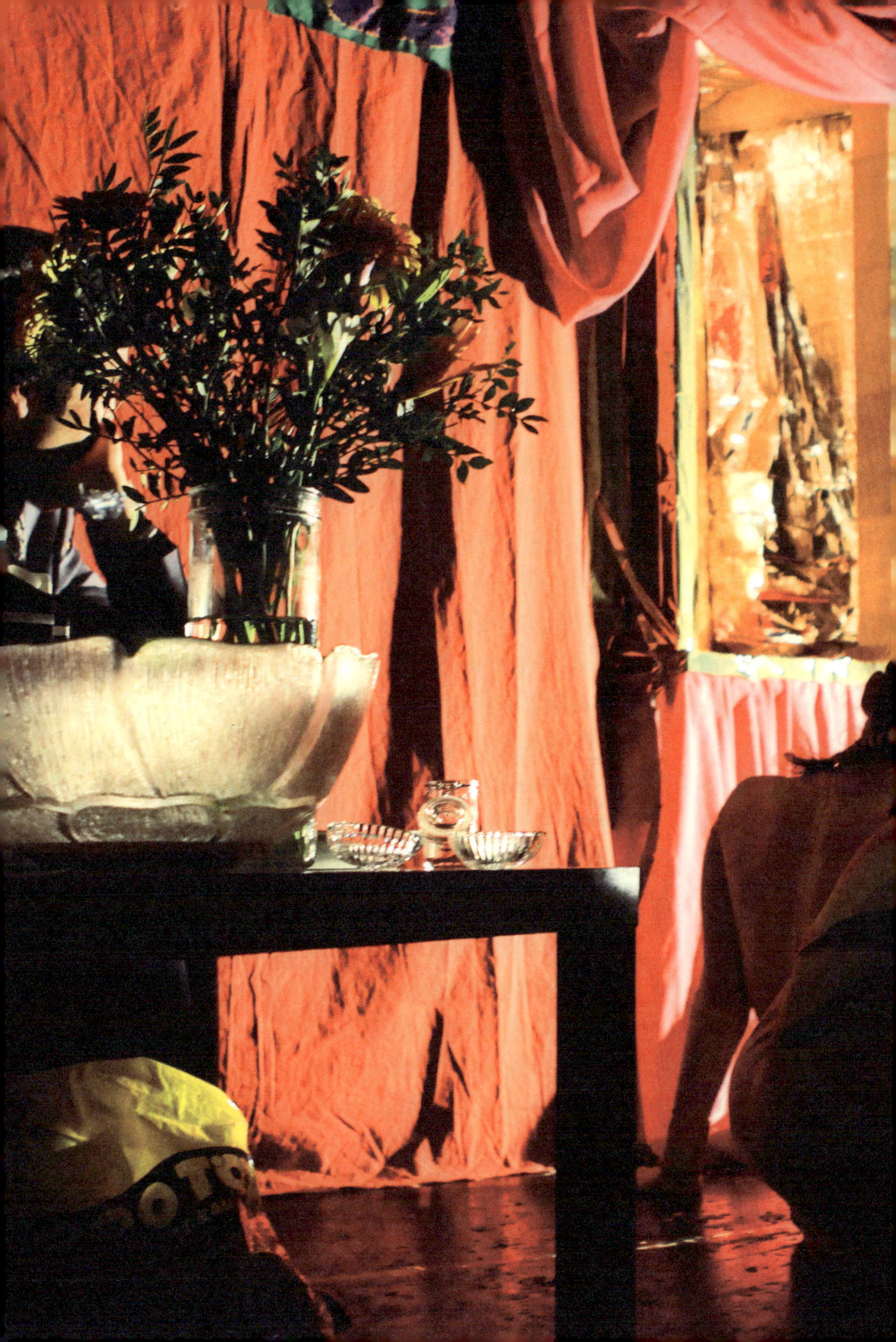

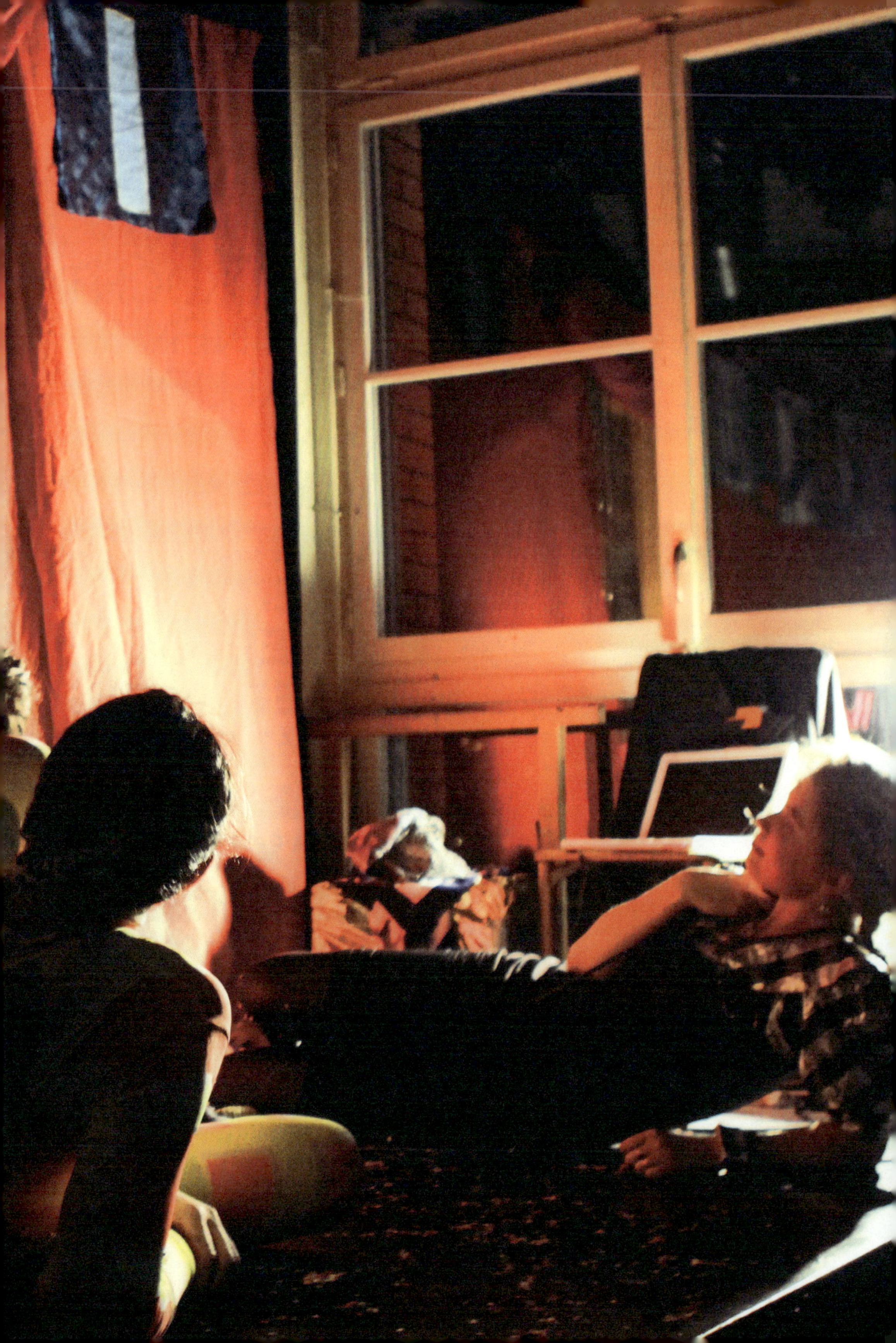

FORMEN DER BETEILIGUNG. TELLERVO KALLEINEN/ OLIVER KOCHTA-KALLEINEN, JOKAKLUBI UND YKON

FORMS OF PARTICIPATION: TELLERVO KALLEINEN/ OLIVER KOCHTA-KALLEINEN, JOKAKLUBI AND YKON

Das in Finnland lebende Künstlerpaar Oliver Kochta-Kalleinen (*1971) und Tellervo Kalleinen (*1975) nahm bereits an unserem ersten Ausstellungsprojekt *Un/Mögliche Gemeinschaft* teil. Wir zeigten die Videoarbeit *The Making of Utopias*, die aus der engen Zusammenarbeit mit vier verschiedenen Aussteiger-Communities in Australien entstand und ein lebendiges Portrait über utopische Gemeinschaften liefert. Und wir produzierten einen *Beschwerdechor* für Zürich (vgl. S. 228), eines der erfolgreichsten Projekte von Kalleinen/ Kochta-Kalleinen, das sich mittlerweile von ihnen als verantwortliche Künstler_innen abgelöst und verselbständigt hat. Aufgrund dieser spannenden Begegnung und dem Eindruck, dass die beiden eine ganz eigenständige Weise gemeinschaftlicher und kommunikativer Praktiken entwickeln, entstand der Wunsch, ihre auf Partizipation, Kollektivität und wechselnde Konstellationen gründenden Arbeitsweisen genauer zu thematisieren und einige Arbeiten speziell mit dem Zürcher Publikum weiter zu entwickeln. Im Mittelpunkt der gezeigten Ausstellung standen Kalleinen/Kochta-Kalleinens neue Videoinstallationen: *I love my job* (Abb. S. 249), *People in White*, *Dreamland*, *Beschwerdechöre* und *Archipelago Science Fiction* (Abb. S. 244/245), welche für die Ausstellung fertig gestellt wurde. Ergänzt wurden sie durch die für Zürich produzierte Performance *Off Art Talent Show* der Gruppe JOKAklubi (Abb. S. 240/241) sowie eine Installation und ein partizipatives Spiel der Gruppe YKON (Abb. S. 316). Beide Künstler_innen sind Teil dieser Gruppen. Im Gegensatz zum intendierten Werkcharakter der Videos und ihres aufwändigen und lange dauernden Prozesses fokussieren die Gruppen auf das Momenthafte und die Inputs der Teilnehmer_innen vor Ort.

Wie teilhaben?

Obwohl die Videos durch einen scheinbar geschlossenen ‚Werkcharakter' gezeichnet sind, sind es keine Filme im herkömmlichen Sinn. Vielmehr sind sie das ästhetisch reflektierte Endprodukt eines bewusst langwierigen, kollektiven und partizipativen Prozesses mit verschiedenen Menschen, die sich durch ein bestimmtes Thema

The Finland-based artist couple Oliver Kochta-Kalleinen and Tellervo Kalleinen already participated in our first exhibition project, *Im/Possible Community*. We presented the video *The Making of Utopias*, which resulted from a close collaboration with four different dropout communities in Australia, providing a vital portrait of utopian communities. And we produced a *Complaints Choir* for Zurich (see p. 228): one of the most successful of their projects, which now has taken on a life of its own independent of the artists themselves.

Due to this exciting encounter and the impression that both develop community and communicative practices in a very idiosyncratic way, the wish emerged to explore more precisely their way of working, based on participation, collectivity and altering constellations, and to develop several works with the Zurich audience in particular. Central to the exhibition were nine video installations, *I love my job* (fig. p. 249), *People in White, Dreamland, Complaints Choirs* and *Archipelago Science Fiction* (fig. p. 244/245), which was completed for the exhibition. They were complemented by the performance produced for Zurich, *Off Art Talent Show* of the group JOKAklubi (fig. p. 240/241), as well as an installation and a participatory game by the group YKON (fig. p. 316). The two artists are members of each of these groups. In contrast to the intended work character of the video and its elaborate and long-lasting process, the groups focus on the momentary aspect and the input of participants on site.

How to Participate?

Although the videos are marked by an apparently closed 'work character', they are not films in the ordinary sense. Rather, they are the aesthetically reflected final product of a consciously protracted, collective, and participatory process with various people who feel addressed by a certain topic and are prepared to get involved. The degree of participation varies depending on the project and respective individual needs. In *Dreamland*, for example, Kalleinen and Kochta-Kalleinen used so-called crowd sourcing, a form of collaborative knowledge generation that comes from the open source community and is intended to provide a non-monopolistic solution to a problem. They issued a public call that sketched out the topic and collected material submitted by participants. Sought were dreams in which the Finnish president at the time played a central role. From the eighty dreams submitted, the artists made a selection, transformed them into a script and shot a film using them, in which those interested could also participate. In this form, participation is 'limited' to submitting content and the performance. Other projects like *People in White, Archipelago Science Fiction* and *I love my job* are more dialogical in structure. Despite the respective differences, certain approaches have repeatedly proven themselves: for example, the two artists seek out participants by way of issuing a public call. This is followed by a differentiated catalog of questions that is carried out in writing, but above all discussed in a personal conversation and recorded. Using these individual conversations, Kalleinen/Kochta-Kalleinen either formulated their first suggestions for scripts or held continuous workshops in which the participants worked on possible stories and scripts together or in various interest groups. Those who do not want to participate in the film (usually due to reasons of anonymity or a lack of time) are played by professional actors.

In terms of the range of possible decisions, these projects are intended in a grass roots and anti-authoritarian sense, and in their execution recall projects like Summerhill from the 1920s, where inventing and discussing stories played a role, or the anti-psychiatry movement from the 1970s. The role of artists is one of hosts and moderators that inspire discussion and sum them up. For example, in the *Complaints Choir* project, they need not be personally present, because select participants, like the initiators or the chorus director, take on the responsibility for their realization. Besides the notion of participation, this project is more about community building and thus the experience of temporary communality.

Tellervo Kalleinen/Oliver Kochta-Kalleinen, Henrik Andersson: *Archipelago Science Fiction*, 2012

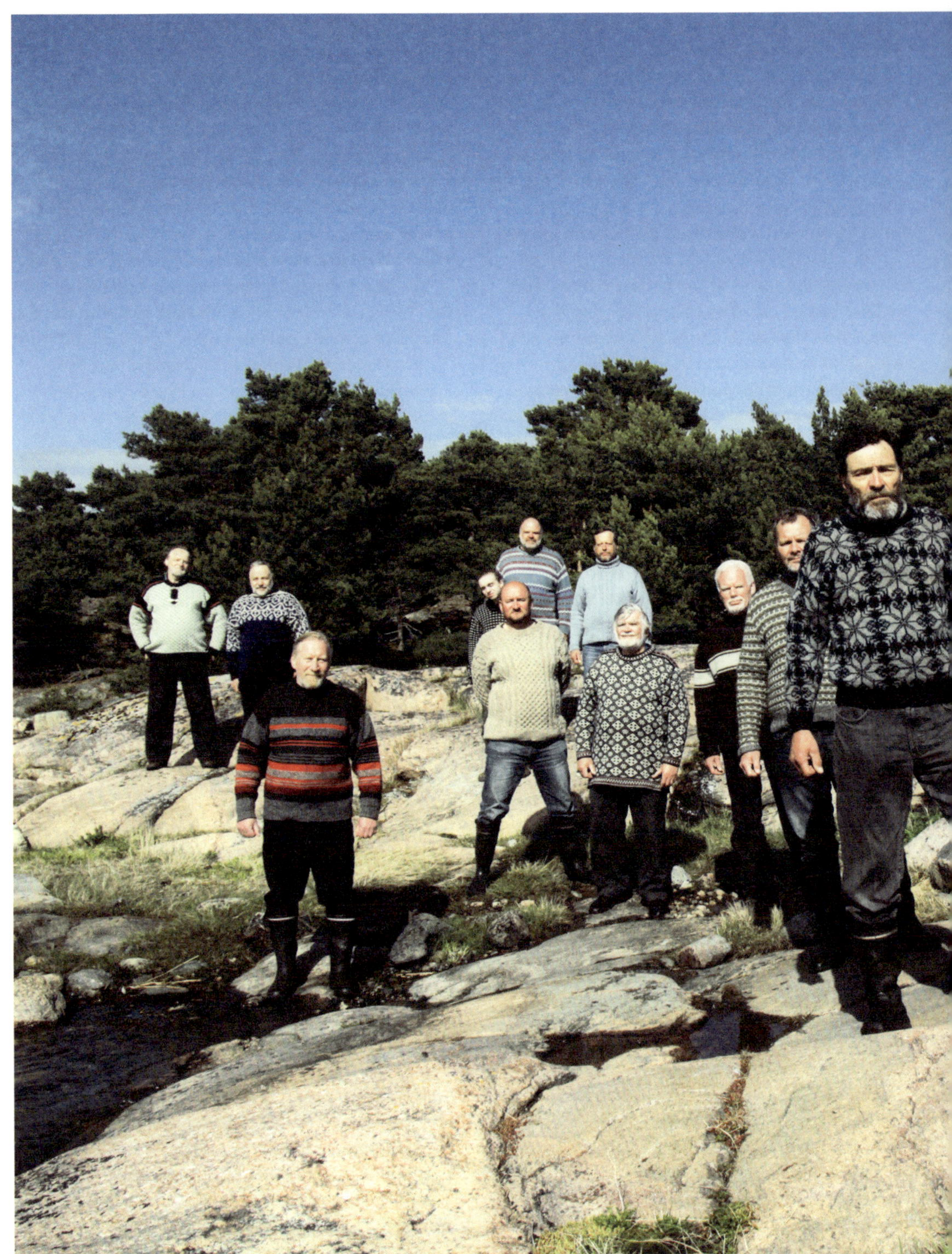

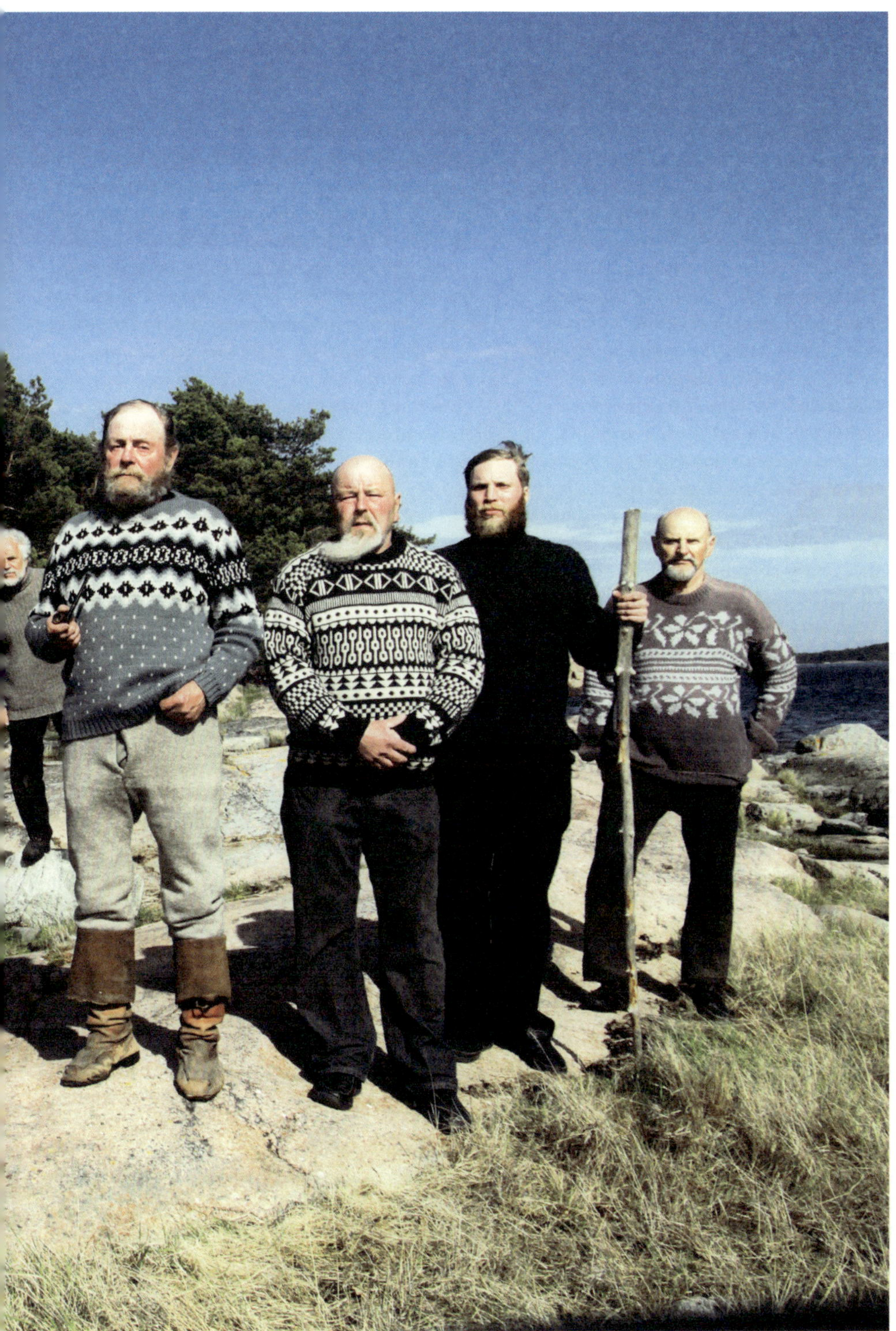

A Theme in Variations

It is only logical that this dialogical production process results in a large number of possible stories: the video works never include just one story or version. Each 'work' is, in its final phase as well, a heterogeneous mixture of many narratives or variants. While the installation *I love my job* consists of eight case studies from Helsinki and Göteborg, *Archipelago Science Fiction* combines four different fantasies about a possible future on the islands near Turku; longer films such as *The Making of Utopias*, *Dreamland* or even *People in White*, a film in feature length format, always consist of various scenarios that reflect the various different or individual points of view and experiences of those affected. In most films, moments of repetition and modification (similarity) play an important role. The repetition of the subject, the situation treated, the feeling that could be experienced or the respective filmic structure show that under certain circumstances and despite all individuality certain hierarchical structures, experiences of power and powerlessness, fear or pleasure can repeat. Making this visible and palpable is a key goal of these repetitions. The variability and principle openness of the films thus represent not only the sum of individual perspectives, but rather is the result of a collective, multi-vocal process that opposes aesthetically an appropriating 'we' identity and simple representation. This corresponds to what Gilles Deleuze, quoting Félix Guattari, formulates in the following way: 'A good group does not take itself to be unique, immortal, and significant, unlike a defense ministry or homeland security office, unlike war veterans, but instead plugs into an outside that confronts the group with its own possibilities of non-sense, death, and dispersal "precisely as a result of its opening up to other groups". In turn, the individual is also a group.'[1] In other words: although these projects aim at moments of solidarity and community, they insist on a form of singularity that is both more and less than is suggested by the word 'individual'. This 'uniqueness' is only possible at certain times, in very particular sites, with very particular actors; it is situational and not repeatable.

The exhibition display also represents a conscious staging of moments of presence and absence. Scenographically, this is expressed by the fact that the eight episodes from *I love my job* were shown on eight different screens, but that only a single 'case' could be watched at a time. The remaining screens were black, only showing the title of the film not being shown. The four-part installation *Archipelago Science Fiction* never showed all future fantasies at the same time: here too, one scenario was shown after another on a single monitor. The remaining monitors remained empty: a temporal continuum that is translated to space as a continuous monitor series that suggests lucidity and linear order and at the same time counteracts it. The space itself generates moments of absence and emptiness (so much room with so little going on), but also the unforeseen and erratic. It is impossible to be sure when the next film begins; there are always a few seconds missing from the beginning— there will never be a moment of absolute clarity. Our movement in space, to get a grasp on the films, becomes a symbolic crossing of spaces, times and voids where almost nothing happens.

Between Therapy and Art

Regardless of the subject, moments of narrative and acting are given an important significance. This approach, which relies on moments of the event-aspect and the present instead of representation, recalls therapeutic processes in which it is assumed that the narrative of a problematic or traumatic situation creates an initial awareness that something is fundamentally not right and that something must be undertaken to change it. With the option of participating in a game or making a film together, the described problem, as banal or traumatic as it might seem to be, contains a seriousness and an importance, but at the same time by way of the playful and artistic approach becomes a limited subject that can be mastered, which

1 ....Gilles Deleuze, 'Three Group-Related Problems', *Desert Islands and Other Texts, 1953–1974* (New York, 2004), p. 193.

angesprochen fühlen und bereit sind, sich einzubringen. Der Grad der Teilhabe variiert, je nach Projekt und persönlichem Bedürfnis. Für *Dreamland* etwa benutzten Kalleinen/Kochta-Kalleinen das sogenannte Crowdsourcing, eine Form kollaborativer Wissensgenerierung, die aus der Open-Source-Community stammt, und dem nicht-monopolistischen Lösen eines Problems dient. Sie lancierten einen öffentlichen Aufruf, der das Thema umriss und sammelten das Material, das ihnen die Beteiligten zukommen liessen. Gesucht wurden Träume, in denen die damalige finnische Präsidentin eine Hauptrolle spielte. Aus den 80 eingesandten Träumen trafen die Künstler_innen eine Auswahl, verwandelten sie in ein Skript und machten einen Film daraus, bei dem Interessierte mitspielen konnten. Bei dieser Form ‚beschränkt‘ sich die Beteiligung auf das Liefern des Inhalts sowie die Aufführung. Andere Projekte, wie *People in White*, *Archipelago Science Fiction* und *I love my job* sind dialogischer angelegt. Trotz der jeweiligen Unterschiede haben sich bestimmte Vorgehensweisen bewährt: So suchen auch hier die beiden Künstler_innen mögliche Beteiligte durch einen öffentlichen Aufruf. Auf diesen folgt ein differenzierter Fragenkatalog, der schriftlich, vor allem aber in einem mehrstündigen, persönlichen Gespräch diskutiert und aufgezeichnet wird. Aus diesen Einzelgesprächen formulieren Kalleinen/Kochta-Kalleinen entweder erste, gemeinsam zu diskutierende Vorschläge für Skripte, und/oder es gibt weiterführende Workshops, bei denen die Beteiligten gemeinsam bzw. in verschiedenen Interessensgruppen mögliche Geschichten und Skripts erarbeiten. Wer bei den Filmen nicht mitspielen will (zumeist aus Gründen der Anonymität oder mangelnden Zeit), wird durch professionelle Schauspieler_innen vertreten.

Vom Grad der Entscheidungsmöglichkeiten sind diese Projekte basisdemokratisch und antiautoritär angelegt und erinnern in ihrer Ausführung an Projekte wie etwa Summerhill seit den 1920er Jahren, wo das Erfinden von Geschichten und deren Diskussion auch eine Rolle spielt(e), oder an die Anti-Psychiatriebewegung in den 70er Jahren des 20. Jahrhunderts. Die Rolle der Künstler_innen besteht in einer Art Gastgeber- und Moderator_innenrolle, die die Dinge anstösst und

zusammenfasst. So müssen sie etwa beim *Beschwerdechor*-Projekt gar nicht mehr persönlich anwesend sein, weil spezielle Beteiligte, wie die Initiant_innen oder der/die Chorleiter_in die Verantwortung für die Realisation übernehmen. Neben dem Partizipationsgedanken geht es bei diesem Projekt aber noch stärker um die Community-Bildung und damit verbunden die Erfahrung einer temporären Gemeinschaftlichkeit.

Ein Thema in Variationen

Es ist nur logisch, dass aus diesem dialogischen Produktionsprozess eine Vielzahl an möglichen Geschichten resultiert; nie umfasst eine Videoarbeit nur eine einzige Geschichte oder nur eine Version. Jedes ‚Werk‘ ist auch in seiner Endphase eine heterogene Mischung aus vielen Erzählungen oder Varianten: Während die Installation *I love my job* aus acht Fallbeispielen aus Helsinki und Göteborg besteht, vereint *Archipelago Science Fiction* vier unterschiedliche Fantasien über eine mögliche Zukunft auf den Inseln bei Turku; auch längere Filme wie *The Making of Utopias*, *Dreamland* oder sogar *People in White*, ein Film im Kinoformat, besteht stets aus verschiedenen Szenarien, die die jeweils unterschiedliche oder individuelle Sicht und Erfahrung der Betroffenen widerspiegeln. In den meisten Filmen spielen Momente von Wiederholung und Abwandlung (Ähnlichkeit) eine wichtige Rolle. Diese Wiederholung des Sujets, der verhandelten Situation, des nach-erlebbaren Gefühls oder der jeweiligen filmischen Struktur zeigt, dass sich unter bestimmten Umständen und bei aller Individualität gewisse hierarchische Strukturen, Erfahrungen von Macht und Ohnmacht, Angst oder Lust wiederholen können. Diese sicht- und erlebbar zu machen, ist ein wesentliches Ziel dieser Wiederholungen.

Die Variabilität und prinzipielle Offenheit der Filme stellt somit nicht nur die Summe individueller Perspektiven dar, vielmehr ist sie das Ergebnis eines kollektiven, vielstimmigen Prozesses, der sich auch ästhetisch einer vereinnahmenden Wir-Identität und simplen Repräsentation widersetzt. Es entspricht dem, was Gilles Deleuze, Félix Guattari zitierend, folgendermassen formuliert:

„Das Kriterium für eine gute Gruppe besteht darin, dass sie sich nicht vormacht, einzigartig, unsterblich und signifikant zu sein wie ein Verteidigungs- oder Sicherheitssyndikat, wie ein Ministerium der Kriegsveteranen, sondern sich auf ein Aussen bezieht, dass sie mit ihren Möglichkeiten des Unsinns, des Todes oder des Zerspringens konfrontiert, und zwar, ‚gerade wegen ihrer Öffnung gegenüber anderen Gruppen‘. Das Individuum seinerseits ist eine solche Gruppe."[1]

Mit anderen Worten: Obwohl Momente von Solidarität und Gemeinschaft eines der Ziele dieser Projekte sind, wird doch auf einer Form von Singularität bestanden, die zugleich mehr oder weniger ist als es das Wort ‚Individuum‘ suggeriert. Diese ‚Einzigkeit‘ ist immer nur zu ganz bestimmten Zeiten, an ganz bestimmten Orten, mit ganz bestimmten Akteur_innen möglich, sie ist situativ und nicht wiederholbar.

Auch das Ausstellungsdisplay stellt ein bewusstes In-Szene-Setzen solcher ereignishafter Momente von Präsenz/Absenz dar. Szenografisch äussert sich dies dadurch, dass z.B. die acht Episoden aus *I love my job* zwar auf acht verschiedenen Screens gezeigt werden, dass aber im Moment immer nur ein verhandelter ‚Fall‘ angeschaut werden kann. Die übrigen Screens sind schwarz und geben lediglich den Titel des nicht gezeigten Filmes an. Auch die vierteilige Installation *Archipelago Science Fiction* strahlt nie alle Zukunftsfantasien gleichzeitig aus; auch hier wird immer nur ein Szenario nach dem anderen, an nur gerade einem Monitor gezeigt. Die restlichen Monitore bleiben leer: ein zeitliches Kontinuum, das als kontinuierliche Monitorreihe in den Räum übersetzt wird, das Übersichtlichkeit und lineare Ordnung suggeriert und gleichzeitig durchkreuzt. Der Raum selbst generiert so Momente der Abwesenheit und der Leere (so viel Platz und so wenig los), aber auch des Unvorhersehbaren und Sprunghaften: Nie kann man sich ganz sicher sein, wo der nächste Film beginnt, immer wird man ein paar Sekunden lang den Anfang verpasst, den Durchblick nicht gehabt haben. Unsere

Bewegung im Raum, um der Filme habhaft zu werden, wird zu einem symbolischen Durchqueren von Räumen, Zeiten und Abgründen, wo fast nichts geschieht.

Zwischen Therapie und Kunst

Egal, um welche Themen es geht, den Momenten des Erzählens und Durchspielens kommt eine wichtige Bedeutung zu. Dieses Vorgehen, das auf Momente des Ereignishaften und der Aktualisierung statt der Repräsentation setzt, erinnert an therapeutische Prozesse, bei denen man davon ausgeht, dass das Erzählen einer problematischen oder traumatischen Situation ein erstes Bewusstsein darüber schafft, dass etwas fundamental nicht in Ordnung ist und etwas dagegen getan werden muss. Mit der Option, an einem Spiel teilzunehmen oder gemeinsam einen Film zu drehen, erhält einerseits das geschilderte Problem, so banal oder traumatisch es zu sein scheint, eine Ernsthaftigkeit und eine Wichtigkeit, wird andererseits aber durch den spielerischen und künstlerischen Umgang damit auch zu einem abgrenzbaren, zu bewältigenden Thema, das zugleich innerhalb als auch ausserhalb von einem selbst liegt. Das gemeinsame Filme-Machen dient also nicht nur dazu, ein ästhetisches, autonomes Werk zu produzieren, sondern ein abgeschlossenes, überschaubares und erreichbares Ziel vor Augen zu stellen und dies in einer temporären Gemeinschaft zu erreichen suchen.

In einer informellen Dienstleistungsgesellschaft wie unserer heutigen, in der immer weniger Fassbares hergestellt wird oder fassbar ist, und wo fast nur noch Daten herumgeschoben und Papiere geschrieben werden, kommt diesem Aspekt des ‚Kreierens‘ eines konkreten Produkts eminente Bedeutung zu: Erfolgserlebnisse, Stolz, Zufriedenheit über das erreichte Ziel und die Erfahrung, dass sich über geteilte Arbeit Dinge erreichen lassen, die allein nicht erreichbar wären, führen zu grundlegenden Gefühlen von Glück und Befriedigung; Gefühle, die selbstredend die Voraussetzung dafür sind, dass man sich selbst als entscheidungsfähiges und verantwortliches Subjekt empfindet.

---

1 .... Deleuze, Gilles: Vorwort. Drei Gruppenprobleme. In: Guattari, Félix: *Psychotherapie, Politik und die Aufgabe der institutionellen Analyse.* Frankfurt a.M. 1976, 7.

Tellervo Kalleinen/Oliver Kochta-Kalleinen: *I love my job*, 2008–2010

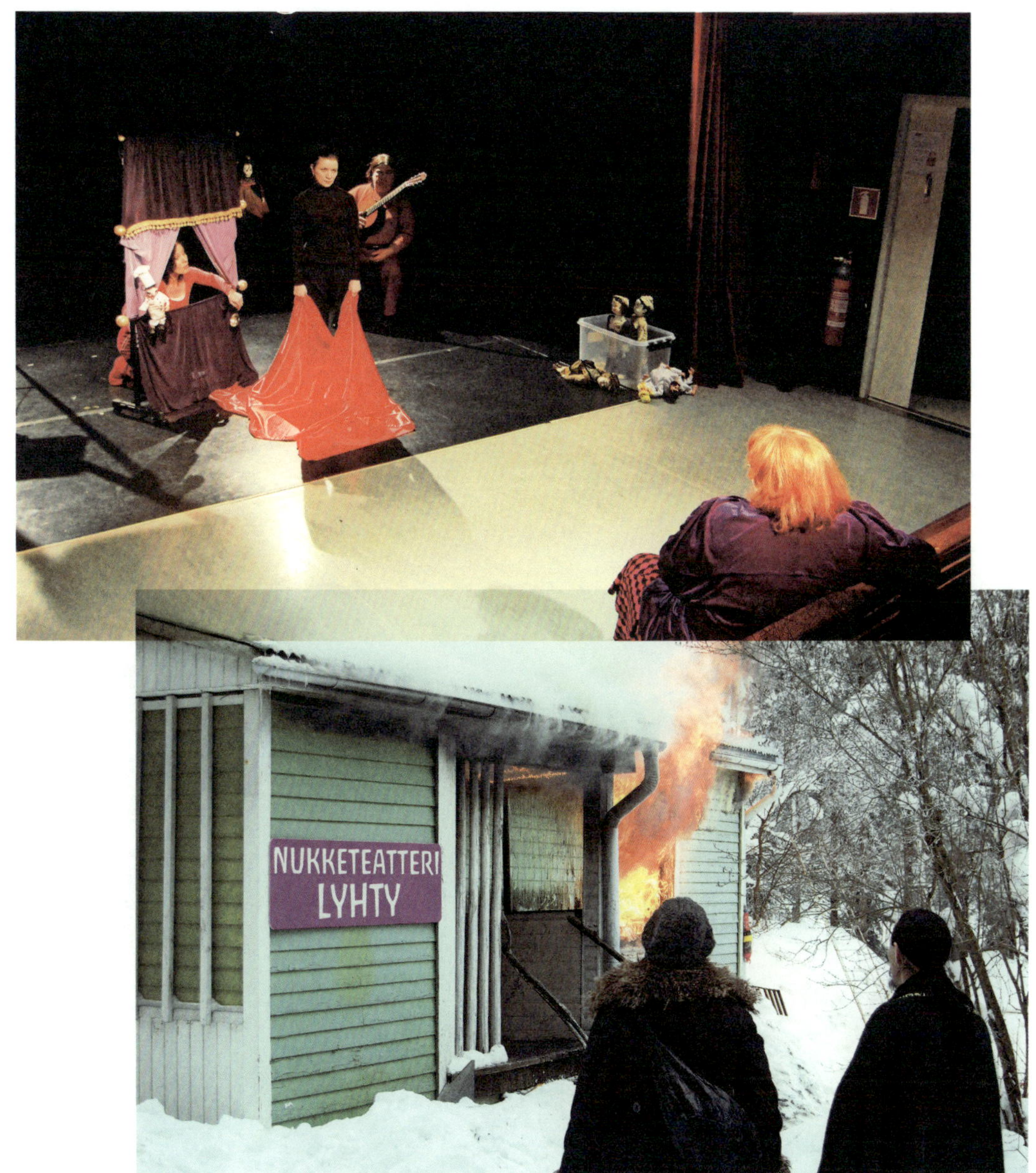

Tellervo Kalleinen/Oliver Kochta-Kalleinen, Henrik Andersson: *Archipelago Science Fiction*, 2012

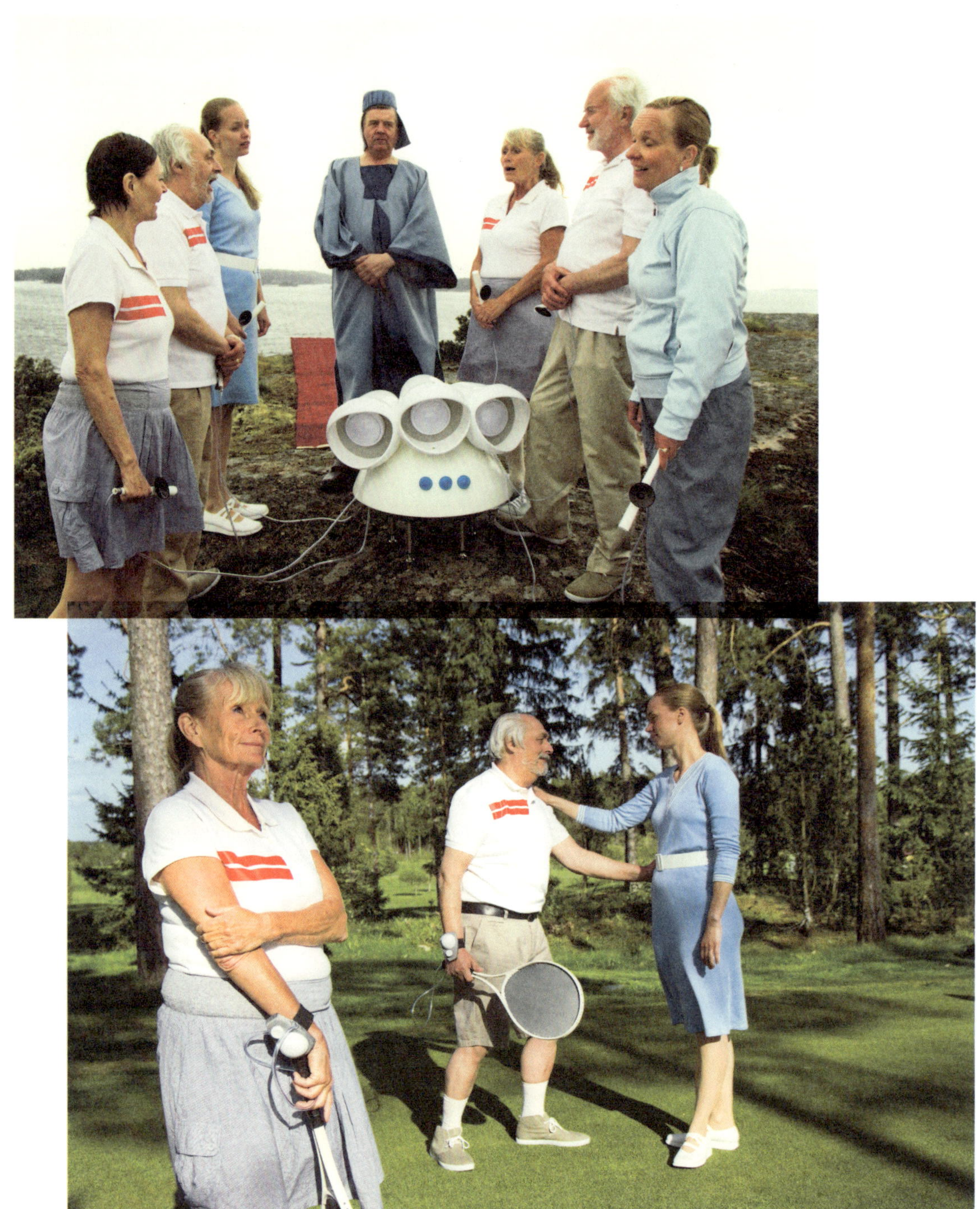

at the same time lies outside of ourselves. The shared act of filmmaking not only serves to produce an aesthetic, autonomous work, but also presents a closed, manageable and achievable goal, and seeks to achieve this in a temporary community.

In an informal service society like ours, in which less and less is being actually created, and where only data is being pushed around and papers are written, this aspect of 'creating' a concrete product takes on eminent importance.Experiences of success, pride, satisfaction in a goal accomplished and the experience that things can be achieved through shared work that would not be achievable on our own can lead to profound feelings of happiness and satisfaction, feelings that naturally are the requirement for feeling capable of making a decision like a responsible subject.

The artwork and/or the film here becomes a means in the dialogical process with the others and ourselves to the extent that we ourselves are all groups, as Deleuze puts it. The work as a goal of a group process makes it possible to think about forms, about the translation of (formless) emotions and states in abstract contexts and visible things. In my opinion, this corresponds to a profoundly human pleasure in transcending ourselves in the other, the artificial, the formal. Seen in this way, the fact that ultimately the how of the form interests the artists more than the participants is not a betrayal of the notion of participation: it accounts rather for the variety of people and their various interests and motivations. And it ultimately guarantees that the amateur level (that is important as the starting point) can also be passed in terms of the professionalisation of expression and aesthetics. This means that it guarantees that something will result that is interesting for the artistic context from which it was also created. (Recall here the accusations of lacking aesthetics made at the social art of the 1990s.) The artists not only account for this state of affairs, but, as mentioned, also the human need for aesthetics and for turning their own life into something artificial, artful, that means into art, but regardless of questions of professionalism, distinction or good taste. This need is taken up by reality programmes on

television and perverted in a way that allows for no possibility for abstraction. The practices collected here attempt to return transcendental meaning to this longing for metamorphosis.

My Acting's Fine

The moments of play and acting, in opening other paths, are also central to the other forms of participation presented by the performance group JOKAklubi and YKON as part of the exhibition project. The primary concept behind YKON was to develop other formats for meetings and conferences to enter into conversations with one another in an unconventional way or to trigger action. In this way, the participants developed and discussed their ideas for several hours and played out possibilities of how the world could be changed. In JOKAklubi's *Off Art Talent Show* the idea of the show and the subversion of competitive structures was placed in the foreground.[2] Local artists and people who enjoy performing were invited to present something on stage, while the three women from JOKAklubi decided as jurors whether something was 'in' or 'out' with unusual, revealing methods. In so doing, they took the competition format that dominates at talent shows to absurd ends, and at the same time created a different form or perception where the issue is not selecting the best, but sharing and giving among the group. All three groups share the notion that moments of self-abandon and community can emerge in play that explodes the individualised, capitalist notion of achievement and the primacy of (apparent) reason. By performatively revealing, playing through and acting out other sides of humanity (both 'dark' and 'light'), accomplishes something that only has little room in our postmodern society even though today everything and everyone is exhibitionist in a media sense or can be discussed

2...... Originally, the *Off Art Talent Show* was about the question of belonging and possible appropriation, as implied by the word 'off' which is used in German speaking countries to refer to the alternative art world. When the show was first developed for the Subvisions-Festival in Hamburg in 2009, it was also about discussions on gentrification that could use the alternative scene.

intellectually. The non-hierarchical and non-chalant experiments that they achieve, accelerate the basic feeling that is central for the understanding as an acting subject. I am good enough, even if I'm 'off' and not 'on'.

People's Stories

'One of the most central experiences in my life was the book *Amerikanische Portraits* by Studs Terkel. It was an edited and perhaps censored version of his *Working: People Talk About What They Do All Day and How They Feel About What They Do* from 1974. In the book, people like housewives, firemen or bank managers spoke about their everyday life and their working day. I was twelve years old, and it was one of my best reading experiences from my youth. Of course the West or the US was something like an exotic fairy tale land for us in the GDR, but I think it was rather the roughness of the text, the emotions, the humour and the tragedy of everyday life that was most impressive. That was much better than *Treasure Island* or the other literature for boys. I think that something of this reading experience continues to resonate in our projects.'[3]
Central to all the projects discussed here are the people, their hidden stories, their abysses, their dreams and desires and their engagement with the social world. The motto of *Forms of Participation* thus applies also to the artists themselves. They want to participate, with the people, the world, their hierarchies, and they want to develop adequate aesthetic forms for this purpose. Although each of the projects presented here was marked by a varying form of interaction and participation, and although in each the world is not shown as 'easy going', humor and a kind of absurd, surrealist comedy is a principle throughout: humor and ease as a survival strategy. They are a capacity to perceive gridlocked systems in different ways and to experience them anew so that we can encounter them in different ways, in real life as well.

Translated by Brian Currid

3................ Oliver Kochta-Kalleinen in an e-mail, March 2012.

Das ,Kunstwerk' bzw. der Film wird hier also auch zu einem Mittel für den dialogischen Prozess mit den anderen und sich selbst, insofern man, wie Deleuze sagt, selbst eine Gruppe ist. Das Werk als Ziel eines Gruppenprozesses erlaubt es, über Formen nachzudenken, über die Übersetzung von (formlosen) Emotionen und Zuständen in abstrahierbare Zusammenhänge und sichtbare Dinge. Es entspricht meiner Meinung nach einer zutiefst humanen Lust nach Transzendenz des Eigenen in etwas Anderes, Artifizielles, ,Formales'. Dass letztlich das Wie der Form wiederum die Künstler_innen mehr interessiert als die Teilhabenden, ist so gesehen kein Verrat am Partizipationsgedanken: Es trägt vielmehr der Verschiedenheit der Menschen und deren unterschiedlicher Interessen und Motivationen Rechnung. Und es garantiert letztlich auch, dass die Ebene der Amateure (die als Ausgangspunkt wichtig ist) auch durchbrochen werden kann in Hinblick auf eine Professionalisierung des Ausdrucks und der Ästhetik. Das heisst, es garantiert, dass etwas auch für den künstlerischen Kontext, aus dem heraus es mit geschaffen wurde, wieder interessant wird. (Erinnert sei hier an die Vorwürfe der mangelnden Ästhetik, mit denen sich die Sozialkunst der 1990er Jahre konfrontiert sah). Die Künstler_innen tragen nicht nur diesem Umstand Rechnung, sondern wie gesagt auch dem humanen Bedürfnis nach Ästhetik und Umsetzung des eigenen Lebens in etwas Künstliches, Kunsthaftes, das heisst in Kunst, unabhängig jedoch von Fragen der Professionalität, Distinktion oder des guten Geschmacks. Dieses Bedürfnis ist von den Reality-Sendungen des Fernsehens aufgenommen und dadurch, dass es keine Abstraktionsmöglichkeiten erlaubt, pervertiert worden. Die hier versammelten Praktiken versuchen, diesem Begehren nach Verwandlung seine transzendente Bedeutung zurückzugeben.

Ich spiele gut genug

Die Momente von Spiel und Spielen, als Eröffnen anderer Wege, sind auch bei den weiteren im Rahmen des Ausstellungsprojekts vorgestellten ,Formen der Beteiligung', nämlich bei der Performancegruppe JOKAklubi und YKON, zentral. Beim YKON-Game stand ursprünglich der

Gedanke im Vordergrund, andere Formate für Treffen und Konferenzen zu entwickeln, um auf unkonventionelle Weise miteinander ins Gespräch oder eben – ins Handeln – zu kommen. So entwickelten und diskutierten die Teilnehmer_innen während mehrer Stunden Vorstellungen und spielten Möglichkeiten vor, wie die Welt geändert werden könnte. Bei JOKAklubis *Off Art Talent Show* steht der Showgedanke und die Subvertierung kompetitiver Strukturen im Vordergrund.[2] So werden jeweils lokale Künstler_innen und Menschen, die gerne auftreten, für eine kurze Darbietung auf die Bühne eingeladen, während die drei Frauen von JOKAklubi als Jurorinnen mit ungewöhnlichen und selbstentblössenden Methoden darüber entscheiden, ob etwas ‚in' oder ‚out' ist. Dadurch führen sie das Format des Wettbewerbs, wie es an Talent-Shows vorherrscht, ad absurdum und schaffen gleichzeitig eine andere Form der Teilhabe, bei der nicht die Auslese aus den Besten, sondern das Miteinander-Teilen und Geben bestimmend werden.

Alle drei Gruppen eint die Idee, dass im Spiel Momente von Selbstvergessenheit und Gemeinschaftlichkeit entstehen können, die den individualisierten, kapitalistischen Leistungsgedanken und das Primat von (scheinbarer) Vernunft sprengen. Im performativen Hervorholen, Durchspielen und Abstrahieren anderer (‚dunkler' und ‚heller') Seiten des Menschseins gelangt etwas zur Darstellung, das in unserer nachmodernen Gesellschaft nur noch wenig Platz hat; und dies, obgleich heute alles und jedes medial exhibitioniert oder intellektuell durchdiskutiert werden kann. Die nicht-hierarchischen und gleich-gültigen, im Sinne von gleichwertigen Versuchsanordnungen, die sie auf die Beine stellen, beschleunigen jenes grundlegende Gefühl, das zentral ist für das Verständnis von sich als handelndem Subjekt: Ich bin gut genug, auch wenn ich vielleicht nur ‚OFF' statt ‚ON' bin.

People's Stories

„Eine meiner grundlegendsten Erfahrungen war das Buch *Amerikanische Portraits* von Studs Terkel. Es war eine redigierte und womöglich zensurierte Fassung von *Working: People Talk About What They Do All Day and How They Feel About What They Do* aus dem Jahre 1974. Darin sprachen Leute wie Hausfrauen, Feuerwehrmänner oder Bankmanager über ihren Tagesablauf und ihr Arbeitsleben. Ich war zwölf Jahre alt, und es war eine meiner besten Leseerfahrungen in der Jugend. Natürlich waren der Westen oder die USA so etwas wie ein exotisches Märchenland für uns aus der DDR, aber ich glaube, es waren trotzdem eher die Rohheit des Textes, die Emotionen, der Humor und die Tragödie des Alltagslebens, die mich am stärksten beeindruckten. Das war viel besser als *Die Schatzinsel* oder andere Literatur für Jungen. Ich glaube, dass etwas von dieser Leseerfahrung in unseren Projekten weiterwirkt."[3]

Im Mittelpunkt aller hier diskutierten Projekte stehen Menschen, ihre verdeckten Geschichten, ihre Abgründe, Träume und Wünsche, ihre Auseinandersetzungen mit der sozialen Welt. Das Motto der *Formen der Beteiligung* gilt somit auch für die Künstler_innen selbst: Sie wollen sich beteiligen, an den Menschen, an der Welt, an ihren Hierarchien, und sie wollen adäquate ästhetische Formen dafür entwickeln. Obwohl sich jedes der hier vorgestellten Projekte durch eine variierende Form der Interaktion und Teilhabe auszeichnet und obwohl bei jedem die Welt nicht als ‚easy going' gezeigt wird, sind Humor und eine Art von absurder, surrealistischer Komik ein durchgängiges Prinzip: Witz und Leichtigkeit als Überlebensstrategie. Sie sind ein Vermögen, festgefahrene Systeme anders wahrzunehmen und zu erleben, sodass wir ihnen auch in der Realität anders begegnen können.

2............. Ursprünglich ging es bei der *Off Art Talent Show* auch um die Frage von Zugehörigkeit und möglicher Vereinnahmung, wie sie dem Wort ‚Off' bzw. Off-Art-Szene inhärent ist. Als die Show 2009 erstmals für das Subvisions-Festival in Hamburg entwickelt wurde, ging es auch um Diskussionen von Gentrifizierung, die sich der Off-Szene bedienen könnte.

3.................... Kochta-Kalleinen, Oliver in einer E-Mail, März 2012.

THE F-WORD. SIND WIR ALLE TOP GIRLS ODER BRAUCHEN WIR DEN FEMINISMUS HEUTE NOCH?

THE F-WORD: ARE WE ALL TOP GIRLS, OR DO WE STILL NEED FEMINISM?

Bist du ein Feminist? Bin ich eine Feministin? Feminismus ist seit fast 15 Jahren eine grosse heisse Kartoffel. Feminismus ist zum Unwort, zum F-Word geworden. Nur wenige Frauen und Männer bezeichnen sich heute als Feminist_innen. Feminismus wird „verschmäht oder sogar gehasst, diffamiert und musealisiert"[1]; bei den meisten herrschen „Unkenntnis und Berührungsängste"[2]; oder „Feministin, vermuten wir, wird man nur aus einer Notlage, aus einer Frustration heraus"[3]. Feminismus wird als historisches Kapitel betrachtet, das seine Schuldigkeit getan habe. Frauen wie Männer glauben zu wissen, wie sie sich geschlechtsstereotypen Vorurteilen erwehren können. Feminismus, das ist ein Thema für islamistische Gesellschaften, meint frau und man. Denn rechtliche Gleichberechtigung in unseren Breiten[4] ist auf mehreren Ebenen erreicht worden: Geschlechtsspezifische Freiheitsbeschränkungen wurden in Gesetzen nivelliert, Frauen betrachteten sich nicht als blosses Sexualobjekt, haben ein Recht auf Erwerbsarbeit und können selbst entscheiden, wann sie Mutter werden. Frauen können, wollen, müssen ihr eigenes Leben gestalten. Es scheint, als haben sich feministische Forderungen durch gleichstellungspolitische Realitäten abgeschafft. Politische Machtspitzen, wie der IWF, werden erstmals von einer Frau geführt, die Schweiz hat drei Bundesrätinnen und Deutschland eine Bundeskanzlerin. Lady Gaga ist Aushängeschild einer sexuell-selbstbewussten Generation von jungen Frauen und populäre Fernsehserien, wie die *Lindenstrasse* oder *The L-Word,* in denen Stigmata von Homosexualität aufgeweicht werden, sind beinahe schon historisch. Dem Unterhaltungspotential von Genderfragen in Mainstream- und Popkultur stehen die realen Alltagsantipathien und Diskriminierungen allerdings entgegen. Warum werden 2011 Forderungen europäischer Politikerinnen nach einer Frauenquote im Top-Management aktualisiert?

1............ Vgl. McRobbie, Angela: *Top Girls. Feminismus und der Aufstieg des neoliberalen Geschlechterregimes.* Wiesbaden 2010.

2............. Eismann, Sonja (Hg.): *Hot Topic. Popfeminismus heute.* Mainz 2007, 10.

3........................ Roten, Michèle: *Frau sein.* Basel 2011, 4.

4............... Ich beziehe mich auf west-europäische Gesellschaften, mit nationalen Spezifika, dort wo sie erwähnt werden.

Are you a feminist? Am I a feminist? For almost fifteen years now, feminism has been a red hot potato. Feminism has become a negative buzzword, the F-word. Only a few women and men would today call themselves feminists. Feminism has been maligned, defamed or turned into something of a museum piece[1]: the great majority are 'uninformed or have extreme reservations' about it,[2] or 'people become feminists, so it is thought, only out of necessity or a sense of frustration'[3].

Feminism is considered a historic movement that has played its part. Women and men alike believe that they can defend themselves against gender stereotypes. Feminism: that's a subject for Islamic societies, or so the logic goes. For legal equality has already been achieved on several levels in our latitudes[4]: gender specific limitations on freedom have been legally abolished, women are no longer considered a mere sex object, they have a right to waged labour and can decide for themselves when they want to become a mother. Women can, want and need to shape their own lives. It seems as if feminist demands have been met by the realities of equal rights. Seats of political power, like the IMF, are today being led by a woman for the first time; Switzerland has three federal councillors and Germany has a female chancellor. Lady Gaga is the spearhead of a sexually self-confident generation of young women, and popular television series, such as *Lindenstrasse* or *The L-Word*, in which the stigma of homosexuality is weakened, now seem almost historic. The entertainment potential of gender issues in the mainstream and popular culture, however, stands alongside real everyday antipathy and discrimination. Why is it necessary for European women in politics to renew the demand for a quota for top management positions in 2011? Why do the statistics repeatedly show the relationship of the number of female students to female professors as that of a mountain to a valley? Why is the average gender pay gap[5] across Europe still 21.6%? Why do women continue to give up their professions or work part time when they have children? Why are single women of retirement age in danger of poverty? Why do biologistic explanations for gender-based behaviour repeatedly meet with popularity? Why do men who take extended parental leave or who refuse to accept the role as family provider continue to meet with social scorn? Why do male role models in particular seem to be so without an alternative?

Our short-term historical memory, which allows us to suppress all these issues, can on the one hand be linked to the self-evident way in which we take advantage of the achievements of feminism. Correctives in terms of legal rights and freedoms have made possible a pluralisation of female roles and gender identities. At the same time, neo-liberal policies have emphasized the projection of our own destiny as an individual, purely private responsibility, and thus the rejection of the notion of any structural disadvantages as a woman. 'At all costs, nobody wants to be considered part of a victim group. The neo-liberal ideology that there are no structural disadvantages, but just individual failure, that is, there are no longer any victims, but only losers who are themselves to blame, has shaped our own self-image without our noticing', as film scholar Gertrud Koch analyses.[6] Everything is under control: we women are the ones making our own life decisions. This is the coaching provided by the great majority of women's magazines. In the recent preface to a special edition of *Texte zur Kunst* on the subject of feminism, the editors critically sum up: 'The mood has never been more " post-feminist" or "post-gender" than today.'[7]

---

1 ... For a discussion of this, see Angela McRobbie, *The Aftermath of Feminism: Gender, Culture and Social Change* (London, 2009).

2 ..... Sonja Eismann (ed.), *Hot Topic: Popfeminismus heute* (Mainz, 2007), p. 10.

3 .... Michèle Roten, *Frau sein* (Basle, 2011), p. 4.

4 .... I am here referring to Western European societies with specific national characteristics.

5 ..... See for example www.destatis.de/DE/PresseService/Presse/ Pressemitteilungen/2012/03/PD12_101_621.html.

6 .... Gertrud Koch, 'Feminismus nach der Identitätspolitik', *Feminismus. Texte zur Kunst*, 84 (Berlin, 2011), p. 69.

7 .... Sabeth Buchmann, Isabelle Graw and Juliane Rebentisch, 'Preface', trans. Karl Hoffmann, *Feminismus. Texte zur Kunst*, 84 (Berlin, 2011), p. 4.

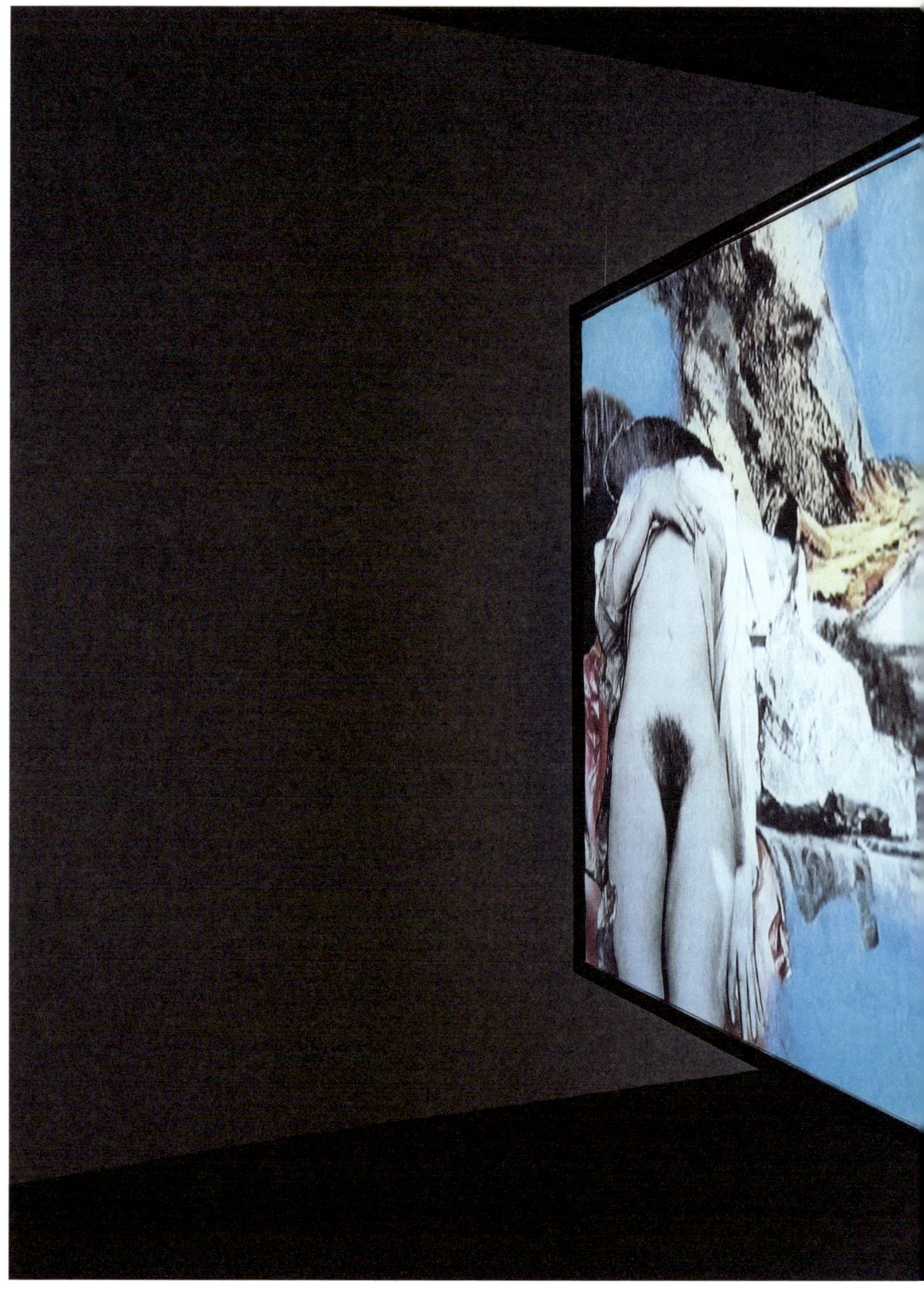

Michaela Melián: *Sarah Schumann und Silvia Bovenschen*, 2012 (Ausstellungsansicht / Exhibition view)

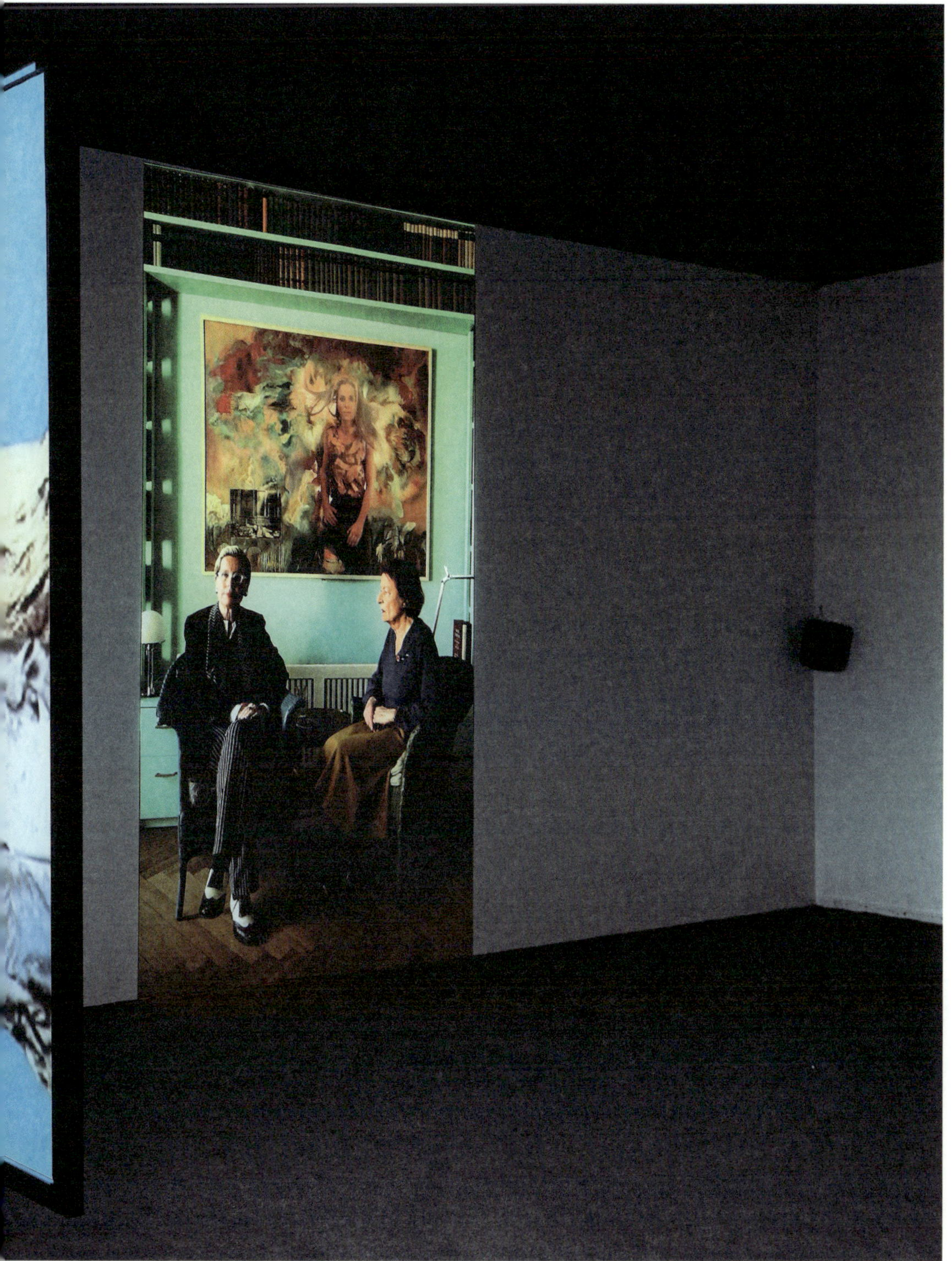

These statements follow the analysis of the British cultural sociologist Angela McRobbie in her study *The Aftermath of Feminism: Gender, Culture and Social Change*: capitalism sells us a pseudo-feminism in which personal freedom, mobilisation and flexibility seem to be promoted to our own advantage, and only ambition, competition, a drive to achieve and luck will guarantee success in life. Society with its inherent structures and rewards is negated and subject to 'retraditionalisation' by negating a system of hegemonic masculinity.[8] In her examples, McRobbie looks at a generation of younger women who are convinced that they have no need of feminism. But McRobbie shows that they still move within a narrow definitional frame of femininity and beauty. Within this atmosphere, the provocative book *Die Feigheit der Frauen* (The Cowardice of Women) by journalist Bascha Mika strikes a nerve. She charges women with being cowardly, cushy, mousy, and of subordinating themselves of their own accord, in the end cheating themselves.[9] So the battle lines are drawn once again: What can or should women want?

Nothing better could happen to feminism than becoming something to talk about once again. And not just within the academic framework, where feminism has indeed been continuously developed in theoretical and analytical terms, but in a way that rarely achieves social publicity. The division between the academy and real-life experience promotes the mistrust of feminism as an emancipatory project for those not interested in demonizing a gender, but rather in the culturally and politically attentive interrogation of rigid gender roles and hegemonic heterosexual gender identities in places where we no longer suspect them, because gender relations remain power relations. Nobody wants to be constantly reduced to a gender identity or to judge everything according to that basis. And this is precisely the goal of feminist politics: the abolition of gender stereotypes linked to expectations and limitations. It is necessary to develop an awareness of the category of gender, for without it social patterns and ascriptions and conceptual boxes like those of biological gender, but also ethnicity, religion or class cannot be decoded and deconstructed.

So what should a modern feminism accomplish, and above all how can it represent itself? In the English-speaking West, there has been a lively critical engagement with the media and entertainment industry, often carried out by people who are still quite young. For example, the American blogger Anita Sarkeesian, who in *Feminist Frequency*[10] offers a refreshing view of the codes and kings of American popular culture. Another example of this is the Bechdel Test[11], which evaluates feature films according to the presence of female characters and analyses music videos, TV series or even toys. This younger generation decodes global media and popular culture because they have grown up as part of its mass audience and the sense of 'anything goes'. In her reader *Hot Topic: Popfeminismus heute* and as co-founder of *Missy Magazin*, German cultural theorist Sonja Eismann focuses on feminist subjects in (pop) culture and society. On the field of tension between popular culture and feminism, she writes:

'While on the one hand the feminist movement, still seen with mistrust or hate due to constantly reanimated associations of "unattractiveness" or "grimness" seems like the last bastion of unmarketability, on the other hand the "cool" codes of feminists in popular culture, emptied of all content, can be fed to the market with no difficulties whatsoever.'[12]

Eismann's critique rings similar to that of Angela McRobbie: capitalism and neo-liberalism trump with the fulfilment of promises of equality

---

8......... See Angela McRobbie, *The Aftermath of Feminism*, p. 43.

9........ See Bascha Mika, *Die Feigheit der Frauen: Rollenfallen und Geiselmentalität. Eine Streitschrift wider den Selbstbetrug* (Munich, 2011).

10...... 'Conversations with Pop Culture: Feminist Analysis of Race, Gender, Class, Sexuality and Privilege in the Media', www.feministfrequency.com.

11..... The so-called Bechdel-Test, often referred to in a comic way, comes from Alison Bechdel's queer comic *Dykes to Watch Out For* (begun in 1983). The Bechdel Test is used in American blogs also to study racist representations in entertainment.

12.............................. Sonja Eismann (ed.), *Hot Topic*, p. 9.

Michaela Melián: *Ignaz Guenther House*, 2002 (Ausstellungsansicht / Exhibition view)

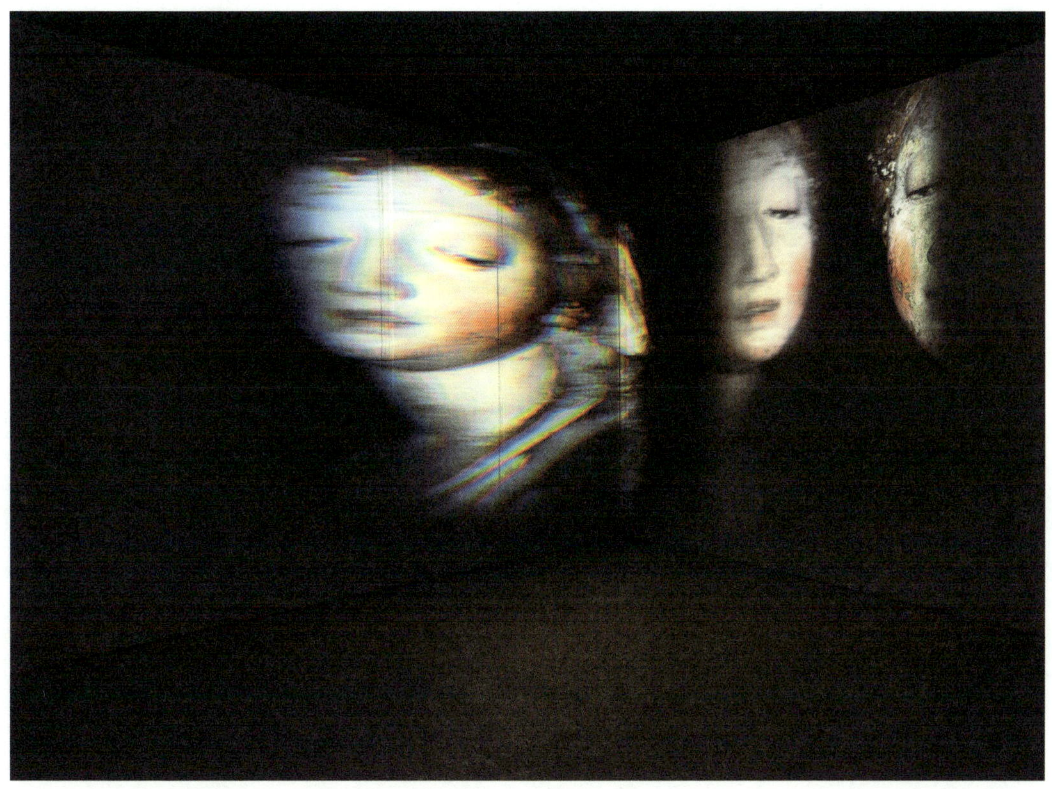

Nevin Aladağ: *Leaning Wall*, 2012 (Ausstellungsansicht / Exhibition view)

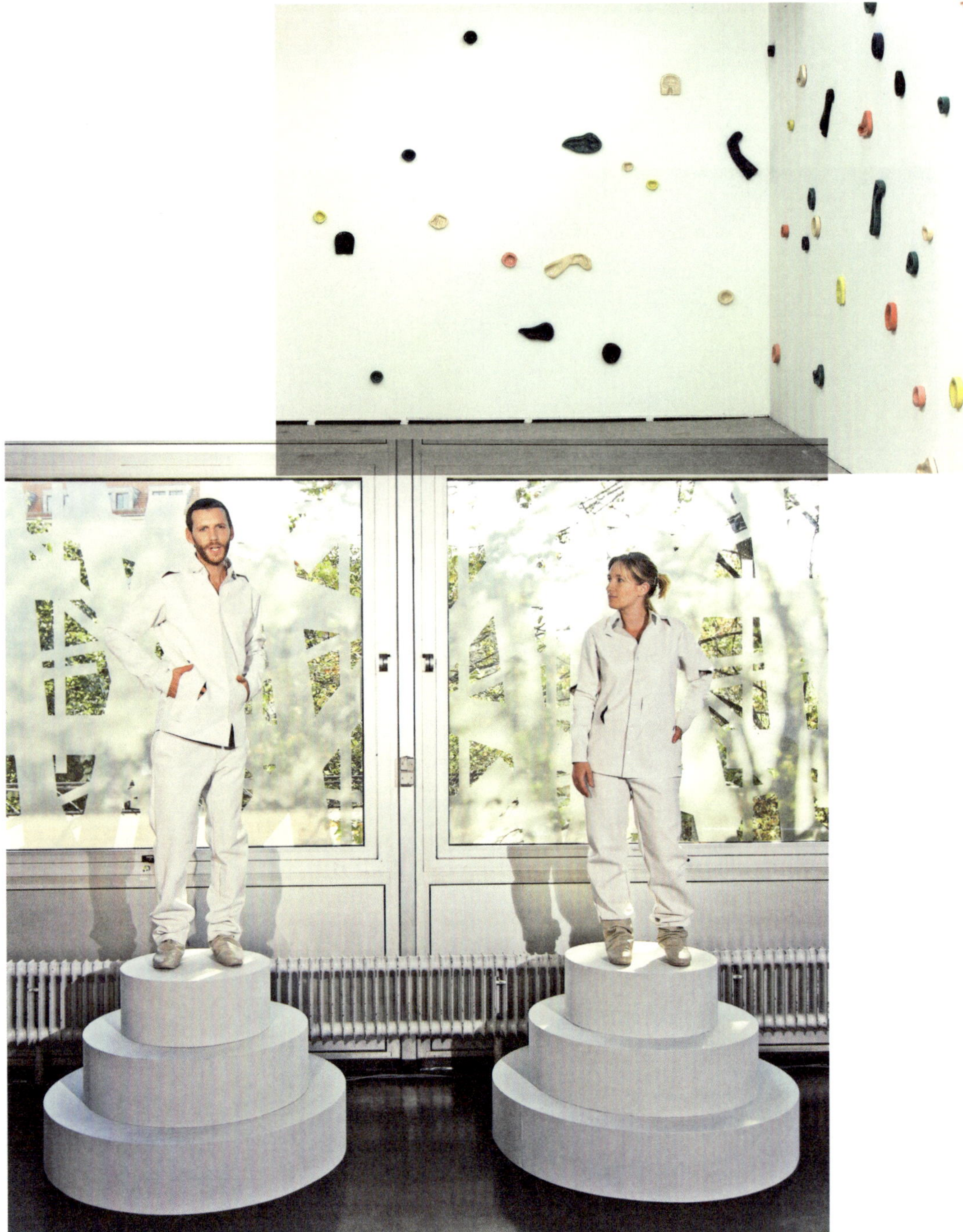

Nevin Aladağ: *Significant Other*, 2011

Warum wiederholen sich Statistiken, die das Verhältnis der Anzahl von Studentinnen gegenüber der von Professorinnen als Berg-zu-Tal-Fahrt visualisieren? Warum macht der Gender Pay Gap[5], das Lohngefälle zwischen Frauen und Männern im europäischen Vergleich immer noch einen Unterschied von 21,6 % aus? Warum geben Frauen ihren Beruf auf oder wechseln in Teilzeit, wenn sie Kinder bekommen? Warum sind alleinstehende Frauen im Pensionsalter von Armut betroffen? Warum haben biologistische Erklärungen für geschlechtsdifferente Verhaltensweisen immer wieder aufs Neue Konjunktur? Warum erwartet Männer, die durch eine Elternzeit von ihrem Job länger pausieren oder sich der Rolle als Familienernährer widersetzen gesellschaftliche Häme? Warum scheinen gerade männliche Rollenmuster so alternativlos?

Das historische Kurzzeitgedächtnis, das uns all diese Fragen verdrängen lässt, kann einerseits mit der Selbstverständlichkeit verbunden werden, mit der wir die Errungenschaften des Feminismus für uns in Anspruch nehmen. Die juristischen Gleichheits- und Freiheitskorrektive haben eine Pluralisierung von weiblichen Rollen und Genderidentitäten ermöglicht. Gleichzeitig aber verstärkt neoliberale Politik die Projektion des Lebensschicksals als individuelle, rein private Verantwortung und damit die Ablehnung einer strukturellen Benachteiligung als Frau. „Auf keinen Fall wollte irgendwer noch zu irgendeiner Opfergruppe gerechnet werden. Die neoliberale Ideologie, dass es keine Benachteiligung gebe, sondern nur noch individuelles Versagen, also keine Opfer mehr, sondern nur selbstverschuldete Verlierer, hat unbemerkt das Selbstbild markiert", analysiert die Filmwissenschaftlerin Gertrud Koch.[6] Alles ist unter Kontrolle – allein frau selbst ist es, die die Lebensentscheidungen trifft. So coacht uns der Grossteil der Frauenzeitschriften. Im Vorwort der Ausgabe *Texte zur Kunst* zum Thema Feminismus fassen die Herausgeberinnen kritisch zusammen: „Noch nie war die Stimmung so ‚postgender', so ‚postfeministisch' wie heute."[7] Diese Aussagen folgen der Analyse der britischen Kultursoziologin Angela McRobbie in ihrer Studie *Top Girls – Feminismus und der Aufstieg des neoliberalen Geschlechterregimes*: Der Kapitalismus verkauft uns einen Pseudo-Feminismus, in der persönliche Freiheit, Mobilisierung und Flexibilität scheinbar zum eigenen Vorteil gefördert werden und allein Ehrgeiz, Kompetenz, Leistungswille und Glück für den Erfolg im Leben garantieren. Gesellschaft mit seinen inhärenten Strukturen und Belohnungen wird negiert und so kann sich qua der Negation ein System hegemonialer Männlichkeit „re-traditionalisieren"[8]. In ihren Beispielen blickt McRobbie auf eine Generation junger Frauen, die selbstbewusst davon überzeugt ist, einen Feminismus nicht zu brauchen. McRobbie zeigt aber auf, dass sie sich immer noch in einem engen Definitionsrahmen von Weiblichkeit und Schönheit bewegen. In dieser Stimmung trifft die provokante Schrift *Die Feigheit der Frauen* der Journalistin Bascha Mika einen Nerv. Sie beklagt: Frauen sind feige, bequem, vermaust, ordnen sich freiwillig unter und betrügen sich damit letztlich selbst.[9] Die Fronten sind also (wieder) offen. Was wollen, sollen, können Frauen sollen und wollen?

Es könnte dem Feminismus eigentlich nichts Besseres passieren, als dass er wieder mehr Gesprächsstoff bietet. Und nicht nur in akademischen Räumen, in denen er sich seit 15 Jahren zwar theoretisch und analytisch weiterbildet, aber selten gesellschaftliche Öffentlichkeit erreicht. Die Trennung zwischen Akademie und realer Lebenserfahrung fördert das Misstrauen gegenüber dem Feminismus als emanzipatorisches Projekt für alle, dem es nicht um die Dämonisierungen einer Geschlechtsgruppe geht. Sondern um ein kulturell und politisch aufmerksames Hinterfragen etablierter Geschlechterverhältnisse, unbeweglicher Rollenbilder von Männern und Frauen und hegemonialer hetereosexueller

5............ Vgl. z.B. www.destatis.de/DE/PresseService/Presse/ Pressemitteilungen/2012/03/PD12_101_621.html.

6............... Koch, Gertrud: Feminismus nach der Identitätspolitik, in: *Feminismus. Texte zur Kunst* 84 (2011), 69.

7........... Buchmann, Sabeth/Graw, Isabelle/Rebentisch, Juliane: Vorwort, in: *Feminismus. Texte zur Kunst* 84 (2011), 4.

8........... Vgl. McRobbie, Angela: *Top Girls – Feminismus und der Aufstieg des neoliberalen Geschlechterregimes*. Wiesbaden 2010.

9.............. Vgl. Mika, Bascha: *Die Feigheit der Frauen. Rollenfallen und Geiselmentalität. – Eine Streitschrift wider den Selbstbetrug*. München 2011.

Genderidentitäten, da, wo wir sie vielleicht schon lang nicht mehr vermuten. Weil Geschlechterverhältnisse immer noch Machtverhältnisse sind. Niemand von uns möchte ständig auf eine Geschlechtsidentität reduziert werden oder alles daraufhin beurteilen. Und genau das ist die Absicht einer feministischen Politik: die Abschaffung von Geschlechtsstereotypen, die mit Erwartungen und Einschränkungen verbunden ist. Zur Bewusstwerdung ist die Kategorie Geschlecht notwendig, ohne die gesellschaftliche Muster und Zuweisungen nicht zu decodieren sind und ohne die Denk-Schubladen, wie die des biologischen Geschlechts, aber auch die der Ethnizität, Religion oder Klasse, nicht geschlossen werden können.

Was soll ein moderner Feminismus also leisten und vor allem, wie kann er sich repräsentieren? In der englischsprachigen, westlichen Welt gibt es eine kritisch-lebendige Auseinandersetzung mit der Medien- und Unterhaltungsindustrie, getragen von oft recht jungen Menschen. Zum Beispiel die amerikanische Kulturwissenschaftlerin Anita Sarkeesian, die mit ihrem Blog *Feminist Frequency*[10] einen erfrischenden Blick hinter die Codes und Kings amerikanischer Popkultur liefert: vom *Bechdel-Test*[11], der Spielfilmproduktionen nach der Anwesenheit von weiblichen Charakterrollen bewertet, zu Analysen von Musikvideos, TV-Serien oder auch Spielzeug-Editionen. Diese jüngere Generation decodiert globale Medien- und Popkultur, weil sie als Teil deren Massenpublikums und des Anything Goes aufgewachsen sind. Die deutsche Kulturwissenschaftlerin Sonja Eismann widmet sich in ihrem Reader *Hot Topic. Popfeminismus heute*, wie auch als Mitbegründerin des *Missy Magazin*, feministischen Inhalten in (Pop-)Kultur und Gesellschaft. Sie konstatiert zum Spannungsfeld von Pop und Feminismus:

„Während auf der einen Seite die immer noch misstrauisch bis hasserfüllt beäugte Bewegung des Feminismus aufgrund stets neu befeuerter Assoziationen von ‚Unattraktivität' und ‚Verbissenheit' wie die letzte Bastion der Unvermarktbarkeit wirkt, werden auf der anderen Seite die ihrer Inhalte entleerten ‚coolen' Codes der popkulturell aktiven Feministinnen unbekümmert in den Markt eingespeist."[12]

Eismanns Kritik liest sich ähnlich wie die einer Angela McRobbie: Kapitalismus und Neoliberalismus trumpfen mit der Einlösung von Gleichheitsversprechen und Genderpluralisierung auf, aber hinter dem Glamourvorhang und dem Erfolgstreppchen verbergen sich oftmals manifeste Verteilungsmechanismen. Daher lohnt sich der Blick zurück und nach vorn. Was kann man vom Feminismus der 1970er Jahre noch lernen? Was haben wir zu Unrecht verdammt und vergessen? Was können heute erfolgreiche Strategien sein, um neoliberale Pseudo-Wahrheiten zu entziffern? Welches sind adäquate Haltungen gegenüber einer prognostizierten Re-Traditionalisierung hegemonialer Geschlechterverhältnisse? Sind kulturell-künstlerische Formate wirksame Sprachen für einen kritischen Umgang mit einer differenz-affirmativen Marktlogik?

Die Ausstellung *The F-Word*

Das Projekt *The F-Word* positioniert vier ausgewählte Künstlerinnen in einen offenen Dialog verschiedener Formate und individueller Perspektiven. Nevin Aladağ, Ariane Anderegg, Alexandra Bachzetsis, Michaela Melián sind Künstlerinnen, deren Arbeiten Befragungen zur Aktualität und Verhandlung feministischer Haltungen ausdrücken, ohne einem Label von feministischer Kunst verpflichtet zu sein. Kunst oder künstlerische Praktiken mit Labeln zu versehen, kann problematisch, weil einengend sein und weitere Lesarten einschränken. Ob diese Künstlerinnen sich selbst als Feministinnen verstehen oder nicht, bleibt offen. Die Auswahl

---

10 .... Conversations with Pop Culture – Feminist analysis of race, gender, class, sexuality and privilege in the media. www.feministfrequency.com.

11 .... Der sogenannte Bechdel-Test, als kritisch-humoristische Anwendung vielfach zitiert, stammt aus Alison Bechdels queerem Comicstrips *Dykes to Watch Out For* (seit 1983). Der Bechdel-Test wird in US-amerikanischen Blogs auch für die Untersuchung rassistischer Repräsentationen in Unterhaltungsformaten angewendet.

12 .... Eismann, Sonja (Hg.): *Hot Topic*, 9.

and gender pluralisation, but manifest mechanisms of distribution hide behind the glamour curtain and the stairway to success. So it is worth taking both a look backwards and forwards. What can we learn from the feminism of the 1970s? Has it been judged unfairly and forgotten? What might successful strategies for decoding neo-liberal pseudo truths today look like? What are adequate responses to the threatening re-traditionalisation of hegemonic gender relations? Are cultural artistic formats effective languages for a critical approach to a market logic that affirms difference?

The Exhibition: *The F-Word*

The project *The F-Word* positions four artists in an open conversation of various formats and individual perspectives. Nevin Aladağ, Ariane Andereggen, Alexandra Bachzetsis, Michaela Melián are all women artists whose works express questions about the current relevance of feminist attitudes, negotiating them without being committed to a label of feminist art. Trying to affix labels to art or artistic practices can be problematic because it is narrowing and limits other readings. Whether these artists understand themselves as feminists or not remains an open question. The selection of these artists in their individual variability with the subject reflects the reality of the engagement with the public ambivalence and unpopularity of feminism as a critical form of social and political consciousness. From intense discussions between myself, the curator, and the artists, constellations of works resulted that engage with pop feminism, neo-liberalism, visual culture, gender issues, self-reflection and the feminist legacy. In so doing, the collaboration between the curator and artists was intended as a framework that enabled and demanded granting the artists liberties in choosing the positions presented. A key starting point of the exhibition was the constellation of artists who differ not only in terms of their media expression, but also in their thematic contexts. What they share is a productive mixing of genres and formats of contemporary art, exploring the outer reaches of performative and visual art in the combination of performance, acting, dance, music, video and audio installation, drawing, photography and sculpture. The project *The F-Word* is an exhibition, a performance platform and a concert event all at the same time.

Blind Spots and Forgotten Heroines

The Berlin exhibition *Künstlerinnen international 1877–1977*, which was held in 1977 and showed works by 265 artists, was the first art exhibition in Europe with exclusively female participation. Central to Michaela Melián's new work *Sarah Schumann und Silvia Bovenschen* (fig. p. 256/257) is a lengthy interview with two of the co-initiators of the exhibition: the artist Sarah Schumann and writer Silvia Bovenschen, who met at the time. In its spatial staging, the combined audio-video installation seems like a visit to the home of the couple Schumann/Bovenschen: captured in a *tableau vivant*, we see the two sitting beneath a painting made by Schumann in 1977 depicting Bovenschen life-sized. A second film shows a hand leafing through the catalogue of the exhibition from 1977. Now and again, as if we were walking through the Berlin pre-war apartment of the two, we see paintings by Sarah Schumann. The voices of the two tell of challenges and obstacles they experienced: it is a visit with a generation of activists from the German women's movement from the 1960s and 1970s which decisively shaped feminist discourse. And it is a visit with two artists who promote a public shift of perception with their texts and images. As an artist, like many of her contemporaries, Sarah Schumann never received much recognition for her work. Her collages were, even for the women's movement, too provocative in their affirmation of female eroticism and beauty. In their refusal to conform, Bovenschen and Schumann attest to the multivocality of feminism. Using the example of the now forgotten exhibition *Künstlerinnen international 1877–1977*, Silvia Bovenschen puts it this way:

'An exhibition creates a communicative space that takes up a tradition and passes it on. But what did not happen is … Somehow just a short while after the exhibition nobody was talking about the show anymore, even the women themselves. It's almost spooky. And that seems to confirm the history of the lack of a woman's history. It's like a hiccup.'[13]

In her artistic research, Michaela Melián once again undertakes a journey to the recent history of the twentieth century and illuminates the forgotten and marginalised, the brief memory of our generation of those who have gained from the past and how this memory produces simplifications and gaps. Michaela Melián (born in 1956, lives near Munich) is a visual artist and musician, and in her work she has repeatedly concerned herself with forgotten female figures from the history of medicine, industry or art. In her installational stagings, she creates highly aesthetic spaces of tension and multilayered systems of reference by way of drawing and sculpture, film and sound. As a musician she has released two albums and is cofounder of the band F.S.K. (founded in 1980). Her work *Ignaz Guenther House* (fig. p. 259), an audio-slide installation, consists of a house music piece produced by Melián and 80 slides of a Rococo sculpture of St. Mary Magdalene (1755), carved in 1755 by Ignaz Guenther. Maria Magdalene is worshiped and interpreted in various ways: as a sinner, as a repentant woman and the patron saint of prostitutes. The images of Mary Magdalene are refracted by a prism rotating before the lens in semicircles and projected into the space in constant movement. The saint becomes a dancer. Her image oscillates between shyness, ecstasy and trance, between a girl, a Mad(d)onna and a disco queen. Melián fragments and multiplies this ambiguous Magdalene figure and combines it with her own house piece that is based on a piano prelude sample by Johann Sebastian Bach: 'to give the music a body, something sculptural'.[14] House, a form of electronic dance music that began in the 1980s at Chicago's' Warehouse, knows neither start no end: 'House radicalises soul by taking recourse to the oldest gospel sources, that always, as an unseverable Möbius strip, spiritualised the erotic and eroticised the spiritual … House music is utopian transgender/race/class music of salvation … My house is your house.'[15] House, with its many influences and origins, from gospel, Latin, soul, funk, and disco, is also a social music in which the heterogeneity of culture, ethnicity, class and gender reverberates.

The Search for Identity without Pitfalls

Around 70 negative prints of female and male bodies have been burned into ceramic and glazed in various colours. The prints in their original sizes are installed as grips or rocks on a wall, like a climbing wall. *Leaning Wall* (fig. p. 260) is the title of this work by Nevin Aladağ, which as a generous gesture that appropriates space, promises footing where there is none. The body imprints seem like a perfect fit, at the same time supra-individual and individual. In so doing, female and male knee, chin, elbow or hand can hardly be distinguished from one another. The body imprints become a puzzle of non-gender-specific traces, and point out that we are all individuals with 'male' and 'female' components and attributes. The sculptural composition of real body overlays questions the determinism of biological gender in terms of its theoretical deconstruction. *Leaning Wall* positions identity in the antagonism between gender stereotypes and the desire to dissolve these borders. The symbolic reliance of the work on a sport from the world of Alpine mountain climbing, which today speaks equally to body and agility as modern self-discipline, refers to our lives in a high-performance society, in which the tuning of the body is just as important as the tuning of the self. And this is true for all genders and

13...... Silvia Bovenschen and Sarah Schumann, quoted in the work discussed.
14...... 'Freundliche Übernahme: Ein Interview mit Michaela Melián von Aram Lintzel', *Sounds. Texte zur Kunst*, 60 (Berlin, 2005), p. 128.

15........ Didi Neidhardt, 'Ignaz Guenther House ... Fäden ziehen ...', *Michaela Melián: Triangel*, eds. Bettina Dziembowski, Silvia Eiblmayr, Nicolaus Schafhausen (New York, 2003), p. 117.

Ariane Andereggen: *Second Art World (S.A.W.) – Myself as Popfeminist-Artist: 5 Confrontation-Dress: Astrofeminist*, 2009

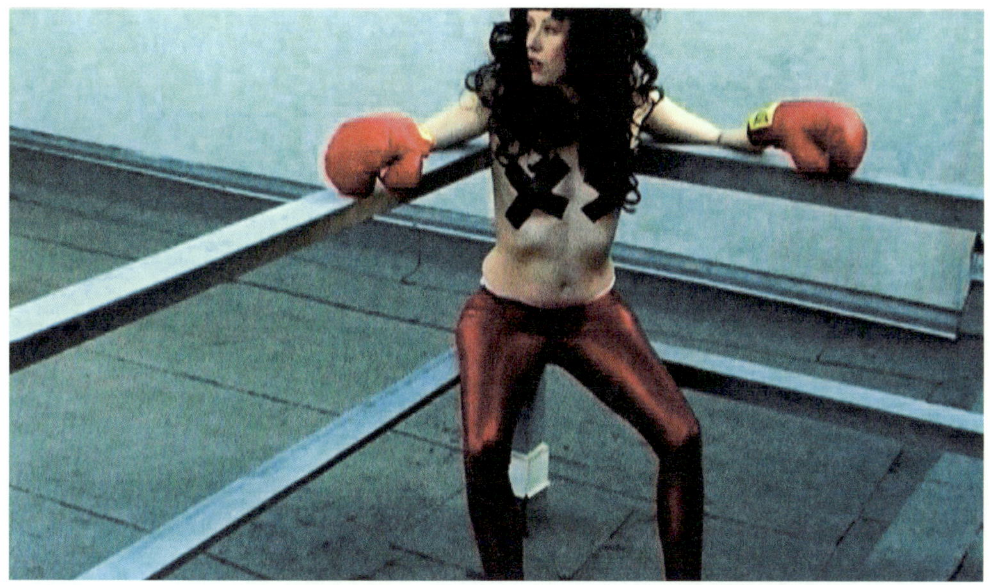

ANKE HOFFMANN

Ariane Andereggen: *Second Art World (S.A.W.) – Myself as Popfeminist-Artist, 2009–2012*
(Ausstellungsansicht / Exhibition view)

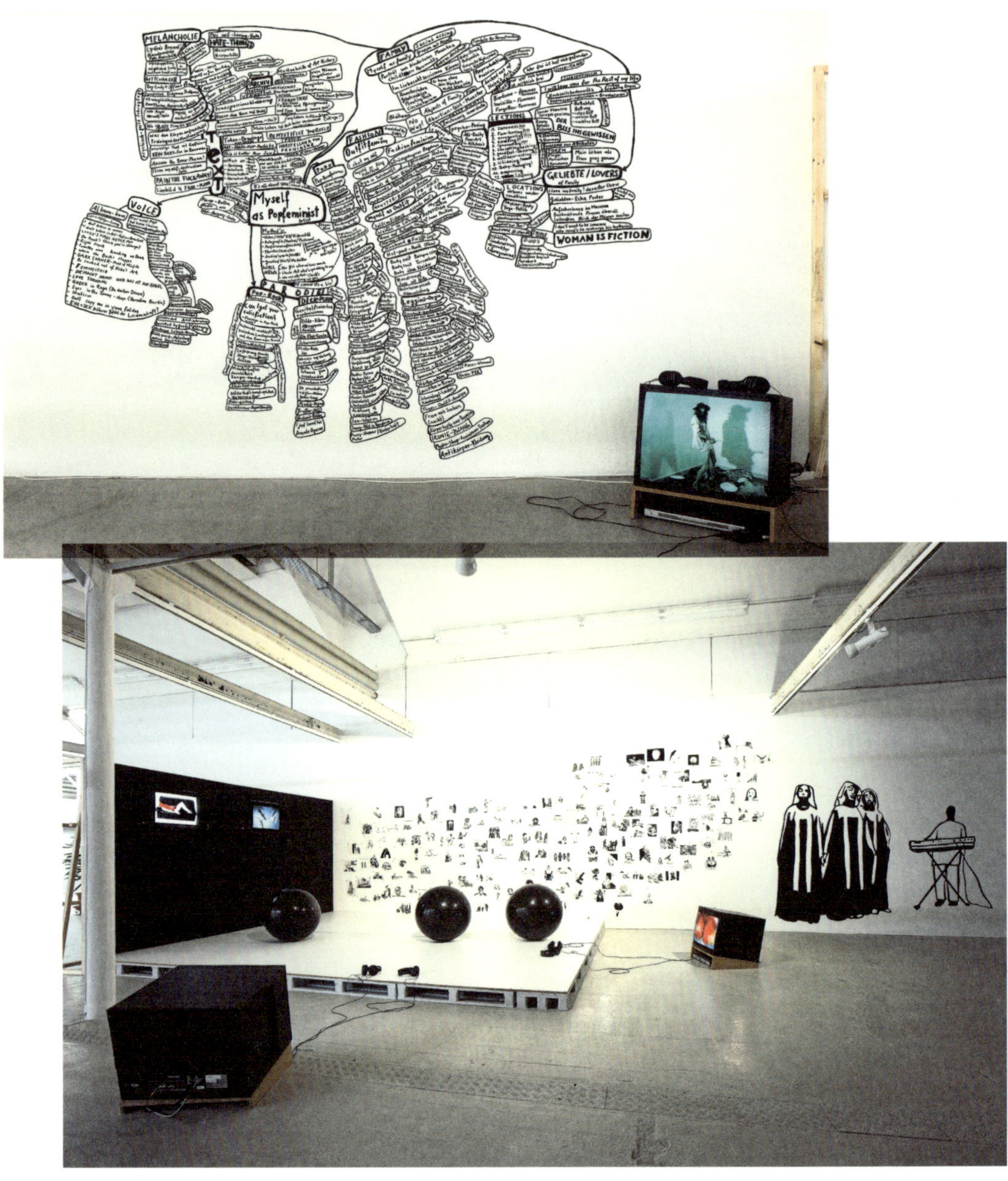

Ariane Andereggen: *Second Art World S.A.W. – Myself as Popfeminist-Artist, 2009–2012*
(Ausstellungsansicht / Exhibition view)

der Künstlerinnen in ihrer individuellen Unterschiedlichkeit mit dem Thema umzugehen, spiegelt auch die Realität in der Auseinandersetzung mit der öffentlichen Ambivalenz und Unpopularität des Feminismus als kritisches soziales und politisches Bewusstsein. Aus den intensiven Dialogen zwischen mir, der Kuratorin, und den Künstlerinnen haben sich Konstellationen von Arbeiten ergeben, die sich mit Popfeminismus, Neoliberalismus, Visual Culture, Genderfragen, Selbstreflexion und dem feministischen Erbe auseinandersetzen. Dabei war die Zusammenarbeit zwischen Kuratorin und Künstlerinnen als Setzung angelegt, die den Künstlerinnen Freiraum in der Auswahl ihrer präsentierten Positionen ermöglichte und einforderte. Ein wesentlicher Ausgangspunkt der Ausstellung war die Konstellation von Künstlerinnen, die sich in ihrem medialen Ausdruck, wie in ihren inhaltlichen Kontexten unterscheiden. Was sie verbindet, ist das produktive Vermischen von Genres und Formaten zeitgenössischer Kunst, das Ausloten von Grenzen darstellender und bildender Kunst in der Kombination von Performance, Schauspiel, Tanz, Musik, Video- und Audioinstallation, Zeichnung, Fotografie und Skulptur. Das Projekt *The F-Word* ist eine Ausstellung, eine Performanceplattform und ein Konzertevent.

Blinde Flecken und vergessene Heldinnen

Die Ausstellung *Künstlerinnen international 1877–1977,* die 1977 in Berlin stattfand und Werke von 265 Künstlerinnen zeigte, war die erste Kunstausstellung mit ausschliesslich weiblicher Beteiligung in Europa. Im Zentrum von Michaela Meliáns neuer Arbeit *Sarah Schumann und Silvia Bovenschen* (Abb. S. 256) steht ein längeres Interview mit zwei Mitinitiator_innen dieser Ausstellung: der Künstlerin Sarah Schumann und der Autorin Silvia Bovenschen, die sich damals kennenlernten. Die kombinierte Audio-Video-Installation wirkt in ihrer räumlichen Inszenierung wie ein Besuch beim Paar Schumann/Bovenschen: In ein Tableau vivant gebannt, sieht man beide lebensgross sitzend, unter einem Gemälde Schumanns von 1977, das Bovenschen zeigt. Ein zweiter Film zeigt eine Hand, die im Katalog

der Ausstellung von 1977 blättert. Ab und zu, als schritten wir die Berliner Altbauwohnung der beiden ab, erscheinen Bilder von Sarah Schumann. Die Stimmen der beiden erzählen von Herausforderungen und Hindernissen. Es ist ein Besuch bei einer Generation von Aktivist_innen der deutschen Frauenbewegung der 1960/1970er Jahre, die den feministischen Diskurs massgeblich mit prägten. Und es ist ein Besuch bei zwei Künstlerinnen, die mit ihren Texten und Bildern für eine öffentliche Wahrnehmungsverschiebung eintreten. Sarah Schumann hat als Künstlerin, wie viele ihrer Zeitgenossinnen, nie die grosse Anerkennung erhalten. Ihre Collagen waren selbst für die Frauenbewegung zu provokativ in ihrer Bejahung von weiblicher Erotik und Schönheit. In ihrer Unangepasstheit erzählen Bovenschen und Schumann von der Vielstimmigkeit des Feminismus. Am Beispiel der in Vergessenheit geratenen Ausstellung *Künstlerinnen international 1877–1977* formuliert Silvia Bovenschen:

„Eine Ausstellung schafft einen kommunikativen Raum, der eine Tradition aufnimmt und weitergibt. Was aber nicht geschehen ist [...] Irgendwie haben alle nach kurzer Zeit nicht mehr über die Ausstellung geredet, auch die Frauen selbst nicht. Es ist geradezu unheimlich. Und das scheint mir die Geschichte der weiblichen Geschichtslosigkeit zu bestätigen. Es ist wie ein Schluckauf."[13]

Michaela Melián unternimmt in ihrer künstlerischen Recherche einmal mehr eine Reise in die junge Geschichte des 20. Jahrhunderts und beleuchtet Vergessenes und Marginalisiertes, das kurze Gedächtnis unserer Generation von Gewinner_innen und den Umstand, wie dieses Gedächtnis Simplifizierungen und Auslassungen produziert. Michaela Melián (*1956, lebt bei München) ist bildende Künstlerin und Musikerin und hat sich in ihren Arbeiten immer wieder mit vergessenen Protagonistinnen der Medizin-, Industrie- oder Kunstgeschichte beschäftigt. In ihren installativen Inszenierungen schafft sie mittels Zeichnung und Skulptur, Film und Sound hochästhetische Spannungsräume und vielschichtige Verweissysteme. Als Musikern hat

---

13 .... Silvia Bovenschen und Sarah Schumann, zitiert aus dem Interview mit Michaela Melián, 2012.

sie zwei Alben veröffentlicht und ist Mitgründerin der Band F.S.K. (seit 1980). Ihre Arbeit *Ignaz Guenther House* (Abb. S. 259), eine Audio-Dia-installation, besteht aus einem von Melián produzierten House-Musikstück und 80 Dias einer Rokoko-Frauenskulptur, der *Heiligen Magdalena*, 1755 von Ignaz Guenther geschnitzt. Die Bilder der Magdalena werden mittels eines sich vor dem Objektiv drehenden Prismas halbkreisförmig aufgefächert und in ständiger Bewegung in den Raum projiziert. Die Heilige wird zur Tänzerin. Ihre Erscheinung changiert permanent zwischen Schüchternheit, Ekstase und Trance, zwischen Mädchen, Mad(d)onna und Disco Queen.

Melián fragmentiert und multipliziert diese vieldeutige Magdalena und kombiniert sie mit einem eigenen House-Stück, das auf einem Klavier-Präludium-Sample von Johann Sebastian Bach basiert, „um der Musik einen Körper, etwas Skulpturales zu geben".[14] House, eine basslastige elektronische Tanzmusik, die in den 1980ern im Warehouse in Chicago entstand, kennt weder Anfang noch Ende. „House radikalisiert Soul durch Rückgriffe auf älteste Gospel-Quellen, die schon immer als undurchtrennbares Möbiusband das Erotische spiritualisierten und das Spirituelle erotisierten. [...] House Musik ist utopische trans-gender/race/class-Erlösungsmusik [...] My house is your house."[15] House ist mit seinen vielen Einflüssen und Ursprüngen, von Gospel, Latin, Soul, Funk und Disco auch eine soziale Musik, in der die Heterogenität von Kultur, Ethnizität, Klasse und Geschlecht mitschwingt.

Identitätssuche ohne Fallstricke

Etwa 70 Negativabdrücke von weiblichen und männlichen Körpern sind in Keramik gebrannt und verschiedenfarbig glasiert. Die originalgrossen Abdrücke sind als Haltegriffe oder Boulder an einer Wand installiert, einer Kletterwand nachempfunden. *Leaning Wall* (Abb. S. 260) heisst die

Arbeit der Künstlerin Nevin Aladağ, die als grosszügige, Raum aneignende Geste Halt verspricht, wo kein Halt ist. Passformen gleich wirken die Körperabdrücke, die überindividuell und individuell zugleich sind. Dabei sind weibliches und männliches Knie, Kinn, Ellbogen oder Hand kaum bis überhaupt nicht zu unterscheiden. Die Körperabdrücke werden zu einem Puzzle von geschlechtsunspezifischen Spuren und weisen darauf hin, dass wir alle Individuen mit ‚männlichen' und ‚weiblichen' Anteilen und Attributen sind. Die bildhauerische Komposition aus realen Körperfolien hinterfragt den Determinismus des biologischen Geschlechts hinsichtlich seiner theoretischen Dekonstruktion. *Leaning Wall* positioniert Identität im Widerstreit zwischen Geschlechtsstereotypen und dem Wunsch, diese Grenzen aufzulösen. Die symbolische Anlehnung der Arbeit an einen Sport aus der alpinen Bergsteigerwelt, der heute als moderne Selbstertüchtigung Körper und Geschicklichkeit gleichermassen anspricht, verweist auf unser Leben in der Hochleistungsgesellschaft, in der Body-Tuning genauso wichtig ist wie Ego-Tuning. Und dies für alle Geschlechter und Identitäten gleichermassen. Die Gleichsteuerung aller Individuen unter den kompetitiven Erfolgsdruck gilt heute als vermeintliche Einlösung von Gleichberechtigungsforderungen. So lässt *Leaning Wall* auch Reflexionen über Spielregeln gesellschaftlichen Erfolgs mittels Körperertüchtigung und Fitness-Wahn zu.

Nevin Aladağ (*1972, lebt in Berlin) ist bildende Künstlerin mit einem Hintergrund in Bildhauerei. Als solche arbeitet sie in konzeptuellen und mehrdeutigen Installationen aus skulpturalen Objekten, deren ursprünglichen Gebrauchswert die Künstlerin pointiert und in oft minimal-ästhetischer Zurückhaltung aus dem alltäglichen Bedeutungszusammenhang herausnimmt und neu akzentuiert. Eine ähnliche Komposition und Verschiebung von realer und übertragener Bedeutung liegt sowohl ihren urbanen Interventionen und Arrangements, als auch den seit einigen Jahren entwickelten performativen Choreographien zugrunde, die Aladağ von Schauspieler_innen und Tänzer_innen aufführen lässt. In ihren medial vielfältigen Arbeiten wird untersucht, welches die Trieb- und Ziehkräfte sozialer Gemeinschaften

---

14 .... Freundliche Übernahme. Ein Interview mit Michaela Melián von Aram Lintzel. In: *Sounds. Texte zur Kunst* 60 (2005), 128.
15 .... Neidhardt, Didi: Ignaz Guenther House ... Fäden ziehen ... In: Dziembowski, Bettina/Eiblmayr, Silvia/Schafhausen, Nicolaus (Hg.): *Michaela Melián – Triangel*. New York 2003, 117.

Alexandra Bachzetsis: *Rehearsal (Ongoing)*, 2011 (Ausstellungsansicht / Exhibition view)

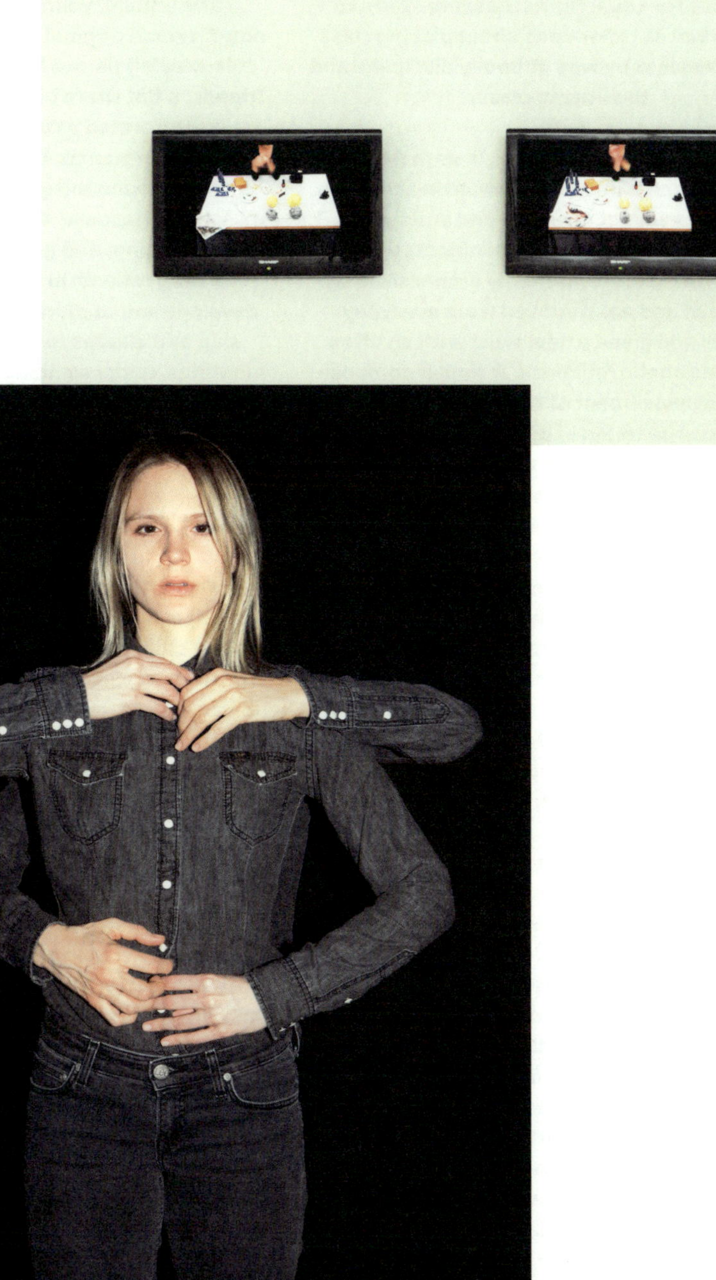

Alexandra Bachzetsis: *A Piece Danced Alone*, 2011

identities. The equal control of all individuals under the competitive pressure to succeed is today considered the supposed redemption of demands for equal rights. *Leaning Wall* can thus be read as reflections about playing rules of social success by way of bodily discipline and the fitness craze.

Nevin Aladağ (born in 1972, lives in Berlin) is a visual artist with a background in sculpture. She works with conceptual and ambiguous installations using sculptural objects whose original use value is pointedly emphasised by the artist and are removed from everyday contexts and given a new twist with an often minimal aesthetic reticence. A similar composition and displacement of real and metaphorical meaning can be found in her urban interventions and arrangements, as well as the choreographies that have been developed over the past few years that Aladağ has had actresses and dancers perform. Her varied media works explore what are the driving forces and forces of dissolution in social communities and how individual interests and counter representations are articulated within normative social contexts.

The video installation *Significant Other* (fig. p. 260) is the implementation of an original live performance. Two actors, a woman and a man, each stand on a pedestal, whose shape recalls a wedding cake. Audible are voices of individuals with whom Aladağ carries out interviews on their private social relationships and which differ according to age, gender, origin and their familial status. Both actors now 'speak' these monologues and dialogues by simply synchronically moving their lips, mimicking moves and facial expressions. As a refrain, just as in a song, we can hear the Milli Vanilli hit and playback scandal 'Girl, You Know It's True', sung in a new version and performed by the musician couple Joy Denalane and Max Herre. Both performers are dressed in identical loose-fitting white leather suits that have openings or gaps in numerous places. The actresses, depending on which person is speaking at the moment, reach into the openings in various ways, and thus negotiate the different variants of coded body language. In so doing,

the gender-attributing gestures and poses are exchanged back and forth between the two performers, just as the attributions of male and female, young and old, German and non-German original sounds are mixed. In these role-playing games between the fictional duo, friends, a flat share or a married couple, identity is interpreted as an object of negotiation and performance. The title *Significant Other* comes from the gender-neutral term for a partner or spouse. Playing with sound collage, body staging, and gender indifference, Nevin Aladağ reflects in an entertaining way the development of pluralized patterns of relationship and alludes to the desire for subjective identities, understanding difference as a constitutive characteristic.

Popular Feminism as Self-Experimentation

Ariane Andereggen (born in 1969, lives in Basel) is an actor, media artist and performer: she calls herself a visual performer and a performing artist. Formats used by the artist include theatre and performance, video, photography, drawing and text. In her artistic engagement, she is interested in the contradictions between conscious reflection and appropriate and unconscious action, that which motivates social action and self-representation at its deepest level. With her long term project *Second Art World (S.A.W.)* she seeks a point of access to the collective mediatised subconscious of the past avant-garde. A semi-internalised universe, where the individual projects such as *Myself as Post-Punk-Artist*; *Myself as Outsider-Artist*; *Myself as Media-Artist* and *Myself as Global-Artist* serve as strategies of self-appropriation.

Her current series of works *Myself as Popfeminist-Artist*[16] (fig. p. 266) consists of five videos, a live performance, drawings and photographs

16......... Installation, diverse materials, five videos: *1 Psycho-Pop Subjection; 2 Discursive Limits and detailed Artwork of Free-Jazz-Rockmonster; 4 Living in female Drifts (In the Style of Fakelore); 5 Confrontation-Dress: Astrofeminist; 6 The Depression-Gala; Woman is an Art-Show Part 1* (live performance).

sind und wie sich individuelle Interessen und Gegen-Repräsentationen innerhalb von normativen Sozialgefügen artikulieren.

Die Videoinstallation *Significant Other* (Abb. S. 260) ist die Umsetzung einer ursprünglichen Live-Performance. Zwei Schauspieler_innen, eine Frau und ein Mann, stehen auf je einem Podest, deren Form an eine Hochzeitstorte erinnert. Zu hören sind Stimmen von Personen, mit denen Aladağ Interviews zu ihren privaten sozialen Beziehungen führte und die sich nach Alter, Geschlecht, Herkunft und Familienstand unterscheiden. Beide Schauspieler_innen ‚sprechen‘ nun diese Monologe und Dialoge nach, indem sie lediglich ihre Lippen synchron bewegen und als Interpret_innen mimisch und körperlich agieren. Als Refrain, wie bei einem Song, ertönt der Milli Vanilli-Hit und Playback-Skandal „Girl, you know it's true", neu eingesungen und interpretiert durch das Musiker_innen-Paar Joy Denalane und Max Herre.

Beide Performer_innen sind mit denselben weissen, locker sitzenden ledernen Anzügen bekleidet, die an mehreren Stellen Öffnungen oder Eingriffe tragen. Die Schauspieler_innen greifen, je nach dem, welche Person gerade spricht, auf ganz unterschiedliche Art in die Öffnungen und tarieren so die verschiedenen Varianten von codierter Körpersprache aus. Dabei wechseln die geschlechtszuweisenden Gesten und Posen zwischen beiden Interpret_innen hin und her, wie auch die Zuweisungen von männlichen und weiblichen, jungen und alten, deutschen und nicht-deutschen O-Tönen vermischt werden. In diesen Rollenspielen zwischen fiktivem Paar, Freund_innen, Wohngemeinschaft oder Eheleuten wird Identität als Verhandlungsgegenstand und Performance gedeutet. So steht auch der Titel *Significant Other* für den genderneutralen englischen Begriff des oder der Lebenspartner_in. Im Spiel mit Soundcollage, Körperinszenierung und Genderindifferenz spiegelt Nevin Aladağ auf unterhaltsame Weise die Entwicklung von pluralisierten Beziehungsmustern wider und lässt den Wunsch nach subjektiven Identitäten, die Differenz als konstitutives Merkmal begreifen, anklingen.

Popfeminismus als Selbstversuch

Ariane Andereggen (*1969, lebt in Basel) ist Theaterschauspielerin, Medienkünstlerin und Performerin und bezeichnet sich selbst als bildende Schauspielerin und darstellende Künstlerin. Formate der Künstlerin sind neben Schauspiel und Performance, Video, Fotografie, Zeichnung und Text. In ihrer künstlerischen Auseinandersetzung interessiert sie sich für die Widersprüche zwischen bewusster Reflexion und Aneignung und unbewusstem Agieren, für das, was soziales Handeln und Selbstrepräsentation im Innersten motiviert. Mit ihrem Langzeitprojekt *Second Art World (S.A.W.)* sucht sie nach einem Zugriff auf das kollektiv-mediatisierte Unterbewusstsein der vergangenen Avantgarde. Ein halberinnertes Universum, deren einzelne Projekte wie *Myself as Post-Punk-Artist*; *Myself as Outsider-Artist*; *Myself as Media-Artist* und *Myself as Global-Artist* Selbstaneignungsstrategien sind.

Ihre aktuelle Werkserie *Myself as Popfeminist-Artist*[16] (Abb. S. 266) umfasst fünf Videos, eine Live-Performance, Zeichnungen sowie Fotografien, die Ariane Andereggen kontinuierlich produziert. Alle unterschiedlichen Teile sind in einer von der Künstlerin inszenierten Bühneninstallation zu sehen. *Myself as Popfeminist-Artist* oszilliert ein fiktives Ich der Künstlerin inmitten popkultureller Muster, geschlechtsstereotyper Medienbilder und (pop-)feministischer Klischees. In ihren Performancevideos agiert Andereggen als Schauspielerin, die als „Kunst-Vorturnerin" (Andereggen) Themen wie Sexualität, Einsamkeit, Aggressivität, Verweigerung, Depression und Identitätssuche durchspielt. In ihren Videos zeigt sie offene, kreative Prozesse, die Theater und Kunst verbinden, und hinterfragt darin weibliche Rollen zwischen Authentizität und Projektion. Dabei steht das Sichtbare dem Unsichtbaren gegenüber und wird zu einem Instrument subjektiver Befreiung vor einer Konsumkultur, die durch Vereinnahmung leere Parolen identifiziert.

---

16 .... Installation, diverse Materialien, fünf Videos: *1 Psycho-Pop Subjection*; *2 Discursive Limits and detailed Artwork of Free-Jazz-Rockmonster*; *4 Living in female Drifts (In the Style of Fakelore)*; *5 Confrontation-Dress: Astrofeminist*; *6 The Depression-Gala*; *Woman is an Art-Show Part 1* (Live–Performance).

Mit einer unerschrockenen Körpersprache, einer Liebe zu Absurdität und Komik, einer grossen Spielfreude und Selbstironie unternimmt Andereggen einen Parcours der Gesten, Körperbilder und Zitate der Popkultur und Kunstavantgarde. Im Video *Living In female Drifts* ist es ein weiblicher Cowboy *(In the Style of Fakelore)*, ‚der' sich mit einem Stein unterhält, schlecht gelaunt aufs Meer schaut und sich immer wieder offensiv der Kamera zuwendet. Andereggens Monologe bestehen aus einem Referenzsystem von pseudo-feministischen Sprüchen und richten sich immer wieder an die Betrachter_innen: „It's not about me, it's about – YOU." In *Confrontation-Dress: Astrofeminist* tritt Andereggen als eine Lady mit knallroten Boxhandschuhen und roten Glitzerleggins auf, die mit ihrem eigenen Schatten kämpft, oder verwandelt sich in einen Stern, der in einer Parkgarage auf seine Entdeckung wartet. Immer spielt Andereggen mit Projektionen und Karikaturen von Weiblichkeit, die wir selbst produzieren. Neben der Körpersprache ist es auch ihre Sprachakrobatik, die den Rhythmus der Videos bestimmt. Zitate und Sätze wie „Wir sind das erste studierte Zeitalter der Kostüme" (nach F. Nietzsche) oder „Then I became a woman in the style of penetrating culture" sind aphoristische Wortbilder. Erweitert werden die Videos in der Installation durch eine Vielzahl an zeichnerischen Studien von Szenen, die Andereggen im Internet und in Zeitungen recherchiert und miteinander re-kombiniert. Die dichte Bilderwand bietet unterschiedlichste Assoziationen und Dialoge und wird zu einem Eintritt in den Anderegg'schen Kosmos von Bedeutungszusammenhängen. In der Performance *Woman is an Art-Show Part 1*, die zur Eröffnung der Ausstellung live aufgeführt wurde, performt die Künstlerin in einer „sprachlich-fieberhaften Ver- äusserung allen pop-feministischen Halbwissens eine Art widerständiges Selbstgespräch".[17]

Sich der eigenen Performanz bewusst werden

Alexandra Bachzetsis (*1974, lebt in Basel) arbeitet als Künstlerin, Choreografin und Performerin im Kontext darstellender und bildender Kunst. Sie ist Solo-Tänzerin ihrer eigenen Stücke als auch Choreografin von Tanz-Performances mit einem Ensemble von Tänzer_innen und Musiker_innen. Bachzetsis untersucht in ihren choreografischen Arbeiten visuelle Codes von Dress- und Körpersprache und im Zentrum dessen oft weibliche Stereotype, wie sie uns die Bildwelten der populären Kultur einspeisen. Gegenstand ihrer aufs Genaueste ausgearbeiteten Analysen und kritisch-reflexiven wie ästhetisch-komplexen Spiegelungen sind Medienformate wie Musikvideos, TV- und Kinoproduktionen, aber auch Alltagskommunikation sowie Mode- und Sexindustrie. Ihr Zwei-Personen Stück mit dem Titel *A Piece Danced Alone* (Abb. S. 269) untersucht eben jene Alltagsgesten und das Repertoire von kulturell codierter Körpersprache und inwieweit sich Authentizität und Performance noch voneinander unterscheiden. Alexandra Bachzetsis stellt sich mit einem fiktiven Künstlerinnen-Ego und einer Doppelgängerin vor, deren biografische Überhäufungen von Engagements im Vergleich zu ‚ihrem' Alter Fragen nach beruflicher (Künstler_innen-)Selbstdarstellung und gesellschaftlichen Erwartungshaltungen eröffnet. Beide Performerinnen tanzen in dem 40-minütigen Stück verschiedene Soli, die mal als Wettbewerb, mal als Nachahmung, als Interpretation und als Duett angelegt sind. Kompetitives Verhalten konkurriert hier mit dem Sujet der Freundinnen und spielt schliesslich mit der Ununterscheidbarkeit der beiden Personen. Alexandra Bachzetsis und Anne Pajunen tanzen in erotisch-neutralen und unisex-konformer Jeanskombi und Turnschuhen, die ihren modischen Hintergrund im Diskozeitalter der 1970er Jahre hat. Die Choreografie *A Piece Danced Alone* zitiert ein Vokabular der Körpersprachen, die auf Alltagsgegenwart, modernem Tanz und unserem kollektiven medialen Gedächtnis der Mainstreamunterhaltung beruhen. Bachzetsis und Pajunen interpretieren das geschlechtsstereotype Idealbild einer Marilyn Monroe und Jane Russell aus *Gentleman Prefer Blondes* (1953), oder die Brechung solcher

17 ....Ariane Andereggen in einer E-Mail, 22.04.2012.

that Ariane Andreggen continuously produces. The various parts can be seen in a stage installation by the artist. *Myself as Popfeminist-Artist* oscillates a fictional self of the artist in the midst of popular cultural patterns, gender stereotypical media images and (pop) feminist clichés. In her performance videos, Andereggen works as an actor who as an 'art acrobat' (Andereggen) plays through subjects such as sexuality, loneliness, aggression, refusal, depression and the search for identity. In her videos, she shows open, creative processes that combine theatre and the arts, and therein questions female roles between authenticity and projection. In so doing, the visible is contrasted with the invisible and becomes an instrument of subjective liberation from a consumer culture that identifies empty slogans by way of their appropriation. With an unflinching body language, a love of the absurd and comedy, a great joy in play and self-irony, Andereggen takes up a series of gestures, body images and quotations from popular culture and the art avant-garde. In the video *Living in female Drifts*, a female cowboy (*In the Style of Fakelore*) speaks with a stone, looks in a foul mood across the ocean and turns repeatedly with an offensive facial expression towards the camera. Andereggen's monologues consist of a system of references of pseudo-feminist slogans and are directed repeatedly at the beholders: 'It's not about me, it's about YOU.' In *Confrontation-Dress: Astrofeminist*, Andereggen appears as a woman wearing bright red boxing gloves and sparkling red leggings who fights her own shadow or transforms herself into a star who awaits discovery in a parking garage. Andereggen always plays with projections and caricatures of femininity that we produce ourselves. Beside this physical language, her linguistic acrobatics also define the rhythm of the video. Quotations or statements such as 'We are the first studied age of the costume', (after F. Nietzsche), or 'Then I became a woman in the style of penetrating culture', are aphoristic sayings. The videos of the installation are complemented by a large number of situations of drawings of scenes that Andereggen researches in newspapers and the Internet and recombines with one another.

The dense wall of images offers various associations and dialogues and becomes a point of entrée into the Andereggian universe of contexts of meaning. In the performance *Woman Is an Art-Show Part 1,* which was performed live at the exhibition opening, the artist performs in a 'linguistically-feverish expression of all pop-feminist semi-knowledge a kind of restive conversation with oneself'.[17]

Becoming Aware of Our Own Performance

Alexandra Bachzetsis (born in 1974, lives in Basel and Zurich) works as an artist, choreographer and performer. She performs her own dance pieces and choreographs performances with an ensemble of dancers and musicians. In her choreographic works, Bachzetsis explores visual codes of dress and body language, often centering on female stereotypes as fed to us by the visual worlds of popular culture. The object of her analyses, critically reflexive as well as aesthetically complex reflections worked out in the most precise terms, are music videos, television and cinema productions, as well as everyday communication and the fashion and sex industry. Her two-person piece with the title *A Piece Danced Alone* (fig. p. 269) explores these very gestures of everyday life and the repertoire of culturally coded body language and to what extent authenticity and performance still differ from one another. Alexandra Bachzetsis presents herself with a fictional artist ego and a *doppelgänger*, whose biographical excess of engagements in comparison to 'her' age raise questions of professional artistic self-presentation and social attitudes of expectation. In the 40-minute piece, the two performers dance various solo parts that are conceived in part as competition, in part as imitation, as interpretation and as duet. Competitive behaviour here vies with the theme of friendship and ultimately plays with the impossibility of distinguishing the two individuals. Alexandra Bachzetsis und Anne Pajunen dance in erotically neutral and unisex

17.............. Ariane Andereggen in an e-mail, 22 April 2012.

jeans outfits and trainers that have their background in the fashion of the disco era during the 1970s. The choreographed *A Piece Danced Alone* cites a vocabulary of body languages that rely on the everyday present, modern dance and our collective media memory of mainstream entertainment. Bachzetsis and Pajunen act out the gender-stereotypical ideal image of a Marilyn Monroe or Jane Russell from *Gentleman Prefer Blondes* (1953) or the refraction of such manifest gender images in the androgynous role models of the singer Ian Curtis from Joy Division or the role of Alex Owens in *Flashdance.* In interpreting titles such as 'She's Lost Control', they explore the studying of movements in contrast to supposedly authentic ecstasy and exuberance, and thus the individual tension between freedom and conformity. In these studies of gestures and codes, also visually confrontational for the audience, Bachzetsis presumes the voyeurism of the beholders as a concept, by performing without a stage or distance from the audience.

The video installation *Rehearsal (Ongoing)* (fig. p. 269) is a choreographed piece divided into exactly parsed events at a table with various utensils. A woman uses and shifts various things on the table: a cigarette, nail polish, skin cream, a fashion magazine, a Polaroid camera, pills, a sponge, a ball of wool, paper with holes punched in it. From this arrangement on a table that combines everything—work, leisure, reflection, household chores, personal hygiene—a possible microcosm of female existence emerges. By repeated, minimal interventions, she changes the still-life slowly, but remains in a closed world. The loop of the scene's events, coupled at two adjacent screens, underscores the act as a permanent practicing, a constant rehearsal. In the endless series of attempts to appropriate that never reach completion and that due—to their doubling—cannot be separated into authentic and imitated actions, interpretations of individual adaptations and socially normative codes can be read that also leave open the act of self-empowerment and breaking this deterministic cycle.

The F-Word

The F in F-Word stands for a way of avoiding saying something vulgar and unspeakable, something that has been adapted as a curse word and cannot be named directly, because the speakers are afraid of 'sullying' themselves by using it. Feminism has become just such a word, where speakers are afraid of outing themselves as behind the times or somehow frustrated by using it. That this is due to a social denigration and the distortion of facts is something that I tried to make clear at the start. This exhibition constellation is intended to underscore the fact that art and culture with its exploration of identity politics and logics of representation provide an impulse to actualise attention and arguments in favour of a feminist politics. In the works discussed here, all four artists explore the challenges of being a female-connoted individual in particular social and normative contexts. Michaela Melián targets the emancipation of a feminist belief beyond distortions and simplifications. She does this by using real biographies and superimposing temporally disparate culture content. Nevin Aladağ takes on the heterogeneous, non-hierarchical representation of the individual to reflect on the subject of identity politics before the dictum of stereotypes and determinism. With a choreographic anthropology of popular culture Alexandra Bachzetsis creates an instrument for de-coding hegemonic patterns of female representation and reflects them in an act of performative aesthetic self-empowerment as a cliché of control from outside. And Ariane Andereggen reveals with her exaggeration of art methodology, popular culture and 'liberated femininity' the affirmation of difference in today's marketing logics. The artists examine in very particular ways contemporary mainstream culture, everyday representations, but also the system of art history for structures of hegemonic gender relations. In their transdisciplinary positions, the artists thus produce strategies of critical, feminist attitudes that are presented confidently, attentively, seriously and reflexively, but also aesthetically, pleasurably, comically and in an easygoing fashion.

Translated by Brian Currid

manifester Geschlechterbilder in den androgynen Rolemodels des Sängers Ian Curtis von Joy Division oder der Rolle der Alex Owens aus *Flashdance*. In der Interpretation von Titeln wie zum Beispiel *She's lost control* wird das Einstudieren von Bewegungsabläufen im Gegensatz zur vermeintlich authentischen Ekstase und Ausgelassenheit thematisiert und damit die individuelle Spannung zwischen Freiheit und Konformität. In diesen für das Publikum auch visuell konfrontativen Studien von Gesten und Codes nimmt Bachzetsis den Voyeurismus der Betrachter_innen als Konzept vorweg, indem sie ohne Bühne oder Abstand zu demselben performt.

Die Videoinstallation *Rehearsal (Ongoing)* (Abb. S. 269) ist eine in genaue Abläufe geteilte Choreografie an einem Tisch mit verschiedenen Utensilien. Eine Frau benutzt und verschiebt abwechselnd Dinge auf dem Tisch: Zigarette, Nagellack, Creme, Modemagazin, Polaroid-Kamera, Pillen, Schwamm, Wollknäuel, ausgestanztes Papier. Aus dieser Anordnung auf einem Tisch, der alles vereint – Arbeit, Müssiggang, Reflexion, Haushalt, Körperpflege – entsteht ein möglicher Mikrokosmos weiblicher Existenz. Durch wiederholte, minimale Eingriffe verändert sich das Stillleben langsam, bleibt aber eine in sich geschlossene Welt. Die Ereignisschleife der Szenen, auf zwei nebeneinander justierten Bildschirmen verdoppelt, unterstreicht die Handlung als permanente Probe, als Rehearsal. In der unendlichen Aneinanderreihung von Aneignungsversuchen, die nie zur Vollendung gelangen und die aufgrund ihrer Dopplung nicht in authentische und nachgeahmte Handlungen zu unterscheiden sind, lassen sich Deutungen von individuellen Anpassungsleistungen und sozial normativen Codes herauslesen, die aber auch den Akt von Selbstermächtigung und Brechung dieses deterministischen Kreislaufes offen lassen.

The F-Word

Das F in F-Word steht eigentlich für eine Umschreibung von etwas vulgär Unaussprechlichem, von etwas, das zum Schimpfwort adaptierte und nicht beim Namen genannt werden kann, weil die Sprechenden sich fürchten, sich damit zu ‚beschmutzen'. Feminismus ist zu einem solchen Un-Wort geworden, mit dem man und frau fürchtet, sich als ewig gestrig oder verkrampft zu outen. Dass dem jedoch eine gesellschaftliche Verunglimpfung und Verdrehung von Tatsachen zugrunde liegt, haben meine Argumente eingangs deutlich zu machen versucht. Dass Kunst und Kultur mit ihren Erkundungen von Identitätspolitik und Repräsentationslogiken Anreize schaffen, um Aufmerksamkeiten und Argumente im Sinne einer feministischen Politik zu aktualisieren, soll mit dieser Ausstellungskonstellation unterstrichen werden. Alle vier Künstlerinnen widmen sich in ihren hier besprochenen Arbeiten der Bearbeitung von individuellen Herausforderungen als weiblich konnotiertes Individuum unter ganz bestimmten gesellschaftlichen und normativen Rahmenbedingungen. Michaela Melián zielt auf die Emanzipation eines feministischen Bekenntnisses jenseits von Verdrehungen und Simplifizierungen. Sie tut dies anhand realer Biografien und Überblendungen von zeithistorisch disparaten kulturellen Inhalten. Nevin Aladağ nimmt sich der heterogenen, unhierarchischen Darstellung des Individuums an, um das Thema von Identitätspolitik vor dem Diktum von Stereotypisierung und Determinismus zu reflektieren. Alexandra Bachzetsis erarbeitet sich mit einer choreografischen Anthropologie der Popkultur ein Instrument zur De-Codierung hegemonialer Muster von weiblichen Darstellungen und spiegelt sie in einem Akt performativ-ästhetischer Selbstermächtigung als Klischee der Fremdsteuerung. Und Ariane Andereggen bringt mit ihrer Überzeichnung von Kunstmethodik, Popkultur und ‚befreiter Weiblichkeit' die Affirmation von Differenz in den heutigen Marketinglogiken zu Tage. Die Künstlerinnen untersuchen auf ganz spezifische Weise zeitgenössische Mainstreamkultur, Alltagsrepräsentationen, aber auch das System Kunstgeschichte auf Strukturen hegemonialer Geschlechterverhältnisse. So erarbeiten sie in ihren genreübergreifenden Positionen Strategien kritischer, feministischer Haltungen, die selbstbewusst, aufmerksam, ernsthaft und selbstreflexiv, aber auch ästhetisch, lustvoll, witzig und gelassen daherkommen.

EINE EXTRA-RUNDE NACH-DENKEN, ODER: WIDER EINE VORSCHNELLE FUNKTIONALI-SIERUNG VON KUNST

AN EXTRA ROUND OF THINKING, OR AGAINST FUNCTIONALIS-ING ART TOO QUICKLY

Die Vorbehalte gegenüber dem insbesondere in Kunst und Kultur allgegenwärtigen Topos der produktiven Unentschiedenheit und Bedeutungsoffenheit ist verständlich – insbesondere aus einer politischen Perspektive: Nicht selten dienen ambivalente Strategien dazu, sich einer klaren Stellungnahme zu entziehen, sich also nicht eindeutig und damit mit den entsprechenden Konsequenzen festlegen zu müssen. Während eine solche künstlerische Geste im Fall von Malerei, wie etwa derjenigen von Neo Rauch, verlustfrei als ästhetisches Kokettieren auf intellektuell hohem Niveau – dies suggeriert zumindest die kunstwissenschaftliche Rezeption – bezeichnet werden kann, wirkt der Bedeutungsentzug, dann wenn es um künstlerische Arbeiten mit der Absicht eines politischen Engagements geht, irritierend, mitunter gar störend. So ist es beispielsweise Vertreter_innen einer politisch linken Kulturkritik immer wieder wichtig, auf die sogenannten blinden Flecken in Thomas Hirschhorns partizipativen Arbeiten hinzuweisen. Sie werfen ihm vor, im Austausch mit dem „nicht-exklusiven Publikum" (Hirschhorn) nur scheinbar einen egalitären Raum herzustellen. Stattdessen, so die Skeptiker_innen, würde er seine Position als diskursbestimmender Mittelschichtangehöriger unkritisch reproduzieren, ja vielmehr sogar auf dem Rücken der involvierten Statist_innen seine Karriere ausbauen.[1] Hirschhorns Versuch, die gesellschaftlichen Wirkungsmächte für die Zeitdauer und den Ort seiner Intervention auszuhebeln, wird ihm von seinen Kritiker_innen als lediglich fadenscheiniges Engagement ausgelegt. Dies ist eine Interpretation, die davon ausgeht, dass die gesellschaftlichen Richtkräfte im Feld der Kunst ungebrochen weiterwirken und Künstler_innen diese kaum einzig und alleine mit und durch Kunst ausser Kraft zu setzen vermögen. Ich meine,

1 .... Vgl. dazu etwa Hummer, Bernhard/Kaufmann, Therese/ Minichbauer, Raimund/Raunig, Gerald im Intro zu dem von ihnen herausgegebenen Bericht *republicart practices* zum europäischen Forschungsprojekt *republicart*. Online einzusehen unter: http://republicart.net/art/practices.pdf, 11/12. Darin werfen sie Hirschhorn vor, in seinem 2002 im Rahmen der Documenta11 realisierten Bataille Monument nahezu alle „Problempunkte der Partizipationskunst der 1990er" unkritisch zu reproduzieren. Ähnlich grundlegend ist die Kritik von Michaela Pöschl. Dies.: Hirschhorns Wurst. In: *Kulturrisse. Zeitschrift für radikaldemokratische Kulturpolitik* 4 (2002).

The reservations about the subject of productive indecision and the openness of meaning, especially omnipresent in art and culture, are understandable especially from a political perspective. Often, ambivalent strategies are used to evade taking a clear position, thus avoiding the relevant consequences. While such an artistic gesture in the case of painting, like that of Neo Rauch, can easily be called an aesthetic flirting on an intellectually high level—at least its reception in art history suggests just this—when dealing with artistic works with the intention of a political commitment, the removal of significance can be disconcerting, even disturbing. For example, practitioners of a left-leaning cultural critique have repeatedly found it important to point out the so-called blind spots in Thomas Hirschhorn's participational works. They accuse him of creating an only apparently egalitarian space in exchange with the 'non-exclusive audience' (Hirschhorn). Instead, according to the sceptics, he uncritically reproduces his position as a discourse-defining member of the middle class, even building up his career at the expense of the extras involved.[1] These critics see Hirschhorn's attempt to suspend the social powers for the time and location of his intervention as a merely specious commitment. This is an interpretation that presumes that the social forces in the artistic field have a continuous impact and that artists can hardly suspend them solely with and through art. I would argue that this is precisely the point to localise and discuss the question of whether politics and artistic ambivalence can coincide.

In recent years, quite a few participants in the world of politically invested art have chosen dis-ambiguity, and thus not rarely for primarily activist practices in the field of art.[2] In the following, however, and with a programmatic intention, I would like to turn to those artistic positions that make use of ambivalent strategies to make specific political statements. It is these efforts whose decided interest in ambivalence or blatant ambiguities is not due to current fashionable talk, but represent a serious attempt to wrest a moment of reflexive pause and the potential for expanded room to manoeuvre from overly quickly and rigid positionings—the latent reverse side of dis-ambiguity.

knowbotiq

knowbotiq (Yvonne Wilhelm and Christian Huebler) has been experimenting on the possibilities of the blatant withdrawal from fixation and categorisations for several years in various artistic works. The starting point of this form of action is the realisation that the visibility and transparency demanded in political debates in recent years has turned from an emancipatory promise[3] into its opposite, that is, a 'technically controlled becoming' and 'an administrative availability'.[4] knowbotiq's declared goal is to reveal this transformation, far from harmless, exploring possibilities of where and how omnipresent attempts at control can be escaped. Towards this end, the artist duo developed a figure that has been used in very different contexts, the MacGhillie (fig. p. 279). In terms of material, this is a standard full body camouflage suit, covered with usually

1 ...... For more on this, see Bernhard Hummer, Therese Kaufmann, Raimund Minichbauer, Gerald Raunig, 'Intro', http://republicart.net/art/practices.pdf, p. 11–12. Here, they criticise Hirschhorn for uncritically reproducing 'nearly all problematic aspects of participation art of the 1990s' in his Bataille monument, realised as part of Documenta11. See also Micaela Pöschl's throrough critique: 'Hirschhorns Wurst', *Kulturrisse: Zeitschrift für radikal-demokratische Kulturpolitik* 4 (Vienna, 2002).

2 ..... At the intersection of artistic practice and political resistance, art scholar and curator Marius Babias locates only three options for action: 'Activism as an art form, cooperation between artists and activists, art as an activist manifestation.' See Marius Babias, *Kunst in der Arena der Politik: Subjektproduktion, Kunstpraxis, Transkulturalität* (Cologne, 2008). Oliver Ressler in turn can be seen as an artist who dedicates his entire artistic TUN to political resistance, where a significant portion consists of activism. See www.ressler.at/category/projects.

3 .... In her dissertation *Ambivalenzen der Sichtbarkeit: Über die visuellen Strukturen der Anerkennung* (Bielefeld, 2008), Johanna Schaffer explores deconstructing the political topos that visibility leads automatically to mere recognition, using examples from the political and artistic field.

4 .... knowbotiq quotes an unpublished text with the title 'Nicht Ereignishaft, Undurchschaubar, datenlos. Innerlichkeit des Gesellschaftlichen' (February 2012).

es ist just an dieser Stelle, wo die Frage danach, ob Politik und künstlerische Ambivalenz sich vertragen, zu lokalisieren und entsprechend zu diskutieren ist.

Nicht wenige Akteur_innen einer politisch engagierten Kunstszene haben sich in den letzten Jahren angesichts dieser Ausgangslage für die Eindeutigkeit und darin nicht selten hauptsächlich für aktivistische Praktiken im Feld der Kunst entschieden.[2] Ich will mich aber im Folgenden und in durchaus programmatischer Absicht denjenigen künstlerischen Positionen zuwenden, die sich gerade ambivalenter Strategien bedienen, um damit spezifische politische Aussagen zu machen. Es sind dies Bestrebungen, deren dezidiertes Interesse an Ambivalenzen oder offensiven Vieldeutigkeiten nicht dem allseits wahrnehmbaren modischen Reden darüber geschuldet ist, sondern einen ernsthaften Versuch darstellen, voreiligen und starren Positionierungen – dies die late nt mitschwingende Kehrseite der Eindeutigkeit – einen Moment des reflexiven Innehaltens abzuringen und Potentiale eines erweiterten Handlungsspielraums auszutesten.

Z.B. knowbotiq

knowbotiq (Yvonne Wilhelm und Christian Huebler) experimentieren bereits seit mehreren Jahren entlang unterschiedlicher künstlerischer Arbeiten zu Möglichkeiten des offensiven Entzuges von Festlegungen und Kategorisierung. Ausgangspunkt dieser Form des Agierens ist die Feststellung, dass die gerade auch in politischen Debatten eingeforderte Sichtbarkeit und Transparenz sich in den letzten Jahren von einem emanzipatori-

schen Versprechen[3] in ihr Gegenteil, nämlich in ein „technisch gesteuertes Werden" und „eine administrative Verfügbarkeit"[4] verwandelt hat. Diesen durchaus nicht harmlosen Wandel offenzulegen und Möglichkeiten auszutesten wo und wie den allgegenwärtigen Kontrollversuchen entkommen werden kann, ist erklärtes Ziel des Schaffens von knowbotiq. Dazu entwickelte das Künstler_innenduo u.a. eine seit 2009 in sehr verschiedenen Kontexten eingesetzte Figur, den MacGhillie (Abb. S. 279). Materiell gesehen handelt es sich dabei um einen handelsüblichen Tarnanzug, ganzkörperlich übersät mit meist gräulichen und herunterhängenden Fetzen, die aus der Figur einen schwierig einzuordnenden Typus machen. Mit der Bezeichnung „just a void" titulieren knowbotiq diesen Umstand in der Schilderung des MacGhillie programmatisch als Leerstelle,[5] die Weise wie sie ihn in der Öffentlichkeit auftreten und agieren lassen, testet denn auch aus, wie viel „Opakheit"[6] in dem scheinbar demokratischen Raum zugelassen ist. So wird er einmal als Utensil für einen getarnten Spaziergang auf Bestellung für jedermann_frau eingesetzt, während ein anderes Mal eine ganze Truppe von MacGhillies sich am Äusseren und schliesslich auch im Inneren der Grossbank UBS als Ganzkörper-Wischmob zu betätigen beginnt. knowbotiq sprechen von diesen Interventionen als von semi-fiktiven Testfällen, semi-fiktiv deshalb, weil sie einerseits zwar innerhalb einer Alltagsrealität stattfinden, dabei aber jeweils nur für den kurzen Moment der Aufführung eine spezifische Realität herstellen und danach nur mehr in deren Nacherzählung existieren.

2......... In der Gemengelage von künstlerischen Praxen und politischem Widerstand ortet etwa der Kunstwissenschaftler und Kurator Marius Babias einzig drei Optionen des Handelns: „Aktivismus als Kunstform; Kooperationen zwischen KünstlerInnen und AktivistInnen; Kunst als aktivistische Manifestation." Vgl. Marius Babias: *Kunst in der Arena der Politik*, 2008. Oliver Ressler wiederum kann als Künstler bezeichnet werden, der sein gesamtes künstlerisches Tun dem politischen Widerstand widmet, worin ein beachtlicher Teil aktivistische Betätigungen sind. Vgl. www.ressler.at/category/projects.

3................. Die Kulturwissenschaftlerin Johanna Schaffer hat in ihrer Dissertation *Ambivalenzen der Sichtbarkeit. Über die visuellen Strukturen der Anerkennung* (Bielefeld 2008) den politischen Topos, dass Sichtbarkeit automatisch zu mehr Anerkennung führt, an Beispielen aus dem politischen und künstlerischen Feld dekonstruiert.

4................. Zitiert nach: nicht ereignishaft, undurchschaubar, datenlos. Innerlichkeiten des Gesellschaftlichen unter post-medialen Konditionen, Text von knowbotiq, März 2012, einzusehen unter: http://krcf.org/krcf.org/?page_id=220.

5..................... Vgl. http://krcf.org/krcf.org/?p=249.

6........... *Opaque Presence. Manual of Latent Invisibilities* ist der Titel der jüngsten Publikation von knowbotic research (nebst Wilhelm und Huebler gehört zu dieser Konstellation auch Alexander Tuchaček) in Zusammenarbeit mit Andreas Broeckmann. Zürich 2010.

knowbotiq: *MacGhillie – just a void* (ongoing)

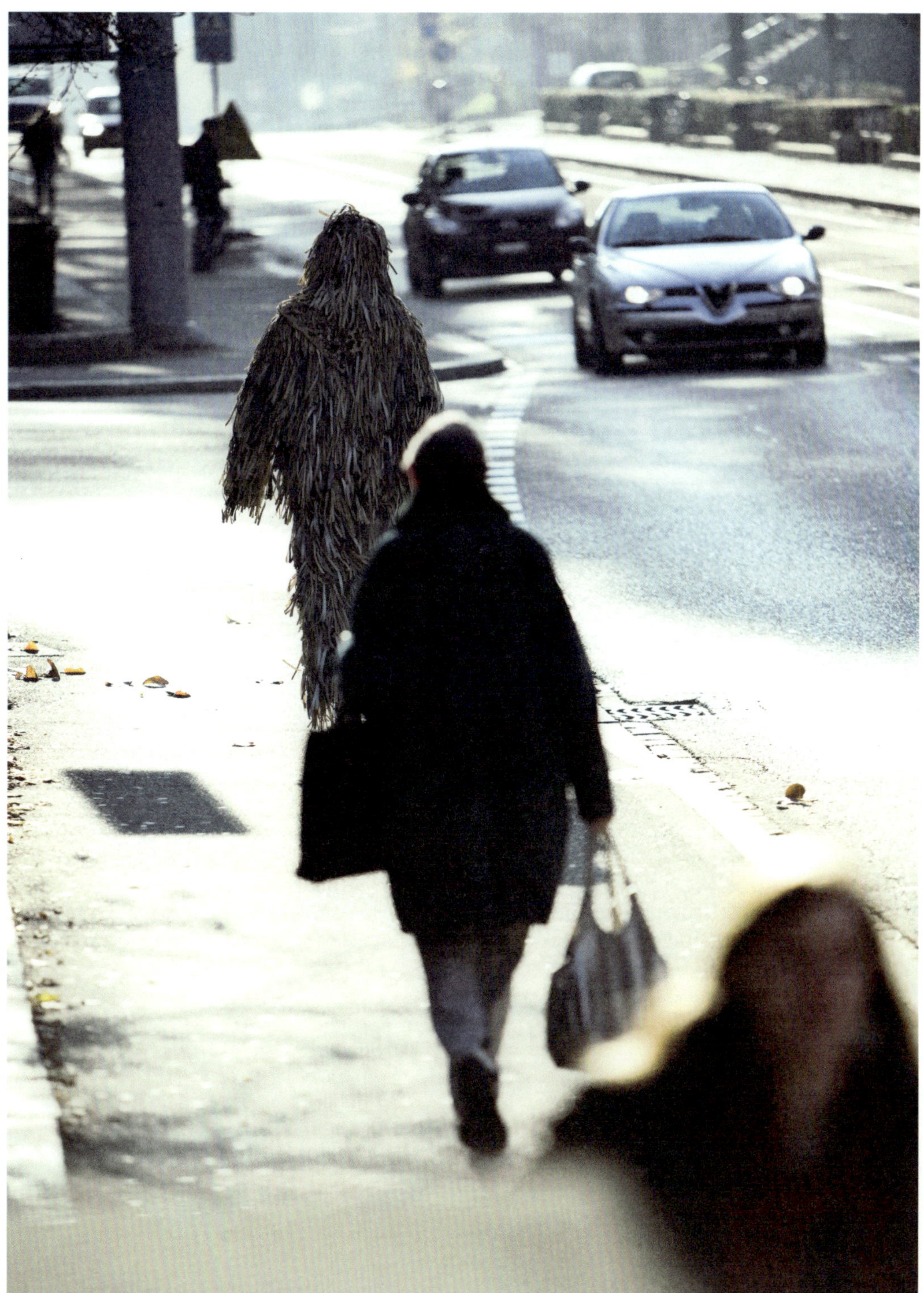

Z.B. Uriel Orlow

Uriel Orlow untersucht in zahlreichen seiner Arbeiten, wie Erinnerung durch die Formen der Erzählung zu Geschichte verarbeitet und diese entsprechend repräsentiert und wirksam wird. In der Videoarbeit *Remnants of the Future* (vgl. S. 104) etwa filmte Orlow in langsamen und mitunter irritierend schönen Aufnahmen die lediglich halbfertig gebaute grosse Wohnsiedlung Mush am Rande der armenischen Stadt Gyumri. Nach der Öffnung der Sowjetunion, wenige Jahre nach Beginn des Baus, wurden die Arbeiten an dieser modernistischen Architekturutopie gestoppt. Heute leben in diesen Ruinen allem voran Tiere und lediglich vereinzelt auch Menschen, die sich ihren Lebensunterhalt mit dem Recyceln von Bauschutt verdienen. Orlows Video arbeitet mit präzisen Mitteln die dieser Konstellation inhärenten Paradoxien heraus: Das Leben in der einstigen Modellarchitektur ist zum Überleben geworden – und dies wegen einer sozialen und politischen Revolution, die die Menschen eigentlich der Freiheit hätte zuführen sollen. Dass der Künstler zur Schilderung dieser Reihe von gescheiterten gesellschaftlichen Entwürfen einen Reigen von betörend schönen Gesamt- und Detailansichten zusammenstellt, schält nicht nur das aktuelle Potential dieser Stätte hervor, sondern verweist ebenso auf die einst auf sie zugeschnittene Projektion einer schönen neuen Welt.

Testfelder, Möglichkeits- und Reflexionsräume – Potentiale der Kunst jenseits utopischer Projektionen

Trotz sehr unterschiedlicher Themen und Vorgehen zeigen künstlerische Positionen wie knowbotiq und Uriel Orlow ernsthafte und ernstzunehmende Versuche, ein politisches Engagement in Absetzung von festgefahrenen Kategorisierungenm zu formulieren. Das Feld der Kunst – und darin im Besonderen Institutionen wie etwa die Shedhalle – bieten ihnen einen Ort potentieller Handlungsspielräume, innerhalb dem ebendiese Kategorisierungen – dazu gehören

auch diverse politische Aspekte – einer kritischen Sichtung unterzogen werden können.[7]

Das ist nun beileibe kein neuer Gedanke: Bereits seit der künstlerischen Moderne wird der Topos von der Kunst als Ort der Reflexion bemüht und ihr damit auch eine neue Rolle im gesellschaftlichen Ganzen zugestanden. Auch in Adornos absolutem Diktum von Kunst als dem ‚Anderen der Gesellschaft' klingt das Potential eines Reflexionsraumes an, innerhalb dem durch Kunst eine unabhängige kritische Sicht auf das gesellschaftliche Gefüge ermöglicht würde. Mit Jacques Rancières Überlegungen zu Politik und den Möglichkeiten ihrer Reformulierung angesichts aktueller Verhältnisse möchte ich aber keinesfalls für Kunst als einem gesellschaftlichen Anderen, Utopischen und damit Gegenüber plädieren. Vielmehr will ich auf den vielschichtigen und komplexen Verschränkungen der Felder Kunst, Politik und Gesellschaft insistieren, innerhalb der Positionen wie knowbotiq und Orlow sich sehr gezielt und präzise bewegen.

In seiner kleinen Schrift *Die Aufteilung des Sinnlichen. Die Politik der Kunst und ihre Paradoxien* (2006) schlägt Rancière vor, die Idee des Politischen neu zu fassen. Er versteht darunter die grundlegende Möglichkeit, als Stimme im gesellschaftlichen Ganzen gehört und wahrgenommen zu werden. Gleichzeitig weist er die anerkannten Sphären und Kategorien des Politischen dezidiert zurück, Apparaturen und verwaltende Strukturen bezeichnet er als ‚Polizei'. Ihm geht es darum, die Vorstellung eines Spielraums des Agierens zu eröffnen, innerhalb dem die Polizei nicht bereits reglementierend wirksam ist.

Ich meine, dass Arbeiten wie diejenigen von knowbotiq oder Uriel Orlow just in der grundsätzlichen Weise, wie dies Rancière skizziert, an den Möglichkeiten von politisch relevanter Sicht- und Hörbarkeit arbeiten. Beide Positionen

---

7 .... Selbstverständlich ist die Kunst in keinster Weise der einzige Ort oder die einzige Handlungsmöglichkeit, innerhalb der diese kritische Reflexion unternommen werden kann. Kunst ist allerdings insofern ein privilegierter Ort solcher Auseinandersetzungen, als ihre gesellschaftliche Funktion und die ihr gesetzlich zuerkannte Freiheit ihr tatsächlich einen relativ grossen Handlungsspielraum zubilligt.

greyish hanging shreds that make the figure into a type that is difficult to classify. knowbotiq uses the phrase 'just a void' to refer to this state of affairs in their description of MacGhillie,[5] that way in which they allow him to appear in public and act, testing how much 'opacity'[6] is allowed in the apparently democratic space. In one case, it is used as a utensil for a camouflaged walk that can be ordered by anybody, while in another case a whole group of MacGhillies become active outside and ultimately inside the major bank UBS as a whole body 'wiping mob'. knowbotiq refers to these interventions as semi-fictional test cases: semi-fictional because they take place within an everyday reality, but create a specific reality only for the brief moment of the performance and then exist solely in their reporting.

Uriel Orlow

In numerous works Uriel Orlow explores how memory is processed and represented through forms of narrative as history—and becomes effective accordingly. In the video work *Remnants of the Future* (fig. p. 104), Orlow filmed in slow and disturbingly beautiful shots the only half-completed housing complex Mush on the outskirts of the Armenian city of Gyumri. After the fall of the Soviet Union a few years after construction was begun, work on this modernist architectural utopia was stopped. Today, the ruins are inhabited primarily by animals and a few people who earn a living from recycling the construction materials. Orlow's video uses precise means to show the paradoxes inherent in this constellation. Life in the former model architecture has become a question of survival, and all this due to a social and political revolution that was supposed to provide people with freedom. That the artist assembles a collection of enchantingly beautiful views—both large scale and details—to describe a series of failed social models, exposes

not only the current potential of these locations, but also refers to the projection of a beautiful new world once tailored to match.

Test Fields, Spaces of Possibility, and Reflection: Potentials of Art Beyond Utopian Projections

Despite very different subjects and approaches, artistic positions like those of knowbotiq and Uriel Orlow illustrate serious attempts—or attempts that should be taken seriously—to formulate political commitment while rejecting fixed categorisations. The field of art, and especially institutions like Shedhalle, offer them potential room to manoeuvre, within which these very categorisations—including various political aspects—can be subjected to critical inspection.[7]

This is naturally nothing new: ever since artistic modernism, the topos of art as a site of reflection has been revisited over and over, thus providing it a new role in the social whole. Adorno's absolute dictum of art as society's other also alludes to the potential of a space of reflection within which art makes possible autonomous critical views of the social configuration. With Jacques Rancière's considerations on politics and the possibilities of its reformulation in light of current relations, I would not like to argue for art as a social other, utopian and thus as something alongside society. Rather, I want to insist on the multilayered and complex intersections of the fields of art, politics and society, within which the positions like knowbotiq and Orlow move in a very targeted and precise fashion.

In his book *The Politics of Aesthetics*, Rancière proposes reconceptualising the idea of the political. He understands the political as the foundational possibility of being heard as a voice in the social whole. At the same time, he

---

5 .... See http://krcf.org/krcf.org/?p=249.

6 ... See the most recent publication, knowbotiq, *Opaque Presence: Manual of Latent Invisibilities* (Zurich, 2010). This constellation includes not only Wilhelm and Huebler but also Alexander Tuchaček in collaboration with Andreas Broeckmann.

7 .... Naturally, art is by no means the only site or the only possibility of action within which this critical reflection can be undertaken. But art is a privileged site of such engagements only to that extent that its social function and its legally recognised freedom actually grants it a relatively large space of action.

vermeiden es aber zugleich, utopische Entwürfe (Kunst verändert die Welt) zu lancieren, oder den gesellschaftlich bereits gesetzten Kategorien (Kunst als lediglich spezifischer Ausdruck bestehender) zuzudienen. Der Ort ihrer künstlerischen Interventionen spielt strategisch und gekonnt mit der Zurückweisung solcher Erwartungen, um sich dadurch einen Raum und damit Themen, Fragen und Positionen zu erobern, die einen kleinen Moment lang frei von Interpretation und definitorischem Zugriff sind. Damit eröffnen sie einen produktiven Raum, der – das zeigen die Beispiele anschaulich – in keinster Weise losgelöst ist von gesellschaftlicher Realität, vielmehr ebenso die scheinbar gesetzten Leitplanken politischen Agierens in Kunst und Gesellschaft einer kritischen Sichtung unterziehen. Und die gesellschaftlichen Realitäten scheinen mir heute auf eine Weise komplex organisiert, dass es durchaus angebracht scheint, in einer Extrarunde Nachdenken darüber zu reflektieren, welche Richtkräfte adaptiert oder aber zurückgewiesen werden sollen.

decidedly rejects recognised spheres and categories of the political, calling apparatuses and administrative structures within it the 'police'. At issue for him is opening the notion of a playing field of action within which the police is not always already regulating.

I think that work like that of knowbotiq or Uriel Orlow intervenes in the possibilities of a politically relevant visibility and audibility in the very fundamental way that Rancière sketches. Both positions avoid proposing utopian models (art changes the world) or serving the socially already set categories (art merely a specific expression of the existent). The site of their artistic interventions plays strategically and ably with the rejection of such expectations, thus capturing a space and with it issues, questions and positions that remain free of interpretation and definitional access for just a moment. In so doing, they open a productive space that, as the examples illustrate, are by no means divorced from social reality. Rather, the apparently fixed guide rails of political action in art and society are subjected to critical inspection. And the social realities seem to me today so complexly organised that it is quite appropriate to think some more about what adjusting forces are to be adapted or rejected.

Translated by Brian Currid

SPRENGENDE EINDEUTIG-KEITEN. DAS EINE ALS SINGULARITÄT IN DER VIELDEUTIGKEIT

Eine erste Version dieses Textes entstand für einen Vortrag anlässlich der Tagung *Radikal ambivalent*, veranstaltet von Rachel Mader und dem Institut für Gegenwartskunst an der Zürcher Hochschule der Künste am 1. und 2. Dezember 2011.

SUBVERSIVE DIS-AMBIGUITIES: THE ONE AS SINGULARITY IN AMBIGUITY

The first version of this article was written as lecture for the conference 'Radikal Ambivalent', held by Rachel Mader and the Institute for Contemporary Art Research at Zurich University of the Arts, 1–2 December 2011.

I.

Auf einem Symposion in Petersburg zum Thema *Politics of the One* hielt Jean-Luc Nancy im April 2010 einen Vortrag mit dem Titel *Plus d'un* mehr als eins, mehr als eines. Nancy wies in einem zunächst etwas kryptischen Satz darauf hin, dass „Mehr als eines" auf die Unterscheidung zwischen zwei grundsätzlich verschiedenen Bedeutungen des Einen verweist. „Mehr als eines", schreibt er, „das heisst in Wahrheit einfach Eines, eine beliebige Ein-heit." Was meint Nancy hier mit der scheinbar paradoxen Wendung, dass „Mehr als eines" eine beliebige Ein-heit sei, eine beliebige Eins-heit, einfach Eins? Er weist implizit auf eine philosophische Unterscheidung hin, bei der es im wahrsten Sinn des Wortes ‚ums Ganze' geht oder eben gerade nicht ums Ganze.

Einerseits Eins-Sein im Sinne einer Ganzheit, einer Identität, einer vollen, einer vollendeten und vollständigen Einheit. Dieser Einheit ist nichts hinzuzufügen. „Mehr als eines" wäre hier ein Widerspruch. Addition ist unmöglich – mögliche Verfahren, die von einer ganzen, vollen, einheitlichen Identität ausgehen, sind die Entzweiung, die Distinktion, die Subtraktion. Andererseits ein ganz anderes Eines im Sinne von Einzigkeit, Einzigartigkeit, einer Singularität. Diese zweite Bedeutung der Ein-heit im Sinne einer Singularität meint Nancy mit seiner Rede vom „Mehr als eines".

Mehr als eins, mehr als zwei, mehrere. Ein Mehr-Sein, ein Mehr-Werden, Ver-mehrung. Keine Mehr-heit, denn es geht nicht um die Herrschaft einer Mehrheit über die Minderheiten, eines ebenso universellen wie leeren Standardmasses über die Akzidentien, einer konstanten Hauptsache über die flüchtigen Nebensachen. Statt der Unterscheidung und Feststellung von Mehrheit und Minderheit geht es um Vielheit, Vermehrung, Addition, Multiplikation, Vervielfältigung.

Nancy betont in seinem Vortrag gerade den Unterschied zwischen Vervielfältigung und Distinktion: „Die Pluralität der Vielen ‚Einen' eröffnet zugleich die Frage nach ihrem Wesen: ist sie Addition, Multiplikation oder ist sie Wohlunterschiedenheit, Unähnlichkeit?" In meine Sprache übersetzt geht die Frage so: Stehen die Vielen als Singularitäten in Beziehung und Austausch mit einem Masse-Einen, einer Multitudo, einer molekularen Mannigfaltigkeit – oder beugen sie sich als identitäre Differenzen einem All-Einen, einer Identität, einer universellen Einheit? Und nochmal ein längeres Stück Nancy:

„Wenn die Pluralität Addition oder Multiplikation bedeutet, kann ‚mehr als eines' sich unbegrenzt ausdehnen, und zwar als die Reihe der Zahlen, die Aneinanderreihung aller möglicher Auf-zählungen [...]. Ihr Prinzip ist die Auf-zählung, die Viel-zahl: Mehr als eines, das bedeutet nicht einfach mehrere, einige, etliche, sondern Viele. Oder genauer: Es gibt nie Mehrere, ohne dass Viele am Horizont sind. Vieles, die Vielheit, die Multitude, das ist die Multiplikation der Einsen, die nicht auf die Rechtsprechung des einen Einen zurück-geführt werden kann, schlichtweg weil es keine Rechtsprechung und kein Eines mit grossem E gibt, sondern nur die Auf-zählungen der Einsen. Es ist die Auf-zählung, die das Prinzip der Menge ist, das Zahlreiche, dessen Zahl nicht aufhört zu wachsen. Die Addition verlängert allzeit weiter die unbegrenzte Summe, die niemals selbst eine Einheit sein wird."[1]

Das Mehr verweist auf den Horizont des Vielen. Mehr als eines bedeutet immer auch mehr als zwei, mehr als mehrere. Es bedeutet eine Vielzahl, eine Ver-Mehrung des Zahlreichen, eine Verviel-fältigung, es bedeutet eine Verkettung der Einsen, eine spezifische Verkettung, die diese Einsen nicht zu beherrschen oder gar aufzuheben sucht, die das Singuläre nicht unter das Kommando eines ganzen, vollen, einen Einen stellt.

II. „Sie repräsentieren uns nicht!"

Mehrdeutigkeit, Ambiguität, Ambivalenz sind spätestens mit dem 20. Jahrhundert ubiquitär geworden, das stellt Verena Krieger in der Einleitung des von ihr gemeinsam mit Rachel Mader herausgegebenen Bands *Ambiguität in der Kunst* klar.[2] Diese Allörtlichkeit gilt nun nicht nur für die Kunst, sondern für sehr verschie-dene Diskurse, doch – und das ist für mich Ausschlag gebend – unter je unterschiedlichen Vorzeichen. Deswegen möchte ich im Weiteren auch die zuvor angedeutete philosophische Problematik auf zwei verschiedene soziale Felder – jenes des Aktivismus und jenes der Kunst – beziehen, die unterschiedliche, ja sogar gegenläufige Auslegungen des Verhältnisses von Mehr- und Eindeutigkeit, des Vielen und des Einen nahelegen.

Mein erstes Beispiel stammt aus dem Bereich der sozialen Bewegungen. Hier hat sich, zunächst mit 1968, dann in den 1990er Jahren im zapatis-tischen Umfeld, schliesslich verstärkt in den 2000er Jahren in der Antiglobalisierungsbewegung, den Social Fora, queer-feministischen Aktivismen und der Euromayday-Bewegung der Prekären eine Vielzahl an Praxen gegen die Vereinheitl-ichung der Kämpfe, gegen die Repräsentation durch Staatsapparate wie Parteien und Gewerk-schaften, gegen die Unterwerfung unter identitäre Positionen entwickelt. In der Auseinanderset-zung und Verkettung der sozialen Maschinen mit den foucaultianischen und deleuzianischen Strömen der 1970er Jahre, später mit neuen feministischen Theorien um und nach Judith Butler, dann mit der populären Verknüpfung von Marxismus und Poststrukturalismus in den Bestsellern von Antonio Negri und Michael Hardt, fanden auch in den sozialen Bewegungen Molekularität, Vieldeutigkeit und Vielheit ihren Niederschlag.

Gegen diese Tendenzen gibt es allerdings in den letzten Jahren wieder identitären Gegenwind. Das eine Eine kehrt zurück und mit ihm auch die Rechtsprechung des Einen. Den molekularen Kämpfen, Bewegungen und Diskursen wird – in wiederkehrender Simplifizierung – Kulturali-sierung, antimaterialistische Haltung und Entpolitisierung vorgeworfen: Antideutsche erproben eine antifaschistische, negative

---

1 .... Nancy, Jean-Luc: Plus d'un. Vortrag im Rahmen der Konferenz *Politics of the One*, Smolny Institute of Liberal Arts and Sciences. Petersburg, 8.–10. April 2010.

2 .... Krieger, Verena/Mader, Rachel (Hg.): *Ambiguität in der Kunst: Typen und Funktionen eines ästhetischen Paradigmas*. Köln/Weimar/ Wien 2010.

I.

At the 'Politics of the One' conference held in St. Petersburg in April 2010, Jean-Luc Nancy presented a talk entitled 'Plus d'un', or 'More Than One'. In a statement that initially seems rather cryptic, Nancy argued that 'more than one' refers to the difference between fundamentally different meanings of the one. 'More than one', he writes, 'in truth, it simply means "one", any given unit.' What does Nancy mean by this apparently paradoxical turn of phrase that 'more than one' is 'any given unit', any given one-ness, simply one? He is implicitly referring to a philosophical distinction whereby the whole is at issue—or perhaps precisely not the whole.

On the one hand, being one in the sense of a wholeness, an identity, a fullness, a complete and perfect unity: nothing can be added to this unity. 'More than one' would here be a contradiction. Addition is impossible, possible techniques that presuppose a whole, full, unified identity are division, distinction, sub-traction.
At the same time, a very different one in the sense of particularity, uniqueness, singularity: The second meaning of oneness in the sense of a singularity is what Nancy is referring to when he speaks of 'more than one'.

More than one, more than two, several; being more, becoming more, multiplication; not a majority, for it is not about the domination of a majority over minorities, a universal as well as standard measure over the accidentals, a constant central issue over fleeting coinci-dences. Instead of distinguishing and establish-ing a majority and a minority, at issue is multiplicity, multiplication, addition.

In his lecture, Nancy emphasised the distinction between multiplication and distinction. 'But the plurality of "ones" opens straight away the question of its nature: is it addition, multiplica-tion or else distinction, dissimilarity?' Translated into my own terms, the question is: Do the many as singularities stand in a relationship and

exchange with a mass-one, a multitude, a molecular manifoldness—or do they subject themselves as identitarian differences to an all-one, an identity, a universal unity? To quote Nancy more extensively:

'If plurality results from addition or multipli-cation, "more than one" may extend indefinitely like the series of numbers, of all possible numerations … The principle is that of numera-tion or numerality: more than one, which is to say not only some ones but also many. More precisely, there are never "some ones" without there having "many" at the horizon. Many, the multitude, i.e., the multiplication of the ones that are not brought back to the jurisdiction of a One, simply because there is neither a jurisdiction nor a "One" with a capital, but only the enumeration of "ones". Enumeration is the principle of the crowd, the numerous, the number of which continually increases. Addition brings always further the indefinite sum that will never make up a unity.'[1]

The more refers to the horizon of the many. Being more than one always already means more than two, more than several. It indicates a plurality, a multi-plication of the numerous, it signifies a concatenation of ones, a specific concatenation that does not seek to dominate or even to sublate them, that does not place the singular under the command of a whole, a fullness, a one One.

II. 'They Don't Represent Us!'

By the twentieth century, at the latest, ambi-guity and ambivalence had become ubiquitous: Verena Krieger makes this point in her introduc-tion to *Ambiguität in der Kunst,* a collection of essays she co-edited with Rachel Mader. This ubiquity is not only true of art, but of many discourses, but nonetheless—and I think this is decisive—it takes on a different valence in various realms. In the following, I would like

1 .. Jean-Luc Nancy, 'Plus d'un', lecture at the conference 'Politics of the One', Smolny Institute of Liberal Arts and Sciences, St. Petersburg, 8–10 April 2010.

to relate the philosophical problematic discussed above to two different social realms—that of activism and that of art—suggesting different, even contrary interpretations of the relationship between ambiguity and disambiguity, the many and the one.

My first example comes from the realm of social movements. Here—at first in 1968, then in the 1990s around the Zapatist movement, and finally increasingly in the first decade of the new century with the anti-globalisation movement, the social fora, queer-feminist activisms, and the Euro Mayday movement of the precarious—multiple practices have developed against the unification of struggles, against representation by state apparatuses such as parties and unions, against subjection under identitarian positions. In the conflict and concatenation of social machines with the Foucauldian and Deleuzian currents of the 1970s, later with new feminist theories around and after Judith Butler, then with popular linkage of Marxism and post-structuralism in the international bestsellers by Antonio Negri and Michael Hardt, molecularity, ambiguousness and multitude found their expression in the social movements as well. But counter to trends, in recent years there has been an identitarian opposing wind. The one One is returning, and with it, a jurisdiction of the one. The molecular struggles, movements and discourses are—in a returning simplification—accused of culturalisation, an anti-materialist attitude and depoliticisation: the Anti-Germans try out an anti-fascist, negative identity policy, feminist identitarianisms surface against the queer movement, German-speaking representatives of critical-whiteness studies tend towards an anti-racist identitarianism.

I am rather sceptical of those in the art context who exercise a fundamental critique of political activisms, who undertake aesthetic critique of political posters at art history conferences instead of intervening at the activist meetings and work groups in the process of aesthetic political production. It is partially for this reason that my example is explicitly not intended as a critique of identitarianism, but as an affirmation of a renewed movement against disam-

biguation, identity politics and the domination of the one One.

Radical inclusion and representational critique are two outstanding components of the new occupy movements, especially the Spanish 15-M movement—founded around the demonstrations on May 15, 2011—and the Occupy movement since September 2011: 'No nos representan!', 'They don't represent us!', is one of the most important slogans of the movements. This not only means that 'they', the politicians, are doing something wrong or that they are the wrong politicians, but rather something more fundamental: that the politics of representative democracy do not work or not longer function, that its hegemonic model of organic representation is necessarily based on the logic of the one One, the identity. I would like to discuss something from the recent past in more detail, for in my view the specific genealogy of the occupations of 2011 can be directly linked to the university occupations from 2008 and 2009.

Not unlike the re-appropriation of the smooth, deterritorialised spaces in the centres of the Arab, Spanish, Israeli and US-American cites, the movement of reterritorialisation that took place in the years prior at the universities of Europe could be seen as similarly para-doxical. Already in the fall of 2008, the Italian onda anomala triggered a wave of protests, strikes, blockades and demonstrations that here and there spilled across the borders as well, emerging in different forms in France, Greece and Spain. In April 2009, however, something new emerged. The protests over education policy turned into an occupy movement. Zagreb students did not just occupy a lecture hall, but took over the entire division of the humanities and the social sciences. It remained under student control for 35 days, and the occupation then expanded to other cities in Croatia. Especially interesting when it came to subsequent developments was the trend toward the broad introduction of representational critique and non-representational practices. What was alluded to in the social movements of the 1990s and 2000s already on a smaller scale

Identitätspolitik, gegen die queere Bewegung entstehen neuerdings wieder feministische Identitarismen, deutschsprachige Vertreter_innen der Critical-Whiteness-Studies tendieren zu einem antirassistischen Identitarismus.

Ich bin einigermassen skeptisch jenen gegenüber, die im Kunstkontext Fundamentalkritik an politischen Aktivismen üben, die ästhetische Kritik an politischen Plakaten auf kunsthistorischen Tagungen unternehmen, statt auf den aktivistischen Versammlungen und Arbeitsgruppen selbst kritisch in die ästhetisch-politische Produktion zu intervenieren. Unter anderem deswegen fungiert mein Beispiel nicht als Kritik an den genannten Identitarismen selbst, sondern als Affirmation einer neuerlichen Gegenbewegung gegen Vereindeutigung, Identitätspolitik und die Herrschaft des einen Einen.

Radikale Inklusion und Repräsentationskritik sind die zwei herausragenden Komponenten der neuen Besetzungsbewegungen, vor allem 15-M seit dem 15. Mai in Spanien und der Occupy-Bewegung seit September 2011. „No nos representan!", „Sie repräsentieren uns nicht!" ist einer der wichtigsten Slogans der Bewegungen, und das meint hier nicht nur, dass sie, die Politiker_innen, etwas falsch machen oder dass sie überhaupt die Falschen sind, sondern noch grundsätzlicher: dass die Politik der repräsentativen Demokratie nicht oder nicht mehr funktioniert, dass ihr hegemoniales Modell der organischen Repräsentation zwangsläufig auf die Logik des einen Einen, der Identität, zurückführt. Ich möchte hier etwas in die jüngere Vergangenheit aus- und zurückgreifen, weil aus meiner Sicht die spezifische Genealogie der Besetzungen von 2011 unter anderem auch eine Linie ziehen lässt zu den Universitätsbesetzungen der Jahre 2008 und 2009.

Ähnlich paradox wie die Wiederaneignung der glatten, deterritorialisierten Räume im Zentrum der arabischen, spanischen, israelischen und US-amerikanischen Städte könnte man jene Bewegung der Reterritorialisierung interpretieren, die sich in den Jahren zuvor an den europäischen Universitäten ereignete. Die italienische onda anomala hatte schon im Herbst 2008 eine nicht abreissen wollende Welle von Protesten, Streiks,

Blockaden und Demonstrationen in Gang gesetzt, die auch da und dort über Italien hinaus schwappte, unter unterschiedlichen Vorzeichen nach Frankreich, Griechenland, Spanien. Im April 2009 entsteht jedoch etwas Neues. Aus den Bildungsprotesten wird eine Besetzungsbewegung. Zagreber Student_innen besetzen nicht einfach einen Hörsaal, sondern übernehmen die gesamte philosophische Fakultät. Sie bleibt 35 Tage unter der Kontrolle der Student_innen, die Besetzung weitet sich in diesen Tagen auch auf andere Städte in Kroatien aus. Besonders interessant für die nachfolgenden Entwicklungen ist die Tendenz zu einer breiten Einführung repräsentationskritischer und nicht-repräsentationistischer Praxen. Das, was sich in den sozialen Bewegungen der 1990er und 2000er schon im Kleinen immer wieder andeutete, dehnt sich nun aus und wird zentraler Fokus von Sozialität und Organisation.

In Zagreb kann man das zunächst vor allem an der Verfassung der plenaren Versammlungen erkennen. Das Plenum ist grundsätzlich offen, auch für Menschen, die nicht Studierende oder Angestellte der Fakultät sind, und es ist der einzige Ort, an dem Entscheidungen getroffen werden. Das Plenum ist selbst weder Territorium noch Gemeinschaft, sondern eine temporäre Versammlung, die nur besteht, solange die Versammlung währt. Es gibt dementsprechend keine Mitglieder, sondern nur den Akt des Versammelns, Diskutierens und Beschliessens, ohne Identifizierung und organische Repräsentation.

Der andere Komplex der Repräsentationskritik der Zagreber Besetzung besteht in der Medienstrategie der Besetzer_innen. Ganz bewusst umgehen sie die mediale Falle der Identifizierung und Instrumentalisierung als junge, naive und politisch etwas verwirrte Protestbewegung. Üblicherweise wird dieses Bild von den Mainstream-Medien routinemässig mit immergleichen Statements eingeführt, in den ersten Wochen durchaus affirmativ („Die jungen Leute sollen ruhig mal protestieren!"), mit „menschlichen" Features von Protagonist_innen garniert, um dann nach einiger Zeit – auch nach den immer gleichen Mustern – in das Gegenteil umzukippen: Die Besetzer_innen seien „verantwortungslos", weil keine gleichbleibenden Gesichter und Namen sie vertreten, „planlos", weil sie keine konkreten Forderungen präsentieren, und schliesslich am Ende „gewaltbereit".

Die Zagreber Besetzer_innen unterlaufen diese massenmediale Logik, indem sie ihre Repräsentation selbst bestimmen; vor allem mit den Mitteln der ‚Entpersonalisierung' und der permanenten Rotation der Pressesprecher_innen, die prinzipiell nur einmal auftreten dürfen. Die genaue Artikulation der Bewegung wird vor allem durch das tägliche Verfassen von schriftlichen Presseerklärungen ermöglicht, die Darstellung der Ziele der Besetzung möglichst unter Kontrolle des Kollektivs gehalten.

Während die Zagreber Student_innen ihre Fakultät besetzen, veranstaltet an der Wiener Kunstakademie ein vorerst kleines Häuflein Studierender und Assistent_innen Diskussionen mit Mitgliedern der transnationalen universitätskritischen Plattform edu-factory und kleinere Aktionen gegen die bevorstehende Einführung der Bologna-Reform. Im Oktober 2009, vier Monate nach dem Ende der Zagreber Besetzung, wird zuerst die Aula der Wiener Akademie der bildenden Künste besetzt, zwei Tage später dann der grösste Hörsaal Österreichs, das Audimax an der Wiener Universität. Diese Besetzung wird zwei Monate andauern, so lang wie noch nie in Österreich. Unter dem Slogan #unibrennt gibt es selbstorganisierte Bildung, Essen, Wohnen, Schlafen in der besetzten Universität. Nach fünf Tagen weitet sich die Besetzungsbewegung auf andere österreichische Städte aus, Anfang November kommt es zu einer unglaublichen Kette von Audimax-Besetzungen in Deutschland, der Schweiz, in anderen europäischen Ländern, aber auch in Kalifornien.

Die Audimax-Besetzer_innen in Wien agieren von Anfang auf der Basis von radikaler Inklusion, Repräsentationskritik und der Forcierung von singulären Stimmen, erklären das Plenum zum zentralen Ort der Entscheidungen und richten eine beträchtliche Menge an Arbeitsgruppen ein. Waren in Zagreb Klarheit und Einheitlichkeit der Rede, Primat des Kollektivs und Anonymität der Aussagen die zentralen

Errungenschaften, so gehen die Audimax-Besetzer_innen einen Schritt weiter. Die singuläre Qualität der vielen Einen von Vielen verbirgt sich nicht hinter Kollektiv und Anonymität, sondern trägt die Vielheit der Positionen innerhalb des Plenums und selbst die Differenzen über Organisationsformen oder Umgangsweisen mit sexistischen und rassistischen Praxen mehr oder weniger deutlich nach aussen. Als exemplarisch für diesen Aspekt der Vervielfältigung von Positionen können die schon in den ersten Wochen der Besetzung geführten Diskussionen über die Notwendigkeit der Einrichtung eines queer-feministischen Raums als Konsequenz von sexuellen Übergriffen gelten.

Und noch ein Unterschied ereignet sich zwischen Frühling und Herbst 2009, zwischen Zagreb und Wien: Während die Zagreber Besetzer_innen nur geringe Teile des Plenums filmen oder fotografieren lassen, gehen die Wiener den Weg der radikalen Veröffentlichung. Der permanente Dauer-Livestream aus dem Audimax ermöglicht es nicht nur Menschen ausserhalb Wiens, die Besetzung und ihre Selbstverwaltung zu verfolgen, sondern auch den lokalen Protagonist_innen dem Aspekt der direkten Kommunikation weitere Schichten hinzuzufügen. Soziale Maschinen und technische Maschinen wirken zusammen, das An-hängen an den elektronischen Gadgets hat diesmal nicht den Charakter der Abhängigkeit, und die technischen Verfahren der Tweets, Livestreams und Social Media schaffen einen gewissen Grad an Unabhängigkeit von den spektakulären Strömen der grossen Mainstream-Medien.

In den aktuellen Kämpfen lässt sich also die Forcierung singulärer Stimmen und ihre Vervielfältigung erkennen. Das Verhältnis von Mehr- und Eindeutigkeit nimmt die Form des Kampfes gegen politische Einheiten, gegen die eindimensionalen Programme der repräsentativen Demokratie, gegen Hauptwidersprüche aller Arten an. Vielheit repräsentiert nicht die Singularitäten. Die Vielheit, das ist die Vervielfältigung der Einsen, „die nicht auf die Rechtsprechung des einen Einen zurückgeführt werden kann".[3] Die Mehrdeutigkeit, um die es hier geht, steht

3... Nancy: Plus d'un.

now expanded and became a central focus of sociality and organisation.

In Zagreb, this could be seen firstly in the constitution of the plenary assemblies themselves. The plenum was fundamentally open, even to those who were not students, staff or members of the faculty, and it was the only location where decisions were made. The plenum was neither a territory nor a community, but a temporary assembly that only existed as long as the assembly lasted. There were accordingly no members, but just the act of assembly, discussion and decision, without any identification or organic representation.

The other complex of representational critique at the Zagreb occupation consisted in the occupiers' media strategy. Quite consciously, they avoided the media trap of being identified and instrumentalised as a protest movement that was young, naïve and politically somewhat confused. This image is routinely introduced in the mainstream media to describe new protest movements: in the first weeks quite affirmatively (the young should protest, after all!) decorated with 'human' features of the activists, and then, after some time—and always according to the same patterns—turning into the opposite: the occupiers are irresponsible, because there are no constant faces or names representing them, they have no plan, because they present no concrete demands, and ultimately they are 'ready for violence'.

The Zagreb occupiers subvert this mass media logic by defining their representation themselves: above all, by way of depersonalisation and permanently rotating spokespersons. As a rule, each spokesperson only appeared before the press once. The exact articulation of the movement was secured primarily by the press releases written daily, making it possible to keep the representation of the occupation's goals under the control of the collective. While the Zagreb students occupied the division of arts and social sciences, at Vienna's Kunstakademie an initially small number of students and young faculty members began holding discussions with members of the transnational

platform Edu-Factory, critical of university education, and smaller actions directed against the imminent implementation of the Bologna reform. In October 2009, four months after the end of the Zagreb occupation, the main lecture hall at Vienna's Akademie der bildenden Künste was occupied, and two days later the largest lecture hall in all of Austria, the Audimax at Universität Wien. This occupation lasted for two months, longer than any other in the history of Austria. Using the slogan #unibrennt, the movement organised its own teaching, meals and secured places to live and sleep at the occupied university. After five days, the occupation movement spread to other Austrian cities, and by early November there was an unbelievable chain of Audimax occupations all across Germany, Switzerland, in other European countries and in California as well.

The Audimax occupiers in Vienna acted from the very start on the basis of radical inclusion, representational critique and promoting individual voices, declaring the plenum to be the central location of decision making and establishing a large number of working groups. While in Zagreb the central achievements were clarity and unity of speech, the primacy of the collective and anonymity of statements, the Audimax occupiers went a step further. The singular quality of the many ones of many was not hidden behind the collective and anonymity, but took the multiplicity of positions within the plenum and even differences over forms of organisation or approaches to sexist or racist practice toward the outside in more or less clear ways. Exemplary for this work of multiplication of positions was the discussion held already during the first weeks about the necessity of the establishment of a queer-feminist space as the result of incidents of sexual harassment.

And yet another difference between the spring and fall of 2009, between Zagreb and Vienna: while the Zagreb occupiers only allowed small parts of the plenum to be filmed or photographed, the Vienna occupiers radically opened themselves up to the public. The permanent live-streams from the Audimax not only allowed people outside Vienna to follow the occupation and its self-administration, but also allowed local protagonists to add additional layers to the aspect of direct communication. Social machines and technological machines operated together: being plugged into electronic devices this time did not have the character of dependence, and the technological procedures of tweets, live streams and social media created a certain degree of independence from the spectacular currents of the mainstream media.

In recent struggles, the promotion of singular voices and their multiplication can be recognised. The relationship between ambiguity and disambiguity takes the form of a struggle against political unities, against the uni-dimensional programmes of representative democracy, against central contradictions of all kinds. The multitude does not represent the singularities. The multitude, that is the multiplication of the ones, that cannot be 'brought back to the jurisdiction of a One'.[2]

The ambivalence intended here is not meant in the sense of a juxtaposition resistant to concatenation or even a hierarchical differentiation, but rather as the always already new attempt to concatenate singularities without an identitarian claim.

III. *What Would It Mean to Win?*

In her introduction to *Ambiguität in der Kunst*, Verena Krieger discusses in extremely clear terms how ambiguity in the field of art has become a quasi-natural, stereotypical, ultimately 'normative' category. Whether as an 'aesthetic paradigm' of modernism, as a 'postmodern metanarrative', ambivalence becomes a 'programme' (30), the 'absolute criterion for judging the actual art character of each work' (36), an 'all-encompassing principle' (41), finally a fetish (48). Alongside earlier positions, above all Theodor W. Adorno's aesthetic theory—with its focus on the artwork as a riddle—as a question mark, is taken as a main point of

reference for the different variants of an ambiguity that is declared to be a norm.[3]

In comparison to the recurrent political attempts at disambiguation or unification that the variety of social movements is repeatedly subject to, in the realm of art the situation is almost the inverse. In the discourse about the bourgeois art world, ambiguity seems to be the norm, and disambiguity seems to be something of a criterion of exclusion. The question mark becomes imperative. With the 'assertion of a tolerance of ambiguity', as Tom Holert (243) describes this tendency in his contribution to *Ambiguität in der Kunst*,[4] Adorno's elitist-authoritarian gesture becomes a hegemonic perspective in the field of art, a normativity, sometimes gently concealed, sometimes aggressive, that for its part causes closure.[5] In an extreme case, this closure leads to denunciatory evaluations of non-ambiguous art practices as 'bad art' or 'non-art'. Particularly when ambiguity and the manifold have become a ubiquitous norm in the art field (and at the same time an object of post-Fordist value creation), it is a good idea to explore the one as a singularity, as a manifold uniqueness that triggers multitude, to reinvent a singularity on the non-foundation of ambiguity, that does not oppose the many as a one, subjecting it, but emerges from it and will collapse into it. Here, several positions from the historical avant-garde would apply, above all the post-revolu-

---

2 .... Ibid.

3 .... Verena Krieger, ' "At War with the Obvious": Kulturen der Ambiguität', *Ambiguität in der Kunst: Typen und Funktionen eines ästhetischen Paradigmas*, eds. Verena Krieger and Rachel Mader, (Vienna, 2010), pp. 13–49.

4 .. Tom Holert, 'Resonanzen, Streifen, Scherenschnitte. Formen und Funktionen von Ambiguität seit 1960', *Ambiguität in der Kunst*, pp. 241–259.

5 ... In recent decades, these closures can also and primarily be seen as components of economic developments. The imperative towards ambiguity takes on a structural analogy to contemporary forms of production. Ambivalence and ambiguity are here by no means to be understood as weapons of the bourgeoisie in the sense of the old and rather static Bourdieuian mechanism of distinction between classes and social strata, but as a variously hierarchised differentiation. In recent years, this complicated analogy has been made clear by queer/feminist positions such as that of Antke Engel and Brigitte Bargetz: If today post-Fordist economics operates as a capitalism of difference, differences of all kinds are substantialised and hierarchised. In this settting, the flows between the singularities, their exchange, their being placed in relation to one another are converted into value.

allerdings nicht im Zeichen einer verkettungs-resistenten Juxtaposition oder gar einer hier-archischen Differenzierung, sondern dient als immer neuer Versuch, die Singularitäten ohne identitäre Anmutung zu verketten.

III. *What would it mean to win?*

Verena Krieger hat in ihrer Einleitung zu *Ambiguität in der Kunst* äusserst klar herausgearbeitet, dass Mehrdeutigkeit im Kunstfeld zur „quasi naturhaften", „stereotypen", schliesslich „normativen" Kategorie geworden ist. Ob als „ästhetisches Paradigma" der Moderne, ob als „postmoderne Metaerzählung", Ambivalenz wird zum „Pro-gramm" (30), zum „absoluten Kriterium für den eigentlichen Kunstcharakter jedes Werks" (36), zum „alles erfassenden Prinzip" (41), schliesslich zum „Fetisch" (48). Neben früheren Positionen wird vor allem Theodor W. Adornos ästhetische Theorie mit ihrem Fokus auf das Kunstwerk als Rätsel, als Fragezeichen zu einem Haupt-referenzpunkt für die verschiedenen Varianten einer zur Norm erhobenen Uneindeutigkeit.[4]

Im Vergleich zu den wiederkehrenden politischen Vereindeutigungs- und Vereinheitlichungsan-mutungen, denen die Vielheit der sozialen Bewegungen immer wieder ausgesetzt ist, ist im Kunstfeld also fast eine inverse Situation vorzufinden. In den Diskursen des bürgerlichen Kunstbetriebs scheint Mehrdeutigkeit die Norm, und Eindeutigkeit so etwas wie ein Ausschlusskri-terium geworden zu sein. Das Fragezeichen wird zum Imperativ. Mit der „Durchsetzung der Ambiguitätstoleranz", wie Tom Holert (243) diese Tendenz in seinem Beitrag für *Ambiguität in der Kunst* bezeichnet,[5] wird der elitär-autoritäre Gestus Adornos zur hegemonialen Perspektive im Kunstfeld, zu einer manchmal sanft verschleier-ten, manchmal aggressiven Normativität, die

ihrerseits Schliessungen verursacht.[6] Im Extrem-fall führt diese Schliessung zu einer denunzieren-den Bewertung von mit Eindeutigkeiten hantierenden Kunstpraxen als ‚schlechte Kunst' oder ‚Nicht-Kunst'.

Gerade wenn Mehrdeutigkeit und Mannigfaltigkeit zur im Kunstfeld ubiquitären Norm (und zugleich zum Objekt postfordistischer Inwertsetzung) werden, tun wir gut daran, das Eine als Singularität, als vielfältige und Vielheit entfachende Einzigkeit zu untersuchen, vor dem Ungrund der Vieldeutig-keit eine Singularität zu erfinden, die sich nicht als Eines der Vielheit entgegenstellt, sie unter-wirft, sondern – wie Kafka das formuliert – „aus ihr entsteht und in sie zurückfallen wird". Hierher würden einige Positionen der historischen Avant-garde passen, vor allem die postrevolutionären Praxen und Theorien von Tretjakov, Arvatov und Eisenstein oder auch das epische Theater und vor allem die Lehrstücke von Bert Brecht. Ich möchte aber zum Abschluss auf ein neueres künstlerisches Beispiel eingehen, eine filmische Zusammenarbeit der australischen Künstlerin Zanny Begg mit dem österreichischen Künstler und Filmemacher Oliver Ressler.

Begg und Ressler haben ihren Film über die Anti-G8-Proteste im deutschen Heiligendamm im Sommer 2007 ziemlich zeitnah publiziert und haben damit auch in die Diskurse der sozialen Bewegung interveniert. Am Ende des Titels ihrer Arbeit steht ein Fragezeichen, wiewohl gar nicht in Adornos Sinn. Der Titel lautet *What would it mean to win?* In der Arbeit findet sich implizit aber auch ein Rufzeichen, ein singulärer Imperativ, eine Eindeutigkeit.

4............ Krieger, Verena: ‚at war with the obvious' – kulturen der ambiguität. In: Krieger/Mader: *Ambiguität in der Kunst*, 13–49.

5............ Holert, Tom: Resonanzen, Streifen, Scherenschnitte. Formen und Funktionen von Ambiguität seit 1960. In: Krieger/Mader: *Ambiguität in der Kunst*, 241–259.

6............ Diese Schliessungen sind in den letzten Jahrzehnten auch und vor allem als Komponente ökonomischer Entwicklungen zu verstehen. Das Mehrdeutigkeitsgebot gewinnt eine strukturelle Analogie zu zeitgenössischen Produktionsformen. Ambivalenz und Mehrdeutigkeit sind hier keinesfalls nur mehr als Waffen der Bourgeoisie im Sinne des alten und recht statischen bourdieuschen Distinktionsmechanismus zwischen Klassen und sozialen Schichten zu verstehen, sondern als vielfach hierarchisierte Differenzierung. In der letzten Zeit hat diese komplizierte Analogie vor allem die queer-feministischen Positionen etwa von Antke Engel und Brigitte Bargetz deutlich gemacht: Wenn heutige postfordistische Ökonomie als Differenzkapitalismus funktioniert, werden Differenzen aller Art substanzialisiert und hierarchisiert. In diesem Setting werden sogar die Flüsse zwischen den Singularitäten, ihr Austausch, die Verhältnissetzungen in Wert gesetzt.

Eine Grundaussage des Films besteht darin, dass ‚Gewinnen' in den Figuren eines einheitlichen revolutionären Subjekts und der Übernahme der Staatsmacht keine grosse Zukunft hat. Vielmehr muss die Vielheit der Aktivist_innen von Heiligendamm, die sich diese Frage nach der Bedeutung des Gewinnens stellt, selbst die Form einer Frage annehmen, die Form einer undefinierten Bewegung, holpernd und stotternd vielleicht, wie die Musik zu den Zeichentrick-Fragmenten in Beggs und Resslers Film, die die Bilder von Aktionen und die theoretischen Kommentare ergänzen. Wie diese fragmentierte, molekulare Vielheit sich jeder Definition und jeder organischen Repräsentation entzieht, macht es auch Sinn, dass Begg und Ressler, statt die spektakulären Riots in Rostock am Beginn des Gipfels zu thematisieren oder die medienträchtigen Greenpeace-Aktionen an den Küsten von Heiligendamm, sofort in die dichten Tiefen der mikropolitischen Gefüge in den Feldern und Camps um den G8-Gipfel eintauchen. Die Bilder und Originaltöne, die die beiden Künstler_innen von den Aktionen und sozialen Organisationsformen um Heiligendamm eingefangen haben, sind poetische Aktualisierungen der Blockaden und der Versuche, die Polizeilinien im weiten Hinterland von Heiligendamm zu durchbrechen, vor allem der Effektivität der ‚Fünffingertaktik' in den weiten Wiesenlandschaften an der Ostsee, jener Strategie der wiederholten Aufteilung grösserer Gruppen beim Kontakt mit Polizeilinien, bis deren Lücken schliesslich zum Durchbruch führten.

Das Rufzeichen, das auf dem Ungrund des Fragezeichens entsteht, erscheint als ereignishafte Affirmation einer neuen politischen Praxis, nicht als rechthaberische Rechtsprechung. Der Film fügt dieser Praxis etwas hinzu. Er ist ein Stück Gegeninformation, und insofern ein Rufzeichen. Er berichtet über eine Praxis, die in der gängigen medialen Berichterstattung nicht vorkommt. Er affirmiert die kleinen Aktionen, die Organisationsformen, die Ästhetik und die Diskurse der Aktivist_innen um Heiligendamm.

Diese Zerstreuungen, Auffaltungen, Vervielfältigungen entsprechen auch der aus dem Zapatismus entliehenen Forderung des Films, dass das Leben nicht jeden Tag denselben Film bedeuten müsse, sondern im Gegenteil jeden Tag einen neuen. Statt die eine Welt des maschinischen Kapitalismus zu affirmieren, aber auch statt sich damit zu bescheiden, dass eine andere Welt möglich sei, geht es darum, viele Welten zu erfinden. Das impliziert zum einen die Vervielfältigung der einen anderen Welt in eine Vielheit anderer Welten, aber zugleich auch die konkrete Aktualisierung der Möglichkeit im Hier und Jetzt, als singuläres Rufzeichen. Hierin liegt auch die Stärke der Arbeit von Begg und Ressler im Vergleich mit anderen Beispielen visueller Repräsentation der Antiglobalisierungsbewegung: Aspekte der Gegeninformation und Gegenpropaganda weiterzutreiben, daneben aber auch mehrere Ebenen der Reflexion einzubauen, die es vermeiden, eine allzu einfache Lösung der Fragen nach dem ‚Wir', nach ‚der Macht', nach der Qualität des Gewinnens vor- und einzuschlagen …

Hier geht es also nicht um eine Verwerfung der Eindeutigkeit zugunsten einer im Kunstfeld forcierten und als Norm fungierenden Vieldeutigkeit, Ambivalenz, Ambiguität, sondern um ereignishaft eindeutige Singularitäten, die vor dem Ungrund der Vielheit ihre Sprengwirkung erzielen. Die Eindeutigkeit, um die es hier geht, steht nicht im Zeichen der Identität und des All-Einen. Sie entsteht als riskante Singularität, die etwas aufs Spiel setzt, der Vielheit etwas hinzufügt. Sie sprengt das All-Eine. Das Rufzeichen ist hier kein moralischer Zeigefinger, sondern ein singulärer Imperativ, eine Anrufung zur Verkettung und Ansteckung, die die vielen Fragezeichen nicht verschluckt, sondern sie aktualisiert. Ein-deutigkeit, Ein-heit nicht als Identität, sondern als Singularität, die mehr als eines ist.

tionary practices and theories of Tretjakov, Arvatov and Eisenstein, but also the epic theatre and above all Bert Brecht's *Lehrstücke*. I would like to conclude with a more recent example, a film collaboration between the Australian artist Zanny Begg and the Austrian artist and film-maker Oliver Ressler. Begg and Ressler first presented their film about the Anti-G8 protests at Germany's Heiligendamm in the summer of 2007 soon after the protests themselves, and in so doing intervened in debates within the social movement itself. The title of their work ends in a question mark, but not in Adorno's sense: *What Would It Mean to Win?* But in the work itself, there's also an implicit exclamation mark, a singular imperative, a disambiguity.

A core statement of the film is that 'winning' in the figure of a unified revolutionary subject and taking over state power has no great future. Instead, the multitude of the activists of Heiligendamm that pose this question of the significance of winning takes the form of a question— the form of an undefined movement, a stumbling and perhaps stuttering—like the music used for the animation fragments in Begg and Ressler's film that complement the actions and the theoretical commentaries. Just as this fragmented, molecular multitude refuses all definition and all organic representation, it also makes sense that Begg and Ressler, instead of exploring the spectacular riots in Rostock at the start of the summit or Greenpeace's actions on the shores of Heiligendamm, immediately immerse themselves in the depths of the micro-political assemblages in the fields and camps around the G8 summit. The images and sounds that both artists captured from the actions and social forms of organisation around Heiligendamm poetically summon the block-ades and the attempts to break though the police lines near Heiligendamm itself, above all the effectiveness of the 'five finger' tactic in the broad fields along the Baltic, the strategy of the repeated division of larger groups upon making contact with police lines, until their gaps ultimately lead to a breakthrough.

The exclamation point that stands against the non-foundation of the question mark appears as the affirmation of a new political practice in the event, not as dogmatic jurisdiction. The film adds something to this practice. It is a piece of counter information, and to that extent an exclamation point. It reports on a practice that did not surface in the media reporting at the time. It affirms the little actions, the organi-sational forms, the aesthetics and the debates among the activists around Heiligendamm.

These distractions, bifurcations, multiplications correspond to the film's demand, borrowed from Zapatism, that life need not mean the same film each day, but rather that each day should be a new film. Instead of affirming the one world of machinic capitalism, but also without just being satisfied that another world is possible, at issue is inventing many different worlds. This implies on the one hand the multiplication of the one other world in a multiplicity of other worlds, but at the same time the concrete actualisation of possibilities in the here and now, as a singular exclamation point. Herein lies the power of Begg and Ressler's work in comparison to other examples of visual representation of the anti-globalisation movement: it furthers aspects of counter-information and counterpropaganda, but also integrates several layers of reflection that avoid suggesting and taking an all too simple solution to questions of the 'we', of 'power', of the nature of winning.

At issue here is not dismissing disambiguity in favour of the ambiguity and ambivalence that is promoted by the art world, but disambiguous singularities with an event character that seek their explosive power against the non-foundation of the multitude. The disambiguity, the clarity at issue here does not promote identity and the all-one. It emerges as a risky singularity that sets something at stake, adding something to the multiplicity. It explodes the all-one. Here, the exclamation point is not a scolding finger, but a singular imperative, a plea for concatenation and contagion that does not devour the many question marks, but actual-ises them. Disambiguity, oneness not as identity, but as a singularity that is more than one.

Translated by Brian Currid

FORMEN DER BI

ROLLE DES/DER KÜNSTLERIN

AUTORIN
INITIATORIN
☐ MODERATORIN
☐ ANIMATORIN
☐ DIKTATORIN
☐ PRODUZENTIN

GRAD DER PUBLIKUMSBETEILIGUNG

MITDENKENDE BETRACHTERIN
☐ ERWEITERTES ENGAGEMENT
☐ ZULIEFERER VON IDEEN GESCHICHTEN
☐ AM PROZESS DIREKT BETEILIGT
☐ "JEDER MENSCH IST EIN KÜNSTLER"

DAS PROJEKT IST EINE KOLLABORATION MIT

☐ KUNST-INSTITUTION
☐ LOKALER BEHÖRDE
☐ KOMMUNALEN ENTWICKLUNGSVORHABEN
☐ KUNST-FERNER INTERESSENGRUPPE
☐ "ALLE KÖNNEN MITMACHEN!"

TEILNEHMERINNEN FINDEN SICH ÜBER

☐ OPEN CALL
☐ MASSENMEDIEN
☐ PERSÖNLICHE EINLADUNG
☐ SOZIALEN DRUCK
☐ ZWANG

DAS PROJEKT FINDET STATT

☐ IM INTERNET
☐ IN DER STADT
☐ IN DER NACHBARSCHAFT
☐ IN EINER SUBKULTUR

TEMPORALITÄT

☐ TEMPORÄR BEFRISTET
☐ SITUATIV
☐ OFFENER ZEITHORIZONT
☐ ZIEL STRUKTURVERÄNDERUNGEN
☐ AUFBAU (ALTERNATIVER) INFRASTRUKT

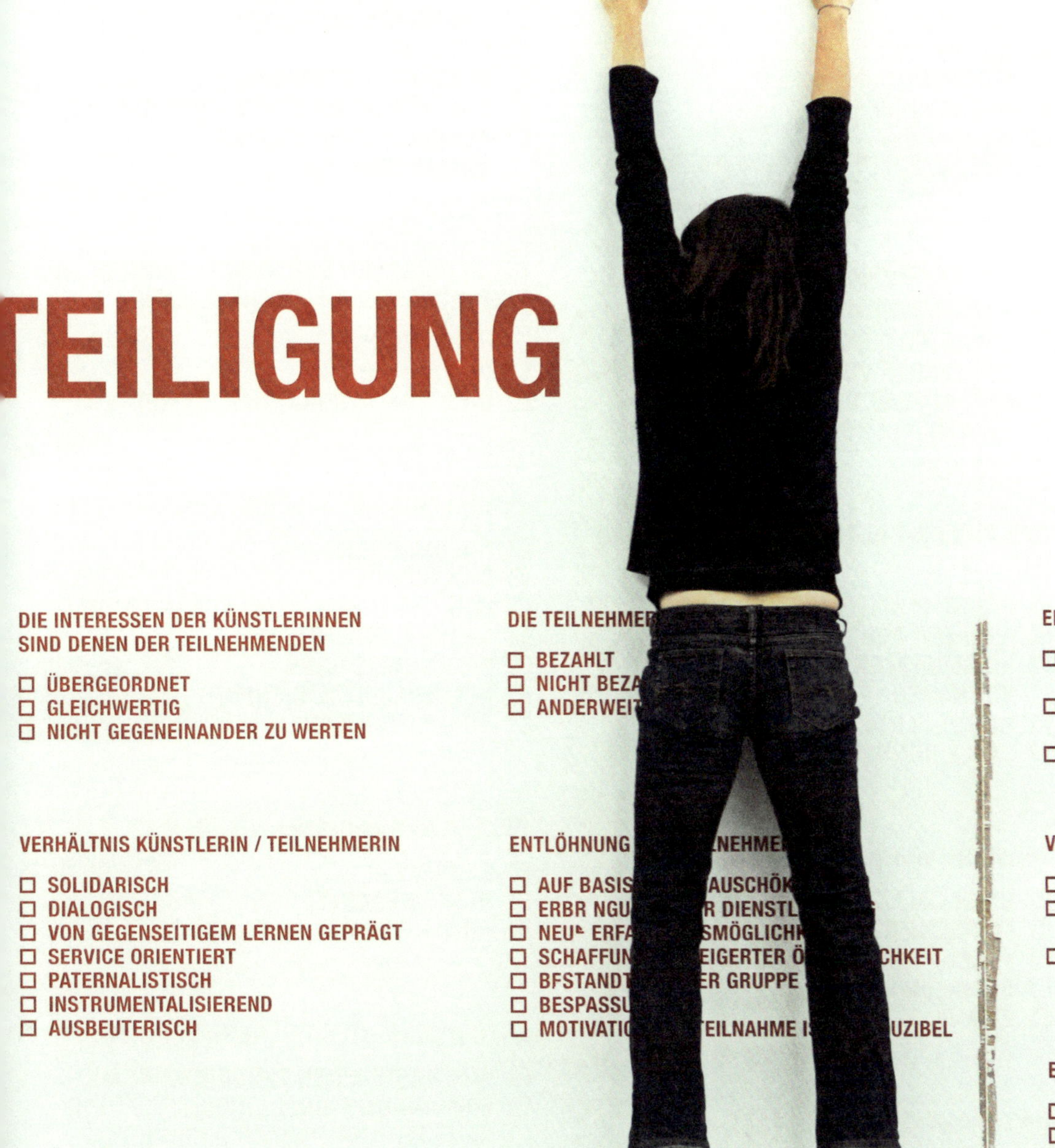
TEILIGUNG

DIE INTERESSEN DER KÜNSTLERINNEN
SIND DENEN DER TEILNEHMENDEN

☐ ÜBERGEORDNET
☐ GLEICHWERTIG
☐ NICHT GEGENEINANDER ZU WERTEN

VERHÄLTNIS KÜNSTLERIN / TEILNEHMERIN

☐ SOLIDARISCH
☐ DIALOGISCH
☐ VON GEGENSEITIGEM LERNEN GEPRÄGT
☐ SERVICE ORIENTIERT
☐ PATERNALISTISCH
☐ INSTRUMENTALISIEREND
☐ AUSBEUTERISCH

DIE TEILNEHMER

☐ BEZAHLT
☐ NICHT BEZA
☐ ANDERWEIT

ENTLÖHNUNG   LNEHME

☐ AUF BASIS   AUSCHÖK
☐ ERBR NGU   R DIENSTL   G
☐ NEU ERFA   SMÖGLICHK
☐ SCHAFFUN   EIGERTER Ö   CHKEIT
☐ BFSTANDT   ER GRUPPE
☐ BESPASSU
☐ MOTIVATIC   TEILNAHME IS   UZIBEL

ENT

☐
☐
☐

VER

☐
☐

☐

ES

☐
☐
☐
☐

ROLLE DES/DER KÜNSTLERIN

- ☐ AUTORIN
- ☐ INITIATORIN
- ☐ MODERATORIN
- ☐ ANIMATORIN
- ☐ DIKTATORIN
- ☐ PRODUZENTIN

GRAD DER PUBLIKUMSBETEILIGUNG

- ☐ MITDENKENDE BETRACHTERIN
- ☐ ERWEITERTES ENGAGEMENT
- ☐ ZULIEFERER VON IDEEN/GESCHICHTEN
- ☐ AM PROZESS DIREKT BETEILIGT
- ☐ „JEDER MENSCH IST EIN KÜNSTLER"

DAS PROJEKT IST EINE KOLLABORATION MIT

- ☐ KUNST-INSTITUTION
- ☐ LOKALER BEHÖRDE
- ☐ KOMMUNALEN ENTWICKLUNGS-VORHABEN
- ☐ KUNST-FERNER INTERESSENGRUPPE
- ☐ „ALLE KÖNNEN MITMACHEN!"

TEILNEHMERINNEN FINDEN SICH ÜBER

- ☐ OPEN CALL
- ☐ MASSENMEDIEN
- ☐ PERSÖNLICHE EINLADUNG
- ☐ SOZIALEN DRUCK
- ☐ ZWANG

DAS PROJEKT FINDET STATT

- ☐ IM INTENET
- ☐ IN DER STADT
- ☐ IN DER NACHBARSCHAFT
- ☐ IN EINER SUBKULTUR

TEMPORALITÄT

- ☐ TEMPORÄR BEFRISTET
- ☐ SITUATIV
- ☐ OFFENER ZEITHORIZONT
- ☐ ZIEL STRUKTURVERÄNDERUNGEN
- ☐ AUFBAU (ALTERNATIVER) INFRASTRUKTUR

DIE INTERESSEN DER KÜNSTLERINNEN SIND DENEN DER TEILNEHMENDEN

- ☐ ÜBERGEORDNET
- ☐ GLEICHWERTIG
- ☐ NICHT GEGENEINANDER ZU WERTEN

VERHÄLTNIS KÜNSTLERIN / TEILNEHMERIN

- ☐ SOLIDARISCH
- ☐ DIALOGISCH
- ☐ VON GEGENSEITIGEM LERNEN GEPRÄGT
- ☐ SERVICE ORIENTIERT
- ☐ PATERNALISTISCH
- ☐ INSTRUMENTALISIEREND
- ☐ AUSBEUTERISCH

DIE TEILNEHMERINNEN WERDEN

- ☐ BEZAHLT
- ☐ NICHT BEZAHLT
- ☐ ANDERWEITIG ENTLÖHNT

ENTLÖHNUNG DER TEILNEHMERINNEN

- ☐ AUF BASIS EINER TAUSCHÖKONOMIE
- ☐ ERBRINGUNG EINER DIENSTLEISTUNG
- ☐ NEUE ERFAHRUNGSMÖGLICHKEITEN
- ☐ SCHAFFUNG GESTEIGERTER ÖFFENTLICHKEIT
- ☐ BESTANDTEIL EINER GRUPPE SEIN
- ☐ BESPASSUNG
- ☐ MOTIVATION ZUR TEILNAHME IST IRREDUZIBEL

ENTSCHEIDUNGEN

- ☐ TEILNEHMERIN AGIERT AUF GLEICHER ENTSCHEIDUNGSEBENE WIE KÜNSTLERIN
- ☐ TEILNEHMERIN KANN DEN PROZESS KOMMENTIEREN UND BEEINFLUSSEN
- ☐ MEINUNG DER TEILNEHMERIN HAT NUR GERINGEN EINFLUSS

VERANTWORTUNG

- ☐ KÜNSTLERIN DEFINIERT DIE SPIELREGELN
- ☐ KÜNSTLERIN IST FÜR DAS ENTSTEHENDE WERK LETZTLICH VERANTWORTLICH
- ☐ TEILNEHMERINNEN SIND EIGENVERANTWORTLICH

ES BESTEHT GEFAHR

- ☐ STIGMATISIERUNG DER TEIL-NEHMERINNEN
- ☐ ÜBERNAHME VON SOZIALARBEIT
- ☐ NORMATIVER GEMEINSCHAFTSBEGRIFF
- ☐ FIXIERUNG EINER BEWEGLICHEN SITUATION
- ☐ NUR SCHEINBARE TEILHABE

PROZESS

- ☐ IST ZIEL ORIENTIERT
- ☐ MIT OFFENEM AUSGANG

DAS AUS DEM PROZESS RESULTIERENDE KUNSTWERK IST

- ☐ DAS EINZIGE KRITERIUM FÜR ERFOLG/MISSERFOLG
- ☐ NUR VON ZWEITRANGIGER BEDEUTUNG
- ☐ IRRELEVANT, NUR PROZESS IST VON BEDEUTUNG
- ☐ ENTSTEHT AUS UND LEITET DIALOGISCHEN PROZESS

DIE MOTIVATION DER KÜNSTLERIN

- ☐ GEGENSEITIGES LERNEN
- ☐ TEILHABE AN LEBENSWIRKLICHKEIT
- ☐ BESTANDTEIL EINER GRUPPE SEIN
- ☐ DIE WELT VERBESSERN
- ☐ ANERKENNUNG
- ☐ "ICH WEISS NICHT"

DAS PROJEKT KATEGORISIERT SICH ALS

- ☐ COMMUNITY ART
- ☐ DIENSTLEISTUNGSKUNST
- ☐ AKTIVISTISCHE KUNST
- ☐ NEW GENRE PUBLIC ART
- ☐ SOZIAL ENGAGIERTE KUNST
- ☐ DIALOGISCHE KUNST

DAS PROJEKT HINTERFRAGT

- ☐ DAS ELITÄRE VON KUNST
- ☐ DIE AUSKLAMMERUNG SOZIALER FRAGEN VON KUNST
- ☐ DER KOMMODIFIZIERUNG VON KUNST
- ☐ DIE PASSIVE ROLLE DES PUBLIKUMS
- ☐ SONSTIGES

DAS ZIEL DES PROJEKTES IST

- ☐ BEDÜRFNISSE DER TEILNEHMERINNEN ZU BEFRIEDIGEN
- ☐ EINE AUSSERGEWÖHNLICHE SITUATION ZU KONSTRUIEREN
- ☐ SOZIALE FRAGEN AUFZUWERFEN
- ☐ SOZIALE VERÄNDERUNGEN HERVORZURUFEN
- ☐ MENSCHEN ZU ERMÄCHTIGEN
- ☐ MARGINALISIERTE GEMEINSCHAFTEN ZU UNTERSTÜTZEN
- ☐ DIE REVOLUTION ZU BEGINNEN

- ☐ ICH NEHME TEIL
- ☐ ICH NEHME NICHT TEIL

TOWARDS TRANSVERSAL INTERSECTIONS

An e-mail exchange between Gluklya (Factory of Found Clothes) and Yvonne Volkart

Yvonne Volkart: *In your ongoing project* Utopian Unemployment Union *(since 2009) you usually assemble different people in subaltern or pre-carious situations, such as unemployed men in Russia for workshop no. 1, or asylum-seekers in Switzerland for workshop no. 4, combined with ballerinas and artists struggling to make a living. I have the impression that a lot is about the idea of learning from each other and sharing experiences and skills. Can you tell me something about your ideas behind and experience with bringing together people with such different cultural, social and gender backgrounds?*

Gluklya: The main idea behind my work is uniting all of those we refer to as 'the weak' in our FFC Manifesto (factoryoffoundclothes.org). By that we mean all of those people who are deprived of their voices by the authorities, who are socially excluded in different ways. Women belong among them, too. We introduce the term 'weak' to emphasize a 'universalist' attitude towards those people. A person of any class can become weak at any moment, which is why I don't think it's appropriate to call them 'poor' or 'oppressed'. The FFC's view of classes is different than that of the Chto Delat.

Obviously, artificially alienating people from one another benefits those in power, so the goal of art is to help them find a common language and join together, becoming stronger in their resistance. Such efforts have been made by many leftists: for example, in Augusto Boal's theatre of the oppressed, attempts were made to unite anti-racist and anti-sexist movements. The more numerous such 'transversal intersections' of different kinds of fighters are, the better.

Yvonne Volkart: *In your projects, you not only coop-erate with different people, but you also try to develop a work of art with them, an artwork that deals with their wishes and hopes, translating their (sometimes traumatic) experiences into*

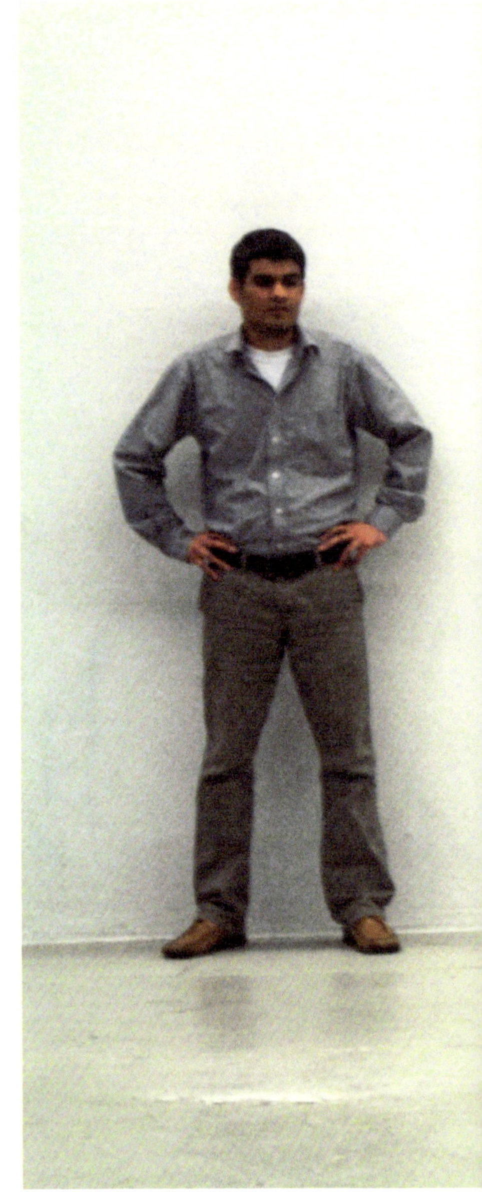

Factory of Found Clothes/Gluklya: *Dumped Dreams (Utopian Unemployment Union N4)*, 2011

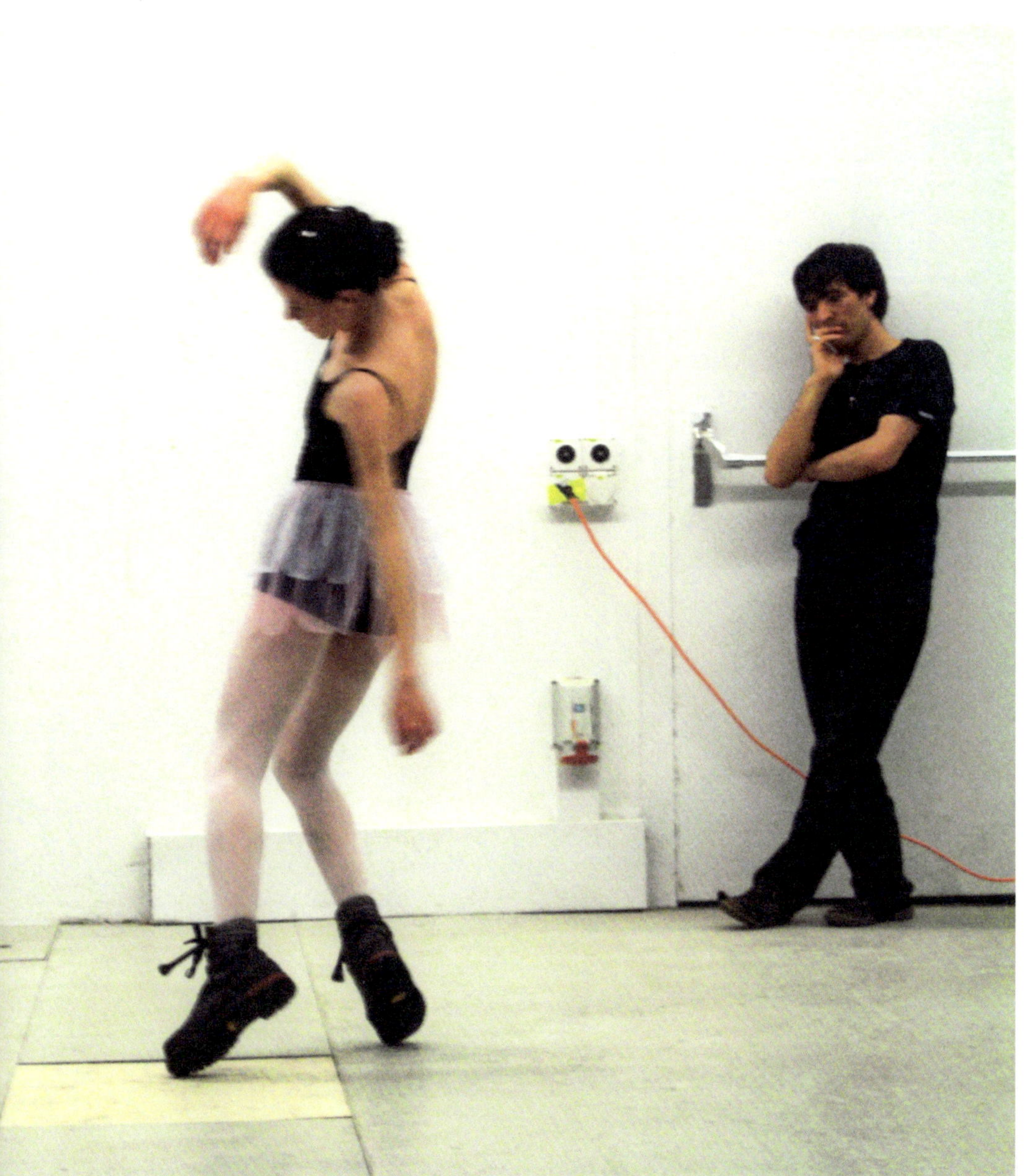

Factory of Found Clothes/Gluklya: *Dumped Dreams (Utopian Unemployment Union N4)*, 2011

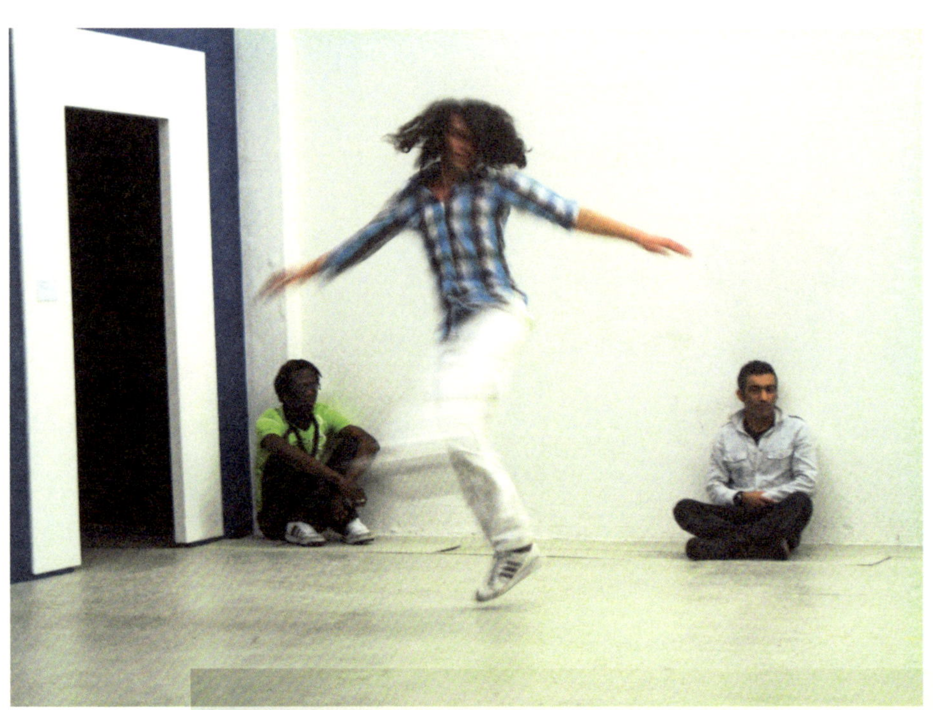

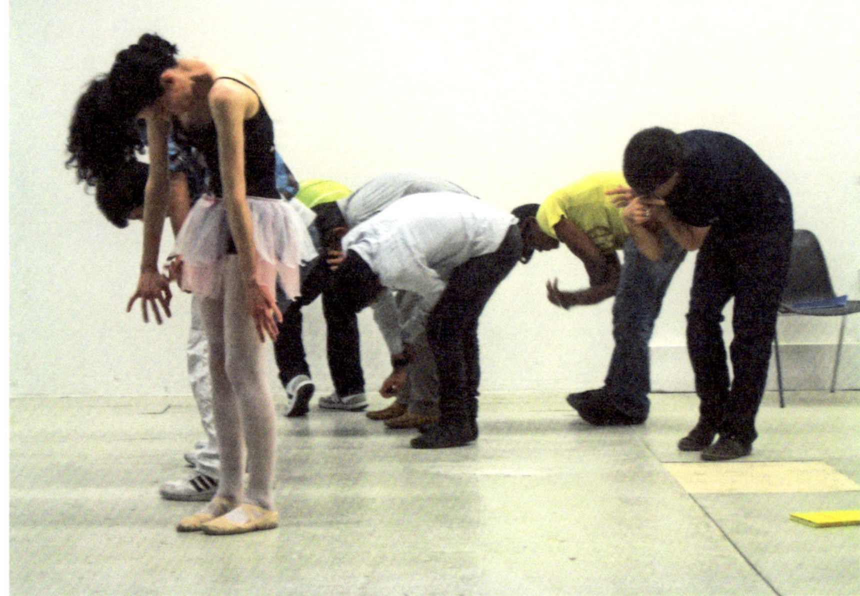

something abstract and artificial. I was deeply touched by the multi-layered performance Dumped Dream, which presented not only the dreams asylum-seekers have, but also acted out various hierarchies, e.g., the gender gaps between the young male asylum-seekers and beautiful young ballerina, as well as the middle-aged female artists acting as jurors. Can you tell us something about your basic ideas behind these workshops and which role the final performance plays?

Gluklya: Performance is one of the most powerful strategies of bringing people together and transforming their phobias and fears into a constructive capacity in order to comprehend the flows of their desires and anxieties. Moreover, it is a very good means for dealing with such stereotypes as 'a not exactly young female artist', for instance. The contemporary art system is designed for a sort of male robot, a super-tough guy who is single and an egoist. How can artists-cum-mothers fit in with that standard if they have to digress from serving the contemporary art machine to give birth and raise their children? Who will wait for the poor mummy to come back to the machine and work? Nothing to do, that ship has sailed, new trends have emerged, and to catch up with them you can travel to conferences and talks, taking your baby with you—all this if you have a successful businessman for a husband and no artist brother with a biography similar to yours. And we all know that the vast majority of artists have such a life. How is it possible to resist that order?

I invited my wonderful friends, bright and subtle artists and great mothers to assume the role of judges of asylum-seekers' dreams. An artist must always help a fellow artist, resisting the capitalist manner of causing everybody to quarrel because of competition in the art world.

In our performance *Dumped Dreams,* my Swiss friends, two of them are themselves migrants from Russia and exactly the kind of mothers-cum-artists trying to catch the ship that is sailing away, embodied three typical positions in the art world: an activist who calls out theatrically leftist clichés, an art dealer who is concerned with nothing save aesthetics and a poet reciting a very long poem no one can absorb. The performance was interrupted by their commentaries; every position was exaggerated to show by means of irony the insufficiency of the art community's efforts to understand the other, to overcome indifference and narcissism. It was important for me to make two very distant worlds clash in the same performance space so as to uncover the system's controversy that is smooth at first sight but hideously overwhelming in reality.

Similarly, the mental stereotypes of a male asylum seeker from Morocco and of a young female dancer from Zurich who studied in London and cannot find a place for her knowledge of modern dance are unlikely to intersect in real life. But we give them that opportunity and create a performance situation for them in which, through the use of the utopian realism methodology, they can rethink their experience and develop their own behavioural codes and frames of mind. In that sense performance is first of all a practice of liberation and of personal make-up. It is an emancipatory project.

The structure of the performance is an invitation to a game. Usually I suggest that participants perform a simple task in free format, for example: 'Try to follow the ballerina and repeat all of her movements, but when she gets strongly carried away, you make some unexpected move that will confuse her, so that you switch roles after that.' Thus I set the beginning of the game, and then all the participants are free to complete or alter the performance structure at will. All I ask them is to maintain the equity, and if anybody in the group feels a lack of voice or some other sort of discomfort, they should express it as soon as they can, sharing their alarm with the others.

Yvonne Volkart: *Although I had the impression that there was a respectful as well as challenging atmosphere during your workshops, the role of the artist in such projects is not easy. How would you depict your role? What do you think prompts people to participate, and what do you do to not become paternalistic or dictatorial?*

Gluklya: I have a very clear feeling, a confidence that all people are equal on some level, on some layer of their complex machine structures. (Which does not imply that there aren't any differences or that all human beings are angels.) I've had that feeling ever since I can remember. And that's something that makes you happy: you just know that all the people are initially brothers and sisters and that everything else is illusion. And then I realised that if that feeling fades in you, it means you're sick. That is the only thing that should be called a real sickness. You are responsible for that state of equality and happiness inside you.

It is that feeling of equality that makes me move towards defying existing hierarchies. I was happy to see a description of transversal strategies by Guattari; it gave me this nice feeling that my artistic intuition has pointed me in the right direction. I also like the Volxtheater Favoriten concept, where the plays are interpreted freely, the collective production process rejects the power of names altogether, the staging turns into plena and experimental rehearsals: 'We all know that it's much easier to live with a boss and a hierarchy, within a system of sticks and carrots, and we spit upon that knowledge.'

Yvonne Volkart: *What was your experience working at Shedhalle and during your workshop?*

Gluklya: For me it was extremely exciting to work with your institution. It's wonderful to have faced the true reality: to go to this Autonomous School where they teach German for free to asylum-seekers, *sans-papiers* and everyone who wants to learn something or share their knowledge. It has been an adventure and a real challenge, because in order to implement something you have to come very close to the 'object' of your interest. That is the artist's research that must precede every performance or video.

So we came to the Autonomous School for free education. The building is single-storied, like a big garage. We entered classroom after classroom, packed with people, stuffy (they didn't dare open windows because some neighbours said it bothered them), and made our speech. It really was similar to the experiments in the 1920s: agitation among workers, teaching reading and writing skills to the kolkhoz members in the young country of the USSR. As soon as you enter, silence and tension set in, black and tanned faces turn to you, and it depends on you, on how you speak about the project, on your ability to calm down and convince people, whether they are going to come and take part in your project or not. It's a challenge and a responsibility. In one classroom I felt they all were going to come and we were going to build a new world. It was a very clear feeling that everything was going to be right. Then some people confirm that they'll come and then on the first day, they don't show up. And it's like you fall face down on the ground. I remember even crying at night, afraid that nothing would come out of all that. But I understood that they didn't come because they were afraid and unsure, not because they didn't want to be part of the experiment. Angela and I (it's very important to have such an angel-helper, it guarantees you about 70 % of the success) went there again, took them all with us in our car and went together to Shedhalle, making more stops by some relatives. I mean, you must try to walk in their shoes, albeit for a little while, try to live their lives alongside them.

We took them to Shedhalle and they liked it there straight away and felt at ease. Not all of them really wanted to retell their dreams—some of the dreams were too traumatic and frightful—but they liked repeating the ballerina's weird movements very much. Somebody preferred singing. It took my breath away when they crawled after her like snakes on the floor; it was overwhelming because it

depicted so clearly their actual position within
the society: slaves who serve the rich class,
doing all the dirty work. And at the same time
they made me think about coiling snakes
that will slither up into the trees and into the
sky someday.

All such projects have a painful aspect: time is
too short. It's nervous work, when you activate all your reserves and do in 10 days what
should have been done in 6 months minimum.
Of course it's no good at all; it's like a kind of
drug. On the other hand, I'll never forget these
people and I'm deeply grateful to them for
that experience, because they helped me a lot
to learn how to interact myself with that level
of happiness-bringing equality which tends
to disappear from time to time, immersing the
conscience into twilight but only to return
again.

But how do we know what impact our project
had on them? Is that not the institution's task
to watch over asylum-seekers in the future?

That's why I think an asylum-seekers'
theatre should be organised as a platform
for longer periods of interaction with them.

ANHANG
APPENDIX

KURZ-BIOGRAFIEN VON AUTOR_INNEN UND KÜNSTLER_IN-NEN

SHORT BIOGRAPHIES OF AUTHORS AND ARTISTS

Nevin Aladağ............(*1972 in Van, TR) lebt und arbeitet in Berlin. Internationale Ausstellungen: MOT – Museum of Contemporary Art, Tokio; Haus der Kunst, München; Hayward Gallery, London; XIV Biennale Internazionale di Scultura, Carrara; 11. Istanbul Biennale; 8. Taipeh Biennale, Taiwan; Kunsthalle Fridericianum, Kassel; Museo Tamayo, Mexiko u. a.

www.wentrupgallery.com, www.rampaistanbul.com

.........................(*1972 in Van, Turkey) lives and works in Berlin. She has exhibited internationally, at institutions including MOT – Museum of Contemporary Art Tokyo; Haus der Kunst, Munich; Hayward Gallery, London; The XIV Biennale Internazionale di Scultura, Carrara; The 11th Istanbul Biennial; The 8th Taipei Biennial, Taiwan; Kunsthalle Fridericianum, Kassel and Museo Tamayo in Mexico City, among others.

Ariane Andereggen............(*1969 in Aigle, CH) ist Schauspielerin, Performance- und Videokünstlerin. Sie studierte Schauspiel an der Hochschule der Künste Bern und schloss 2002 ihr Studium der Medienkunst an der HfG Karlsruhe ab. In Form von Kunstausstellungen, Videos, Fotografien, Zeichnungen, Sound, Texten oder Live-Performances zeigt sie Artefakte, die sie während ihrer Forschungsarbeit geschaffen hat.

www.videostar.ch

.................(*1969 in Aigle, Switzerland) is an actress, performer and video artist. She studied at Bern University of the Arts, HKB, at the Department of Theatre and the University of Applied Arts HfG, Karlsruhe, Department of Media-Arts where she graduated in the year 2002. She presents artefacts created in the course of her research work in the form of art-shows, videos, photographs, drawings, sound, text or live performances.

Alexandra Bachzetsis...................(*1974) ist Performancekünstlerin und Choreographin. Lebt und arbeitet in Zürich und Basel (CH). Studium an der DasArts Amsterdam. Autorin/Choreographin zahlreicher Stücke; 2008 und 2010 konzipierte sie Solo-Ausstellungen für die Kunsthalle Basel und das Kunsthaus Glarus. 2009 erhielt sie ein Werkstipendium für Choreographie von der Stadt Zürich, und 2011 wurde sie mit dem Swiss Art Award ausgezeichnet.

www.alexandrabachzetsis.com

.........................(*1974) is a performance artist and choreographer based in Zurich and Basel, Switzerland. She graduated from DasArts, Amsterdam. She has authored numerous pieces in the last years, 2008 and 2010 she conceived solo exhibitions at the Kunsthalle Basel and Kunsthaus Glarus. In 2009 she received a grant for choreography of the city of Zurich and 2011 the Swiss Art Award.

Zbyněk Baladrán........(*1973 in Prag, CZ) ist Autor, bildender Künstler und Kurator. Studium am Institut für Philosophie an der Karls-Universität Prag und an der Prager Akademie der Bildenden Künste. Seine Kunstwerke können als Suche nach Verbindungen zwischen der Vergangenheit und ihrer Konstruktion in Bezug auf die herrschenden epistemologischen Muster beschrieben werden. Zusammen mit Vít Havranek kuratiert er *Monument to Transformation*, ein dreijähriges Forschungsprojekt über gesellschaftliche Transformation.

www.zbynekbaladran.com, www.monumenttotransformation.org

.................(*1973 in Prague, Czech Republic) is an author, visual artist and curator. He studied at the Charles University Philosophical Faculty in Prague and at the Prague Academy of Fine Arts. His artworks can be characterised as the search for links between the past and its construction in relation to the prevailing epistemological patterns. He is the co-curator, with Vít Havranek, of *Monument to Transformation*, a 3-year research project on social transformation.

Sabina Baumann............ (*1962 in Zug, CH) lebt und arbeitet in Zürich und studierte 1987 bis 1991 bildende Kunst an der Höheren Schule für Gestaltung in Zürich (heute ZHdK), seit 1992 Ausstellungen, sowie Auslandstipendien u.a. in New York und Berlin. Seit 2001 Dozentur für plastisches Gestalten, an der F+F Schule für Kunst und Mediendesign in Zürich, 2006–08 Dozentur für Kunst an der haut école d'art et de de design HEAD in Genf und seit 2010 Z-Module an der ZHDK.

http://sabinabaumann.ch

...............(*1962 in Zug, Switzerland) lives and works in Zurich. Studied visual arts from 1987 to 1991 at what is now the Zurich University of the Arts (ZHdK). Since 1992 she has had exhibitions and been awarded scholarships to work abroad, including New York and Berlin. Her lectureships include sculptural design at the F+F School of Art and Media Design in Zurich since 2001, art at the Geneva University of Art and Design HEAD (2006–08) and Z-Modules at the ZHdK since 2010.

Elke Bippus............ lehrt Kunsttheorie und Kunstgeschichte und ist stellvertretende Leiterin des Institut für Theorie an der Zürcher Hochschule der Künste. Ihre Forschungsschwerpunkte sind: Moderne und zeitgenössische Kunst, Bild- und Repräsentationstheorie, künstlerische Produktions- und Verfahrensweisen, Kunst als epistemische Praxis, Ästhetik und Politik.

http://people.zhdk.ch/elke.bippus

.... teaches art theory and art history and is the assistant director of the Institute for Critical Theory at the Zurich University of the Arts. Her fields of research include modern and contemporary art, theory of images and representation, artistic production techniques and procedure and art as epistemic practice, aesthetics and politics.

Rossella Biscotti .... (*1978 in Italien). Ihre Arbeiten wurden in zahlreichen Ausstellungen gezeigt, u. a. CAC, Wilna; Museu de Serralves, Porto; MAXXI Museum, Rom; Presentation House Gallery, Vancouver; Fondazione Sandretto Re Rebaudengo, Turin; Witte de With, Rotterdam. Sie wurde mit dem Premio Italia Arte Contemporanea (2010); Premio Michelangelo, Carrara (2010); und dem 2. Platz beim niederländischen Prix de Rome (2009), ausgezeichnet.

www.rossellabiscotti.com

...............(*1978 in Italy) has shown her work in various exhibitions: CAC, Vilnius; Museu de Serralves, Porto; MaXXI Museum, Rome; Presentation House Gallery, Vancouver; Fondazione Sandretto Re Rebaudengo, Torino; Witte de With, Rotterdam, among others. She won the Premio Italia Arte Contemporanea (2010), the Premio Michelangelo, Carrara (2010), the second prize of the Prix de Rome in Amsterdam (2009).

Igor und Ivan Buharov .... (Kornél Szilágyi *1971; Nándor Hevesi *1974) leben und arbeiten in Budapest. Zusammenarbeit als Experimentalfilmemacher, Komponisten und bildende Künstler seit 1994. Ausstellungen 2011: Manifesta 8, Murcia; Svit Gallery, Prag; Shedhalle, Zürich; Moravian Gallery, Brünn; Ungarische Nationalgalerie, Budapest; Transit Display, Bratislava.

http://buharov.hu/portfolio

.... live and work in Budapest. They have been working together since 1994 as experimental filmmakers, composers and visual artists.

Exhibitions 2011: Manifesta 8, Murcia; Svit Gallery, Prague; Shedhalle, Zurich; Moravian Gallery, Brno; Hungarian National Gallery, Budapest; Transit Display, Bratislava.

Matthew Fuller .... ist Autor mehrerer Bücher, u. a. *Media Ecologies: Materialist Energies in Art and Technoculture* (MIT), *Behind the Blip: Essays on the Culture of Software* und *Elephant & Castle* (beide bei Autonomedia), sowie Koautor von *Urban Versioning System v1.0* (ALNY) und der demnächst erscheinenden Publikation *Evil Media* (MIT). Sein Tätigkeitsbereich umfasst Kunst-, Medien- und Softwareprojekte; er arbeitet am Centre for Cultural Studies, Goldsmiths, University of London.

www.spc.org/fuller

.... is author of various books including *Media Ecologies: materialist energies in art and technoculture* (MIT), *Behind the Blip: essays on the culture of software*, *Elephant & Castle* (both Autonomedia) and is co-author of *Urban Versioning System v1.0* (ALNY) and the forthcoming *Evil Media* (MIT). He is involved in projects in art, media and software and he works at the Centre for Cultural Studies, Goldsmiths, University of London.

Karen Geyer ..... ist Klangkünstlerin und Musikerin, die Soundobjekte entwickelt und mittels ihres Oral History Archivs performativ und installativ arbeitet. 1976 in Konstanz (D) geboren, studierte sie Bildende Kunst in Zürich. 2007 erhielt sie das Atelierstipendium der Stadt Zürich in New York und lebt und arbeitet seither an beiden Orten. Sie erhielt zahlreiche Auszeichnungen für Ihre künstlerische Arbeit und ist mit Ausstellungen und Soundperformances in Europa und Amerika präsent.

.... is a sound artist and musician who develops sound objects and draws on her oral history archive for her performances and installations. Born in Constance (Germany) in 1976, she studied visual arts in Zurich. In 2007 the city of Zurich awarded her a grant for the use of a studio in New York, and since then she has been living and working in both cities. She has won numerous prizes for her artistic work, and her exhibitions and sound installations can be seen in Europe and America.

Gluklya (Natalia Pershina-Yakimnanskaya) .... (*1969 in Leningrad, RUS) lebt in Amsterdam und St. Petersburg. Studium an der St. Petersburger Muhin Akademie. Begründerin von Factory of Found Clothes (FFC), 1996 Mitbegründerin von Chto Delat. Teilnahme an den 53., 55. und 56. Internationalen Kurzfilmtagen Oberhausen; ICA London (Chto Delat); Spezialprojekt der 4. Moskauer Biennale; MUSAC, Leon, Spanien; MUMOK Wien; Tate, London (2012).

http://factoryoffoundclothes.org, http://chtodelat.org

...............(*1969 in Leningrad, Russia) lives in Amsterdam/St. Petersburg. Studies at Muhina Academy of Art and Design, St. Petersburg. Founder of Factory of Found Clothes (FFC), 1996 co-founder of Chto Delat. 53rd, 55th , 56th Internationale Kurzfilmtage Oberhausen; ICA London (Chto Delat); special project 4th Moscow biennale; MUSAC, Leon, Spain; MUMOK Wien; Tate, London (2012).

Graham Harwood und Matsuko Yokokoji ....leben und arbeiten seit 1994 zusammen. Als YoHa sind sie die treibende Kraft hinter mehreren Projekten, u.a. Mitbegründer der Künstlergruppe Mongrel (1996–2007) und Begründer des Labors für freie Medien, Mediashed, in Southend-on-Sea (2005–2008). 2008 produzierte YoHa zusammen mit Richard Wright *Tantalum Memorial* (Transmediale 1. Preis, 2009), das bei der ZERO1 Biennale in San Jose, Manifesta 7 in Bozen, Ars Electronica Linz und im Science Museum

London gezeigt wurde. Harwood unterrichtet am Centre for Cultural Studies, Goldsmiths, University of London.

www.yoha.co.uk

.... have lived and worked together since 1994. YoHa has powered several collaborations including co-founding the artists group Mongrel (1996–2007) and establishing the Mediashed, a free-media lab in Southend-on-sea (2005–2008). In 2008 they produced *Tantalum Memorial* (Transmediale first prize, 2009) with Richard Wright which featured at ZERO1 Biennial San Jose, Manifesta7 Bolzano, Science Museum London, Ars Electronica Linz. Harwood teaches at the Centre for Cultural Studies, Goldsmiths, University of London.

Christina Hemauer ......(*1973 in Zürich, CH), studierte Bildnerisches Gestalten an der Hochschule für Gestaltung und Kunst in Zürich und Freie Kunst an der Kunstakademie Gent.
Roman Keller .... (*1969 in Liestal, CH) schloss ein Studium der Umweltnaturwissenschaften an der ETH Zürich ab und bildete sich in Zürich (Gaf), New York (SVA, ICP) und in Karlsruhe (HfG) zum Fotografen aus. Die Zusammenarbeit besteht seit 2003. Christina Hemauer und Roman Keller proklamierten 2006 ein neues Kapitel der Kunstgeschichte – den Postpetrolismus.

www.hemauer.ch, http://romankeller.info

.........................(*1973 in Zurich, Switzerland), studied visual design at the University of Art and Design, Zurich, and liberal arts at the Academy of Art, Ghent.
.... (*1969 in Liestal, Switzerland) graduated in environmental studies at the Swiss Federal Institute of Technology, Zurich, and studied to become a photographer in Zurich (Gaf), New York (SVA, ICP) and Karlsruhe (HfG). The two artists have been collaborating since 2003. In 2006 Christina Hemauer and Roman Keller proclaimed a new era in art history—Postpetrolism.

Anke Hoffmann .... studierte Kulturwissenschaften an der HU Berlin und am Goldsmiths, University of London und war von 2009–2012 Kuratorin an der Shedhalle Zürich. Zuvor tätig in kuratorischer Verantwortung und Kulturmanagement bei der transmediale Berlin (1999–2001), Zentrum für Kunst und Medientechnologie Karlsruhe, ZKM (2001–2004) und als freie Kuratorin unter anderem bei der Neue Gesellschaft für Bildende Kunst, NGBK, Berlin (2004–2009), Werkleitz Biennale Halle (2006).

.... studied cultural studies at Humboldt-Universität, Berlin, and at Goldsmiths, University of London and was a curator at Shedhalle, Zurich (2009–2012). Previous curatorial and cultural management activities include positions at transmediale Berlin (1999–2001) and the Zentrum für Kunst und Medientechnologie, ZKM Karlsruhe, (2001–2004) and freelance curatorial work at the Neue Gesellschaft für Bildende Kunst, NGBK Berlin (2004–2009) and Werkleitz Biennale, Halle (2006), among others.

Hannah Hofmann ....(*1971 in Hameln, D) und
Sven Lindholm .... (*1968 in Hamburg, D) studierten Angewandte Theaterwissenschaft in Giessen. Sie realisieren als Hofmann & Lindholm Projekte an den Schnittstellen von szenischer, bildender und akustischer Kunst. 2009 / 2010 hatten Hofmann & Lindholm eine Gastprofessur an der Universität der Künste UdK Berlin inne. Div. Ausstellungen und Interventionen, darunter Frankfurter Kunstverein (2012), Schauspiel Köln (2011), ZKM Karlsruhe (2010/11), HAU Berlin (2010), Neuer Berliner Kunstverein (2010).

www.hofmannundlindholm.de

.................................(*1971 in Hameln, Germany) and
..................(*1968 in Hamburg, Germany) studied applied theater studies in Giessen. As Hofmann & Lindholm they realise projects at the interface of scenic, visual and acoustic arts. In 2009 / 2010 Hofmann & Lindholm held a visiting professorship at the Berlin University of the Arts. Various exhibitions and interventions, including at the Frankfurter Kunstverein (2012), Schauspiel Köln (2011), ZKM Karlsruhe (2010/11), HAU Berlin (2010), Neuer Berliner Kunstverein (2010).

Ute Hörner ....(*1964 in Karlsruhe, D) studierte Bildhauerei an der Kunstakademie Stuttgart und Medienkunst an der Kunsthochschule für Medien Köln.
Mathias Antlfinger ......(*1960 in Limburg, D) studierte Freie Kunst und Kybernetik an der Kunstakademie Düsseldorf. Seit 1991 Zusammenarbeit Hörner/Antlfinger, seit 2009 lehren beide im Bereich Medienkunst an der Kunsthochschule für Medien Köln. Zahlreiche Ausstellungen und Festivalbeteiligungen, zuletzt Shift, Basel; Videonale 13, Kunstmuseum Bonn; National Taiwan Museum of Fine Arts, Taichung.

www.h--a.org

.... (*1964 in Karlsruhe, Germany) studied sculpture at the Academy of Art and Design, Stuttgart, and media arts at the Academy of Media Arts, Cologne.
.................(*1960 in Limburg, Germany) studied fine arts and cybernetics at the Kunstakademie Düsseldorf. Hörner/Antlfinger have been collaborating since 1991; both have been teaching in the field of media arts at the Academy of Media Arts, Cologne since 2009. Numerous exhibitions and participation in festivals, most recently Shift, Basel; Videonale 13, Kunstmuseum Bonn; National Taiwan Museum of Fine Arts, Taichung.

JOKAklubi: Niina Lehtonen Braun (MFA), Tellervo Kalleinen (MFA) und Mirka Raito (MFA) .... alle wurden 1975 in Finnland geboren und leben und arbeiten in Berlin, Helsinki und Hamburg. JOKAklubi hatte ihren ersten Auftritt 2009 in Subvision, Hamburg. Seitdem ist die Gruppe u. a. in folgenden Veranstaltungsorten aufgetreten: W139, Amsterdam; Baltic Circle, Helsinki; KW, Berlin; West Germany, Berlin; Fluc, Wien; Atelier Frankfurt, Frankfurt.

http://jokaklubi.blogspot.com

.... all born 1975 in Finland – live and work in Berlin, Helsinki and Hamburg. JOKAklubi had its first performance 2009 in Subvision, Hamburg. Since then the group has performed in venues such as W139, Amsterdam; Baltic Circle, Helsinki; KW, Berlin; West Germany, Berlin; Fluc, Wien; Atelier Frankfurt, Frankfurt.

Tellervo Kalleinen ......(*1975 in Lohja, FIN) studierte an der Abteilung für Zeit & Raum der Akademie der Bildenden Künste in Helsinki, und
Oliver Kochta-Kalleinen ....(*1971 in Dresden D) geboren, studierte an der HFBK Hamburg. Sie leben in Helsinki (FIN). Mitbegründer von complaintschoir.org, YKON und der Speech Karaoke Action Group.

www.tellervo.net, www.ykon.org, www.ykon.org/kochta-kalleinen

.... (*1975 Lohja, Finland) Studies at the Department of Time & Space, Academy of Fine Arts, Helsinki and
......................(*1971 Dresden, Germany) Studies at HFBK, Hamburg live in Helsinki (Finland). Co-founders of: complaintschoir.org, YKON, Speech Karaoke Action Group.

Hassan Khan .... (*1975) ist Künstler, Musiker und Schriftsteller. Er lebt und arbeitet in Kairo, Ägypten.

www.hassankhan.com

.... (*1975) is an artist, musician and writer. He lives and works in Cairo, Egypt.

Korpys/Löffler ....(*1966 und *1963 in Bremen, D) leben und arbeiten in Berlin und Bremen. Zusammenarbeit seit 1989. Lehren seit 2009 an der Hochschule für Künste HfK Bremen.

www.meyer-riegger.de

.... (*1966 and *1963 in Bremen, Germany) live and work in Berlin and Bremen. Collaboration since 1989. They have been teaching at the University of the Arts in Bremen since 2009.

Heimo Lattner .... (*1968 in Eisenstadt, A) lebt in Berlin. Er studierte Kunst an der Akademie der Bildenden Künste in Wien und am Whitney Independent Study Program New York. Ist Mitbetreiber des Projektraums General Public in Berlin und Teil des Künstlerkollektivs e-Xplo (mit Erin McGonigle und Rene Gabri). Realisierte Projekte und Ausstellung u.a. *Die Stadt von Morgen*, Akademie der Künste Berlin 2007; *Same Time Tomorrow*, Kunstpavillion Innsbruck 2012.

.................(*1968 in Eisenstadt, Austria) lives in Berlin. He studied art at the Academy of Fine Arts, Vienna, and at the Whitney Independent Study Program, New York. Along with others he jointly runs the project space General Public in Berlin and is a member of the artist collective e-Xplo (with Erin McGonigle and Rene Gabri). Realised projects and exhibitions include *Die Stadt von Morgen*, Academy of Fine Arts, Berlin, 2007; *Same Time Tomorrow*, Kunstpavillion Innsbruck 2012.

Rachel Mader .... ist Kunstwissenschaftlerin; 2009–2013 Projektleitung *Die Organisation der Innovation – Künstlerische Praxis und Kulturpolitik im Grossbritannien der Nachkriegszeit*, dazu Tätigkeiten als Mentorin an Kunsthochschulen und als Kritikerin (springerin, camera austria, etc.); Organisation von Tagungen (*Radikal ambivalent*, ZHdK, 2011; *Das Kunstprojekt*, Bern 2011) und Künstlergesprächen; seit 2008 Stiftungsratsmitglied Stiftung GegenwART, Kunstmuseum Bern, seit 2011 Associate Editor beim Journal for Artistic Research.

.... is an art historian; 2009–2013 she was the director of the project *Organisation of Innovation—Artistic Practise and Cultural Politics in Postwar Great Britain*, she is also active as a mentor at art universities and as an art critic (springerin, camera austria, etc.), organises congresses ('Radikal Ambivalent', ZHdK, 2011; 'Das Kunstprojekt', Bern 2011) and conducts artist discussions; since 2008 she has been a member of the Foundation Board of the Stiftung GegenwART, Kunstmuseum Bern; since 2011 associate editor of the Journal for Artistic Research.

Maurice Maggi .... (*1955 in Zürich, CH) ist ausgebildeter Landschaftsgärtner, Künstler und Küchenchef in Zürich/New York. £Seit 1984 macht er Ansaaten mit Malven im öffentlichen Raum Zürichs. Führungen und Referate, Ausstellungen u.a. im Message Salon, Zürich und O.K. Centrum für Gegenwartskunst, Linz. 2009 ist der Film *Floraler Anarchist* von Roland Achini über Maurice Maggi erschienen.

www.maurice-maggi.ch

.... (*1955 in Zurich, Switzerland) is a trained landscape gardener, artist and cook in Zurich/New York. He has been sowing hollyhocks as flower graffiti in Zurich's public space since 1984. Guided tours and lectures, exhibitions at venues such as Message Salon, Zurich, and O.K. Centrum für Gegenwartskunst, Linz. In 2009 Roland Achini made a film about Maurice Maggi entitled *Floraler Anarchist*.

Michaela Melián .... Künstlerin und Musikerin, lebt in München und Hamburg. Sie ist Mitglied der Band F.S.K. (Freiwillige Selbstkontrolle) und seit 2010 Professorin an der HFBK Hamburg. Zahlreiche

Gruppen- und Einzelausstellungen, zuletzt *30 Künstler / 30 Räume*, Neues Museum Nürnberg.

www.galerie-karin-guenther.de, www.memoryloops.net, www.diskob.com/artists/fsk/modeundverzweifelung.html

.... artist and musician, lives in Munich and Hamburg (Germany). She is a member of the band F.S.K. (Freiwillige Selbstkontrolle) and has been a professor for time-based media at the University of Fine Arts in Hamburg (HFBK) since 2010. Numerous group and solo shows, most recently *30 Artists / 30 Rooms*, Neues Museum Nürnberg.

Sebastian Diaz Morales........... (*1975 in Comodoro Rivadavia, AR) lebt und arbeitet in Amsterdam. Studium an der Universidad del Cine de Antin, Argentinien, der Rijksakademie van Beeldende Kunsten, Amsterdam und am Le Fresnoy in Roubaix, Frankreich. Seine Arbeiten wurden international gezeigt, u. a. in der Tate Modern, London; im Centre Pompidou, Paris; in der Fundació Joan Miró, Barcelona, und im Stedelijk Museum Bureau Amsterdam.

www.sebastiandiazmorales.com

.... (*1975, Comodoro Rivadavia, Argentina) lives and works in Amsterdam. He attended the Universidad del Cine de Antin in Argentina, the Rijksakademie van Beeldende Kunsten in Amsterdam, and Le Fresnoy in Roubaix, France. His work has been exhibited widely, including solo shows at Tate Modern, London; Centre Pompidou, Paris; Joan Miró Fundation, Barcelona and Stedelijk Museum Bureau Amsterdam.

Uriel Orlow .... (* in Zürich, CH) lebt in London. Forschungsstelle University of Westminster, London. Einzelausstellungen 2012: Oslo Kunstverein, Prefix ICA Toronto, Saint Gervais Geneva, ACAF Alexandria, Centre PasquArt Biel. Weitere Ausstellungen und Film-Screenings: Manifesta 9, Belgium; Chewing the Scenery, Schweizer Beitrag für 54. Biennale Venedig; 3. Guangzhou Trienniale, Tate Modern und Whitechapel Gallery, London.

www.urielorlow.net

.... (* in Zurich, Switzerland) lives and works in London, where he is a senior research fellow at the University of Westminster. Solo exhibitions in 2012 include Oslo Kunstforening, Prefix ICA Toronto, Saint Gervais Geneva, ACAF Alexandria, Centre PasquArt Biel. Other exhibitions and screenings include Manifesta 9, Belgium; Chewing the Scenery Swiss off-site Pavilion at the 54th Venice Biennale; 3rd Guangzhou Triennial, Tate Modern and Whitechapel Gallery London.

Stefan Panhans .... (*1967 in Hattingen/Ruhr, D) ist Künstler und lebt in Hamburg, Berlin und anderen Orten. 2010/2011 wurden seine Arbeiten unter anderen im Folkwang Museum, Essen; Kasseler Kunstverein; Kunstverein Medienturm, Graz; Experimenter, Kalkutta und am Goethe Institut Rom gezeigt. Einzelausstellungen im Museum für Gegenwartskunst in Siegen, im W 139 Amsterdam und im Rahmen des Steirischen Herbst 2012 bei Camera Austria, Kunshaus Graz.

www.dorotheaschlueter.com

.... (*1967 in Hattingen/Ruhr, Germany) is an artist and lives in Hamburg, Berlin and other places. In 2010/2011 his work was shown at the Folkwang Museum, Essen; Kasseler Kunstverein; Kunstverein Medienturm, Graz; Experimenter, Calcutta, and at the Goethe Institute, Rome, among other venues. Solo exhibitions at the Museum für Gegenwartskunst, Siegen; W139, Amsterdam, and as part of the Steirischer Herbst Festival 2012 at Camera Austria, Kunsthaus Graz.

Alexei Penzin .... ist Forscher am Institut für Philosophie, Moskau. Seine Interessensbereiche umfassen philosophische Anthropologie,

Marxismus und kritische Theorie sowie Verknüpfungen zwischen Kunst und politischer Praxis. Er arbeitet zurzeit an einem Buch über die kulturellen Repräsentationen von Schlaf im Zusammenhang mit den biopolitischen Verordnungen im Alltag des Spätkapitalismus – Arbeitstitel: *Rex Exsomnis. Towards a Political Economy of Sleep*. Alexei Penzin ist Mitglied der Gruppe Chto Delat/What is to be done?

www.chtodelat.org

.... is a researcher at Institute of Philosophy, Moscow. His fields of interest are philosophical anthropology, Marxism and critical theory, concatenations of art and political praxis. His current project is a book on cultural representations of sleep in context of biopolitical regulations of life under late capitalism with the working title *Rex Exsomnis. Towards a political economy of sleep*. Alexei Penzin is a member of the group Chto Delat/What is to be done?

Gerald Raunig .... ist Philosoph und Kunsttheoretiker. Er arbeitet an der Zürcher Hochschule der Künste und am eipcp. Seine Bücher sind ins Englische, Serbische, Spanische, Slowenische, Russische und Italienische übersetzt, u.a. *Tausend Maschinen. Eine kleine Philosophie der Maschine als sozialer Bewegung*, Turia+Kant 2008; *Fabriken des Wissens. Streifen und Glätten 1; Industrien der Kreativität. Streifen und Glätten 2*, beide: diaphanes 2012.

.... is a philosopher and art theoretician. He works at the Zurich University of the Arts and at the eipcp. His books have been translated into English, Serbian, Spanish, Slovenian, Russian and Italian. Monographs available in English: *Art and Revolution. Transversal Activism in the Long Twentieth Century*, Semiotext(e)/MIT Press 2007; *A Thousand Machines*, Semiotext(e)/MIT Press 2010, both translated by Aileen Derieg.

Emily Richardson .... (*1971) lebt und arbeitet in London. Studium an der Londoner Middlesex University und am San Francisco Art Institute. Ausstellungen: The Wapping Project, London; Arprojx Cinema at The Armory Show, New York; Tate Modern; Tate Britain sowie Filmfestivals in Venedig, London, Rotterdam und New York. Für ihre Filme wurde sie 2009 mit dem Gilles-Dusein-Preis, Paris, ausgezeichnet.

www.emilyrichardson.org.uk

.... (*1971) lives and works in London. Studied at Middlesex University, London and San Francisco Art Institute. Exhibitions: The Wapping Project, London; Arprojx Cinema at The Armory Show, New York; Tate Modern; Tate Britain; and Venice, London, Rotterdam and New York Film Festivals. She was awarded the Gilles Dusein Prize, Paris, 2009 in recognition of her films.

Kathrin Röggla .... (*1971 in Salzburg, A) geboren, lebt als Schriftstellerin in Berlin. Sie verfasst Prosa, zuletzt *die alarmbereiten* (S. Fischer, 2010), Theaterstücke, zuletzt *Kinderkriegen* (Uraufführung: Residenztheater München, 2012) und Hörspiele (z.B. *die unvermeidlichen*, BR2, 2012). 2012 erhielt sie den bekannten Stadtschreiber-Literaturpreis der Stadt Mainz.

www.kathrin-roeggla.de

.... (*1971 in Salzburg, Austria) lives as a prose writer in Berlin. Her most recent work includes the novel *die alarmbereiten* (S. Fischer, 2010), the play *Kinderkriegen* (premiere: Residenztheater, Munich, 2012) and the radio play *die unvermeidlichen*, (BR2, 2012). In 2012 she received the renowned Stadtschreiber literature prize awarded by the city of Mainz.

Jan-Peter E.R. Sonntag .... (*1965 in Lübeck, D) studierte Kunst, Kunstgeschichte, Musikwissenschaft, Komposition, Philosophie und Kognitionswissenschaft u.a. bei Rudolf zur Lippe, Ivan Illich, Umberto Maturana, Gert Selle, Gertrud Meyer-Denkmann und Gustavo Becerra Schmidt. Er nahm an zahlreichen internationalen Ausstellungen und Festivals teil und erhielt zahlreiche Stipendien und Preise u.a. 2012 Villa-Aurora in Los Angeles.

www.sonarc-ion.de

.... (*1965 in Lübeck, Germany) studied art, art history, musicology, composition, philosophy and cognitive science with Rudolf zur Lippe, Ivan Illich, Umberto Maturana, Gert Selle, Gertrud Meyer-Denkmann and Gustavo Becerra Schmidt, among others. He has participated in many international exhibitions and festivals and been awarded numerous grants, scholarships and prizes, including the Villa Aurora L.A. Artist Grant 2012.

Mladen Stilinović .... (*1947 in Belgrad, SRB) lebt und arbeitet als Künstler in Zagreb. Er war Mitglied der Group of Six Artists (1975 – 1979) und führte die PM-Galerie in Zagreb (1982 – 1991). Seine künstlerische Tätigkeit spannt den Bogen von Collagen über Fotografien, Künstlerbücher, Gemälde, Installationen, Aktionen, Filme und Videoarbeiten. Seit 1974 zeigt er seine Werke in zahlreichen Solo- und Gruppenausstellungen, u. a. im Museum für zeitgenössische Kunst, Zagreb; Centre for Contemporary Art, Glasgow; VOX, Montreal; E-flux, New York; Museum für moderne Kunst, Warschau; Ludwig Museum, Budapest.

.... (*1947, Belgrade, Serbia) is a Zagreb-based artist. He was a member of the Group of Six Artists (1975–1979). He ran the PM Gallery in Zagreb (1982–1991). His works include collages, photographs, artist books, paintings, installations, actions, films and video. He has been exhibiting since 1974 in numerous solo and group shows including Museum of Contemporary Art, Zagreb; Center for Contemporary Art, Glasgow; VOX, Montreal; E-flux, New York; Museum of Modern Art, Warsaw; Ludwig Museum, Budapest.

Alexander Tuchaček .... (*1962 in Wien, A) studierte Elektroakustische Musik und Medienkunst in Wien und Köln. Er unterrichtet seit 2001 an der ZHdK im Studienbereich Mediale Künste. Als Mitglied von knowbotic research Teilnahme an internationalen Ausstellungen, darunter Biennale di Venezia, Österreichischer Pavillon,1999; *Synthetic Times*, NAMOC Beijing, 2008; *Enter Action—Digital Art Now*, Aarhus Kunstmuseum, 2009.

www.krcf.org

.... (*1962 in Vienna, Austria) studied electroacoustic music and media art in Vienna and Cologne. He has been teaching media arts at the Zurich University of the Arts since 2001. As a member of knowbotic research he has participated in numerous international exhibitions including the 48th Venice Biennale, Austrian Pavillon,1999; *Synthetic Times*, NAMOC Beijing, 2008; *Enter Action—Digital Art Now*, Aarhus Kunstmuseum, 2009.

Yvonne Volkart .... war Kuratorin an der Shedhalle Zürich (2009–12). Sie ist Dozentin für Kultur- und Kunsttheorie an der Hochschule für Gestaltung und Kunst FHNW Basel, freie Kuratorin und Autorin, u.a. für *springerin*. Ihre Dissertation *Fluide Subjekte. Anpassung und Widerspenstigkeit in der Medienkunst* erschien 2006 bei [transcript]. Schwerpunkte: ökologische und politische Ästhetik, Queer Theory, kuratorische Praktiken, Repräsentationskritik.

.... was curator at Shedhalle, Zurich (2009–12). She is a lecturer in cultural studies and art theory at the Academy of Art and Design FHNW in Basel, freelance curator and author for *springerin* and others. Her dissertation *Fluid Subjects. Adaptation and Defiance in Media Art* was published (in German only) by [transcript] in 2006. Main fields of interest: ecological and political aesthetics, queer theory, curatorial practices, representational critique.

Ute Vorkoeper .... Hamburg, Autorin, Kuratorin und Kunstvermittlerin, u.a. künstlerische Leitung der Akademie einer anderen Stadt, Kunstplattform der Internationalen Bauausstellung Hamburg (2009–2011); Gastprofessorin an der Kunsthochschule Berlin Weissensee (2007–2009), Promotion 1997; internationale Ausstellungsprojekte, Veranstaltungen, Buch- und Textpublikationen zu zeitgenössischer Kunst.

www.deponat.de, www.mitwisser.net

.... Hamburg, author, curator and art educator, artistic director of the Academy of Another City, art platform of the International Building Exhibition Hamburg (2009–2011); visiting professor at the Berlin Weissensee School of Art (2007–2009), PhD 1997; exhibition projects on an international scale, events, publications of books and texts on contemporary art.

Angela Wittwer .... (*1987) studierte Theorie an der Zürcher Hochschule der Künste ZHdK und Kulturwissenschaften an der Kunstuniversität Linz. Aktuell Studium in Fine Arts, ebenfalls an der ZHdK. Kuratorische Assistenz an der Shedhalle Zürich (2010–11), Arbeiten und Projekte in kollektiven und künstlerisch-theoretischen Zusammenhängen.

.... (*1987) studied theory at the Zurich University of the Arts and cultural studies at the The University of Art and Design, Linz, and is currently studying Fine Arts at the Zurich University of the Arts. Assistant curator at Shedhalle, Zurich (2010–11), works and projects in collective and artistic-theoretical contexts.

YKON .... wurde im Jahre 2004 gegründet, um das 1. Gipfeltreffen der Mikronationen zu organisieren. YKON ist ein Künstlerkollektiv, dessen Hauptinteressensgebiete in praktischen Utopien, alternativen Staaten und im gemeinsamen Handeln liegen. Mitglieder: Oliver Kochta-Kalleinen, Tellervo Kalleinen, Ulu Braun, Pekko Koskinen, Christina Kral und Tomas Träskman.

www.ykon.org

.... was founded in the year 2004 in order to organise the first summit of micronations. YKON is an artist collective with key interest in practical utopias, alternative nations and participation. Members are: Oliver Kochta-Kalleinen, Tellervo Kalleinen, Ulu Braun, Pekko Koskinen, Christina Kral and Tomas Träskman.

Juliane Zelwies .... (*1976 in Berlin, D), Studium Bildhauerei in Stockholm und Philadelphia, Medienkunst an der UdK Berlin. Zahlreiche Einzel- und Gruppenausstellungen, Filmfestivals und Performances, zuletzt Momenta Art, Brooklyn (2012), Deutsches Technikmuseum, Berlin (2011); Simultanhalle, Köln (2011); Projektraum Uqbar, Berlin (2010); Galerie Sans Nom, Moncton, Kanada (2010).

www.juliane.de

.... (*1976 in Berlin, Germany), studied sculpture in Stockholm and Philadelphia, graduated in media arts at the UdK Berlin. Numerous solo and group exhibitions, film festivals and performances, most recently Momenta Art, Brooklyn (2012), Deutsches Technikmuseum, Berlin (2011); Simultanhalle, Cologne (2011); Projektraum Uqbar, Berlin (2010); Galerie Sans Nom, Moncton, Canada (2010).

VERAN-STALTUNGEN SHEDHALLE 2009–2012
SHEDHALLE EVENTS 2009–2012

07.11.2009–31.01.2010 .... Ausstellung / Exhibition
Un/Mögliche Gemeinschaft / Im/Possible Community
Kuratiert von / Curated by Anke Hoffmann und / and Yvonne Volkart
Künstler_innen / Artists: Nevin Aladağ, Ulf Aminde, Sabina Baumann,
Perry Bard, Bureau d'Etudes, Hassan Khan, Korpys/Löffler,
Heimo Lattner, Naeem Mohaiemen, p-r-o-x-y, Isabelle Stever, Tellervo
Kalleinen/Oliver Kochta-Kalleinen, Juliane Zelwies

06.11.2009 ....Performance **Occupation Shedhalle 2009**
von / by Nevin Aladağ
Konzert / Concert **The Big One** von / by Hassan Khan

19.11.2009 .... Vortrag / Lecture **Spielball des Mit-Seins /
Plaything of the Mit-Sein** von/by Krystian Woznicki

20.11.2009........... Workshop **Politik–Ästhetik / Politics–Aesthetics**
mit / with Iris Dressler, Oliver Marchart, Krystian Woznicki

03.12.2009........ Workshop **Geschichte–Erzählung / History–Narration**
mit / with Jörn Etzold, Eran Schaerf, Bea Schlingelhoff

17.12.2009 .... Workshop **Identität–Ethnizität / Identity–Ethnicity**
mit / with María do Mar Castro Varela, Christian Ritter

07.01.2010 .... Diskussion / Discussion **Gemeinschaft im
Gespräch / Community in Conversation**
mit / with Sabina Baumann, Elke Bippus, Anke Hoffmann, Jörg Huber,
Oliver Kochta-Kalleinen, Dorothee Richter, Yvonne Volkart und dem
Publikum / and the audience

Die Veranstaltungsreihe **Politik–Ästhetik**, **Geschichte–Erzählung**,
Identität–Ethnizität und **Gemeinschaft im Gespräch** wurde
konzipiert und organisiert von Elke Bippus unter Mitwirkung von Anne
Schuh, Chantal Küng und David Lanz, Institut für Theorie ith, ZHdK.
The series of events **Politics–Aesthetics, History–Narration, and
Community in Conversation** was initiated and organised by Elke
Bippus in collaboration with Anne Schuh, Chantal Küng, und David Lanz,
Institute for Critical Theory ith, ZHdK.

13.12.2009.................. Filmscreening **Unheilige Familie / Unholy Family**
Einführung und Auswahl / Introduction and selection von / by
Anke Hoffmann
mit / with Alina Rudnitskaya: **Civil Status** (2005), Maria Mohr:
Cousin Cousine (2005), Renata Poljak: **Great Expectations** (2005),
Mohammed Ossama: **Step by Step** (1979), Guy Ben-Ner: **Wild Boy** (2005)

30.01.2010.................... Aufführung / Performance **Erster Zürcher
Beschwerdechor / First Zurich Complaints Choir**
in der Stadt Zürich und im Fabriktheater Rote Fabrik / in the city of
Zurich and Fabriktheater Rote Fabrik. Eine Koproduktion von
Shedhalle Zürich und Fabriktheater Rote Fabrik / A co-production
of Shedhalle Zurich and Fabriktheater Rote Fabrik

20.03.–16.05.2010................................ Ausstellung / Exhibition
**Lands End. Landschaft zwischen Bild und Raum / Lands End.
Landscape as Image and as Space**
Kuratiert von / Curated by Anke Hoffmann und / and Yvonne Volkart
Künstler_innen / Artists: Ulu Braun, Eva Castringius, Matthew Fuller/
Graham Harwood, Gabriela Gerber/Lukas Bardill, Dirk Haupt,
Verena Maas, Maurice Maggi, Achim Mohné, Sebastian Diaz Morales,
Emily Richardson, Michaela Schwentner, Christian Vetter,
Jana Winderen

19.03.2010.............. Kochperformance des Guerilla-Gärtners Maurice
Maggi / Cooking performance by the guerilla gardener Maurice Maggi

08.05.2010 .... CrossTalk **Lands End**
Referent_innen / Speakers: Maurice Maggi, Yvonne Volkart,
Philipp Felsch, Sibylle Omlin
Ortsbegehung um das Gelände der Roten Fabrik / On-site inspection
tour of Rote Fabrik mit / with Maurice Maggi und / and Sebastian Mundwiler

17.09.–19.09.2010...................... Jubiläumsfestival / Jubilee festival
**30 Jahre sind genug! – 30 Jahre Rote Fabrik /
30 Jahre are enough!—30 Years Rote Fabrik**
ein Gemeinschaftsprojekt der Kultur- und Kunstschaffenden auf dem
Gelände der Roten Fabrik / a common project of all those presenting,
producing, facilitating and mediating art on the site of Rote Fabrik
Künstler_innen / Artists supported by Shedhalle: Christoph Franz/
Michael Meier, Pascale Grau, Damian Jurt, Georg Keller

09.10.2010–30.01.2011 .... Ausstellung / Exhibition
**Überblendungen. Das Zukünftige rekonstruieren /
Cross-fades. Reconstructing the Future**
Kuratiert von / Curated by Anke Hoffmann und / and Yvonne Volkart
Künstler_innen / Artists: Zbyněk Baladrán, Rossella Biscotti,
Daniela Comani, Christoph Draeger, Karen Geyer, Hofmann & Lindholm,
knowbotic research, Uriel Orlow, Suzanne Treister, Sarah Vanagt,
Miriam Visaczki

12.11.2010.................... Film-Gespräch / Filmscreening and discussion
mit / with Sarah Vanagt
Begin Began Begun (2003), **Boulevard d'Ypres / Ieperlaan** (2010),
beide von / both by Sarah Vanagt

13.11.2010................ CrossTalk **Kunst, Wissenschaft, Geschichte /
Art, Science, History**
Referent_innen / Speakers: Raffael Dörig, Christoph Draeger,
Beat Näf, Suzanne Treister, Ute Vorkoeper, Sarah Vanagt,
Miriam Visaczki, Anke Hoffmann und / and Yvonne Volkart

20.01.2011 .... Performance & Lecture **Atlas of Transformation**
von / by Zbyněk Baladrán, Vít Havránek, Vera Krejcová

05.03.–15.05.2011 .... Ausstellung / Exhibition
**Dump Time. Für eine Praxis des Horizontalen / Dump Time.
For a Practice of Horizontality**
Kuratiert von / Curated by Anke Hoffmann und / and Yvonne Volkart
Künstler_innen / Artists: Alex Antener, Igor und / and Ivan Buharov,
Cristina David, Johanna Domke, Factory of Found Clothes/Gluklya,
Eiko Grimberg, Yolande Harris, Petra Elena Köhle/Nicolas Vermot
Petit-Outhenin, Stefan Panhans, Mladen Stilinović, Anna Zaradny

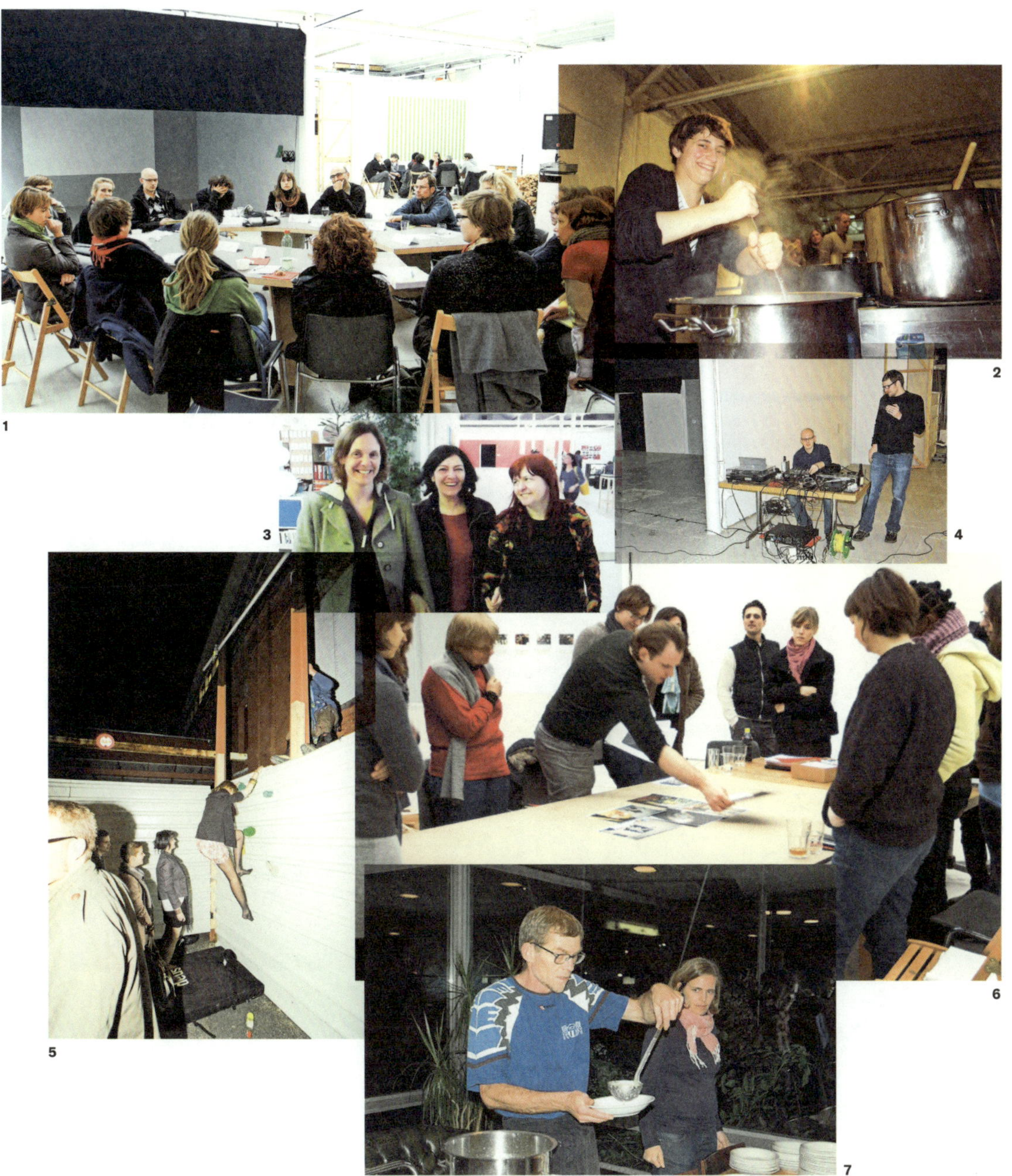

1 .... Vortrag / Lecture **Spielball des Mit-Seins** von / by Krystian Woznicki, **Un/Mögliche Gemeinschaft / Im/Possible Community**, 2009
2 .... Mitgliederfest Verein Shedhalle / Member party Verein Shedhalle 2010, Andrea Thal
3 .... v.l.n.r. / f.l.t.r.: Sarah Mehler, Maria Mosayebi, Yolanda Hug, 2009
4 .... Mitgliederfest Verein Shedhalle / Member party Verein Shedhalle 2010, Tim Zulauf und / and Markus Bösch
5 .... Christoph Franz / Michael Meier: **30 Jahre sind genug!, 30 Jahre Rote Fabrik / 30 Years Rote Fabrik**, 2010
6 .... Workshop **Identität–Ethnizität / Identity–Ethnicity** mit / with Christian Ritter, María do Mar Castro Varela, **Un/Mögliche Gemeinschaft / Im/Possible Community**, 2009
7 .... Kochperformance / Cooking performance von / by Maurice Maggi, 2010

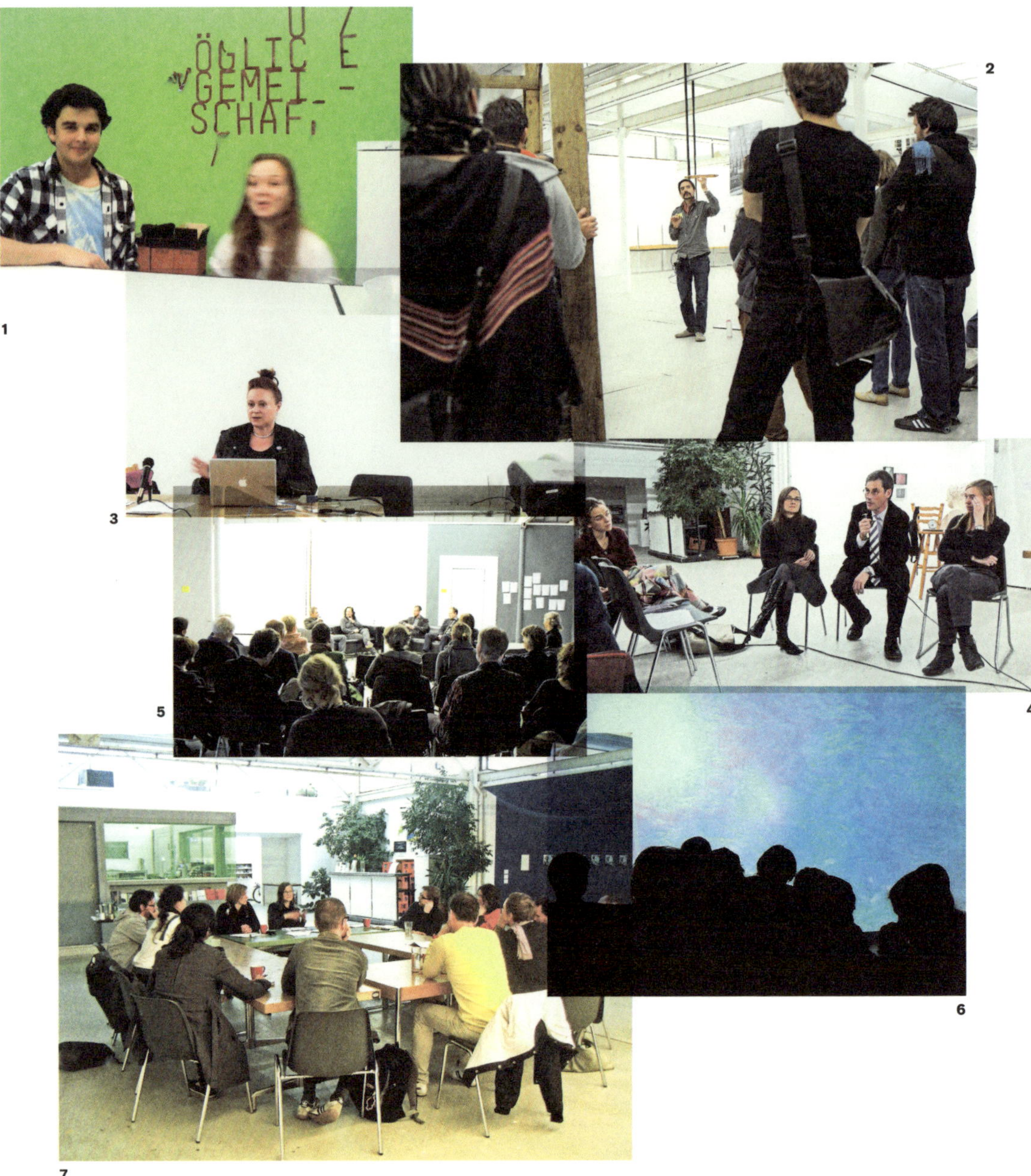

1 .... Shedhalle Bar, Hannah Mehler und Freund / and friend
2 .... Führung in der Shedhalle / Guided tour at Shedhalle von / by Christian Ratti, **30 Jahre Rote Fabrik / 30 Years Rote Fabrik**, 2010
3 .... CrossTalk **Überblendungen / Cross- fades**: Suzanne Treister, 2010
4 .... CrossTalk **Überblendungen / Cross-fades** (v.l.n.r. / f.l.t.r.): Sarah Vanagt, Yvonne Volkart, Beat Näf, Ute Vorkoeper, 2010
5 .... CrossTalk **Quo vadis Schweiz? / Quo vadis Switzerland?** mit / with Marion Mertens, Marcel Hänggi, Franz Baumgartner,
Frank Rutschmann, 2011
6 .... Performance Yolande Harris: **Pink Noise/Fishing for Sound, Dump Time**, 2011
7 .... Offenes Gespräch / Open discussion mit den Künstler_innen / with the artists, **Dump Time**, 2011

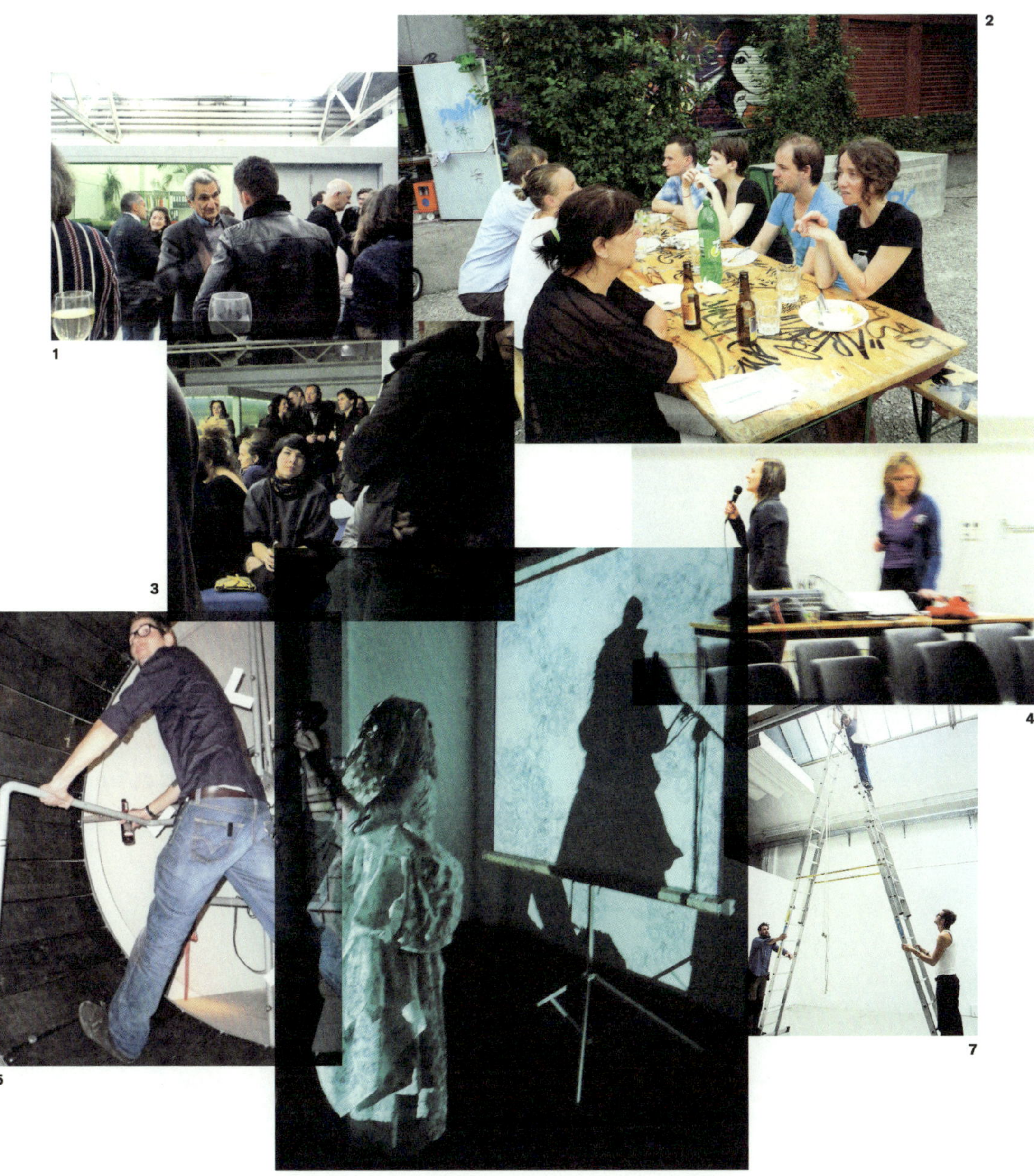

1 .... Inventionen 03.05.2011 mit / with Antonio Negri
2 .... Barbecue mit den Künstler_innen von / with the artists of **Connect**. Vorne / Front: Teres Wydler, Brigitte Renz Sonko, 2011
3 .... Publikum / Audience **Dump Time**
4 .... Ausstellungseröffnung / Opening reception: Yvonne Volkart und / and Anke Hoffmann
5 .... Techniker / Technician Markus Bösch moving the energy
6 .... Performance knowbotiq, *__kotomisi – non essential mix Vol 1, Connect__*, 2011
7 .... Aufbau / Setting up *__Unter Strom / Live Wire__*, (v.l.n.r. / f.l.t.r.:) Tobias Borup, Karen Geyer, Markus Bösch

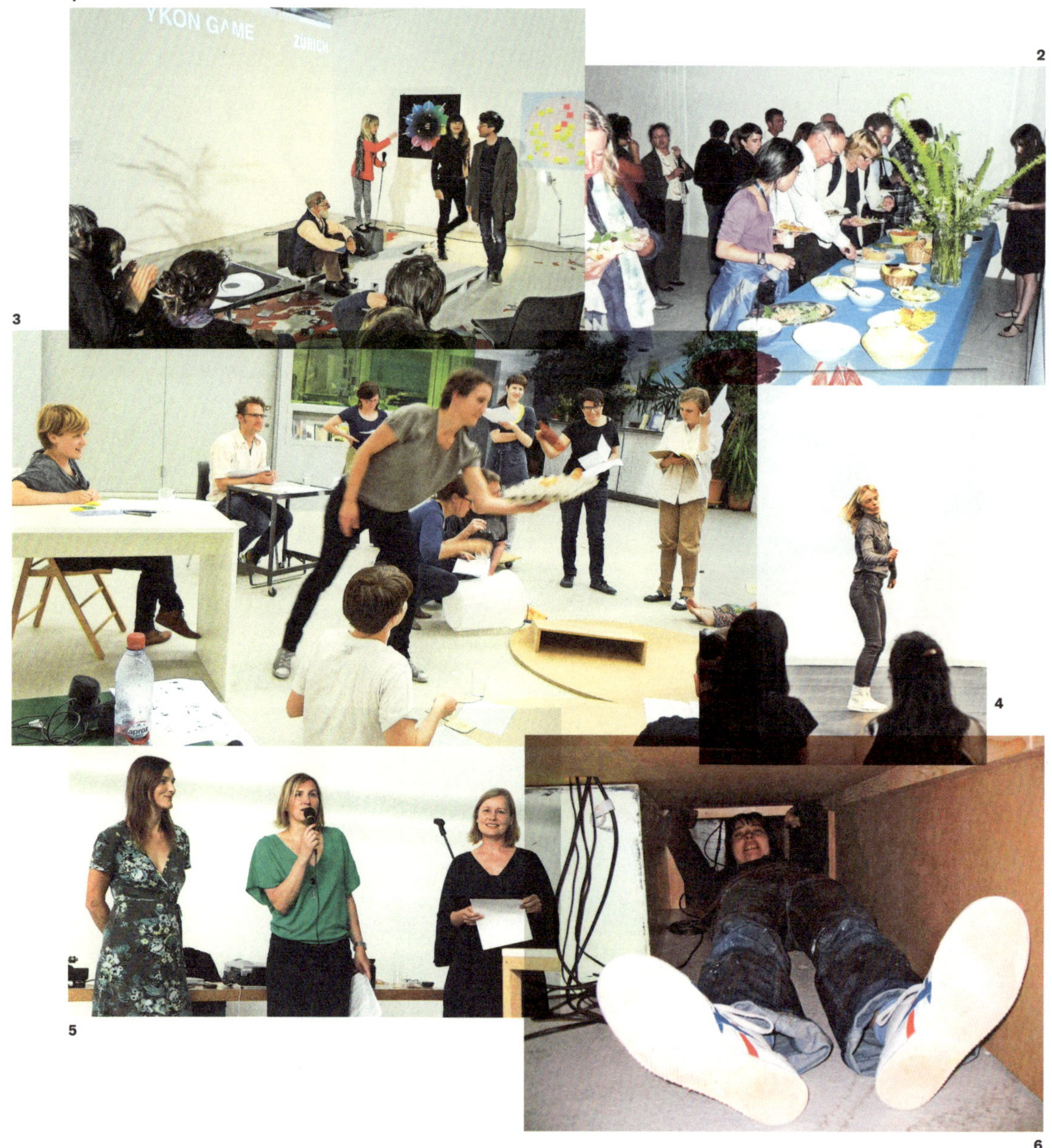

1 .... YKONgame, *Formen der Beteiligung / Forms of participation*, 2012
2 .... Buffet von / by Riglehof Densbüren
3 .... bolwerK, mit / with Marthe Van Dessel: *Screensavers, sleep mode, hibernate, standby or off*, *Dump Time*, 2011
4 .... Performance Alexandra Bachzetsis: *A Piece Danced Alone*, Shedhalle 2012
5 .... Ausstellungseröffnung / Opening reception *Connect*: Yvonne Volkart, Anke Hoffmann, Aurelia Müller, 2011
6 .... Technikerin / Technician Karen Geyer searching for solutions

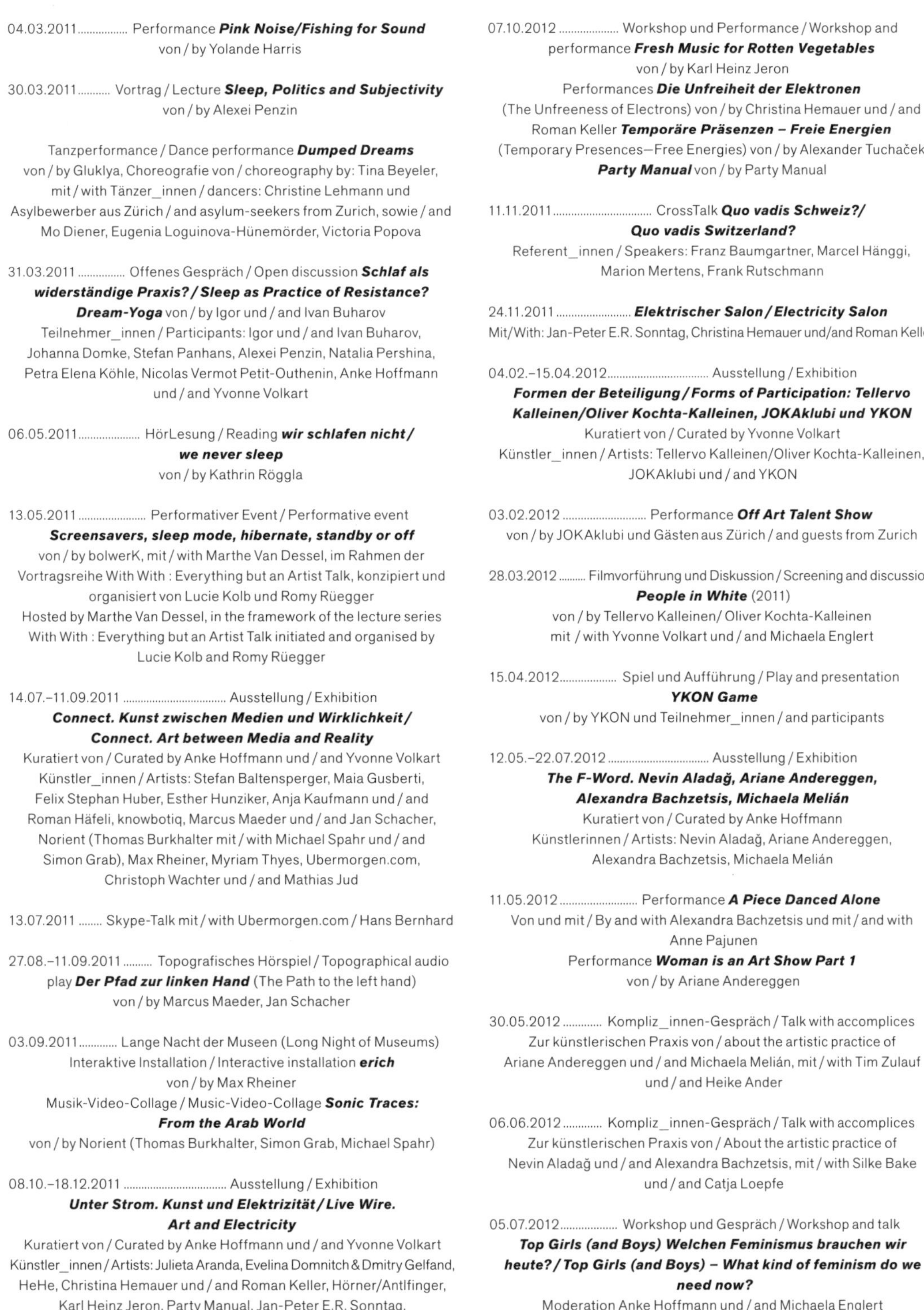

04.03.2011................ Performance *Pink Noise/Fishing for Sound*
von / by Yolande Harris

30.03.2011........... Vortrag / Lecture *Sleep, Politics and Subjectivity*
von / by Alexei Penzin

Tanzperformance / Dance performance *Dumped Dreams*
von / by Gluklya, Choreografie von / choreography by: Tina Beyeler,
mit / with Tänzer_innen / dancers: Christine Lehmann und
Asylbewerber aus Zürich / and asylum-seekers from Zurich, sowie / and
Mo Diener, Eugenia Loguinova-Hünemörder, Victoria Popova

31.03.2011 .... Offenes Gespräch / Open discussion *Schlaf als
widerständige Praxis? / Sleep as Practice of Resistance?*
Dream-Yoga von / by Igor und / and Ivan Buharov
Teilnehmer_innen / Participants: Igor und / and Ivan Buharov,
Johanna Domke, Stefan Panhans, Alexei Penzin, Natalia Pershina,
Petra Elena Köhle, Nicolas Vermot Petit-Outhenin, Anke Hoffmann
und / and Yvonne Volkart

06.05.2011.................... HörLesung / Reading *wir schlafen nicht /*
we never sleep
von / by Kathrin Röggla

13.05.2011 .... Performativer Event / Performative event
Screensavers, sleep mode, hibernate, standby or off
von / by bolwerK, mit / with Marthe Van Dessel, im Rahmen der
Vortragsreihe With With : Everything but an Artist Talk, konzipiert und
organisiert von Lucie Kolb und Romy Rüegger
Hosted by Marthe Van Dessel, in the framework of the lecture series
With With : Everything but an Artist Talk initiated and organised by
Lucie Kolb and Romy Rüegger

14.07.–11.09.2011 .... Ausstellung / Exhibition
Connect. Kunst zwischen Medien und Wirklichkeit /
Connect. Art between Media and Reality
Kuratiert von / Curated by Anke Hoffmann und / and Yvonne Volkart
Künstler_innen / Artists: Stefan Baltensperger, Maia Gusberti,
Felix Stephan Huber, Esther Hunziker, Anja Kaufmann und / and
Roman Häfeli, knowbotiq, Marcus Maeder und / and Jan Schacher,
Norient (Thomas Burkhalter mit / with Michael Spahr und / and
Simon Grab), Max Rheiner, Myriam Thyes, Ubermorgen.com,
Christoph Wachter und / and Mathias Jud

13.07.2011 .... Skype-Talk mit / with Ubermorgen.com / Hans Bernhard

27.08.–11.09.2011 .... Topografisches Hörspiel / Topographical audio
play *Der Pfad zur linken Hand* (The Path to the left hand)
von / by Marcus Maeder, Jan Schacher

03.09.2011............. Lange Nacht der Museen (Long Night of Museums)
Interaktive Installation / Interactive installation *erich*
von / by Max Rheiner
Musik-Video-Collage / Music-Video-Collage *Sonic Traces:*
From the Arab World
von / by Norient (Thomas Burkhalter, Simon Grab, Michael Spahr)

08.10.–18.12.2011 .... Ausstellung / Exhibition
Unter Strom. Kunst und Elektrizität / Live Wire.
Art and Electricity
Kuratiert von / Curated by Anke Hoffmann und / and Yvonne Volkart
Künstler_innen / Artists: Julieta Aranda, Evelina Domnitch & Dmitry Gelfand,
HeHe, Christina Hemauer und / and Roman Keller, Hörner/Antlfinger,
Karl Heinz Jeron, Party Manual, Jan-Peter E.R. Sonntag,
Alexander Tuchaček (knowbotic research), Clemens Winkler

07.10.2012 .... Workshop und Performance / Workshop and
performance *Fresh Music for Rotten Vegetables*
von / by Karl Heinz Jeron
Performances *Die Unfreiheit der Elektronen*
(The Unfreeness of Electrons) von / by Christina Hemauer und / and
Roman Keller *Temporäre Präsenzen – Freie Energien*
(Temporary Presences—Free Energies) von / by Alexander Tuchaček
Party Manual von / by Party Manual

11.11.2011 .... CrossTalk *Quo vadis Schweiz? /*
Quo vadis Switzerland?
Referent_innen / Speakers: Franz Baumgartner, Marcel Hänggi,
Marion Mertens, Frank Rutschmann

24.11.2011 .... *Elektrischer Salon / Electricity Salon*
Mit/With: Jan-Peter E.R. Sonntag, Christina Hemauer und/and Roman Keller

04.02.–15.04.2012.................................. Ausstellung / Exhibition
*Formen der Beteiligung / Forms of Participation: Tellervo
Kalleinen/Oliver Kochta-Kalleinen, JOKAklubi und YKON*
Kuratiert von / Curated by Yvonne Volkart
Künstler_innen / Artists: Tellervo Kalleinen/Oliver Kochta-Kalleinen,
JOKAklubi und / and YKON

03.02.2012 .... Performance *Off Art Talent Show*
von / by JOKAklubi und Gästen aus Zürich / and guests from Zurich

28.03.2012 .... Filmvorführung und Diskussion / Screening and discussion
People in White (2011)
von / by Tellervo Kalleinen/ Oliver Kochta-Kalleinen
mit / with Yvonne Volkart und / and Michaela Englert

15.04.2012.................... Spiel und Aufführung / Play and presentation
YKON Game
von / by YKON und Teilnehmer_innen / and participants

12.05.–22.07.2012 .... Ausstellung / Exhibition
The F-Word. Nevin Aladağ, Ariane Andereggen,
Alexandra Bachzetsis, Michaela Melián
Kuratiert von / Curated by Anke Hoffmann
Künstlerinnen / Artists: Nevin Aladağ, Ariane Andereggen,
Alexandra Bachzetsis, Michaela Melián

11.05.2012 .... Performance *A Piece Danced Alone*
Von und mit / By and with Alexandra Bachzetsis und mit / and with
Anne Pajunen
Performance *Woman is an Art Show Part 1*
von / by Ariane Andereggen

30.05.2012 .... Kompliz_innen-Gespräch / Talk with accomplices
Zur künstlerischen Praxis von / about the artistic practice of
Ariane Andereggen und / and Michaela Melián, mit / with Tim Zulauf
und / and Heike Ander

06.06.2012 .... Kompliz_innen-Gespräch / Talk with accomplices
Zur künstlerischen Praxis von / About the artistic practice of
Nevin Aladağ und / and Alexandra Bachzetsis, mit / with Silke Bake
und / and Catja Loepfe

05.07.2012.................... Workshop und Gespräch / Workshop and talk
*Top Girls (and Boys) Welchen Feminismus brauchen wir
heute? / Top Girls (and Boys) – What kind of feminism do we
need now?*
Moderation Anke Hoffmann und / and Michaela Englert

21.07.2012 .... Buchpräsentation / Booklaunch *Eindeutigkeiten sprengen – Shedhalle 2009–2012 / Subverting Disambiguities—Shedhalle 2009–2012*

Konzert / Concert von / by *F.S.K. (Freiwillige Selbstkontrolle)*
Djane Fred Hystère & Ginger Drops Downstairs
Abschlussfest des Teams Shedhalle 2012 / Farewell party of the Shedhalle team 2012
Konzert und Fest in Kooperation mit Konzeptbüro Rote Fabrik, IGRF / Concert and party in cooperation with Konzeptbüro Rote Fabrik, IGRF

Gastprojekt / **Guest project**
auf Einladung des Vorstands des Vereins Shedhalle / at the invitation of the Board of Verien Shedhalle

10.07.–08.08.2010................. Faculty of Invisibility: *Versammlung /* Faculty of Invisibility: *Assembly*
Kuratiert von / Curated by Sönke Hallmann und / and Inga Zimprich
mit / with Benjamin Cölle, Laurie Cohen, Maaike Engelen, Clemence Freschard, Jeanne van Heeswijk, Ingela Johansson, Achim Lengerer, M7red (Mauricio Corberlan, Pio Torroja), p-r-o-x-y, Dagmar Reichert, Darren Rhymes, Jan Rolletschek, Elske Rosenfeld, Simone Schardt, Johan Siebers, Tanja Widmann und anderen / and others

09.07.2010.................. Konzert von / Concert by Singer/Songwriter
Clemence Freschard

16.07.–18.07.2010................. Faculty of Invisibility: *Versammlung /* Faculty of Invisibility: *Assembly*
mit / with Benjamin Cölle, Laurie Cohen, Maaike Engelen, Jeanne van Heeswijk, Ingela Johansson, Dagmar Reichert, Darren Rhymes, Johan Siebers und anderen / and others

23.07./24.07.2010................ Workshops *Der Zentrale Runde Tisch der DDR / The Central Round Table of the GDR*
mit / with Faculty of Invisibility (Inga Zimprich, Sönke Hallmann), Elske Rosenfeld und Teilnehmer_innen / and participants

30.07.–01.08.2010.......... Department of Reading: *Masse, Bewegung, Bild /* Department of Reading: *Mass, Movement, Image*
mit / with Helmut Draxler, Achim Lengerer, p-r-o-x-y, Jan Rolletschek, Johan Siebers, Tanja Widmann

07.08.2010................. Diskussion und Gespräch / Discussion and talk
Die Shedhalle als Archiv politischer Begehren / Shedhalle as an Archive of Political Desire
mit / with Dagmar Reichert, Simone Schardt, Eva von Wartburg, Yvonne Volkart

Gastvorträge / **Guest lectures**

Ästhetik@Subversion
Ästhetik@Subversion ist eine Vortragsreihe des BA Kunst & Medien / Vertiefung Theorie in Zusammenarbeit mit dem Master of Fine Arts des Departements Kunst & Medien an der Zürcher Hochschule der Künste ZHdK.

www.zhdk.ch/index.php?id=inventionen

Aesthetics@Subversion
Aesthetics@Subversion is a series of lectures by BA Media & Art / Specialization in Theory in cooperation with the Master of Fine Arts of the Department of Art & Media at the Zurich University of the Arts.

13.01.2010: *Dialectics of Subversion / Subverting Dialectics*
Referent_in / Speaker: Dmitry Vilensky, Chto Delat

14.04.2010...................... *Kunst als Anti-Copyright-Aktivismus / Art as anti-copyright-activism*
Referent_in / Speaker: Cornelia Sollfrank

Inventionen
Inventionen ist eine Reihe von Doppelvorträgen zur Aktualisierung poststrukturalistischer Theorie, koordiniert von Isabell Lorey, Roberto Nigro und Gerald Raunig. Organisation: ith und BA Kunst & Medien / Vertiefung Theorie, ZHdK in Kooperation mit der Shedhalle Zürich und dem European Institute for Progressive Cultural Policies eipcp.

www.zhdk.ch/index.php?id=aesthetik_subversion

Inventions
Inventions is a series of double lectures actualising post-structuralist theory, coordinated by Isabell Lorey, Roberto Nigro, and Gerald Raunig. Organisation: ith and BA Media & Art / Specialization in Theory at the Zurich University of the Arts in cooperation with Shedhalle Zurich and the European Institute for Progressive Cultural Policies eipcp.

25.03.2010 ...... *Construire le Commun / Constructing the Common*
Referent_innen / Speakers: Roberto Nigro & Gerald Raunig, Judith Revel

06.04.2010......... *Prekarität, Prekariat, Prekarisierung / Precarity, Precariat, Precarization*
Referent_innen / Speakers: Isabell Lorey, Angela Mitropoulos

06.05.2010.................... *Politics of Potentiality*
Referent_innen / Speakers: Thomas Seibert, Katja Diefenbach

12.10.2010............... *Das politische Ereignis / The Political Event*
Referent_innen / Speakers: Maurizio Lazzarato, Stefan Nowotny

09.11.2010 .... *Transversalität / Transversality*
Referent_innen / Speakers: Encarnación Gutiérrez Rodríguez, Boyan Manchev

07.12.2010........................... *Queer Assemblages*
Referent_innen / Speakers: Antke Engel, Jasbir Puar

05.04.2011.. *Krise / Crisis*
Referent_innen / Speakers: Rita Casale, Ida Dominijanni

03.05.2011...................... *Wiederaneignung (‚Ceci est à moi') / Reappropriation ('Ceci est à moi')*
Referent_innen / Speakers: Sandro Mezzadra, Antonio Negri

25.10.2011 .... *Exodus*
Referent_innen / Speakers: Klaus Neundlinger, Paolo Virno

15.11.2011 .... *Immanenz / Immanence*
Referent_innen / Speakers: Thomas Hippler, Anne Sauvagnargues

13.12.2011.................................... *Territorium / Territory*
Referent_innen / Speakers: Anne Querrien, Ludger Schwarte

12.04.2012........................... *Real Democracy*
Referent_innen / Speakers: Montserrat Galcerán, Raúl Sánchez Cedillo

24.05.2012... *Cognitive Capital*
Referent_innen / Speakers: Silvia Federici, Christian Marazzi

DANKSAGUNG / ACKNOWLEDGEMENTS

Die Publikation ***Eindeutigkeiten sprengen – Kuratorische Praxis Shedhalle 2009–2012 / Subverting Disambiguities—Curatorial Practice Shedhalle 2009–2012*** wurde ermöglicht durch die freundliche Unterstützung von / The publication was kindly supported by

Präsidialdepartement Stadt Zürich
Cassinelli-Vogel-Stiftung

Stiftungen und Sponsoren / Foundations and Sponsors

Die Projekte der Shedhalle zwischen 2009 – 2012 wurde ermöglicht durch die freundliche Unterstützung von / The Shedhalle programme 2009 – 2012 was kindly supported by

Präsidialdepartement Stadt Zürich
Bundesamt für Kultur (BAK)
Migros Kulturprozent

Arts Council of Finland
G. und J. Bloch-Stiftung
Cassinelli-Vogel-Stiftung
Dr. Georg und Josi Guggenheim-Stiftung Zürich
Ernst Göhner Stiftung
Ernst&Olga Gubler-Hablützel Stiftung
EWZ Zürich
Fondation Nestlé pour l'Art
FRAME Finnish Fund for Art Exchange
Finnland-Institut in Deutschland
KoKo Rote Fabrik
Institut für Auslandsbeziehungen (ifa)
Stiftung Corymbo
Victorinox
Zürcher Kantonalbank

Anke Hoffmann und Yvonne Volkart möchten darüber hinaus für das Zustandekommen dieses Buches und für die engagierte Unterstützung der Projektarbeit in der Shedhalle danken / Anke Hoffmann und Yvonne Volkart would like to thank all contributors to this publication and all supporters of the project work at Shedhalle:

Allen Künstler_innen und Autor_innen und dem S. Fischer Verlag Frankfurt für die freundliche Erlaubnis des Wiederabdrucks eines Auszuges von Kathrin Röggla: *wir schlafen nicht* © S. Fischer Verlag, 2004 / all artists, authors and the publishers of the S. Fischer Verlag for the kind permission to reproduce an excerpt from Kathrin Röggla, *wir schlafen nicht* © S. Fischer Verlag, 2004;

Dem gesamten Team und Vorstand der Shedhalle und allen Künstler_innen / the entire team and board of Shedhalle, all artists und / and also Heike Munder und / and Moni Schori (Migros Museum Zürich), allen Leihgeber_innen und Galerien der Künstler_innen / to all lenders and the artists' galleries and Susi Bodmer, Fränzi Keller, Roger Studer, Franziska Rütimann, Christian Frick, Rebecca Vonlaufen, Jasmin Phasuk, Patrik Riemann, Kyros Kikos, Rahel Leupin, Eveline Gfeller, Elke Bippus, Silvia Jaklitsch, Christoph Franz, Michael Meier, Hannah Horst, Aurelia Müller, Sybille Omlin, Werner Hegglin, Juan Widmer, Silvia Hofer, Team Ziegel oh Lac, allen Beteiligten des ersten Zürcher Beschwerdechores / all participants of the First Zurich Complaints Choir: Regina Steiner, Niels van der Waerden, Stefanie Ressin, Jan Theiler, Alexandra Papadopoulos, Ajana Calugar, Anca Sinpalean, Bea Schwager, Bice Aeberli, Boris von der Burg, Celia Bachmann, Claudia Trachsler, Debora Gerber, Eva Lauper, Gabor Doka, Eugenia Loguinova-Hünemörder, Geronimo Hiestand, Hans Gamma, Kristina Schönwälder, Mo Diener, Regula Rüst-Walcher, Res Hotz, Rezia Krauer, Sibylle Aeberli, Suzanne Zahnd, Sven Hünemörder, Thomas Rüdisühli, Tobias Hoffmann, Yvonne Christ und / and Petra Wild und / and Volker Schmiedchen, sowie allen Beteiligten der Performance Dumped Dreams / also all participants of the performance Dumped Dreams: Tina Beyeler, Mo Diener, Eugenia Loguinova-Hünemörder, Sergej Nikokoshev, Victoria Popova, Christine Lehmann, Siavash Namehsini, Karim Khider, Mohammad Ghasem Reza, Hoseini Mohammad Kasem, Diams Silla, Lama Diallo, Aziz Mohamadi and special thanks to Trixa Arnold und Ilja Komarov.

Danke euch allen!
Thanks to all of you!

IMPRESSUM / IMPRINT

Diese Publikation basiert auf der dreijährigen Zusammenarbeit der Kuratorinnen Anke Hoffmann und Yvonne Volkart, die von 2009 bis 2012 als kuratorisches Team der Shedhalle Zürich arbeiteten. Das Buch vereint die Projekte dieser Zusammenarbeit und stützt sich dabei auf Beiträge von beteiligten Theoretiker_innen, Autor_innen und Künstler_innen. / This book was published on the basis of a three-year cooperation between the curators Anke Hoffmann and Yvonne Volkart, who both worked at Shedhalle Zurich from 2009 to 2012. The book joins the projects realised in this cooperation and draws on the contributions by participating art theorists, authors and artists.

Herausgegeben von / Edited by Anke Hoffmann und / and Yvonne Volkart für den Verein Shedhalle / for the Verein Shedhalle
Gestaltet von / Design by Claudia Klein & Emanuel Tschumi, Zürich
Redaktion und Koordination / Editing and Coordination:
Anke Hoffmann, Yvonne Volkart, Angela Wittwer
Lektorate / Proofreading: Yvonne Volkart, Ingrid Fichtner, Angela Wittwer
Übersetzungen / Translations:
Brian Currid, Berlin / Fiona Elliott, Edinburgh / Ingrid Fichtner, Zürich / Christopher Langer, Berlin / Rebecca van Dyck, Hannover / Kimi Lum, Wien (S. 306–311)
Deutsches Schlusslektorat / German Proofreading
Anke Hoffmann, Silvia Jaklitsch, Angela Wittwer
Englisches Schlusslektorat / English Proofreading
Christopher Langer
Druck / Printing / Buchbinderei / Bookbinding
Karl Grammlich GmbH, Pliezhausen

Copyrights
© alle Texte / all texts die Autor_innen / the authors
© für das Buch / for the book Shedhalle Zürich, Verlag für moderne Kunst Nürnberg

Bildnachweise / Image credits
Alle Ausstellungsansichten aus der Shedhalle, falls nicht anders vermerkt / All exhibition views from Shedhalle exhibitions, if not stated otherwise.
© Die Künstler_innen / the artists und/ and:
Susi Bodmer, Zürich: S. 20/21, 26 (3), 65 oben, 66 oben, 70 oben, 79 oben, 80 oben, 85 unten, 112 mitte, 128 unten, 134, 141 oben, 147 oben, 188 (2), 194 unten, 219, 224, 256/257, 259, 260 oben, 266 (2), 269 oben
S. 4/5, S. 298–300 (3): Anke Hoffmann/Angela Wittwer
S. 65 unten, 103: Courtesy of Rossella Biscotti and Wilfried Lentz, Rotterdam
S. 123: Julia Barclay
S. 160, 161 oben: Kai Ziegner
S. 169 unten links: Anke Hoffmann
S. 175 oben, S. 240/241: Michaela Englert
S. 182/183: Sarah Mehler
S. 229–230 (4) Thomas Rüst
S. 260 unten: Tobi Altertshofer
S. 269 unten: Melanie Hofmann
S. 294/295: Tobias Borup
S. 313– 316: Seán Kennedy (S. 313: 1, 6), Shedhalle Team (S. 313: 2, 3, 4, 7; S. 314: 1; S. 315: 3, 4, 6), Gunnar Meier (S. 313: 5), Anke Hoffmann (S. 314: 2, 3, 4, 6; S. 315: 1, 2, 5, 7; S. 316: 2), Gérôme Grollimund (S. 314: 5), Angela Wittwer (S. 314: 7), Ulu Braun (S. 316: 1), Romy Rüegger (S. 316: 3), Michaela Englert (S. 316: 4), Jörg Weule (S. 316: 5), Juliane Zelwies (S. 316: 6)
© 2012, VG Bild-Kunst Bonn: Ulu Braun, S. 216/217

Verein Shedhalle
Seestrasse 395
PF 771
CH-8038 Zürich
www.shedhalle.ch

Shedhalle Team 2009–2012

Geschäftsleitung / General Management: Sarah Mehler (2009 - 2011) Brigitte Renz Sonko (2011 - 2012)
Buchhaltung / Accounting: Yolanda Anastasia Hug
Kuratorisches Team / Curatorial Team:
Anke Hoffmann, Yvonne Volkart
Praktika und Assistenzen / Assistant Curators (2009 - 2012):
Anca Sinpalean, Angela Wittwer, Gérôme Grollimund, Michaela Englert
Technik und Aufbau / Technicians: Markus Bösch, Karen Geyer, Tobias Borup
Archiv / Archive: Maria Mosayebi
IT Support: Thomas Schmidt (emso)
Webdesign: Esther Hunziker
Webprogrammierung / Web programming: Michi Mauch
Gute Seele / Good soul: Francis
Vorstand / Board: Alice Cantaluppi, Irene Jost (bis 2010), Kurt Maeder (bis 2010), Carmen Moersch, Federica Gärtner (bis 2011), Peter Haerle, Jean-Pierre Hoby (bis 2010), Simone Schardt, Andrea Thal, Eva von Wartburg, Eva Wille, Teres Wydler, Tim Zulauf (bis 2011)
Aufsichtskräfte / Museum supervision: Verena Doerfler, Ann Nelson, Anna Staehle, Christina Ramsauer

Erschienen im / Published at Verlag für moderne Kunst Nürnberg
Königstrasse 73
D-90402 Nürnberg
www.vfmk.de

ISBN 978-3-86984-355-1

Printed in Germany

Bibliografische Information Der Deutschen Nationalbibliothek:
Die Deutsche Nationalbibliothek verzeichnet diese Publikation in der Deutschen Nationalbibliografie; detaillierte bibliografische Daten sind im Internet abrufbar über http://dnb.ddb.de

Bibliographic information published by Die Deutsche Nationalbibliothek:
Die Deutsche Nationalbibliothek lists this publication in the Deutsche Nationalbibliografie; detailed bibliographic data is available on the Internet at http://dnb.ddb.de

Distributed in the United Kingdom: Cornerhouse Publications

Distributed outside Europe:
D. A. P. Distributed Art Publishers, Inc.